COLOUR-CODED

A LEGAL HISTORY OF RACISM IN CANADA
1900–1950

Historically Canadians have considered themselves to be more or less free of racial prejudice. Although this perception has been challenged in recent years, it has not been completely dispelled. In *Colour-Coded*, Constance Backhouse illustrates the tenacious hold that white supremacy had on our legal system in the first half of this century, and underscores the damaging legacy of inequality that continues today.

Backhouse presents detailed narratives of six court cases, each giving evidence of blatant racism created and enforced through law. The cases focus on Aboriginal, Inuit, Chinese-Canadian, and African-Canadian individuals, taking us from the criminal prosecution of traditional Aboriginal dance to the trial of members of the 'Ku Klux Klan of Kanada.' From thousands of possibilities, Backhouse has selected studies that constitute central moments in the legal history of racism in Canada. Her selection also considers a wide range of legal forums, including administrative rulings by municipal councils, criminal trials before police magistrates, and criminal and civil cases heard by the highest courts in the provinces and by the Supreme Court of Canada.

The extensive and detailed documentation presented here leaves no doubt that the Canadian legal system played a dominant role in creating and preserving racial discrimination. A central message of this book is that racism is deeply embedded in Canadian history despite Canada's reputation as a raceless society.

CONSTANCE BACKHOUSE is Professor of Law at the University of Western Ontario and author of *Petticoats and Prejudice: Women and Law in Nineteenth-Century Canada*.

PATRONS OF THE SOCIETY

Aird & Berlis

Blake, Cassels & Graydon

Davies, Ward & Beck

Fasken Campbell Godfrey

Fraser, Milner

The Law Foundation of Ontario

McCarthy Tétrault

Osler, Hoskin & Harcourt

Tory Tory DesLauriers & Binnington

Weir & Foulds

BENEFACTORS OF THE SOCIETY

Bastedo Stewart Smith

Kathleen, John, and Stephen Risk

The Society also thanks The Law Society of Upper Canada for its
continuing support.

COLOUR-CODED

A Legal History
of Racism in Canada
1900–1950

CONSTANCE BACKHOUSE

Published for The Osgoode Society for Canadian Legal History by
University of Toronto Press
Toronto Buffalo London

ISBN 0-8020-4712-2 (cloth)
ISBN 0-8020-8286-6 (paper)

Printed on acid-free paper

Canadian Cataloguing in Publication Data

Backhouse, Constance, 1952–
Colour-coded : a legal history of racism in Canada, 1900–1950

Includes bibliographical references and index.
ISBN 0-8020-4712-2 (bound)   ISBN 0-8020-8286-6 (pbk.)

1. Race discrimination – Law and legislation – Canada – Cases.
2. Race discrimination – Law and legislation – Canada – History –
20th century.   I. Osgoode Society for Canadian Legal History.
II. Title.

KE4395.A7B32 1999   342.71'0873   C99-931104-2
KF4483.C58B32 1999

University of Toronto Press acknowledges the financial assistance to its
publishing program of the Canada Council for the Arts and the
Ontario Arts Council.

University of Toronto Press acknowledges the financial support for
its publishing activities of the Government of Canada through the Book
Publishing Industry Development Program (BPIDP).
Canada

Contents

Foreword

THE OSGOODE SOCIETY
FOR CANADIAN LEGAL HISTORY

The purpose of The Osgoode Society for Canadian Legal History is to encourage research and writing in the history of Canadian law. The Society, which was incorporated in 1979 and is registered as a charity, was founded at the initiative of the Honourable R. Roy McMurtry, a former attorney general for Ontario, now Chief Justice of Ontario, and officials of the Law Society of Upper Canada. Its efforts to stimulate the study of legal history in Canada include a research support program, a graduate student research assistance program, and work in the fields of oral history and legal archives. The Society publishes volumes of interest to the Society's members that contribute to legal-historical scholarship in Canada, including studies of the courts, the judiciary and the legal profession, biographies, collections of documents, studies in criminology and penology, accounts of significant trials, and work in the social and economic history of the law.

Current directors of The Osgoode Society for Canadian Legal History are Jane Banfield, Tom Bastedo, Brian Bucknall, Archie Campbell, J. Douglas Ewart, Martin Friedland, Charles Harnick, John Honsberger, Kenneth Jarvis, Allen Linden, Virginia MacLean, Wendy Matheson, Colin McKinnon, Roy McMurtry, Brendan O'Brien, Peter Oliver, Paul Reinhardt, Joel Richler, James Spence, Harvey Strosberg, and Richard Tinsley.

The annual report and information about membership may be obtained by writing The Osgoode Society for Canadian Legal History, Osgoode Hall, 130 Queen Street West, Toronto, Ontario. M5H 2N6.

In 1990 The Osgoode Society was delighted to publish Constance Backhouse's first book, *Petticoats and Prejudice*, an important and innovative study of women and law in nineteenth-century Canada. Using a case-study method and presenting her material in a lively style which attracted a wide range of readers, Professor Backhouse won great acclaim for her path-breaking scholarship in a relatively new field of historical inquiry.

In *Colour-Coded: A Legal History of Racism in Canada, 1900–1950*, she maintains the same high standards as she continues to break new historiographical ground. Shifting her interest from gender to race, and maintaining her case-study approach, her mission in *Colour-Coded* is to capture the role played by the law in shaping the definition of race and shoring up racial repression and stereotypes. Professor Backhouse weaves a spell-binding storyline in her depiction of a series of court cases that focus on Aboriginal, Inuit, Chinese-Canadian, and African-Canadian individuals. From the criminal prosecution of traditional Aboriginal dance, to the trial of members of the "Ku Klux Klan of Kanada," Backhouse demonstrates the deep and abiding legacy of racism that suffused Canadian legal structures and society.

R. Roy McMurtry
President

Peter N. Oliver
Editor-in-Chief

Acknowledgments

Colour-Coded grew out of work that was intended to produce a sequel to my first book of legal history, *Petticoats and Prejudice: Women and Law in Nineteenth-Century Canada*, published in 1991.[1] My initial plan was to examine the intersection of gender and law across the first half of the twentieth century. As I embarked upon *Colour-Coded* I was committed to improving upon the research methodology I had used for *Petticoats*. One of the shortcomings of that book is its failure to interrogate fully how gender relates to race in historical terms. In an effort to prevent this happening again, I commenced my research by attempting to compile and analyse all the racialized cases and statutes in Canada that arose between 1900 and 1950.

Almost immediately, it became abundantly clear that 'race' is a complex and variable historical construct. For example, the situation of Aboriginal peoples is not uniform across the diversity of nations. The situation of Asian Canadians differs from that of the First Nations. Black communities experience the law differently yet again. The concept of a 'white' race, although significantly more muted in the historical record, also permeates and complicates racial divisions. The materials I was able to compile were so rich and plentiful that it soon became clear that many books on the subject could, and should, be written. I have now worked on this research for seven years. Although I have merely begun to scratch the surface, I have decided to publish what I have completed.

Writing a book about the legal history of race is an exercise that is fraught with difficulties for a woman who is the beneficiary of 'white' privilege. I am indebted to the men and women of colour whom I have been privileged to teach in my classes in history, women's studies, and law at the University of Western Ontario, the Native Law Centre in Saskatoon, and the Nunavut Arctic College on Baffin Island. It was their insistence that race had centrality in Canadian legal history which brought me to pursue this research, and their questions and ideas which persuaded me to write this book. As some of them embark upon graduate studies and academic careers of their own, I know that they will produce books that far outdistance my initial efforts here.

I am also indebted to the many scholars of colour who have begun to publish works of critical race theory, whose ideas have helped me to begin to understand more about race and racism.[2] The recognition that racism is perpetuated through institutionalized and systemic practices, rather than through the idiosyncratic behaviours of isolated individuals, is fundamental to the accurate assessment of Canadian racial history. The academy will be far richer when it is pushed to include a true diversity of race within the ranks of its professoriate and student body, when funding bodies begin to make research monies available equally to whites and racially diverse peoples. I am acutely aware that the books that Aboriginal, Asian-Canadian, and African-Canadian scholars will write about Canadian legal history will most probably differ from mine.[3]

I am greatly obliged to the many individuals who have helped to locate and interpret the legal records that appear in this book. Betty Brewster, Susan Enuaraq, Sandra Inutiq, Leetia Janes, Eric Joamie, Bernadette Makpah, Julia Olayuk, Sarah Papatsie, Pauline Pemik, Louisa Pootoolik, Paul Quassa, and Helen Tologanak, students of the Jump-Start Inuit Legal Studies Program in Iqaluit in 1997, helped to analyse the Re Eskimo materials. Wendy Whitecloud of the University of Manitoba and Albert Angus of Turtleford, Saskatchewan, made efforts to locate information from the Sioux Valley Dakota Territory and the Thunderchild Territory for the chapter on Aboriginal dance. Tracey Lindberg, an assistant professor at Athabasca University, also offered richly detailed suggestions on this chapter. Audrey Chisholm, Ike Hill, Shirley Maracle, Ron Green, Earl Hill, Laura Green, Evelyn Ross, Lyle Leween, Phyllis Green, Gloria Smith, and Shirley Benett of the Tyendinaga Mohawk Territory assisted me in locating material for the chapter on Eliza Sero's case. Erica Tao, Lisa Mar, Imogene Lim, and Henry Yu provided assistance that helped me to interpret the Yee Clun case. Pearleen Oliver, Jack Desmond, Wanda Robson, Mrs S.A. Clyke, David Woods, Tanya Hudson, Gwen Jenkins,

Diba Majzub, Barrington Walker, and Sherry Edmunds-Flett provided information and assistance on the Viola Desmond chapter.

I am also indebted to Brenda Mowbray and Gayle Jessop of the Nunavut Arctic College Library, Nunatta Campus; Sylvie Côté of the Avataq Cultural Institute; Sheila Staats of the Woodland Cultural Centre; Ruth Thompson of the Native Law Centre of the University of Saskatchewan; Karen Lewis of the Ka:nhiote Library at Tyendingaga; David Maracle of the Centre for Iroquoian Studies, University of Western Ontario; Delmor Jacobs of the Six Nations Land Research Office; Phil Monture of the Six Nations Grand River; Darlene Johnston of the Chippewas of Saugeen First Nation Land Claims Office; Michael Sherry, Legal Advisor Fishing Rights, Chiefs of Ontario; Sally Houston of the Ontario Black History Society; Debra Moore of the Hudson's Bay Company Archives; Tina Sangris of the Northwest Territories Archives; Patricia Kennedy, Trish Maracle, and Helen De Roia of the Public Archives of Canada; Barry Cahill and Allen B. Robertson of the Public Archives of Nova Scotia; Indiana Matters of the Archives of British Columbia; Elizabeth Kalmakoff and Tim Novak of the Saskatchewan Archives Board; Lynne Champagne and Jocelyn McKillop of the Provincial Archives of Manitoba; John Choules, Mary Ledwell, Sharon Fleming, and Joseph Solovitch of the Archives of Ontario; Sheila Redel of the Law Society of Manitoba; Ann-Marie Langlois and Susan Lewthwaite of the Law Society of Upper Canada Archives; Margaret Northam of the Museum of Rapid City, Manitoba; Anne-Marie White of the Halifax *Herald*; Dean Jobb of the Halifax *Mail-Star*; Glen Curnoe of the London Room, London Public Library; Lisa Russell of the Anglican Diocese of Ontario Archives; Harry Buxton of the Oakville Historical Society; John Kromkamp, Registrar of the Ontario Court of Appeal with the Court of Appeal of Ontario Archives; the Halton Region Museum/Archives and Halton Regional Police Service; the Town of Oakville; and Special Collections at the Toronto Reference Library.

Many scholars have generously shared their sources and taken time from their own research to answer my questions: Vijay Agnew, James Benincasa, Joan Brockman, Ian Bushnell, Agnes Calliste, Dorothy Chunn, Richard Diubaldo, Alan Grove, DeLloyd Guth, Sidney Harring, Elizabeth Higginbotham, Doug Leighton, Ken Leyton-Brown, Peter S. Li, Tina Loo, Sheila McIntyre, John McLaren, Robert Menzies, Elizabeth Mitchell, Patricia Monture-Angus, Mary Jane Mossman, David Philips, Jim Phillips, Joy Parr, Bruce Ryder, Carolyn Strange, Georgina Taylor, James Walker, and John R. Wunder.

Bruce Feldthusen and Diana Majury, two people who provide me with encouragement and sustenance beyond imagining, leave me in their indescribable debt.

I continue to benefit from the unparalleled expertise and supportiveness of the staff at the Law Library at the University of Western Ontario: Linda Aitkins, John Eaton, Barb Fetchison, Debbie Grey, Leslee Ingram, John Sadler, and Marianne Welch. I owe much to the supportive secretarial assistance of Jean Fisher, Janette Henry, and Amy Jacob. I have had the good fortune to be able to call upon the resources of an exceptionally skilled group of research assistants: Shelly Avram, Michael Boudreau, Linda Charlton, Kristen Clark, Susan Dawson, Anne Eichenberg, Anna Feltracco, Jennifer Hall, Alexandra Hartmann, John Hill, Paul Holmes, Bev Jacobs, Michelle McLean, Kevin Misak, Debbie Rollier, and Signa Daum Shanks.

I am substantially indebted to Marilyn MacFarlane and Peter Oliver of the Osgoode Society, and Gerry Hallowell, Bill Harnum, Jill McConkey, Melissa Pitts, Anne Forte, and Beverley Beetham Endersby at the University of Toronto Press, for their advice, assistance, and support in the preparation of this book. Two anonymous reviewers of the manuscript offered thoughtful and detailed suggestions for revision. Funding from the Law Foundation of Ontario and the Social Sciences and Humanities Research Council of Canada was pivotal to the completion of this research.

In the acknowledgments to my previous book, *Petticoats*, I confessed that at least some of the twelve years that it took me to complete that manuscript were attributable to the perils, tribulations, and fascinations of birthing and raising two young children. Many of the female readers of *Petticoats* later admitted to spontaneous self-recognition and bemused humour over my ruefully frank assessment of the complexities of mixing scholarly research with child-caring responsibilities. (Others, if truth be told, seem to have been slightly scandalized and less amused.) There is a certain sense of buoyancy over completing this book in seven years. The children have grown. The colic and ear infections are behind us. We are charting a new phase between the eclipse of toddlerhood and the advent of adolescence in the perennial saga of parent–child trajectories. These days, unexpected intrusions on scholarly work come in the form of endless chauffeuring to youth sporting events and shopping malls. The emotional drain tends to encompass squabbles over wearing apparel, hair styles, table manners, and telephone marathons. On the whole, however, I can report a net gain. To all scholarly parents of infants and toddlers, take heart in knowing that life's impossible pace and burdens do ease up somewhat.

It seems only fitting, then, that this book should be dedicated to my daughter, Diana, and my son, Mark. I hope they come to represent in some small measure the world of the future, in which Canadians will begin to confront issues of race and racial discrimination with greater knowledge of our history and a renewed commitment and energy to work for change.

Constance Backhouse
London, Ontario
December 1998

COLOUR-CODED

A LEGAL HISTORY OF RACISM IN CANADA
1900–1950

1

Introduction

The year was 1901, the eve of the first Canadian census of the twentieth century. The federal government dispatched a tidy and compact set of instructions to the faithful civil servants charged with surveying the nation. 'The races of men will be designated by the use of "w" for white, "r" for red, "b" for black, and "y" for yellow.' Missing was the colour brown, which was sometimes also linked to race, but including it would have mucked up the short-form letter categories, leaving two 'b's' in a polyglot of confusion. What was eminently clear, however, was that colour and race, two twin conceptions, were inseparably intertwined.

In case the census-takers were unable to make immediate colour distinctions when they canvassed door to door, the instructions expanded upon the business at hand:

The whites are, of course, the Caucasian race, the reds are the American Indian, the blacks are the African or Negro, and the yellows are the Mongolian (Japanese and Chinese). But only pure whites will be classed as whites; the children begotten of marriages between whites and any one of the other races will be classed as red, black or yellow, as the case may be, irrespective of the degree of colour.[1]

White, red, black, and yellow. *Of course.* The prepositional phrase is oddly positioned right after the opening three words. Is it meant to imply that race is universally and matter-of-factly identified by colour? Except, of course, for those who cross colour lines and are more accurately categorized 'as the case may be'? That colour is definitive, except when it becomes a question of 'purity' and 'degree'? That one smudge of anything other than snowy white 'tints' the colourization beyond reckoning? The precedence that is bestowed on the white race is vividly conveyed in so many ways. It is obvious from the order of the listings, with the white race featured first. It is suggested with the use of the adjective 'pure,' which appears as descriptive of only the white race. The colours 'red,' 'black,' and 'yellow' must encompass not only their named pigments, but all manner of variegated tones.

The primary colour scheme selected by the officials, with bold brush strokes of reds and yellows, was a curious choice. The census palette stretches beyond these vivid hues right to the margins of the colour charts. It splashes literally off the spectrum to the black tones, representing the absorption of all the colours of the rainbow, and the white tones, incapable of colour absorption at all. As most observers would likely have admitted if pressed, the categories are also highly inaccurate. Human beings simply do not come in any of these colours.

Yet the designation of race by colour was ubiquitous in early twentieth-century Canada. Everyone – from novelists and poets to politicians, public commentators, and historians – commonly portrayed racialized peoples in the luminous hues catalogued by the census officials. Despite the artificiality of classifying people by colours that bore little resemblance to their skin tones, the census proceeded confidently. In 1901, official records portray Canada's racial composition as a brightly painted, if uneven, graph of colour. Whites weigh down the charts, at 96.2 per cent of the official Canadian population. Reds tally in at 2.4 per cent. Yellows comprise 0.41 per cent. Blacks total 0.32 per cent. The few who defied all powers of classification at the hands of the census-takers, simply designated 'various origins' and 'unspecified,' total 0.66 per cent.[2]

Half a century later, the matters of race and colour are more delicately inscribed. Gone is the reference to the brash white, red, black, and yellow colour scheme. Now the enumerators are instructed to ask people about their 'origins.' The 1951 census report concedes that the results of such a survey reveal information that is 'partly cultural, partly biological, and partly geographical.' Recognizing that the mechanisms of classification have changed over time, the report takes care to assure Canadians that the overall objectives have not:

The word 'origin' in census terminology has, in the past, been variously qualified by such attributes as 'racial' and 'ethnic,' but the purpose of the inquiry has remained essentially the same. Fundamentally, it is an attempt to distinguish groups in the population having similar cultural characteristics, based on a common heritage.[3]

And the census data themselves remained largely intact. Those of 'European origins' – formerly the 'whites' – represent 96.95 per cent of the Canadian population. Those claiming 'Native Indian and Eskimo' origins total 1.18 per cent. Those of 'Asiatic origins,' now described as 'Chinese,' 'Japanese,' and 'Other Asiatic,' comprise 0.52 per cent. 'Negroes' constitute 0.13 per cent. The only non-white group to increase during the half-century is elusively described as 'Other and Not Stated.' It totals 1.22 per cent. Trying to account for the increase, the census reports that this group represents 'persons who stated that, because of mixed ancestry or other reasons, they did not know the origin group to which they should be classified.' Forebodingly, the report continues: 'This is a problem which can be expected to increase in magnitude ...'[4]

THE SHIFTING DEFINITION OF THE CONCEPT OF 'RACE' AND THE HISTORICAL CONSISTENCY OF 'RACISM'

The meaning of the word 'race' has changed substantially over the past several centuries. A concept with roots extending as far back as the Enlightenment, it was originally intended to mark differences of class within European society. During the eighteenth and nineteenth centuries, when empires stretched to the far corners of the globe, Europeans began to exploit the idea of 'race' as a convenient justification for their right to rule over 'uncivilized' peoples, a rationale for the creation of colonial hierarchies. With the rise of 'science' on the heels of the Industrial Revolution, newly emerging disciplines such as ethnology, anthropology, eugenics, psychology, and sociology began to offer 'professional' help in this task.

Many different scientists, all of them white, undertook the complex work of delineating 'racial' categories and speculating about the multiple distinctions between human beings that might be drawn from 'racial' data. Skin colour was only one of a long list of human variables drawn into service. Others included stature, head shape, cranial capacity, hair colour, hair texture, eye shape, eye colour, nasal index, and miscellaneous other facial features. There is nothing inherently important about any of these aspects of human physique to warrant singling them out for particular focus. The wonder is that human beings were not divided up into 'big-eared' and 'little-eared' races. Even despite the multiplicity of physical characteristics delineated, there were worrisome anomalies. Some individuals who 'looked' white chose to identify themselves as members of racially oppressed groups, or were classified as such by others. In order to resolve such inconsistencies, characteristics such as language, religion, geographic residence, manner of dress, diet, intelligence, reputation, and name were added to the list of identifying 'racial' elements.[5]

Racial classification functioned as the hand-servant for many disparate groups as they sought to explain why they were entitled to hold inequitable resources, status, and power over others. The adoption of the notion of 'race' in aid of the institution of Black slavery is well known. It is equally evident that 'racial' ideology was pressed into service as an excuse for the seizure of First Nations lands. 'Race' was offered as a definitive explanation for the punitive treatment of Asian immigrants in the late nineteenth century. 'Racial' terminology was also used to rationalize exploitation between whites. 'Racial' distinctions have historically been drawn between Saxon, Celtic, Norman, Irish, Welsh, Scottish, and English communities. Immigrants from southern and eastern Europe, Syria, Armenia, Arabia, India, and the Philippines often found their claim to 'whiteness' contested in North America. The discriminatory treatment meted out to Canadian francophones, to individuals who practised religions other than Protestantism, and to groups who emigrated to Canada from eastern and southern Europe has also been ideologically fastened to notions of 'race.'[6]

Historians who study the intellectual theories underlying the concept of 'race' have suggested that major shifts in thinking occurred during the first half of the twentieth century. Their research suggests that the white scientific community reached something of a pinnacle in the measurement, quantification, and description of the physical distinctions between 'races' during the first two decades. In the 1930s, a new breed of anthropologists began to dismantle the carefully constructed pyramid of knowledge, poking criticism at the failure of an earlier generation of researchers to arrive at any uniform data or conclusions.

The younger scholars ventured that racial distinctions were amorphous. Although they did not completely disavow the existence of races, they introduced the concept of 'ethnicity' and argued that human differences were better explained by social, political, economic, and geographic factors than by biology. A sense of this new thinking is evident from the 1951 Canadian census, where references to 'culture' and 'geography' appear, joining 'biology' as defining features of human organization. As the 1951 census report stresses, however, the change was more semantic than substantive. The belief that humanity is divided into discrete groups, and that such groups can be differentiated by specific characteristics, remained unshaken.[7]

By the late 1930s and early 1940s, it is generally conceded, the apogee of racial thinking arrived in the 'Aryan' philosophy of the 'Master Race' that served as the bedrock for Hitler's Nazism. Rather belatedly, the Allied powers began to recognize some of the horrendous implications of racial discrimination. Under the aegis of the newly created United Nations during the late 1940s, Western governments ushered in a host of policies that proclaimed an intent to eliminate discrimination on the basis of race. Even this transformation was more theoretical than practical, however. Most acts of racial discrimination continued to go unaddressed, but it became unfashionable to be characterized as racist.[8]

IS 'RACIAL' HISTORY POSSIBLE, GIVEN THE EPHEMERAL NATURE OF 'RACE'?

The study of the concept of 'race' through time illustrates beyond controversy that the very notion is built upon shifting sands. The impermanence and transmutability of 'race' is never clearer than when examined against the backdrop of the past. Does it follow, then, that any inquiry into 'racial' history is doomed from the outset? Given the artificiality of racial designations, can one presume to study the historical implications of 'race'? Some might argue that it is virtually impossible to make any credible assessments about the extent of racism through history, that all talk of racial categories ought to be abandoned. This would be, in my view, the gravest of errors. 'Race' is a mythical construct. 'Racism' is not.

Canadian history is rooted in racial distinctions, assumptions, laws, and activities, however fictional the concept of 'race' may be. To fail to scrutinize the records of our past to identify the deeply implanted tenets of racist ideology and practice is to acquiesce in the popular misapprehension that depicts our country as largely innocent of systemic racial exploitation. Nothing could be more patently erroneous.

Terms such as 'white,' 'Eskimo,' 'Indian,' and 'Chinese,' for example, are obviously problematic in view of the historically impermanent, social construction of the concept of 'race.' Despite the artificiality of such terminology, however, racial designations such as these were routinely utilized in Canada during the first half of the twentieth century. What was more, racial concepts had significant economic, social, and political implications for the people who drew these distinctions. Exploring the meanings attached to racial designations is part of the task of the race historian.

One of the most remarkable consistencies throughout this period was the prevailing assumption that, however it might be described, defined, or utilized, 'race' was a distinct attribute that served to differentiate human beings. In the face of dramatically fluctuating classifications and intellectual theorizing, the vast majority of commentators from the ranks of academia, government, the legal system, the press, and the general populace stood firm. They refused to budge from their sense that racial distinctions were a factual certainty. Influential school texts depicted 'black,' 'red,' and 'yellow' races well into the 1960s and 1970s. Pressed to define their understanding of 'race,' people might be twisted into paroxysms of confusion. But everybody seems to have believed, in some visceral sense, that they knew it when they saw it.[9]

Canadians were wedded to the belief that race was, for whatever disparate reasons, a valid categorization. Certain groups might move in and out of specific racial groupings, depending on a multiplicity of factors such as class, geographic location, language, behaviour, culture, or physical attributes. The racial groupings themselves might shift around over time. Towards the end of the period, some began to tout the term 'origins' over the words 'race' or 'colour.' What remained glaringly constant, however, was the continued utilization of 'race' as a phenomenon to differentiate some people from others. And 'racism' – the use of racial categories to create, explain, and perpetuate inequalities – remained hauntingly static. The omnipresence of racism underscores the significance of research into racial matters, despite the appalling emptiness of racial categories themselves.

DESIGNATING 'RACE' AND 'RACISM'

The terminology I have chosen to describe the racialized groups who appear in the cases discussed in this book is 'Aboriginal,' 'First Nations,' 'Black,' 'Chinese,' and 'white.' I have capitalized all but 'white,' following the practice of many critical race scholars.[10] Obviously, given the slippery fictions of racial designation, these labels are not meant to imply any definitive or fixed groupings. At particular times, however, these classifications enveloped certain individuals and communities, ushering in substantial legal, political, economic, and social consequences in their wake. It is critical to study how racial designations, whether accepted or resisted in the circumstances, functioned in historical context.

Canadians have become accustomed to describing most individuals without adverting to their race. Sporadically, labels are attached to members of oppressed racial groups, but usually only when the speaker or writer intends to make a specific point about matters of race. I believe that this practice is problematic. Racism so permeated Canadian society during the first half of the twentieth century that it is important to inquire about the racial designation of all historical actors. I think it is helpful to depart from the customary convention and attribute racialized status to all individuals on a regular basis.

Many readers may find this particularly disconcerting with respect to the 'whites' who figure in the cases examined in this work. Some will argue that the individuals I have designated as 'white' probably did not understand themselves as 'white,' and preferred to think of themselves as having a particular country of origin. If pressed to define themselves, they would likely have said they were 'of English heritage' or 'Scottish descent,' for example. From their perspective, 'whiteness' would have come into play only when they juxtaposed themselves against individuals and groups categorized as 'non-white.' It is true that the racial identity of the dominant white group was splintered in many directions (not unlike the racial identity of other groups), and that multiple subgroups formed distinct rankings (which would themselves shift over time). At certain points in the chapters that follow, I have adverted to this in some detail. However, I have typically chosen to make use of the label 'white' in an effort to denote the racial chasm that separated such groups from 'Aboriginal peoples,' the 'Chinese,' and 'Blacks.'

Some readers may also take issue with the overt depiction of the 'whiteness' of well-known historical figures. They may object that the 'whiteness' of persons such as Prime Minister Sir John A. Macdonald or Archbishop Adélard Langevin, for example, is beyond debate and unworthy of specific declaration. Unaccustomed as we are to designating white people by race, the repeated insertion of the adjective 'white' is undeniably jarring. Several of the readers who reviewed this work prior to publication even suggested that some might view the practice as 'tendentious' and 'polemical.' However, there is a growing literature that analyses the tendency of whites not to perceive themselves in racial terms. The transparency of 'whiteness' is misleading and contributes to an erasure of the privileges that attach to membership in the dominant race.[11] I think it is important to designate the race of the judges, legislators, lawyers, litigants, witnesses, community advocates, moral reformers, and other commentators who appear throughout these pages, to underscore the centrality of a full racial configuration in the legal disputes.

Although historians disagree about many things, it is almost universally accepted within the discipline that it is ahistorical to utilize our current understandings of the concept and practice of racism to evaluate and assess the past. The derogatory label 'presentist' is meant to suggest that the writer/speaker has infected her historical analysis by overlaying the historical record with assumptions, knowledge, and ideology drawn from present-day life. It is common for scholars – from the most established and senior to the most adventuresome of graduate students – to state that modern-day understandings of racism are distinct from those of earlier decades and centuries. Many will also state that it is unfair to tag historical actors with late twentiethth-century labels such as 'racist.'

Statements such as these litter the landscape of Canadian historical analysis:

Indeed, the racism of the [writings of X] was so customary for the day that it was virtually invisible to contemporaries.

[Y] seems to have simply accepted the [racial perspective] of his time and culture in a totally uncritical manner. One can't blame him for being a totally nineteenth-century person.

The major social thinkers of the second half of the nineteenth century did not articulate any critique of racial theories; even for self-proclaimed egalitarians, the inferiority of certain races was no more to be contested than the law of gravity was to be regarded as immoral.

The subject of race inferiority was beyond critical reach in the late nineteenth century.

Until about the third decade of the present century, most people in the so-called western world, including most social scientists and historians, took for granted the hereditary inferiority of non-white peoples.

The various victims of racism had internalized much of the oppressive ideology … They shared much of the racist world view, including conceptual thinking and language. In hindsight, it is difficult to locate non-racist views, since race was viewed as a scientific fact both in its philosophical and popular versions.

Generally speaking the times in which [these accounts] were written made prejudice and ignorance inevitable.[12]

The intellectual, cultural, economic, political, social, and legal history of race in Canada is still in its infancy. Surely it is foolhardy to make such sweeping declarations without the benefit of fuller inquiry and analysis. Societies are far more multitextured and complex than such monolithic observations suggest.

Some of the authors who wrote these statements 'normalizing' racism from the past appear to have been thinking primarily of the beliefs of the dominant racial group. The failure of historians to flesh out the understandings and activities of racially subordinate communities contributes to this unidimensional sense of the world. But at least some of the comments also purport to cast the same observational net over those who suffered directly from racist conditions. Undoubtedly racism infected the communities that were victimized by its devotion to power imbalance and inequality. But many First Nations, Inuit, Black, and Chinese communities in Canada never accepted the premise that they were 'inferior.' As Evelyn Brooks Higginbotham has noted, 'racial meanings were never internalized by blacks and whites in an identical way.'[13] People subordinated by race understood that they were disadvantageously situated and treated because of racial discrimination, but this did not necessarily equate with 'inferiority.' Many opposed racist ideology and struggled against racist policies. Their challenges gave energy and sustenance to their communities, and helped them to withstand and survive conditions of smothering adversity. Some whites, including some lawyers and judges, also dissented from racist ideas and practices. The suggestion that racism was like the air one breathed, that there was no space for countervailing perspectives, is simply not credible.

Nor is it helpful to suggest that one cannot label past actors and events as 'racist.' The concept of 'race' is undeniably a moving target through time and space. But the nineteenth and twentieth centuries witnessed a surprising, sticky constancy in outcomes generated by racial distinctions. Groups were defined and categorized. Then some capitalized on their 'race' to assert their 'rights' over property, education, employment, religion, social position, access to services, and so on. Others were prevented from asserting similar 'rights.' The resulting disparities might shift over time and place. Issues of education might take precedence in one period, and then become supplanted by issues of employment, to give but one example. In some decades, racialized groups might be barred from immigration; in others, barred from hiring white women. From the historical records I have examined, however, it seems to me that the use of racial hierarchy to foster privilege and maintain subordination is remarkably similar across past decades.

Eliza Sero, who advanced the claim to Mohawk sovereignty before sceptical Canadian legal authorities in 1921 (see chapter 4), would immediately have understood the demands of Wanduta, a Dakota Heyoka, of his right to celebrate a traditional Grass Dance in 1903 (see chapter 2). Ira Johnson, who faced the wrath of the Ku Klux Klan over his desire to contract an interracial marriage in 1930 (see chapter 6), would have had much to say to Yee Clun, a Chinese-Canadian restaurateur who was denied the right to hire white women in 1924 (see chapter 5). Anti-racist activists, who describe being hounded in the 1990s by sales-clerks who suspect racialized shoppers of shoplifting, will find Viola Desmond's treatment at the hands of theatre staff who refused to allow her to be seated in the 'whites only' section in 1946 (see chapter 7) only too painfully recognizable.

Some historians have suggested that the word 'racism' was not coined until the 1930s.[14] Does this make it inappropriate to attach the term to events that took place prior to its articulation? The word 'feminism' was coined a lot later than the emergence of the ideals and behaviour that bear its analytical imprint. Why is there so little objection to historical research that seeks to locate and explicate feminist forebears from centuries afar, and so much resistance to attributing 'racism' to generations from the past? Is the resistance in part a reflection of the late twentieth-century revulsion over the label itself? Is it evidence of the lack of sophistication of historians generally about matters of race? Is it emblematic of the infancy of Canadian race history as a subdiscipline? Whatever the underlying rationale, it is simply, in my opinion, wrong. Individuals and groups from Canada's past acted in identifiably 'racist' ways, causing actual and substantial damage to those they perceived as racially subordinate. These acts reinforced a wider social structure that was permeated with racism.

A DISTINCTIVE CANADIAN HISTORY OF RACE?

Is there a distinctive Canadian history of 'race' and 'racism'? Historians have been slow to recognize the importance of race in Canada's past, despite the efforts of many from racialized communities to draw this to our attention.[15] Most of the individuals and groups described in Canadian historical publications are not identified by race or ethnicity. Race is generally understood as something that affixes itself only to marginalized groups, and, by definition, these have not been the focus of Canadian historical writing. The vast majority of historical renderings have chronicled the lives of politicians, civil servants, intellectuals, diplomats, and soldiers with nary a mention of their designations on the racial hierarchy. Indeed, whiteness is completely beyond the powers of observation in most historical texts. The initial efforts of social historians, labour historians, and women's historians to expand the scope of historical research have been almost equally silent on the matter of race. When racialized communities are mentioned at all, it is typically in cursory and stereotypical fashion.[16]

The first public glimmer of historians' interest in race is often marked by the release of Robin Winks's book *The Blacks in Canada: A History* in 1971.[17] Since then, a host of authors have begun to publish books on the histories of Black, Asian, and First Nations communities in Canada.[18] Although there is as yet no book explicitly devoted to a study of 'whiteness' in Canadian history, some publications have begun to explore the history of white supremacy and white racism.[19]

It is still too early in the process of reclaiming these lost histories to be able to comment with any comprehensiveness or certainty on the question of whether Canada has a distinctive racial past, but some preliminary observations can be offered. One of the features that is discernible right at the outset is the largely erroneous presumption that our country is primarily 'raceless.' The sense of 'racelessness' that pervades Canadian thought.is, in part, a reflection of our unique position in juxtaposition to the United States and Britain. Given the centrality of Black–white racial divisions, past and present, in the United States, historians and contemporary commentators rarely characterize the American nation to the south of us as 'raceless.' Prior to 1950, Britain had more of a claim to racial homogeneity in its population at home, but the imperial mission of the British Empire irresistibly drew matters of race into the forefront of national consciousness. In contrast with these two countries, who share much of our culture and legal tradition, Canada maintained a strong sense of its 'racelessness.' Despite remarkable evidence to the contrary, despite legislation that articulated racial distinctions and barriers, despite lawyers and judges who used racial constructs to assess legal rights and responsibilities, the Canadian legal system borrowed heavily from this mythology, and contributed to the fostering of the ideology of Canada as a 'raceless' nation.

'Race' does not appear as a recognizable legal category of classification between 1900 and 1950. Legal cases were not indexed by reference to race. Statutes drawing all manner of racial distinctions were frequently 'raceless' in title. Legal commentary in treatises and periodicals rarely adverted to race. Consequently, a serious inquiry into the legal history of race means starting from scratch. It is necessary to wade laboriously through the welter of legal materials page by page, looking through each paragraph for references to 'Indians,' 'half-breeds,' 'Negroes,' 'Orientals,' 'Chinese,' 'Japanese,' and 'Hindus,' as well as the more elusive 'Caucasians' or 'whites,' the racialized terms that appear in the legal documents of the time. Sometimes these terms do not appear on the surface of the texts, but do show up in the commentary of newspaper reporters or legal writers who discussed the cases and statutes at a later date. Some racialized cases are simply irretrievable, lost in the 'racelessness' of the Canadian legal records.

Even where cases are identifiable as important legal precedents in the field of race, it is often the case that the primary sources that should be housed in archival collections are missing. The explanations offered for such gaps provide further manifestations of a society that seems determined to ignore issues of race. Archivists report that legal officials often failed to record and turn in written reports on these cases.[20] And in the periodic episodes of documentary culling that have imperilled archival files, racialized legal records are often the first to be jettisoned as 'unworthy of retention.'[21]

The ideology of racelessness, a hallmark of the Canadian historical tradition, is very much in keeping with our national mythology that Canada is not a racist country, or at least is much less so than our southern neighbour, the United States. Dionne Brand, an African-Canadian historian, poet, and writer, recounts that she still gets asked in interviews: 'Is there racism in this country?' Her response: 'Unlike the United States, where there is at least an admission of the fact that racism exists and has a history, in this country one is faced with a stupefying innocence.'[22] A 'mythology of racelessness' and 'stupefying innocence'– these would appear to be twin pillars of the Canadian history of race.

THE DESIGN OF THIS STUDY AND THE SELECTION OF CASES

This book seeks to examine what can be learned about the realities of race and racism from the study of Canadian legal history during the first half of the twentieth century. The research for this book began with a detailed search through every legal decision published in a Canadian law report between 1900 and 1950, and a sample of unreported decisions from the Archives of British Columbia, Saskatchewan, Ontario, and Nova Scotia. Next came a review of every federal and provincial statute enacted in Canada from 1900 to 1950. Despite the difficulties of locating the records of Canada's racial past within a legal system that professes racelessness, the time-consuming process of sifting through papers and texts has elicited hundreds of statutes and thousands of judicial decisions that use racial constructs as a pivotal point of reference.

Collectively, these legal documents illustrate that the legal system has been profoundly implicated in Canada's racist history. Legislative and judicial sources provide substantial evidence to document the central role of the Canadian legal system in the establishment and enforcement of racial inequality. Legislators and judges working in combination nipped, kneaded, and squeezed artificial classifications into rigid, congealed definitions of race under Canadian law. They jointly erected hierarchies of racial grouping and delineated segregated boundaries based on race. In their hands, the law functioned as a systemic instrument of oppression against racialized communities. When the individuals and groups who bore the brunt of racism sought to turn the tables and call upon the legal system for redress, the resisters typically failed in their quest. It was only on the rarest of occasions that certain legislators, lawyers, and judges attempted to stem the systemic discrimination that permeated Canadian law, refuting the excesses of Canadian racism.

It is essential to recognize that racism is located in the systems and structures that girded the legal system of Canada's past. Racism is not primarily manifest in isolated, idiosyncratic, and haphazard acts by individual actors who, from time to time, consciously intended to assert racial hierarchy over others. The roots of racialization run far deeper than individualized, intentional activities. Racism resonates through institutions, intellectual theory, popular culture, and law. Immigration laws shaped the very contours of Canadian society in ways that aggrandized the centrality of white power. Racialized communities were denied the right to maintain their own identities, cultures, and spiritual beliefs. Education, employment, residence, and the freedom of social interaction were sharply curtailed for all but those who claimed and were accorded the racial designation 'white.'

The systemic outlines of historical Canadian racism are thrown into sharp relief through an examination of specific cases that exemplify how the law fostered the inequality of racialized groups. I believe that the 'case study' method is particularly well suited to explaining the intricate and fascinating legal record of the past. The opportunity to excise one particular legal dispute from the larger framework lends itself to a detailed and multifaceted probing of the role of law. The 'case study' permits the pinpointing of the concrete impact of legal rules upon real people at specific times. The thick description of a microscopic event allows a fuller dissection of how the law interacts with the wider social, political, economic, and cultural surroundings. It also provides a more accurate reflection of some aspects of legal history than can often be produced in the abstract recounting of a lengthy series of statutes and cases that span years and decades.

In an effort to make this book as accessible to the reader as possible, I have used a narrative format that tries to keep the intricacies and complicating details of the underlying legal frameworks away from the storyline. However, it is important to recognize that these 'case studies' took place against a larger backdrop of many other trials, appeals, legislative activities, and commentaries. To ensure that the details of these statutes and cases are not relegated to a raceless dustbin, I have included extensive documentation of the wider legal framework within the notes. The adoption of this rather unconventional format ultimately resulted in a mass of scholarly apparatus that dwarfed the text in terms of length. In the end, it seemed best to sever many of these long and intricate research notes from the book itself, and post them on the University of Toronto Press Web site, www.utpress.utoronto.ca. The computerization of the bulk of the notes is designed to assist historical researchers who may find it useful to have access to portions of these references in electronic form. My hope is to accommodate the needs of distinct groups of readers without infringing on the interests of any.

From the thousands of cases I have reviewed that deal with issues of race between 1900 and 1950, I have selected six that I think serve well to exemplify how Canadian law addressed matters of race in this period. While it is always an exercise in risk-taking to prioritize some cases over others, I have chosen these cases because they meaningfully illustrate the complexity of race under Canadian law. The cases encompass constitutional questions, issues of religious freedom, international matters, conflict of laws, municipal law, criminal law, and the response of law to social and economic discrimination. I have also tried to ensure that the cases represent some degree of balance with respect to gender. The law sometimes had different impacts for racialized men and women, but both genders actively participated in racial discrimination and both persisted in resisting racial inequality. The cases were also selected, in part, to reflect the geographic diversity of Canada and to emphasize that race discrimination spanned the full length and breadth of our nation. The legal decisions canvas the racial status of the Inuit in northern Quebec, the racial oppression of Aboriginal peoples in rural Manitoba, and the resistance of Chinese Canadians to economic racism in Regina, Saskatchewan. They examine Aboriginal sovereignty claims in eastern Ontario;

the prosecution of the Ku Klux Klan in Oakville, Ontario; and the racial segregation forced upon Blacks in Nova Scotia.

The *Re Eskimos* case (which appears first, chronologically out of order in relation to the other cases) was positioned first because it provides a foundational framework for dissecting racial classification. Before one can evaluate the legal enactments and judicial opinions that affected racialized communities in early twentieth-century Canada, one must first try to grapple with contemporary understandings of the concept of 'race.' The *Re Eskimos* case is particularly helpful in this regard, because the legal documentation that was compiled during the litigation was unusually comprehensive and richly detailed. Others cases, such as *Wanduta* and *Sero* v *Gault*, are less fully documented in the surviving records. However, these were chosen because they represent transformative and defining moments in the legal history of Aboriginal peoples, who fought to maintain their cultural and political traditions. The case of *Yee Clun* permits some analysis of the efforts of Chinese Canadians to activate legal proceedings to challenge racism. The *Phillips* case allows some assessment of the penetration of racist organizations such as the Ku Klux Klan into Canadian culture and law. The case involving Viola Desmond was singled out because of the interest it has provoked in the Black community in Nova Scotia historically and in the present.

I have not done justice to all of the multiple strands of racial legal history that are interwoven through Canada's past. Because of the sheer immensity of the task, I have restricted my discussion to sources relating to the Inuit, First Nations, Blacks, Chinese Canadians, and whites. Aboriginal issues are often considered apart from those involving other visible minorities in writings on race, but I believe that their inclusion in this discussion permits a fuller, more rounded analysis of the multiple ways in which 'race' impinged upon the history of Canadian law. Due to constraints of time and space, I have not touched on matters relating to the Japanese, South Asian and eastern European communities, nor laws affecting Jews and French Canadians, all groups which were frequently 'racialized' throughout this period. All deserve extensive further treatment.

The research that supports the narratives that follow proves, beyond debate, that the Canadian legal system played a principal and dominant role in creating and preserving racial discrimination. Racism is a deeply embedded, archly defining characteristic of Canadian history. This is a legacy that has contributed in tenaciously rooted and fundamental ways to the current shape of Canadian society.

2

Race Definition Run Amuck:
'Slaying the Dragon of Eskimo Status' in *Re Eskimos*, 1939

At the time, the decision that the Supreme Court of Canada issued on 5 April 1939 was derisively labelled 'an absurd little mouse.' Diamond Jenness, a leading white Canadian anthropologist, coined the phrase, which he borrowed from the Latin poet Horace. In the original Latin, the sentiment was 'Parturiunt montes; nascetur ridiculus mus,' meaning: 'The mountains are in labour. From their womb will issue an absurd little mouse.' Such was Jenness's disdain for the ruling that he could find no better way to sum up his scorn for the reasoning of the eminent judges.[1]

The impetus for Jenness's sarcasm was the Supreme Court's *Re Eskimos* decision, in which the judges definitively held that 'Eskimos' were 'Indians' within the Canadian constitutional framework. A landmark judicial opinion on racial definition, the most noteworthy feature of the case is the breathtaking sense of certitude that accompanied the Court's pronouncement.[2]

The legal definition of 'Indian' had long occupied Canadian legislators and judges, who tinkered and fretted over the language in the successive enactments of the Indian Act. Now the perplexing question of whether the word 'Eskimo' was subsumed within the word 'Indian' was at last resolved. And Jenness was properly irked. As well he might have been, since he had testified as an expert witness that 'Eskimos' and 'Indians' were 'racially' distinct.

Diamond Jenness was, by all accounts, a fascinating and irrepressible scholar, possessed of a bitingly funny wit and apt to dispense disarmingly frank, droll comments on any range of intellectual issues. Born in Wellington, New Zealand, he obtained his academic degrees at the University of New Zealand and Oxford, where he trained in classics. Towards the end of his studies, he embraced the subject of anthropology and picked up a 'diploma' in the newly emerging discipline. In 1911, he began his fieldwork in the steamy jungles of Papua New Guinea, and then in 1913, looking for a change of pace, he hired on with Vilhaljmur Stefansson's Arctic expedition. Jenness spent an extraordinary period of three years travelling and living among the Arctic peoples, examining their culture, and recording his observations for posterity. In 1926, he was appointed chief anthropologist for the National Museum of Canada, where his steady stream of papers, articles, and books inspired others to christen him 'Canada's most distinguished anthropologist' and 'one of the world's most respected Eskimologists.'[3]

Testifying before the Supreme Court, Diamond Jenness had offered his opinion that both 'Eskimos' and Indians had 'a very strong infusion or percentage of Mongoloid blood,' and that there was a 'strong racial resemblance, a strong community of race between all the inhabitants' of North and South America. There were, however, sharp distinctions. In addition to different language, customs, and religion, the 'Eskimo' 'diverge[d] considerably from the other aborigines' in physical appearance. 'The Eskimo may well have inherited some of the same racial elements as the Indians,' noted Jenness, 'but may have deviated so greatly, owing to his peculiar environment, that he now forms a distinct sub-type.'[4]

Trying to clarify matters, one of the lawyers had asked Jenness whether the difference between the 'Eskimo' and the Pacific Coast Indians, for example, could be compared 'with the difference between the Englishman and the Hindu.' Although he was careful to qualify his answer, noting that it was 'hard to define the uniform Englishman or the uniform Hindu,' Jenness had no difficulty formulating a reply. A man with a genius for calculating his words, Jenness may have gazed steadily out at the bench of six white Supreme Court judges when he offered up this astute assessment: 'I should think the difference between the Eskimo and your Siwash [Indians] on the Pacific coast would be about as great as between, say, an Englishman and an Italian or Greek; possibly between an Englishman and certain Hindus.'[5]

This evidence must have given some pause. The judicial panel was composed of Sir Lyman Poore Duff, Patrick Kerwin, Oswald Smith Crocket, Henry Hague Davis, Albert Blellock Hudson, and Lawrence

Cannon. They were a bit out of their league in trying to assess the racial affinity between the 'Eskimo' and the 'Indian,' lacking any personal reference base from their own sense of the world. Now the litigants were attempting to lob the problem back onto more familiar territory. All of the judges knew instinctively what an 'Englishman' was. Some of them were such. Had they glanced down the bench, they would have found no one of Italian or Greek heritage. Nor was there anyone who professed the Hindu religion. With the exception of Lawrence Cannon, whose mother, Aurelie Dumoulin, was francophone, all of them came from a homogeneous English, Scottish, and Irish background.[6] What ran through their minds as they pondered the difference between their own ethnic heritage and that of a Hindu? Did they surreptitiously scan the faces of their colleagues, searching for skin pigmentation, skull shapes, nostril alignment, and eye characteristics? Just how distinct did they feel themselves, linguistically, socially, economically, culturally, and physically, from Hindus, Italians, and Greeks?

Diamond Jenness meant the judges to recognize intuitively the vast chasm between themselves and the specific groups he chose for comparison. He wanted the judges to draw a legal distinction between the 'Eskimo' and the 'Indian' on a racial basis:

The Eskimo of the Arctic and sub-Arctic coast-line diverges considerably from the other aborigines. His skin is lighter in colour, verging towards a yellowish white, his head longer and often keel-shaped, the face wider and flatter, the eyes more often and more markedly oblique, and the nasal aperture unusually small. The cranial capacity slightly exceeds that of the average European, whereas the capacity of Indian skulls is slightly less.[7]

The reference to skin colour alone ought to have scored a few points. The official Canadian census divided the 'races' into four: white, red, black, and yellow. The 'red' were the 'American Indian,' and the 'yellow' the 'Mongolian (Japanese and Chinese).' When Jenness characterized the skin colour of Arctic peoples as 'yellowish white,' it was a pigmentation resistant to any simple amalgamation within the four tidy boxes. Jenness summed up the anthropological data with confidence and certitude. The 'Eskimos' were 'a people distinct in physical appearance, in language, and in customs from all the Indian tribes of America.'[8] What possessed the Supreme Court justices in unanimous agreement to sweep aside the conclusions of Canada's pre-eminent 'Eskimologist,' and collapse the two 'racial' groups into one under the law?

THE LEGAL DEFINITION OF 'INDIAN'

The preliminary issue of how to define 'Indian' had posed a conundrum for years. The earliest statute on record, passed for Lower Canada in 1850, included four categories of individuals: 1 / persons of Indian blood, reputed to belong to the particular body or tribe, and their descendants; 2 / persons intermarried with any such Indians and residing among them, and their descendants; 3 / persons residing among such Indians, whose parents on either side were or are Indians, or entitled to be considered as such; and 4 / persons adopted in infancy by any such Indians, and residing in the village or upon the lands of such tribe or body of Indians, and their descendants.[9] This is a fulsome description by any reckoning, and it provides some glimpse into the racial understanding of the time. The concept of 'Indian blood' suggests that the legislators believed there was a biological difference between 'Indians' and other races. Yet the definition is not restricted to the 'bloodline' alone. Reputation is sufficient to garner Indian status. And for those who choose to reside among 'Indians,' intermarriage and adoption are also passable.

The history of race definition shows a remarkable mutability, with terms no sooner articulated than they come under pressure for displacement. One year after the first legislative formulation, the sweeping definition was pinched and squeezed a bit. Adoptees were stricken from the record, and status through intermarriage was reduced to women only, defying centuries of Aboriginal tradition.[10] The first federal statute passed in 1868 temporarily embraced this version of racial designation.[11] One year later, the central government began to whittle deeper into the constricting definition. In 1869, federal legislation stipulated that no person 'of less than one-fourth Indian blood' could share in any annuity monies, interest or rent owing to a band.[12]

By 1876, the Indian Act defined an 'Indian' as 'any male person of Indian blood reputed to belong to a particular band, any child of such person, and any woman who is or was lawfully married to such person.'[13] The unabashed male chauvinism clearly in the ascendancy here makes Indian status pivotal to one's relationship with an Indian man.[14] Other provisos began to erode the status of children born out of wedlock and individuals who had resided for more than five years in a foreign country.[15] For the first time, the concept of a 'half-breed' was given reification in a statute, but only to indicate that 'no half-breed in Manitoba who has shared in the distribution of half-breed lands shall be accounted an Indian.' Curiously, the act contained no definition for 'half-breed.'[16]

The 1876 Indian Act also contained the rather startling statement that the word 'person' did not include an 'Indian.'[17] The arrogance of the federal government knew no bounds in taking upon itself the unilateral authority to draw such definitions. In 1887, Parliament purported to make the superintendent general of Indian Affairs the complete arbiter of 'membership in an Indian band.'[18] There was no consultation with First Nations communities on definitional matters. Aboriginal spokespersons might have advised on the multiplicity of indigenous ways of defining identity, devised across centuries of political, economic, and spiritual experience. Aboriginal history and culture went dismissively unheeded in the development of the legal definitions.[19]

The provincial governments were inclined to use slightly different race formulations. None seemed prepared to embrace the decision taken by the federal government to exclude Aboriginal people from the definition of 'person.' Yet the phrasing of provincial legislators proved little more edifying than that of their federal counterparts. British Columbia, concerned to ensure that First Nations peoples were prohibited from voting in provincial elections, defined an 'Indian' in 1903 as 'any person of pure Indian blood, and any person of Indian extraction having his home upon or within the confines of an Indian reserve.'[20] In the 1922 statute that barred Indians from voting at public school meetings, the British Columbia legislature described an 'Indian' as 'any person who is either a full-blooded Indian, or any person with Indian blood in him who is living the Indian life on an Indian reserve.'[21] To clarify what was meant by the phrase 'Indian woman or girl' in another statute, the same legislators proclaimed it to encompass 'any woman or girl of pure Indian blood or Indian extraction.'[22]

The fascination with blood is no significant departure from the federal perspective, but the British Columbian legislators seem to have been particularly interested in the purity of that blood. The notion that race definition has something to do with residence on a reserve is also familiar, but the phrase 'living the Indian life' signifies a whole new point of definitional departure. Exactly what could the legislators have had in mind here? What thinking went through their collective mind as to the peculiarities and racially distinctive features of the Aboriginal 'lifestyle'? A 1950 statute authorizing an inquiry into 'Indian rights' defined 'Indian' somewhat more sweepingly as 'a person resident in this Province of the North American Indian race.'[23] Here the dozens of Aboriginal nations, from the interior Salish to the plateau Athapaskans to the coastal Haida, were simply conflated into one amorphous mix.[24]

Saskatchewan and Alberta were more content to follow the lead of the federal government, albeit in a relatively simplified formula. In their early twentieth-century statutes prohibiting First Nations peoples from voting, the two Prairie provinces defined 'Indians' as 'all persons of Indian blood' who 'belong or are reputed to belong' to a band.[25] Blood and reputation seem to mix in an uneasy blend of disparate clues and characteristics. Alberta took greater care with its designations of racial intermixture than the federal government. 'Métis' was defined in a 1938 statute as 'a person of mixed white and Indian blood' who was not 'an Indian or a non-treaty Indian as defined in The Indian Act.'[26] Obviously worried that this might be too encompassing, the Alberta legislature amended the definition in 1940 to stipulate that only individuals who had 'not less than one-quarter Indian blood' were meant.[27] The province of Ontario refrained from making any legislative pronouncements about the definition of 'Indian,' but was anxious to indicate that the word 'person' in the context of its game and fisheries legislation definitely encompassed an 'Indian,' whatever that might be construed to mean.[28]

The tangled legal definitions were surpassed only by the tangled evidence that often emerged before the courts. Despite the complexity of people's lives, the courts typically took a no-nonsense approach to sorting out the confusing welter of data. Rex v Tronson, a 1931 British Columbia case, involved a man named George Tronson who had been born on the 'Okanagan Indian Reserve.'[29] The evidence on Tronson's parentage is fragmentary, but he apparently had an 'Indian' grandmother, an 'Indian' uncle, and an 'Indian' wife. The court described his father as 'a white man' who was 'one of the old-time large cattle ranchers of the Okanagan District.' The evidence also indicated that Tronson had exercised certain racial privileges available only to whites – voting in provincial elections and filing for land grants not open to 'Indians.' Although Tronson was reputed to belong to the 'Head of the Lake Indian Reserve,' and had lived on and off the 'Okanagan Reserve' throughout his life, the superintendent general had not seen fit to list his name on the membership rolls, and the government challenged his right to reside there. First Nations witnesses expressed their agreement to having Tronson reside with his First Nations wife in their community. The court would have none of it. Tronson 'cannot in one breath say in effect that he is a white man, and in the next say that he is an Indian,' railed the judge. He 'cannot blow hot and blow cold.' Without further explanation of why, the judge concluded it was 'abundantly clear' that Tronson was not an 'Indian,' and ordered him off the 'reserve.'[30]

Some of the legal debates regarding racial definitions were provoked by alcohol prosecutions. Liquor had long functioned as a staple of the fur trade, a bartering tool used by unscrupulous white traders to inflate profits and crush Aboriginal resistance to European control.[31] The overwhelming problems of violence and social dislocation wrought by alcoholism caused successive provincial and federal governments to enact a series of statutes prohibiting the sale of liquor to First Nations peoples.[32] Court after court encountered defendants accused of selling alcohol to Indians who tried to avoid conviction by tangling up the authorities with questions of racial definition. Who could be certain that the individual to whom the accused had sold liquor was in fact an 'Indian'?

One of the most famous cases to rule on this was *Regina* v *Howson*, an 1894 decision of the Northwest Territories Supreme Court.[33] The accused had sold liquor to Henry Bear, described in the case as a 'half-breed' residing on the 'Mus-cow-equan reserve.' Bear's father was described as a 'Frenchman' and his mother 'an Indian.' Defending himself against conviction, the accused argued that Henry Bear was not 'an Indian of pure blood,' and as such did not count. That Bear's father was 'white' was another plank in the accused's argument, and his lawyer insisted that paternal racial inheritance ought to be definitive.

Turning to the Indian Act definition, 'any male person of Indian blood,' the Court held that this must mean 'any person with Indian blood in his veins, whether such blood is obtained from the father or mother.' Forcing the prosecution to prove purity of the bloodline, or patriarchal Aboriginal lineage, would be a stark impossibility in vast numbers of cases. Skin colour ought to play a distant second to the characteristics of language and 'lifestyle,' according to the Court: '[T]he alleged Indian might so far as his skin was concerned be as white as a Spaniard or an Italian or as many Englishmen or Frenchmen for that matter, and yet not understand a word of any European language, and be in thought, association and surrounding altogether Indian.' Throwing up its hands in despair over this problematic line-up of pigmentation, the Court eschewed skin colour, insisting that 'reputation' ought to prevail instead:

It is notorious that there are persons in those bands who are not full blooded Indians, who are possessed of Caucasian blood, in many of them the Caucasian blood very large predominates, but whose associations, habits, modes of life, and surroundings generally are essentially Indian, and the intention of the Legislature is to bring such persons within the provisions and object of the Act ...[34]

Directly on the heels of this decision, Parliament amended the definition of 'Indian' in the Indian Act as it related specifically to the liquor prohibition. 'In addition to its ordinary signification,' the meaning was extended to include 'any person, male or female, who is reputed to belong to a particular band, or who follows the Indian mode of life, or any child of such person.' The 'mode of life' phrase was lifted straight out of the *Howson* decision.[35]

The concept of an 'Indian mode of life' being rather nebulous, clarification awaited further judicial pronouncements. Affirmed in its definitional prowess, the Northwest Territories Supreme Court branched out even further in *The Queen* v *Mellon* in 1900.[36] The man to whom the liquor had been sold, Charles Pepin, conceded that he was a 'half-breed.' But he spoke English 'fluently,' 'never dressed like an Indian,' 'never wore moccasins,' and had been employed to move freight between Calgary and Edmonton for several summers. The judge took one look at the man and pronounced that he 'dress[ed] better than many ordinary white men.' In fact, he said, 'there is no indication whatsoever in his appearance, in his language, or in his general demeanour, that he does not belong to the better class of half-breeds.' With some despatch, the judge dismissed all charges, ruling that it was nonsense to convict a liquor seller who could not have known his customer was an 'Indian.' The Indian mode of life seems to be deftly fashioned from attire, linguistic facility, demeanour, and employment history.[37]

The Edmonton District Court had an opportunity to pursue this further in *The King* v *Pickard* in 1908.[38] In that case a shop-owner sold a bottle of liquor to an individual named Ward. The legal question was whether the shop-owner ought to have known or suspected that Ward, who resided at Stony Plain, was 'Indian.' In contrast with the absence of 'Indian' characteristics in *Mellon*, here there was a surfeit of pointers. There was the now familiar reference to moccasins, which Ward wore. The linguistic signs were definitive, for Ward 'could speak little or no English.' In fact, he purchased a calendar from the shop-owner by 'pointing' and 'asking in Cree.' Skin colour seems to have been equally determinative, with the judge noting that Ward was 'fairly dark.' Without further elaboration, he concluded that the man looked 'a good deal like an Indian.' The judge's certainty is belied in part by a shrewd tactic employed by the defence lawyer, who brought into court that day a number of individuals whose race was difficult to discern from appearance. 'It is true that there are many half breeds that look like Indians,' the judge admitted,

and the counsel for the accused brought into Court many for that purpose, but to my mind, this makes my contention all the stronger that Pickard, knowing how difficult it was to distinguish the Indian from the half-breed, should have been on his guard and refused the liquor till he found out whether they were Indians or half breeds.[39]

In what seems the most far-fetched variable to date, racial status seems also to have been ascertained by the company Ward kept. The judge reconstructed in depth the racial designation of Ward's companion, a man named Bonenose, who had accompanied him into the store: he also wore moccasins; he, too, bought a calendar by asking for it in Cree; he 'was rather darker than Ward' and was 'very much like an Indian, in appearance, even more so than Ward.' Since the shop-owner was not charged with selling liquor to Bonenose, there was no need to delve into his racial attributes. It was solely his value as companion to Ward that was under appraisal. One's racial status seems to turn here in part on the racial designation of one's friends and acquaintances. In the end, the court concluded Ward was indeed 'Indian,' and that the shop-owner had unlawfully sold him alcohol.[40]

Once having determined the meaning of an 'Indian mode of life,' it behooved the court to consider when someone could be held to have 'abandoned the Indian mode of life.' *Rex* v *Verdi* offered the Halifax County Court the opportunity to dwell on this fine point at length in 1914.[41] Mr Lambkin was born of mixed heritage, and the court pronounced his father 'French,' and using the most racist appellation available, his mother a 'squaw.'[42] Raised in a Mi'kmaq community in New Brunswick, Lambkin left his reserve and moved to Nova Scotia. Although he conceded that he 'lived amongst Indians in Nova Scotia,' and had spent short periods on a Nova Scotia 'Indian reserve,' for the previous ten years he had been living away. He was employed in farming and 'travelling for a living,' and testified that he lived 'like a white man' and paid municipal taxes. The court was poised to classify him as non-Indian until it determined that Lambkin had voted at the last election of a Mi'kmaq chief. This tipped the balance the other way, and the liquor seller was convicted.[43]

The complexity of defining what is meant by 'Indian' is baldly obvious. The intricate ways in which people group themselves and live their lives presents a host of enigmatic possibilities. To try to capture such a dizzying array of human combination with a watertight definitional framework is destined for disaster, no matter how earnest or multitextured the effort. The multiplicity of legislative formulae, inconsistent between governments and over time, is reflective of the insoluble difficulties. What is most remarkable is the apparent readiness of Canadian authorities to use the law to draw racial boundaries, cutting through the morass, in case after case, to concretize distinction and to create a hierarchy of racial designation.

SEPARATE RECOGNITION OF 'ESKIMO' STATUS

The origin of the word 'Eskimo' is often attributed to an Algonquian term (from Plains Cree), 'a'yaskime'w,' meaning 'eater of raw meat.' Others claim that the term was derived from a completely different Montagnais word, 'ayassime'w,' meaning 'those who speak a strange language,' which was disseminated through Spanish-speaking Basque whalers as 'esquimaos.' Europeans who tried to capture the word in writing fashioned a multiplicity of possible spellings, ranging from 'Eskeimoes' through 'Iskemay,' to 'Usquemaw' and 'Huskemaw.'[44] None of these terms bore the slightest resemblance to the name the Aboriginal people of the Arctic had given themselves: 'Inuit' (meaning 'the people') and 'Inuk' (for the singular 'person') in their Inuktitut language.[45]

Various European spellings of 'Eskimo,' 'Esquimau,' and 'Eskimaux' made their way into Canadian statutes during the first half of the twentieth century. In 1919, the Quebec legislature enacted an exemption for 'Eskimos' under the fish and game laws.[46] The Northwest Territories passed an ordinance in 1930 to protect 'Eskimo ruins' from unauthorized excavation.[47] The federal government used the term 'Esquimau' when it disqualified the group from voting in 1934.[48] The Northwest Territories barred sales of liquor and prohibited drinking for 'Eskimos,' or 'any person, male or female, who follows the Eskimo mode of life,' as well as 'any child of such person.'[49] An 1882 Newfoundland statute baldly conflated two terms when it prohibited the sale and delivery of intoxicating liquors 'to any Esquimaux Indian.'[50]

The federal government never enacted an Eskimo Act to be the counterpart of the Indian Act, and seemed to be of two minds whether to include 'Eskimos' under the latter. In 1924, Parliament debated whether it should bring 'Eskimos' into the Indian Act, and resolved not to do so.[51] Instead, the legislators specified that the superintendent general of Indian Affairs was to have 'charge of Eskimo affairs.' Speaking for the federal government at the time, the Liberal Minister of the Interior, Charles Stewart, pronounced definitively on the racial status of 'Eskimos.' 'No,' he posited, 'Eskimos are not Indians. While they may be of a somewhat similar character, they are not looked upon as Indians in the real sense of the word.'[52]

Six years later, 'Eskimo affairs' was brusquely separated from 'Indian affairs' once more, with Stewart advising that it was administratively more efficient to transfer the responsibility back to the Department of the Interior. The move occasioned further debate in the House of Commons over racial designation. All seemed to agree that 'Eskimos' were not 'Indians,' but opinions divided on the variables of distinction. Challenged to delineate the differences, Charles Stewart itemized three: 'appearance,' 'language,' and 'habits.' Sir George Halsey Perley, Conservative Opposition MP for the Quebec riding of Argenteuil, remained sceptical. 'The minister says that a person could tell the difference between them by their appearance, but the minister himself is not going to decide which of these thousands of people are Eskimos and which are Indians,' he fussed. 'I do not see how the minister can draft a definition which will hold water in all cases.' The response from Charles Stewart was dismissive and peremptory: 'There is no doubt that the racial distinction between even the most northern Indian and the Eskimo is very marked. I do not think anyone would have a great deal of difficulty in distinguishing one from the other.'[53]

Endeavouring to get to the root of the matter, Hugh Guthrie, Conservative MP from an Ontario riding near Guelph, asked his parliamentary colleagues a simple question. If 'Eskimos' are not Indians, 'what race are they?' This provoked some hesitation. Some of the legislators ventured that 'Eskimos' were originally 'Mongolian.' Others jocularly adverted to substantial sexual intermingling in the North by speculating that 'some people say they are Scotch.'[54]

The issue of racial purity seems to flutter at the margins of debates over racial designation. Most anthropologists conceded that racial intermixture flourished virtually everywhere. The Arctic was perhaps something of an exception, as Diamond Jenness pointed out, in that 'two grim sentinels, Cold and Silence, guarded the retreats of the Eskimos,' repelling most European adventurers who tried to 'storm their gates.' Relying on the male lexicon of his generation, Jenness pronounced it 'a land where the climate demanded that men be men.' By the late nineteenth century, however, intrepid whalers from Britain, Holland, Spain, France, Russia, and the United States showed they had the stamina to 'breach the walls.'[55] Tracking the changes the whalers wrought to 'Eskimo' culture, Jenness discovered that the commanders, officers, and crews of the whaling ships routinely 'frequented with local Eskimo women.' The racial blending was dramatic: 'In the veins of increasing numbers [of Eskimos]

coursed European blood that modified their forms and their features.'
On the heels of the whalers came fur-traders, police, missionaries, and
anthropologists, many of whom continued to contribute to the cross-
fertilization.[56]

In the eastern Arctic, for centuries the Inuit had 'jostled and intermarried' with neighbour Algonkian peoples. On the west coast, there was
also interbreeding between Inuit and some Africans, Asians, and
Polynesians.[57] What is more, anthropologists had discovered in France
an ancient skull that they believed came from 'Eskimo' stock. Another
find of an alleged 'Eskimo skull' at Obercassel, near Bonn in Germany,
created more consternation. 'Theoretically, it would seem not impossible
that the generalized Eskimo type established itself somewhere in the Old
World towards the close of the Glacial period, and that some of its
representatives penetrated to western Europe,' explained Jenness.[58] But
if 'Eskimos' had migrated to France and Germany, what were the implications for the purity of racial theory? Racial blending made mincemeat
of the already imponderable task of quantifying and delineating racial
characteristics. The most bizarre thing was how few seemed to recognize
that, before one could articulate racial definitions, one had to be certain
exactly whom one was measuring.

None of this seemed to bother Canadian legislators, who tossed about
racial terminology, without even a semblance of reflection. Statutes drew
multiple distinctions between 'Indians' and 'Eskimos' without clarifying
what the difference encompassed.[59] In fact, few of the enactments attempted to define their terms at all. When the legislators tried their hand
at the task, they came up with circular depictions. The Newfoundland
legislature defined 'Esquimaux' in 1911 to mean 'native residents of the
Coast of Labrador who are commonly known as Esquimaux.'[60] The
Northwest Territories defined 'Eskimo' under the game law as including
'a half-breed of Eskimo blood leading the life of an Eskimo.'[61] The
notions of 'blood' and 'lifestyle' are reminiscent of earlier pronouncements relating to 'Indians.' The Indian Act of 1951 made reference to 'the
race of aborigines commonly referred to as Eskimos.' Here the federal
Parliament seemingly contemplated the group as a distinct 'race' but
remained helpless to delineate the individuals within it, except by using
the term others customarily applied to them.[62]

INUIT HISTORY

The Inuit had inhabited the northern reaches of Canada for centuries by
the time European explorers first recorded contact. Aboriginal peoples

migrated across the Arctic in waves, from the 'Palaeo-Eskimo' group (around 2000 B.C.) to the 'Pre-Dorset' (until 800 B.C.) to the 'Dorset' (until A.D. 1000) and 'Thule' (until A.D. 1600), spreading west from Alaska to Greenland.[63] Scattered across the coastal areas of a vast geographic panorama, the hallmark of the Inuit became their common language, Inuktitut, spoken in a number of distinct dialects.[64] Despite the harsh climate, the Inuit subsisted on a rich bounty of sea mammals, caribou, musk oxen, polar bears, birds, and fish.

Diamond Jenness, who claimed an intimacy with Inuit culture atypical of most whites, picturesquely recorded the expertise of the indigenous hunters. He described how they tracked the 'breathing holes of the seals in the ice that mantles the winter sea,' how they approached their quarry 'within harpoon range' as the seals 'drowsed in the sun on the surface of the ice,' how they drove 'whole herds of caribou into snares or ambushes, or into lakes and rivers where the hunters could pursue the swimming animals in their kayaks and slaughter them with their lances.' He marvelled at how the Inuit seemed to thrive in the face of 'howling blizzards,' recounting the example of an Inuk woman, 'crouched down in the lee of her sled, during a winter migration,' who withdrew 'her naked baby from under her fur coat,' and calmly changed 'its tiny caribou-fur diaper, although the temperature was 30 degrees fahrenheit below zero and a thirty-mile-an-hour gale was whipping the snow against our faces.'[65]

The first contact between Europeans and Inuit came when the Norse skirted the coast of Labrador around A.D. 1000, and fought with a mysterious people they called 'Skraelings.' The Norse perished or retreated, and it would take another five hundred years before European cod-fishing boats returned. Moravian missionaries established permanent religious settlements in the eighteenth century, and the romantic search for the Northwest Passage to the Orient brought renewed attention from explorers in the nineteenth. Shortly thereafter, commercial whalers began to arrive from Europe and the United States, often 'wintering over' with Inuit communities in the Arctic. When the whaling industry began to erode after 1910, due to overfishing and the collapse of the market for baleen, fur traders took up the slack.[66] The demand for Arctic fox fur intensified in the 1920s, and white traders set up additional outposts to expand a booming business. According to Jenness, a number of regions began to 'ooze prosperity,' permitting the Inuit to exchange igloos for 'wall-board and dressed lumber,' skin bedding for 'brass and iron spring beds,' and skin umiaks for 'highly powered motor schooners.' The Canadian government's desire to assert sovereignty over the North also sparked an accelerating white presence, with police posts dropped sporadically throughout the Arctic wherever Inuit populations seemed to congregate.[67]

The impact of white intrusion into the Arctic was predictable. Commercial trapping began to displace subsistence hunting, with the concomitant loss in traditional knowledge. The Inuit found it increasingly difficult to return to a lifestyle of wilderness survival without the aid of firearms, manufactured clothes, boats, tools, and southern foods such as flour, sugar, butter, jam, canned fruit, and tea. Nomadic band settlement patterns gave way to dispersed hunting camps, and then concentrated villages populated by both Inuit and whites. Alterations in migration patterns put accelerating pressure on the wildlife, which began to thin out. Influenza, measles, tuberculosis, syphilis, and alcoholism, all introduced by Europeans, took a dramatic toll, often carrying off up to one-third of local Inuit populations. A formerly egalitarian society began to experience an increase in the differentiation of functions, wealth, and status. When the financial crash of the 1930s smashed the bottom out of fur prices, severe economic dislocation ensued.[68]

THE IMMEDIATE DISPUTE THAT SPARKED THE REFERENCE

Although the majority of the Inuit in Canada lived along the Arctic and sub-Arctic coasts and islands of the Northwest Territories and the Yukon, a smaller population settled on lands that eventually became part of Quebec. A geographic expanse initially referred to as the Ungava Peninsula, this area later came to be known as 'Nouveau Québec,' and then 'Nunavik.' Inuit spokespersons still register surprise as they describe how their traditional lands seemed to change hands at the stroke of a pen, without any consultation with the Native inhabitants. Zebedee Nungak writes:

If I go back to 1670, when King Charles issued a proclamation naming not only this vast geographic area, indeed all the area where the rivers flow into Hudson and James Bay as Rupert's Land, I can describe that as the first political earthquake that happened. This act gave a political status to a geographic area that did not involve the consent or involvement of the people who lived there. It was known as Rupert's Land for the next two hundred years. In 1870, three years after the Dominion of Canada was proclaimed as a country, this geographic area was transferred ... to the Dominion of Canada ... gaining the label of the Northwest Territories ... This was the second political earthquake that took place without the involvement or even the information of our forefathers. Then in 1912, another event took place, where the Parliament of Canada extended the bounda- ries of what was then Quebec to the geographic area that it is now. The third political earthquake that happened in the time of my great-grandfather was when he woke up one morning in 1912, a newly minted citizen of La Belle province – not ever having been informed of such.[69]

In 1870, Britain transferred all of the Indian and Inuit lands purport- edly under the jurisdiction of the Hudson's Bay Company to the new dominion of Canada, which named the area 'the Northwest Territories.' In 1898, the Canadian Parliament unilaterally transferred to Quebec jurisdiction over the lands west of the coast of Labrador, north to Church- ill River, over the divide to James Bay, and north to the Eastmain River, in an effort to ensure political equity between Quebec and Ontario. In 1912, Robert Borden's Conservative government conveyed the Ungava district to Quebec, along with an area from the Eastmain north to Hudson Straits, a transaction measuring approximately half a million square miles of land.[70]

The transfers were more notional than anything else, since there was little government presence or intervention in the area. The first Quebec government functionary did not arrive until the 1960s. In the 1920s, the federal government assigned its Eastern Arctic Patrol to include the Ungava Inuit in its annual police and health inspections.[71] The police officers making these rounds were authorized to distribute food, clothing, and medicines 'to needy Eskimos' in dire circumstances, although the federal government was quick to disclaim any legal respon- sibility for the Inuit on the grounds that they were really citizens of Quebec. Generosity not being a trademark of government largesse, the cost of such relief was minimal and nothing came of the interjuris- dictional uncertainty until an economic upheaval brought matters to a head.[72]

During the depression of the 1930s, the Inuit in the Ungava area of northern Quebec were some of the hardest hit. Of the estimated 6,000 Inuit in Canada, official counts placed 1,589 in the Ungava district of Quebec, and 715 on the coast of Labrador.[73] The inhabitants of the south shore of Hudson Strait and the east coast of Hudson Bay had already experienced major cultural disruption. The proselytization of Anglican missionaries in Little Whale River, Fort Chimo (now Kuujjuaq), and Poste-de-la-Baleine, often in competition with Roman Catholic priests, greatly undermined the Native shamanism, a traditional source of spir-

Map of Northern Quebec and Labrador, Provincial Boundaries/Aboriginal Distribution.

ituality and cultural identity. The establishment of outposts run by the Hudson's Bay Company and its intermittent competitor, Revillon Frères, drew concentrations of population into the nearest trading posts, inspiring infectious epidemics. Proximity to trading posts meant a growing dependence on manufactured tools, cloth, firearms, steel traps, metal, lumber, tobacco, and tea. In 1930, the average price of a white arctic fox fur fell from around $39 to $17, and then to $12.[74]

Returning to a completely traditional lifestyle was out of the question, since the caribou herds had disappeared and marine game resources were increasingly scarce. A particularly severe winter in 1934–5 brought starvation in its wake. Diamond Jenness, ever vivid in his depictions, wrote agonizingly of 'lonely Eskimo trappers' who died of starvation while their tents 'overflowed with furs.' 'From Coronation Gulf to the Magnetic Pole,' Jenness declared, 'the Eskimos had lost their bearings and were drifting through unfamiliar waters without a compass or a friendly star.'[75]

Stepping in to forestall starvation, the federal government targeted the relief to Inuit living mainly along the shores of Hudson Bay and Hudson Strait. Parsimonious bureaucrats selected dried buffalo meat for distribution, aware that 'the Eskimos are not particularly fond of it and consequently are not likely to ask for it unless they are in real need.' Another problem was the fat content. Buffalo meat did not contain enough fat to be much use in the Arctic climate, but federal officials hoped that the Inuit might supplement it with 'seal or walrus meat [to] provide a very nourishing diet.' Secure in the knowledge that the relief bill was thrifty and pared to the bone, the Department of the Interior set forth to make the recalcitrant government of Quebec pick up its fair share.[76]

In early 1929, the two governments struck a deal that authorized the federal government to provide minimal subsistence to the Inuit in Quebec, with the province agreeing to reimburse for expenses incurred. Between 1929 and 1932, Quebec forwarded a total of $54,660.16. Diamond Jenness wise-cracked that, if this 'dreadful amount' was actually broken down, it came to the grand total of 'an exorbitant sum of nearly $9 per head.' The politicians in Quebec were less impressed by the meagreness of the sum. In 1932, not to be outdone on penny-pinching, the newly elected Taschereau government in Quebec announced that this would be the final transfer of funds.[77]

The true legal responsibility for the Inuit, argued Quebec, lay with the federal government under the British North America Act, 1867.[78] Section 91(24) of that constitutional statute allocated jurisdiction over 'Indians and Lands Reserved for the Indians' to the federal government. Insisting that the Inuit were 'Indians,' the Taschereau government declared its intention to wash its hands of provincial responsibility. In an effort to settle the stand-off, the federal government resolved to seek a legal opinion from the Supreme Court of Canada.

THE REFERENCE POWER AND THE LAUNCHING OF THE CASE

Since the creation of the Supreme Court in 1875, the federal government had been empowered to 'refer' questions to the Court for resolution. The 'reference' power, as it became known, permitted the government to obtain advisory rulings on important matters of law or fact pre-emptively, before a concrete lawsuit had arisen. Consequently the federal government put the question squarely to the Court: 'Does the term "Indians" ... include "Eskimos"?'[79]

In reference cases, the Supreme Court is specifically authorized to direct that all 'interested parties' be heard, and it can appoint counsel to represent interests otherwise unrepresented.[80] In this pivotal proceeding, no one seems to have thought that representatives of the Inuit or First Nations communities constituted 'interested parties.' The only groups represented at the hearing were the federal government and the province of Quebec.[81] Had the Court taken proper care to solicit the perspectives of Aboriginal peoples, it might have sought input from any number of First Nations with whom it had negotiated treaties in the past. The collective view of the Inuit might have been somewhat more difficult to discern, since there had as yet been no treaty-making, and there were no hierarchically situated 'chiefs' or associations to approach among the scattered camps and outposts in the North. However, there were many elders, shamans, and other leaders whose ideas would have been invaluable to the proceeding.[82]

Even some contemporary observers must have felt that restricting the carriage of the case to government lawyers was a grave mistake. Diamond Jenness was contemptuous of the role played by governments in Inuit affairs. 'Bureaucracy in inaction,' he christened it, 'steering without a compass,' 'shamelessly passing the buck.' He accused the federal government of a wickedly transient perspective, one moment donning 'the mantle of the witch of Endor' to 'exorcise the spectre of foreign interference' with an 'incantation and a majestic wave' of the flag, and then settling 'back into her armchair again to forget the region and its Eskimos.' The cabinet members and their advisers couldn't be bothered to 'raise their eyes from their long mahogany table' to contemplate the real issues unsettling the Arctic.[83]

In its selection of counsel, the federal government demonstrated how utterly remote it was from the North. Undeniably, there were few prominent barristers living in northern regions or practising in Inuit territory. However, Ottawa selected an individual who seems to have had no connections to the North or Aboriginal affairs whatsoever. A white man, James McGregor Stewart, KC, was born in 1889 in Pictou, Nova Scotia, and studied law at Dalhousie University. Called to the Nova Scotia bar in 1914, he became a senior partner in the Halifax firm of Stewart, Smith, MacKeen, Covert, and Rogers. Stewart was well linked to diverse busi-

James McGregor Stewart, CBE, QC, DCL, of Stewart, Smith, Mackeen,
Covert and Rogers, 1930s.

ness interests, and sat on the boards of companies such as Maritime Steel,
National Sea Products, Mersey Paper, Canada Cement, Sun Life Assurance, Montreal Trust, the Royal Bank, and Nova Scotia Light and Power.
A widely respected leader at the bar, in 1941 he would be elected president of the Canadian Bar Association. A Conservative by politics and a
Presbyterian by religion, Stewart was a 'bookish' man who listed his sole
recreational interest as reading.[84]

The Quebec government retained Auguste Desilets, QC, a white man
whose professional background was not dissimilar from Stewart's. Desilets
was born in Trois-Rivières, Quebec, in 1887, the son of Alfred Desilets
and Georgine (Decoteau) Desilets. A lifelong bachelor, he made his home
in Grand'Mère, Quebec, where he practised law with Desilets, Crête &
Lévesque. Desilets was as well-connected to the corporate world as was
Stewart, boasting directorships with Siscoe Gold Mines, Siscoe Metals,
Suzorite Company, Banque Canadienne Nationale, Shawinigan Water &

Auguste Desilets, QC, of Desilets, Crête & Lévesque, Grand-Mère, Quebec.

Power, Mudiac Gold Mines, and Bazooka Mines. Bâtonnier of the Quebec Bar from 1933 to 1935, Desilets would go on to play a fundamental role in the reform of Quebec law in the late 1930s and 1940s. He also maintained a lifelong passion for historical research, and published a history of Grand'Mère in 1933.[85]

No one seems to have been in any great hurry to conclude the case. Although the federal government initiated the reference on 2 April 1935, it took the parties until the spring of 1937 to prepare their cases. They produced voluminous exhibit books, filled with extracts from the notes of geographers, explorers, anthropologists, cartographers, historians, missionaries, compilers of dictionaries, and government papers. Each side laced their documentation with beautiful reproductions of scores of hand-scripted historical maps.[86]

The Quebec lawyers seem to have had more fun with their submissions. Quebec's sixty-four-page factum is inspired in its choice of words and reads like a tightly structured oratorical summation. Even though Auguste Desilets was writing in his second language, his factum is replete with dramatically posed rhetorical questions, and filled with metaphorical imagery that cajoles and entices the reader. Tongue in cheek, while evoking terms of great respect for scholarly research, the Quebec factum 'humbly' pokes a bit of fun at the failure of science's 'most brilliant adepts' to pronounce definitively on racial theory, while 'a student in Logics would not be embarrassed to draw the conclusion.'[87] Where anthropologists take sides against them, the Quebec factum dissects their writing line by line, characterizing them as 'distinguished opponents – if they really are opponents,' and twisting their words until it can be argued that even the recalcitrant scholars are actually 'flirting with our thesis.' The federal government's star witness, Dr Jenness, is not spared either. 'We would like to state candidly that he seems to us to be more than half won to our cause,' they hazard. Mocking their opponents, the Quebec lawyers assert that the Dominion government has only one 'solid (?) authority in the lexicological field.' 'We have geographers,' crows the Quebec brief, 'we have cartographers,' 'we have travelers and explorers,' 'we have historians.' Flourishing a list of more than 140 sources that equate 'Eskimos' and 'Indians,' the factum avows it to be 'a chain where no link is missing.'[88]

The federal government's factum is considerably more flat-footed. Content to quote at length from a host of historical documents and other primary sources, James Stewart's passive prose is buried beneath the endless citations. There is little evidence of flamboyant locution or energetic vocabulary, as the brief repetitively resorts to the leaden, if traditional lawyerly, phrases 'it is submitted,' 'hereinafter set out,' 'for such other reasons as may be urged,' 'the inferences to be drawn,' and 'it is to be observed.' Not one attempt at impassioned exhortation lurks throughout the twenty-eight pages of sluggish narration. James Stewart's relatively uninspired factum seems to have been an uncanny reflection of his own doubts about the case. At the very outset, Stewart advised his client that he was inclined 'more and more to the view that the Courts will find that the term "Indian" … includes the "Eskimos".' Predicting that Quebec would 'win the day,' Stewart even questioned the wisdom of pursuing the file. 'On the whole,' he wrote to the Department of Justice, 'I would seriously consider whether it is wise to incur the expense incidental to bringing this matter before the Court.' Evidently, the federal government disagreed with its external counsel's misgivings, and instructed him to push forward.[89]

The case itself took only four days of oral argument, but the pedestrian pace of scheduling meant that the submissions stretched across nine months, from June 1937 to February 1938. James Stewart began by conceding that Christopher Columbus had made something of a 'mistake' in classifying North American Aboriginal peoples as 'Indians.' Nevertheless, the federal lawyers claimed that 'Eskimos' had never been confused under the rubric of such terminology. Tracing back to the Royal Proclamation of 1763, which referred to 'Indians' as 'the several nations or tribes of Indians with whom We are connected and who live under Our protection,' Stewart argued that the 'Eskimo' were never 'organized or commonly spoken of as "nations or tribes".' Nor had they ever been conceived of as allies of Great Britain or France. The Crown had never entered into any treaties with them, nor had it designated any 'reserves' in their name. The Instructions issued to Governor Guy Carleton in 1775 set forth a 'comprehensive plan for the management of Indian Affairs,' and listed all of the 'Indian tribes' living in North America without any reference to the 'Eskimo.' An 1845 report of Commissioners of the Province of Canada on the Affairs of Indians in Canada likewise failed even to mention 'any tribe or settlement that can include Eskimo.'[90]

Stewart cited the 1842 edition of the *Encyclopaedia Britannica*, describing it as a 'standard reference work' available to legislators in 1867, when the Constitution was enacted. The entry on 'Esquimaux' defined the Inuit as 'a people of North America, inhabiting the vast tract of land known by the name of *Labrador*. They differ very considerably, both in aspect and manners, from the other American nations, and agree in most respects with the inhabitants of West Greenland.' Advancing a veritable avalanche of memoirs and journals from explorers, traders, and missionaries published between 1733 and 1861, Stewart insisted that all knowledgeable sources drew 'a sharp distinction' between the two groups, and the words 'Indian' and 'Eskimo' conjured up distinctly different images.[91]

In their efforts to prove that 'Indians' included 'Eskimos,' the Quebec lawyers were placed off-kilter a bit at the outset by distinctions between French and English terminology for First Nations peoples. The French language contained multiple references to 'sauvages,' a word frequently used in preference to 'aborigènes,' 'indigènes,' or 'Indiens.' Explaining the discrete francophone terminology, Auguste Desilets advised the court that, from the first contact between the First Nations and the French,

'Frenchmen were wont to use the word "sauvages" to designate the Indians.' Quebec counsel noted that the term appeared in the French translations of *Hansard* of the House of Commons and in the French texts of federal statutes, but hastened to emphasize that the term did not imply 'that the *sauvages* are barbarous, ferocious or savage.' The word was simply chosen 'in opposition to the appellation of civilized people.' One is left wondering whether anyone thought such explication actually bettered the situation.[92]

Auguste Desilets was able to point to a host of historically important occasions when the words 'sauvages' or 'Indiens' had been used in connection with 'Eskimos.' Champlain wrote of 'une nation de sauvages … qui s'appellent Exquimaux.' Documents compiled by Jesuit and Récollet priests referred to 'Sauvages nommez Esquimaux.' In the eighteenth century, the governor and intendant of New France, as well as the King of France, described the Inuit as 'Sauvages Esquimaux.' French geographers referred to the Esquimaux as 'les tribus indiennes.' The *Dictionnaire Larousse Complèt* of 1932 defined 'Esquimaux' as 'Indiens qui habitent le nord du Canada depuis la baie d'Ungava jusqua'à l'Alaska.'[93]

Begging to differ from the definition in the *Encyclopaedia Britannica* cited by Stewart, Desilets quoted from the *Encyclopedia Americana*, which defined 'Eskimos' as 'an Indian nation of North America,' and *Webster's American Dictionary*, which defined 'Esquimaux' as 'a nation of Indians inhabiting the north-western parts of North America.' Desilets was able to point to numerous occasions when the federal government's own census publications, annual reports of the Department of Indian Affairs, and atlases issued by the Department of the Interior included 'Eskimos' in tables and population graphs regarding Indians.[94]

Quebec counsel slyly pointed out that even Mrs Eileen Jenness, the 'wife of the well known ethnologist Diamond Jenness,' had published a 1933 anthropological treatise titled *Indian Tribes of Canada*, in which she 'designated the Eskimos as one of the seven groups of Indian Tribes of Canada.'[95] This was skilful sleight of hand indeed, citing Diamond Jenness's wife to contradict him. Had the court taken the trouble to review the actual treatise, it would have become apparent that the Jenness partners were not actually at odds. Eileen Jenness, a white woman, may have devoted a portion of her book on 'Indians' to 'Eskimos,' but she went to great pains to note the differences:

All the native tribes of Canada (with the exception of the Eskimo) … though they often understand not a word of one another's language (there are eleven different languages and many distinct dialects), are one and all called 'Indians' ... The Eskimo differ from the Indians in many respects; probably they inherit some of the same racial blood, but they should be regarded as a special type, that has changed considerably owing to the severe climate of the Arctic and the harsh diet its inhabitants endure.

These little known Eskimo, who lived from Coronation Gulf to the Magnetic Pole, were but one group of the people who inhabited the Arctic coastline, at intervals, all the way from the Alaskan boundary to the southern edge of the Labrador Peninsula. All spoke dialects of a common language, and though each group had, with time and isolation, developed slightly different manners and customs, they were originally one people, and probably the last of the American aborigines to reach this continent from the Siberian shore. So different were they from Indians in appearance, dress and manner of life, that many scientists believe they belonged to a distinct race.[96]

Undeterred, Auguste Desilets cursorily dismissed these passages of Eileen Jenness's text as 'one or two mild reservations' respecting the equation of 'Eskimos' and 'Indians.' He was prepared to concede that 'Eskimos' differed from other 'aborigines' in their clothing, food, fuel, winter dwellings, and hunting practices. However, if one scrutinized the 'main characters of their life,' Desilets insisted, it was clear that 'Eskimos' were exactly like Indians. Both groups exhibited 'the same dependence upon fish and game for subsistence, the same lack of any organization for agricultural or industrial production, the same absence of exchange of wealth by way of money, the same poverty, the same ignorance, the same unhygienic mode of existence.'[97]

Counsel's acute ethnocentricity is obvious, as centuries of Inuit expertise regarding survival in the Arctic is reduced to 'ignorance,' and the entire sweep of northern communities dismissed as 'unhygienic.' The argument also introduces several novel characteristics of racial definition. Economic factors have surfaced here, as occupational mode of life, system of monetary exchange, and even the indicia of wealth begin to take precedence.

Auguste Desilets postulated that the court was really faced with a binary proposition. Evoking the vivid spectre of the trenches during the First World War , he insisted that 'Eskimos' had to be slotted into one of two racial groupings:

The definition of Indians as including all aborigines is only logical. Otherwise, how would the Eskimos be classified? They would be neither Indians nor white people. They would not belong to the category of natives inhabiting America at the time of its discovery nor to the group of new-comers who settled in America since. In a figurative way, the Eskimos would be in the no man's land so much spoken of during the Great War.[98]

Desilets's either–or proposition – Indian or white – is a rather simplistic rendering of the contemporary anthropological understanding of race. Professor Otto Klineberg, a white Canadian who had studied under the tutelage of the famous white American anthropologist Franz Boas, and gone on to attain a prestigious appointment at Columbia University in New York, published a book titled *Race Differences* in 1935. In this, he asserted that 'the universal interest in racial problems has so far not been accompanied by anything like universal agreement as to the meaning of race.'[99] The word 'race' originally denoted 'family,' and was applied only to noble or important dynasties – the race of the Bourbons and the race of David, for example. The term underwent 'a semantic journey of extraordinary proportions' when it expanded during the nineteenth century to categorize large groups of people who were not related directly through kinship, but who shared specified traits.[100] Early classifications, based almost exclusively on skin colour, had enumerated four separate races: *Europaeus albus, Asiaticus luridus, Americanus rufus,* and *Afer niger*.[101] Professor Klineberg noted that later scholars (most of them cited in the voluminous exhibits produced before the Supreme Court) had bumped up the number of distinct races considerably higher:

Blumenbach's widely used classification changed the terminology slightly and added one more race: his groups were the Caucasian, Mongolian, Ethiopian, American, Malayan. Nott and Gliddon kept these five under the names of European, Asiatic, Negro, American and Malay, and added to them the Australian and the Arctic. On the other hand, F. Muller, using hair texture as a criteria, reached a classification which naturally gave results entirely different. [...] Deniker ... used a combination of hair texture, skin color, eye color and shape of nose to arrive at no less than seventeen main races and twenty-nine sub-races.[102]

The doctrines of natural selection and 'survival of the fittest,' promulgated by Charles Darwin and Herbert Spencer, laid the intellectual framework for an intensified stratification of racial typology. Those who claimed descent from western European stock fancied themselves representative of the highest plane of 'civilization,' well above the more 'primitive' racial stages of 'simple savagery' and 'barbarism.' 'Civilization' itself was regaled as a racial trait, inherited by Anglo-Saxons and other 'advanced' white races.[103]

With so much at stake in racial classification, the emerging social sciences endeavoured to bring precise empirical data to bear on the question. Dismissive of the early racial theorists, who catalogued and classified largely on the basis of anecdotal commentary from world travellers, the new scholars showed themselves anxious to demonstrate the superiority of 'scientific method.'[104] Physicians, biologists, psychologists, and ethnologists conducted scores of studies on specific racial criteria. The deluge of researchers combing sites as remote as the polar North ultimately provoked the Inuit to coin the joke that 'the ideal family in the arctic consists of a husband and wife, four children and an anthropologist.'[105] They measured head length, head width, face height, nose height, nose width, facial angle, stature, eye colour, hair colour and form, thickness of lips, and beard characteristics.[106] Debates erupted over gradations of skin colour. The original idea that the 'American race' was properly designated as 'red' gave way to scholarly critique, with some conjecturing the real shade was 'bronze,' 'coppery,' 'burnt coffee,' or 'cinnamon,' while others continued to hold that 'there is a tinge of red in some tribes amid the almost universal brown colour of the Amerind races.'[107] One British scientist, anxious to bring the respectability of mathematics to bear on the problem, created an 'index of nigrescence,' a curious algebraic equation that purported to measure the darkness of skin.[108] Even the most astute researchers blanched a bit when one anthropologist postulated that there were no fewer than thirty-four shades of skin colour differentiating the races.[109]

Then there was always the question of whether the skin being measured had been properly cleaned, with some fretting that smoke and dirt could sully the accuracy of findings.[110] Others struggled over precisely where on a subject's body skin colour should be tested. Data had traditionally been based on facial colouration, but more reflective minds suggested that researchers should examine a spot better protected from the elements. H.L. Shapiro, a white anthropologist whose writings were cited by counsel in *Re Eskimos*, tried to compare the 'Alaskan Eskimo' with the 'Chipewyan Indians of central Canada' in a 1928 study, and thoughtfully recorded 'the skin colours of the inner side of the upper arm' as well as 'the cheek.'[111] Classifications of hair type were also broken out in surprisingly picayune ways: 'Lophokomoi (woolly haired, like "pepper corns"); Eriokomoi (woolly haired, closely embedded); Euthykomoi (straight-haired); and Euplokomoi (curly-haired).'[112]

Skull measurement was touted as a quintessential characteristic, since scientists noted that 'the chief difference between man and the lower animals is in the development of the reasoning faculties.' The logical construct, they concluded, was that intelligence was correlated with brain size. 'As the reasoning powers become of greater value (as man evolves),' noted one expert, 'and the power of the jaw of less importance, we can see that the sides of the skull would tend to bulge out and the front of the skull tend to become less prominent.'[113] The celebrated, white Philadelphia physician Samuel George Morton, whose writings were also cited by counsel in Re Eskimos, collected thousands of human skulls between 1820 and 1851. Dr Morton filled the cranial cavity with sifted white mustard seed, poured the seed back into a graduated cylinder, and read the skull's volume in cubic inches, on the theory that the cranial cavity provided a faithful measure of the brain it once contained. Published in lavish, beautifully illustrated volumes and touted as irrefutable 'hard' data, Morton's findings ascertained that the 'races' descended in mental worth in the following order: 1 / 'whites' ranked into subgroups, in descending order, of 'Teutons and Anglo-Saxons,' 'Jews,' and 'Hindus'; 2 / 'Indians'; and 3 / 'blacks.'[114]

The industrious measurers of cranial characteristics soon ran into problems when their theories ran afoul of their data. Shaken researchers discovered that 'Eskimos, Lapps, Malays, Tartars and several other peoples of the Mongolian type' had larger cranial capacity than 'the most civilized people of Europe.'[115] In fact, Klineberg advised that 'the Eskimo have on the average larger heads than the Parisiens ...' Instead of reordering the racial hierarchy, anthropologists circumvented the problem, claiming that 'brain size and intelligence' might not correlate 'at the upper end of the scale,' because 'some inferior groups have large brains.'[116] Others speculated that 'almost all the peculiarities of the [Eskimo] skull' might hearken back 'to the masticatory apparatus,' which had seen extraordinary development as a result of their 'flesh and fish diet and the energetic uses to which they put their teeth.' A steady diet of chewy, raw seal and whale had purportedly distorted the facial size and shape with enormous chewing muscle.[117]

Comparable problems developed with the measurement of the arms. The famous white French scientist Paul Broca surveyed the ratio of the size of the radium bone in the lower arm to the humerus bone in the upper arm, on the theory that a long forearm was 'more characteristic of the ape.' His studies showed 'blacks' to have relatively longer forearms than 'whites,' but 'Eskimos and Australian Aborigines' to have shorter forearms than either. Some suggested that, at least in the case of the

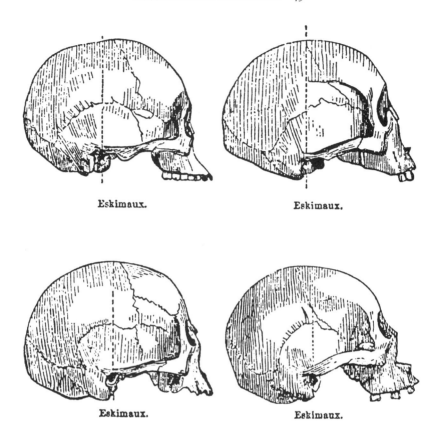

Eskimaux.   Eskimaux.

Eskimaux.   Eskimaux.

Dr Samuel George Morton's drawings of 'well-characterized' Eskimo skulls, allegedly found near Davis Inlet, off the coast of Greenland, and at Icy Cape. Sketch produced as exhibit for the Government of Canada in the *Re Eskimos* case, 1939.

'Eskimos,' the frigid Arctic weather might have stunted arm growth. But Broca simply concluded that 'it seems difficult for me to continue to say that elongation of the forearm is a character of degradation or inferiority.'[118]

Blood, although commonly adverted to in the terminology of statutes and courts, seems to have come under research scrutiny less frequently. Professor Ruggles Gates was one of a few exceptions, and his work was produced in evidence before the Supreme Court of Canada. The white scientist had journeyed to the Mackenzie Delta to test the blood of the

Inuit for a reaction to 'agglutinogen B,' an agglutinogen more dominant in eastern Asia than in Europe. An inconclusive 50 per cent of his admittedly small sample reacted, although Diamond Jenness pointed out that 'since pure-blood Indians appear to possess neither this agglutinogen, nor agglutinogen A, its presence in nearly pure-blood Eskimo, if substantiated, would suggest a separate origin for the two peoples.'[119] Renowned white anthropologist Kaj Birket-Smith, known as the 'doyen of Danish Eskimologists,' was another authority whose writing was produced for the judges in *Re Eskimos*. Birket-Smith took the position that racial classification through blood testing was 'far from clear.' He reported that, although 'some authorities contend that the "O"-[blood] type is the most original among the Eskimos,' the 'Eskimo and some Indians as e.g. the Blackfoot and Shoshone' showed a high percentage of type A blood, while 'Eskimos' in East Greenland had a fairly high reading for type B blood. Both 'Eskimos and Indians' also showed 'a high frequency of M and a corresponding low of N.'[120] Blood groupings fell out of favour with some researchers after numerous studies failed to show differences between the serological classification of 'white' and 'American negro' blood, and no discernible differences in 'the degree of relationship between the blood of various races and that of the anthropoid apes.'[121]

Some researchers maintained that racial characteristics could differ by gender. Birket-Smith confided that 'Eskimo women' had 'a more Mongoloid appearance than the men,' attributing this strange finding to 'the fact that they are fuller in the face and more frequently show the peculiar formation of the eyelid fold which gives the eye its oblique appearance.' Nor did he stop with the eyes. 'The breasts of quite young women are often conical,' recounted Birket-Smith, 'but soon begin to hang and before long resemble a pair of long, loose bags.' One wonders what comparison base he was using when he drew this particular assessment.[122]

Gender distinctions enthralled the scientific gaze, as white male anatomists, zoologists, and physiologists alike sketched, poked, and prodded the buttocks, pelvises, and genitalia of African women to prove their assorted theories about the evolutionary ladder of racial development. Saartje Baartman, popularly known as the 'Hottentot Venus,' was a Khoisan woman lured from South Africa to Europe, where she was put on display before spellbound crowds who ogled her body during the early nineteenth century. In a horrifying example of anthropological excess, the white French naturalist Georges Cuvier dissected her body after her untimely death from smallpox or syphilis, and presented her anus and genitalia to the French Academy of Medicine.[123]

With all the testing, measuring, weighing, and plotting of graphs, no one seemed to recognize that it was virtually impossible to ascertain whether the subject under scrutiny was 'racially pure.' The reluctance to admit the obvious is puzzling, since the scientists themselves allowed that the concept of 'racial purity' was 'anthropological nonsense.'[124] 'It is many thousands of years too late, not only for Europe and Europeans, but for other parts of the world as well,' concluded Professor Klineberg. 'There are no longer any pure races to be kept pure.'[125] Even the Inuit, who must have been as 'protected' from racial mixture as any group on the continent, were not undiluted.[126] 'The Eskimo peoples ... appear to mix readily with neighbouring peoples,' conceded researchers; 'hence we may assume that the more remote eastern Eskimo were purer than the western, at any rate until the Danish settlers arrived.'[127] When one recalls that the first Norse arrivals date from the tenth century, 'purity' becomes an elusive artefact indeed.

The 'discovery' of 'blonde Eskimos' scattered from the Bering Strait to the Atlantic set anthropological tongues to wagging in earnest until scientists discovered that some Inuit women washed their hair 'in stale urine' with a pronounced bleaching effect, while the red beards of the men were attributable to the daily drinking of 'scalding blood soup.' 'Blue eyes' were ultimately diagnosed as 'pathological,' brought on by 'frequent attacks of snow-blindness.' Despite the corrective revelations, experts such as Birket-Smith were at pains to stress that certain 'Eskimos' had skins with 'somewhat lighter pigmentation than usual,' chiding those who expressed surprise with the reminder that 'comparatively blonde individuals are far from unknown in Central and Northern Asia.'[128]

At the other end of the spectrum, Diamond Jenness located some 'rarer types' among the Copper Inuit who reminded him of 'Melanesians,' a 'Negroid population' from New Guinea and the islands to the northeast of Australia.[129] This caused others to speculate that 'some strain of Negroid blood' might be present in certain Inuit communities.[130] Nor was there any widespread agreement on how to classify individuals of mixed heritage. Did the least trace of African origins make someone 'Black'? What of individuals who could 'pass' between racial lines, 'Indians' who could 'pass for white,' and 'whites' who could 'pass for Indian'?[131] Even the most knowledgeable of physical anthropologists had to confirm that there is 'no homogeneity within each race' and 'no sharp

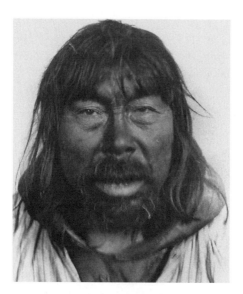

Portrait of Pijausuittuq, Inuk from Southampton Island, 1926. (Photograph provided by Avataq Cultural Institute.)

Portrait of Lucassie Uvua, Inuk from Kangiqsujuaq, 1926. (Photograph provided by Avataq Cultural Institute.)

Portrait of Qajakjuaq, Inuk from Southampton Island, 1926. (Photograph provided by Avataq Cultural Institute.)

Portrait of unidentified Inuk, Sanikiluaq, 1927. (Photograph provided by Avataq Cultural Institute.)

line between one race and another.'[132] Given that within 15 generations, one individual could trace back 32,000 direct ancestors, this is not surprising.[133]

With all the uncertainty over classification and the indisputable evidence of sexual activity across groups, one can be forgiven for wondering why no one ventured to whisper 'the Emperor has no clothes.' To the contrary, prominent 'Eskimologists' piled up report after report on the defining characteristics of the 'Eskimo race.' Diamond Jenness, one of the foremost authorities, concluded:

Their nearly white skin, lighter than that of most Indians, their dark-brown eyes with frequent epicanthic fold, their black nearly straight hair, broad, high cheekbones, and rather stocky build attach them most closely to the peoples of northeastern Asia. Yet they present some striking peculiarities, the most noticeable being the extremely narrow nose and, except in the Bering Sea region, the disharmony in face and head; for while the face is as broad or broader than the head, the head itself is relatively long. Other peculiarities are the unusually high skull capacity, the frequency of scaphecephaly, the strong development of the lower jaw and of the temporal muscles that govern its movement, the size of the teeth, the relative shortness of the forearms and of the legs below the knees, and the smallness of hands and feet. The stature fluctuates between medium and low, with a tendency to lowness; but it becomes higher in Alaska, where the head is also rounder and the nose less narrow.[134]

On the racial origin and affinities of the Inuit, Jenness professed that, although the experts had proffered multiple theories, the verdict was still out:

Some scholars, following Boas and Steensby, consider them but an offshoot of the Indians. According to this theory their original home was the inland country around Great Bear and Great Slave lakes, whence for some reason they moved out to the coast, developed a peculiar littoral culture, and spread east and west over the shores of the Arctic and sub-Arctic. Bogoras, on the other hand, places their earlier home on the Siberian side of Bering Strait, and believes that they did not enter America until about a thousand years ago. Archaeology appears rather to support the latter theory, but with the date of entry into America pushed back another two or three thousand years.[135]

According to Kaj Birket-Smith, the Inuit represented a complex racial puzzle.

Portrait of unidentified Inuit children, Kangirsukallak, 1930s–40s.
(Photograph provided by Avataq Cultural Institute.)

The racial position of the Eskimos then may be approximately expressed thus, that the face is Asiatic Mongoloid and the brain-case of the 'Lagoa Santa-type,' while the exceedingly narrow nose places them outside both categories. Their blood group may or may not place them on the same level of development as the American Indian. Not much more can be said until the science of genetics has advanced farther than at present.[136]

Even today, when modern scholars have the benefit of advanced genetic knowledge, researchers remain divided over the classification of the Inuit.[137]

The lawyers on both sides of the case were aware that the 'scientific' verdict was still out. Stewart advised the court that anthropological experts entertained 'the widest differences of opinion' as to 'the origins and racial affinities of the Eskimo.' Desilets agreed that the Supreme Court of Canada ought to be cautious about arbitrating definitively on the matter, 'especially at a time when [scientists'] investigations do not seem to be concluded.' Yet counsel forged ahead with their own summations. Stewart urged the bench to draw a legal distinction between 'Eskimos' and 'Indians,' stressing that no one could deny that, hundreds of years before Confederation, 'the Eskimo had evolved a distinct civilization and that in physical characteristics, culture, customs, habits and language he forms a group highly differentiated from any of the other aborigines.' Desilets claimed that 'Eskimos' were Indians 'by their blood' and 'by definition,' and that 'the majority of ethnologists' were 'not in the least adverse to Eskimos being Indians.' 'In a zoological sense,' he pronounced, 'our eastern Eskimos of the Province of Quebec' can reasonably be believed to be Indians, 'in bones, flesh and blood.'[138]

THE SUPREME COURT'S CONCLUSION

Getting out the final decision took the Supreme Court another fourteen months, further stretching out an already time-encrusted lawsuit. An impatient Diamond Jenness mockingly suggested that the Court must have needed 'the fullness of time' to review the evidence of the witnesses 'long and patiently.'[139] He may have been particularly taken aback to discover that the fullness of time had not endeared the judiciary to his testimony. In fact, none of the anthropological exhibits was cited in the Court's decision. The judges based their judgment upon sources that predated Confederation, on the theory that they should focus on 'what was in the minds of those responsible for the drafting of the Resolutions leading to the passing of the *British North America Act*.'[140]

The key factors, in the Court's reasoning, were the following:

1 / an English House of Commons committee, investigating the affairs of the Hudson's Bay Company in 1856–7, placed the 'esquimaux' under the general designation 'Indians' in census documents and a map;
2 / the officials of the Hudson's Bay Company regarded the 'Eskimo' as 'an Indian tribe';
3 / General Murray, the governor of Quebec, classified the 'Eskquimaux' as 'Savages' in 1762;
4 / proclamations from governmental officials, journals from explorers,

and reports from missionaries, clergymen, cartographers, and geographers that made reference to the term 'Esquimaux Indians';

5 / terminology from the dictionaries cited by Quebec counsel, that defined the 'Esquimaux' as 'Indians';

6 / correspondence between Prime Minister Sir John A. Macdonald and Sir Hector Langevin, in 1879, in which the federal government promised to provide money for the relief of the 'Eskimo on the north shore of the St. Lawrence.'

Item 6 resulted in the expenditure of $2,000 to aid the 'Montagnais and Eskimaux Indians' in the Lower St Lawrence in 1880, prompting the judges to conclude that

these two Fathers of Confederation always understood that the English word 'Indians' was to be construed and translated as 'sauvages' which admittedly did include *all* the aborigines living within the territories in North America under British authority, whether Imperial, Colonial, or subject to the administrative powers of the Hudson Bay Company.[141]

A rather dry and laboured judgment, the only passage that seemed somewhat at odds with the overall tone was a lengthy quotation from the colourful report of a Newfoundland bishop who had travelled in Labrador in the mid-nineteenth century. The legal relevance of the document seems to have been the fact that the bishop used the words 'Esquimaux' and 'Indians' interchangeably. However, Chief Justice Lyman Poore Duff recited detailed extracts, which spoke of punishingly high seas, heavy rains, and blowing winds. Apart from his dismay over the climate, the things that stood out in the bishop's mind were the changing dress of the Inuit women (previously garbed in sealskin cloaks, but now 'rejoic[ing] in European dresses, shawls and gowns of many colours') and the Inuit ability to 'compress into the smallest possible compass' when they were corralled together in little wooden huts, placing the poor bishop 'into painfully close proximity.' The most fascinating comment reflects the bishop's evident self-satisfaction with the results of racial mixing. 'In the race of mixed blood, or Anglo-Esquimaux,' wrote the chief justice, quoting from the bishop, 'the Indian characteristics very much disappear, and the children are both lively and comely.' The complacent racial superiority is outdone only by the ultimate ruling, in which six white judges conclude without hesitation that 'Eskimos' are 'Indians' according to law.[142]

Why did the Court completely disregard the avalanche of anthropological studies cited in argument? Were the judges dismayed by the complexity and ambiguity of the 'racial' data before the Court? Were 'Eskimos' and 'Indians' so obviously on a different social and cultural plane from other Canadian groups that there was no need to call up 'scientific' data before equating them? Had the judges earnestly contemplated the difference between an Englishman, an Italian, a Greek, and 'certain Hindus' and measured the distinctions insufficient to warrant separate legal categorization? Had they rejected the comparison altogether?

In designating 'Eskimos' to be 'Indians,' the Supreme Court of Canada relied on nineteenth-century pronouncements and opinions promulgated exclusively by persons of European heritage. Colonial representatives of the imperial British power led the pack, supplemented by the compilers of U.S. dictionaries. No persons of Aboriginal heritage were consulted or permitted to speak to an issue that would have an enormous impact on their status in law. Indeed, no one seems to have thought their omission worthy of comment.

The correspondence between Prime Minister Macdonald and Sir Hector Langevin in 1879 was arguably a decisive factor. That the white, federal leaders who drafted the constitution were prepared to shoulder the costs of administering relief to Inuit people residing in Quebec seems to have resonated with the bench, for the question posed in the instant reference concerned precisely the same issue. The allocation of the costs of distributing relief supplies appears to have been the engine driving the coupling of Inuit and 'Indian' peoples. The federal government had been prepared to act unilaterally in the nineteenth century. Quebec counsel had adverted to the indisputably 'vaster resources' currently available to the federal government for bailing out indigent Aboriginal peoples. As a matter of practical politics, the Court may have felt it wiser to equate 'Eskimos' with 'Indians' under section 91(24). Alternatively, the judges may simply have been persuaded to side with Quebec after comparing the legal arguments produced by both sides. Quebec counsel had indisputably outlitigated their opponents.[143]

In the end, the judges shrank from entangling themselves with the morass of variables that had been used in the legal classification of race in the past. Legal decisions had been based on an amazing array of factors: language, customs and habits, mode of life, manner of dress, diet, demeanour, occupation, wealth, voting history, religion, blood, skin colour, head shape, hair texture, thickness of lips, beard characteristics, facial features, teeth size, eye shape and colour, nasal aperture, cranial capacity, stature, intermarriage, adoption, legitimacy at birth, place of residence, reputation, and the racial designation of one's companions, to offer just a few examples. Perhaps wisely, the Supreme Court made no attempt to sort through this profuse and rambling list of variables, or to offer guidance on matters of racial designation for the future. It simply declared that, as a matter of Canadian constitutional law, the Inuit were 'Indians' because the framers of the British North America Act had regarded them as such.

The federal government was initially alarmed over the outcome of the case, particularly since it feared that the Quebec government might try to seek reimbursement for funds expended on the Inuit prior to the reference. The Ottawa bureaucrats consulted extensively over whether to appeal the decision to the Privy Council in England, but the looming horizons of the Second World War put an end to the prospect. Government officials remained divided over whether it was useful to integrate the Inuit into the Indian Act or pass an entirely separate Eskimo Act. In the end, they did neither.[144] The policy of benign neglect continued until well past the mid-century mark, when the prospect of exploitable natural resources and Cold War defence strategy peaked interest once more, generating renewed intervention and expenditures, from both the federal and Quebec governments.[145] From the benefit of hindsight, the designation of federal jurisdiction may have proven salutary for the Inuit. Negotiations regarding sovereignty and land claims, which would ultimately produce the new Inuit territory of Nunavut in 1999, for example, could be contracted primarily with one political regime, rather than a multiplicity of provincial and territorial powers. Even Diamond Jenness would eventually come to accept the outcome of *Re Eskimos*, if not the reasoning. Characteristically claiming the final word, Diamond Jenness quipped that the powers that be had 'unweariedly fought the dragon of Eskimo status,' but the 'august body' of the Supreme Court of Canada had decided the question 'once and for all.'[146]

3

'Bedecked in Gaudy Feathers': The Legal Prohibition of Aboriginal Dance: Wanduta's Trial, Manitoba, 1903

Rapid City, Manitoba, was swaggering with civic pride over its annual fair, scheduled for 17 July 1902. Flag waving, ceremonial cannon shots, town meetings, camaraderie, and social mingling had been a hallmark of the annual July festivities since the days of the earliest white settlement in the small southwestern Manitoba town. Located on the Minnedosa River about 150 miles west of Winnipeg and 24 miles north of Brandon, Rapid City was first settled by white homesteaders in 1872. Named in 1878 for the abundance of rapids on the Saskatchewan River, the town was populated by white farmers transplanted from the United States and Eastern Canada. Having weathered the setback of losing the main railway line to Brandon, the town established a school in 1882, a church in 1884, and a Masonic Hall in 1888. It held its first annual agricultural exhibition in 1888.[1]

In 1897, the local newspaper ran a promotional insert boasting about Rapid City's four general stores, three hotels, three hardware stores, four livery barns, three blacksmith shops, four churches, two barbershops, a harness shop, a tinsmith shop, a drug store, a millinery shop, a jewellery store, a bakery, a banking house, and four fraternal organizations. As was the case in all prairie towns during this period, population ebbed and flowed, from a small handful of families in 1872 to a high of 1,200 in 1881, steadying at 564 people in 1902.[2]

The opening up of the Canadian prairies to intensive agriculture was an operation fraught with difficulty. The combination of uncertain weather, pests, and lack of resources to invest in agricultural technology

Rapid City, aerial view, *circa* 1895.

plagued all those who sought to make a success of farming. After several decades of mixed results, the summers of 1901 and 1902 brought forth some of the largest grain crops in history, ushering Manitoba into an unprecedented farming boom and an uncontested spot on the world's agricultural map.[3]

So there was much to celebrate in July 1902, with land prices low, grain prices high, and rapidly expanding rail and shipping routes to carry the crops to ever-widening destinations. The annual July fair was an event that provoked great excitement and anticipation in Rapid City, as crowds of up to 2,000 people swelled the city boundaries. A ritual of summer, a conspicuous gathering that celebrated display, consumption, and competition, the fair was one of the great events of the season. For farming families weary of their back-breaking labours, the July festival brought temporary relief from the day-to-day schedule, simultaneously acknowledging and renewing the life-stream of the community.[4]

One of the central organizers of the 1902 celebration was Malcolm Turriff, the clerk of the municipality and a local businessman. Originally from Little Métis, Quebec, Turriff had been one of the first white men to settle in Rapid City in the 1870s. In 1881, he married a white woman, Ellen Henry, who had travelled from Ontario to Manitoba with her family in a Red River cart. The couple built a log house in the expanding town, and as Ellen birthed a succession of nine children, Turriff tried his hand at a series of businesses – owner of a meat market, grain elevator, and the Rapid City Lime Kiln; town auctioneer; issuer of marriage licences; river-ferry operator; licence inspector; insurance agent; and the first real estate agent in the entire Little Saskatchewan Valley. Turriff brought the first significant capital into Rapid City, and used it to establish businesses, invest in local real estate, and lend to other townspeople. He played the role of 'pioneer town-builder,' donating time and energy to community undertakings.[5]

THE DAKOTA GRASS DANCE

Annual holidays such as the July fair highlighted racial distinctions, constituting one of the few occasions when white settlers came face to face with large groups of Aboriginal people.[6] At the July fair in Rapid City, whites competed in the farming events, and then stood back to watch in stark fascination as the First Nations danced to traditional drumbeats. One of Malcolm Turriff's responsibilities in setting up the annual fair was to arrange for some Aboriginal presence. He contacted

Chief James Antoine, of the Dakota Nation from the nearby Oak River Territory (known today as Sioux Valley), and requested that a contingent of Dakota dancers perform at the fair.[7]

Chief James Antoine, who was fondly recalled by old-time townsfolk as 'a most amazing personality,' maintained an almost legendary stature within the local white community until his death in 1917.[8] The Oak River Dakota had been attending the Rapid City annual fairs since the late 1870s.[9] About a dozen of the Dakota in traditional ceremonial dress would engage in Aboriginal dancing and drumming before the enthralled throngs of white fair-goers. White old-timer Ellerton Hopper, reminiscing about the spectacle more than seventy years later, recalled:

One of the highlights of that time for me was to be on hand to witness the Indian Pow-wow. This event usually took place on a grassy plot of land adjacent to the drugstore … The Indians, about a dozen in number, were part of the Sioux tribe, under the leadership of Chief Antoine, an outstanding and attractive individual. I always managed somehow to get a closeup view of him and his warriors, to me an exciting event.[10]

In 1901, the Aboriginal participation in the town's first Citizens' Day parade had been particularly memorable, according to the whites who observed it:

The Town's first Citizens' Day in 1901 saw townspeople, country cousins, and the Sioux tribe led by Chief Antoine, all join together to celebrate. A lengthy parade followed by Indian games, pow-wow demonstration, pony races, baseball, football, trapshooting and other events were part of the excitement. In particular, the parade offered to the public an impressive display of Indian costumes and Indian braves decked out in warpaint and feathers as they depicted scalp hunters returning from a successful hunt. Another highlight was the Indian dance which was proclaimed a sight worth waiting for and rarely seen again. Throughout the exciting celebration, the Rapid City Brass Band provided instrumental entertainment.[11]

The fascination of whites with First Nations traditions was pervasive and long-standing. European Canadians were transfixed with what they understood to be the warlike and violent aspects of Aboriginal culture. What appeared to whites to be doomed societies, on the edge of extinction, garnered an almost guilty and voyeuristic attention. The newspaper reporters who wrote about the dances at stampedes sensationalized their copy. Ascribing racially laden words such as 'savage' and 'barbarous' to the dances, they also demonized the dancers with highly judgmental adjectives such as 'revolting,' 'gaudy,' 'weird,' 'torturous,' 'cruel,' and 'frightful.'[12] The conflicting emotions such performances could evoke in whites were captured by an account in the *Lethbridge Herald*, describing the First Nations presence at the Lethbridge Exhibition in 1911: 'There in full war paint, with totem poles waving in mid air, bedecked in gaudy feathers, and amid the merry music of jingling bells, beating drums and singing braves, the parade presented a sight that was at the same time awe-inspiring and amusing.'[13] Shrewd white businessmen identified First Nations dancers as a 'drawing card,' a premiere attraction to be marketed for the benefit of local fairs and exhibitions.[14]

All of the Dakota from Oak River apparently attended the July fair in 1902, expanding the crowd of visitors to the town by between 200 and 300 people.[15] The Dakota intermingled with the white fair-goers a bit, and the younger members of both races participated heartily in a variety of sports and athletic competitions. Shortly before the event commenced, the Dakota advised the July fair organizers that they had chosen the Grass Dance for the exhibition. Ever the entrepreneur, Malcolm Turriff charged fifteen cents per person to see the Dakota dance. He contracted to pay the Dakota with groceries and other foodstuffs along with a portion of the take at the admission gate. The net revenue from the admission fare is unknown, but the Dakota, who received only a portion of the proceeds, were paid with ten bags of flour, four pounds of tea, five pounds of sugar, six dollars' worth of meat and beef, one dollar's worth of tobacco, and $43.60 in cash.[16]

The Grass Dance lasted three days, beginning on 17 July 1902, the day of the fair, and continuing two full days after the fair was over, through 19 July. Although the Grass Dance was renowned for its 'gorgeous costumes,' 'beauty,' and 'picturesqueness,' no one at the time attempted to describe the ceremonial dancing or its relationship to the people. Indeed, First Nations spokespersons warn against the futility of giving 'a simplistic rendition of ceremonies.' 'It is impossible to capture the essence of traditional ways in a moment or on paper. It is a lifelong commitment to learn these ways,' observes Patricia Monture-Angus.[17]

THE 'CRIMINALIZATION' OF ABORIGINAL DANCE

Most of the white onlookers who paid to watch the Grass Dance seem to have been blissfully unaware that the dance they were observing would

Pow Wow at Virden, *circa* 1886.

The Stoney performing a Grass Dance, at Joe Peacemaker's camp near Morley, Manitoba, 13 October 1917.

ultimately result in the prosecution of criminal charges. The Canadian government first began to pass criminal laws prohibiting the ceremonial dancing of the First Nations in 1884, when the Indian Act outlawed the Potlatch and Tamanawas dances native to the west coast.[18] The prohibition was extended in 1895 to encompass all festivals, dances, and ceremonies that involved the giving away of money or goods, or the wounding of humans or animals. The federal legislation, which would remain substantially intact until 1951, was remarkably comprehensive. The statute proclaimed it an indictable offence for 'Indians' or 'other persons' to engage in, or assist in celebrating, or encourage anyone else to celebrate, either directly or indirectly:

any Indian festival, dance, or other ceremony of which the giving away or paying or giving back of money, goods or articles of any sort forms a part, or is a feature, whether such gift of money, goods or articles takes place before, at, or after the celebration of the same, and every Indian or other person who engages or assists in any celebration or dance of which the wounding or mutilation of the dead or living body of any human being or animal forms a part or is a feature ... [19]

Violations carried a prison sentence ranging anywhere from a minimum term of two months to a maximum term of six months.

It was a matter of common agreement that horses and blankets were exchanged between participants at the Rapid City Grass Dance.[20] This potentially brought all of the Oak River Dakota dancers in conflict with the statute. Malcolm Turriff and the other organizers of the July fair, and possibly even the paying onlookers, were also at risk for 'encouraging' the celebration of an illegal dance contrary to the Indian Act, section 114. In addition, section 112 of the act made it a separate crime to 'incite any Indian to commit any indictable offence.' If convicted of 'inciting' the Oak River Dakota to commit the indictable crime of dancing, the fair organizers would have been liable to an even longer term of imprisonment, up to a maximum of five years.[21] The legislation contained a specific exemption, which provided that 'nothing in this section shall be construed to prevent the holding of any agricultural show or exhibition or the giving of prizes for exhibits thereat.' This proviso had never been considered by judicial authorities, and it was unclear exactly what was exempted.[22]

Most Aboriginal dancing was not done at agricultural shows or exhibitions, of course, but within the private sanctity of First Nations communities as part of the traditional heritage and religion. The Dakota were particularly renowned for the large number, frequency, and variety of their dances. Written records indicate that the Dakota, who settled at Oak River in 1875, had been conducting Give-Away Dances regularly since 1879. The Oak River Dakota made continuing and substantial efforts to preserve their Aboriginal culture, and dancing was pivotal to these efforts. Members of the community had constructed a sizeable round house to serve as a meeting place for the spiritual and ceremonial dances that played a central role in maintaining relationship and kinship ties.[23] Oak River remained something of a traditional stronghold, and many of its members resisted Christianity long after those in the neighbouring communities converted.[24] Ceremonial practices were inextricably linked with the social, political, and economic life-blood of the community, and dances underscored the core of Aboriginal resistance to cultural assimilation.[25]

Some Aboriginal leaders were reluctant to display their ceremonial dances before crowds of white viewers. They were understandably resentful of the role they were expected to play before crowds of curious onlookers, most of them woefully ignorant of the spiritual and symbolic meaning of the dances.[26] Others took great delight in performing, using the opportunity to inject sarcastic humour into the dances to satirize the behaviour and proclivities of whites. Still others achieved international fame touring with 'wild west' shows to great box-office acclaim.[27]

The dancing at prairie exhibitions was not, as many white spectators mistakenly thought, an example of 'quaint primitivism,' but sophisticated manifestations of centuries-old Aboriginal culture. White anthropologists who tried to document the ceremonial rites were at pains to indicate that the 'dances and feast' were 'not amusements,' that they had 'object and meaning,' and were celebrated year after year 'under a belief that neglect will be punished by the Great Spirit by means of disease, want, or the attacks of enemies.' The dances entailed large gatherings of Aboriginal peoples, and provided invaluable opportunities for the elders to pass on their memories of the buffalo hunts, the intertribal wars, the Rebellion of 1885, the signing of the treaties, indigenous songs, legends, and ceremonies.[28]

The distribution of goods that occurred during some of the ceremonies reflected an Aboriginal world view which took the accumulation of material goods, motivated by pure acquisitiveness, as deeply immoral. It was also part of a sophisticated affirmation of kinship ties, which enhanced the prestige and status of those households with surplus material wealth. Give-Away Dances functioned as a cooperative pooling of labour and goods within an interdependent community. Certain of the traditional practices also required the participants to fast from food and water and to undergo spiritual purification through various means of self-mortification, such as body piercing and the like. On occasion, the sacrifice, offering and consumption of designated animals was also utilized. These forms of religious expression were used to demonstrate self-sacrifice, courage, and conviction, and to assist in the development of spiritual power.[29]

It was Canada's white prime minister Sir John A. Macdonald who first introduced the legislation to make Aboriginal dancing a crime. On 24 March 1884, the Conservative prime minister rose in the House of Commons to advance the racist argument that the 'Indian festival' known as the 'Potlatch' was a 'debauchery of the worst kind.' The white Liberal leader of the Opposition, Edward Blake, likewise agreed that the dance was an 'insane exuberance of generosity,' but questioned the harshness of a minimum two-month term of imprisonment. Prime Minister Macdonald bowed to Blake's demands and advised Parliament that he would delete the minimum penalty from the bill.[30]

Not all of the legislators were convinced that the dances ought to be made the subject of criminal prosecution. William Johnston Almon, a Nova Scotia member of the Senate, tried to explain the ethnocentric nature of the bill:

Supposing a savage were to go to England, and visit Buckingham Palace, and see a number of Highlanders dancing a sword dance in the garb of old Gaul, would he not say that that was as crazy as any potla[t]ch he had ever seen? We can imagine him saying 'you people put down our potla[t]ches, yet you dance in petticoats over naked swords.'[31]

Almon had been appointed to the Senate in 1879, after a distinguished career as a Halifax doctor, chair of the Dalhousie Faculty of Medicine, and Conservative politician. A white man who was reputed to be 'one of the kindest-hearted men in the Senate,' he was famous for backing renegade causes.[32] Almon's vivid imagery failed to sway the gathered politicians, who voted the prohibition into force in April 1884. Prime Minister Macdonald seems to have forgotten about his promise to delete the minimum penalty from the bill, and the enactment that passed retained the mandatory two-month provision.[33]

Advocates of the anti-dancing law soon discovered that the initial wording of the prohibition was problematic in two ways. First, the white judges who were asked to apply it complained that it was too vague to enforce. In 1889, Sir Matthew Begbie, Chief Justice of British Columbia, disparaged the legislation for its ambiguity and the failure to include any statutory definition of the dances involved.[34] Second, the original geographic scope of the law was quite narrow, with the only two dances listed restricted to the west coast. Proponents for change wished to see the reach of the provision extended nationwide, and government officials were convinced that an amendment was required to effect this.[35]

In 1895, another white prime minister, Mackenzie Bowell, introduced a bill designed to address both deficiencies. The new legislation attacked the dances not by name, but by describing their specific features in broad terms that would potentially encompass dances stretching across the continent. A wider definition captured all Give-Away Dances or other celebrations involving 'wounding or mutilation' of humans or animals. The very wording of the provision illustrated that the character, nature, and components of Aboriginal peoples' ceremonies were as culturally misunderstood as the spiritual dimensions of the dances. Prime Minister Bowell was not aware of the full panoply of First Nations dances, which he referred to generically as 'orgies,' but he did single out for explicit censure the Omas-ko-sim-moo-wok, or 'Grass Dance,' which he believed was commonly known as the 'Giving away dance.'[36]

During the parliamentary debates, Thomas Mayne Daly, the white Minister of the Interior, erroneously categorized the newly defined offence as a 'misdemeanour.' In fact, the bill he was discussing specifically characterized the anti-dancing prohibition as an 'indictable' offence. This sloppiness reflects a breezy carelessness on the part of the legislative officials, similar to Prime Minister Macdonald's failure to delete the two-month mandatory penalty during the 1884 debates. Senator Almon continued to oppose the legislation, and warned that such a prohibition might spark First Nations 'insurrections.' His anxiety again failed to strike a chord with the legislative body, which passed the amendment that summer.[37]

The federal Department of Indian Affairs, which was the driving force behind the enactments, viewed the retention of Aboriginal traditions with alarm. Department officials, all of them whites, sought to establish residential schools, eradicate First Nations languages, and encourage speedy conversion to Christianity. The goal was to supplant Aboriginal religions with acculturating influences, to replace Sun Dances, Grass Dances, and Give-Away Dances with square dances and quadrilles.[38] In correspondence, Indian Affairs officials indicated their sincere desire that the churches would convince the Dakota of the 'immorality' of their traditional dances. A Church of England mission had been established on Oak River Dakota Territory in 1880, and various Presbyterian ministers were also vying for converts. White missionaries who reviled Aboriginal spiritual practices complained that the dances posed a 'challenge to our common Christianism principles and a setting up of the old barbarian order on the ruin of our common civilization.' Victorian Christianity inculcated notions of European cultural superiority, which spawned a wave of religious repression.[39]

The non-religious reasons that whites tendered for opposing Aboriginal dance were many and varied. Some of the more spurious included claims by the superintendent general of Indian Affairs that 'Indians raised dust with their dancing and the women's failure to clean it up spread diseases such as tuberculosis.'[40] Deputy Superintendent General of Indian Affairs Frank Pedley advanced the theory that dancing caused 'physical deterioration' and 'mental instability.' One Indian Agent went so far as to postulate that it was a 'principal cause' of 'destitution and misery' of the aged and 'a great deal of sickness and deaths among the children.'[41] A sergeant of the North West Mounted Police despaired that Indians worked themselves into 'a complete frenzy' at the dances, which rendered them incapable of resuming farm work for a long time afterwards. Another Indian Agent insisted that Aboriginal peoples were quite distinct from white people in the degree to which they could become 'excited' and 'unsettled' by dancing. Unlike whites who would go back to tending their farms without incident after a parade or exhibition, he believed Aboriginal people were 'incapable' of settling down.[42]

Other whites claimed that the 'excitement of [the] celebrations' exposed the dancers to 'temptation,' although the precise nature of such allurements went unspecified. Hayter Reed, an Indian Agent who would eventually be promoted to Indian Commissioner, pinpointed the dangers such dances posed to 'young braves.' The dances 'attracted those from all parts to witness acts of endurance,' he charged, 'and to hear recounted deeds of valour committed by those now more advanced in years, which, of course, acted upon the young braves as a dime novel of a thrilling nature would upon the susceptible youth of our own race.'[43] The practice of giving away food, horses, and other material goods also struck observers from European countries as profligate and spendthrift behaviour. In their eyes, it served to divert potential workers from the waged labour market, to remove property from commercial trade, and to impede the private accumulation of wealth in the hands of individuals. As Alberta MP, and former Minister of the Interior, Frank Oliver put it, 'ownership [and] selfishness, which is foreign to the mind of the Indian in his normal condition, is really the foundation of civilization.'[44]

The first arrest under the anti-dancing law took place in 1889, when a Kwakiutl chief of the Mamalillikulla, Hamasak, was convicted and sentenced to six months' imprisonment for performing the Potlatch.[45] Almost immediately after the enactment of the 1895 amendment, the Department of Indian Affairs used the provision to halt a ceremonial dance taking place that summer, and to charge Matoose, a Cree from the Touchwood Hills community of Saskatchewan.[46] In 1896, a white Indian Agent arrested Kah-pee-cha-pees of the Ochapowace First Nation in Saskatchewan and sentenced him to two months of hard labour for sponsoring a Sun Dance.[47]

In 1897, Chief Thunderchild of the Thunderchild First Nation was sentenced to two months in the Battleford Gaol in western Saskatchewan, along with two other Cree dancers, for participating in the Mahtah-e-to-win, a traditional Give-Away Dance.[48] Speaking to a large gathering of Cree from his log-house on the Thunderchild Territory some years later, Chief Thunderchild explained his sense of the injustice inherent in the criminal prosecution of Aboriginal spirituality:

[I]t is heartrending. [...] Can things go well in a land where freedom of worship is a lie, a hollow boast? To each nation is given the light by which it knows God, and each finds its own way to express the longing to serve Him. It is astounding to me that a man should be stopped from trying in his own way to express his need or his thankfulness to God. [...]

I have listened to the talk of the white man's clergy, and it is the same in principle as the talk of our Old Men, whose wisdom came not from books but from life and from God's earth. Why has the white man no respect for the religion that was given to us, when we respect the faith of other nations?

The white men have offered us two forms of their religion – the Roman Catholic and the Protestant – but we in our Indian lands had our own religion. Why is that not accepted too? It is the worship of one God, and it was the strength of our people for centuries.[49]

In 1897, a white North West Mounted Police officer in Battleford, Saskatchewan, arrested Pas-ke-min, Baptiste, Sake-pa-kow, and Ky-ass-i-kan from the Sweet Grass Cree Territory on the occasion of another Give-Away ceremony.[50] Also in 1897, Yellow Bird of File Hills was arrested and sentenced to three months in the Regina prison for his role in assembling a dance lodge on the Okanese territory.[51] In 1901, Chief Piapot, a Cree elder from the Qu'Appelle Valley of southeastern Saskatchewan, was imprisoned for two months in a Regina prison for participating in a Give-Away Dance and encouraging six others to resist arrest.[52] Although virtually none of the records of such criminal proceedings survives, one authority has estimated that between 1900 and 1904 there were fifty arrests and twenty convictions for dancing in contravention of the Indian Act.[53]

THE CENTRAL PROTAGONISTS IN THE *WANDUTA* PROSECUTION

Long before they concluded their Grass Dance at Rapid City, the Dakota must have been aware that Aboriginal dancing had come under strident attack. They expressed some concern to the organizers of the fair about the potential for prosecution, but Malcolm Turriff apparently advised them that if any individuals were imprisoned, he would 'see they were released forthwith.'[54] Turriff was a man of some reputation and substance, and the Dakota probably took him at his word. Vigorous land speculation was rife during the first decades of Rapid City's existence, and Turriff had prospered substantially. A man of increasingly prominent status within the expanding prairie town, Malcolm Turriff used letterhead that boasted of his position as 'agent for the Canadian Pacific Railway and the Hudson's Bay Company,' a businessman with 'money to loan.' His position as clerk of the municipality would remain secure for twenty years running.[55]

No arrests were made during or immediately after the July fair, and Turriff and the Dakota were probably relieved that the exhibition had unfolded so successfully and without incident. Nothing could have been further from the truth. News of the Rapid City event eventually reached the ears of several officials from the federal Department of Indian Affairs, who decided action must be taken. Three white men appear to have been key figures in the decision to marshal criminal law resources against the Dakota.

The first was David Laird, the Indian Commissioner for Manitoba and the Northwest Territories. A native of Prince Edward Island by birth and a Presbyterian Scot by heritage, Laird had come to his position by way of newspaper publication and elected office. A Liberal MP who served as Minister of the Interior, David Laird had introduced the Indian Act into the House of Commons in 1876. Although Laird preferred the classical

David Laird, Indian Commissioner for Manitoba and the Northwest Territories, n.d.

intellectual pursuits of Greek and Hebrew to any effort to familiarize himself with Aboriginal languages and culture, he was assigned a substantial role in governmental–Aboriginal relations, and represented the Crown during the extensive negotiation of Treaties Four through Ten. Stationed in Winnipeg from 1899 on, Laird has been variously described as 'austere,' 'formal,' 'stiff-necked,' and 'a stickler for propriety.' Aged sixty-nine in 1902, the six-foot four-inch, teetotaling commissioner was a force to be reckoned with.[56]

David Laird was incensed to learn that Aboriginal religious rites were still taking place in Manitoba, convinced that 'almost all Sioux dances' had 'illegal features,' and of the belief that stopping them was fundamental to the centralization of power in the hands of the white Indian Agents. Denouncing the dances as 'foolish practices,' 'gatherings of a very injurious character,' and 'vestiges of savage life,' Laird insisted that, while these wretched excesses continued, the best efforts of the farming instructor, the teacher, and the missionary to 'civilize' the 'Indians' would remain 'comparatively at a stand-still.'[57]

G.H. Wheatley, the white Indian Agent from the Oak River Dakota community, was equally adamant about the need to prosecute the danc-

ers. Wheatley was a relative newcomer to the area, having been transferred from the Blackfoot agency in November 1900.[58] His white predecessor, John A. Markle, had made the prohibition of Aboriginal dance a
personal crusade, railing that the Give-Away Dances at Oak River were
'neither elevating, refining nor profitable,' and that those most 'zealous'
to retain such traditions were 'those strongly opposed to educational and
Christian advancement.'[59] In his former posting, Agent Wheatley had
tried to replace the traditional Sun Dance of the Blackfoot with an 'Indian
Fair,' complete with agricultural displays, sports competitions, and cash
prizes. His efforts with the Blackfoot had failed abysmally, but he was
determined to make greater headway with the Dakota.[60]

Wheatley seems to have been gravely concerned that the majority of
the Oak River Dakota still refused to attend Christian church services,
and that the day school that Rev. J.F. Cox had operated within the
community had been closed due to lack of pupils. 'A great number of the
Indians take no interest in the education of their children and are quite
indifferent as to sending them to either boarding or industrial schools,'
he grumbled.[61] Agent Wheatley drew a direct link between the Dakota
resistance to acculturation and traditional dancing. Just months after the
events of the July fair, Wheatley would file his annual report with the
Department of Indian Affairs, taking the occasion to insist that 'pow-
wows' and 'heathen dances' be prohibited altogether. This time he based
his argument on the potential for the abuse of liquor when large numbers
of 'Indians' were drawn to prairie towns to perform for the 'amusement
of the public.'[62]

The third person to spearhead the legal attack on the dancers was E.H.
Yeomans, the farming instructor from the Oak River Dakota community.
The farming instructors assigned to the agencies by the Department of
Indian Affairs were all white. They were typically selected on the basis of
political, familial, and religious affiliations; few knew much about Western agricultural practices, and fewer still could speak Aboriginal languages.[63] Like Wheatley, E.H. Yeomans was quite new to his position,
having been appointed only a year earlier after a string of his predeces-
sors had been fired or departed voluntarily for better opportunities
elsewhere. A long history of strife between the farming instructor and
the Oak River Dakota made the job rather unenviable, as such posts
went.[64] Yeomans must have pointed this out to his superiors, for he
managed to bargain a salary increase from $480 to $600 per annum
within a year of his arrival. Yeomans would soon become one of the
department's most adamant opponents of Aboriginal dancing.[65]

The individual the three white men targeted as the central culprit in the prohibited ceremony was a Dakota Elder named Wanduta (Red Arrow). Wanduta was a 'Heyoka,' an esteemed member of one of the sacred Dakota societies. When the Department of Indian Affairs learned that Wanduta intended to sponsor dances at all of the annual exhibitions across southwestern Manitoba, they determined to curtail the Heyoka's plans. They probably chose to single out Wanduta, the only individual charged after the Rapid City Grass Dance, because of his prominence within the Dakota community.[66]

THE DAKOTA COMMUNITY

Wanduta's home community, the Oak River Dakota, had originally been part of a loose confederation known as the Oceti Sakowin, or Seven Council Fires, made up of three main divisions of people: the Dakota, Nakota, and Lakota. 'Sioux' was a name used by people from outside the confederation to describe the group, and was probably a short form of an Ojibwa word, 'Naddowissi' ('lesser snake,' 'adder,' or 'enemy') with the French plural ending '-ioux,' becoming 'Naddowissioux,' which was shortened over time to 'Sioux.' The ancestors of the Oak River people had fought as allies with England in the War of 1812, assisting in the capture of Michilimackinac and Detroit.[67] Originally the Dakota had ranged across western Wisconsin, Minnesota, Iowa, North and South Dakota, northwestern Ontario, and eastern Manitoba. By the mid-nineteenth century, after considerable 'racial intermixture' and economic and social interaction with English and French settlers, they had been confined to the central American states. In 1862, war broke out between the Dakota and the white settlers in Minnesota, and in the aftermath of the violence many Dakota fled north.[68]

Approximately 1,500 Dakota escaped to Canada, where they set up camps near Fort Garry, Manitoba, and then dispersed more widely. In 1875, when the Dakota were negotiating with the Canadian government for a specified grant of land in return for their earlier military support, approximately one hundred families from the bands of Wambdiska (White Eagle), Choate (the Crow), and Dowaneya (the Singer) settled on the Oak River 'reserve.' Although the property allotted to the Oak River Dakota was smaller than the tracts set aside for white immigrant home-steaders, and smaller also than other Aboriginal allotments in Western Canada, the land itself was of high quality. The 'reserve' was located where the Oak River joins the Assiniboine River, five miles north of where the main line of the Canadian Pacific Railway crossed through the town of Griswold, in one of the finest wheat-growing districts in Western Canada.[69]

Despite almost continuous waves of illness from consumption and scrofula which spread through the community, many Oak River Dakota took up labouring jobs, haying, fencing, and harvesting for other settlers; working on survey crews and on railway construction; or cutting wood for steamers. They began cultivation of their own lands in the summer of 1877, initially making steady progress with crops of turnips, potatoes, and carrots. From the mid 1880s to 1892, the Oak River Dakota made outstanding agricultural advances, investing substantially in farm machinery and implements, and producing abundant crops of wheat to sell in the market. Contemporary observers pronounced them 'in the van[guard] of Indian farmers in this country.'[70]

All of this the Dakota accomplished without the 'assistance' of any farming instruction from the Department of Indian Affairs. By 1891, the department was becoming increasingly nervous about the runaway success of the Oak River agricultural output. The policy of the department was to encourage subsistence-level farming among Indians, in which they produced for their own needs and did not attempt to compete with white settlers in the wider agricultural markets. In 1891 the first farm instructor was placed at Oak River.[71]

The white farming instructor took over the financial management of the community through the strict enforcement of the permit system under the Indian Act, which authorized him to regulate all sales of crops. Combined with the pass system, which required any Dakota who wished to leave the 'reserve' to obtain a pass from the farm instructor or Indian agent, the encumbrances upon First Nations liberty were all-encompassing.[72] The Oak River farm instructor restrained the Dakota from purchasing any more labour-saving machinery and actively interfered with their ability to market their produce efficiently. The Dakota complained about this to the department constantly over the next three years, sending letters, petitions, and even a three-man delegation to Ottawa, with many openly defying departmental regulations. The department officials rejected all complaints.[73]

Despite the heavy-handed interference, the Dakota continued to produce bumper wheat crops, more than 19,000 bushels in the summer of 1901. Their cattle and horse livestock were 'in first-class condition,' with the grade improving yearly. The Dakota generated earnings from the sale of ponies, fish, skins, bead-work, baskets, rush mats, and wild fruits to farmers and storekeepers. They also worked as hourly waged workers for whites in the vicinity. Income from such labour bought shingled roofs, frame and log houses, good doors, windows, and newly sunk wells to add to the general sense of material well-being. The official reports depicted them as 'industrious and law-abiding, and ... fairly well-to-do, from an Indian standpoint.'[74]

In fact, the deadlock with the Department of Indian Affairs had caused significant factionalization of the Dakota. The majority continued to protest the actions of the Department of Indian Affairs, the farming instructor, and the permit system. But a smaller group began to advocate conciliation and compliance with the rules and regulations of the department. Capitalizing on the division, the Department of Indian Affairs moved to appoint a new chief at Oak River who would offer less resistance to governmental policy. The man they settled upon was Tunkan Cekiyana. Over the objections of the 'reserve's leading men,' Tunkan Cekiyana was called to Regina, presented with a medal, and installed as chief.[75]

The whole matter of designating 'chiefs' had become contentious. Traditional Dakota leadership was based on accomplishment and internal politics. Different individuals exercised leadership authority across fairly fluid and overlapping functions, which historically included such diverse matters as warfare, buffalo hunts, and dispute resolution. None of these leaders exercised significant hierarchical authority, since before taking decisions on important issues Dakota leaders would canvass the community to determine the opinion of the members.[76] White government officials seemed incapable of appreciating these sophisticated political structures, and tried to reduce all Aboriginal leadership mechanisms to the level of an individual 'head chief' for each band.[77]

The Indian Act of 1869 authorized the government to pre-empt traditional forms of selecting leaders by ordering triennial elections at which only Aboriginal males over the age of twenty-one could vote. The government was also empowered to depose elected chiefs on the grounds of 'dishonesty,' 'intemperance,' or 'immorality.'[78] 'Incompetency' was added to the list in 1876.[79] In 1895, Parliament specified that, however selected, whether through election or 'according to the custom of the band,' chiefs could be deposed by the governor-in-council.[80]

Not content merely to supplant centuries of traditional leadership selection, the Department of Indian Affairs also began actively to intervene in the election process, nominating individuals known to be supportive of departmental policies, attempting to co-opt traditional chiefs, and removing from office certain leaders who displeased government officials, including those who had been involved in traditional ceremonies.[81] In Western Canada, the government simply abandoned the electoral system and began to appoint chiefs who would toe the departmental line.[82]

Indian Commissioner David Laird was one of the key proponents of removing chiefs from office as a mechanism to suppress Aboriginal dancing.[83] Keen to exploit the factionalization within Oak River, he may have felt that the newly designated Dakota chief, Tunkan Cekiyana, would be more amenable to promulgating departmental policies than Chief James Antoine had been. When he learned of the dancing in Rapid City, Laird must have seen it as an opportunity to test the strength of the Department of Indian Affairs, and another wedge to drive deep into the heart of the Dakota community.

THE ARREST, CHARGE, AND TRIAL OF WANDUTA

Although Laird, Wheatley, and Yeomans hoped to charge Wanduta immediately, they were initially stymied by their inability to locate the Heyoka. Both the farming instructor and the Indian Agent were taken by surprise to learn that, before they could arrest him, Wanduta had left Oak River to collect his son from the Brandon Industrial School.[84]

At first blush, it might seem surprising that Wanduta, who was being targeted in a campaign to eradicate Aboriginal opposition to white assimilationist education, had a son attending industrial school. One explanation may be that Wanduta's son's residence in the industrial school was not voluntary. In 1894, the federal government had begun to pass legislation to coerce Aboriginal children to attend residential, industrial, boarding, and day schools run by whites.[85] It is also possible, however, that Wanduta made a deliberate choice to place his son at the Brandon Industrial School. While some Aboriginal people resisted Euro-Canadian schooling, others sought education selectively, hoping to obtain practical advantages in dealing with whites without losing contact with their own culture.[86]

The white principal of Brandon Industrial School, Rev. Thompson Ferrier, had campaigned vigorously against the 'evils of dancing,' stressing the dangers this posed for his pupils and graduates.[87] He seems not to have convinced Wanduta's son. The young man cut short his educational semester to accompany his father to Ottawa, where the two lodged a pre-emptive complaint with the white secretary of Indian Affairs,

Wanduta, Oak River Dakota Nation, 10 July 1909.

J.D. McLean, about the injustice of the efforts to prohibit Aboriginal dancing. That Wanduta's son might be utilizing the language and political skills he had acquired at the industrial school to argue for the rights of Aboriginal peoples to practise traditional customs must surely have pleased the Dakota Heyoka.[88]

When David Laird got wind of the twosome's journey to Ottawa, he wrote to Secretary McLean to complain that Wanduta was 'not a Chief, but ... a mischief-maker among the less industrious element of the Sioux, who wish to keep up the dances.' What was worse, advised Laird, was that he was one of the Indians who was 'mixed up in the dance affair at Rapid City last summer.'[89] Shrewdly, Laird also rallied support from the newly elevated chief. Tunkan Cekiyana forwarded a lengthy letter to the Department of Indian Affairs, apologetic in tone and condemnatory of Wanduta. It is difficult to assess Tunkan Cekiyana's position. One interpretation is that he was primarily an 'Indian Affairs chief,' completely beholden to the department and eager to serve as Laird's mouth-piece. Another possibility is that he genuinely reflected the views of a group within the Dakota community who had consciously chosen specific aspects of acculturation. Tunkan Cekiyana may have concluded that, given the undeniable progress the Dakota had made in housing, farming, and managing livestock, the Oak River community stood to benefit from aligning itself more fully with Euro-Canadian ways. He may have worried that the spectacle and display of traditional dance would stall the growing economic security of the Dakota, exacerbating racial divisions in dangerous directions.[90]

Describing himself through an interpreter as a chief who had 'tried to follow as near the footsteps of the white man as possible,' Chief Tunkan Cekiyana explained that he had 'put aside all the bad and useless customs of my former life.' Singularly supportive of the Indian Affairs officials, he noted: 'The assistance given us [through] the Commissioner, Agent and Instructor has been of great benefit to those who wished to profit by it.'

Chief Tunkan Cekiyana praised Farming Instructor E.H. Yeomans in particular, stating: 'I am pleased with our present Instructor. [H]e has been a great help to us and we are commencing to farm now. [We] also get up good buildings and live more like white men and women.' Chief Tunkan Cekiyana advised that the recent appointment of Indian Agent Yeomans as constable for the 'reserve' was also beneficial, lamenting that 'some of my people do not wish to have a constable on the reserve and try to make complaints against him.'

Chief Tunkan Cekiyana was at pains to place blame for any discontent directly upon Wanduta:

[D]uring the summer he took many of the Band away from their work to attend a Pow-wow at Rapid City at which a number of the school children took part. I was sorry for this. [...] This Wanduta is not a credit to the Band. [H]e is only on the reserve a short time during the year and while here causes as much trouble as he possibly can. [A]lso his former record was not good. [...]

About the first [unclear] new year some of the people were induced to make up a sum of money by one Wanduta for the purpose of sending him to Ottawa to make certain complaints and I think misrepresent the state of affairs. [E]ven some of the poor women were induced to pay money for this purpose.[91]

The involvement of the women in Wanduta's Ottawa petition seems to have irked Chief Tunkan Cekiyana particularly, perhaps because some Aboriginal leaders from the Canadian plains have described the traditional role of women as 'more or less silent partners.' However, the Dakota women were central to the economic success of the community during this period. They maintained the small livestock and gardens, and the income women contributed from the sale of handicraft items at market was indispensable in years of crop failure. Aboriginal women seem always to have played a critical role in preserving and celebrating the stability, culture, and religion of their communities. Some have suggested that women's efforts became even more visible in the years after the 1885 rebellion, when the state and the clergy increasingly deprived men of their roles as 'defenders, providers and decision makers.' Aboriginal women's traditional roles as caregivers for the children and the sick remained more intact, allowing them to exercise a defining and obvious influence in the defence of the culture.[92]

Chief Tunkan Cekiyana took great umbrage at what he felt was Wanduta's effort to usurp his proper authority as chief of the community, insisting that 'Wanduta has no right to the title of chief as he claims. [T]he medal he has was purchased from a son of one of the former Chiefs who died some years ago.' That some of the Dakota looked upon Wanduta as an important and esteemed leader prompted Chief Tunkan Cekiyana to apologize to the department on their behalf. 'I am sorry some of my people follow Wanduta instead of looking at the work of the white man,' he wrote. Anxious for the intercession of governmental officials to diminish Wanduta's status, he added: 'His visit to Ottawa had not my approval and I think he should be prevented from making such trips at the expense of the hard working members of the band.'[93]

Chief Tunkan Cekiyana's letter evoked little interest from departmental officials. Frank Pedley, the white deputy superintendent general, acknowledged the letter with an inscrutable response: 'Your observations with reference to Wandutta [*sic*] have been noted, and that in case the Department considers that action is necessary some shall be taken.' The necessary action, it appears, was to enforce the law against Aboriginal dance. In Winnipeg, Commissioner David Laird was jubilant, writing to congratulate J.D. McLean and to express his happiness that the department 'gave [Wanduta] no encouragement in his mission.'[94]

Upon his return to Oak River in January 1903, Wanduta was arrested by Farming Instructor E.H. Yeomans, and charged with hosting a dance which involved the giving away of merchandise and a number of horses, contrary to section 114 of the Indian Act. On 26 January 1903, he was brought before a white police magistrate, R. Lyons, in Griswold, Manitoba. There being no courtroom in the tiny prairie town, the trial was held in a room in the Manitoba Hotel. There is no record of whether Wanduta was allowed to have his son or another interpreter present to assist with the problems of language translation.[95]

The trial was remarkable in its brevity: no witnesses appear to have been called, no legal counsel were present, and there appears to have been no consideration of any defence arguments that might have been available to the accused. Magistrate Lyons simply recorded that Wanduta 'acknowledged his guilt,' and entered a conviction. Wanduta was sentenced to four months at hard labour and incarcerated in the Brandon Jail. There was no press coverage of the trial, so the many white citizens who had flocked to the Rapid City Annual Fair had no notice that they may have witnessed an event that was contrary to criminal law.[96]

Many Dakota, however, were incensed and alarmed at the verdict. A number approached Malcolm Turriff, the Rapid City businessman who had invited them to present their dance and promised them no trouble would ensue. Turriff took immediate steps to try to make good on his commitment. Within three days, he had fired off a letter to the Department of Indian Affairs, in which he endeavoured to explain that the Dakota had merely given 'an exhibition of their national dance' for the benefit of those attending the Rapid City Annual Fair. The use of the term 'national' suggests that Turriff may have been attempting to equate the Dakota with the many other diverse groups of immigrants who had arrived over the past decades from Iceland, Denmark, Sweden, Belgium, Holland, Germany, Poland, Russia, and the Austro-Hungarian Empire.[97]

'I can say that the Indians who came to Rapid City at that time were quiet and well conducted,' added Turriff. The real trouble-maker, in

Turriff's opinion, was Farming Instructor E.H. Yeomans: 'A good many complaints have been made to me by these Indians of the arbitrary manner in which Mr. Yeomans has dealt with them. He appears to be very much disliked by them.' Shaping his argument to emphasize the modernization of the Oak River Dakota, Turriff continued: 'Many of these people are getting along well in their farming operations; they seem to be improving steadily under these circumstances and from a humane standpoint, I think your department should investigate into the matter of the Chief's imprisonment and other complaints.'[98]

This plea was unlikely to have much resonance within the offices of the Department of Indian Affairs. That it came from a highly placed, white town official who had initiated the request that the Dakota dance at the fair could only have inflamed matters. For years government officials had been griping that the fixation of prairie townspeople like Turriff upon Aboriginal pageantry frustrated efforts to wipe out traditional dance. The former Indian Agent at the Oak River Dakota community, John A. Markle, fumed that the 'Indians' under his 'charge' had received far too many 'invitations from the whites to attend celebrations, picnics and other gatherings to give such exhibitions.' 'The more uncivilized they appear,' stormed Agent Markle, 'the more they please the public.'[99]

The spectre of whites provoking 'Indians' to put on 'heathen dances' that might never have occurred had they been left to their own devices was one of the main factors driving the legislative amendment of 1895. The new provision expressly enlarged the potential pool of offenders to include those who 'encouraged' either 'directly or indirectly' the celebration of illegal festivals or dances.[100] In 1896, the white Indian Commissioner, Amédée E. Forget, described the curiosity of whites as 'one of the most serious impediments' in the struggle to eradicate 'heathen rites.' Lambasting the 'class of whites' responsible, Forget fumed about

the encouragement given to the Indians on reserves adjacent to towns and settlements by that element of the white population which is ever ready to assist in the creation or maintenance of anything which panders to an appetite for the sensational and novel and to whom the resultant effect on the actors therein is a matter of perfect indifference.

How could the criminal law ever be successfully implemented while the salacious appetites for 'buckskins,' 'beadwork,' 'feathers,' and 'war paint' kept the 'gate-money' mounting so precipitously?[101]

The Department of Indian Affairs conducted no investigation into

Turriff's allegations except to forward the letter to Commissioner David Laird. Laird was quite agitated that Turriff had intervened, and quoted Indian Agent Wheatley's view that 'this Mr. Malcolm Turriff deserves censure more than the Indians, as he has undoubtedly assisted in getting up the dance and induced the Indians to visit Rapid City during Fair time for that purpose.' The government made no move to prosecute Turriff for his role in the dancing, possibly because of his race and standing within the prairie community. The full force of Laird's displeasure was concentrated on Wanduta:

The Indian referred to ... is not a Chief, but the ring-leader of all the discontented Indians on the Oak River Reserve and the leader in the illegal dances held at Rapid City in July last. [...] Wanduta was given a fair trial before Mr. Police Magistrate Lyons and was sentenced to four months in jail with hard labour, which sentence he should serve in full to give himself and his followers an example and to teach them that the law must be respected.[102]

As for the aspersions cast upon the farming instructor and Indian Agent, these were malicious falsehoods according to Laird. Farming Instructor E.H. Yeomans simply 'acted upon instructions from me given through Mr. Agent Wheatley in this matter, and he simply did his duty without fear or favour.' Laird insisted that Yeomans was 'painstaking' and 'succeeds very well in his position.' Complaints against him could only come 'from such worthless Indians as Wanduta and his followers.'[103]

RETAINING LEGAL COUNSEL

When nothing further was heard from Indian Affairs about Malcolm Turriff's protestations, the Oak River Dakota decided to fight back. Fourteen days after Wanduta's conviction, on 9 February 1903, five Dakota men – Akisa, Pazaiyapa, Wasticaka, Kiyewakan, and Hoksidaska – travelled to the nearby city of Brandon to retain a lawyer. In their quest to free Wanduta, the five undoubtedly spoke on behalf of those within the Dakota community who treasured their spiritual heritage and were determined to assert their rights to follow traditional ways. Yet there is evidence that they also represented the group that had achieved significant economic prosperity, even as defined by whites. At least one of the five men had been singled out by the Indian Agent only a year earlier as one of the 'better farmers' in the community, with between fifty and ninety acres of wheat under cultivation. What the faction represented by

Chief Tunkan Cekiyana thought of the intervention by the five Dakota, and whether it provoked intensified division within the Dakota community, is not clear.[104]

The legal firm selected by the five Dakota men was Coldwell and Coleman, a promising partnership active in real estate, civil litigation, and matrimonial practice. The Coldwell and Coleman law partners, like Malcolm Turriff, proudly displayed the names of their prominent clients alongside the masthead of the letterhead: 'Coldwell and Coleman, Solicitors to the Imperial Bank of Commerce, the Bank of British North America, the Imperial Loan and Investment Co. of Canada.' Why Coldwell and Coleman was the firm to which the Dakota turned is unknown. Possibly, as one of the largest law firms in Brandon, it was the most visible. There were no Aboriginal barristers or solicitors to retain, and it may have seemed prudent to select the biggest firm in town.[105]

George Robson Coldwell was one of only two barristers in Brandon holding the prestigious 'King's Counsel' designation. The forty-five-year-old, white lawyer grew up on a farm in the township of Darlington, near Bowmanville, Ontario. He was a graduate of public school in Kinburn, Ontario, Clinton grammar school, Trinity College School in Port Hope, and Trinity College in Toronto. He became a student-at-law for several years in Seaforth and Toronto, and then moved out to Winnipeg in 1882, where he completed his legal studies at the law firm of Kennedy and Sutherland. Called to the Manitoba bar in November 1882, he resettled in Brandon in February 1883. Initially, Coldwell took up practice with Thomas Mayne Daly, the local mayor who would later go on to become a conservative MP, Minister of the Interior, and Superintendent General of Indian Affairs. When Daly left Brandon for Winnipeg, Coldwell forged a new partnership with George B. Coleman, an association that would continue profitably for decades.

Coldwell was an Anglican by religion, a man who spent his leisure time shooting and gardening. A Conservative by party affiliation and a sitting member of the Brandon City Council for years, Coldwell held a bit of a mixed bag of political positions: he supported fair wages and worker's compensation legislation, was non-committal on women's suffrage, and was touted as the personification of Brandon's business and professional community. In 1907, he would be elected as an MLA for Brandon, and in 1908 he would be appointed the first Minister of Education for Manitoba.[106]

In retaining counsel, the Dakota set a pattern that many Aboriginal protestors would follow in future. Wherever possible, it seems that First

George Robson Coldwell, 1907.

Nations individuals who were charged with illegal dancing sought legal representation. Despite their lack of direct personal connections with members of the bar, they exhibited great acumen in selecting counsel who were highly regarded for their advocacy skills.[107] The expertise that First Nations communities amassed in defending themselves from dance prosecutions might have paid off handsomely in other areas, such as the bringing of land claims before the courts. However, federal politicians would eventually move to defuse such potential. In 1927 Parliament made it a crime to raise money from First Nations communities for the prosecution of Aboriginal claims, unless the Department of Indian Affairs had given prior written consent.[108]

Although there are no surviving records of what George Coldwell charged the Dakota, it is reasonable to assume that they were paying clients. The Dakota probably had the wherewithal to hire counsel that winter because their community was almost as flush as the white neighbouring townsfolk. The Dakota had harvested one of their best crops ever in the summer of 1902. The records also indicate that they drew considerable income that year from the sale of ponies, cattle, baskets, beaded articles, and mats to new settlers, and that they sold over $2,000 worth of wild berries as well. A number of the Dakota had opened bank accounts in Brandon with their growing investments.[109]

Like most of his white counterparts in the community, Coldwell probably knew little about the legislative prohibition on Aboriginal dance. So he would first have reviewed the section of the Indian Act under which Wanduta had been convicted. Reading this, Coldwell must have been struck by two things. First, the dances that were prohibited were ones that entailed 'the giving away or paying or giving back of money, goods or articles of any sort' or 'the wounding or mutilation of the dead or living body of any human being or animal.' The Grass Dance in question involved no 'wounding' or 'mutilation' whatsoever, and according to his Dakota clients, Wanduta himself had not given away anything during the ceremony. Second, the section contained an exemption: 'nothing in this section shall be construed to prevent the holding of any agricultural show or exhibition or the giving of prizes for exhibits thereat.' The dancing at the annual fair might be interpreted to fall squarely within the exempted 'agricultural shows' or 'exhibitions.'

Once convicted by a police magistrate, there were several avenues of redress. It was too late to file an appeal from the conviction, because more than ten days had elapsed from the police magistrate's verdict.[110] However, it was possible to attack Wanduta's conviction through the courts by bringing a writ of *habeas corpus*, an action that required a judicial review of the legality of the imprisonment of the accused person. Another option was a writ of *certiorari* challenging the jurisdiction of the convicting magistrate.[111] It was also possible to request a pardon through the exercise of executive clemency, which would have provided for Wanduta's immediate discharge from jail.

For reasons that are not entirely clear from the records, George Coldwell chose to pursue executive clemency. While judicial remedies required court appearances, appealing for executive clemency involved a rather different campaign of letter-writing, the filing of declarations of support, and the exercise of political influence. Working through an interpreter from Portage la Prairie, Coldwell got his Dakota clients to sign five identical statutory declarations attesting to their presence at Rapid City during the holiday for the annual fair. The statements stressed that the Dakota had been invited to the fair and asked to 'give a Dance for the white people' as part of the celebration. The declarations continued:

[T]he Indians gave a dance there on that day and there was no gambling, immorality with women, drinking of intoxicating liquors, feasting on dogs [*sic*] flesh, giving presents of money or goods or cutting or wounding of the body in connection with such dance.[...] [O]n that occasion two or three Indians traded coats and some print or cotton but Wanduta did not trade or give away anything.[112]

George Coldwell must have concluded that making an appeal to the Department of Indian Affairs was a waste of time, for he forwarded the declarations directly to the minister responsible for the department, Clifford Sifton, who held the post of Minister of the Interior in Ottawa. Coldwell's former law partner, Thomas Mayne Daly, had also served as the Minister of the Interior some years back, and this may have been another factor that prompted Coldwell to go directly to the top. Clifford Sifton was the most powerful politician ever to represent the Brandon constituency, a white, Liberal cabinet minister who controlled the distribution of federal patronage in the West. A forty-one-year-old lawyer of British descent who had previously held the position of Manitoba attorney general, Sifton represented the economic and social elite of Manitoba's 'second city.' A Methodist in religion, Sifton was equally at home in the temperance movement as he was playing sports such as lacrosse and polo, or entertaining from his opulent new residence in Ottawa and his summer retreat in the Thousand Islands district of the St Lawrence. As

Clifford Sifton, *circa* 1896.

Minister of the Interior, he was responsible for the early twentieth-century wave of East European immigration, a group he depicted as stalwart 'peasants in sheep-skin clothing,' who were rapidly filling up the prairie plains.[113]

When Coldwell wrote to Sifton, he included a lengthy letter of his own containing a number of distinct arguments, in which he requested Sifton exercise 'executive clemency' and order the immediate release of Wanduta. For starters, Coldwell claimed that the Dakota Grass Dance should be distinguished from the Potlatch, the Sun Dance, and 'other objectionable dance[s]' which he conceded might be prohibited under the Indian Act. Coldwell's letter was certainly no out-and-out attack on the criminalization of Aboriginal dance, but a much more cautious attempt to separate out 'permissible' dances from the impermissible. He seems to have been unaware of Prime Minister Mackenzie Bowell's explicit reference to the Grass Dance during his classification of all First Nations dances as 'orgies.' Whether he was seeking a generalized exemption for all Grass Dances, or just this one in particular, is not entirely clear.

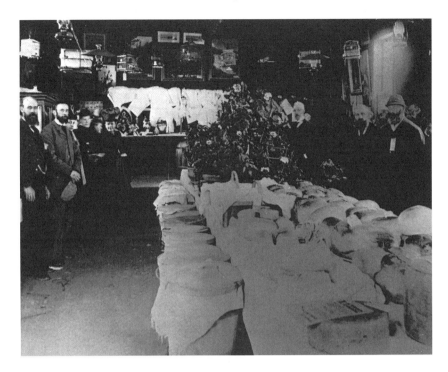

Rapid City Agricultural Society Exhibition, *circa* 1898.

In addition, Coldwell insisted that Wanduta's individual actions during the Grass Dance had been above reproach since he had not taken part 'in the giving away of anything.' To the extent that there had been any giving away, Coldwell advised that 'certain Indians who took part in it exchanged with one another some articles of clothing or bits of money during the dance.' This was not, Coldwell emphasized, 'a promiscuous giving away of property without some reasonable return.' Once again, Coldwell threw down no challenge to the legislative provision, but endeavoured to emphasize that Wanduta was not the sort of individual who should have been convicted under the law as properly administered.

Next, Coldwell stressed that the Dakota had been 'invited' to dance: 'They were procured to go there as an attraction to help out the Entertainment being furnished' in Rapid City during 'some sort of holidays.' This was surely not the sort of situation encompassed by a law devised to criminalize Aboriginal dances. All the Dakota were doing was helping their fellow townsfolk celebrate the annual fair. The presence of the white fair-goers seemed to symbolize the innocuousness of the ceremony in Coldwell's view. Furthermore, there was the matter of the legislative exemption covering agricultural shows and exhibitions, which had never been addressed at trial.

Lastly, Coldwell laid claim to principles of due process. He complained of procedural irregularities in the trial, some of which were so grievous that a higher court would most certainly quash the conviction and grant the release of Wanduta under a *habeas corpus* proceeding: 'We find from inquiry of Mr. Lyons, the Magistrate, that no evidence was taken down at the trial but he says that Wanduta acknowledged his guilt. We believe that the circumstances connected with this trial were quite irregular and that had this Indian been advised he would not have been convicted at all.'[114] In the alternative, Coldwell argued that the sentence was entirely out of line with the crime: 'If he was guilty of an offence against the Indian Act a trifling penalty would have been sufficient under the circumstances.' Given Wanduta's imprisonment since 26 January, Coldwell argued that he should be granted an immediate pardon. He emphasized the 'large number' of Dakota who were 'very much dissatisfied at the conviction and sentence of Wanduta,' and described the five who had submitted statutory declarations as 'very respectable looking Indians.'

In case the testament of Indians, respectable though they might be, was insufficient, George Coldwell also dispatched four additional statutory declarations from leading white citizens, representatives of the early founders of Rapid City. Coldwell seems to have selected the four white men because they were personal acquaintances of Clifford Sifton, and he offered their statements as corroboration for the statements of the Indians. Edmund Cecil Gosset-Jackson, who had established a lumbering and implement business in the early years of the settlement, had served as the elected councillor and mayor of Rapid City. John Bowen Mowatt Dunoon, the son of one of the earliest white settlers, rose to local prominence after his appointment as postmaster in 1898 and election as secretary of the Citizens Committee and secretary-treasurer of the Driving Park Association. Edward Soldan, a director of the Rapid City Agricultural Society, was the reeve of the municipality. Alexander McKellar was a well-established lumber dealer.[115]

All four attested to their involvement in arranging for the Dakota to 'give a dance for the amusement of the people visiting the town.' All four insisted that a 'great many people' watched the dancing, which was 'perfectly harmless and inoffensive,' and that 'nothing of an immoral,

Store-fronts in Rapid City, including McKellar & Jackson Implement Dealers, *circa* 1900. Alexander McKellar and Edmund Cecil Gosset-Jackson, who owned the lumbering and implement business, swore out statutory declarations on behalf of Wanduta.

improper or dangerous character' occurred. Each swore that he had observed no giving away of horses or blankets, and that the small exchanges that did take place were of goods such as 'a coat or piece of money but were not matters of any consequence.' The four leading citizens demanded that Clifford Sifton release Wanduta from jail, since 'the said Indians committed no offence whatever.'[116]

These testaments from some of the most prominent white men of Rapid City suggest that it was not only the Dakota who were at odds with the prosecution of Aboriginal dance. Powerful sectors of the white population were joining the protest.[117] It is noteworthy, however, that the white protesters who signed the sworn statements were all male. Presumably Coldwell had restricted his quest for signatories to male community leaders, thinking that in the male-dominant world of law, politics, and government, male voices would be more influential. But the absence of female perspective on the record does provoke pause.

Did prairie townswomen hold different views from their menfolk? Did gender have an impact on the white gaze, as it feasted upon the 'thrilling' elements so salaciously favoured by those who wrote about Aboriginal dance? Did the cross-cultural response to Aboriginal ceremonial dress, often described as 'half-naked attire' by white reporters, differ by gender?[118] Elite white women's organizations such as the National Council of Women of Canada were on record complaining about the 'gross immoralities' of Aboriginal dance to the Department of Indian Affairs.[119] Such sentiments may have deterred Rapid City's leading white female citizens from adding their names to Coldwell's list of declarants. Yet there were significant ties between women's organizations and Aboriginal leaders as well. The Brandon Imperial Order Daughters of the Empire, for example, would bestow a ceremonial and honorary 'Union Jack' upon Dakota Chief Antoine when he reached the age of ninety in 1915.[120] And presumably, women fair-goers stood cheek by jowl with their male relatives as they craned their necks for a better glimpse of the Aboriginal dancers. Notions of respectable female decorum and modesty seem to have succumbed to the romantic lure of 'Indian' pageantry, at least for some women at prairie exhibitions.

Whatever their gender, the white citizens of Rapid City who protested the prosecution of Aboriginal dance posed no arguments on the basis of freedom of religion, or the inherent right of Aboriginal peoples to preserve their own culture and traditions, as some of the federal politicians who opposed the legislation had done.[121] The white community was in fact quite intolerant of First Nations individuals who failed to abandon egalitarian economic practices for more accumulative ethics. These sentiments, laced with racial stereotyping, were frequently expounded in the local press. The Brandon *Western Sun* carried a feature titled 'The Indian Is Naturally Lazy' on 5 June 1902, which asserted that 'even though encouraged to work, the Indian is naturally lazy and if he can get out of work on any paltry excuse he will do so.'[122]

The thrust of the Rapid City leaders' objection to Wanduta's conviction was not based on Aboriginal rights, but rather on an insistence on their own prerogative to schedule entertainment at local fairs as they saw fit. To the extent that Aboriginal parades and dances were a resource that could be exploited for the amusement of fair-goers and the profit of fair organizers, these men felt that the federal government had no right to intervene. The law against Aboriginal dancing thwarted the ability of the newly emerging entertainment industry to realize the highest returns possible through the exploitation of white nostalgia over the loss of the 'wild west' frontier. Laws prohibiting Give-Aways also made a dent in

Dakota arriving at Brandon Fair, drawing great attention from white women, 1907.

the earnings of local store-keepers who wished to furnish the food, clothing, and other articles used in the ceremonies. It was likely no accident that the white petitioners included some of the leading retailers in the town. The irony of it was that a law enacted to ensure that the First Nations would adopt the Protestant work ethic of calculated thrift and accumulation was having a detrimental impact upon the cash revenues of prairie businesses.[123]

The other irony is that, despite their clear authority to press charges against Turriff, Gosset-Jackson, Dunoon, Soldan, and McKellar, the officials at the Department of Indian Affairs sat on their hands. David Laird had already expressed his rage about Turriff, convinced that the Rapid City businessman had 'induced' the Indians to dance. Now the department had before it four written admissions from Turriff's cronies, openly admitting that they had 'arranged' for the illegal dance to take place.[124] Why did Indian Affairs not pounce upon such confessions with glee? For years the department had been griping that dancing would never be stamped out while the unruly 'class of whites' whose appetites feasted on

Aboriginal 'war paint' and 'exotica' were allowed to pursue their pleasures unhindered. The 1895 legislative amendment expanding the scope of prosecution to all those who 'encouraged' these dances, either 'directly or indirectly,' had been designed precisely to encompass such troublemakers. So what was holding David Laird and Frank Pedley back?

In fact, the surviving records suggest that no whites were ever prosecuted under the Aboriginal dance provisions, from the date of the first legislative enactment to 1951, when the law was finally repealed.[125] The Indian Agents, the police, and the higher authorities within the Department of Indian Affairs seem to have ruled out laying any charges against the multitude of white townsfolk, stampede organizers, and fair hucksters who jockeyed among themselves to book Aboriginal dancers for their annual festivities. This must signify some tacit recognition that the goal of eradicating traditional dance, so dear to the hearts of Indian Agents, farming instructors, and Christian missionaries, was substantially at odds with the popular views of most white farmers and townspeople in the Canadian West. If the authorities had gone so far as to place white civic leaders on trial, it might even have provoked some criticism of their program of cultural eradication. In what seems to be an implicit recognition of the lack of support for their policies, the department backed off any effort to enforce the law against non-Aboriginal people.

It is equally remarkable that the four men's admission of lawbreaking was contained in formal, written statements drawn up by the lawyer George Coldwell. These were not declarations secured through coercion or trickery, but open statements attesting to personal responsibility. It seems surprising that a lawyer, who must have been fully aware of the potential for criminal prosecution against anyone who 'encouraged' the celebration of an illegal dance, or 'incited any Indian' to commit an indictable offence, had solicited these signed declarations, and then distributed them to the department. It underscores the sense of immunity and privilege that infused middle-class, white prairie politicians and businessmen. They seem to have been surprised that a Dakota man was in jail for participating in an Aboriginal dance. They could not begin to imagine that they might be put behind bars on related charges.

Apart from the sense of immunity that allowed white businessmen to make such declarations to the Minister of the Interior, was there any potential for a coalition of interests between the First Nations and white civic leaders? Might it have been possible for the Dakota and other Aboriginal communities to forge an alliance with the organizers of prairie town fairs and agricultural exhibitions to protest the prosecution of First Nations dance? Given the disparity in motivation, the differences in language and culture, and the generalized suspicion and distrust that decades of racial tension had wrought, it is difficult to imagine the two groups effectively combining forces. Had they done so, the federal politicians whose voices had been in the minority in Parliament might have mustered the support necessary to repeal the legislation.

The other potential alliance that might have been forged was with the British Crown. White representatives of the British Crown always seemed to glory in the parade and pageantry of First Nations display during their visits to Canada. The Marquis of Lansdowne positively revelled in what he probably perceived as Aboriginal 'spectacle' during his tour of Western Canada in February 1899, as did the Earl and Countess of Minto in September 1900, and the Duke and Duchess of Cornwall and York in September 1901. When the white Rev. Slocken of the Blackfoot Mission wrote to Governor General Lord Minto in 1900, calling upon him to cancel the Blackfoot dance display, the white governor general wrote back indicating that he considered the dances 'harmless.'[126]

A delegation of First Nations chiefs took their complaints directly to Governor General Lord Minto on 16 October 1902, when a viceregal party was hunting in the district north of Qu'Appelle. The Brandon *Western Sun* described the encounter:

A few days ago a large deputation of Indians waited on the governor-general. The Red Skins, learning who the distinguished personage was, who was shooting game in 'their country,' took the advantage of his presence in the west by appearing before him to make a few requests. His Excellency listened in an earnest and patient manner to long harangues from the chiefs, who were decked out in honor of the occasion. [The] chief complaint was for more rations and for permission to hold 'give away' dances.[127]

The newspaper's characterization of the demands of the First Nations leaders as a deferential seeking of 'permission' to carry on their traditional spiritual ceremonies, suggests that here, too, the potential for effective alliance between Aboriginal communities and powerful whites was more illusory than real. Although Governor General Lord Minto subsequently raised a concern about the prosecution of native dancing with white Prime Minister Sir Wilfrid Laurier, nothing further came of this intervention.[128]

THE OFFICIAL RESPONSE TO THE PETITION FOR PARDON

Clifford Sifton's involvement in the petition for executive clemency seems to have stirred up the bureaucrats at the Department of Indian Affairs somewhat. Deputy Superintendent General Frank Pedley ordered a legal opinion on the trial forthwith. The white law clerk from the Department of Indian Affairs who investigated the case noted that it was 'undoubtedly the policy of the Department to entirely suppress such dances.' The clerk emphasized that Wanduta had been convicted on a 'plea of guilty,' a straightforward admission of guilt. This, of course, sidestepped the question of whether Wanduta would have 'acknowledged' his guilt if he had had legal counsel at the trial or been properly advised of the defences available to him. It also ignores the more fundamental question of whether Wanduta understood the concept of guilt under Canadian law, and whether he fully appreciated the significance of his plea and the ensuing proceedings. The law clerk also dismissed Coldwell's position that Wanduta had not himself given anything away at the dance. The statutory declarations had established 'that Wanduta was present at the dance and there was some exchange of goods amongst the Indians thereat,' noted the clerk. The conviction was 'for assisting at a dance of which the giving away of articles formed a part.' This conclusion, while attempting to draw Wanduta into the words of the section that penalized an individual who 'assists in celebrating' an Aboriginal dance, failed to indicate exactly what the Court had found to constitute such assistance.

Thus the law clerk perfunctorily dismissed some of Coldwell's arguments and ignored others. There was no discussion of the complaint that Wanduta had been allowed to plead guilty without anyone ascertaining whether he understood the charge. The clerk disregarded Coldwell's objection that the police magistrate made no record of the evidence against Wanduta. There was no response to the question of whether the punishment fit the crime. The issue of an exemption for agricultural shows or exhibitions went unaddressed. There was no examination of Coldwell's query as to whether the Grass Dance was included in the statutory prohibition. In fact, it remained an open question whether all Aboriginal dances were prohibited under section 114 or whether it was only specific features of the dances that ran afoul of the law.

This very debate had occupied both David Laird and J.D. McLean only weeks before Wanduta's trial. David Laird telegraphed McLean in Ottawa on 9 January 1903 that he had learned that the 'Indians of Standing

Buffalo's reserve were about to hold a dance,' and that he had sent the farming instructor to warn them to stop. J.D. McLean telegraphed back the next day to ask whether the farming instructor had prohibited the dance entirely, and why, or whether he had prohibited only the 'illegal features.' Somewhat flummoxed by the question, Laird replied only hours later: 'Cannot give precise terms of [the farming instructor's] prohibition, but almost all Sioux dances have illegal features. Dances have been stopped in the agency for eighteen months, and agents [*sic*] influence will be much weakened if they are allowed to resume.' This seems to be something of a reversal of opinion for Laird, who had taken an official position in 1898 that the Indian Act did not prohibit ceremonies as a whole, but only the objectionable features such as the making of gifts and so forth. Now Laird's hasty exhortation to ban the dances themselves, and not just their illegal features, seems to have carried the day. In any event, no one from Indian Affairs was prepared to make further inquiry into the legality of this wide-ranging interpretation of section 114.[129]

On one matter, however, the law clerk registered a serious concern. He was worried that the magistrate may have overstepped his jurisdiction by hearing the trial at all:

I think it is possible that the Indian could obtain his release under habeas corpus proceedings. Under Section 114 of the Indian Act ... the offence with which he was charged is an *indictable offence* for which he is liable to imprisonment for a term not exceeding six months and not less than two months. There is no provision in the Indian Act giving a police magistrate power to dispose of the case in a summary manner; and the offence does not appear to be one in which he is given jurisdiction to hear and determine the charge ... I incline to the opinion that the case is one for appeal to the courts rather than for application for executive clemency.[130]

On the jurisdictional point, the law clerk was quite correct.[131] Furthermore, this matter was one that had been of long-standing concern amongst Aboriginal communities, where people were often subjected to conviction and sentence at the hands of lowly judicial personnel who processed complaints with little concern for the rules of evidence, the presumption of innocence, or access to legal counsel. Whether higher-level courts, with their more formal procedures, would have been able to provide fairer hearings across such vast cultural chasms is, of course, an open question.

The clerk's suggestion that the case was one for appeal to the courts rather than the exercise of executive clemency seems to be a bit of a dodge. He was apparently well-versed in the bureaucratic shuffle, since he also appended to his opinion letter the following notation: 'On the suggestion of clemency, the matter is one for the consideration of the Justice Department to which application should have been made. It would perhaps be well to refer the papers there. I don't think the case is one in which this department should recommend any line of action.'[132] Clearly, the Department of Indian Affairs was miffed that Coldwell had tried to exercise influence through Clifford Sifton's Ministry of the Interior. Indian Affairs wanted to wash its hands of the executive clemency application, without deigning to make any recommendation at all. This seems a dereliction of responsibility in the face of the clerk's conclusion that Wanduta had not been convicted by a court of competent jurisdiction. If anything, the jurisdictional improprieties should have enhanced the case for Wanduta's immediate discharge from jail.

Frank Pedley seems to have been delighted with the idea of shifting the matter to Justice. He forwarded the entire file to E.L. Newcombe, KC, the white Deputy Minister of Justice, on 10 March 1903 and advised Clifford Sifton's department that the matter was now under review at Justice. Pedley indicated he would provide the Minister of the Interior with further information as soon as possible, but couldn't resist closing with: 'Personally, I may say, I think the cause of justice is not going to suffer very much by keeping this Indian in jail for the full term of his sentence.'[133]

Over at the Department of Justice, the file languished for more than two months. Despite the passage of time, the only investigation pursued was to request a report from the convicting magistrate, Mr Lyons. Not surprisingly, Lyons pronounced himself seriously opposed to any exercise of executive clemency in the case, indicating that 'it would have a very bad effect, not only on Wanduta but also on his followers.' When J.D. McLean received this news back at Indian Affairs, on 15 May 1903, he drafted a reply for Clifford Sifton to send to George Coldwell. The letter was brief, paternalistic, and completely silent on the breach of jurisdictional process that the inquiry had uncovered:

I beg to inform you that the Department of Justice made inquiry into the matter and obtained a report from the convicting Magistrate, Mr. Lyons, who is of the opinion that should the Department take any action in this matter in the direction of clemency it would have a very bad effect not only on Wanduta but also upon his followers. Under the circumstances, therefore, the Department of Justice states that the case would not appear to be one for executive interference.[134]

The failure to address the jurisdictional matter was no mere oversight, but a profound flouting of duty. Only a few weeks earlier, David Laird had cabled the secretary of Indian Affairs to inquire whether it was an excess of jurisdiction for an Indian Agent to convict Aboriginal dancers using the informal procedure of summary conviction. J.D. McLean's reply, succinct and to the point, advised Laird that there was 'no jurisdiction to try summarily.'[135]

Whether Clifford Sifton was aware that his departmental officials were papering over a major departure from proper legal process is not clear. He forwarded the draft letter prepared by his underlings to Coldwell almost verbatim on 15 May 1903. Sifton may have failed to intervene further because of his preoccupation with other matters; he was deeply embroiled in the Alaska boundary dispute between 1902 and 1903, to the detriment of increasing demands from Manitoba party organizers for more of his personal attention. His main interest in Indian Affairs seems to have been devoted to reducing its budget. 'Economy is the Watchword' was how the Regina *Leader* described Sifton's efforts at departmental reorganization.[136] Another explanation may have been that he simply agreed with the tenor of Indian Affairs' response. Sifton would write a letter seven months later to Adélard Langevin, the white Roman Catholic Archbishop of Saint Boniface, indicating that he 'fully sustained' the efforts of the department to eradicate Aboriginal dancing.[137]

The reaction of the Dakota and their lawyer, George Coldwell, to the receipt of the letter only days before Wanduta's full prison sentence was complete, was anger and disgust. Coldwell wrote to both Clifford Sifton and the Department of Indian Affairs on 20 May 1903, to register substantial dismay. Although the letter began courteously enough, it soon began to stray somewhat from the even tone that typically characterized professional correspondence:

Dear Sir –
Your letter of May 15th is received for which we are much obliged. We are sorry that you have taken the view that you do in this matter. From inquiries we have made into the matter we are satisfied that the representations made to us are correct and it is the harshest kind of treatment that this Indian has received. We do not see why any different justice should be meted out to them than to a white man and certainly no white man has been treated in the way this Indian has. We

wrote to Mr. Lyons, the Magistrate for evidence on which he convicted this Indian and he hasn't even the scratch of a pen to show the grounds upon which he convicted him. It is a sentimental matter between him and Mr. Yeomans, the Indian Agent. We think that under the circumstances the executive clemency should at once have been meted out to this Indian instead of leaving him to serve his term and answering a letter about the time his term is up. When another matter of this kind occurs we shall not take the trouble to appeal to you but will apply for a habeas Corpus and bring the matter before the Courts, where redress can be got in a reasonable way.

Again thanking you for your delayed reply, we are,

Yours truly,

Coldwell & Coleman[138]

It is rare to see lawyers excoriating judicial personnel for their offhand, turnstile approach to criminal trials involving Aboriginal accused. It is still rarer to see white lawyers drawing such stark conclusions about racial bias in the criminal justice system and the lacklustre governmental response to a petition for executive clemency on behalf of an Aboriginal man. Given the passage of time, there was no longer any point in bringing a writ of *habeas corpus*, so Coldwell could only spew threats of such action in the future. Nor did he seem aware that a fundamental jurisdictional error had been committed and that the original committal of Wanduta to the Brandon jail was without legal force.

Back in Rapid City, the white civic leaders appear to have lost whatever interest they may have had in the legal struggle. Just as there was no local press coverage of the original trial, neither was there any report of the failure of the Dakota and their lawyer, George Coldwell, to secure Wanduta's release. The chroniclers of Rapid City local history, while waxing exuberant over the spectacular pageantry of the Dakota dances up to and including the year 1901, remain completely silent about the controversy stirred up over the 1902 dance. The accounts indicate that the 1903 July fair dazzled spectators with horse racing, baseball, football, and an aquatic program, but the absence of the Dakota dancers is not even documented.[139] A local paper, the Marquette *Reporter*, indicated in August 1903 that a number of Aboriginal communities continued to dance on their own reserves, despite concerted opposition from the Department of Indian Affairs.[140] The 1905 annual summer fair in Brandon featured a parade of Aboriginal people, described by one white observer as 'noble red men attired in all their gorgeousness,' who marched by the grandstand to the sound of drumming. They did not dance.[141]

First Nations and white fair organizers, Brandon Fair, 1916.

The enforcement arm of the criminal justice system gathered momentum over the next few decades as hundreds of First Nations dancers across the country were arrested, convicted, and jailed.[142] Federal politicians, intent upon expanding the scope of the law, brought in a series of amendments to facilitate prosecution. A 1914 enactment criminalized all 'Indian dances' outside the bounds of a 'reserve,' and 'Indian participation' in any 'show, exhibition, performance, stampede or pageant' in 'aboriginal costume' unless the Department of Indian Affairs had given its express consent. The amended offence was carefully designated a 'summary conviction' offence, eliminating any troublesome jurisdictional debates of the sort that had been swept under the rug in Wanduta's case.[143] In 1918, the summary jurisdiction procedure was expanded to encompass the original prohibition on Aboriginal dance as well. By striking out the word 'indictable' and substituting the phrase 'on summary procedure,' Parliament ensured that all dancing prosecutions could be dispatched with ease and speed, far from the higher courts with their fussy insistence upon legal niceties.[144]

A 1933 amendment expanded the offence again, deleting the words 'in aboriginal costume' from the section and making it possible to charge any Aboriginal participant, however attired. The Right Hon. Arthur Meighen explained that the amendment was 'intended to render it a little more difficult for Indians to evade the ban by making a slight change in their costume.' Although some legislators expressed reservations about keeping such a sweeping prohibition on the books, Meighen insisted that the dances were 'pretty wild affairs,' having a tendency to 'take them back to jungle conditions.'[145] One wonders whether the 'jungle' appellation struck any of his listeners as a bit off-kilter. In 1936, the white superintendent of Indian Affairs, Thomas Alexander Crerar, tabled another amendment to the Indian Act that would have enabled the authorities to seize and confiscate any property connected with Give-Away Dances. After vociferous challenge from several of the newly elected white Co-operative Commonwealth Federation MPs, including J.S. Woodsworth, Crerar agreed to pull the amendment from further consideration.[146]

In the face of distended legislation and the feverish pitch of prosecutions, Aboriginal peoples continued to register objections. Some retained counsel to mount vigorous defences against the charges laid against them.[147] Some resorted to subterfuge to trick or elude the authorities.[148] Others used political channels to petition legislators for surcease, initially through the representations of individual chiefs, and eventually capitalizing on the growing strength of the Pan-Indian movement to campaign through organized associations of Aboriginal peoples.[149]

Still others attempted to sway opinion through literary means. Pauline Johnson, a poet and orator from the Grand River Six Nations territory, was 'one of the most popular stage performers' in Canada at the turn of the century.[150] During a whirlwind tour of London, England, she wrote and published 'A Pagan in St. Paul's Cathedral,' depicting an Aboriginal person who stumbles upon a scene of worship in the English Protestant cathedral. The church with its altar-lights, organ music, sonorous boys' choir, and vestment-clad bishop, fades out of vision only to be replaced by the smouldering campfires of a starlit ceremony in the Onondaga longhouse, pulsing with drumming and rattles. Pauline Johnson makes explicit the parallel spiritual significance of the two scenes:

The deep-throated organ and the boys' voices were gone; I heard instead the melancholy incantations of our own pagan religionists. The beautiful dignity of our great sacrificial rites seemed to settle about me, to enwrap me in its garment of solemnity and primitive stateliness.

The atmosphere pulsed with the beat of the Indian drum, the eerie penetrations of the turtle rattle that set the time of the dancers' feet. Dance? It is not a dance, that marvellously slow, serpentine-like figure with the soft swish, swish of moccasined feet, and the faint jingling of elks'-teeth bracelets, keeping rhythm with every footfall. It is not a dance but an invocation of motion. Why may we not worship with the graceful movement of our feet? The paleface worships by moving his lips and tongue; the difference is but slight.[151]

The daughter of a Mohawk chief and an English-born white woman, Pauline Johnson divided her stage orations into two parts, the first delivered in a fringed buckskin dress and the second in an elaborate evening gown. Caught between two worlds, Pauline Johnson was well situated to draw the comparison between religious practices, and to make the implicit critique of the criminal sanctions being taken against the Aboriginal ceremonies.[152] Despite the tenacity, defiance, and determination of the First Nations, however, the prohibition on Aboriginal dance would remain in the Indian Act until 1951.[153]

The perseverance of the Aboriginal community, evident throughout the country, found particular personal expression in Wanduta. Following his release from jail, the Dakota Heyoka continued to carry on his spiritual activities. Wanduta's reputation as a healer spread well beyond the boundaries of the Oak River community, and his fame came to the attention of Wilson D. Wallis, a white anthropologist from the National Museum in Ottawa. On a mission to research the 'Canadian Dakota Sun Dance' in Manitoba, Wallis was sent to interview Wanduta in Brandon in 1914.[154]

Wallis's publications describe Wanduta's important role as a participant in the annual Dakota War Dances at the Brandon Exhibition. He recounts how Wanduta managed to cure a sick individual from the Dakota community in Portage la Prairie, when the medical expertise of other Native healers and white doctors from the nearby towns had failed. Under Wanduta's care, the sick man conducted a Sun Dance under cover of night darkness to avoid the detection of the authorities, and recovered immediately and completely.[155] Wallis records that the Dakota were resisting the efforts of criminal authorities to prosecute their religious expression, and that they continued to participate in ceremonial dances.[156] One can only wonder what Wanduta must have thought about Wallis's anthropological endeavours. He must have been both perplexed and amazed at the audacity of the federal government, wielding the club of the criminal law with one hand, while financing the academic exploration and transcribing of Aboriginal culture with the other.

4

'They Are a People Unacquainted with Subordination': First Nations Sovereignty Claims: *Sero* v *Gault*, Ontario, 1921

It was an unusual court exhibit. A forty-foot seine fishing net, with a mesh of about three inches, had become the centre of a storm of controversy before the Ontario Supreme Court in Belleville, in the spring of 1921. The net was owned by Eliza Sero, a fifty-two-year-old Mohawk widow from the Tyendinaga Mohawk Territory. She had woven a good portion of the mesh netting herself. The net was designed to be anchored by a 'spool' on the north shore of the Bay of Quinte on Lake Ontario, loaded onto a small rowboat, stretched out across the waters of the bay, and fastened securely to a second 'spool' down the shoreline. Several hours later, the Mohawk fishermen who operated the boat would rotate the spools to wind the net back into shore, along with the day's catch.[1]

Fish stocks were declining precipitously in the Great Lakes, due to environmental pressures from the burgeoning urban populations and persistent overfishing. Many desirable species, including Atlantic salmon, had entirely disappeared from Lake Ontario, but whitefish, herring, and pike stocks remained relatively plentiful. The Tyendinaga side of the Bay of Quinte was very flat and shallow, ideal for spawning. The Mohawk fished there, for sale to the nearby fresh-fish markets in Deseronto, for subsistence, and in keeping with traditional practices.[2]

Spring came early to eastern Ontario in 1921. A Deseronto reporter announced that the ice bridge across the Bay of Quinte had already broken up, the earliest this had happened in forty years, according to the old-timers. Today, however, Eliza Sero's seine net was not being cast over the waters of the Bay of Quinte. Today, it was the item that had catapulted the matter of Mohawk sovereignty before the Canadian courts.[3]

SEIZURE OF THE NET

Some months earlier, Thomas Gault, a white fishery inspector employed by the government, had entered the Tyendinaga Territory, seized the seine net, and confiscated it. He claimed lawful authority to do this, based on federal and provincial statutes making it illegal to fish without a licence. The legislation provided that all nets used in violation of the regulations should be 'confiscated to His Majesty.'[4] The enactments originally contained various forms of potential exemption for 'Indians,' but all of these had been deleted by 1914.[5] And there was no dispute about the licences. All parties agreed that neither Eliza Sero nor the Mohawk fishermen who used her seine net had taken out fishing licences.

Most cases of fishing violations were framed as criminal prosecutions, with the Crown pursuing the defendant for fines or imprisonment. The novel feature of this case was that the party originating the lawsuit was not the Crown, but the individual alleged to have breached the fishing regulation. Eliza Sero was the plaintiff who brought the case to court. She filed for $1,000 in damages from Thomas Gault, whom she named as a personal defendant. Claiming sovereignty over Mohawk lands on the Tyendinaga Mohawk Territory, Eliza Sero took issue with the seizure of her net, arguing that the ordinary provincial laws were not applicable to the Mohawk within Mohawk territories. Eliza Sero took the position that she was not a 'subject of the King,' but a member of the Mohawk Nation, also known as 'Kanienkehaka,' 'Gon-yon-gay-hah-gah,' or the people of the 'Land of the Flint,' an independent and sovereign nation.[6]

THE TYENDINAGA MOHAWKS OF THE HODENOSAUNEE CONFEDERACY

The claim of Mohawk sovereignty was not a novel one. The Tyendinaga Mohawk were members of the Six Nations Confederacy of the League of the Iroquois, composed of the Mohawk, Oneida, Onondaga, Cayuga, Seneca and Tuscarora peoples.[7] The confederacy was one of the oldest and most successful political unions on the continent, established well before the seventeenth century and functioning continuously for four centuries. The name the people of the confederacy used for themselves was 'Hodenosaunee,' from the Seneca language, meaning 'People of the Long House.'[8]

Iroquoian-speakers had long inhabited the area that would become the provinces of Ontario and Quebec – according to their oral histories, from 'time immemorial.'[9] Jacques Cartier left the first written records of meeting St Lawrence Iroquoians in 1534. French accounts place members of the confederacy, whom they called the 'Iroquois du Nord,' in year-round settlements dotting the north shore of Lake Ontario in the mid-seventeenth century. As was the case in other Aboriginal communities, however, the imported diseases and warfare generated by contact with white Europeans ravaged the Iroquoian peoples, displacing them from their hunting grounds and forcing many south into what is now New York State.[10]

There the members of the confederacy, skilled in agriculture, hunting, and fishing, resided in relative prosperity in semi-sedentary villages in the Mohawk Valley, surrounded by white American settlers who described the native communities as 'unequalled in townsite neatness.'[11] Forging diplomatic ties with other nations constituted a vital part of Iroquois culture, and one of their most important allies was the English. The alliance negotiated between English political and military leaders and the League of the Iroquois came to be known as the 'Covenant Chain,' represented in beaded wampum belts reciprocally exchanged in formal ceremony. One of the most important of these belts, the Gus-Wen-Qah, or Two-Row Wampum, is described as follows:

When the Haudenosaunee first came into contact with the European nations, treaties of peace and friendship were made. Each was symbolized by the Gus-Wen-Tah, or Two Row Wampum. There is a bed of white wampum which symbolizes the purity of the agreement. There are two rows of purple and those two rows have the spirit of your ancestors and mine. There are three beads of wampum separating the two rows and they symbolize peace, friendship and respect.

These two rows will symbolize two paths or two vessels, travelling down the same river together. One, a birch bark canoe, will be for the Indian people, their laws, their customs and their ways. The other, a ship, will be for the white people and their laws, their customs and their ways. We shall each travel the river together, side by side, but in our own boat. Neither of us will make compulsory laws or interfere in the internal affairs of the other. Neither of us will try to steer the other's vessel.[12]

The white officials who came into contact with the Mohawk in the eighteenth century were well aware of their claims to independence. Sir William Johnson, Northern Indian Superintendent, fully understood the relationship of equality symbolized in the 'Covenant Chain.' Writing in 1763 to the Lords of Trade, he noted: 'The English never conquered the Six Nations nor subjected them to English laws.' Four years later, he wrote to the Earl Shelburne: 'One who would call the Six Nations our subjects needs a good army at his back.' Colonel Daniel Claus, designated by the English as Superintendent to the Six Nations, put it succinctly in his letter to Governor Haldimand of 15 December 1783: '[T]hey are a people unacquainted with Subordination.'[13]

From the perspective of the English, alliances with the independent Iroquois were critical to their imperialistic goals. Some researchers have concluded that it was Iroquois support that ultimately tipped the balance of power in favour of the English during the Anglo-French colonial struggles. Others even refer to British North America as 'England's gift from her loyal Mohawks.'[14] When the British were faced with the American Revolution, they turned again to their traditional allies, the Six Nations Confederacy, to join them in mustering arms against the rebels. Several Mohawk chiefs, who would later play a pivotal role in founding the Tyendinaga Mohawk community, were among the first to take up the call. Joseph Brant (Thayendanegea), John Deserontyon, Isaac Hill (Anoghsoktea), and Aaron Hill (Kanonraron) led the warriors from the Mohawk communities of Canajoharie and Fort Hunter into active battle.[15]

When their own settlements came under attack by American troops and Oneida forces sympathetic to the rebels, the Mohawk residents of Canajoharie fled west to Niagara, while the Fort Hunter Mohawks escaped north to Lachine. Quebec governor Sir Guy Carleton and British general Sir Frederick Haldimand gave their Mohawk allies specific assurances that their property in western New York would be fully restored after the war. The displaced Mohawks continued to mount small-scale attacks on American settlements, using scouting parties to capture prisoners and undertake intelligence activities. In 1782, much to the chagrin and consternation of their Aboriginal allies, the British commanders ordered a halt to the fighting. In 1783, the Treaty of Versailles recognized an independent American republic, comprising the territory south of the Great Lakes and the 45th parallel, including the lands formerly belonging to the Mohawk communities.[16]

The Mohawk were seriously affronted that the British had purported to give up Six Nations territory to the Americans without consulting them, an injustice that several declared 'Christians *only* were capable of doing, that the Indians were incapable of acting so.' The treaty terms flew in the face of the unwavering promises Haldimand had made to Brant and Deserontyon during the hostilities. The British were cognizant of the betrayal in their failure to restore the Mohawk to their former villages and hunting grounds. Allan Maclean, the white Superintendent of Indian Affairs at Niagara, noted as much in his letter to Governor Haldimand: '[The Six Nations] Indians were a free People Subject to no Power upon Earth ... [T]hey were the faithful Allies of the King of England, but not his Subjects ... [H]e had no right Whatever to grant away to the States of America, their Rights or properties without a manifest breach of all justice and Equity, and they would not Submit to it.'[17]

On 27 May 1783, Brant and Deserontyon travelled to Quebec to lodge a protest with Governor Haldimand over the cession of their lands. In recompense for their losses and in recognition of their steadfast military support, General Haldimand advised Brant and Deserontyon to relocate their communities. He recommended Canada West land between the Gananoque and Trent rivers, which the British had recently purchased from the Mississauga nation.[18] The two Mohawk chiefs accompanied a surveyor up the St Lawrence to examine the area in May 1783, but Brant subsequently rejected the proposal. He contracted instead for a land grant on the Grand River near Brantford, which would become known as the Six Nations Grand River Territory. Deserontyon preferred the original offer, and settled his followers on a 7,000-acre tract of land on the Bay of Quinte, at the Tyendinaga Territory. The location on the Bay of Quinte was historically significant to the Mohawks. According to their oral traditions, this was the same area where Deganwidah, also known as the Peacemaker and founder of the Six Nations Confederacy, had been born.[19]

Deserontyon and approximately one hundred Mohawks from sixteen families landed at the present site of the village of Deseronto on the Bay of Quinte on 22 May 1784. Isaac Hill and Aaron Hill joined them with an additional group somewhat later. At Tyendinaga the Mohawks established a school; erected farm houses; cleared the land to sow grain; and began to rear horses, cattle, and sheep.[20] Various acculturating pressures influenced many to join Christian churches, learn English, and accept waged labour in the towns of Deseronto and Belleville that grew up beside the Tyendinaga Mohawk Territory. However, the Mohawk had migrated to Ontario to ensure the survival of their culture and to maintain their political and territorial independence. As Joseph Brant wrote shortly before his death in 1807, the Mohawk also retained a distinct preference for their own legal system:

Among us we have no prisons, we have no pompous parade of courts; we have no written laws, and yet judges are revered among us as they are among you, and their decisions are as highly regarded.

Property, to say the least, is well guarded, and crimes are as impartially punished. We have among us no splendid villains above the control of our laws. Daring wickedness is never suffered to triumph over helpless innocence. The estates of widows and orphans are never devoured by enterprising sharpers. In a word, we have no robbery under color of law.[21]

The original position of the Mohawk, that they had always been and remained a sovereign nation, continued unshaken.

ELIZA SERO, MOHAWK WOMAN

It is not surprising that it was a woman, Eliza Sero, who put forth the sovereignty claim in the courts. The Mohawk were traditionally a matrilineal society, in which women had more social freedom, more economic autonomy, and more political power than their white female counterparts. Since property was 'owned' by those who used or occupied it, women, who were historically responsible for agriculture, held primary authority over the village, the land, and the food supply. Upon marriage, a Mohawk woman continued to control her own property, maintained full custody of all children, and possessed the right of divorce. Chieftainships were determined through female lines of descent, selected by the senior women of the clan. The 'matrons,' the women of the lineage's eldest living generation, functioned as dominant figures within Mohawk society. Indeed, they were equal signatories to the earliest treaties, along with the chiefs.[22]

Pauline Johnson, the Mohawk poet from Six Nations Grand River who visited London, England, as an internationally acclaimed poet and dignitary in 1906, stated: 'I have heard that the daughters of this vast city cry out for a voice in the Parliament of this land. There is no need for an Iroquois woman to clamour for recognition in our councils; she has had it for upwards of four centuries.'[23] It is true that traditional matrilineal customs faced erosion through juxtaposition with the male-dominant white society during the nineteenth and early twentieth centuries. But those who struggled to maintain Iroquois culture guarded the role of women with care.[24]

Eliza Sero, n.d.

Eliza Sero's unmarried name was Eliza Brant (her Mohawk name has been lost). She was the daughter of two Tyendinaga Mohawks, Margaret Brant and Jacob Oak Brant. She was born into the Turtle Clan in 1869, on the Tyendinaga Mohawk Territory, where she would live all her life. Most Mohawk women married young during the nineteenth century, and Eliza was no exception. On 5 October 1882, at the age of fourteen, she was married in the Anglican Christ Church to Israel Sero, also a Mohawk from the Tyendinaga Territory. Israel was then twenty-five years old, and listed his occupation as a 'labourer.' The couple took up residence together, on Sero property between Dawson Creek and Sucker Creek, on the shoreline of the Bay of Quinte. There they constructed a two-storey wooden, two- or three-bedroom house on the point of Eagle Hill.[25]

The Sero family grew slowly but steadily, with Eliza giving birth to eight children over the course of the next twenty-eight years. Clara Bella was born in 1883, Theresa in 1885, Rosa in 1888, Maud in 1892, Earl Reuben in 1897, Annie Elfreda in 1899, James in 1902, and Nelson Lorne

Eliza Sero's two-storey, wood-frame house on Eagle Hill, Tyendinaga Mohawk Territory, *circa* 1930.

in 1910. Eliza Sero's great-granddaughter Audrey Chisholm recalls her great-grandmother as short in stature and plump, her hair 'tied back in a knot,' and always attired in calf-length 'high-button boots.' Fluent in Mohawk, Eliza Sero was able to converse to some degree in English as well. Although Eliza's husband, Israel, must have done some work for wages away from Tyendinaga, the family also continued the traditional Mohawk way of life: farming, fishing, and trapping. The community grew corn, tomatoes, and peas, and raised cattle, chickens, and pigs. They fished for pickerel, eels, and mudcats in the spring, and whitefish in the fall. They trapped muskrats and beaver for pelts, and hunted ducks for food. It was a labour-intensive means of obtaining a livelihood, one that required all members of the family to contribute.[26]

Tragedy struck the Sero family twice only a few years after the birth of Eliza's last child. Israel Sero died at the age of fifty-seven, on 21 November 1914. Then Eliza's eldest son, Earl Reuben, was killed in France in 1917, while on active military service during the First World War. Three of Eliza's daughters had already married and left home, but Eliza struggled to support her remaining children with the help of neighbours. She arranged with other members of the band to continue fishing on a share basis. As the owner of the valuable seine net, she was entitled to half the catch. The fishermen who operated the net took the other half of the catch

Reuben Sero (who died in the First World War), seated on lower right-hand side, with fellow soldiers, *circa* 1917.

Clara Brant, Registered Nurse, Eliza Sero's daughter, n.d.

and split it among themselves. The net was extremely valuable to Eliza Sero, and its seizure by government officials represented a significant financial loss. Her legal claim would have been motivated by a desire to secure the economic livelihood of her family, as well as to attest to the long-standing sovereignty of the Mohawk people.[27]

THE LAUNCH OF THE LAWSUIT

The timing of the legal challenge suggests that it may have been inspired, in part, by the 'pan-Indian consciousness' that welled up in the wake of the First World War. First Nations individuals from across Canada were brought together to serve militarily overseas. When they returned from active service, many were convinced that they needed collective pressure to resolve long-standing grievances. From 1914 on, First Nations communities began to embark upon a wave of agitation that stretched across the country. Some were inspired by Chief Thunderwater (Oghema Niagara), a resident of Cleveland, Ohio, who had been highly successful in revitalizing First Nations cultural and political activism internationally. Thunderwater campaigned throughout southern Quebec and Ontario for Aboriginal autonomy and improvements in education, health, and living conditions. He advocated political and legal action to fight 'the white man' with 'his own weapons.' In 1918, he managed to initiate a private member's bill in the House of Commons to incorporate the Council of the Indian Tribes of Canada.[28]

The strength of Chief Thunderwater's organization peaked in 1919, when the Department of Indian Affairs began to counterattack, accusing him of fraudulent motives and 'Black ancestry.' War veteran Frederick Ogilvie Loft, a Mohawk from the Six Nations, took over the leadership of First Nations political activism, helping to found the League of Indians of Canada, an organization whose reach extended west to Alberta by the early 1920s. The concerted commitment to change represented by these organizational breakthroughs may have encouraged Eliza Sero to bring her legal claim. Chief Thunderwater visited Tyendinaga during his excursions and garnered some support there. Eliza Sero may also have been aware of the charismatic Loft, whose ancestors would have been among the Six Nations group that settled with Joseph Brant at Grand River near Brantford, Ontario, the same year that Eliza Sero's ancestors settled at Tyendinaga.[29]

Eliza Sero retained Edward Guss Porter, KC, as counsel to represent her in the case, which was scheduled to be heard in both Belleville and

Ottawa. Porter was a sixty-two-year-old, white lawyer with the law firm of Porter, Butler and Payne in Belleville, who also served as the mayor of Belleville and the Conservative member of Parliament for West Hastings. Porter was probably selected to act on this case because of his knowledge of the political momentum within First Nations communities. He was the MP who introduced the private member's bill to incorporate the Council for the Indian Tribes of Canada.[30] Utilizing centuries-old English common-law doctrines, Porter framed the action in 'trover,' demanding $1,000 satisfaction for the value of Eliza Sero's seine fishing net. 'Trover' is a legal action in tort, traditionally brought by an owner whose property has been wrongfully seized, to recover the value of the lost goods.[31]

Although the transcript of the proceedings of the trial has not survived, it is probable that Eliza Sero, the plaintiff, was called as the first witness. Edward Guss Porter would have wanted her to give evidence concerning the seine net, her ownership of it, and how it came to be taken from her. Canadian courts had historically expressed some scepticism about the testimony of Aboriginal people, especially if they were not Christians and could not swear to the truth of their evidence by taking the oath on the Bible. It seems clear that there was some hesitation to admit the testimony of 'Indians' at all, for statutes passed in 1874, 1876, 1880, and 1886 had to specify that 'Indians shall be competent witnesses.'[32]

Legislation had also been enacted to regularize the testimony of 'any Indian or aboriginal native or native of mixed blood, who is destitute of the knowledge of God, and of any fixed and clear belief in religion or in a future state of rewards and punishments.' Such individuals could testify without the customary oath, so long as they gave a 'solemn affirmation or declaration to tell the truth,' and the presiding judge cautioned them that they would 'incur punishment' if they did not tell the truth. Eliza Sero would have had to explain to the judge that she was a confirmed member of the Anglican Church, in order to be spared this indignity.[33]

No fewer than three white male lawyers appeared to argue against Eliza Sero's claim. William Carnew and Malcolm Wright represented Thomas Gault, the fishery inspector, and Deputy Attorney General Edward J. Bayly, KC, intervened on behalf of the attorney general for Ontario.[34] All three argued that Thomas Gault was fully authorized to seize the net by virtue of various statutes that made it illegal to fish without a licence. They bolstered their position by proving, in laborious detail, that both the federal and the provincial government had constitutional jurisdiction to pass the respective game and fisheries statutes.

The remaining and more complicated question was whether there was 'power in either Dominion or Province or in both together to pass such legislation in respect of these Indians.' Eliza Sero's lawyer maintained that, 'from the time of Joseph Brant,' the Mohawk had been an 'independent people.' As allies rather than subjects of the Crown, they were 'exempt from the civil laws governing the true subject.'[35]

Sero's lawyer was assisted in this argument by a second white lawyer, Andrew Gordon Chisholm, who intervened in the case on behalf of the Six Nations of Grand River. Andrew Chisholm was a fifty-eight-year-old London lawyer who had acquired a reputation as a leading expert on Aboriginal legal issues. He was held in such regard that he had even been named an honorary chief. Chisholm represented the Mississauga of the Credit, the Chippewa of the Thames, the Onyota'a:ka (Oneida) of the Thames, and the Six Nations Grand River on a variety of legal claims. He was expert in many aspects of First Nations legal concerns, from the enforcement of treaty rights to land disputes. For several years, he had been working with Chief Deskeheh of the Six Nations Grand River, compiling historical evidence to support the claim of Six Nations sovereignty.[36]

Chisholm filed a lengthy petition with the court, in which he asserted that the Six Nations were 'a perfectly independent people,' with every right 'to continue in the enjoyment of all their national rights and privileges.' The most fundamental was the right to 'self-government of their own internal and domestic affairs.' 'From the time of their earliest contact,' Great Britain had recognized Six Nations 'rights and sovereignty':

She considered them as nations competent to maintain the relations of Peace and War and governing themselves in their own way, with a distinct country of their own ... There was a mutual recognition of sovereignty, each acknowledging the natural and primordial rights of the other party. Political status was on each side conceded. Each covenanted for the members of its own community. The power to govern, to punish, to be responsible for the actions of individuals forming the respective governments, was assumed and acknowledged by each.[37]

The Six Nations based their sovereignty claim not only upon their long-standing diplomatic and military relationship with Britain, but also upon their status as 'aborigines of this country.' While they maintained that the situation of the Six Nations presented 'unique features,' they insisted that sovereignty was inherent to all 'Indian tribes' that continued to reside on 'lands or territory not surrendered to the Crown.' Claiming

Andrew Chisholm.

'their ancient right of self-government,' the Six Nations asserted control over most areas of legal affairs:

The Six Nations were absolute owners of their original possessions and were a self-governing people in every way, adjudicating both civil and criminal offences, but at a subsequent period a deputation from the government of Canada appealed to the chiefs in council to allow the judiciary of Canada to deal with the crimes of rape and theft committed by their people on the reserve, to which the chiefs in council acceded, but were never asked to make any other concession whatsoever.

They also claim the right to settle all controversies themselves re title to lands, membership of band, descent, alienations, incumbrances and the settlement of estate, and the right to determine as to who is and who is not a desirable tenant on their reserve, the selection of such officers as are paid out of their funds.

The Six Nations contested the legitimacy of the Canadian judiciary, noting that their people 'should not be placed under the judicial authority of which they have no voice in selection.' The concept of representative voice was integral to Six Nations government, and in this they argued they were 'in advance of their English allies' in some ways, for their political structures 'recognize[d] their women as having a part in legislation.' Using imagery from ancient Wampum belts conveying alliance – not subjugation – between two sovereign peoples, they concluded:

Therefore the Six Nations feel that they should not be compelled nor snared into accepting a position and condition inconsistent with the solemn covenants and assurance made with and to them and which were to continue as long as the sun continued to shine, the grass to grow and the waters in the rivers to run, on the honor of the British Crown.[38]

The white lawyers representing the Crown ought not to have been surprised by these claims. The Six Nations position had never wavered from the times of earliest contact. Chiefs from the Six Nations presented multiple petitions to the British and Canadian governments in 1839, 1890, 1920, and 1921, demanding the right to be governed by their own laws and customs.[39] The Department of Indian Affairs dismissed these claims as 'highly amusing' and a 'hopeless project,' and the Wampum belts as 'so called treaties,' setting the stage for the arguments that the government lawyers would make in *Sero*.[40]

The Six Nations also premised their claim on the distinct and exhaustive rights they obtained over the lands originally granted to them at the culmination of the American Revolutionary War. Mohawk Chief Deserontyon had wisely insisted that the Haldimand land grant of 1784, which transferred the Tyendinaga lands on the Bay of Quinte to the Mohawk, be formalized, which it was on 1 April 1793, in a deed issued by the white lieutenant-governor, John Graves Simcoe. The 'Simcoe Deed' granted

unto the Chiefs, Warriors, Women and People of the said Six nations and their Heirs for ever ... for the sole use and behoof of them and their Heirs forever ... confirming the full and entire possession, Use, benefit and advantage of the said District or Territory of Land to be held and enjoyed by them in the most free and ample manner and according to the several Customs and usages ... securing to them the free and undisturbed possession and enjoyment of the same.[41]

And these were the precise words that Eliza Sero quoted to the Ontario Supreme Court that spring. She was entitled to use her seine net however she pleased on lands she 'held and enjoyed' in the 'most free and ample manner,' according to the Mohawk 'several customs and usages.'[42]

A HISTORY OF LITIGATION CLAIMING SIX NATIONS SOVEREIGNTY

This was not the first time that the matter of First Nations sovereignty had been litigated in Ontario courts.[43] An 1823 case, *The King* v *Phelps*, considered a sovereignty claim in the context of a dispute over the Crown's right to seize the lands of Epaphrus Phelps for treason. The land originally belonged to the Six Nations of Grand River. It had been assigned by Joseph Brant for a term of 999 years to Phelps, a white man, in trust for the support of Phelps's Mohawk wife and three children. Phelps was indicted for treason in the aftermath of the War of 1812, and fled to the United States. Esther Phelps, his Mohawk wife, contested the Crown's right to forfeit her husband's lands in the normal manner. Her argument was that Epaphrus Phelps's entitlement to the land amounted to no more than a trust limited to providing for his wife and children. The Six Nations of Grand River continued to maintain their rights over the property, pursuant to the original Haldimand land grant, which the chiefs characterized as a 'binding treaty' made with a 'distinct' and 'independent' people, who were 'not subject to mere positive laws.' The Crown's white lawyer hotly contested these assertions, labelling the claim of immunity from British law 'absurd.' The white judges of the Upper Canada King's Bench ruled for the Crown, without giving any reasons.[44]

More fulsome treatment could be found in an 1852 decision concerning the legal rights of the Six Nations over their Grand River land. *Sheldon* v *Ramsay* also involved a dispute over lands seized by the Crown from a white man who had been convicted of treason. The traitorous white man originally held the land through a lease granted by Joseph Brant. The issue was whether Brant had the legal right to lease the land in the first place. The actual lawsuit involved only white litigants: the white man who purchased the land from the Crown after forfeiture, and the white squatters who inhabited the lands after the traitor fled to the United States. The squatters claimed that the traitor could not have legally forfeited the lands because he could not acquire a legal title from Brant. The position that members of the Six Nations might have taken on their land rights and sovereignty was argued only indirectly by the white men concerned.

The white chief justice, John Beverley Robinson, made no attempt to canvass Six Nations views on sovereignty. This did not stop him from issuing a devastating judgment against their interests, ruling that the Six Nations could not hold legal title to their lands. Robinson even went so far as to question General Haldimand's authority to grant the original tract of land. He insisted upon the applicability of the British law of real property to Aboriginal peoples, noting that 'the common law is not part savage and part civilized.' The most that the Upper Canada Court of Queen's Bench was willing to concede was that the Six Nations were a 'distinct race of people,' but the judge's myopic powers of observation accorded them 'no national existence, nor any recognized patriarchal or other form of government or management, so far as we see in any way.'[45]

This type of muddled thinking seems to have been entrenched in the ideology of European colonizers. As Olive Dickason has noted, the Spaniards, Portuguese, French, and English all proceeded to colonize the New World 'on the basis that this region was *terra nullius*, uninhabited land.' The gist of the argument is that 'since the Amerindians led a mobile life without settled abode, "ranging" the land "like beasts in the woods" rather than inhabiting it, they could not be classified as inhabitants according to European law.' Refusing to recognize the distinct and varied forms of Aboriginal political structures, the colonizers concluded that they were 'savages' who lived without the benefit of any organized national state. Furthermore, Europeans seem to have believed that Christians ought to prevail over non-Christians, using their religious preferences to disavow Aboriginal rights as well.[46]

European ideology, as well as the earlier cases of *Phelps* and *Sheldon*, weighed heavily against the claim that Eliza Sero was attempting to make. Yet none of this stopped Eliza Sero from taking her assertions of Mohawk sovereignty into the judicial forum. There are no surviving records to indicate why she chose to seek vindication within the Canadian legal system, dominated exclusively by Euro-Canadian, white men. Speculation presents several possible motives. At the most practical level, she was missing a valuable net. To obtain reimbursement, Eliza Sero was forced, by necessity, to make her arguments before the legal authorities who administered the laws within which the fishery inspector purported to act. On a more idealistic plane, Eliza Sero and the lawyers representing her may have felt that the Canadian courts might benefit from reviewing the full documentary evidence of Mohawk sovereignty. Presumably they believed that Eliza Sero's claim, bolstered by the supporting legal argument from the intervening Six Nations community, had a realistic chance of success.

Theoretically, there was some risk in bringing the action before the Canadian courts. Some might have viewed the mere launching of the claim as a formal recognition of the lawful jurisdiction of Canadian judges over Mohawk litigants. Those who viewed Aboriginal self-government as a matter of inherent right might have remarked upon the irony of seeking support for Mohawk sovereignty within the ranks of the legal system of the 'colonizers.' To use the symbolism of the Two-Row Wampum, was it an exercise in folly for one of the occupants from the 'canoe' to cross over to the 'ship' and ask one of the ship's occupants to rule on the navigational course of the two vessels?

Another way of looking at the problem is to suggest that Eliza Sero was not asking the occupants of the ship to chart the course of the birchbark canoe. She was merely asking them to alter the ship's navigational course, because it had strayed from its proper path on the river and was in danger of swamping the canoe. In the spirit of the beads of wampum separating the two rows – symbolizing peace, friendship, and respect – Eliza Sero was attempting to reach across to the Canadian judicial authorities. She was seeking to communicate Mohawk resistance to the unlawful intrusions on First Nations culture and way of life. If this analysis accurately captures Eliza Sero's motivation, it was a mark of diplomatic respect that brought her into the Ontario Supreme Court. It

Left to right: Clara Sero Brant (Eliza's daughter), Eliza Sero, Theresa Sero Green (Eliza's daughter), *circa* 1930.

was a continuation of the traditional expression of courtesy that First Nations peoples had always extended to outsiders. It was by no means an expression of submission, deference, or capitulation.

JUSTICE RIDDELL OF THE ONTARIO SUPREME COURT

The white Ontario Supreme Court judge appointed to hear the *Sero* case was William Renwick Riddell. Reputed to be an 'ardent imperialist,' a man more unlikely to be supportive of Aboriginal sovereignty claims could hardly have been found. William Renwick Riddell had long-standing and established ties to the political, social, and economic elite of the province. He was born in Cobourg, Ontario, in 1852, to Presbyterian parents who emigrated from Dumfries, Scotland, in 1833. Riddell obtained a bachelor of arts and science from Victoria College, Cobourg, and carried off the gold medal from Osgoode Hall Law School in Toronto in

1883. He married Anna Hester Kirsop Crossen in 1884, a 'generously dowered' member of Toronto's white 'well-to-do gentry,' who would maintain a lifelong interest in the charitable works of the Imperial Order Daughters of the Empire. The couple took up residence in 'sumptuous' premises at 109 St George Street, down the street from Premier Oliver Mowat in a neighbourhood of 'Victorian residential splendour.' A member of the Toronto Club, the London Club, and the Ontario Jockey Club, Riddell was named a Queen's Counsel in 1899, and served as a bencher of the Law Society from 1891 until 1906, when he received his appointment to the Ontario Supreme Court. A lifelong supporter of the Liberal party, he was on a first-name basis in his correspondence with Prime Ministers Wilfrid Laurier and William Lyon Mackenzie King, whom he petitioned incessantly for judicial elevation.[47]

Riddell cultivated a reputation as an avid classicist, prided himself on being able to use Latin daily in his work, and claimed to read the entire *Iliad* and *Odyssey* each year in their original form. He was a much sought-after speaker. During the course of his career, he gave hundreds of speeches to different bar associations, university convocations, and organizations such as the Empire Club of Canada and the Canadian Society of New York. A prodigious writer, he published more than 1,200 articles on various aspects of early Canadian history, law, and international relations. Riddell's biographer acclaims him as one of Canada's great publicists for the 'loyalist, imperialist heritage.' His reputation as a judge is that of a rather stuffy specimen of the old school, caught up with the prestige of his position, who brooked no 'slang in his court.' Partially deaf in his later years, the petulant Riddell would occasionally stop counsel in mid-flight to register his disapproval of their arguments by removing his hearing aid, plunking it down on the table, and insisting rancorously: 'I don't want to hear that.'[48]

Somewhat surprisingly, Riddell seems to have fancied himself something of a progressive on certain racial issues. The history of Black slavery fascinated Riddell, and he was an unequivocal supporter of abolition. He wrote a number of historical papers on slavery in Canada, expressing pride in the steps taken to free British slaves at Niagara-on-the-Lake before the English Parliament had abolished slavery. Riddell contributed historical articles to *The Dawn of Tomorrow*, a Black newspaper published in London, Ontario, in the 1920s and 1930s. His research earned him an honorary editorship of the journal. Riddell's apparent dislike for the institution of slavery did not, however, extend to a wider comprehension of the evils of racism. His various articles and speeches suggest that he viewed Blacks as distinctly inferior, 'incompetent,' and 'uncivilized.'[49] He took time out of his busy schedule to serve as president of the Canadian Social Hygiene Council, a group that promoted eugenics as a mechanism for 'racial improvement' and whose publications admonished 'The Race is to the Strong.'[50]

Something of Riddell's attitudes towards Aboriginal peoples may be discerned in an article he would publish some years later, in the *Journal of Criminal Law, Criminology and Police Science* in 1929. In it he describes the importance of extending British criminal law to the Inuit and First Nations of Western and northern Canada, whom he describes as people with 'savage appetites,' having 'little conception of government by law,' who 'seldom considered themselves to be bound by anything but their own desires.' He contrasts whites, whom he labels a 'higher race,' as surpassing 'such forms of humanity and grades of civilization as were represented by the Esquimaux and the wandering Indian tribes.'[51]

A review of the other articles Riddell published that touch on Aboriginal matters reveals an explicit and unwavering colonial mentality and paternalistic bias.[52] Two of his publications deal with the *Phelps* case. Writing in *The University Magazine* in 1913, Riddell describes the Mohawks as 'a distinct though a feudatory people,' and Esther Phelps as 'a Mohawk maiden rejoicing in the name of Esther,' who had 'captured the fancy of a white man, a schoolmaster called Epaphrus Lord Phelps.' On the sovereignty question, Riddell expresses considerable satisfaction over the anti-Mohawk resolution of the *Phelps* case:

The solicitor-general took the ground, which has ever since been held good law, that the Indians are bound by the common law and have no rights higher than those of other people. [...] In the United States there has been from time to time question as to the legal status of Indians and Indian land; in Ontario there never has been any doubt that all the land, Indian or otherwise, is the king's, and that Indians are subjects in the same way as others. There are no troublesome subtleties in Canadian law.[53]

In 1920, he published a revised version of the article in the *Canadian Law Times*. This time, he offhandedly labels the Haldimand grant 'a so-called treaty.' In the earlier article he had dismissed it as 'not a treaty in any accurate sense of the term.' Judge Riddell, then, had already published articles which suggest he was predisposed to favour the arguments made by the Crown in the *Sero* case.[54]

An additional factor in the allocation of Judge Riddell's predilections may have related to the gender of the plaintiff. Riddell's position on women's rights is well known. He had disrupted a meeting of the Law Society of Upper Canada in 1892 in an unsuccessful attempt to prevent the admission of Clara Brett Martin, the first woman seeking entrance to the profession of law. Contemporaneously with hearing the *Sero* case, Riddell was preparing a manuscript titled 'An Old-Time Misogynist,' which he would publish one year later in the *Canadian Magazine*. The article offered Riddell the opportunity to translate at length, and with obvious gusto, long passages from ancient Latin texts describing women variously as 'a daily injury,' 'perpetually complaining,' 'a constant liar,' 'fondling and caressing deceit,' 'a filthy bedmate,' and 'a piece of hell.' Commenting that the passages had been 'well selected,' Riddell sanctimoniously suggests that the 'advance made by woman toward obtaining simple justice' meant that no modern country would allow such a book to be published. Profoundly ignorant of the centuries of Iroquoian tradition that celebrated the economic, political, cultural, and spiritual power of women, William Renwick Riddell probably wondered why in the world such weighty legal litigation had been relegated to an ageing widow.[55]

Equally unsettling to Judge Riddell must have been the presence of Andrew Chisholm in the courtroom. The lawyer intervening for the Six Nations of Grand River had considerable previous dealings with Judge Riddell. Before Riddell's appointment to the bench, the two had squared off on opposite sides of the courtroom in 1904 in the *Jones* v *Grand Trunk Railway* case. That dispute centred on the right of 'Indians' to travel on the Grand Trunk Railway on reduced-fare tickets. An agreement signed between the railway company and the Six Nations in 1875 contracted for a right-of-way across Six Nations lands in exchange for a commitment that Aboriginal people could travel at half-fare on the line. Chisholm represented Charlotte Jones, who claimed entitlement to the reduced fare, and Riddell represented the railway. The case had been a bit of a draw. Chisholm won recognition that the railway wrongly ejected Charlotte Jones in the incident under dispute. But Riddell succeeded on the larger question, getting the court to rule that the Six Nations had no right to make binding agreements about the alienation of their land without the approval of the Superintendent General of Indian Affairs. The thrust of the argument Riddell made as the counsel in *Jones* was undeniably inimical to the claims the Six Nations were pressing before him in the *Sero* case.[56]

William Renwick Riddell.

Chisholm was also forced to appear as supplicant in Judge Riddell's court in 1909, when he attempted to recover payment owing to him for legal services rendered on behalf of the Mississauga of the Credit. Chisholm acted for the Mississauga in the landmark case of *Henry* v *The King* in 1905, when he convinced the Exchequer Court to rule that the federal government was delinquent in paying out treaty monies. Although he was successful in *Henry* in obtaining a decree for a large sum of money for the Mississauga, Chisholm was never paid for his legal services. A meeting of the band council in 1909 decided to consent to judgment for the more than $10,000 owed, an amount which the council conceded was a fair and honest assessment of the worth of the services rendered. A court order was subsequently registered in favour of Chisholm. Shortly thereafter, six members of the band joined with the Superintendent General of Indian Affairs and the Minister of Justice to oppose payment. After hearing from all of the parties, Judge Riddell ruled that the original decision of the band council to consent to the order could not bind all of the members of the band, and ousted the order for Chisholm's payment.[57]

What Judge Riddell and Andrew Chisholm must have thought about being thrown together again in the context of another First Nations legal dispute is unrecorded. Judge Riddell heard out the arguments from all of the lawyers involved, and reserved on his decision for some months after the hearing. He released his decision in March 1921.

THE DECISION IN *SERO* V *GAULT*

Of Chisholm's petition, Judge Riddell was curtly, almost surreptitiously, dismissive: 'Mr. A.G. Chisholm, counsel for the Six Nations, whom I heard as *amicus curiae*, made a very able and interesting argument, chiefly on historical grounds; but, for the reasons stated, I am unable to accede to it.' The reasons Riddell offered for his rejection of Eliza Sero's claim were not significantly more forthcoming. A clue to the frame of mind that lay behind the ruling may rest in the judge's vocabulary. Riddell was unable to bring himself to refer to treaties between the Mohawk and the Crown – painstakingly placing the word 'treaties' in quotation marks, or inserting the adjectival phrase 'so-called' before any such reference. Although he professed to have conducted extensive research on the matter – even going to the lengths of searching through the files in the Canadian Archives, files he was notorious for failing to return – Riddell found little to guide him.[58] He made reference to one statement from a white judge, William Dummer Powell, in 1837, to the effect that 'Indians, so long as they are within their villages, are not subject to the ordinary laws of the Province.' This, stressed Riddell, is merely an 'unofficial opinion,' which Judge Powell later recanted.[59] The only case law to which Riddell referred was the murder conviction of a member of the Ottawa nation in 1822, and the manslaughter conviction of a member of the Six Nations of Grand River over which Riddell himself had presided.[60]

Riddell failed to make reference to either the *Phelps* or the *Sheldon* case, possibly a deliberate oversight in view of his pre-trial pronouncements on the *Phelps* matter. Nor, despite his self-acknowledged resort to the dusty tomes of the archives looking for precedents, did he cite a string of earlier legal cases which examined the applicability of various statutory regulations to Aboriginal peoples. He might have referred to the 1907 Ontario case of *Rex* v *Hill*, which upheld the conviction of George W. Hill, an 'unenfranchised treaty Indian' of the Brant and Haldimand Territory, for practising medicine without a licence. Although the *Hill* court specifically declined to say what would have been the result if Hill had confined his practice to 'Indians' on an 'Indian reserve,' it concluded that dealings outside the 'reserve' were to be governed by the applicable provincial law.[61] Following *Hill*, the 1917 Ontario case of *Rex* v *Martin* ruled that the Ontario Temperance Act applied to Indians beyond the limits of an Indian 'reserve.'[62] Strictly speaking, one might have distinguished *Hill* and *Martin* from the *Sero* case, in that the events in *Sero* all took place on Mohawk Territory. However, many later courts were quick to expand *Hill*, citing it as authority for imposing provincial law to incidents on the 'reserve' as well.[63]

Riddell might also have considered the 1908 Ontario case of *The King* v *Beboning*, which held that the theft provisions of the Criminal Code could be enforced against 'Indians' on a 'reserve.' Failing to provide reasons or to cite authority for its conclusion, the *Beboning* court made the sweeping assertion that 'the suggestion that the Criminal Code does not apply to Indians is also so manifestly absurd as to require no refutation.'[64]

Although Judge Riddell did not make reference to any of them, there are also several cases that dealt with Native hunting and fishing rights. The British Columbia case *Rex* v *Jim* held in 1915 that a North Saanich chief could not be convicted for hunting deer for his own use on North Saanich lands, because the provisions of the provincial game-protection statute did not apply to 'Indians.' The usefulness of this case to Eliza Sero was limited, however, because the British Columbia case focused exclusively upon the constitutional division of powers, with the court holding that the federal government had exclusive jurisdiction over the management of Indian 'reserves.' The *Jim* court conceded that, although the province could not restrict the hunting rights of 'Indians,' the federal government could.[65]

The difficulty for Eliza Sero was that one of the regulations under which her net was seized was issued by the federal government. Moreover, a Quebec court had actually upheld the right of the province to impose hunting restrictions upon First Nations communities. The 1917 case *Dion* v *La Compagnie de la Baie D'Hudson* cited the Ontario *Hill* decision, and ruled that 'Indians in Canada are British subjects and ... subject to all provincial laws which the province has power to enact.'[66]

None of the earlier cases provided much solace to Eliza Sero, with several potentially damaging opinions tending to weigh against her claim. With the exception of *Phelps*, however, none of the cases considered full legal argument from the Mohawk or other First Nations on the question of sovereignty. And the failure of the *Phelps* court to give reasoned analysis for its decision did much to limit the persuasiveness of its holding. Indeed, *Phelps* set the trend for what would emerge as a marked and disturbing pattern. Canadian courts had a pronounced tendency to issue sweeping decisions in Aboriginal matters without much attention to the complexity of the legal niceties before them.[67]

In *Sero*, unlike most of the earlier cases, Judge Riddell was confronted with comprehensive and lengthy presentations regarding Mohawk claims to legal sovereignty. The Mohawk arguments resonated within the legal framework of international law, an area with which Judge Riddell was quite familiar, since he had served as an international law examiner for Osgoode Hall Law School for years, and was 'particularly noted for his expertise' in the field. Like most early twentieth-century imperialist thinkers, however, Riddell did not take it upon himself to consult references to the law of nations, or international perspectives on legal sovereignty when confronted with Aboriginal claims. Instead, he selected as his definitive legal authority a white jurist, Sir William Blackstone, whose *Commentaries on the Laws of England* had served as the dominant legal treatise in nineteenth-century England. With strikingly ethnocentric horizons, Riddell quoted Blackstone on the matter of 'allegiance':

Natural-born subjects (as distinguished from aliens) are such as are born within the dominions of the Crown of England ... and aliens, such as are born out of it. Natural allegiance is such as is due from all men born within the king's dominions immediately upon their birth. Natural allegiance is therefore a debt of gratitude; which cannot be forfeited, cancelled, or altered by any change of time, place, or circumstance, nor by anything but the united concurrence of the legislature.[68]

The circularity of his reasoning seems unclear to Judge Riddell. The precise point that Eliza Sero was arguing was that she had *not* been 'born within the dominions of the Crown of England.' Mere recitation of the law regarding the obligations of individuals who had been born 'within the king's dominions' fails to settle the more fundamental question. The legislation Riddell cited governing 'nationality, naturalization and aliens' also begs the point, defining 'natural-born British subjects' as 'any person born within His Majesty's dominions and allegiance.'[69]

Nor did Judge Riddell deign to advert to the lack of reciprocity in Canadian political thinking, which claimed allegiance from First Nations peoples while denying them the modern hallmark of citizenship, the right to vote. 'Indians' were denied the suffrage federally until 1960, with the exception of a brief interlude between 1885 and 1898.[70] The province of Ontario barred 'Indians' from voting until 1954.[71] British Columbia barred them until 1949, Manitoba until 1952, Saskatchewan until 1960, Prince Edward Island and New Brunswick until 1963, Alberta until 1965, and Quebec until 1969.[72]

Finally homing in on the link that Eliza Sero was trying to make between the 'Simcoe deed' and Mohawk sovereignty, Riddell conceded that any 'rights the Indians have in the land' flowed from the wording of the original land grant. It was true, he allowed, that the deed granted lands 'to be held and enjoyed' in the 'most free and ample manner and according to the several customs and usages.' But the words 'customs and usages' were plainly 'words of tenure,' noted Riddell, 'not indicative of the manner in which they are to use the land.' This analysis premised a lengthy and speculative excursion into how the Mohawk actually did utilize the Tyendinaga Territory:

For example, suppose that the custom of the Indians was to grow corn and not wheat, could it be contended that growing wheat would be beyond their rights under the grant – if to make maple syrup from the sap of the maple, would they be wrong to chop down the trees and form arable land? Or, if they were wont to break up land with mattocks or hoes, were they precluded from using ploughs?

The implied reference to the impact of modern agricultural methods upon traditional Mohawk practices reveals just how little Judge Riddell knew of the history of the Six Nations peoples, whose agricultural knowledge dominated the St Lawrence River and Great Lakes region for centuries.[73]

Then, as if in contradiction to his earlier remarks, Riddell added, 'moreover, there is no evidence that fishing with a seine was one of the customs of the Indians in 1793.' If Judge Riddell had done a little more research into the matters about which he spoke so brazenly, he might have discovered that fishing nets, including beach seines, had been employed by Iroquoians and other North American indigenous peoples for centuries. Indeed, Lord Dorchester made provision to outfit the Six Nations allies with seine nets in 1789, several years after they settled into their new Upper Canadian homes. Riddell's misplaced conjecture intimates that the Mohawk were too 'primitive' to have had any knowledge of seine-net fishing methods at the time of the establishment of the Tyendinaga settlement. With this false theory he shored up his disdainful dismissal of the Mohawk claim to fishing rights generally.[74]

In the final result, Judge Riddell was uncompromising. 'I can find no justification for the supposition that any Indians in the Province are exempt from the general law – or ever were,' he announced, going far beyond the terms of the case before the bar. Unable to restrain himself from chastising Eliza Sero and her Six Nations allies, he quoted a passage from John Beverley Robinson, written in 1824 when he was attorney general for Upper Canada: 'To talk of treaties with the Mohawk Indians, residing in the heart of one of the most populous districts of Upper Canada, upon lands purchased for them and given to them by the British Government, is much the same, in my humble opinion, as to talk of making a treaty of alliance with the Jews in Duke street or with the French emigrants who have settled in England.' Dripping contempt, Riddell's decision concluded: 'I cannot express my own opinion more clearly or convincingly.'[75]

The judgment seems to have caught the immediate interest of the Department of Indian Affairs. Right on the heels of its release, the white Deputy Superintendent General, Duncan Campbell Scott, wrote personally to Judge Riddell, noting that the 'claim of the Six Nations Indians that they are not British subjects ... but a nation allied to the British Crown' was 'very much to the fore just now.' Exchanging pleasantries about the upcoming elections of the Royal Society, a matter of some mutual interest, Scott also asked for a full copy of Riddell's judgment. Judge Riddell complied two days later, offering his frank opinion that the claim that 'the Indians were not British subjects' but 'a Nation allied to the British Crown' was entirely without merit. 'The matter as a question of law, is not arguable – the authorities are so perfectly plain that anyone born in his Majesty's territory is his Majesty's subject.' Adding that he hoped to see Deputy Superintendent General Scott at the meeting of the Royal Society in May, Judge Riddell signed off. The easy familiarity of the correspondence between the Indian Affairs bureaucrat and Judge Riddell is highly revealing. Riddell's breezily offered legal opinion underscores the barriers impeding Eliza Sero in her efforts to assert Mohawk sovereignty before Canadian courts.[76]

Even the unmitigated victory embodied in Riddell's decision was insufficient to quell Duncan Campbell Scott's uneasiness. The deputy superintendent general was incensed that Aboriginal people were able to hire lawyers to make such insurgent arguments before the courts, and equally angered that there were some lawyers willing to represent such claims. After some consideration, Scott hit upon a plan to nip the bothersome lawsuits in the bud. He began to lobby the legislators to enact a law prohibiting Aboriginal peoples from paying lawyers to pursue claims without government approval. In 1927, Parliament amended the Indian Act to make it a crime to raise money from First Nations communities for the prosecution of Aboriginal claims, unless the Department of Indian Affairs gave prior written consent.[77]

What the First Nations thought of the outcome in *Sero* v *Gault* is difficult to decipher. The surviving legal and archival documents contain no documentation of Eliza Sero's response to Riddell's decision. The sentiments expressed years later by Irving Powless, Jr, one of the Onondaga chiefs of the Hodenosaunee Grand Council, may capture something of the Mohawk reaction. Powless wrote:

Court hearings, jurisdiction, judges sitting in the courtrooms, making decisions that formulate or change our lives. […] And the people who are making these decisions don't even know who we are. […] The rights of the Houdenosaunee do not come from any treaty. They do not come from any court decision or law. The rights of the Houdenosaunee came long before your people came here. We have not changed. […] It must be set down today, solid, as it was three, four thousand years ago, that we are the landowners. This house is ours. This must be set down, so that my grandchildren's grandchildren will be safe, and they will still be able to conduct the ceremonies of our people. They will still be able to sing their songs and speak their language. And they will still be able to teach you people about peace and harmony and living together.[78]

The ruling in *Sero* v *Gault* was undoubtedly of concern to the members of the Six Nations and other Aboriginal peoples. But neither the Mohawks nor other First Nations ever ceded to Canadian courts the right to make the ultimate determination regarding their sovereignty. The legal challenge was only one strategy among many. The judgment was a loss, without question. However, decisions such as Judge Riddell's simply reinforced Aboriginal suspicions that Canadian courts served the colonial interests of white officials. The ruling did nothing to dissuade the Mohawks of their belief in their own inherent right to sovereignty.[79] Eliza Sero died in 1937, at the age of sixty-eight.[80] Her battle for Six Nations sovereignty lived on.[81]

5

'Mesalliances' and the 'Menace to White Women's Virtue': Yee Clun's Opposition to the White Women's Labour Law, Saskatchewan, 1924

It was late in the day at the peak of midsummer on 6 August 1924. The elected members of the Regina City Council must have been chafing at the timing as they found themselves faced with the troublesome application. Yee Clun, the Chinese-Canadian proprietor of the Exchange Grill and Rooming House, had filed an application for a special licence – one that would allow him to employ 'white women.'[1]

The town of Regina, Saskatchewan, was initially named 'Pile of Bones,' after the accumulations of skeletal debris from historically bountiful buffalo hunts. As the original Cree, Assiniboine, Blackfoot, Chipewyan, and Salteaux communities were displaced to ever-diminishing 'reserves' by an influx of white settlers, the town was prompted to adopt a more dignified title. Settling upon 'Regina,' the Latin word for 'Queen,' the ambitious townsfolk boasted of their home as the 'Queen City of the Plains.' Their determination was rewarded in 1883, when Regina was designated the capital of the North-West Territories. Disgusted by the choice, the *Manitoba Free Press* snidely remarked that the town was 'in the midst of a vast plain of inferior soil ... with about enough water in the miserable little creek ... to wash a sheep.'

Undeterred by such peevishness, the citizens of Regina began to fashion their city into the governmental and policing centre of the district, an urban anchor for a network of rural villages and agricultural towns. In 1905, Regina was selected to be the capital of the newly created province of Saskatchewan, despite spirited competition for the title from Saskatoon, Moose Jaw, and Prince Albert. A cyclone in 1912 destroyed 500 buildings and rendered 2,500 homeless, but proved to be only a temporary setback to burgeoning growth and construction. By 1921, with advances in mixed farming, industrial activity, and mechanization, Regina's population mushroomed to 34,432, making it the fifteenth-largest city in Canada.[2]

Regina's population was drawn from Eastern Canada, the United States, and Europe. Its citizens were predominantly British, with small clusters of German, Jewish, Romanian, Austrian, French, and Russian communities present on the peripheries of the dominant Anglo-Saxon society. Fewer in number than all of these groups were the Chinese, who represented only 250 in a city of 34,432 people.[3] The low number of Chinese reflected harsh and discriminatory immigration laws that imposed punitive 'head taxes' on Chinese immigrants to Canada.[4]

Most prairie cities contained miniature 'Chinatowns' populated by tiny groups of Chinese immigrants, predominantly male, who settled along the railway line. The Chinese newcomers moved eastward from the West Coast, where they first landed, in the hope that race relations on the prairies might be less antagonistic than in British Columbia. The Chinese opened hand laundries, restaurants, and grocery stores in well-defined, segregated areas of Calgary, Edmonton, Lethbridge, Red Deer, Medicine Hat, Moose Jaw, Saskatoon, and Winnipeg. Regina was something of an exception. The Chinese population in the 'Queen City' was simply too small to establish a full-scale 'Chinatown.' Furthermore, the earliest Chinese immigrants mutually agreed to disperse throughout the city core, on the theory that they might avoid competition by setting their businesses apart from each other. Instead of being clustered in a confined neighbourhood, the Chinese residents and their small businesses were scattered throughout Regina's downtown area.[5]

Despite the desires of the several hundred Chinese settlers for a harmonious environment, their mere presence appears to have provoked a strong sense of racial disjunction in the flourishing capital city. Some of the hostility was directed at the newly established Chinese business ventures. In October 1911, the Regina *Leader* recounted that a group of white citizens objected to the existence of a Chinese laundry on Cornwall Street. The *Daily Province* indicated in November 1912 that white Reginans in residential neighbourhoods generally complained of having to live in proximity to the 'yellow' proprietors of Chinese laundries. That year the Regina City Police Commission voted to restrict Chinese laundries to an

Two unidentified Chinese men outside a laundry, probably Regina, 1931.

unpopulated, isolated district near the exhibition grounds. Some of the white aldermen who spoke to the issue argued that 'all places of business conducted by the Chinese' should be similarly relegated to a segregated geographic area.[6]

Reflecting the vocabulary of its white prairie readers, the Saskatchewan press thought nothing of adopting the derogatory and racist term 'Chink' in its copy. 'Chinks Lose Car of Goods' headlined the Regina *Morning Leader* in April 1911. 'Chink Follows Pick-Pocket and Gets Back $1,400 Wallet' was a featured news item in the Regina *Evening Province* on September 1916. The Moose Jaw *Evening Times* felt perfectly free to use remarkably racist rhetoric when it described the Chinese as a 'stagnant race,' an untrustworthy, 'sterile and barren' people, and warned readers against the 'moral and intellectual decadence' posed by 'the Yellow Peril.'[7]

The use of the term 'yellow' to describe those who traced their ancestry to China was commonplace in Canada at this time. While ethnologists usually preferred to use the racial classification 'Mongolian,' many people were more comfortable with the word 'yellow.' Those who cast racial aspersions on the Chinese often resorted to the concept of colour to separate individuals and communities, relying upon the adjective 'yellow' to draw definitive lines between the Chinese and others. Whether blazoned across newspaper headlines or shouted across street corners, colour seems to have been a hallmark of Canadian racial characterization.

Few seem to have questioned whether the colour 'yellow' was any more accurate a description of the Chinese than the designation of 'red' applied to First Nations people. Unlike the host of ethnologists who purported to measure the colour tone of Inuit people's skin, there were few 'scientific' treatises on Asiatic skin colour. And although the Chinese seem to have been consistently tagged as 'yellow,' there was some uncertainty about Asian people generally. At the turn of the century, individuals born in Japan were sometimes described as 'brown-skinned,' but by the mid-twentiethth century, they seem to have been lumped in with the Chinese and depicted as 'yellow' as well.[8]

The colour designated for Chinese Canadians was not a value-neutral one. 'Yellow-belly' was a term used to describe a coward, a 'yellow streak' signified a 'trait of cowardice,' and 'yellow dog' was an epithet coined within the trade union movement to label a 'scab,' or someone who flouted solidarity with fellow labourers. Unscrupulous and sensational newspapers were dubbed the 'yellow press.' The unsavoury label 'yellow' that was affixed to the Chinese was undeniably both artificial and fallacious. Yet the majority of early twentieth-century Canadians seem to have gravitated complacently towards the concept of colour as a defining racial attribute.

Within this enveloping and poisonous social climate, discriminatory licensing strategies such as the one debated in Regina in 1912 were a considerable thorn in the side of Chinese entrepreneurs. Yet few of them had as substantial an impact as the statute Yee Clun was attempting to challenge. By bringing his application in 1924, Yee Clun sought to subvert the infamous 'White Women's Labour Law.'

THE 'WHITE WOMEN'S LABOUR LAW'

First enacted in 1912, An Act to Prevent the Employment of Female Labour in Certain Capacities is politely titled in racially neutral phraseology. The actual text, drafted in rather ponderous prose, reads: 'No person shall employ in any capacity any white woman or girl or permit any white woman or girl to reside or lodge in or to work in or, save as a *bona fide* customer in a public apartment thereof only, to frequent any restaurant, laundry or other place of business or amusement owned, kept or managed by any Japanese, Chinaman or other Oriental person.'[9] The statute is anything but racially neutral in its text, with the Japanese, Chinese, and 'other Oriental' communities explicitly targeted because of their race. The designated female group is also defined by race, as the prohibition is expressly restricted to 'white women.' Prior to this act, most racial designations in Canadian statutes purported to classify peoples of colour. Various enactments dealt with 'Indians,' 'colored people,' the 'Chinese, Japanese, and Hindu.'[10] Racial designations in law are typically assigned by whites to non-whites. While the property of 'whiteness' is clearly a definable asset from which all manner of privilege and power flows, it usually tends to disappear into invisibility in legal terminology. The 'White Women's Labour Law' thus constitutes a rather startling development. It appears to mark the first overt racial recognition of 'whiteness' in Canadian law.[11]

Although Canadian legislatures were known to borrow liberally from other jurisdictions as they pursued their legislative agendas, the 'White Women's Labour Law' seems to have been the first of its kind, a thoroughly homegrown manifestation of racial legislation. As Saskatchewan's white attorney general, William Ferdinand Alphonse Turgeon, would announce proudly, the measure was 'without precedent in Canada.'

William F.A. Turgeon.

Even across the border, where many American states promulgated statutes prohibiting intermarriage between white women and Asian males, there appear to have been no laws quite like this one. What provoked the Saskatchewan government to produce such an unusual piece of legislation in 1912?[12]

Turgeon was quite evasive on the question during the legislative debate.[13] Although he did not acknowledge it, one of the prime motivations was to satisfy the demands of organized labour. The Saskatchewan Trades and Labor Council (TLC) presented a formal petition calling for such legislation months before the bill was introduced.[14] The Saskatchewan TLC came into being in July 1906, when representatives of the Trades and Labor Congress of Canada convinced a group of three hundred working men in Regina of the need for a working-class lobby group. A successful period of union organizing followed, with the number of Saskatchewan trade unions doubling from fifteen to thirty between 1910 and 1912. Demands to restrict the immigration of foreign labourers, who were thought to depress the wages of Canadian workers, met with great enthusiasm among the new trade unionists. In particular, white workers believed that Chinese labourers offered perilously dangerous competition, due to their purported 'diligence, sobriety, cleverness and low standard of comfort.'[15]

Although the racial stratification of the Canadian labour market meant that whites and Asians were rarely in direct competition for jobs, Asian men had on occasion been used as strike-breakers to subvert the trade union activities of whites. Race prejudice combined with economic fears to mobilize the white male labour movement. Trade unionists sought to exclude Asian men from their trade unions, boycott businesses employing Asian labour, press for legislation to protect jobs for white men, and spearhead the movement to eradicate further Asian immigration.[16] At the 1911 convention of the Trades and Labor Congress of Canada, the official agency representing organized labour throughout Canada called upon the federal government to make it a criminal offence across the nation for Asian employers to hire white women.[17]

Whites who owned small businesses also joined forces with organized labour to campaign for anti-Asian measures, their concerns magnified as growing numbers of Chinese and Japanese immigrants began to branch into businesses of their own. One such group was the Saskatchewan Retail Merchants' Association, which joined with the TLC to support the bill.[18] The white owners of steam laundries in Saskatchewan complained ceaselessly about the competitive pace set by Chinese-operated hand laundries. White restaurateurs expressed similar anxiety about the remarkably low prices in Chinese restaurants.[19] The new law was intended to hinder the ability of Asian entrepreneurs to compete with white proprietors. It would be a useful addition to the provincial and city laws that restricted the location of Asian-owned businesses and dampened their competitive edge with early-closing and other regulatory provisions.[20]

The statute did not directly bar Asian entrepreneurs from operating restaurants, laundries, or other businesses. It merely enjoined them from hiring a certain group of employees: white women and girls. Presumably this left open the possibility of employing 'non-white' women and girls, whatever that might be construed to mean, and men of all races. Despite the apparent options, the legislation had an undeniably anti-competitive impact because of the gendered and racially segmented nature of the Canadian labour market.

Discriminatory legislation, social customs, and attitudes all coalesced to create a complex stratification of jobs and pay scales on the basis of race and gender.[21] White males had access to the widest range of occupations and the highest wages. Consequently, although the statute permitted Asian businessmen to hire white males, doing so was simply too costly.[22] Males and females of colour were cheaper to employ, but in relatively short supply. Asians and Blacks were artificially restricted in number by racist immigration policies. First Nations communities were largely inaccessible due to their geographic isolation and the confinement of the pass system.[23]

White women, who were restricted in the types of jobs they could obtain, typically earned wages that were one-half those of white males, and slightly less than those of male Asian immigrants.[24] The gender factor is obvious, as one Chinese restaurant owner stressed at the time. It was essential to hire white women, he pointed out, because 'we cannot have our own women here to act as waitresses.' The new legislation denied Chinese businessmen access to these less expensive employees, and would result in a significant blow to their competitive position.[25]

Moreover, in a racially discriminatory society, it was an advantage to have white employees waiting tables. Some white proprietors directly pandered to the racist sentiments of their customers by promoting their restaurants with advertisements that proclaimed 'None but white help employed.' Others suggested that 'the stomach of a person of refined tastes must revolt at the mere idea that his dinner has been cooked by a Chinaman.' In such a climate, legislative restrictions that left Chinese employers no access to white serving staff could have a substantial dampening effect on profit margins.[26]

Labour-market concerns were not the only motivation behind the new law. Social reformers also lobbied for the passage of the statute as critical to 'moral' interests. Reverend T. Albert Moore, the white general secretary of the Methodist Social and Moral Reform Department, published a copy of a letter he received from a 'prominent citizen of Saskatoon' in the 5 September 1912 edition of the Regina *Morning Leader*. The letter is an appalling example of anti-Asian hatred and hysteria. Describing the Chinese as 'harpies' and 'Oriental almond-eyed anthropoids,' the writer decries the Asian ownership of 'a large proportion of our eating houses' across Western Canada, where they work 'side by side with white women' for up to 'eighteen hours a day.' 'To my certain knowledge,' the writer continues, many of these white women are lured 'into the underworld to suffer a fate worse than death.' Urging speedy passage of a law barring the employment of white women, the letter predicts that 'each day's delay means scores of Canadian women lost to decency, and shames our country in the eyes of all moral nations.'[27]

Racist whites in late nineteenth- and early twentieth-century Canada depicted Chinese men as subject to 'loathsome diseases' and 'demoralizing habits,' despite the lack of any firm evidence upon which to ground their assertions. The very vocabulary of social reformers, who incessantly equated 'whiteness' with 'cleanliness' and 'purity,' contributed to racial prejudice against non-whites.[28] Such sentiments invigorated the Saskatchewan Social and Moral Reform Council, one of the key proponents of the 'White Women's Labour Law.' Founded in Regina in December 1907, with representation from churches, labour, medical, and educational associations, this organization also included prominent white women's groups such as the Woman's Christian Temperance Union, the Local Council of Women, and the Young Women's Christian Association (YWCA). While there were many men who supported the bill on 'moral' grounds – as community activists, members of the press, and legislators – white women were by no means absent from the debate.[29]

One of the most noteworthy aspects of the campaign for the 'White Women's Labour Law' is the certainty that appears to underlie the Canadian understanding of the concept of 'race.' That the world was divided into a number of discrete, clearly defined, distinct 'races' appears to have been an indisputable fact. A 'ladies' debate' sponsored by the Regina Metropolitan Church in February 1912 selected as its topic whether Asiatics should be excluded from Canada. The all-white group advocating exclusion won handily with the following arguments:

that the Asiatics being a different race and one which could not be assimilated with the white races, would be a menace to the unity of Canada, that they could not appreciate the aims and ideals of the westerner and that while they might be of great benefit to the world by staying in China and working to realize the ideals of their own race in conjunction with the teaching of Christianity, in Canada they tend to promote strife.

The Regina ladies were simply echoing statements made in the House of Commons by Canada's white prime minister John A. Macdonald as early as 1882, that the 'Mongolian' and white races could never combine. Macdonald was emphatic on the question of racial distinction, and he designated the Chinese a 'semi-barbari[c],' 'inferior race.'[30]

Many of these derogatory images were spread by white, Protestant clergymen eager to secure financing for their China missions. They found a ready audience for their vociferous condemnation of Chinese plural marriage and concubinage among women's rights organizations in North America.[31] Christian missionaries developed a highly negative opinion of the status of women in China, deploring practices such as female infanticide, child-brides, and marital arrangements that they equated with 'female slavery.'[32] White women's organizations back home were horrified by the reports. Further, they were not averse to exploiting the condition of women in China as an example of the 'immorality and social decay' that would follow in the wake of unjust treatment of women.[33] The National Council of Women of Canada demanded at the turn of the century that 'conscientious citizens should ... drive out foreign importations like white slavery and oriental concubinage which, by their example, seduced Canadians away from higher Anglo-Saxon standards.' By 1912, the National Council of Women of Canada called for the revision of Canadian immigration policy 'to exclude all members of the "yellow race".'[34]

Significantly, the 'White Women's Labour Law' was also a gendered construct. It was the horror of female sexual slavery that the act was meant to remedy. The protection of white women, as the symbolic emblem of the 'white race,' became a crucial cornerstone in the attempt to establish and defend white racial superiority and white racism. White women were called into service in their reproductive capacity as the 'guardians of the race,' a symbol of the most valuable property known to white men, to be protected at all costs from the encroachment of other races.[35]

Sexuality was often intertwined with racism, as racists linked coloured skin pigmentation to excessive sexual desires.[36] Their perspective on the sexuality of Chinese men was less definitive. Some whites made use of manipulative images to construct mythical stereotypes depicting Chinese males as more 'feminine' than white men.[37] By logical extension, white female employees working for Chinese men ought to have been seen as relatively immune from coercive sexual advances. Yet ironically, some worried that the 'asexuality' of the male Chinese could lure white women to their ruin. The muckraking Toronto newspaper *Jack Canuck* put this prospect squarely before its readers in 1911:

The bland smiling Oriental and his quaint pidgeon English does not appear very formidable to the young woman who enters his store for a weekly wash. She does not notice the evil leer lurking in the almond eyes as she accepts the silk handkerchief or other trifling Oriental knick-knack 'just for a plesant.' A few weeks later she is induced to drink a cup of 'leal Chinese tlea' whilst examining his Oriental treasures. A drowsy feeling and when she returns to her senses the evil deed has been consummated.

Fear-mongering journalists fretted that, shrouded from view in the booths of Chinese restaurants or hidden behind the partitions erected in Chinese laundries, unsuspecting white women might be tricked into interracial sexual liaisons.[38]

Toronto Presbyterian minister John G. Shearer, the white founder of the Moral and Social Reform Council of Canada, toured the Western provinces in 1910 and announced that 'most of the dens of vice are owned by Chinese and Japanese.'[39] Reverend T. Albert Moore reported in 1912 that 'the question of whether Chinese restaurant keepers and laundrymen should be allowed to employ white women' was 'one of the most vital ones before the country.' Advising that 'only girls of the lowest type' would work for Asian Canadians, the white clergyman stressed that 'the results of the close intimacy of this class of white girls and their Oriental employers' was 'appalling.' The Regina *Leader* commented upon Reverend Moore's opinion in detail: 'Many disastrous things have occurred when young girls have been employed by Chinks ... and we should bring to bear on the Chinese the way of our civilization. Every time anything occurs, punishment should be meted out. It is clear that some definite action should be taken at once.'[40]

Narcotics play a central role in such racist imagery. Whites who were eager to draw links between the Chinese and opium rarely admitted that it was British traders who first introduced opium to China, where the drug served much the same function as alcohol had with respect to the Aboriginal peoples of North America. Over the strenuous objections of the Chinese, British imperialists deliberately fostered the consumption of the addictive narcotic in order to enhance their own trading position in the quest for tea, silk, and porcelain.[41] Nor did Canadians generally admit that the Chinese, who were by no means the only users of opium in early twentieth-century Canada, were often singled out for prosecution. Chinese residents found their convictions given great prominence in the newspapers, without any apparent recognition of the racially selective enforcement that often led to their detection and capture. Despite the absence of concrete evidence for such assertions, the press carried stories speculating that the Chinese opium peddler had a particular predilection for white women, whom he intended to 'enslave with the poppy,' 'defile with his embraces,' and 'prostitute to his countrymen.' Racist press

'A Pound of Prevention – or an Ounce of Cure?' Illustration from *Chatelaine* magazine, December 1928.

reports inspired increasing anxiety among white Canadians that opium would fuel 'flagging sexual energies,' transforming the 'asexual' Chinese man into a sexually dangerous adversary. Many feared that the indiscriminate use of drugs would dissolve boundaries between the races and encourage sexual contact across colour lines.[42]

Canada's first white female magistrate, Emily Murphy, published an influential anti-narcotics book in 1922, in which she profiled Chinese involvement in drug trafficking and chronicled 'the amazing phenomenon' of 'an educated gentlewoman, reared in a refined atmosphere, consorting with the lowest classes of yellow and black men,' and producing 'half-caste' infants. Entrapment was likely to occur, warned the renowned feminist, in Chinese 'chop-suey houses' and 'noodle parlors.' White women who sought work in Chinese restaurants were at particular risk.[43] Unless opium were driven from the country, Murphy suggested, 'the black and yellow races may yet obtain the ascendancy.' The promotional literature for the book emphasized the threat to 'Anglo-Saxon supremacy,' and the book contained pictures of white women in bed with non-whites, inscribed with the notation: 'When she acquires the habit, she does not know what lies before her; later she does not care.'[44]

Another of Canada's first white female judges, feminist Helen Gregory MacGill, would take a different position. MacGill, who had travelled in Asia as a journalist, told *Chatelaine* magazine in 1928 that 'laws prohibiting women working for a particular race ... should have the whole-hearted endorsement and support of every good citizen' *only if* there were concrete evidence that such laws would 'solve the problem.' The real issue, she asserted, was 'protection [of women] from exploitation, moral or financial.'[45] With her latter point, MacGill was on strong feminist footing, since concerns about sexual coercion perpetrated upon female workers were legitimate and long-standing. When feminists directed their attack solely at employers of one race, however, their racial motivation usurped any claim they had to be protecting women. Helen Gregory MacGill seemed to have recognized this, and argued that laws should focus on conduct, not race. Averse to legislation that singled out the Chinese, she concluded: 'What is needed is protection against recognized danger, not restriction directed against a race.'[46]

The National Council of Women of Canada, which studied the need for such legislation in the mid-1920s, thought otherwise, even though the results of its investigation revealed 'no evidence of girls receiving harmful treatment' at the hands of Chinese employers. Mindless of the inconsistencies in its analysis, the powerful feminist lobby group concluded that the legislation was vital 'not for the purpose of discriminating against an Oriental race,' but for the 'protection [of white girls] only.' The report noted that employment bureaus discouraged white women from taking such positions, and that social-service workers were 'emphatic in desiring the bar raised against such employment.'[47] Some were also concerned that 'timid,' 'unmuscular' Chinese employers would be unable to protect their female staff from the untoward behaviour of white patrons. As *Chatelaine* magazine acknowledged in 1928, the problem was 'the ability of the Chinese employer to surround female employees with security and good influences.' Its conclusion: 'It is believed by persons who have made a survey of the subject that no white man intent on mischief would respect the authority of a Chinaman.' The hypocrisy of penalizing Chinese employers for the sexual improprieties of white men is not mentioned.[48]

Some of the anxiety over interracial mixing seems to have been spawned by the absence of Chinese women among the immigrant community. Immigration laws, highly restrictive for Asians generally, were particularly onerous for Asians wishing to immigrate with their families. The legal barriers and the hostile treatment accorded Asian newcomers in Canada combined to create Chinese-Canadian communities that were overwhelmingly male.[49]

Few whites gave voice to the obvious solution of reducing discrimination and easing immigration restrictions to admit more Chinese women. Indeed, the few Chinese women who arrived in Canada were unfairly denounced as slaves, concubines, or syphilitic prostitutes, thought to be 'more injurious to the community' even than 'white abandoned women.' White Canadian legislators were unwavering in their belief that it was imperative to exclude Chinese women from Canada to contain the growth of any settled Chinese population.[50]

Nor were the sexual imbalances of the Asian community to be lessened by racial intermarriage, a phenomenon that seems to have been regarded as both rare and outrageous.[51] White brides who married Asian grooms were 'better off in their coffins,' exclaimed one Canadian news editor in 1904. A sense of horrified fascination attends the press account of several marriages between white American women and Asian-American men that appeared in the Regina *Leader* in November 1911. 'Don't Wed Oriental Says Woman Who Did' was the headline of a Regina *Morning Leader* news item in January 1912.[52]

Despite the absence of laws prohibiting interracial marriage in Canada, various news reports suggest that other legal barriers were set up to impede such unions. In some instances, couples were simply denied marriage rites. Dr T.E. Bourke, the white secretary of the United Methodist Social and Moral Reform Committee, proudly informed the Regina *Morning Leader* in September 1912 that he had refused as a matter of principle to perform the wedding ceremony for a Chinese man and his 'fine looking English-speaking' white fiancée several months earlier.[53] Lethbridge police locked up a Chinese man from Diamond City, Alberta, in September 1911, after learning that he had proposed marriage to his white female employee.[54] Some have even suggested that, for Chinese men on the prairies, dating a white female could be enough to provoke talk of a lynching.[55]

This was the context within which a widely diverse range of constituents joined forces to secure the anti-Chinese statute. An all-white coalition of labour organizations, small businessmen, Protestant moral reformers, and women's groups forged a common ground. Their alliance transcended gender and class in an archly racist campaign to secure passage of the 'White Women's Labour Law.'[56]

ASIAN RESISTANCE AND LEGISLATIVE RESPONSE

Members of the Chinese and Japanese communities in Saskatchewan were appalled and disheartened over the new legislation. Stressing that many had taken out naturalization papers and that they provided employment for a number of white Canadians, they urged swift retraction of the act.[57] Dr Yada, the Japanese consul general in Vancouver, travelled to Regina to meet with Attorney General Turgeon. He complained that Japanese merchants would be unable to open businesses in Saskatchewan if the new law remained in force, mentioning specifically the need to employ white women as stenographers. Shortly thereafter, Dr Yada returned to Tokyo to address the Japanese government on the matter of anti-Japanese legislation in Western Canada generally. Japan was an imperial power of relatively greater military and commercial significance than China. Within months, strong protests from the Japanese government resulted in a legislative amendment deleting all references to 'Japanese' or 'other Oriental persons.'[58]

Just as the Saskatchewan legislature appeared to be backing down a bit, legislators in other jurisdictions were forging ahead. The province of Manitoba was so impressed by the Saskatchewan initiative that it adopted identical legislation on 15 February 1913. Due to opposition from the Chinese community, the law was never proclaimed.[59] In 1914, the Ontario legislature passed a similar enactment, although it was not proclaimed until 1920.[60] British Columbia sallied forth with its own version of the 'White Women's Labour Law' in 1919.[61] In Alberta and Quebec, despite expressions of interest, no such act was passed.[62] There was discussion from Nova Scotia municipal politicians about drafting a similar measure, but nothing came to fruition in the Atlantic provinces either.[63]

Test-case prosecutions of the Saskatchewan 'White Women's Labour Law' were brought first in Moose Jaw. Quong Wing and Quong Sing, Chinese-Canadian men who operated two restaurants and a rooming house in Moose Jaw, were charged in 1912 with employing three white women: Nellie Lane and Mabel Hopham as waitresses, and Annie Hartman as a chambermaid. The cases were hotly contested at trial. The white defence lawyer rather sensibly argued that it was impossible to know with any certainty what the legislature meant by the term 'Chinese.' Various witnesses offered suggestions that the designation might relate to birth in China, birth of one's parents in China, physical presence such as 'standing on Chinese soil,' citizenship, reputation within the community, proficiency in the Chinese language, and visual appearance. Defence counsel insisted that the absence of any racial definition within the statute rendered it too vague to enforce. He was backed up by the testimony of waitress Nellie Lane, who stubbornly refused to make any racial designation of her employer, Quong Wing. Instead, she insisted tenaciously: 'I treat him as myself.'[64]

The defence argument laid bare the nonsense of racial classification, challenging those who believed the notion of 'race' to be an immutable, natural concept. 'Race' is not a biological or transhistorical feature, but a sociological classification situated in a particular time and context. It is shaped and moulded by economic, political, and cultural forces as well as resistances and challenges.[65] Racial categories form a continuum of gradual change, not a set of sharply demarcated types. There are no intrinsic isolating mechanisms between people and, given the geographic dispersion of populations over time, the concept of 'pure' human 'races' is absurd. It is almost impossible to define 'Chineseness' as a fixed concept, transported without variation across generations and location. How can the single label 'Chinese' serve as a monolithic identifier for the multiplicity of communities that make up the richly varied diaspora of peoples originating from China? How potentially misleading it is to adopt one term to signify equally a person born in China, an immigrant of Chinese origin living in Saskatchewan, a second-generation person of

Chinese origin living in Africa, and a third-generation Canadian of Chinese origin living in Vancouver. The term 'racialization,' a concept of much greater utility than race, refers to 'the process by which attributes such as skin colour, language, birthplace and cultural practices are given social significance as markers of distinction.'[66]

The prosecutions in Moose Jaw represent a successful effort on the part of the state to 'racialize' Quong Wing and Quong Sing, who were pronounced 'Chinese' by the presiding police magistrate without serious consideration of any of the defence arguments. Although the witnesses might have had difficulty articulating what they meant by 'Chinese,' most were adamant in their observations that the two defendants were such. Rooted in a particular historical context, racial distinctions take on a certain 'common sense' quality, an unconscious and visceral reflection of community assumptions and prejudice. The white magistrate felt so certain of his ground that he saw no need to offer any rationale or analysis of the matter in his judgment. Nor did the appellate courts disagree. A number of Chinese merchants organized to raise money to finance a constitutional challenge to the convictions of Quong Wing and Quong Sing. The legislation and convictions were upheld by the Supreme Court of Saskatchewan in 1913 and the Supreme Court of Canada in 1914.[67]

An equally significant test case was tried in 1912, when charges were laid against the Asian-born proprietor of a Saskatoon restaurant. The 'whiteness' of the three female waitresses employed by Mr Yoshi, an immigrant from Tokyo, was the major dilemma in that case. The question was complicated by the ethnic origins of the women concerned, who were described as 'Russian' and 'German.' As such, the waitresses represented two immigrant groups that had not been fully accepted by the Euro-Canadian elite. On the other hand, they were also difficult to classify as 'non-white.' Since the statute contained no definition of 'white woman,' the Crown endeavoured to supply one, arguing that the court should 'give these words the meaning which is commonly applied to them; that is to say the females of any of the civilized European nations.' Professing great confusion, the white police magistrate in Saskatoon reserved on the issue and adjourned the trial.[68]

Racial visibility can change dramatically over time. People objectified as racially different in one place and time may find themselves shuffled and recategorized, or rendered racially invisible in others. The divisions in Canada between the English and French, and Jews and Gentiles have been depicted in 'racial' terms.[69] In the late nineteenth century, British officials referred to natives of India as 'niggers,' but by the first decade of the twentieth century the Canadian press described them as 'Orientals' and 'Asiatic.'[70] One witness who testified before the 1902 Canadian Royal Commission on Chinese and Japanese Immigration announced: 'I never call Italians white labour.' A Saskatchewan historian, writing in 1924, claimed that Slovaks (or Polaks), Germans, Hungarians, Scandinavians, Finns, and Serbians were each discrete groups in a 'racial sense.'[71] In early twentieth-century Saskatchewan, residents of English or Scottish origin would have been hard-pressed to identify racially with Russian or German immigrants in matters of employment or social intermingling. What was at stake in this trial was whether the latter should be 'racialized' as 'white' in distinction to Asian immigrants, in the context of the 'White Women's Labour Law.'[72]

Endeavouring to provide some assistance to the court, one resident wrote to the editor of the Saskatoon *Daily Star*. A sense of arrogant self-importance suffuses the letter:

Sir – Having in mind the adjournment of the [Yoshi] case ... I take the liberty of offering enlightenment as to the definition of the term 'white'... Fingier, the famous ethnologist, says that the white races or Caucasians include Europeans, Armenians and Russians, other than Tartars who are included in the Yellow or Mongolian class. The white races as defined above, are opposed to the black or Negroids, the brown Malays, the red or American aborigines, and the yellow or Mongolians, including the Chinese and Japanese.

This information can be readily obtained from any good encyclopaedia, and the writer humbly suggests that some reference be supplied the magistrates in this city, as it is deplorable that such culpable ignorance should delay or prevent the dispensation of justice [...]

ONE WHO HAS LIVED IN CHINA[73]

Whether he was prompted to reach a decision by the letter or not, the police magistrate issued his ruling the next day. He had decided to settle the question 'by taking his own opinion,' he announced, and the names of the waitresses turned out to be key. The names revealed Russian and German nationality, claimed the magistrate, and although 'he did not think it necessary to go into the classification of the white race,' he was of the view, by way of 'illustration,' that 'Germans and Russians were members of [the] Caucasian race.' Although the defendant spoke of an intention to appeal his conviction, no further legal records survive. The ruling stands as a hallmark of the utility of law in consolidating various strains of national groups into a central 'white' Canadian identity, constructed in stark opposition to the 'Chinese' other.[74]

The Chinese community in Saskatchewan continued to voice its concern over the 'White Women's Labour Law,' and as the international stature of China improved after the First World War, the protestations ultimately became more forceful. In 1919, the Saskatchewan legislature amended the act again. This time, the intent was to disguise the racial focus. The revised statute deleted all explicit reference to Chinese or other Asian employers, leaving it up to individual municipalities to determine whether to license restaurants or laundries in which 'white women' were employed. Attorney General Turgeon explained that the bill was necessary because of pressures brought to bear for 'the removal of this discrimination on the ground of the racial susceptibility of the Chinese.' The change was one of 'form' only, he assured his fellow legislators. The government intended no substantive alteration in policy, but simply wished to achieve its ends without 'singling out' the Chinese. George Langley, the white member for Redberry and minister of Municipal Affairs, advised that 'it was the hope of those responsible for the bill' that no municipality would 'grant the privilege' contained in the new act.[75]

British Columbia was not far behind Saskatchewan in the drive to replace racially specific terminology with more neutral language. In 1923, the B.C. legislature deleted all reference to Chinese employers, leaving it to the discretion of police officials whether white women were to be allowed to work in restaurants and laundries. 'White' women and girls were still expressly protected by the 1923 act, but for the first time 'Indian women and girls' in British Columbia were specifically included.[76]

YEE CLUN'S APPLICATION

When Yee Clun brought his application before Regina City Council in 1924, he posed a deliberate challenge to the white city politicians. On its face, the revised statute purported to apply to employers on a race-neutral basis. Yee Clun was testing the authorities, hoping to persuade them to take an egalitarian approach to the amended law. One of the strategies adopted by the Chinese-Canadian community to resist racism, it was a singularly bold move.

Fragmentary details survive concerning the man who brought the legal challenge. 'Yee Clun' is how the applicant is identified in the legal documents. Many Canadians appear to have dispensed with concern for accuracy or consistency when they tried to get their tongues around 'foreign' names. Yee Clun is identified variously as 'Yee Clun,' 'Yee Chun,' 'Yee Klun,' 'Yee Kuen,' and 'Yee Klung' by the newspaper reporters and legal authorities, who showed a studied indifference to the spelling of Chinese names.[77]

Yee Clun was among the first Chinese residents in the area, settling in Regina around 1901, during a peak period of Chinese immigration. Yee Clun was one of very few Chinese men who brought their wives over from China to live with them. The 1921 census reveals that only 4 of the 250 Chinese residents in Regina were female. That Yee Clun felt secure enough to settle his family in Regina suggests that he was firmly committed to putting down permanent roots in the new country.[78]

In partnership with another Chinese resident named Jow Tai, Yee Clun purchased property and opened a restaurant that achieved a reputation as 'one of the best' in the city. Located at 1700 Rose Street, the Exchange Grill restaurant contained small apartments upstairs that were let to roomers, some of them Chinese men who could not secure housing elsewhere in the city because of racial discrimination. Despite his extensive family and business responsibilities, Yee Clun was deeply involved in community service. Widely acknowledged as 'the leader of the Chinese community in Regina,' in 1922 he was elected president of the Regina branch of the Chinese National Party, a fraternal organization with a membership of 150 Chinese residents from the city.[79]

Yee Clun's appearance before City Council on 6 August 1924 was a matter of pressing business urgency. According to the newspaper reporters who covered the case with considerable interest, Yee Clun explained that many Chinese restaurateurs required the services of white female employees because 'they can't procure boys of their own nationality on account of the tightening up of immigration laws.' With the passage of the federal Chinese Exclusion Act in 1923, Canadian legislators placed a virtual stranglehold upon Chinese immigration, creating a deplorable situation that dislocated Chinese families for more than twenty years. For Asian employers like Yee Clun, the drying up of the labour pool was equally disastrous. White women became by necessity the only residual group of potential employees available to Chinese restaurateurs.[80]

Yee Clun obviously realized that his application would be a test case, and he staged his request with care. He obtained prior approval from the white city licence inspector. He also persuaded Regina's white chief

Archival sources contain no photographs of Yee Clun or his family in Regina.
One of the few photographs of Chinese-Canadian families, from Moose Jaw
circa 1909, is unidentified.

constable, E.G. Berry, to support his claim. The police backing was
particularly important, since relations between the police and Regina's
Chinese community had not always been harmonious. Some years earlier, the police had trod all over the due-process rights of the city's
Chinese residents. Believing themselves hot on the trail of a Chinese man
suspected of murder in 1907, the chief of police and Regina's mayor
resolved to arrest all the Chinese inhabitants of the city for fear that they
might be 'harbouring' the suspect. The constables rounded up sixty-
seven Chinese individuals in the middle of the night and held them
without warrant for five hours at city hall. No charges were laid, and it
soon became evident that there were no reasonable grounds to believe
that any of the Chinese detainees was giving shelter to the suspect. Later
the authorities tried to justify their actions by claiming that 'special

difficulties arose in this case from the fact that to their eyes all Chinamen looked alike.'

A number of the Chinese individuals arrested in the 1907 Regina raid made a successful claim in court in 1908, on the grounds of unlawful arrest and imprisonment. There are no records indicating whether Yee Clun was one of the men arrested that night, or one of those who launched civil proceedings in consequence.[81] In the wake of the litigation, however, the police seem to have tried to improve their relations with the Chinese, at least as long as they kept to themselves and did not mingle with whites. In 1912, the Regina police chief was quoted as saying that the police 'never had any trouble with the Chinamen, who, as a rule, were very law abiding citizens.' The police 'never interfered with them,' he advised the *Daily Province*, 'unless their dens were also frequented by white men and women.'[82]

As one of the finest restaurants in Regina, Yee Clun's establishment was obviously not a 'den.' However, his application to hire white female employees was an overt attempt to surmount the widespread resistance to racial intermixing. To count Chief Constable Berry as his ally in this quest, Yee Clun must have done more than mend fences with the law enforcement authorities. He must undoubtedly have singled himself out positively among the Chinese community in some noteworthy respect to secure an endorsement from such powerful quarters.

Yee Clun also received support for his application from Alderman Cooksley, who pointed out Yee Clun's twenty-three-year residency in the city, and stressed that he 'had always borne an exemplary character.' The rationale for the 'White Women's Labour Law' seemed to defy Cooksley. The white alderman declared quizzically that it seemed odd that Chinese cooks and waiters were already employed in most restaurants in Regina, where they worked side by side with white women. He seemed unable to comprehend the logic of refusing Chinese employers the right to hire white women.

Alderman Dawson, another white councillor, was less puzzled. He declared that 'there was all the difference in the world between hiring help and being hired help,' and charged that it would be 'a dangerous precedent' for council to 'permit any Chinese to employ white women.' Dawson moved that the matter be tabled until the next meeting to give organizations that might be opposed to the proposal 'an opportunity to express their views.' In an attempt at compromise, the council voted to give preliminary approval to the application, subject to ratification at the next meeting.[83]

Alderman Dawson's delaying tactics were apparently designed to provide local community groups an opportunity to intervene. Some of the most prominent of Regina's white women's organizations nurtured virulent anti-Chinese sentiments. Among the first to debate the matter of Yee Clun's application were the executive members of the Woman's Christian Temperance Union (WCTU), whose concerns revolved around racial intermarriage. The executive of the three Regina WCTU branches called a special meeting on 12 August 1924. There members decried 'instances of girls marrying their Chinese employers,' insisting that 'intermarriage of the races should not be encouraged.'

There were some voices of dissent, with a few arguing that it was unjust to oppose racial intermarriage when immigration regulations made it virtually impossible for Chinese men to bring Chinese wives and families to Canada. At least one woman ventured to assert that she would 'rather marry some Chinaman than some white men,' but the general sentiment of the meeting was that 'there was no desire to see the practice common.' Barring white women from Chinese employment was necessary to deter 'close contact' between the races. Those who expressed concerns about limiting job opportunities for white women were met with brash assurances: 'There was other work to be had which was honest and less fraught with danger.' At the end of the day, the group passed a resolution that 'it was not in the best interests of the young womanhood of the city to grant the request of the restaurateur.' Mrs Rankin was designated to head the delegation to carry the message to city council.[84]

The Regina Local Council of Women (LCW) had been on record as actively opposing such licences since 1920, when it joined with the Regina Trades and Labor Congress in urging the Regina City Council to deny all applications from 'Oriental' men. There was some delay in responding to Yee Clun's particular situation, however, since many members of the LCW were absent from the city on summer vacation. The group more than made up for its tardiness when the meeting was finally held, with members voting unanimously and without discussion to lobby city council to ensure that no licences ever be issued to Chinese men. The LCW would schedule a special lecture on racial intermarriage for later in October, at which time Reverend Hugh Dobson advised them that such liaisons were 'growing in number in Canada.' Although the white reverend would caution that such trends were 'nothing to worry overmuch about,' the women of the LCW were clearly of a different view.[85]

The Regina LCW comprised a coalition of middle- and upper-middle-class women, first founded in 1895. With few exceptions, the LCW women were Canadian-born, of British heritage, well-educated, Protestant, middle-aged, and not employed outside the home. The group made it its mission to confer frequently with government officials on matters of education, social welfare, and labour law. Well known as the founders of the first hospital in Regina and the organizers of the children's aid society, the LCW women also developed reception facilities for immigrant women and a milk fund for needy children. Past efforts to lobby for industrial homes and separate courts for women, as well as the appointment of women to hospital and library boards, had met with substantial success.[86]

The resolution to oppose Yee Clun's licence seems to have been particularly championed by the LCW president, Maude Bunting Stapleford. A native of St Catharines, Ontario, Maude Stapleford graduated from Victoria College, University of Toronto, with an honours in modern languages in 1907. That same year, she married Reverend Ernest W. Stapleford, moving with him to Vancouver, where he took up a post as minister and educational secretary of the Methodist Church in British Columbia. In 1915, they moved to Regina when Dr Stapleford was appointed president of Regina College. The mother of four children, Mrs Stapleford was one of the pre-eminent club women in the province. She served successively as president of the Women's University Club, president of the Women's Educational Club, president of the Regina Local Council of Women, and president and convenor of laws and legislation of the Saskatchewan Provincial Council of Women. She was active as well with the WCTU, the Regina YWCA, the Victorian Order of Nurses, the Imperial Order Daughters of the Empire, the Equal Franchise League, the Liberal party, and the Women's Auxiliary of the Regina Symphony Orchestra. When she urged that a 'strong contingent' of LCW members attend the city council meeting in support of the anti-Chinese lobby, Maude Bunting Stapleford spoke with the authoritative voice of one of the most active leaders of the Saskatchewan women's community.[87]

When City Council reconvened on 19 August 1924, more than twenty representatives of women's organizations were present to speak to Yee Clun's application. Those opposed to granting the licence included groups such as the Gleaners Ladies Orange Benevolent Association of Saskatchewan, the Sons of England Benevolent Society, and the Salvation Army Women's hostel. Most vociferous of all were the spokeswomen from the Regina Women's Labour League.[88]

The Regina Women's Labour League (WLL) was one of a number of

Maude Stapleford.

left-wing organizations established during the second decade of the twentieth century to give women more voice within the labour movement. Loosely affiliated with the Communist Party of Canada, the leagues were primarily made up of middle-aged wives of trade-union men and unmarried career women such as teachers and journalists. Although the WLL's main focus was the economic exploitation of women, the analysis the organization adopted was suffused with the maternal feminism that marked the beliefs and practices of middle-class women's organizations. The primary aim of most Women's Labour Leagues was to support the families of striking workers. Their approval of the concept of a 'family wage' led them to lobby for prohibitions on the employment of married women and an end to night work for all female employees. Some even advocated compulsory medical examination for 'mental defectives' before marriage. The Women's Labour Leagues existed on the fringe of the male trade union world, as the September 1924 decision of the Trades and Labor Congress of Canada to deny their federation membership so eloquently illustrated. But the anti-Asian sentiments that laced the activities of the male labour movement seem to have infected the perspectives of the left-leaning white women from the WLL as well. Crossing class boundaries, the WLL resolutely joined with middle-class women's organizations to resist employment proximity for Asian men and white women.[89]

On behalf of the Regina Women's Labour League, Mrs W.M. Eddy gave the opening address to City Council on the evening of 19 August 1924, flanked by sister members Mrs K. Cluff and Mrs W.J. Vennels. Regina women were proud of the title 'Queen City of the West,' she announced. They had no wish to see their city dubbed the 'Queer City of the West.' Employment of white women by Chinese men was 'not in the best interests of white women or the community in general.' If the Chinese required service, 'they could get it from men.'

The mayor of Regina, a wholesale grocer of mixed Irish, English, and Scottish background named Stewart Coulter Burton, questioned Mrs Eddy intently at this point. The following exchange ensued on the floor of the council chamber:

MAYOR BURTON: Have you any evidence that conditions are not right in other places where white help is employed by Chinese?

MRS EDDY: We are not here as a court of morals, but to voice our protest from the economic standpoint. Judging by the Chinese laundries, conditions are not as good as they might be, and if it is allowed, we feel there will be an influx of an undesirable class of women into the city.

MAYOR BURTON: Your objection is mainly sentimental?

MRS EDDY: Not by any means, Mr Mayor. We feel this is only the thin edge of the wedge and that if this application is granted, there will be an influx into the city of an undesirable class of girl. Male help might just as well be employed. Employment of white women by Chinese might lead to mesalliances. In a rooming house there are many opportunities of temptation, more perhaps than in a restaurant.[90]

Oddly enough for a women's labour organization, the entire focus here is upon the need to deter a group of women workers described as the most 'undesirable class' from taking up residence in the city. It is not entirely clear whence the 'undesirability' stems. Given the reference to 'mesalliances,' the fear may have been of women who flouted prevailing, restrictive sexual mores, particularly proscriptions against crossing racial lines. Another possibility is that the WLL believed that only the most abject of the underclass would opt for these jobs, and resented any influx into Regina of more workers representing the lowest-waged, least-secure employees in the labour market. What is acutely obvious, however, is that the Regina Women's Labour League is archly dismissive of such potential employees.

A few lone voices supported Yee Clun. The city licence inspector held his ground and attested that 'the women of the city had nothing to fear' from Yee Clun. He assured council that, if it granted Yee Clun a licence, he could confidently assert that city bureaucrats would take pains to oversee Yee Clun's operation in the closest manner. He would cancel Yee Clun's licence forthwith, he promised, if 'there was the slightest appearance of wrong' in the future.[91]

Mrs Reninger and Mrs Armour, white teachers from the Chinese Mission in Regina, advised the council that they had come to know Yee Clun personally because he attended the Sunday school classes offered to Chinese residents. The Chinese Mission women declared Yee Clun to be 'a very faithful' and 'conscientious man,' and claimed that 'any girl would be safeguarded in his company.' Indeed, 'more was expected' from the Chinese than 'any other nationality,' they asserted. Their commentary was palpably at odds with the racist rhetoric that was splayed throughout the local newspapers. The Regina *Morning Leader* was given to recounting 'sordid and revolting' stories about young white women who were introduced to Chinese men in Sunday school classes. All too often, the frailer sex fell victim to 'the influence of the stronger personalities' of the would-be converts, and found themselves tragically transformed into 'drug fiends.' What Mrs Reninger and Mrs Armour must have thought of this doggerel can only be imagined. Their first-hand testimonials were sincere efforts to contradict such fear-mongering directly.[92]

The most forceful advocate for Yee Clun was Regina's white city solicitor, George Frederick Blair, KC. It was Blair's opinion that council was wrong to assume that it could arbitrarily grant or refuse a permit except on the ground that the applicant was 'an undesirable character.' 'Whether the applicant was Chinese, Japanese, Irish or Greek,' insisted Blair, 'did not enter into the question.' This went well beyond the submissions of the city licence inspector and the women from the Chinese

Banquet given to Sunday school teachers by their Chinese students, Weyburn, Saskatchewan, n.d.

mission. George Blair's legal advice embodied a simple demand for racial equality. To suggest that Blair's presentation came as something of a shock to the city councillors is an understatement. The Regina *Morning Leader* headlined its coverage of his comments as 'Blair Throws Bomb to Alderman in City Council.'[93]

The sixty-year-old city solicitor was born in Ferguson Falls, Ontario, where he completed high school before obtaining a teaching position in Parry Sound. Turning to the law as a second career, Blair opened up his first law practice in the small village of Brussels, Ontario, in 1901. He linked up with a law firm in Goderich, Ontario, and then moved west in 1910 to Regina, where he joined the legal partnership of Balfour, Martin, Casey and Blair. His appointment as city solicitor came in 1914, and his designation as King's Counsel followed in 1917. Married with four sons, George Blair compiled a record of active community service. He served as chair of the Saskatchewan Boys' Work Board for many years, an organization devoted to the development of sports and other activities for young men. He was a longtime director of the Young Men's Christian Association (YMCA) and sat on the board of the collegiate institute.

Blair was also a member of the board of Knox United Church, whose pastor, Reverend M. MacKinnon, had previously spoken out on behalf of the Chinese community in Regina. Rev. MacKinnon had defended the Chinese laundrymen more than a decade earlier, when racist whites mounted their campaign to impose burdensome taxes on Chinese businesses.[94] So George Blair may have been influenced by his minister. His legal position on the licensing protocol for Asian employers may also, in part, have reflected his personal experience with the Chinese residents of the city. He taught regularly at the Chinese YMCA Sunday school, which was attached to the large brick building on Osler Street where the Chinese National Party was headquartered. Like Mrs Reninger and Mrs Armour, he knew first-hand that the stereotypes that were routinely appended to Chinese men were inaccurate.

It would be incorrect, however, to suggest that George Blair was prepared to ascribe full respect to what he knew of the Chinese culture as a whole. As a Sunday school teacher, Blair was reputed to 'endeavor to instill' in his Chinese students 'the doctrines of Christianity and a love for Western ideals.' No proponent of religious and cultural diversity, Blair was committed to extending the mantle of European civilization and Protestantism to Asian immigrants. Presumably the Chinese individuals who came to the Sunday school classes were prepared to learn about Christianity, even to convert to the Christian religion. They had moved to

Canada, some had made permanent homes here, and they may have been willing to embrace many aspects of the dominant religion and culture. However, it is unlikely that many were anxious to jettison all of their past beliefs, perspectives, and philosophies. Blair's proselytization of 'Western ideals' was part of an overall mission of acculturation.

Unlike many of his fellow Canadians, who were imbued with the fervour of racial separation and inequality, Blair seems to have believed that Chinese immigrants, like others of European origin, could become full citizens if they were given proper training and achieved complete acculturation. His advocacy of the right of Chinese employers to be treated equally under the law seems to have reflected this perspective. For those Chinese immigrants who were prepared to conform to the prevailing norms of Anglo-Canadian society, George Blair believed that legal entitlements should follow.

All of the city councillors in attendance at the meeting seem to have been surprised by Blair's support for Yee Clun's application. Mayor Burton seemed somewhat nonplussed, and asked point blank: 'If this man is a respectable citizen with a good character recommended by public officials, then we have no right to refuse his application?' George Blair retorted: 'You have no right in the world to discriminate.' If the council ruled otherwise, cautioned Blair, it 'would be inviting litigation.' With that, the disconcerted members of council adjourned the matter until October.[95]

Most of Yee Clun's supporters took great pains to characterize the restaurateur as an exceptionally 'moral' individual, who should not be lumped in with other of his countrymen. At points, however, some were prepared to tackle Chinese discrimination head-on. The ladies of the Chinese Mission argued that it was unfair to single out the Chinese as a race. City solicitor Blair was by far the most articulate. He was prepared to expand the debate to encompass the Japanese, the Irish, and the Greek populations, all of whom would have been slotted below the British in the racial hierarchy that gripped the city. According to Blair, discrimination on the basis of race was neither moral nor legal.

When the debate resumed on 7 October 1924, the Local Council of Women took the rather extraordinary step of bringing along legal counsel to put forth their case. The man they selected to represent them was Douglas J. Thom, KC, a white partner with the largest law firm in Regina. The Ontario-born son of a Methodist minister, Thom moved out to Regina after graduating from Osgoode Hall Law School in 1903. He became active in city politics at the same time as he developed a thriving real estate practice at the prestigious firm of Brown, Mackenzie and

Thom. He received his 'King's Counsel' designation the same year as George Blair. Mindful of his religious obligations, Douglas Thom also served as the recording-steward of the Metropolitan Methodist Church for fifteen years.

Thom was no expert on municipal law or Chinese matters, but was probably acting *pro bono* as a favour to Maude Stapleford. Thom and Stapleford had much in common. They had both graduated from Victoria College at the University of Toronto. They shared religious ties. Thom served on the board of governors of Reverend Stapleford's Regina College. And Maude Stapleford must have been well acquainted with Douglas Thom's wife, Mabel Thom, a white woman who was an active member of the LCW and a founder of the University Women's Club in Regina.[96]

LCW solicitor Thom opened by noting that his clients were not asking the council 'to originate any discrimination against the Chinese.' The federal and provincial governments had taken the lead in this, with their long-standing network of legislation that discriminated against the Chinese with respect to immigration, taxation, suffrage, and employment. In 1885, when the completion of the Canadian Pacific Railway reduced the demand for low-waged Chinese construction crews, the federal government placed a head tax of $50 on all Chinese immigrants. In 1900, the tax was doubled, and in 1903 increased to $500.[97] In 1923, Parliament effectively barred all further Chinese immigration for the next two dozen years.[98]

Even when permitted to settle in Canada, many Chinese were denied access to the franchise. British Columbia restricted Chinese, Japanese, 'Hindu,' and 'other Asiatics' from exercising the vote.[99] Saskatchewan excluded the Chinese expressly, while Manitoba impeded their ability to exercise the franchise by way of a more indirect 'language' test.[100] Between 1885 and 1898, the federal government explicitly denied the right to vote to anyone of 'Mongolian or Chinese race.' Subsequently the federal government reinforced racial restrictions, piggybacking on racist provincial statutes through the adoption of provincial voters' lists for federal elections.[101]

The province of British Columbia, with the largest concentration of Chinese workers, enacted sweeping prohibitions against their employment in mines,[102] in the public sector,[103] and in private companies incorporated by the legislature.[104] A series of British Columbia statutes and by-laws impeded the Chinese from obtaining licences for laundries, liquor, mining, pawnbroking, building, and hand-logging.[105] Professions such as law and pharmacy, which required candidates to be on the voters' list, were barred to Asians in British Columbia.[106] Entitlement to unemployment relief was also affected by race, and jobless Chinese applicants in both British Columbia and Alberta were denied assistance provided to whites.[107]

Douglas Thom did not bother to itemize these provisions in his address before the council. In all likelihood, he was not fully aware of the length and breadth of the web of discriminatory legislation that entangled the Canadian legal system. Yet he knew that the LCW request to deny licences to Chinese businessmen was well within the parameters established by other governmental enactments. Taking his cue from the Canadian legislators, Thom mounted an unabashedly racist argument. 'Chinatowns,' he asserted, 'have an unsavory moral reputation,' and 'white girls lose caste when they are employed by Chinese.' As authority for this, he cited Emily Murphy, the Canadian narcotics expert. In December 1922, Emily Murphy had written a letter to the Regina *Morning Leader*, detailing the rapid spread of the narcotics traffic into Saskatchewan and mentioning the interracial nature of opium and cocaine use among both Chinese men and white women. Given information such as this, claimed Thom, regardless of Yee Clun's upstanding character references, 'the reputation of the city was at stake.'[108]

In an attempt to counter the LCW, the Chinese residents of Regina banded together to retain the services of a lawyer. There were no Chinese-Canadian lawyers available for hire. Kew Dock Yip and Gretta Wong, the first to achieve admission to a professional law society, were called in Ontario in 1945 and 1946.[109] Instead, they retained a white lawyer named Andrew G. MacKinnon. Originally from Nova Scotia, the forty-two-year-old MacKinnon obtained a BA from St Francis Xavier University back east in 1905. He served as alderman for the City of Regina from 1908 to 1910, and so would have been reasonably familiar with municipal procedures. MacKinnon entered law practice at the age of thirty-one, when he obtained admission to the Saskatchewan bar in 1913. As a Roman Catholic in Saskatchewan, MacKinnon was no stranger to the dangers of bigotry. When Ku Klux Klan organizers from the United States infiltrated Saskatchewan two years after the *Yee Clun* case, they would target Roman Catholics along with the Chinese, Blacks, and Jews, as the focus of their venomous tirades and intimidation. Klan literature spewed vitriol about the Pope, priests, and nuns, charging them with kidnapping children, murdering babies, and a host of spectacular pornographic sexual acts. As the Klan began to register unparalleled success in Saskatchewan, signing up an estimated 25,000 members across the province, Andrew MacKinnon went on record as abhorring all Klan affiliations. When MacKinnon was subsequently defeated in his bid for election to the House of Commons in 1926, there were some who put it down to his public opposition to the hate-fomenting Klan.[110]

Andrew MacKinnon appeared before the council on behalf of the wider Chinese community, but he did not address the issue of racial discrimination directly. Instead, he focused his arguments primarily upon his client's honourable reputation. Yee Clun was 'the leader of the Chinese in Regina, a man of the highest type and a law-abiding citizen,' claimed MacKinnon. In this, Yee Clun reflected his people, whom MacKinnon asserted tended to be convicted in the courts at a substantially lower rate than people of other nationalities. MacKinnon took a more cautious approach than City Solicitor Blair. He did not argue that it would be unlawful for city council to base their decision on race. Instead, he advised that 'the city was not bound by any law to discriminate' against Yee Clun. In the end, he urged them not to do so.[111]

Under the limelight of this unprecedented public intervention and intense media scrutiny, the city councillors called the question, tallied the result, and announced that they had voted to refuse Yee Clun the licence. Possibly realizing that he should have taken a more forceful legal position in front of the council, Andrew MacKinnon announced his intention to appeal the ruling to the courts. He would seek judicial review of Regina City Council's refusal to grant the licence, on the ground that the councillors had based their decision upon 'an erroneous principle.'[112]

MacKinnon's request to void the ruling of city council was heard by the Saskatchewan Court of King's Bench on 14 November 1925. At the trial, the mayor and various aldermen from Regina's council took the stand to give evidence as to why they had refused Yee Clun a licence. All admitted that the decision was based upon racial grounds.'It was because he employed a number of Chinamen on his premises,' they testified, 'who, owing to the restrictions placed upon them by our federal laws, have not been permitted to bring their wives into this country.' The danger, claimed the witnesses, was that 'such employees would constitute a menace to the virtue of the white women if the latter were allowed to work on the same premises with them.' Yee Clun himself, they conceded, posed no particular threat, given the presence of his wife in Regina and his 'excellent' character. His Chinese employees were another matter entirely.

This reasoning seemed to confound the white Saskatchewan judge, Philip Edward Mackenzie, who sat alone on Yee Clun's application. Like the lawyers who appeared in the *Yee Clun* case, Judge Mackenzie's roots were also back east. He was born in London, Ontario, received his call to the Ontario bar in 1896, practised law for a few years in London, and then moved his practice to Kenora, where he was appointed the Crown attorney of the district of Rainy River until 1910. That year he moved out to Saskatchewan and opened his law practice in Regina. His appointment to the Court of King's Bench in Saskatchewan came in 1921.[113]

Judge Mackenzie appears to have been disconcerted by the testimony of the witnesses who appeared before him. Describing the council's argument as 'fallacious,' Judge Mackenzie concluded: '[I]t suggests that if the plaintiff, instead of employing Chinamen, had employed an equal number of white men, matrimonially unattached, no member of the council would have considered it, though the menace to the virtue of the white women might well be greater in the latter event, since there would exist no racial antipathy to be overcome between them and the white men.'[114]

Judge Mackenzie aligned himself with Helen Gregory MacGill here, seemingly alert to the potential dangers of sexual coercion on the job. The judge was implicitly acknowledging that men who hold power over women in the workplace may exercise it sexually. Like MacGill, he also recognized that such men may come from races other than the Chinese. Both were prepared to take issue with the racially-based focus on Chinese employers.

Oddly enough, since Judge Mackenzie was directing his attention to the efficacy of the law, he missed drawing the next evident conclusion. He appears to have recognizd that sexual overtures on the job might constitute a 'menace to the virtue of white women.' But he neglected to suggest that a more useful remedy would lie in disciplinary sanctions against those who made the coercive advances. He does not seem to have realized that restricting the job opportunities of women was a punitive and ultimately unsatisfactory solution for the women he was purporting to protect.

Judge Mackenzie continued to evaluate the anti-Chinese licensing system, astutely concluding that some of its other features defeated logic: '[I]t is common knowledge that white restaurant keepers do frequently employ Chinamen on their premises, which suggests the seemingly absurd conclusion that when a Chinaman is employed by a Chinaman, however respectable the latter may be, the former is a menace to the white women's virtue, while, when the white man employs him, he is not.' This was clearly a licensing scheme that was both too narrowly and

Andrew G. McKinnon, 1949.

Philip Edward Mackenzie.

too broadly constructed to accomplish what it purported to do, to protect white women's virtue on the job.

If Judge Mackenzie had stopped here, the decision would constitute an interesting illustration of judicial reflection on the utility of licensing measures. However, Judge Mackenzie ventured much further afield, and the final portion of his judgment was more sweeping in its scope. The case prompted Judge Mackenzie to take a closer examination of the 'White Women's Labour Law,' and he found himself searching back into the legislative history of the Saskatchewan statute for guidance. Mackenzie recognized that as it was originally structured, the act overtly discriminated on the basis of race. Consequently, he professed himself brought up short by the legislative amendment in 1913 that removed the 'Japanese' and 'other Oriental persons' from the reach of the law. The 1919 amendment seemed to carry the revising strategy to its ultimate conclusion, erasing all racial references to the employers regulated under the act. Struck by the racial neutrality of the legislative momentum, Mackenzie asserted that the intent behind the statutory revision must have been to 'abolish the discriminatory principle.'

While seemingly straightforward as a matter of logic, this conclusion was wholly at odds with the expressed intentions of the Saskatchewan legislators. The attorney general had announced that the change was not intended to be a substantive one, but a matter of 'form' only. The minister of Municipal Affairs had urged city councils never to grant licences to Chinese entrepreneurs. None of these statements were introduced in evidence at Yee Clun's trial, however, since the law governing statutory interpretation in the early twentieth century was quite restrictive.

Judges who were charged with interpreting the meaning of a particular enactment were instructed to confine their analysis to the words of the statute. They were not permitted to resort to the legislative debates surrounding the statute, or to consider public pronouncements made by the legislators themselves. The prohibition on such extrinsic consultation originated centuries earlier in England, where courts were fond of insisting, rather bizarrely, that 'the person least able to interpret a statute was the drafter, because he is unconsciously influenced by what he meant rather than what he said.' The 'literal' construction of statutes was the strict and governing rule. So the City of Regina was unable to cite Turgeon and Langley's comments suggesting that the racial sanitizing of the 'White Women's Labour Law' was really meant to be a sham.[115]

It is possible that due to this rather odd rule of statutory interpretation, Judge Mackenzie simply did not know that the Saskatchewan legislature meant to continue the racial discrimination against Chinese businessmen as usual. It seems likely, however, that Judge Mackenzie was rather more aware of the politicians' motives and desires than he was allowed to admit. The legislature sat in Regina, where the newspapers of the day carried extensive reports about the positions that politicians took during their legislative debates. Judge Mackenzie must have read the Regina *Morning Leader* along with his morning coffee, as did all the other members of Regina's leading citizenry. He could not have missed seeing the comments of the attorney general and minister of Municipal Affairs, since they were blazoned across the press coverage of the 1919 amendment. It is possible that Judge Mackenzie deliberately decided to repudiate the racial discrimination directed against Chinese businessmen, and that he took a gleeful sense of irony in suggesting that he was merely carrying out the wishes of the legislators themselves.

Judge Mackenzie emphasized that none of the witnesses who testified before him 'questioned' Yee Clun's 'own good character,' and stressed that 'nearly all admitted that it was excellent.' The council refused the licence solely 'upon racial grounds' he held, and this was the fatal flaw in the defendants' position. 'It would be strange,' noted Judge Mackenzie drolly, if municipalities 'could now go on and maintain the discriminatory principle which the Legislature had been at such pains to abolish.' The municipal council's authority to grant licences was a power delegated by the legislature, and the council was required to 'confine its actions strictly within the limits of such authority.' Its error was in refusing a licence simply because Yee Clun failed to satisfy certain preconditions that members of council had unilaterally decided to demand of applicants, based on 'personal character or racial origin.' With this, Judge Mackenzie pronounced Regina City Council's decision to refuse Yee Clun a licence invalid and unlawful. He ordered the councillors to grant Yee Clun his licence forthwith.[116]

The decision to insist upon a racially-neutral interpretation of the statute cut against the prevailing political grain in the province. It departed as well from earlier court rulings that the 'White Women's Labour Law' was constitutional in spite of its discriminatory impact.[117] In the same vein, legislation barring Asians from voting was also upheld as constitutional under Canadian law.[118] The courts rarely supported efforts to resist racism against the Chinese. Mackenzie's judgment, with its direct disavowal of racially discriminatory licensing, stands out as something of a refreshing anomaly.

Judge Mackenzie's ruling was, however, consistent with several earlier decisions from white British Columbia judges who struck down anti-Chinese provincial statutes and municipal by-laws in the late nineteenth century.[119] Although its record was mixed, the English Privy Council also invalidated legislation from British Columbia prohibiting the employment of Chinese men in the mines in 1899.[120] Some have tried to explain these decisions by suggesting that the judges were motivated by a concern to 'check the excesses of "responsible" government,' foster the economic contribution of the Chinese, and protect the formalistic 'rule of law.'[121] Others have argued that where judges ruled against racist legislation and licensing schemes, they typically did so not to advance equality, but to protect the interests of white capital. In the earlier cases, judges frequently took offence to laws that restricted the access of white employers to Asian labourers, while laws that restricted Asians in their right to vote or carry on business as entrepreneurs were left intact.[122]

The suggestion that judges who struck down racist laws were motivated by their own class interests seems not fully explanatory in the *Yee Clun* case. Judge Mackenzie ordered the city to issue a licence to Yee Clun's restaurant, a decision designed to protect the business interests of a Chinese employer. Judge Mackenzie's comments about the 'racial antipathy' that white women might feel towards Chinese men suggest that he was not entirely free from bias against the Chinese. However, he spoke out unabashedly against 'the discriminatory principle.' His curt instructions to the Regina City Council embody a ringing endorsement of racial equality with respect to the right to hire employees. In so ruling, Judge Mackenzie sided squarely with City Solicitor George Blair, who proclaimed that licences should be dispensed on the basis of character, not race.

Judge MacKenzie's decision was an abrupt affront to the Saskatchewan legislators who had tried to design their legislative amendment to achieve racial neutrality on the surface of the statute, while retaining a racist application of the law. The politicians were apprised of the decision by their racist constituents, who were clearly of the view that municipalities ought not to be estopped from applying the neutral language of the 1919 statute in a racially biased manner. Before more than two months passed, the legislature voted in favour of a further enactment. The 1926 statute expanded the scope of the law to encompass lodging houses, boarding houses, public hotels, and cafes, along with the traditional restaurants and laundries. Curiously, this time the off-limit workers were no longer identified by race; the hiring of any 'woman or girl' could subject an employer to municipal scrutiny. Presumably this, too, was a change in form and not in substance, since access to potential employees who were women of colour remained strictly limited.[123]

Although Yee Clun was not mentioned by name, the new enactment explicitly empowered the city council to revoke the court-ordered licence he had been issued. The statute also authorized any municipal council to 'revoke a license already granted,' and admonished that any such revocation 'shall be in its absolute discretion; it shall not be bound to give any reason for such refusal or revocation, and its action shall not be open to question or review by any court.' In one fell swoop, the Saskatchewan legislature voted to shield municipalities from any future judicial review of their licensing decisions.

It is not clear what action, if any, the Regina City Council actually took to revoke Yee Clun's licence. But records indicate that white government officials continued to harass Yee Clun for some time after the litigation was over. Prosecuted and convicted for failing to make proper tax returns for his business, Yee Clun would be forced back to court in 1928, seeking judicial review of this ruling as well. Once again, Andrew MacKinnon represented the Chinese restaurateur and the Saskatchewan King's Bench overturned the initial decision, ruling that the authorities who secured the original conviction failed to follow proper procedures.[124]

As for George Blair, two years after the first Yee Clun trial, he was unexpectedly seized by a heart attack and dropped dead in his office at city hall. Among the many floral tributes that graced his funeral service at the Knox United Church were wreaths from the Chinese YMCA and the Chinese Laundry Association.[125]

The 'White Women's Labour Law,' promoted by a coalition of interests crossing class and gender boundaries, functioned as a critical tool enabling racially dominant groups to prohibit Chinese men from participating freely in the economic and social communities in which they lived. Requiring rigid boundaries to be drawn between races, the statute illustrated the inherent difficulties of race definition, and encouraged the articulation of racist stereotypes in inflammatory ways. Leaders among the Chinese community actively contested the validity of such laws, and although they occasionally found their claims met with some success in the courts, the legal system as a whole was notoriously deficient in response. When Yee Clun's persistent efforts met with a modicum of victory in the courts, political forces superseded judicial opinion to reverse any gains obtained in litigation.

The 'White Women's Labour Law' remained in force for years. Manitoba was the first to repeal its act in 1940, with Ontario following in 1947, but British Columbia let the statute stand until 1968.[126] The Saskatchewan statute, veiled in racially-neutral language, was not repealed until 1969.[127] Working-class white womanhood proved to be a stalwart symbol in the forging of political, social, and economic hierarchies. The enforcement of the 'White Women's Labour Law' illustrates the powerful influence of Canadian law in shaping the historical understanding of race.

6

'It Will Be Quite an Object Lesson': *R. v Phillips* and the Ku Klux Klan in Oakville, Ontario, 1930

It was a spectacle to strike terror into the hearts of 'racialized' people everywhere; the Ku Klux Klan had arrived on a mission. On the night of 28 February 1930, a 'small army' of seventy-five individuals, clad in white gowns and hoods, marched through the town of Oakville. Their movements startled hundreds of alarmed residents, rousing them from their early evening slumbers to see what the commotion signified. The marchers strode to the centre of town, where they planted a massive cross in the middle of the road. Then they set a torch to the oil-soaked rags tied to the huge wooden cross. The cross ignited instantly, shooting fiery flames and blazing sparks across the sky. The hooded band stood by, watching in eerie silence, until it burned down to the last glowing ember.[1]

The Klansmen's next task was to locate David Kerr, Oakville's white police chief, 'to acquaint him with the purpose of their visit.' Given the lateness of the hour, their brief stop at the police station was to no avail; the chief was not in.[2] The gowned and hooded marchers proceeded next to Head Street, several blocks away, to the home of Ira Junius Johnson. The Klansmen had learned that Johnson, 'a Negro,' was living with a 'white girl' named Isabel Jones. Their intent was to discipline the racially upstart Ira Johnson and put an end to the mixed-race liaison. When they learned that the couple was out visiting Ira Johnson's aunt, they motored over to her Kerr Street residence. According to the Hamilton *Spectator*, the KKK members 'thundered on the door and demanded of the negro who answered them that he bring out [the] white girl.' Twenty-year-old Isabel Jones emerged, and was hustled off to the home of her white, widowed mother. After a brief consultation with Mrs Jones, Isabel was put into a car and deposited in the care of Captain W. Broome, a white officer of the Salvation Army.[3]

The Klansmen then returned for Ira Johnson and forcibly removed the terrified man, casting him into another car with 'two stalwarts' as guards on either side. The caravan collected Ira Johnson's elderly aunt and uncle from their home, and drove back to Head Street. The costumed marauders surrounded the house, and turned Ira Johnson and his relatives out in the front yard. Then they nailed a large cross to a post in front of the door and set it on fire. They threatened that, if Ira Johnson was 'ever seen walking down the street with a white girl again,' the Klan 'would attend to him.'[4]

Meanwhile, one of Oakville's Black citizens had located the police chief and alerted him to the situation.[5] Chief Kerr headed out to investigate, and came upon a cavalcade of fifteen cars on Navy Street, all filled with white-robed men. When the chief caught up with the leaders of the procession, several of the gowned men got out and took off their hoods. Chief Kerr recognized them as white residents of the near-by city of Hamilton, whom he 'knew quite well.' They all shook hands. The police chief assured himself personally that 'no damage to property or person warranting his interference' had occurred. Kerr made no arrests, offered no warnings or further complaint, and the Klansmen continued on their way.[6]

THE COMMUNITY RESPONDS

'Ku Klux Klan Cohorts Parade into Oakville and Burn Fiery Cross' was the lead item on page one of next morning's Toronto *Globe*. 'Klan Separates Oakville Negro and White Girl' headlined page one of the Hamilton *Spectator*. The London *Free Press* claimed that the Klansmen had come 'from Toronto and Hamilton by preconceived arrangement.' The Hamilton *Spectator* insisted that the Ku Klux Klan members were all Hamiltonians.[7]

Interspersed with their factual reports, the newspapers seem to have been mostly complacent, even smug, about the fiery episode. The Oakville *Star and Independent* announced that 'it was really impressive how thoroughly and how systematically the klan went about their task,' pointing out that the 'burning of the fiery cross added a realistic touch.' The

London *Free Press* noted: 'At no time during the evening was violence used and the conduct of the "visitors" was all that could be desired, according to Chief of Police David Kerr of Oakville, who said when the men removed their white cloaks he recognized many as prominent Hamilton business men.' The Milton *Canadian Champion* confided: 'If the Ku Klux Klan conducted all their assemblies in as orderly a manner as in Oakville [...] when they separated a negro and his intended white bride, there would be no complaint.' The Brampton *Banner* mused speculatively: 'If the Ku Klux Klan came to Brampton, where would they visit?' The Toronto *Daily Star* noted that the Klansmen had 'escorted' Miss Jones 'courteously and quietly,' referring to the affair as 'a show of white justice.' The *Star* quoted Oakville's white mayor, J.B. Moat: 'There was a strong feeling against the marriage which the young girl and the negro had planned. Personally I think the Ku Klux Klan acted quite properly in the matter. It will be quite an object lesson.' 'There was not [a] semblance of disorder,' concluded the Toronto *Globe*, and the Hamilton *Spectator* added: 'The citizens of Oakville generally seemed pleased with the work accomplished by the visit.'[8]

Described as the 'Saratoga of Ontario,' the town of Oakville was widely reputed to be a 'Canadian Newport,' developed in the late nineteenth century as a splendid and picturesque summer resort for the well-to-do citizens of southwestern Ontario. Situated between Toronto and Hamilton on the shores of Lake Ontario, Oakville became a magnet for weary city-dwellers, long before northern Ontario opened up to cottagers. Even affluent towns like Oakville were affected, however, when the Great Depression hit in 1929, causing unemployment to swell and bread lines to multiply.[9]

In 1930, Oakville's population numbered fewer than 4,000. Almost 93 per cent of the residents traced their heritage from English, Irish, Scottish, or other 'British races.' The largest non-European group to show up in the census data was the Asian Canadians, a community of twenty. Official census records do not list a separate category for Blacks, but Oakville mayor J.B. Moat told the *Star* that 'the colored population' had recently decreased leaving 'not more than forty with women and children.' Ira Johnson, who was 'raised in Oakville,' was one of the steadfast.[10]

The history of Black immigration to Canada is truncated and complex. Although records indicate that the first Black man arrived as early as 1606, substantial numbers did not immigrate until after the American Revolution in 1782. At that time several thousand free Black Loyalists took up land grants from the Crown. Many of the white Loyalists also brought their Black slaves with them. During the War of 1812, several thousand additional Blacks sought refuge with the British, ultimately settling in Nova Scotia between 1813 and 1815. In the 1840s and 1850s, the province of Canada West received an estimated forty thousand American Blacks, who were fleeing the Fugitive Slave Act via the Underground Railroad. Smaller groups of Blacks migrated to the far west, settling on Vancouver Island in 1859, and in Saskatchewan and Alberta in the 1890s, and between 1910 and 1914. Additional numbers continued to come from the United States and the West Indies from the 1920s onward.[11]

Racist whites spearheaded campaigns within several provinces to restrict the entry of Black immigrants.[12] As early as 1864, physicians had been predicting that the harsh Canadian winter would 'efface' the Black population, and this theme was enthusiastically adopted by senior officials from the Department of the Interior at the turn of the century.[13] The federal government responded in 1910 with An Act respecting Immigration that allowed the federal cabinet to issue orders prohibiting the entry of 'immigrants belonging to any race deemed unsuited to the climate or requirements of Canada.'[14] An Order-in-Council was drafted in 1911, to prohibit the landing in Canada of 'any immigrant belonging to the Negro race,' but it was never declared in force. Concerned about the potential diplomatic problems this overtly exclusionary policy might create between Canada and the United States, the authorities opted to utilize unwritten, informal rules to accomplish the same end by more indirect means.[15] Similar legislation was enacted in Newfoundland in 1926.[16]

The Black community in Oakville, primarily descendants of American-born former slaves, dated back to the mid-nineteenth century.[17] It seems safe to suggest that the press commentary on the KKK incident, attributing 'general pleasure' as the predominant community response, did not reflect the views of all the citizens of Oakville. Blacks, Asian Canadians, and the small Jewish and Roman Catholic communities, all groups who suffered from Klan venom, must have been deeply disturbed by the disruption.

Although no one from Oakville was quoted in the press, a delegation of prominent Black Torontonians voiced a challenge to the prevailing sentiment. E. Lionel Cross, one of the few Black lawyers in Toronto, was the most vocal. Originally from Britain, Cross obtained admission to the Nova Scotia bar in 1923, and the Ontario bar in 1924. Cross told the London *Free Press*: 'I call the doings at Oakville last evening an outrage. As a British citizen, I have believed the rule of the law should always prevail. [A man] is free to choose what companions he cares to have.

When anybody under the guise of patriotism or any other "ism" trespasses on the right of any man, no matter who he may be or of what race, it should be the duty of all law-abiding citizens to denounce any such action.'[18]

Cross called a 'mass meeting' of Blacks at the University Avenue First Baptist Church in Toronto on 4 March. The First Baptist, founded in 1826, was Ontario's oldest Black Baptist church, and its pastor, Rev. H. Lawrence McNeil, joined Cross in urging members of the Black community to come out.[19] Adding his voice to Cross's and McNeil's was another prominent Black leader, Toronto lawyer B.J. Spencer Pitt. Born in Grenada into a prosperous mercantile family, Pitt came to Nova Scotia in 1926 to study law at Dalhousie Law School, and continued his legal education at the Middle Temple in London, England. Pitt articled with Lionel Cross and received his Ontario call in 1928.[20]

Cross, McNeil, and Pitt were successful in convincing those assembled to endorse a resolution requesting the government to take action. The three Black leaders confronted the province's senior legal authority, Ontario Attorney General W.H. Price, with their demands the next day. The London *Advertiser* advised that the meeting with the white attorney general constituted 'a most sympathetic interview,' and culminated in a promise that the episode would be 'fully investigated' by the Oakville authorities. The upshot was that Attorney General Price instructed the white Crown attorney from Milton, Ontario, William Inglis Dick, and Police Chief David Kerr to 'conduct the most searching probe.' Dick and Kerr were ordered to 'prepare a full report on the whole affair' for Price's scrutiny.[21]

Then the Toronto *Star* dropped a bombshell in its 5 March edition. 'Has No Negro Blood, Klan Victim Declares' was the startling front-page headline, the fruit of some detailed investigative sleuthing to trace Ira Johnson's heritage. Johnson, who claimed to be descended from white and 'Indian' relations originally from Indiana and Maryland, informed the press that he had 'not a drop of negro blood in his veins.' The perennial conundrum of racial definition floated up out of the morass unbidden and ultimately irresolvable.[22]

The *Star* indicated that Johnson's mother, described by the reporter as 'a refined and intelligent woman,' was the daughter of Rev. Junius Roberts, a 'white,' who 'preached for many years to negro congregations at Guelph, Hamilton and Oakville more than forty years ago.' Johnson explained that 'the reason his grandfather preached in the church for negroes was because Mrs. Roberts was so dark that some objections had been taken to her by members of white congregations.' Either Johnson's maternal grandmother's claim to be 'a Cherokee Indian' had not convinced the concerned parishioners, or else they believed that 'Indian' heritage was as sullying as Black. The *Star* indicated that Rev. Roberts's father was of English and Scottish descent, while his mother was a 'Cherokee half-breed from Indiana.' On his paternal side, Ira Johnson's great-grandfather was another 'Cherokee half-breed,' and his great-grandmother was Irish. For those seeking an immediate and definitive racial designation, this was a confusing welter indeed.[23]

Those who probed the question further discovered that visual identification was equally slippery. The *Star* described Johnson as 'a fine-looking man and nearly white.' Upon closer inspection, the *Star* reporter offered his opinion that Johnson's 'features' portrayed 'his Indian connection.' The major clue seems to have been the Klan victim's hair, which the reporter described as 'black and straight.' Although in demeanour Johnson was 'quiet and unassuming,' he stood 'over six feet in height,' and cut 'quite a figure in the town.' The Toronto *Globe* learned that Johnson had been 'refused liquor because he was an Indian,' but recounted that 'reliable sources' among the Black community insisted he had 'colored blood in his veins.'[24] It is also possible that Ira Johnson's last name may have played some role in racial reputation, since 'Johnson' was the name of several prominent Black families in the area.[25]

The newspapers seemed eager to rehabilitate Ira Johnson's reputation and character, after mistakenly branding him a 'Negro.' The *Star* devoted several columns to describing Johnson's lengthy war service with the 166th Battalion, with the Sussex Regiment in England, and at Vimy Ridge in France. The Hamilton *Spectator* added that the thirty-year-old Johnson had been wounded 'twice' while fighting valiantly during the Great War, had been hospitalized in Burlington for his injuries, and had worked for five years as a motor mechanic for Hillmer Bros. The *Star* also published a detailed history of the Cherokee, inexplicably adjoining a lengthy discussion about the Six Nations in Brantford. Presumably the reporter who attempted to educate the *Star*'s readers about the Six Nations, their claims of 'autonomy,' and their efforts to obtain recognition as 'allies' rather than 'subjects' of the British Crown, believed all First Nations peoples were somehow related.[26]

Meanwhile, Ku Klux Klan members continued to pursue their quarry. The Toronto *Star* advised that 'a large brown sedan motor car' was still stalking Miss Jones. Seemingly unconcerned about detection, night after night four occupants parked the sedan, with 'cowl lights burning,' blocking traffic in front of the Salvation Army home where Miss Jones was stationed. The press let it be known that the Klansmen might also be 'maintaining surveillance over Ira Johnson.'[27]

The editors of the Toronto *Globe* were among the few media sources to express some misgivings about the intimidating nature of the Klan's activities in Oakville. But it was the methods of the Klan, not the philosophy, that the *Globe* denounced on 3 March:

Whatever may have been the merits of the motive prompting a Ku Klux Klan demonstration in Oakville, there can be no compromise with a policy which leads a group of citizens to take the law into their own hands ... [I]ts members may believe their objectives are worthy. If so, they will stand for open discussion in daylight; they should not call for nocturnal visits and disguising costumes. [...]

It is regrettable that men of intelligence, such as many of the Klansmen are, presumably – would associate themselves with such a system for righting what they conceive to be wrongs. If they directed their energy toward policy-making and law enforcement in an open and recognized way they would be serving their country. [...] The work the nocturnal visitors did in Oakville in separating a white girl from a colored man may be commendable in itself and prove a benefit, but it is certain that the methods are wrong.[28]

Rising to the challenge, the Klan delivered a fulsome rebuttal to the office of the *Globe* in the form of a detailed, written statement signed by 'the Scribe': 'Be it understood,' opened the missive, 'that we strenuously oppose any marriage between the white and colored race, regardless of nationality, on the ground of racial purity.' They alleged that they were simply acting at the behest of Isabel Jones's concerned mother:

We, the Knights of the Ku Klux Klan of Canada, received a letter from Mrs. Jones of Oakville, asking for assistance in that her daughter, a white girl, was being detained by a negro ... She stated that she had applied to the police and Magistrate of that town, and also to the Salvation Army, for assistance, and, on account of the doors being barred in the house where this negro held the white girl captive, the Salvation Army having tried on several occasions to enter this house, received no admittance; the police authorities stated that, on account of the girl being over 18 years old, their hands were tied ... Up to the time of the Klan's action, this white girl and the colored man lived alone for five nights, and as no one could gain admittance, and the law being powerless to take its course, the girl's mother was heartbroken and frantic.[29]

What was more, the white girl had had a change of heart, confided the Klansmen. 'We proceeded to take the girl to her mother, where she made a promise in the presence of Klansmen that she would never again associate with a colored man.' The Salvation Army officials greeted them 'with open arms,' and the Klansmen had 'interviewed' the chief of police, 'giving him full details of the case.' Even Ira Johnson's parents, Mr and Mrs Munday Johnson, were described as sympathetic to the Klan's foray. 'His parents are of sterling character and are highly spoken of in their community,' noted the Scribe. 'The Ku Klux Klan extended to them sincere wishes that their son would mend his ways and that this demonstration would be a warning to him.' Most remarkably, the Scribe suggested that a true bond had been forged between the Klan and Ira Johnson's parents. After the cross had been burned, it was emphasized, Johnson's parents had come out to speak to the hooded marauders, and 'made reply in terms of "God bless you all".' 'At no time during this movement was a hand laid upon the girl or the man,' stressed the letter, 'neither did a Klansman enter any of their homes.' In sum, the Scribe insisted, 'these people acted in accordance with their own free will.'[30]

What rankled the Klansmen the most, however, was the *Globe*'s suggestion that the Ku Klux Klan had 'not made great progress in the Dominion.' 'That is a pitiful statement to be made by an outsider who is making statements at random,' complained the Scribe. '[T]he Fiery Cross shines on many of the heads of our Senate and Parliament today, and our growth along with discipline commands thousands of Klansmen in all parts of the Dominion.' The letter insisted that the strength of the Klan was notorious, and that there had never been such a perilous hour of need in Canada:

Canada being a British, Protestant Dominion, where it is evident that British immigration is barred to a great extent in favor of foreign immigration, where again we see the minority controlling the majority, this organization must of necessity protect the interests of the Anglo-Saxon Protestant people against the ever-increasing menace arising from communism, bolshevism, Reds and Orientals, and the peril of racial impurity, together with the international corruption and vice that has moved the Knights of the Ku Klux Klan, as the knights of old, to march forward under the banner of Christ in the fight against foreign domination, crooked politicians, criminals, bootleggers, white slavery, libertines, home wreckers, girl ruiners and all such people who may be opposed to the teachings of our Protestant institutions.[31]

THE HISTORY OF THE KU KLUX KLAN (KKK)

The KKK originated in Pulaski, Tennessee, in 1865. Six white officers of the Confederate army returned home from their unsuccessful campaigns during the American Civil War to form a club they christened the 'Ku Klux Klan.' 'Ku Klux' was their rendition of the Greek word for circle, 'Kuklos.' 'Klan' was added out of deference to the group's common Scottish and Irish heritage. The founders of the organization primarily intended it to be a social club, and initiated an ethos of secrecy, hazing, and ritual that borrowed heavily from a long tradition of male fraternal societies. They gave each other titles such as the 'Grand Wizard,' 'Grand Dragon,' 'Hydra,' 'Fury,' and 'Cyclops.' The members adopted gangly costumes of long, loose-fitting white gowns, decorated with occult symbols such as stars and half-moons cut out of red flannel. Conical hats up to two feet tall, made of white cloth over cardboard with eyeholes punched out, completely concealed their heads.[32]

The Ku Klux Klan initially occupied itself with random acts of nuisance. In the tension-filled postwar American South, this evolved into a focused attack on newly emancipated Black citizens. By 1867, bands of white-robed night prowlers were breaking up Black prayer meetings and social gatherings, intimidating participants and confiscating firearms. Between 1867 and 1871, the reign of terror escalated. Klansmen held vigilante 'trials' and carried out sentences upon their chosen victims under cover of night, wreaking property damage, assault, sexual assault, and murder upon Blacks and whites who resisted their racist onslaught. Klan membership expanded to embrace white Americans from all walks of life, from small farmers and working-class labourers to doctors, lawyers, legislators, and judges.[33]

Klan leaders described their organizational rationale as delivering punishment to 'impudent negroes and negro-loving whites.' Contemporaries described the Klan's purpose: 'by force and terror, to prevent all political action not in accord with the views of the members, to deprive colored citizens of the right to bear arms and of the right of a free ballot, to suppress the schools in which colored children were taught, and to reduce the colored people to a condition closely allied to that of slavery.' The KKK campaign of intimidation was intensely sexualized, both at the ideological level and in practice. Klan propaganda insisted that 'the greatest ambition' of Black men was 'to marry a white wife,' and accused Blacks of using physical coercion to wrangle marriage vows and sex from white female victims. Klansmen understood the abolition of slavery as an unparalleled blow to white male sexual freedom. They lamented the loss of white sexual access to Black female slaves and fretted over the potential loss of exclusive sexual access to their own white female counterparts. In retaliation, the Klan raped and sexually tortured women, some white but mostly Black, as well as castrating and sexually mutilating Black men.[34]

The first wave of Ku Klux Klan activity began to wane in 1871, when a congressional investigation into the unprecedented campaign of violence resulted in the enactment of the Ku-Klux Act. The legislation made it a crime for two or more persons to 'go in disguise upon the public highway or upon the premises of another,' with the intent of depriving anyone of his or her constitutional rights. It also made citizens 'with foreknowledge of Klan violence' liable to Klan victims for any suffering they could have prevented. Although the legislation was not widely or persistently enforced, it was sufficient to drive the organization out of public visibility for several decades.[35]

Little is yet known about the spread of Ku Klux Klan activities to Canada during its first active phase from 1865 to the 1870s. Certainly there must have been some fertile ground for its expansion north of the border, for anti-Black racism permeated areas of Canada well in advance of the creation of the Ku Klux Klan. Susanna Moodie, who emigrated to central Canada from Britain, described in 1852, in her memoirs, *Roughing It in the Bush*, a vicious response to an interracial marriage in the local community. She recounts how a group of white men dragged the newly wed Black man from the home in which he lived with his white wife. Then they 'rode him along the rails' until he died.[36]

It also appears that some Canadians held the American Ku Klux Klan in great esteem. At least one Canadian periodical, published some years later, would sanctimoniously applaud the activities of the Klan in its original phase, explaining the need for such organizations in what seems indicative of remarkable naïvety or outright racial bigotry. '[F]or the Ku Klux Klan, which arose during the era of negro domination after the Civil War, there was excuse if not justification. The coloured people just released from slavery, with no training in self-government, and controlled by rascally Northern politicians, committed every species of folly and offence, and laid intolerable burdens and humiliations upon the white element,' claimed one Canadian journal. 'Only the secret hand of the Ku Klux Klan gave relief and a degree of safety.'[37]

During the 1870s, at least some Canadians were initiated into the Klan in eastern Ontario.[38] There is also some evidence that American Klansmen, fleeing responsibility for their lawless activities, crossed over into Canada to seek refuge. One such case, which ultimately exploded into an international incident, involved a white South Carolina surgeon who was suspected of murdering a Black man during a Ku Klux Klan raid in his home state. Dr James Rufus Bratton, a former surgeon with the Confederate army, crossed the border and took up residence in a London, Ontario, rooming house in 1872. American detectives pursued their suspect there, chloroformed him, put him on a train to Windsor, and charged him with murder as soon as they got him over the border. Outraged that the surgeon had been 'taken with violence from under the protection of the British flag,' Canadian authorities and newspaper publishers called for Dr Bratton's immediate release and return to Canada. Anxious to defuse a politically dangerous international incident, United States marshals dispatched Dr Bratton back to Ontario, where he was welcomed warmly, and where he continued to practise medicine in London without further censure for some years.The public discussion about Dr Bratton's case centred on the procedure for extraditing suspected criminals and the competing sovereignty of the two nations. Canadian commentators seem to have been oblivious to the violent deeds with which Dr Bratton was charged, and unconcerned about his KKK connections.[39]

A mere decade later, a gang of white hoodlums calling themselves the 'Klux Clan' burned down the London, Ontario, residence of a Black family named Harrison. Fortunately, the Harrison family had moved to Windsor two days prior to the razing of the family home. Thus, no one was injured in the blaze, because the Wellington Street house, situated on the banks of the Thames River, stood empty. The first public mention of the incident occurred some fifty years later, when Richard Harrison, who had been a youth of seventeen at the time of the event, returned to London in 1934. During his absence, Harrison had become a celebrated 'Negro actor,' publicly acclaimed throughout the United States, and local London dignitaries lined up to pay their respects. 'Fifty-four years ago they gave us a great celebration when we left London,' he told the London *Advertiser*. 'They burned our house down.' It seems safe to speculate that, given the degree of cross-border movement and communication, other manifestations of the Ku Klux Klan must have expanded to ripple through Canadian territory during this formative period as well.[40]

The reinvigoration of the American Klan dates from 1915, when the 'second phase' of KKK activity commenced. The catalytic event was the publication of a novel, *The Clansman*, written by a southern white author, Thomas Dixon, and the novel's subsequent transformation into one of Hollywood's first cinematic extravaganzas. A racist depiction of the traumatic efforts of the American South to 'redeem its honour' after the civil war, Dixon's novel is designed to 'electrify' readers with the importance of the 'gospel of white Christian supremacy' and the urgent need to forestall 'creeping negroidism.' The implausible plot of *The Clansman* revolves around lust-crazed Black men who chase after terrified Southern white women, who are themselves rescued by the hooded horsemen of the Klan just before their virginal demise. At least one South Carolina white woman jumps over a cliff to her death in an effort to flee her Black pursuer. The Klansmen capture the culprit, conduct a 'fair trial,' and then castrate and lynch the Black man while a wooden cross blazes beside them.

White film director D.W. Griffiths parlayed Dixon's outrageous, racist plot into unparalleled cinematic excess in his movie version, titled *The Birth of a Nation*. The Black men are depicted 'frothing at the mouth,' running 'low to the ground with shoulders thrown back like an ape.' There are flashbacks to pictures of innocent white women, pale and majestical in their coffins. The movie score, to be played by a thirty-piece pit orchestra, ranges from 'hootchy-kootchy music with driving tomtom beats' when Black men appear on the screen, to the triumphant 'Ride of the Valkyries' when the robed Klansmen appear. Frenzied audiences attending the widespread showings of *The Birth of a Nation* 'wept, yelled, whooped, cheered,' and on one occasion 'shot up the screen' with real bullets in an effort to preserve the damsels in distress. Over the vigorous objections of the National Association for the Advancement of Colored People (NAACP), which had been founded six years earlier, the film was viewed by more than twenty-five million people in the United States.[41]

William Joseph Simmons, a white Alabama preacher who is credited with initiating the revival of the second phase of the KKK, coordinated his membership drives with the distribution of the film. He began with a massive rally in Atlanta, Georgia, in 1915, burning a cross on Stone Mountain the night that *The Birth of a Nation* premiered. Simmons ran newspaper advertisements for the Klan, next to those for *The Birth of a Nation*, wherever the film was scheduled to appear. Simmons acclaimed himself the 'Imperial Wizard' and set up a hierarchy of organizers, with a 'King Kleagle' for each state overseeing a corps of 'local Kleagles' who sold memberships and regalia. In order to appeal to a wider audience, the Klan expanded its hate-mongering to include Jews, Roman Catholics, non-Anglo-Saxon immigrants, and socialists. By 1921, the Klan had spread through Texas, Louisiana, Oklahoma, Arkansas, Oregon, the Midwest, the Northeast, and the Atlantic Seaboard, with head-counts totalling 100,000. Murder and mayhem followed, beginning in 1915 with the lynching of a New York Jewish businessman, who had been (wrongly as it would later be learned) convicted of the rape and murder of his fourteen-year-old, Georgia-born female employee. The *New York World* published an account in 1921 of 152 Klan outrages, including arson, tarring and feathering, mutilation, flogging, and murder. The U.S. Congress scheduled hearings into the Klan's activities, but this time the heightened visibility worked to increase the organization's success, with membership mushrooming to four million at its peak in 1924.[42]

White prospective members most eager to sign up were small businessmen and skilled tradesmen, usually middle-aged, married, family men who were 'solid middle-class citizens.' In keeping with its celebration of masculinity, the Klan was a rigidly all-male organization. However, in 1923, a parallel organization called the Women of the Ku Klux Klan (WKKK) was established in Arkansas. Klanswomen embraced the racist, anti-Catholic, anti-Semitic agenda of the Klan, simultaneously as they argued for 'equality for white Protestant women.' Rarely involved in the arson, lynching, and sexual mutilation by the male Klan, the women played a supporting role, serving refreshments, organizing picnics and social outings, and providing transportation to rallies. They also participated in 'poison squads' that 'spread rumor and slander,' and organized consumer boycotts to force Jews, Catholics, and Blacks into financial ruin and out of their communities.[43]

American Klansmen dreamed of spreading their mantle to include 'all Anglo-Saxon, Germanic and Scandinavian portions of the globe.' They made efforts to establish chapters in Hawaii, New Zealand, Shanghai, Lithuania, Czechoslovakia, England, Cuba, and Mexico. However, it was only in Canada that they secured anything other than a precarious foothold. Most accounts date evidence of concerted KKK activities in Canada from the 1920s, as *The Birth of a Nation* began to premiere to positive reviews in Canadian theatres. Sir John Willison, writing in *The Canadian Magazine* in 1923, described the movie as 'a glorified representation of the Klan as an agent of order and security.'[44]

The actual KKK proselytization began with splinter groups, which broke off from the original American organization, and branched out to secure bases in Canada. The Ku Klux Klan of Kanada, the Kanadian Knights of the Ku Klux Klan, and the Ku Klux Klan of the British Empire were the three most successful. All Klan branches required prospective Canadian members to be 'white Gentile Protestants,' who were eighteen years or older, 'of sound mind, good character,' and willing to advocate 'the maintenance of white supremacy.' Those who signed up were mostly drawn from the middling ranks: small businessmen, clerks, salesmen, manual workers, truck drivers, railwaymen, carpenters, plumbers, labourers, and farmers. There were also some Klansmen from the higher strata of society: doctors, lawyers, teachers, clergymen, municipal officials, justices of the peace. Women were drawn to the KKK as well, keen to participate in Klan 'bakes, whist drives, luncheons, theatricals and musicals.' The Canadian Klan devoted itself to a diverse array of targets: Asians on the West Coast; Eastern Europeans on the prairies; French Catholics in Saskatchewan; and Jews, Catholics, and Blacks across the country. The avowed goals were to 'wag[e] war against Roman Catholicism, Judaism, Negroes, the use of the French language in Canada, separate schools and the immigration of foreigners.'[45]

One of the central planks in the KKK platform was the elimination of interracial marriage. Dating and marriage across 'racial' lines signified a racial 'levelling' that evoked, in the minds of Klan members, images of white female exploitation and the usurpation of white male privilege. The Klan called for legislation to ban mixed-race marriages, such as existed in many American states below the border. The Klan also worked informally in a myriad of other ways to destroy such relationships. To the south, the American KKK threatened, whipped, assaulted, kidnapped, and lynched scores of Black, non-Protestant, and immigrant men who dared to consort with white Protestant women. The members physically and sexually tortured white women who took up with non-white men. In Canada, the 'Constitution and Laws of the Invisible Empire' declared it a 'major offence' to be 'responsible for the polluting of Caucasion [sic] blood through miscegenation or the commission of any act unworthy of a Klansman.'[46]

The first public reference to Klan activity in Canada appeared in the Montreal *Daily Star*, which announced the organization of a branch of 'the famous Ku Klux Klan' in Montreal in 1921, and reported that 'a band of masked, hooded and silent men' had gathered in the northwest part of the city behind the Mountain.[47] In 1921, the Klan set up an office in West Vancouver, and British Columbia newspapers began to publish solicitations for Klan membership.[48] KKK crosses were sighted burning across New Brunswick: in Fredericton, Saint John, Marysville, York, Carleton, Sunbury, Kings, Woodstock, and Albert.[49] James S. Lord, the sitting member of the New Brunswick legislature for Charlotte County, became a highly publicized convert.[50] Later the Klan would infiltrate Nova Scotia, burning 'fiery crosses' on the lawn of the Mount Saint Vincent Convent, and in front of St John the Baptist Roman Catholic Church at Melville Cove near Halifax's North-West Arm.[51]

Reports of Klan activities surfaced in Ontario as well, where white American organizer W.L. Higgitt began a tour in Toronto in 1923.[52] In the summer of 1924, a huge Klan gathering took place in a large wooded area near Dorchester. Cross-burning, designed to intimidate the village's few Black residents, was carried out with great pomp and ceremony.[53] In Hamilton in 1924, police arrested a white American named Almond Charles Monteith in the act of administering initiation rites to two would-be Klanswomen. Monteith was later charged with carrying a loaded revolver. Along with the revolver, police confiscated a list of thirty-two new members ('some of them prominent citizens'), correspondence regarding thirty-six white robes and hoods, and a $200 invoice for expenses for 'two fiery crosses.' Monteith denied any involvement in recent cross-burnings on Hamilton Mountain, and was convicted on the weapons charge. The day after Monteith's conviction, the arresting officer received a letter bearing a terse message: 'Beware. Your days are numbered. KKK.'[54] Monteith's conviction did nothing to put a crimp in the Klan's membership drive. Between four hundred and five hundred members paraded through Hamilton in a KKK demonstration in the fall of 1929.[55]

By June 1925 there were estimates of eight thousand Klan members in Toronto; headquarters were installed in Toronto's Excelsior Life Building.[56] The summer of 1925 witnessed hundreds of crosses burned across Chatham, Dresden, Wallaceburg, Woodstock, St Thomas, Ingersoll, London, and Dorchester.[57] A group of hooded Klansmen tried to proceed *en masse* through the chapel of a London church to show their appreciation of the anti-Catholic address that had been delivered to the congregation.[58] At a rally of more than two hundred people at Federal Square in London, J.H. Hawkins, claiming to be the Klan's 'Imperial Klailiff,' proclaimed: 'We are a white man's organization and we do not admit Jews and colored people to our ranks. [...] God did not intend to create any new race by the mingling of white and colored blood, and so we do not accept the colored races.'[59] More than one thousand showed up at a similar rally in Woodstock.[60]

At what was billed as the 'first open-air ceremony of the Klan' in Canada, two hundred new members were initiated at the Dorchester Fairgrounds in October 1925, in front of more than one thousand avid

Four Klansmen with burnt cross, Kingston, Ontario, 31 July 1927.

participants.[61] The 'first Canadian Ku Klux burial' took place in London the next year, as robed and hooded Klansmen, swords at their sides and fiery crosses at hand, showed up to perform a ritual at the graveside of one of the Drumbo Klan.[62] Ontario chapters sprang up in Niagara Falls, Barrie, Sault Ste Marie, Belleville, Kingston, and Ottawa.[63]

New headquarters appeared in a Vancouver mansion in 1925, and local chapters called 'Klaverns' sprang into existence in New Westminster, Victoria, Nanaimo, Ladysmith, and Duncan. Klan bonfires lit up Kitsilano Point. By 1928, the Vancouver Klan was soliciting signatures for a petition to demand that Asian Canadians be banned from employment on government steamships.[64] A 'Great Konklave' was held in June 1927 in Moose Jaw, Saskatchewan, where an estimated ten thousand people stood by as hooded Klansmen burned a sixty-foot cross and lectured to them on the risks of racial intermarriage. Demanding an immediate ban on marriage between white women and 'Negroes, Chinese or Japanese,' the Klan proclaimed: 'one flag, one language, one race, one religion, race purity and moral rectitude.' The Saskatchewan group would later disaffiliate from Eastern Canada, to create an entirely separate western wing that was credited with signing up 25,000 members.[65] In Alberta, 'Klaverns' came into existence in Hanna, Stettler, Camrose, Forestburg, Jarrow, Erskine, Milo, Vulcan, Wetaskiwin, Red Deer, Ponoka, Irma, and Rosebud. Alberta membership peaked between 5,000 and 7,000, but the Klan newspaper, *The Liberator*, produced out of Edmonton, purported to maintain a circulation of 250,000.[66]

Nor were the activities of the Klan restricted to rallies and cross-burnings. In 1922, the Klan was linked to a rash of torchings that wreaked more than $100,000 damage upon three Roman Catholic institutions: the Quebec Cathedral, the rest-house of the Sulpician order at Oka, Quebec, and the junior seminary of the Fathers of the Blessed Sacrament in Terrebonne.[67] In 1922, threatening letters signed by the Klan were delivered to St Boniface College in Winnipeg. Before the year was out, the college burned to the ground, causing the death of ten students.[68] In 1923, similar letters, signed by the Klan, were sent to local police and Roman Catholic authorities in Calgary.[69]

In Thorold, Ontario, the KKK intervened in a local murder investigation in 1922, issuing a warning to the town mayor to arrest an Italian man suspected of the crime by a specified date or face the fury of the Klan. The letter continued: 'The clansmen of the Fiery Cross will take the initiative in the Thorold Italian section. Eighteen hundred armed men of the Scarlet Division are now secretly scouring this district and await the

The London Evening Free Press

WESTERN ONTARIO'S FOREMOST NEWSPAPER

LONDON, ONTARIO THURSDAY, JANUARY 21. 1926 —22 PAGES

THREE CENTS

THE WEATHER: Probabilities—Light Snow; Colder.

FIRST CANADIAN KU KLUX BURIAL HERE

CITY WILL FIGHT MOVE FOR HIGHER PHONE RATES

WOODLAND SCENE OF CEREMONY BY KLAN

ACTION PLANNED TO HALT EFFORT

Definite Steps To Be Taken After Session of Municipal Union At Ottawa.

ONTARIO ASSOCIATION LIKELY TO JOIN BATTLE

Matter Will Probably Be Deferred To Provincial Body By Dominion Group.

The Klu Klux Klan Buries Its Dead

THREATEN TO UNSEAT SEVERAL ALDERMEN

Ealing Residents Declare Vote On Busses Must Accompany One On Street Cars.

CLAIM TWO LAWYERS HAVE BEEN ENGAGED

Committee Appointed By Residents of District Adopt Policy of Watchful Waiting.

Miss A. W. White Leaves Estate of $77,506.00 To Sixteen of Relatives

Accepts Call

Nine Beneficiaries Live In City—Five Nieces Receive $4,059 Each.

First Ritual of Kind In Dominion Conducted At Funeral of Drumbo Man.

UNION JACK, FIERY CROSS, CARRIED TO GRAVESIDE

Ceremony Witnessed Only By Relatives and Few Friends of Deceased.

London's *Free Press* headlines the 'First Canadian Ku Klux Burial,' of Alex Milliken of Drumbo, at London's Woodland Cemetery, 21 January 1926, with an article and photograph of the robed Klansmen and their fiery cross.

word to exterminate these rats.'[70] In 1922, the Mother Superior of a Roman Catholic orphanage in Fort William received a letter signed 'K.K.K.' threatening to 'burn the orphanage.'[71] The mayor of Ottawa was mailed a vitriolic letter, demanding he pay more attention 'to Protestant taxpayers' or the Klan would take 'concerted action.' Two Klansmen stole and destroyed religious paraphernalia from the tabernacle of the St James Roman Catholic church near Sarnia. The Ancaster Klan attempted to intimidate the African Brotherhood of America from erecting a home for 'colored children and aged colored folk.'[72]

The Belleville Klan visited the office of the *Belleville Intelligencer*, demanding that the manager dismiss a Catholic printer employed by the paper. The Sault Ste Marie Klan launched a concerted campaign to force the big steel mills to fire their Italian workers. A rifle bullet was fired at George Devlin during a wedding reception in Sault Ste Marie, with a blazing cross left behind to claim responsibility for the act.[73] In 1924, local Klansmen surrounded the Dorchester home of a white man believed to be married to a Black woman. Threats were made to burn a cross outside the house of a white Bryanstown resident reputed to be involved with a Black woman.[74] In 1927, several crosses were burned on the lawn of a white family believed to be running a brothel in Sault Ste Marie. The family was forced to flee their home.[75]

Klan activities were also responsible for the removal of a francophone Roman Catholic postmaster in Lafleche, Alberta.[76] The Alberta Klan promoted boycotts of Catholic businesses.[77] The Drumheller KKK, which boasted a membership embracing forty of the town's most prominent businessmen and mine owners, burned a cross on the lawn of a local newspaper columnist after he wrote a satirical comment about the Klan.[78] Alberta Klansmen used bullets and flaming crosses to try to intimidate members of the Mine Workers Union of Canada during their bitter labour dispute in the Crow's Nest Pass. Lacombe Klansmen wrote to the editor of the Alberta *Western Globe* after he opposed the Klan, threatening 'severe punishment including the burning of his house and business to the ground.' The same group kidnapped, and tarred and feathered a local blacksmith.[79]

Throughout these activities, white police and fire marshals stood by, often present at the incendiary meetings and cross-burnings, content to reassure themselves there was 'no danger.'[80] Despite the widespread evidence of lawlessness, Klan authorities tended to claim official disengagement whenever there was property damage or personal injury. Eschewing responsibility, they insisted that their organization had nothing to do with such events. Remarkably, the authorities largely respected these assertions of innocence, concluding that, without definitive proof that would tie named Klan officials to specific threatening letters or violent deeds, nothing further could be ascertained.[81] Apart from the arrest and conviction of Almond Charles Monteith for possessing an unauthorized revolver, the only Klan event that attracted legal attention was the dynamiting of St Mary's Roman Catholic Church in Barrie, Ontario, in 1926.

On the evening of 10 June 1926, a stick of dynamite shattered the stained-glass windows and blasted a four-foot hole through the brick wall of Barrie's St Mary's Roman Catholic Church. Buffeted about by the explosion, Ku Klux Klan flyers were scattered throughout the street, strewn among the brick, glass, and wooden debris. Barrie was a major stronghold of Ku Klux Klan activity, and organizers had drawn a crowd of two thousand to watch hooded Klansmen conduct a ritual cross-burning on a hill outside of Barrie several weeks earlier. At that ceremony, thirty-year-old William Skelly, a shoemaker who had emigrated one year earlier from Ireland, swore fealty to the tenets of the Klan, to uphold Protestant Christianity and white supremacy. He was initiated as a member in good standing. It was Skelly whom the police arrested for the bombing days later.

Skelly voluntarily admitted his Klan membership to the police, and confessed that, the night before the bombing, Klan members met to discuss 'a job to be pulled off.' There was a drawing of lots, and when Skelly drew the 'Fiery Cross,' he realized he was the designated man. Skelly claimed that he was intimidated by fellow Klansmen, who 'made [him] drunk with dandelion wine and alcohol,' and forced him to carry out the deed under threat of bodily harm. In fact, he told the police, he had joined the Klan in the first place only because he 'had had considerable difficulty in securing steady work,' and was told that, if he joined, the Klan 'would look after him,' finding him employment. Skelly also implicated two other Barrie Klan officials, Klan 'Kleagle' William Butler and Klan Secretary Clare Lee. Criminal charges of causing a dangerous explosion, attempting to destroy property with explosives, and possession of explosives were laid against all three white Klansmen.[82]

This time the Ontario attorney general's office issued an official statement that 'no group can take into its own hands the administration of the law.' The white deputy attorney general, Edward J. Bayly, became involved personally when he made arrangements for a leading white Toronto barrister, Peter White, KC, to prosecute the trio on behalf of the

Crown. Skelly, Butler, and Lee were all found guilty at a jury trial in October, and sentenced to five, four, and three years, respectively. Officials from the Toronto headquarters of the Ku Klux Klan denied all responsibility, claiming throughout that Skelly 'acted on his own initiative,' despite all the evidence to the contrary.[83]

CRIMINAL CHARGES ARE LAID IN OAKVILLE

The Black community's concerted efforts to pressure the authorities to do something about the Oakville raid resulted in another, rare instance of official legal intervention. On 7 March, two 'leads' brought the Oakville police to the doors of several suspects. Tipped off by the post-office box number that appeared on the Klan's letter to the *Globe*, they also tracked down the licence plates from the motor vehicles that carried the masked men. In all, Crown Attorney William Dick issued summonses to four white men. Dr William A. Phillips, a Hamilton chiropractor, was at the top of the list. Married, with five children, the thirty-seven-year-old Phillips was born in England. He operated his chiropractic business, an emerging new health-care specialty, at 127 1/2 King Street East. Ernest Taylor, of 154 Gibson Avenue, Hamilton, was the second person summonsed. Taylor was also a married man, employed as a pastor at the Hamilton Presbyterian Church, ministering to its Italian mission, and serving as an interpreter for the local police court. Harold C. Orme, of 2 West Avenue North, who worked as a chiropractic assistant, and William Mahony, of unspecified address, were also listed.[84]

All four were charged with a violation of s.464(c) of the Criminal Code: 'Every one is guilty of an indictable offence and liable to five years' imprisonment who is found ... having his face masked or blackened, or being otherwise disguised, by night, without lawful excuse, the proof whereof shall lie on him.'[85]

The section was part of a wider offence making it a crime to be caught possessing burglary instruments under suspicious circumstances. It had been included in the first Criminal Code enacted in Canada in 1892, and was modelled upon a section of the English Larceny Act of 1861. The offence was somewhat different from the one used to prosecute the Klan in the United States, where federal legislation made it a crime for two or more persons to 'go in disguise upon the public highway or upon the premises of another' with the intent of depriving anyone of their rights. Nor was it drafted specifically in response to the Klan, as the American provision had been. The Canadian offence of being 'disguised by night' was a carryover from an old English statute that was aimed at deterring house burglars.[86]

Black barrister E. Lionel Cross was not impressed with the charge. 'Disguised by night' was a trifling offence, he argued, in comparison with other criminal offences that might have been used: 'Seven or eight charges might have been laid against these men – charges of abduction, trespass, violence.'[87] Cross could have added several other possible criminal charges to this list: intimidation, assault, disorderly conduct, common nuisance, unlawful assembly, loitering by night, and kidnapping.[88] Since the Klansmen themselves admitted in their letter to the *Globe* that they kept 'constant watch' over Ira Johnson's home for days before they conducted their raid, they might also have been charged with 'watching and besetting.'[89]

Over the past few years there had been considerable public speculation about the types of criminal sanctions that might be visited upon the Klan. One of the most vociferous proponents of creative criminal law strategies was William Templeton, the white publisher of the *Mercury* in nearby Guelph, Ontario. A notable exception to the general run of Canadian journalists, Templeton used his newspaper to mount a sustained attack on the KKK. On 4 October 1926, two cars filled with Klansmen had driven up to Templeton's home in an attempt to frighten him out of his vocal opposition. In his next-day's editorial, 'Tear Off the Mask from Kowardly Klans,' Templeton lambasted the residents of Guelph for allowing the KKK to operate in their city. He castigated them for renting city hall to the Klan for their meetings. He charged that the organization's membership reached deep into the bowels of the police force and local government. He denounced the cross-burning that the Klan had initiated at the home of a female resident of Guelph several weeks earlier. Recognizing that groups who bore the brunt of Klan hatred faced substantial risks in speaking out, he challenged the authorities to 'ferret out the persons responsible without asking the complainant to do that for them.' Templeton lodged his claim in the language of racial and religious equality, rejecting the Klan for its efforts 'to deny rights to worthy citizens because of their color, their creed and race.'[90]

Templeton advocated extensive legal action against the Klan, and used his newspaper to chart out a number of avenues that ought to be pursued by the Ontario attorney general's office:

The Attorney-General ought to deny the right of any organization to hold masked meetings, under which mask crooks or desperate characters may hide. […] They are guilty of disorderly conduct in setting fires, which fires may easily prove destructive to property and disturbing to the peace. The Klan, officers and individuals, ought to be held individually responsible, to the full extent of their personal property by seizure for damage of any kind. […] There is a by-law against the committing of nuisances. Setting fires that disturb the public quiet is a nuisance. The Chief of Police would be within his rights to arrest the leaders of the Klan here and place every member of their organization under a bond for the preservation of peace.

Several days later, Templeton went further, proclaiming that the activities of the Klan ought not to be protected under the rubric of freedom of speech. 'The law guarantees freedom of speech,' noted the *Mercury*, 'but there are reasonable limitations to that freedom.' Accusing the Klan of 'slander,' the paper continued: 'The freedom to do as one pleases must always first involve consideration of the rights of others who have a claim to be protected against evil speech or unfriendly action.' Had Templeton known of the expansive Ku-Klux Act promulgated in the United States earlier in the nineteenth century, making citizens 'with foreknowledge of Klan violence' liable to Klan victims for any suffering they could have prevented, he might have expanded his list of demands even further.[91]

Templeton's list of legal possibilities is provocative, sweeping, and innovative. Prosecuting the Klan for violations of municipal nuisance by-laws is an interesting suggestion that appears not to have been taken up by Canadian law enforcers. The use of a 'peace bond' to censure the Klan for threatening to commit future harm, deterring them proactively, is even more intriguing.[92] Equally fascinating, considering the advocate is a newspaper publisher, is Templeton's suggestion that the law should be extended to attack 'slander' or 'evil speech' directed at racial and religious minorities. Although Templeton made no reference to it, the only legal avenue currently available was to bring a charge of 'defamatory libel,' an offence carrying a penalty of one to two years' imprisonment under the Criminal Code.

'Defamatory libel' was defined in section 317 as 'matter published, without legal justification or excuse, likely to injure the reputation of any person by exposing him to hatred, contempt or ridicule, or designed to insult the person of or concerning whom it is published.' 'Publication' was defined as 'exhibiting it in public,' 'causing it to be read or seen,' or 'showing or delivering it' to any person. The offence was designed to encompass written matter as well as objects 'signifying such matter

otherwise than by words.' Any letters, leaflets, or other written propaganda connected with the Oakville raid that named Ira Johnson and
insulted or held him up to contempt because of race might potentially
have been caught by this provision. The blazing cross outside Ira Johnson's
home might equally have sufficed.[93]

There were statutory defences to the crime of 'defamatory libel.' Section 324 stated: 'No one commits an offence by publishing any defamatory matter which he, on reasonable grounds, believes to be true, and
which is relevant to any subject of public interest, the public discussion of
which is for the public benefit.' Section 331 also provided: 'It shall be a
defence to an indictment or information for a defamatory libel that the
publishing of the defamatory matter in the manner in which it was
published was for the public benefit at the time when it was published,
and that the matter itself was true.'[94]

These convoluted passages might have furnished grounds for an acquittal of the Klan. Their efforts to bring public notoriety to the marriage
of Ira Johnson and Isabel Jones took place within a social context markedly intolerant of racially mixed marriages. Many authoritative voices
were calling for increased scrutiny of interracial liaisons. Leading newspapers and magazines such as the Toronto *Globe* and *Daily Star*, and
Saturday Night were on record approving the Klan's desire to see racial
mixing reduced. The Klan could argue that its propaganda constituted a
simple exposition of the 'true facts' about an intended interracial marriage,
and that the public debate it sought to generate about the danger of such
relationships was in the 'public interest' and for the 'public benefit.'[95]

What would have gone further to satisfy William Templeton's needs
was a law that expressly restrained racist speech. The first law ever to
focus on racist and anti-Semitic propaganda would be passed in the
neighbouring province of Manitoba, a mere four years after the Oakville
raid. In 1934, the Manitoba legislature authorized the courts to issue
injunctions against 'the publication of a libel against a race or creed'
where such writing was 'likely to expose' persons to 'hatred, contempt or
ridicule,' or 'tending to raise unrest or disorder among the people.' The
definition of 'publication' encompassed circulating or exhibiting such
material in public, but restricted the scope of the law to written communication, rather than verbal hate speech.[96] Canada's first legislative effort
to proclaim 'group defamation' unlawful, the Manitoba enactment was a
reaction to outrageous anti-Semitic newsletters circulated by a fascist
group, the Nationalist Party of Canada, which had formed in Winnipeg
in 1933. Literature and manifestos printed and distributed by the Klan
might well have been enjoined under this law.[97]

A wider prohibition would be enacted in Ontario in 1944, due to the pressure placed on government by Black and Jewish groups demanding the abolition of hateful signs that proclaimed 'No Dogs, No Jews, No Niggers.' The 1944 act prohibited the publication or display of any 'notice, sign, symbol, emblem or other representation' indicating 'discrimination or an intention to discriminate' on the basis of 'race or creed.' Although the listing did not capture verbal speech, its inclusion of 'symbols' and 'emblems' carried the statute far beyond mere words. Whether this would have been sufficient to render unlawful the burning of fiery crosses at Klan rallies is open to debate. The Ontario provision also contained an express disclaimer that it should not be deemed to 'interfere with the free expression of opinions upon any subject by speech or in writing.'[98]

There were no laws specifically prohibiting discrimination in force anywhere in Canada at the time of the Oakville KKK raid. The Ontario legislature did not pass the first such statute until 1932, when it prohibited insurance companies and salespersons from discriminating unfairly on the basis of race or religion when they offered access to insurance coverage.[99] Between 1931 and 1945, British Columbia passed a series of measures to outlaw discrimination in the provision of unemployment relief or welfare because of 'race, political affiliation or religious views.'[100] In 1950, Ontario attempted to outlaw collective agreements negotiated by employers and trade unions that discriminated on the basis of race or creed.[101] That same year, both Ontario and Manitoba passed legislation to prohibit racially restrictive covenants from being registered upon land.[102]

The first comprehensive human rights statute, the Saskatchewan Bill of Rights Act, which barred racial and religious discrimination in employment, business ventures, access to public facilities, housing, and education, was not enacted until 1947. It might have offered some protection from the campaign of intimidation waged by the Klan to oust non-Anglo-Saxon workers from their jobs and to foster economic boycotts of Black, Jewish, and Roman Catholic businesses. The same act contained a section similar to Ontario's, prohibiting the publication or display of any 'notice, sign, symbol, emblem or other representation' likely to 'tend to deprive, abridge or otherwise restrict' a person's rights based on their 'race, creed, religion, colour, ethnic or national origin.' As well, the Saskatchewan provision included an express exemption that it was not to be 'construed as restricting the right to freedom of speech.'[103]

In the absence of legislation specifically aimed at the prevention of racism or religious discrimination, Guelph *Mercury* publisher William

Templeton recommended the outright prohibition of the right of 'any organization to hold masked meetings.' He did not take the next step of calling for a legal ban on the KKK itself.

Would it have been feasible to pass legislation banning 'masked meetings' or explicitly outlawing the Klan as an organization? The legislative response to the formation of the Communist Party of Canada is an interesting point of comparison. Canadian politicians took that organization to pose such a threat that they passed the 'infamous section 98' of the Criminal Code in the wake of the Winnipeg General Strike of 1919. Section 98 defined as an 'unlawful association' any organization whose purpose was 'to bring about any governmental, industrial or economic change within Canada' by advocating the use of 'force, violence, terrorism or physical injury.' Once the court declared an organization to be an 'unlawful association,' the police were authorized to seize and forfeit its property. Officers, representatives, and members were potentially liable for up to twenty years' imprisonment. Publishing, importing, or distributing books, newspapers, or other publications advocating such goals also netted offenders up to twenty years.[104] Contemporaneously with the KKK Oakville raid, substantial lobby campaigns were being initiated 'coast to coast' to expand section 98 to outlaw the Communist Party by name.[105]

The KKK's advocacy of white, Protestant supremacy did not seek to 'bring about any governmental, industrial or economic change within Canada,' and consequently did not run afoul of section 98 of the Code as then written. It is reflective of attitudes about racial and religious equality in Canada in this period that no one seems to have suggested expanding section 98 to encompass the advocacy of violent or terrorist methods in furtherance of racial and religious bigotry. Nor did anyone campaign 'coast to coast' to outlaw the Ku Klux Klan by name.[106]

It was not only the letter of the law that distinguished between Communist and KKK activities. There were striking disparities in enforcement as well. In a spectacular show of criminal justice authority, Tim Buck and eight other white Communist Party leaders and activists were convicted of being 'members of an unlawful association,' contrary to section 98, in September 1931 in Toronto. Their convictions were upheld by the Ontario Court of Appeal in 1932. Prosecutions for seditious libel, disorderly conduct, obstructing police and unlawful assembly were routinely pursued against members of the Communist Party between 1928 and 1932 in Sudbury, Port Arthur, Fort William, and Toronto. The offence of 'disorderly conduct' was also pressed into service, with Communist soap-box orators convicted under the vagrancy law of 'causing a disturbance' in or near a street or public place 'by impeding or incommoding peaceable passengers.'[107] To quell Communist rallies, police and city officials threatened that they would 'read the riot act.' The 'unlawful assemblies and riot' section of the Criminal Code allowed police to invoke 'the riot act' whenever twelve or more persons assembled a meeting that was likely to 'disturb the peace tumultuously.' This offence carried with it possible life imprisonment and permitted the police to shoot to kill.[108]

The readiness of the authorities to use the full force of criminal law against the Communists presents a dramatic contrast to their recalcitrance in the face of Klan activities.[109] When it came down to it, in the end the only charge laid against the four Hamilton Klansmen was 'disguised by night.'

THE FIRST CANADIAN 'KLAN' TRIAL

The 'first trial of a known Klansman in a Canadian court,' as the press heralded it, began on 10 March in Oakville Police Court, a small room constructed over the police station.[110] Well before the proceedings commenced, curious crowds, drawn from the town and surrounding cities of Hamilton and Toronto, thronged the sidewalk outside the station. 'An unidentified man' wandered through the mob, distributing KKK literature. The leaflets described the Klan as 'a great British-Canadian, patriotic, fraternal organization – the most powerful secret order existing in the British Empire.' The overflow crowd parted briefly to make way for Isabel Jones and her mother to enter the courtroom.

Inside, the public area of the courtroom was packed with an overwhelmingly white audience, many of them local farmers. There were also 'groups of Negroes' in attendance, among them Rev. W. Constantine Perry, the pastor of the Oakville African Methodist Church, who had been scheduled to officiate at the marriage of Ira Johnson and Isabel Jones. John Wallace, 'the oldest Negro resident' in the town, was present as well. Ira Johnson sat 'unobtrusively in the back of the room.' Only three of the accused men were present in court. Dr Phillips, Ernest Taylor, and Harold Orme had answered the summons, but William Mahony had managed to evade service, and was nowhere to be found.[111]

Police Magistrate W.E. McIlveen called the courtroom to order. Like most police magistrates, McIlveen was not a lawyer. He was a white businessman, who owned a large dry-goods store on Oakville's main street, where the KKK had torched their cross. Nor was this the first that Magistrate McIlveen had heard of the case. He confided to the *Globe* that Isabel Jones's mother had come to see him some time earlier. 'She asked me to help her in getting her daughter away from Johnson, after it had been discovered that she was living with him,' he told the paper. In his advisory role as police magistrate, McIlveen explained to Mrs Jones that he had 'no power to intervene' since Isabel Jones was over the age of eighteen. Magistrate McIlveen professed not to have witnessed anything of the 'Klan's invasion' on 28 February, learning only of the goings-on with his morning paper. Ten days later, having his courtroom spotlighted in the harsh glare of public scrutiny and with reporters from no fewer than five papers in attendance, Magistrate McIlveen was probably distinctly uneasy.[112]

William Inglis Dick had carriage of the case for the Crown. Born in Brampton, Dick was a graduate of Osgoode Hall Law School, who practised briefly in his home town before moving to Milton in 1894. In 1904, he was appointed to the post of Halton County Crown Attorney, a position he held for forty-five years, until his retirement in 1949. Active on the Milton school board and with the Knox Presbyterian Church, Dick was knowledgeable about criminal prosecution and about local community sentiment.[113]

Magistrate McIlveen called the court to order, and the hearing began. Dr Phillips, Ernest Taylor, and Harold Orme formally registered pleas of 'not guilty' and elected to proceed by summary trial. Crown Attorney Dick chose Police Chief David Kerr to be the first witness for the prosecution. Although he was the senior police official in charge of the investigation, calling Chief Kerr may have been something of a gamble, given his genial reception of the Klansmen on the night of the raid on Ira Johnson's home. Some may have wondered whether the police chief was not only a sympathizer, but a *bona fide* Klan member himself. His open familiarity with the leaders of the cavalcade, all men he admitted knowing 'quite well,' must have raised suspicions in at least some quarters. It was certainly not unheard of for Ontario policemen to be implicated in the activities of local Klan chapters. Four years earlier, William Templeton had disclosed in the Guelph *Mercury* that it was 'the commonest of street rumors' that four Guelph police officers were 'members of the Klan.'[114]

Chief Kerr testified that, when he was first advised of the cross-burning, he and his white assistant, night constable J.W. Barnes, had gone to investigate the cavalcade of cars carrying the Klansmen. 'When I arrived at the front car, Dr. Phillips told me that they had been at the home of Ira

The photographs contain the following text:

TORIES MAY PLEAD DISTILLERS' CAUSE ON EXPORT BILL

May Oppose Ban on Liquor Shipments as Blow to Industry

DEBATE THIS WEEK

By THOMAS WAYLING
Staff Correspondence of The Star
Ottawa, March 10.—Premier King is to move the second reading of the liquor export bill this week and a full-dress debate will be precipitated, which will cut party lines in all directions.

The prime minister will urge passage of the bill by parliament

Photographs from the *Phillips* trial, appearing in the *Toronto Daily Star*, 11 March 1930, identified as follows: 2) Oakville police chief David Kerr with William A. Phillips, accused, 3) Mrs Jones, mother of Isabella Jones, 4) Harold Orme, accused, 5) Crown Attorney William Inglis Dick, 6) Klan outfit picked up by Chief Kerr, 7) Ernest Taylor, accused, 8) Mrs Stuart, Ira Johnson's aunt.

Johnson and had taken the Jones girl to her mother.' Crown Attorney Dick asked Kerr: 'How was he dressed?' 'In a white robe,' replied Kerr. 'He took off his mask and we shook hands. I knew the gentleman quite well.' Chief Kerr then testified that Ernest Taylor and William Mahony had come across the road to shake hands. Neither was masked. Crown Attorney Dick pressed his witness with an important final question: 'Had Taylor been masked before he came across?' 'I think so. They were all masked,' answered Chief Kerr. The police chief then brought forth a 'long, white gown' which he said he had found on the roadway near the outskirts of town. The *Globe* described it as looking 'like a nightshirt but for the singular symbols embroidered upon it.' Dick filed this as the Crown's only exhibit.[115]

C.W. Reid Bowlby appeared as defence counsel for Dr Phillips and Ernest Taylor. A thirty-eight-year-old white lawyer from Hamilton, Bowlby stood up next to cross-examine Chief Kerr.[116] Bowlby's first question was about Ira Johnson's reputation. He pressed the police chief to admit that Ira Johnson had 'always been known as a colored man' around Oakville. Chief Kerr willingly conceded as much. 'Is he colored?' was the follow-up. Clearly Bowlby wanted to make certain that the racial identification was definitive. 'I should say he was,' replied the police chief, more than ready to swear to the racial designation he understood Ira Johnson to bear. 'Has he a savory reputation?' queried Bowlby. 'I should say not,' quipped Kerr, although he added, as if in afterthought, that Johnson had 'never been in police court' before. The exchange continued:

Q. Mrs. Jones approached you on occasions and told you that her daughter was held captive by Johnson?
A. No, not captive. She said Isabel was there.
Q. Well, she was under his power?
A. Yes.
Q. You know that these men went to Johnson's house?
A. Yes.
Q. That no violence was used?
A. Yes.
Q. And that the young lady was taken from Johnson's place and handed over to her mother, later to be taken to the Salvation Army captain?
A. That is what was reported to me.
Q. Don't you think that what was done that night was lawful?
A. I don't care to answer that question.

Crown Attorney Dick objected to this line of questioning, and defence counsel Bowlby replied, to the general merriment of the observers in the courtroom: 'I don't know of any one more fitted than the Chief of Police to say what is lawful or unlawful.' The exchange resumed:

Q. Well, Chief, don't you think it was the humane and decent thing to do?
A. I don't think I ought to answer that.

To this last response, Reid Bowlby laughed out loud, retorting: 'You're pretty hardboiled today.' The spectators were thoroughly enjoying the show by this point; the Toronto *Daily Star* recounted that 'laughter shook the walls of the small room.' Bowlby's final questions were concerned with the reputations of his clients. Police Chief David Kerr vouched for their admirable characters, insisting that they were 'fine types of men.'[117]

Crown Attorney Dick's case was not going well. He tried to recover ground with his next witness, Isabel Jones. She testified that she and Ira Johnson were engaged to be married, that they had taken out a marriage licence in Port Credit, and had planned to wed at the African Methodist Church in Oakville on 2 March. Crown Attorney Dick asked her to describe what transpired on the night of 28 February:

A. They came to the door at about 10:15 p.m. and asked for Mr. Ira Johnson. He went out to the car with them and then they came back for me. They took me to a car and said they'd be back to see Ira. He asked them if they were men of law and they told him I'd be safe.
Q. Why did you get into the car?
A. I thought I had to, there were so many of them. I thought I had to get into the car. I didn't want to contradict them – so I got in.
Q. Can you describe their attire?
A. They had long robes and on their heads they had long caps.

Cross-examination from defence counsel Bowlby came next. Bowlby elicited that Isabel Jones had been living with Ira Johnson alone in his house 'for about a week.' 'Immorally?' pressed Bowlby. 'Yes, I guess so,' was the hesitant reply. Bowlby then had the young woman admit that she knew her mother 'wanted to get her back,' that the robed men 'used no force,' that they did not bother her after leaving her with the Salvation Army, and that they 'conducted themselves as gentlemen.' The ascription of 'gentlemanly' behaviour seems somewhat odd under the circumstances. Presumably the defence counsel was intimating that the Klansmen had not subjected Isabel Jones to physical roughhousing, sexual contact, or sexual innuendo. However, it is hard to see how the intimidation that was so clearly involved here could be characterized as 'gentlemanly.' Perhaps Bowlby was indirectly appealing to concepts of 'chivalry,' hoping to convince the court that the Klansmen were 'saving' Isabel Jones from certain ruination. Whatever his aim, Bowlby had managed to badger Isabel Jones into agreeing that the racist bullying she suffered at the hands of the Klan did not detract from her tormentors' 'gentlemanly' stature.

The most probing questions dealt with the identification of the hooded men:

Q. Did you recognize any of the Klansmen?
A. They were all covered.
Q. Do you think you can recognize any one now?
A. I think I might the driver.

At this point, the *Globe* recounted that Miss Jones cast a glance at the accused men and their lawyers, 'her eyes almost hidden by wisps of chestnut hair.' After a lengthy pause, she answered: 'I can't recognize anybody,' and the courtroom erupted into ripples of laughter. The *Globe* took the liberty of characterizing this answer as 'artless.' The Crown attorney seemed satisfied, however, and announced he had no further witnesses. Why he did not call Ira Johnson or his aunt and uncle is a mystery.[118]

Next Reid Bowlby summoned his client, William Phillips, to the witness box. Described as 'a tall red-headed man, with a small red moustache,' the chiropractor stood, according to the *Globe*, 'almost elegantly clutching a bright silk scarf near the table which served as a witness stand.' Whether this was a decorative addition to his wardrobe or some talisman of sorts was never clarified. When Dr Phillips spoke, it was the hooded cloak of the Klan that occupied his attention. Holding up the gown and headgear that had been entered as an exhibit, Dr Phillips testified that the costume was 'part of the traditional garb of the order to which he belonged,' although he couldn't be absolutely sure of the 'insignia' because he was 'a comparatively new member.' Dr Phillips took offence at the description of the garments as a disguise. The regalia was 'a matter of tradition,' he insisted, 'it was no disguise at all.' Under cross-examination by Crown Attorney Dick, Dr Phillips admitted that he had come to Oakville with other members of the Klan and that he was 'in the motor car' that 'stopped that night at Johnson's door.'[119]

The evidence against Harold Orme was heard next. Constable Barnes testified that they had located Mr Orme by tracing the licence plate of the car he was driving. 'Why had the police singled out this specific car?' asked Harold Orme's defence counsel, another white Hamilton lawyer, named Thomas R. Sloan. To the great hilarity of the audience, Barnes offered that 'it was the cleanest number.' Barnes testified that Dr Orme's car was filled with four or five passengers, all garbed in gowns and hoods. Asked to describe Mr Orme's attire, Barnes stated: 'Mr. Orme had on the regalia, but his face was not covered.' Defence counsel Sloan seized on this with glee:

Q. Did you see Mr. Orme disguised?
A. Well —
Q. Did you or did you not see him disguised? I want an answer, yes or no.
A. No.

With the obvious goal of capitalizing on this damaging admission, defence counsel Sloan eagerly called his client to the stand. Harold Orme proved to be a significantly more exuberant witness than Dr Phillips:

Q. Can you describe how you were dressed?
A. I had a gown on, but I was not hooded at any time. Nor was I in the car which went to Johnson's home. I remained on the outskirts of the town. I drove the car to Oakville, but at no time did I wear a mask, for I don't believe in so doing while driving – and I don't mind who sees my face.

When Crown Attorney Dick asked, in cross-examination, whether Harold Orme was a member of the Ku Klux Klan, the *Globe* described his reply as an emphatic 'Yes, sir, I am.'[120]

No further evidence was called regarding the third accused man, Ernest Taylor, and the legal arguments of counsel came due. Bowlby and Sloan pointed out that there was insufficient evidence to prove that either Harold Orme or Ernest Taylor was 'masked' as required by the section under which they were charged. Crown Attorney Dick admitted as much, particularly with respect to Taylor, whose acquittal he conceded was difficult to oppose. Magistrate McIlveen pronounced both Orme and Taylor 'not guilty' and they were released forthwith.[121]

The decision to charge these two Klansmen with the offence of 'disguised by night' had ultimately proven to be an exercise of bad judgment. To secure a conviction, everything depended upon being able to make out the central fact in issue: that the men were 'masked.' Police Chief David Kerr's evidence on Orme's and Taylor's 'masks' was hesitant and unconvincing. Isabel Jones was unable to identify either man. Constable Barnes expressly denied having seen Orme masked. And Orme himself testified definitively that his face was uncovered throughout. Virtually no evidence had been put forward concerning Taylor's disguise. What was afoot? Did the Crown attorney not appreciate that he had insufficient proof of the disguise when he laid the charges? Or did the witnesses alter their testimony in favour of the accused men when they took the stand? Since the Crown attorney's files and court records of the trial no longer survive, it is impossible to know what really transpired. What is certain is that the choice to lay the charge of 'disguised by night' had proven to be the wrong option with respect to Orme and Taylor.

The situation of Dr William Phillips, for whom there was uncontradicted proof of a mask, was somewhat different. Reid Bowlby took the lead in legal argument, opening with a direct attack on section 464 of the Criminal Code. Bowlby was of the opinion that the crime of going disguised by night was something of an oddity. What, he queried, of 'people at a masquerade ball,' or 'boys and girls who go masked on Hallowe'en night? The police might as well arrest these boys and girls – they are masked.' The section was really intended to trap would-be burglars and house-breakers, Bowlby continued, and his client had been doing nothing of the sort.

Defence counsel Bowlby was obviously discomfited by the criminalization of what seemed to him to be relatively innocuous behaviour. His efforts to raise the spectre of Hallowe'en goblins and gaily attired masqueraders were designed to disconcert the Crown and the court. Imagine putting such revellers to the task of proving 'lawful excuse' for their shenanigans. Indeed, he continued, imagine posing such a challenge to an upstanding citizen such as his client. Emphatically insisting that his client's purpose was anything but unlawful, Bowlby asserted that 'the Klansmen were justified in their action.' To the foot-stamping, hand-clapping, and loud cheers of many members of the audience, Bowlby added: 'I'm sure that there are hundreds of parents throughout the Dominion of Canada who would be eternally thankful that such a step had been taken.' At this point, Ira Johnson must have had enough. He apparently stood up quietly and walked out of the courtroom.[122]

But Bowlby was just gathering steam. He was at pains to stress the good character of his client. Gloating over the testimony from Police Chief Kerr, he continued:

The charge says that they performed this deed without 'lawful excuse.' The chief couldn't do it – his hands are tied. If they had gone there and knocked the furniture about and assaulted people, there would have been an offence. But they did a humane, decent thing in taking her away from that man. […] There can be no doubt that [my client] was hooded, with a lawful excuse. It was no more wrong for him to do that than it is for other lodgemen to wear regalia. Your worship … I ask for a dismissal, and I am sure that thousands of parents, with justice in mind, will back you in your course.[123]

Crown Attorney Dick had a somewhat different perspective. Professing general ignorance about the Klan, Dick was careful not to attack the organization itself, but to focus entirely upon their intimidatory tactics in the case at bar: 'I don't know the Ku Klux Klan – don't know anything about them. […] I am not arguing against the Klan, but we have here the evidence that some men went to the house and got the girl out under circumstances almost amounting to abduction. […] She was in that house with Johnson and his aunt. No person had any right to go to that house and take her out.'

Attempting to distance himself a bit from Isabel Jones, Dick continued:

I put that girl into the box although all I had to prove was that these men were masked. I put the girl into the box only to show that this affair was not a masquerade party. […] They were hooded for the purpose of taking that girl from this home, and not for lodge-room work. They were hooded so that they would not be identified. They were hooded to perform an illegal deed. […] No set of men have the right to set themselves up as administrators of British justice.[124]

At this point, Magistrate McIlveen announced himself ready to issue his findings. He concluded that the evidence proved beyond any doubt that Dr Phillips had gone hooded the night of the Oakville raid. Without much in the way of analysis, the magistrate stated: 'I fail to see that there was any lawful excuse,' and he pronounced the accused man guilty.

Next Magistrate McIlveen called upon counsel to speak to sentence. Crown Attorney Dick noted that the offence carried a maximum penalty of five years. Sentencing law reserves the maximum penalty for the worst instance of the crime in question and the worst type of offender who appears before the court. Given Dr Phillips's stature as a respected community member, he was unlikely to draw the full five years' imprisonment. However, the Crown attorney's submission on sentence was remarkably conciliatory. He advised the court that he would not be seeking any term of imprisonment at all. 'A fine would answer,' Dick indicated, 'the penalty is immaterial. All that the Crown wants to show is that there is a machinery of justice in Canada, and to show it to those persons who may have a different idea.' Magistrate McIlveen fined Dr Phillips fifty dollars and costs. Reid Bowlby announced that he would be filing an appeal forthwith.[125]

Dr Phillips was anything but cowed by his conviction. Emerging from the courtroom, he strode over to speak with Isabel Jones and her mother. 'You go home with your mother,' he warned Isabel sharply, 'or you'll be seeing me again.' The Toronto *Daily Star*, whose reporter overheard the conversation, advised that Isabel Jones's response was: 'All right.' Turning to Mrs Jones, Dr Phillips reassured her: 'Everything will be all right now. Just send for me if there is any further trouble and I'll be right there.'[126]

Crown Attorney Dick seems to have been satisfied with the day's work. Asked by the press whether he contemplated laying any additional charges against other Klansmen, he replied in the negative. 'We don't know who the other members of the raiding party were,' he stated. 'We can't prosecute. For our part, the matter has been cleaned up. We do not propose any further action of any kind.' It seems that Dick was nonchalant about the two losses he had suffered in court that morning. One conviction was enough. And given his explicit request that no prison sentence be imposed, the Crown attorney appears to have been unconcerned about the nominal fine.[127]

REACTIONS TO THE VERDICTS

The reaction of the Black community to the mixed verdicts was predictable. The *Dawn of Tomorrow*, a Black newspaper published out of London, Ontario, applauded the conviction of Dr Phillips, but expressed deep concern about the others who had gone free. '[I]t seems to us that a more rigid exercise of the law would have served our country to a better purpose,' stated the press. '[T]hree Klansmen were tried for assembling for unlawful purpose with their faces masked. Although it was proven that only one wore a mask, still the other two readily and boldly admitted their participation on the occasion. We call upon the magistrate of Oakville to state his reason for not punishing all three men.' The *Dawn of Tomorrow* deplored the Klan's efforts to destroy all that had been accomplished to foster racial tolerance 'through earnest, patient toil and honest endeavour.' It condemned the KKK's goal to 'set one religion at the throat of another, to inoculate the minds of one race with poison against another race, to foster hatred and breed dissension.'[128]

Five days later, the London *Advertiser* reported that more than 3,200 members of the Klan descended upon Hamilton for a meeting to discuss Magistrate McIlveen's decision. They stood solidly behind Reid Bowlby's decision to appeal Dr Phillips's conviction. They also discussed taking legal action against E. Lionel Cross for 'slander.'[129]

Some of the Klan were prepared to do more than appeal to the law. A week after the verdict was rendered, Ira Johnson's home in Oakville burned to the ground. Fortunately, no one was in the house at the time, but the property damage was considerable: the house and its contents were completely demolished. Newspapers from Ontario to Saskatchewan covered the KKK raid. Only one saw fit to report the destruction of Ira Johnson's house. With breathtaking serenity, the London *Free Press* indicated that 'no thought is expressed that the fire was of incendiary origin.' Just to be sure, however, 'an investigation' was to be 'conducted by the police.' Readers who may have wished further elucidation were never offered additional details. Nor would Ira Johnson's razed home result in any further legal action.[130]

Black leaders in Toronto were also targeted. Rev. H. Lawrence McNeil was one who received a string of abusive and threatening phone calls. Police 'are investigating,' soothed the *Daily Star*. Although Rev. McNeil bravely responded that he was 'not the least bit intimidated,' fears for the safety of Rev. McNeil's wife and three young children ultimately provoked the despatch of several police officers to maintain a night-time patrol of McNeil's home. E. Lionel Cross was another who received racist letters and threatening phone calls. Missives signed 'Member of the Ku Klux Klan' vowed to 'put him out of business,' 'burn him out,' and 'put him out of the way' if he did not stop complaining about the KKK. The KKK was well known throughout the United States for resorting to mob violence to discipline Black lawyers who dared to advocate racial equality. When Cross was apprised that the Hamilton KKK had him 'under observation,' he became sufficiently concerned that he complained to Attorney General Price. A man of remarkable courage, Cross advised the attorney general that he 'would not be intimidated' by Klan threats, and demanded that the government take action so that the Klan would be 'shorn of some of its arrogance.'[131]

Lionel Cross was one of a few lone voices to claim that Ira Johnson's and Isabel Jones's right to wed, and that interracial marriage in general, was a positive thing. 'The white people talk of racial purity,' he said scornfully. 'Yet it is a fact that sixty-five percent of the colored people of the South have white blood in their veins.'[132] It was not the *fact* of racial intermixture that caused white consternation, but the legitimizing of the interracial sexual liaisons. Thousands of Black women had been forcibly coerced into sexual relations with whites during and after the decades of slavery in North America. The Klan did nothing to contest those non-consensual sexual connections. It was the voluntary, egalitarian unions between the races that alone provoked their ire. Asserting that there could be 'no biological reason against intermarriage,' Cross objected to the Klan's campaign of terror. The Oakville raid was not merely 'a question of intermarriage,' insisted Cross, 'but of constitutional right.'[133]

Rev. McNeil was considerably less sanguine about this point. McNeil told the Toronto *Daily Star* that he held 'no brief for the promiscuous intermingling of the races,' and directed his complaint solely against 'the substitution of the purely authorized law enforcement agencies by such an intolerant organization as the Ku Klux Klan.'[134] B.J. Spencer Pitt, the other Black lawyer who had pressured the attorney general to prosecute the Klan, was similarly inclined. 'Personally, I do not believe that inter-marriage is advisable,' he indicated. 'Indeed, I would say from my own general experience and observation that such marriages lead more often to discord.' Pitt was even willing to accede to a legislative ban on racial intermarriage: 'If the Canadian government saw fit to prohibit intermar-riage of negroes and whites, I am certain that we negroes would abide by the law.'[135]

Both McNeil and Pitt espoused egalitarian philosophies and demon-strated sustained anti-racist activism in the face of the Oakville raid. It is unlikely that they meant to be understood as suggesting that interracial marriages were problematic because of any inherent hierarchialization of racial groups. Their position is reflective of an affirmative pride in Black identity as a source of community, culture, and solidarity. In the interests of sustaining and strengthening the distinctiveness of the Black commu-nity, single-race Black families have been fundamentally important. Even if McNeil and Pitt had accepted that marital integration ought to be a matter of free choice, given the pervasive racism that suffused Canadian society in employment, housing, schooling, access to public facilities,

NEGRO PASTOR RECEIVES WARNING FROM KLAN

The photographs here show (RIGHT), Rev. Laurence McNeill, negro pastor of University Ave. Baptist church, who received a telephone warning supposedly from the Ku Klux Klan, last night, to "be prepared for a call from some of us who will leave our symbol." On the LEFT is shown the typical garb of the hooded Klansmen when performing a "mission."

'Negro Pastor Receives Warning from Klan,' *Toronto Daily Star*, 7 March 1930.

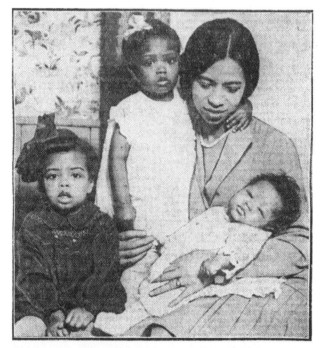

GUARDED BY POLICE IN EDWARD ST. HOME
The photograph here shows Mrs. Laurence McNeill, wife of Rev. H. Laurence McNeill, Edward St., pastor of colored Baptist church, University Ave.,
and her three children, who, since receiving of mysterious telephone warnings,
believed to have been from members of the Ku Klux Klan, have been under
police guard at their Edward St. home. The first telephone message was
received by McNeill two nights ago, when he was warned that he would receive a "visit." Last night two calls were received, allegedly from the Klan.

'Guarded by Police in Edward St. Home,' *Toronto Daily Star*, 8 March 1930.

and social structures, they probably felt that racial mixing caused more
problems than it was worth.[136]

Lionel Cross took a quite different perspective with regard to the most
effective strategy on this question. Speaking also from a commitment to
Black race consciousness, he argued that the white community needed a
transfusion of Black energy. Jabbing right to the heart of white racist
arrogance, Cross told the *Daily Star*:

It is claimed that there is a sort of marasmus afflicting the white race and it
requires some leaven to strengthen it. Scientists who do not permit sentiment to
get the better of their knowledge say that the negro is the best source from which

that leaven might be obtained. [...] The Latins, who are less hypercritical in these matters, have found this out. Shortly after the world war, France was seriously advocating the injection of negro blood from Africa.[137]

Lionel Cross carried his message of racial pride in the legacy of Black heritage to the 'Labour Forum,' when he spoke before a large audience in the Labour Temple in Toronto on 16 March. Making common cause with those branded as 'communists, bolshevists and Reds' by the Ku Klux Klan, he gave a fiery address to the enthusiastic crowd, blasting the bullying tactics of the Klan. 'Seventy-five men, wonderfully brave, started after one man,' he declared, demanding that Attorney General Price force the Klan to make public the names of its members. He ridiculed the hooligans of the Klan, ashamed to reveal their names or faces, who 'boasted' of their 'superior British traditions.'

Cross instructed those who believed Blacks to be intellectually inferior to 'look past [their own] noses' to the richness of African history and civilization. 'Racial difference,' he claimed, 'has been a ruse used by scheming men to subjugate others ... from the beginning of history.' Cross lambasted Canadians for the level of racial discrimination they continued to tolerate: 'Negroes do not enjoy the free rights of citizens in this country no matter what you may say. They are not allowed in certain hotels and theatres. I have been told because I was a negro, people would not give me business fearing I would not get a square deal in the courts.' Labour organizations responded to Cross's address by forwarding resolutions to Attorney General Price demanding more serious charges be pressed.[138]

Other groups condemned by the Klan swelled the ranks of those demanding anti-racist action. Jewish leaders joined forces with Black activists, their interests melded together because of shared persecution. Rabbi Maurice Nathan Eisendrath of Holy Blossom Synagogue in Toronto denounced the Ku Klux Klan as 'a group of law-defying anarchists' inflated with 'bigotry and fanaticism.' No stranger to the southern roots of the Klan, Rabbi Eisendrath had had his first religious posting at the Virginia Street Temple in Charleston, Virginia, whence he was transferred only one year prior to the Oakville incident. A Reform rabbi, who had trained at Hebrew Union College in Cincinnati, Eisendrath would become a leading peace activist in Toronto during the 1930s. Pronouncing himself perplexed that a so-called Christian organization could insist upon the racial supremacy of Nordic peoples, he pointed out that 'Christ, most unfortunately for the purpose of Nordic mythology, seems to have

Photographs from the *Phillips* trial, appearing in the *Toronto Daily Star*, 24 March
1930, identified as follows: 1) Ira Johnson, 2) Rev. Dr. W.C. Perry, pastor of the
African Methodist church, originally scheduled to marry Johnson and Jones, 3) Isabel
Jones, 4) Rabbi Maurice Nathan Eisendrath, 5) E. Lionel Cross.

been a dark-eyed, dark-skinned and dark-haired oriental.' Rabbi
Eisendrath speculated that most Klansmen probably thought of Greeks
as 'alien restaurant owner[s] or popcorn vendor[s],' unfamiliar with 'the
unsurpassed culture of the Greek people.' He challenged Canadian citizens to rouse themselves out of their 'apathetic condonement' of KKK
tactics. 'I fear that the laxity of the law in fining but one individual and
releasing the entire organization without a single reprimand, can but
encourage the Klan to carry further its nefarious pursuits,' he proclaimed.[139]

The Klan seemed buoyed by all of the activity. It stepped up the
campaign of community solicitation in Oakville. Delegations were sent
to distribute Klan pamphlets to schoolchildren, while female Klan members walked door to door, handing out Klan literature. The pamphlets

called upon all 'real redblooded men' to carry on 'that which has been so splendidly conceived and created.' Police Chief David Kerr, apprised of the Klan's actions, shrugged his shoulders and advised the *Globe*: 'No crime has been committed.'[140]

The newspapers that covered these goings-on were, for the most part, fairly intrigued with the Klan. The Toronto *Globe* and *Star* praised the motives of the Klansmen, at the same time as they expressed certain hesitancy about some of the means the hooded messengers used to accomplish their ends.[141] A few reporters appealed to Canadian nationalism, critiquing the Klan as an American import that was out of step with Canadian and British history and culture. They mocked the efforts of the Klan to 'Canadianize' its message, and the membership literature that proclaimed to uphold white Protestant supremacy as a means of 'saving Canada and the British Empire.' Taunting the Klan's top Canadian officials for their American roots, one reporter charged: 'Why a Virginian and a New Yorker should appoint themselves to teach loyalty to Canadians may well be wondered at, and why they should be so particularly concerned in trying to hold the British Empire together is another cause for wonder.'[142]

The reporters who were prepared to oppose the Klan tended to resort to ridicule and sarcasm, rather than to any philosophy of racial or religious equality.[143] Much was made of the financial skulduggery of the Klan organizers, who personally raked off $4 of every $10 membership they sold. Klan officials were simply 'American flim-flam artists,' intent upon 'making a lot of money easily and quickly' and possessing 'a clear view of the main chance.' As for the individuals who signed up, '[t]here is one born every minute,' wagered one reporter. The Welland *Tribune-Telegraph* depicted the whole business as 'a scheme to sell cotton nightgowns to boobs.'[144] A.D. Monk, writing for *The Canadian Magazine*, was the most explicitly satirical:

It is all very splendid for the lads of the village to go tearing about the countryside in flivvers, adorned with flowing cotton, dancing around fiery crosses and the like. After all, when the radio functions not and the movie fails to thrill, the lads must have excitement, exercise and fresh air. Doctors endorse this outdoor life and probably if the members of the Klan went on an excursion every night and returned to bed healthily tired, much good would be the result.[145]

The decision to poke fun at the Klan, to mock their costumes and caricature their adherents, may have been a deliberate ploy to undermine the public stature of the organization. It may even have been a successful strategy that deterred some Canadians from siding with 'buffoons.' The derisive parody was also, however, deeply problematic. It portrayed the Klansmen as foolish oafs rollicking about on harmless larks. It made light of the arson, the economic coercion, the social dislocation, and the pervasive campaign of intimidation and violence that the Klan fostered wherever it took root. It ignored the history of the organization and its legacy of racist terror, assaults, and murders. The persistent belittling also made it far more difficult for anti-Klan activists to gather support for their efforts to stop the spread of Klan activities in Canada.

There also seems to have been a concerted effort to distinguish the Canadian Klan from its American counterpart. Canadian Klansmen were eager to disassociate themselves from the reputation of brutality and mayhem that attached to the KKK in the United States. In a 1925 address in London, Ontario, organizer J.H. Hawkins denied that the Canadian Klan was 'a lawless body, as is often stated.' 'We believe in living up to whatever laws we have on the statute books,' claimed Hawkins, 'but we say "If you have any laws that do not meet the needs of the country, then vote to change them and see that the men you vote for will do what they promise before the elections".' Later that fall, the London *Advertiser* published a photograph of a group of Klansmen fully garbed, noting that the 'distinctive robes' of the Canadian Klan, with 'maple leaves' on the crosses, not only 'added a touch of the picturesque to the meeting,' but also distinguished the group from their American brethren. The Canadian Klan should 'not be judged by the record of the American Klan' was the oft-repeated watchword. A white Saskatchewan member of Parliament, John Evans of Rosetown, defended the Canadian Klan in the House of Commons in 1930: 'As regards the Ku Klux Klan, those people are not in any way what one might call hot-headed, and they are absolutely against any violent or unconstitutional way of doing things.'[146]

It is true that the spectacular level of violent criminality exhibited by the KKK in the United States was not fully duplicated when the organization crossed the border. Historians of the American Klan document an appalling list of scores of shocking atrocities. In the United States, the KKK beat people senseless with horse-whips. They mutilated bodies by pouring boiling pitch over their victims before they shook bags of feathers on top. They cropped people's ears. They drowned and lynched their enemies. They castrated Black men. They raped Black women and set fire to their pubic hair. They tortured their victims, pouring tar into the vaginas of white women reputed to be sheltering Blacks from the Klan.[147]

Compared with this infamous record of depravity, the Canadian record of the Klan can be assessed as relatively less brutal. But continuously setting off the Canadian Klan against its more heinous American counterpart downplays the enormous havoc wreaked by the former. Along with the dismissive and mocking tone taken by many commentators, such a comparison papers over what was actually going on. It erases the ten students who lost their lives when St Boniface College was razed to the ground. It ignores the bullets, the dynamite, and the massive property damage in the multitude of arson-related incidents. It takes no notice of the jobs and businesses lost because the incumbents and candidates were of the wrong race, ethnicity, or religion. It sees no loss in the social relationships destroyed because the Klan would brook no 'sullying' of the white Protestant community. Most of all, such analysis belies the insidious emotional turmoil suffered by all those who felt the impact of Klan threats, whether directed personally at them by name, or because of their membership in specific racial, ethnic, and religious communities.

In the face of the remarkable acquiescence that most Canadian newspapers, politicians, police, and public commentators exhibited towards the Klan, it took persistent and tireless efforts from a host of anti-racist activists to produce significant action. When thousands of Klan members rallied to demand an appeal of Dr Phillips's conviction, Black leaders were ready. Gathering support from the Jewish community and organized labour, they insisted that the authorities stand firm. They claimed not only that the conviction should be upheld, but that the penalty should be strengthened as well. When Reid Bowlby filed notice that he was appealing Dr Phillips's conviction, senior officials in the Toronto office of the Ontario attorney general responded to the pressure and filed a counter-appeal against the penalty issued by Magistrate McIlveen.

APPEAL OF DR PHILLIPS'S CONVICTION AND SENTENCE

The case came on for hearing before the Ontario Court of Appeal on 16 April 1930. Five white appellate judges – Chief Justice Sir William Mulock, James Magee, Frank Egerton Hodgins, William Edward Middleton, and David Inglis Grant – were on the bench. They sat, grey-haired and resplendent in the magnificent courtroom of Osgoode Hall, with its marble lobbies, stately porticos, and polished brass railings. The black-robed judges readied their benchbooks, all set to take notes of the appellate arguments concerning the white-gowned Klansman charged with being 'disguised by night.'

Reid Bowlby began by making a concerted effort to convince the court that his client had been erroneously convicted. He complained again that the wrong offence had been charged, that the crime of being 'disguised by night' was really meant to apply to would-be housebreakers and thieves. Next he squared off on the matter of 'lawful excuse,' repeating his argument from the trial that his client had removed Isabel Jones from Ira Johnson's home without any 'evidence of force.' On the latter point, he received a bit of a grilling from Judge Grant:

Q. There was the strongest kind of force - the force of numbers. Moral force is the strongest kind.
A. They were taking her to the Salvation Army.
Q. What right has any crowd of men to take any woman anywhere, because they think it's where she ought to be? We will not tolerate any group of men attempting to administer a self-made law.[148]

Possibly aware that, as a long-standing member of the Sons of Scotland and the St Andrew's Society, Judge Grant was no stranger to associations that celebrated Anglo-Saxon heritage, Reid Bowlby ventured on.[149] Bowlby continued that there was no evidence of unlawful purpose, that the Klansmen were 'only wearing the regalia of their lodge,' that their actions were 'no more unlawful than holding a masquerade ball.' He repeated his assertions from the trial that the Klan 'acted like perfect gentlemen,' and even went so far as to suggest they behaved 'like clergymen doing a Christian act.' At this point, Judge Grant, who seems to have been more riveted upon the intimidatory force of the Klan than taken with their inherent Christianity, blurted out: 'Oh, oh, oh! They had no right to do it.' Judge Middleton interrupted next to ask rhetorically why there was 'need of a mask' if the 'object of mission was lawful.' Answering his own question, Middleton continued: 'I would say the mask was used for the purpose of avoiding identification and of evading the consequences of their acts.'[150]

Deputy Attorney General Edward J. Bayly, KC, appeared next, for the Crown. Bayly was the highly placed civil servant who had taken such an interest in the criminal trials held in the wake of the Barrie dynamite explosion. Some commentators suggest that he had 'little patience' with the Klan, which he had come to view as a 'disturbing factor in the province's public life.'[151] The deputy attorney general was widely esteemed as one of the most powerful and talented lawyers in the province. A close personal friend of Attorney General Price's, Bayly had an ency-

clopaedic knowledge of criminal and constitutional law that had garnered him a reputation as 'a walking law book,' an 'outstanding lawyer,'
who was at the 'top of his profession.' The grandson of Ontario judge
John Wilson, Bayly had seventeen years of private law practice behind
him when he first accepted a full-time appointment as solicitor with the
attorney general's department in 1907. In 1919, he was promoted to the
post of deputy attorney general, where he represented the province in its
most important legal cases until his death in 1934. Indeed, he had appeared before Judge William Renwick Riddell to argue against Eliza
Sero's claim for Mohawk sovereignty in 1921. A stout figure of a man
with a pronounced 'cleft chin,' Bayly was known as a 'glutton for work'
and 'a compulsive talker.' Intensely conscious of his stature within the
profession, Bayly kept exhibits from his favourite murder trials around
his office, on display as 'trophies,' so that he could 'regale young departmental subordinates' with anecdotal triumphs.[152]

Edward Bayly must have felt quite bucked up by the way the appeal
was progressing. Calling for a jail term to be assessed against Dr Phillips,
the deputy attorney general stressed the sanctity of the 'rule of law' and
denounced the convicted chiropractor for taking the law into his 'own
hands.' In response to Bowlby's insistence that there had been no actual
force used, Bayly took a leaf from Judge Grant's brief, retorting that there
had been 'a great show of potential force.' Significantly, one thing Edward
Bayly did not do was to try to make any reasoned refutation of Bowlby's
argument that the Klansmen had had a 'lawful excuse' for their actions.
Bayly simply asserted that there was no lawful excuse. He did not
challenge Bowlby's depiction of the Klan's mission to prevent interracial
marriage as 'gentlemanly' or 'Christian.' He attacked the Klan's tech-
niques and strategies, not its philosophy or rationale.[153]

Edward Bayly, a graduate of the exclusive Toronto boys' school Upper
Canada College, was a man who was familiar with many social clubs and
organizations that selected their members on the basis of ethnicity and
race. He was a prominent member of the Welsh-based St David's Society
of Canada, and made no secret of his great pride in his Welsh ancestry.
He professed membership in the Zeta Psi Fraternity, the Royal Canadian
Yacht Club, the Albany Club, the Victoria Club, the Toronto Hunt Club,
and the Ionic Lodge. The Klan often defended its racially exclusive
membership criteria by noting how many other fraternal lodges practised race discrimination as well. Few, if any, of Edward Bayly's professional and social acquaintances were likely to have practised or advocated
interracial linkages. Yet the exclusive social clubs Bayly frequented seem

to have been markedly distinguishable, at least in his own mind, from the KKK. They accomplished their selectivity through more mannerly and wealth-based means. They did not resort to mob-enforced intimidation to attain their restrictive focus. They did not march about exhibiting their regalia in public under cover of darkness.[154]

The judges adjourned for lunch following the legal argument, and returned to deliver their decision at the opening of the afternoon session. Chief Justice Sir William Mulock pronounced the unanimous opinion of the court: the conviction would stand. Following Bayly's lead, Mulock declined to respond directly to Bowlby's efforts to portray the Klan's desire to save Isabel Jones from a cross-racial liaison as 'lawful excuse' under Canadian jurisprudence. Instead, the Chief Justice observed that 'the motive of the accused and his companions' was 'immaterial.' In this way, Mulock deftly recharacterized the argument under the legal category of 'motive,' a concept traditionally relegated to the sidelines in the doctrines of criminal law. By classifying the issue as 'motive' rather than the defence of 'lawful excuse,' Mulock avoided making any pronouncement upon the racist philosophy of the Ku Klux Klan.

Instead of attacking their racist ideology, the Chief Justice reserved his ire for the tactics adopted by the hooded men. He announced that Dr Phillips's efforts to intimidate Isabel Jones into leaving her house constituted an interference with 'her rights,' the commission of 'an illegal offence' against her. But the full force of the court's displeasure was not provoked by the unspecified 'illegal offence' against Isabel Jones. It was the flouting of the law generally that inspired the court to a fulsome rebuke:

[T]hey committed not only an illegal offence as regards her, but also a crime against the majesty of the law. Every person in Canada is entitled to the protection of the law and is subject to the law. It is the supreme dominant authority controlling the conduct of everyone and no person, however exalted or high his power, is entitled to do with impunity what that lawless mob did. The attack of the accused and his companions upon the rights of this girl was an attempt to overthrow the law of the land, and in its place to set up mob law, lynch law, to substitute lawlessness for law enforcement which obtains in civilized countries.[155]

These strongly held sentiments inspired Chief Justice Mulock to promulgate a striking metaphor. 'Mob law such as is disclosed in this case' is 'like a venomous serpent,' he exclaimed. Whenever 'its horrid head appears,' it must be 'killed, not merely scotched.' Chief Justice Mulock confirmed Dr Phillips's conviction. Then he pronounced the fifty-dollar fine imposed by Magistrate McIlveen to be 'a travesty of justice.' The Chief Justice struck out the fine, and in its place he substituted a prison term of three months. For good measure, Mulock ended off his remarks in court that afternoon by warning: 'This being the first case of this nature that has come before the Court, we have dealt with the offence with great leniency and the sentence here imposed is not to be regarded as a precedent in the event of a repetition of such offence.'[156]

THE SIGNIFICANCE OF THE APPELLATE RULING

The efforts of E. Lionel Cross, B.J. Spencer Pitt, Rev. H. Lawrence McNeil, and Rabbi Maurice Eisendrath, and all those who rallied to their call, had impelled Attorney General Price to commence criminal proceedings against the Klan. Deputy Attorney General Bayly presented a clarion call for the 'rule of law' before the Ontario Court of Appeal. His legal arguments struck a chord with the white, upper-class judges who presided over the province's highest tribunal. Oakville Police Chief Kerr's initial position, that there was 'no damage to person or property warranting interference,' was unalterably overruled. Defence counsel Bowlby's best efforts to characterize the Klansmen's 'higher motives' as 'lawful excuse' were rejected.

What do we know about the Chief Justice who delivered the court's decision endorsing the conviction and strengthening the penalty? A wealthy member of the Anglo-Saxon elite and an avowed anti-Communist, Sir William Mulock was himself no proponent of progressive social doctrines. Chief Justice Mulock was an eighty-six-year-old jurist of venerable reputation. Born in Bondhead, Ontario, in 1844, he received a gold medal at the University of Toronto in his student years. Called to the bar in 1868, he parlayed family connections and his own ambition and exceptional talent into a distinguished career as a lawyer and federal Liberal politician. Mulock represented North York in the House of Commons between 1882 and 1905, and served as Canada's first minister of Labour. Appointed to the bench in 1905, Mulock held the position of Chief Justice of Ontario from 1923 to 1936. Known as Toronto's 'Grand Old Man,' his six-foot frame unbent well into his late eighties, Mulock was described by the lawyers who appeared before him as 'a God-like figure with his flowing beard [and] high-domed forehead.' He savoured ceremony. During Mulock's last decade, his annual birthday parties offered extravagant occasions for the members of the legal and business elites to line up to pay homage to the Chief Justice.[157]

While it is unlikely that it was a sense of hostility towards the beliefs perpetrated by the Klan that drove Mulock's analysis, the most powerful senior judge in Ontario appears rather to have been incensed at the veiled violence that underlay the Klan's foray to Oakville. The sheer number of hooded Klansmen that made up the 'mob' created an unassailable force which it was not possible to defy. The 'lawlessness' of the Klan's sortie was the magnet that attracted Mulock's censure. The machinery of law was required to forestall the tumultuous rabble that might otherwise unravel orderly relations altogether. Swift police action, no-nonsense prosecution and substantial penalties were the formula to nip such anarchy in the bud.

For all its denunciation of mob-based theatrics and its ringing endorsement of the rule of law, Mulock's decision was notably deficient in certain important respects. In the time-honoured custom of Canadian jurisprudence, the decision contained no overt reference to race. It did not mention the Ku Klux Klan. The Klan was converted into a raceless 'mob of men' wearing no-name 'hoods' that covered the 'top of the head to the knees.' Isabel Jones became a raceless 'girl' who had experienced a violation of unnamed, undefined 'rights.' Ira Johnson was erased from the narrative entirely. Thus, when Chief Justice Mulock stated that 'the motive of the accused and his companions is immaterial,' the uninitiated reader was left floundering. Perhaps this was for the best. The context in which the comment was made left it open to interpretation that the Chief Justice believed that right-thinking citizens might have supported the goals of the KKK marchers that night. In the end, the matter rested with the Chief Justice's vituperative denunciation of raceless venomous serpents.[158]

When news of the Ontario Court of Appeal ruling reached Hamilton, the Klan members were 'stunned,' according to the newspaper reporter who covered their hastily assembled meeting on the night of 17 April. The Klansmen were anxious to pursue any avenue for appeal, although the unanimity of the Court of Appeal ruling meant that recourse to the Supreme Court of Canada was foreclosed. Declaring that the Klan would carry the case 'to the highest court in the land,' some members of the group resolved to explore the possibility of a claim before the Privy Council in England.[159]

Whatever hopes may have rested on this plan were soon dashed. The reporter for the London *Advertiser*, who tried to gather an expert opinion on the advisability of such an undertaking, discovered little legal optimism. 'A high official of the Attorney General's department' assessed the prospect with utter contempt, noting: 'It is almost unheard of for the Privy Council to grant leave to appeal in criminal cases, particularly one where the sentence is so nominal.' Phillips might 'just as well appeal to the Kingdom of Heaven,' continued the source. 'If they are really talking of appeal, they must be intoxicated with the exuberance of their own verbosity.' Even Reid Bowlby was ready to check out of any further involvement. He told the press that, although he had 'previously believed' the law 'wrongly interpreted in the conviction of Phillips,' upon receipt of the Ontario Court of Appeal decision upholding the conviction 'he had nothing further to say or do in the affair.'[160]

Resolving to make the best of a bad situation, the Hamilton Klansmen issued an official statement: 'Mr. Phillips is happy indeed to serve a term in prison for such a cause as this.' Their brave comrade had 'five days' grace' before he had to turn himself in, and when he did, 'it was hinted there would be an escort of brothers in the sheeted fraternity to see Mr. Phillips off.' Proudly purporting to champion the cause of chivalry, the Klan vowed that it would 'care for Mrs. Phillips and [the] five children during the incarceration of their fellow member.' Further afield, Rev. George Marshall, the 'Imperial Wizard of the Klan in Canada' spoke from Belleville, Ontario: 'I don't know what to think. Wonderful things are happening these days. I'm awfully sorry about this, though. It looks vindictive in the face of it. For some time I have thought of recommending that the use of the mask be discontinued, but in view of this bitterness that seems to have crept in, I think it would be advisable to retain the mask for the klansmen's protection.'[161]

On 23 April, Oakville Police Chief David Kerr drove out to Dr Phillips's chiropractic office in Hamilton to take him into custody. 'He had been expecting the officer,' reported the Toronto *Globe*, 'and there was no scene.' The two men quietly departed for the Milton Jail. Someone had apparently thought better of the promised group send-off; it never came to fruition.[162]

The actual jail term, however, was more eventful. Shortly after his incarceration began, Dr Phillips commenced a hunger strike. Although jail guards brought three meals a day into his cell, he refused to partake 'of an ounce of jail fare.' The Milton *Canadian Champion* reported that 'Phillips has been living on water, orange juice, buttermilk and Jersey Milk Chocolate Bars,' and that he refused all jail rations, but was 'suspected of taking the odd snack on the sly.' The Acton *Free Press* advised that Dr Phillips held firm for thirteen days, but by that point he had become so weak that he resolved to end his fast. Jail officials were greatly relieved. Although they sternly advised the press that 'the Klan leader is to be treated the same as any other prisoner, and to receive no favors,' they were jubilant at Dr Phillips's newfound appetite. Governor McGibbon, the white jail supervisor, fervently hoped that Dr Phillips was now 'ready to relish a good meal.' Fellow Klansmen lined up to offer nourishing treats of fresh oranges. There were no further press reports about Dr Phillips's stint in jail, and ninety-one days after his internment, on 22 July 1930, he was released into the community.[163]

The ramifications of the KKK raid, the legal proceedings, Dr Phillips's conviction, and the increased sentence were substantial. Some have pronounced the Oakville trial a symbolic death-knell for the KKK in Canada. They suggest that the glare of publicity, the official intrusion into KKK affairs, and the ringing condemnation of Klan methods from senior governmental and judicial circles, all combined to sap the growth of the hate-mongering movement.[164] Others have suggested that the undeniable diminishment in the strength of the Canadian Klan was due more to its own internal and structural problems.[165] Whatever the reasons, publicly discernible Klan activity dropped off significantly in the 1930s, not to revive until the 1960s.[166]

For their part, in May 1930, Chief David Kerr and Constable J.W. Barnes of Oakville asked for, and were awarded increases in salary 'in recognition of their services.'[167] Dr Phillips returned to his wife, children, and chiropractic business in Hamilton.[168] E. Lionel Cross was found 'guilty of professional misconduct and conduct unbecoming a barrister and solicitor' and was disbarred from law practice in 1937.[169] B.J. Spencer Pitt turned his considerable talents towards the expansion of the Universal Negro Improvement Association, a Black nationalist organization that advocated economic, political, and cultural independence from whites. In 1942, trying to interview a client in jail, Pitt was accosted by a white police officer who seized him by the throat and threw him out of the room. Asked to comment on the incident by the Montreal *Standard*, Pitt exclaimed: 'If I could suffer such an indignity when I was not even in the role of a prisoner, what then?'[170] Reid Bowlby was named a King's Counsel in 1933, elected as a Bencher of the Law Society from 1941 to 1949, and appointed to the Ontario Court of Appeal in May 1949.[171] Edward Bayly dropped dead of a heart attack on 29 January 1934.[172] Chief Justice Mulock continued on in his position as the senior judge in Ontario until his glorious retirement in 1936 at the ripe old age of ninety-two.[173]

The couple at the centre of the controversy married on 22 March 1930, several weeks after Dr Phillips's conviction and prior to the appeal. Rev. Frank Burgess, the First Nations pastor of the United Church from the New Credit Six Nations Territory, conducted the wedding service. Although he was well aware of the danger he placed himself in by performing the nuptials, Rev. Burgess refused to be intimidated, telling the couple: 'I was here before the Klan.' In an ironic twist, the London *Free Press* reported that the marriage took place 'with the consent of the parents,' and that 'Mr. and Mrs. Ira Johnson' announced their matrimonial status at services of the Salvation Army in Toronto on 23 March. 'The couple will take up residence at Oakville,' concluded the account, 'and until they secure a home will reside separately.' The headline for the news item, 'Indian Marries Oakville Girl,' suggests that the newspaper had resolved the question of Ira Johnson's racial ambiguity in favour of a First Nations designation. Whether this was responsible for Mrs Jones's change of heart, and the Salvation Army venue for the announcement, remains unclear.[174]

7

'Bitterly Disappointed' at the Spread of 'Colour-Bar Tactics': Viola Desmond's Challenge to Racial Segregation, Nova Scotia, 1946

The contentious racial incident began on Friday, 8 November 1946, when Viola Irene Desmond's 1940 Dodge four-door sedan broke down in New Glasgow, Nova Scotia.[1] The thirty-two-year-old, Halifax-born Black woman was *en route* to Sydney on a business trip. Forced to wait overnight for repairs, she decided to take in the seven o'clock movie at the Roseland Theatre. Erected on the northeast corner of Forbes and Provost streets in 1913, the theatre was designed in the manner of grand old theatrical halls, and graced with colourful wall murals featuring paintings of 'the land of roses.' In its early days, the Roseland introduced New Glasgow audiences to silent pictures, with enthusiastic local musicians providing background sound with piano, cymbals, sirens, and bass drums. One of the most popular proved to be the American blockbuster *Birth of a Nation*. Outfitted with the latest modern equipment for sound in 1929, the theatre premiered Al Jolson's celebrated Black-face performance in *The Jazz Singer* in the first month of 'talkies.' In time, the Roseland came to be New Glasgow's premier movie theatre.[2]

Handing the Roseland cashier a dollar bill, Viola Desmond requested 'one down please.' Peggy Melanson, the white ticket-seller on duty that evening, passed her a balcony ticket and seventy cents in change. Entirely unaware of what would ensue from her actions, Viola Desmond proceeded into the theatre and headed towards the main-floor seating area. Then Prima Davis, the white ticket-taker inside the theatre, called out after her: 'This is an upstairs ticket, you will have to go upstairs.'

Viola Desmond, after graduation from high school, 1940.

Thinking there must have been some mistake, Viola Desmond returned to the wicket and asked the cashier to exchange the ticket for a down-stairs one. The ticket-seller refused, and when Viola Desmond asked why, Peggy Melanson replied: 'I'm sorry but I'm not permitted to sell downstairs tickets to you people.'

Peggy Melanson never mentioned the word 'Black,' or the other terms, 'Negro' or 'coloured,' which were more commonly used in the 1940s. But Viola Desmond recognized instantly that she was being denied seating on the basis of her race. She made a spontaneous decision to challenge this racial segregation, walked back inside, and took a seat in the partially filled downstairs portion of the theatre. As Prima Davis would later testify, '[When] she came back and passed into the theatre, I called to her. She never let on she heard me. She seated herself below.'[3]

Prima Davis followed Viola Desmond to her main-floor row. Con-fronting the Black woman, who was now sitting quietly in her seat, she insisted, 'I told you to go upstairs.' When Viola Desmond refused to budge, Prima Davis left to report the matter to the white manager, Harry MacNeil. MacNeil was New Glasgow's most prominent 'showman,' his family having constructed MacNeil's Hall in the late 1870s to serve as the town's first theatre. The MacNeils brought in a series of concert artists, ventriloquists, astrologists, musicians, bell-ringers, jugglers, and tum-blers to entertain theatre-goers. Town historians recall innumerable per-formances in MacNeil's Hall of 'Uncle Tom's Cabin,' with 'boozy has-beans of the classic theatre emoting lines of black face roles with Shakespearean declamations.' When moving pictures killed off live theatre, Harry MacNeil built a series of movie houses in New Glasgow, ultimately settling on the Roseland Theatre as the best location in town.[4]

Harry MacNeil came down immediately and 'demanded' that Viola Desmond remove herself to the balcony. She had already 'been told to go upstairs,' MacNeil pointed out, and a notice on the back of the ticket stipulated that the theatre had 'the right to refuse admission to any objectionable person.' Viola Desmond replied that she had not been refused admission. The only problem was that her efforts to purchase a downstairs ticket had been unsuccessful. Politely but firmly, she re-quested the manager to obtain one for her. 'I told him that I never sit upstairs because I can't see very well from that distance,' she later told the press. 'He became angry and said that he could have me thrown out of the theatre. As I was behaving very quietly, I didn't think he could.' The agitated Harry MacNeil turned heel and marched off in pursuit of a police officer.

THE ARREST AT THE ROSELAND THEATRE

In short order, Harry MacNeil returned with a white policeman, who advised Viola Desmond that he 'had orders' to throw her out of the theatre. 'I told him that I was not doing anything and that I did not think he would do that,' advised Viola Desmond. 'He then took me by the shoulders and dragged me as far as the lobby. I had lost my purse and my shoe became disarranged in the scuffle.' The police officer paused momentarily to allow Viola Desmond to adjust her shoe, while a bystander retrieved her purse. Then the forcible ejection resumed. As Viola Desmond recounted:

The policeman grasped my shoulders and the manager grabbed my legs, injuring my knee and hip. They carried me bodily from the theatre out into the street. The policeman put me into a waiting taxi and I was driven to the police station. Within a few minutes the manager appeared and the Chief of Police [Elmo C. Langille]. They left together and returned in an hour with a warrant for my arrest.

She was taken to the town lock-up, where she was held overnight. Adding further insult, she was jailed in a cell alongside male prisoners. Mustering every ounce of dignity, Viola Desmond deliberately put on her white gloves, and steeled herself to sit bolt upright all night long. She later described her experience in the lock-up as follows: 'I was put in a cell which had a bunk and blankets. There were a number of men in the same block and they kept bringing in more during the night. The matron was very nice and she seemed to realize that I shouldn't have been there. I was jailed for twelve hours ...'[5]

THE TRIAL

The next morning, 9 November 1946, Viola Desmond was brought before New Glasgow magistrate Roderick Geddes MacKay. Born and bred in near-by St Mary's in Pictou County, MacKay had graduated in law from Dalhousie University in 1904. He was appointed town solicitor for New Glasgow in 1930, where he managed his law practice while simultaneously holding down a part-time position as stipendiary magistrate. The sixty-nine-year-old white magistrate was the sole legal official in court that day. Viola Desmond had no lawyer; she had not been told of her right to seek bail or to request an adjournment, nor of her right to counsel. Indeed, there was no Crown attorney present either. Harry MacNeil, 'the informant,' was listed as the prosecutor.[6]

Viola Desmond was arraigned on a charge of violating the provincial Theatres, Cinematographs and Amusements Act. First enacted in 1915, the statute contained no explicit provisions relating to racial segregation. A licensing statute to regulate the operations of theatres and movie houses, the act encompassed such matters as safety inspections and the censorship of public performances. It also stipulated that patrons were to pay an amusement tax on any tickets purchased in provincial theatres. Persons who entered a theatre without paying such tax were subject to summary conviction and a fine of 'not less than twenty nor more than two hundred dollars.' The statute authorized police officers to arrest violators without warrant, and to use 'reasonable diligence' in taking them before a stipendiary magistrate or justice of the peace 'to be dealt with according to law.'[7]

The statute based the rate of the amusement tax upon the price of the ticket. The Roseland Theatre's ticket prices were forty cents for downstairs seats, and thirty cents for upstairs seats. These prices included a tax of three cents on the downstairs tickets, and two cents on the upstairs. The ticket issued to Viola Desmond cost thirty cents, of which two cents would be forwarded to the public coffers. Since she had insisted on sitting downstairs, she was one cent short on tax.[8]

This was the argument put forth by Harry MacNeil, Peggy Melanson, and Prima Davis, all of whom gave sworn evidence against Viola Desmond that morning. The trial was short. The three white witnesses briefly testified that the accused woman had purchased an upstairs ticket, paying two cents in tax, and then insisted on seating herself downstairs. After each witness concluded, Magistrate MacKay asked the prisoner if she wanted to ask any questions. 'I did not gather until almost the end of the case that he meant questions to be asked of the witnesses,' Viola Desmond would later explain. 'It was never explained to me of whom I was to ask the questions.' So there was no cross-examination of the prosecution witnesses whatsoever.[9]

At the close of the Crown's case, Viola Desmond took the stand herself. The minutes of evidence from the trial record contain a succinct report of her testimony: 'I am the accused. I offered to pay the difference in the price between the tickets. They would not accept it.' Magistrate MacKay convicted the defendant and assessed the minimum fine of $20, with costs of $6 payable to the prosecuting informant, Harry MacNeil. The total amount of $26 was due forthwith, in default of which the accused was ordered to spend one month in jail.[10]

Viola Desmond was quite properly angry that she was offered no opportunity to speak about the real issues underlying the taxation charges. 'The Magistrate immediately convicted and sentenced me without asking me if I had any submissions to make to the Court on the evidence adduced and without informing me that I had the right to make such submissions,' she later explained. Even a casual observer can see that many arguments might have been raised to preclude a conviction. It was far from clear that Viola Desmond had actually transgressed the statute. According to her testimony, she tendered the difference in the ticket prices (including the extra cent in tax), but the manager and ticket-seller refused to accept her money. It is difficult to find the legally required *actus reus* (criminal act) in Viola Desmond's behaviour here. Indeed, if anyone had violated the statute, it was the theatre owner, who was in dereliction of his statutory duty to collect the tendered taxes and forward them to the designated government board.[11]

Furthermore, the price differential between upstairs and downstairs seats was not prescribed by statute. It was simply a discretionary business policy devised by the management of the theatre. The manager could have decided to collapse the two admission prices and ask one single fee at whim. In this instance, Harry MacNeil chose to charge Viola Desmond a mere thirty cents for her ticket, and on this amount she had paid the full tax owing. She was not charged forty cents, so she did not owe the extra cent in tax. The court might have construed the rules regarding alternate seating arrangements as internal business regulations having nothing whatsoever to do with the revenue provisions in the legislation.

Even more problematic was the prosecution's questionable attempt to utilize provincial legislation to buttress community practices of racial discrimination. The propriety of calling upon a licensing and revenue statute to enforce racial segregation in public theatres was never addressed. Did the legislators who enacted the statute design the taxing sections for this purpose? Were racially disparate ticket-selling practices contemplated when the statutory tax rates were set? Were the penalty sections intended to attach alike to theatre-goers deliberately evading admission charges and Blacks protesting racial segregation? As the press would later attest, Viola Desmond 'was being tried for being a negress and not for any felony.'[12]

Observers of the trial would have been struck by the absence of any overt discussion of racial issues. In the best tradition of Canadian 'racelessness,' the prosecution witnesses never explained that Viola Desmond had been denied the more expensive downstairs ticket on the basis of her race. No one admitted that the theatre patrons were assigned seats on the basis of race. In an interview with the Toronto *Daily Star* several weeks later, Harry MacNeil would insist that neither he nor the Odeon Theatres management had ever issued instructions that main-floor tickets were not to be sold to Blacks. It was simply a matter of seating preferences: 'It is customary for [colored persons] to sit together in the balcony,' MacNeil would assert.[13] At the trial, no one even hinted that Viola Desmond was Black, that her accusers and her judge were white. On its face, the proceeding appears to be simply a prosecution for failure to pay provincial tax. In fact, if Viola Desmond had not taken any further action in this matter, the surviving trial records would have left no clue to the real significance of the case.[14]

VIOLA DESMOND: THE WOMAN ACCUSED

The day of her conviction, Viola Desmond paid the full fine, secured her release, and returned to her home on 4 Prince William Street in Halifax. She was deeply affronted by her treatment at the hands of the New Glasgow officials. Her decision to protest the racially segregated seating practices at the Roseland Theatre had initially been a spontaneous gesture, but now she was resolved to embark upon a more premeditated course of action. She was also 'well known' throughout the Black community in Nova Scotia, and consequently in a good position to do something about it.[15]

Viola Desmond, whose birth name was Viola Irene Davis, was born in Halifax, on 6 July 1914, into a prominent, middle-class, self-identified 'coloured' family. Her paternal grandfather, a Black self-employed barber, had established the Davis Barber Shop in Halifax's North End. Barbering was an occupation within which a number of Canadian Blacks managed to carve out a successful living in the nineteenth and early twentieth centuries. Hair-cutting and -styling were rigorously segregated by race in many portions of the country, with white barbers and beauticians reluctant to accept Black customers. Black barbers were quick to seize the business opportunities rejected by racist whites, and set up shop servicing both Black and white clientele.[16]

James Albert Davis, Viola's father, worked in the Davis Barber Shop for a time, and then took up employment as a shipwright in the Halifax Shipyards. Eventually, he established a career for himself as a businessman, managing real estate and operating a car dealership. Although it was extremely difficult for Blacks to obtain positions within the

James Albert Davis and Gwendolyn Irene Davis, Viola Desmond's parents, in their
Gerrish Street home, March 1948.

civil service, two of Viola's male relatives worked for the federal postal
service.[17]

Viola's mother, Gwendolin Irene Davis, was the daughter of a Baptist
minister who had come to Halifax from New Haven, Connecticut.
Gwendolin Davis's mother, Susan Smith, was born in Connecticut and
identified herself as white. Gwendolin's father, Henry Walter Johnson,
was 'seven-eighths white' and although he is described as being 'of
mixed race,' Gwendolin Davis seems to have been generally regarded as
white.[18]

The question of racial designation, inherently a complex matter, becomes even more problematic when individuals with different racial
designations form blended families. Some have suggested that a fundamental premise of racial ideology, rooted in the history of slavery, stipu-
lates that if individuals have even 'one Black ancestor,' regardless of their

skin colour they qualify for classification as 'Black.' However, it is equally clear that some light-skinned individuals are able to 'pass' for white if they choose, or can be mistaken for 'white,' regardless of their own self-identification.[19]

Viola's parents married in 1908, creating what was perceived to be a mixed-race family within a culture that rarely welcomed interracial marriage. It was not the actual fact of racial mixing that provoked such concern, for there was undeniable evidence that interracial reproduction had occurred extensively throughout North American history. It was the formalized recognition of such unions that created such unease within a culture based on white supremacy. The tensions posed within a racist society by an apparently mixed-race family often came home to roost on the children born to James and Gwendolin Davis. Viola's younger sister recalls children taunting them in the schoolyard, jeering: 'They may think you're white because they saw your mother at Parents' Day, but they haven't seen your father.' Viola self-identified both as 'mixed-race' and as 'coloured,' the latter being a term of preference during the 1930s and 1940s.[20]

Viola Davis was an extremely capable student, whose initial schooling was obtained within a racially mixed student body at Sir Joseph Howe Elementary School and Bloomfield High School. Upon her graduation from high school, Viola took up teaching for a brief period at Preston and Hammonds Plains, racially segregated schools for Black students. She saved all of her teaching wages, since she knew from the outset that she wanted to set up a hairdressing business of her own. Modern fashion trends for women, first heralded by the introduction of the 'bobbed' haircut in the 1920s, created an explosion of adventurous career opportunities for 'beauticians,' who earned their livelihood by advising women on hair care and cosmetics. Beauticians provided much-sought-after services within the all-female world of the new 'beauty parlours,' which came to serve important functions as neighbourhood social centres. Beauty parlours offered steady and socially respectable opportunities to many entrepreneurial women across Canada and the United States.[21]

Despite severely limited employment opportunities in most fields, some Black women were able to create their own niche in this new market, as beauticians catering to a multi-racial clientele with particular expertise in hair design and skin care for Black women. This was Viola Desmond's entrepreneurial goal, but the first barrier she faced was in her training. All of the facilities available to train beauticians in Halifax restricted Black women from admission. Viola was forced to travel to

Montreal, where she was able to enrol in the Field Beauty Culture School in 1936. Her aspirations took her from Montreal to New York, where she enrolled in courses to learn more about wigs and other styling touches. In 1940, she received a diploma from the acclaimed Apex College of Beauty Culture and Hairdressing in Atlantic City, founded by the renowned Black entrepreneur Sarah Spencer Washington.[22]

Shortly before she left for her first training in Montreal, Viola met John Gordon (Jack) Desmond, a man ten years her senior. Their courtship would ultimately lead to her marriage at the age of twenty-two. Jack Desmond was a descendant of generations of Black Loyalists who had settled in Guysborough County in 1783, when several thousand free Blacks took up land grants from the Crown. He was born into a family of eight children in Tracadie, Nova Scotia, on 22 February 1905, and lived for some years in New Glasgow. He moved to Halifax in 1928 and took employment with a construction company, but the loss of his eye to a metal splinter in a work accident in October 1930 cost Jack Desmond his job.[23]

Shifting careers by necessity, in 1932 Jack Desmond opened his own business, Jack's Barber Shop, on Gottingen Street, a central thoroughfare in the 'Uptown Business District' in a racially mixed neighbourhood in the old north end of Halifax. The business attracted a racially mixed clientele, drawn in part from the men who came in on the ships at the naval dockyard. The first Black barber to be formally registered in Nova Scotia, Jack Desmond was popular, with an easy-going personality that would earn him the title 'The King of Gottingen Street.' Jack became romantically interested in the young Viola Davis, took the train up to Montreal to see her while she was in training, and ultimately proposed marriage there. In 1936, the couple was married before a Baptist minister in Montreal.[24]

When Viola returned to Halifax in 1937, she set up Vi's Studio of Beauty Culture alongside her husband's barbershop on Gottingen Street. She offered her customers a range of services, including shampoos, press and curl, hair-straightening, chignons, and hairpieces and wigs. Former customers recall the weekly Saturday trip to 'Vi's' as the social highlight of the week. Viola Desmond amassed a devoted clientele, many of whom still recollect with great fondness her sense of humour, her sympathetic nature, and her cheerful, positive outlook on life. The younger women thought of her as inspirational, someone who 'took all of us kids from this area under her wing, and was like a mother to us all.'[25]

Ambitious and hard-working, Viola Desmond soon developed plans

Grade Three class picture, Joseph Howe Elementary School, Halifax; Viola Davis is in the first row, extreme right.

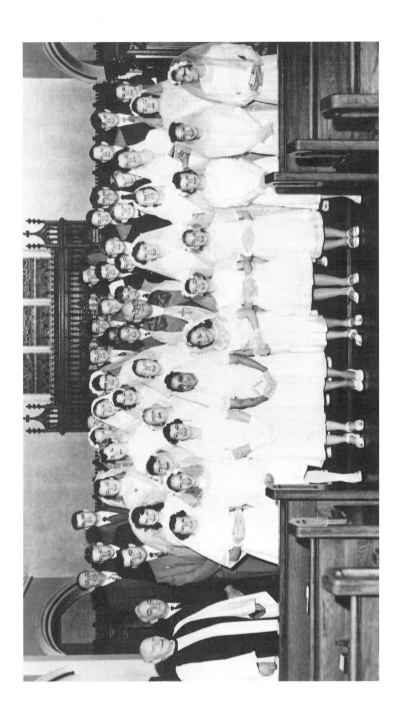

Trinity Church Confirmation Class; Viola Davis is in the front row, fourth from left, n.d.

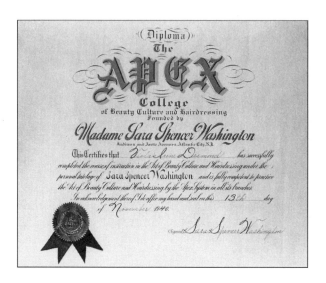

Viola Desmond's diploma from Apex College of Beauty Culture and Hairdressing, founded by Madame Sarah Spencer Washington, November 1940.

DIPLOMA OF GRADUATION

Desmond Beauty Studio

This certifies that

Helen Davis Flint

has completed the regular course of Beauty Culture, and upon a proper examination is found worthy of Graduation and is therefore qualified to practice Hairdressing and all its Branches.

Signed *Viola J. Desmond*

Desmond Beauty Studio

Date *June 4, 1947.*

Helen Davis Flint's diploma of graduation from Desmond Beauty Studio, June 1947.

Desmond's ... 1953

Jack

Your Barber For

21 Years

Vi

Your Beautician For

16 Years

GREETINGS

A thousand times over, we wish you the best
On this first of the year day, and all of the rest.

● ● ●

Fast, Courteous Service Guaranteed when you stop
at
VIOLA'S HAIRDRESSING & JACK'S BARBER SHOP
445 GOTTINGEN STREET　　**Phone 4 - 1 6 8 3**　　　　**HALIFAX, N. S.**

Souvenir calendar, Desmond's, 1953.

to expand her business. She branched out into chemistry and learned how to manufacture many specialized Black beauty powders and creams, which she marketed under the label 'Vi's Beauty Products.' She added facials and ultra-violet-ray hair treatments to her line of services. Viola Desmond's clientele encompassed legendary figures such as the Black classical singer Portia White, who came for private appointments on Sundays because her hectic schedule did not permit regular appointments during the week. Gwen Jenkins, the first Black nurse in Nova Scotia, began weekly visits to 'Vi's Children's Club' for washing and braiding at the age of ten. Despite the hectic pace of business, Viola continued to take courses in the latest hair styles and make-up, travelling to New York every other year to update her expertise. In 1945, she was awarded a silver trophy for hair styling by the Montreal Orchid School of Beauty Culture. Recognizing that there were additional opportunities outside of Halifax, Viola began to travel around the province, setting up temporary facilities to deliver products and services to other members of the Black communities.[26]

Although Jack was initially supportive of his wife's choice of career, her ambitious business plans began to cause him some distress. He became concerned that all of the travel required was inappropriate for a married woman. Both spouses in Black families frequently held down jobs in the paid labour force, contrary to the pattern in white middle-class households. But middle-class Black women who sought work outside the home often faced bitter tensions within their marriages. Their careers tended to clash with society's prevailing ideals of gender, which required that men be masters in their own homes, ruling over dependent women and children. Even women who remained childless, such as Viola Desmond, found themselves subject to pressure to retire from the paid workforce.[27]

At odds with her husband on this point, Viola Desmond held firm convictions that Black women ought to have greater access to employment opportunities outside their traditionally segregated sphere of domestic service. A few years after she set up her own studio, she opened the Desmond School of Beauty Culture, which drew Black female students from across Nova Scotia, New Brunswick, and Quebec. Viola Desmond's long-range plans were to work with the women who graduated from her school to establish a franchise operation, setting up beauty parlours for people of colour across Canada. Her former students recall that she kept the shop immaculately; that all the beauticians, including Viola, wore uniforms and regulation stockings; and that their appearance was rigor-

Demond Beauty Studio Graduation Class, 1947. Viola Desmond is in the front row, extreme left. Her sister, Helen Davis Flint, is in the back row, extreme right.

Desmond School of Beauty Culture, graduation, 1944. Left to right: Rachel Kane, Verna Skinner, Rose Gannon, Joyce Lucas, Nora Dill.

ously inspected each day. Viola Desmond personified respectability to her students, who always called her 'Mrs Desmond' and were struck by the 'way that she carried herself' and her 'strength of character.'[28]

The evidence suggests that most legal challenges to racial segregation in Canada seem to have come from middle-class individuals. This appears not to be a coincidental factor, for class issues are intricately related to such matters. A certain level of economic security furnished a base which enabled such individuals to consider taking legal action against discriminatory treatment. Furthermore, given contemporary class biases, middle-class status appears to have underscored the indignity of racist treatment. Viola Desmond's elite position within the province's Black community was well established. She and her husband, Jack, were often held up as examples of prosperous Black entrepreneurs, whose small-business ventures had triumphed over the considerable economic barriers that stood in the way of Black business initiatives. Yet regardless of her visible financial standing in the community, Viola Desmond remained barred from entry into the more expensive seating area of the New Glasgow theatre. For those who believed that economic striving would eventually 'uplift' the Black race, the response of the manager of the Roseland Theatre crushed all hope of eventually achieving an egalitarian society.[29]

The matter of gender is also important in understanding the significance of Viola Desmond's ejection from the Roseland Theatre. In making her decision to challenge racial segregation in the courts, Viola Desmond became one of the first Black women in Canada to do so. As the controversy spread, Viola Desmond also came to symbolize the essence of middle-class Black femininity. She was a celebrated Halifax beautician, described as both 'elegantly coiffed and fashionably dressed,' a 'fine-featured woman with an eye for style.' Her contemporaries recall that she was always beautifully attired, her nails, make-up, and hair done with great care. Described as a 'petite, quiet-living, demure' woman, who stood four foot eleven inches, and weighed less than one hundred pounds, Viola Desmond was a well-mannered, refined, demonstrably *feminine* woman, physically manhandled by rude and forcibly violent white men. The spectacle would undoubtedly have provoked considerable outcry had the principal actors all been middle-class whites. Customary white gender relations dictated that, at least in public, physically taller and stronger men should exercise caution and delicacy in their physical contact with women. Roughing up a lady violated the very core of the ideology of chivalry.[30]

The extension of traditional white gender assumptions to Black women provoked more pause. Racist practices condoned and nurtured throughout North America during times of slavery denied Black women both the substance and the trappings of white femininity. Slave masters compelled their male and female slaves alike to labour alongside each other, irrespective of gender. Black women found their reproductive capacity commodified for material gain, and frequently experienced rape at the hands of their white owners and overseers. Denied the most fundamental rights to their own bodies and sexuality, Black women were barred by racist whites from any benefits that the idealized cult of 'motherhood' and 'femininity' might have offered white women. The signs on the segregated washrooms of the Deep South, 'white ladies' and 'black women,' neatly encapsulated the racialized gender assumptions. As Evelyn Brooks Higginbotham has described it, 'no black woman, regardless of income, education, refinement, or character, enjoyed the status of lady.'[31]

Whites who ascribed to attitudes such as these were somewhat unsettled by women such as Viola Desmond. Throughout her frightening and humiliating ordeal, she had remained the embodiment of female respectability. Her challenge to the racially segregated seating policies was carried out politely and decorously. Her dignified response in the face of the volatile theatre manager's threat to throw her out was that she 'was behaving very quietly,' and so 'didn't think he could.' Even the white matron from the New Glasgow lock-up recognized the incongruity of exposing a refined woman to the rough-and-tumble assortment of men collected in the cell that night: 'She seemed to realize that I shouldn't have been there,' emphasized Viola Desmond. By the standards of the dominant culture, Viola Desmond was undeniably feminine in character and deportment. The question remained whether the ideology of chivalry would be extended to encompass a Black woman who was insulted and physically mauled by white men.

THE COMMUNITY RESPONDS TO THE CONVICTION

The first to hear about the incident was Viola Desmond's husband, Jack, who was upset but not surprised. Jack was quite familiar with New Glasgow's Roseland Theatre. In fact, he had watched the Roseland Theatre being built while he worked as a child in the drugstore next door. '[T]here were no coloreds allowed downstairs,' he recalled later. 'She didn't know that – I knew it because I grew up there.' A deeply religious man, Jack Desmond held philosophical views that were rooted in tolerance: 'You've got to know how to handle it,' he would counsel. 'Take it to the Lord with a prayer.'[32]

Viola Desmond was considerably less willing to let temporal matters lie, as the interview she gave to the Halifax *Chronicle* shortly afterward indicates:

I can't understand why such measures should have been taken. I have travelled a great deal throughout Canada and parts of the United States and nothing like this ever happened to me before. I was born in Halifax and have lived here most of my life and I've found relations between negroes and whites very pleasant. I didn't realize a thing like this could happen in Nova Scotia – or in any other part of Canada.[33]

The shock that underlies this statement clearly communicates the magnitude of the insult that Viola Desmond experienced in the Roseland arrest. She must have been no stranger to racial segregation. She taught in segregated schools, was denied occupational training on the basis of race, and was keenly aware of segregated facilities in her own business. But unexpectedly to encounter segregated seating in a Nova Scotian theatre seems to have struck Viola Desmond as a startling injustice. The unforeseen discrimination was magnified by the heinous actions of the theatre manager and various officials of the state, who responded to her measured resistance with armed force and criminal prosecution. To see the forces of law so unanimously and spontaneously arrayed against her quiet protest must have struck Viola Desmond as outrageous. Couching her complaint in the most careful of terms, with polite reference to the 'very pleasant' relations that normally ensued between the races, she challenged Canadians to respond to this unconscionable treatment, to side with her against the legal authorities who pursued her conviction.

A considerable portion of the Black community in Halifax seems to have shared Viola Desmond's anger and concern over the incident. Pearleen Oliver was one of the first to take up the case. One of the most prominent Black women in Nova Scotia, Pearleen Oliver was born into a family of ten children in Cook's Cove, Guysborough County, in 1917. She 'put herself through high school by doing housework,' the first Black graduate of New Glasgow High School in 1936. After graduation, she married the young Reverend William Pearly Oliver. The Olivers presided over an almost exclusively Black congregation at Cornwallis Street Baptist Church, where the Rev. Oliver was posted as minister. Viola and

Jack Desmond belonged to the Cornwallis Church, and the morning after her arrest Viola Desmond came over to seek advice from the Olivers. Only Pearleen was home, but she recalls vividly that Viola Desmond was shaken and tearful as she related her experience. 'I said, "Oh Dear God, Viola, what did they do to you, what did they do to you?"' Pearleen Oliver was appalled by what had happened, and told Viola that she should seek legal advice. 'I figured it was now or never,' explained Mrs Oliver, 'Hitler was dead and the Second World War was over. I wanted to take it to court.'[34]

Pearleen Oliver had an enviable record as a confirmed proponent of racial equality. In 1944, she spearheaded a campaign of the Halifax Coloured Citizens Improvement League to force the Department of Education to remove racially objectionable material from its public-school texts. The insulting depiction of 'Black Sambo' in the Grade 11 text should be stricken from the books, she insisted, and replaced by the 'authentic history of the colored people' and accounts of 'their contribution to Canadian culture.' The leader of the Ladies Auxiliary of the African United Baptist Association, who campaigned extensively to eliminate racial barriers from the nursing profession, Pearleen Oliver, also took matters affecting Black women extremely seriously.[35]

When he learned of Viola's treatment later that weekend, the Rev. William Oliver was equally concerned. An influential member of the African United Baptist Association of Nova Scotia, the Rev. Oliver had achieved public acclaim as the only Black chaplain in the Canadian army during the Second World War. A confirmed proponent of racial equality in education and employment, William Oliver was no stranger to humiliating practices of racial segregation himself. He had been refused service in restaurants, barred from social activities organized by whites, and challenged when he attempted to participate in white athletic events. William Oliver was on record as opposing racial segregation in hotels, restaurants, and other public facilities, stressing that businesses should 'cater to the public on the basis of individual behavior, regardless of race.'[36]

The Olivers were shocked by the visible bruises on Viola Desmond's body, and they advised her to get immediate medical attention. The Black physician whom Viola consulted on 12 November treated her for injuries to her knee and hip, and also advised his patient to retain a lawyer to appeal the conviction.[37]

Recognizing that they needed to gather assistance from the wider community, Pearleen Oliver sought public support for Viola's case from the Nova Scotia Association for the Advancement of Colored People (NSAACP). The NSAACP, dedicated to eradicating race discrimination in housing, education, and employment, was founded in 1945. Pearleen Oliver found about half of the NSAACP members supportive of Viola Desmond's court challenge, while half expressed initial reluctance. Divisions of opinion about strategies for change seem to be inherent in all social reform movements, and the NSAACP was no exception. Fears of fostering racist backlash, concerns about using the law to confront racial segregation, and questions about whether equal admission to theatres was a pressing issue seem to have motivated the more cautious.[38]

Pearleen Oliver made a convincing case for supporting a legal claim, however, and all of the members of the NSAACP ultimately backed the case. They pledged to call public meetings about Viola Desmond's treatment and to raise funds to defray any legal costs. As Pearleen Oliver would explain to the Halifax *Chronicle*, the NSAACP intended to fight Viola Desmond's case to prevent 'a spread of color-bar tactics' across the province.[39]

Some dissent continued to linger within the Black community. One individual wrote to *The Clarion*, a bi-weekly Black newspaper founded in New Glasgow in July 1946:

About all we have to say about our Country is 'Thank God' for it. With all its shortcomings it is still the best place on earth. I would like to start complaining about segregation in theatres and restaurants, but as I look around me and see the food stores filled to overflowing while countless millions are starving I just can't get het up over not eating in certain places. I am EATING and REGU-LARLY. Later on, maybe, but not now. Canada is still all right with me.[40]

The argument made here seems partially rooted in economic or class-based concerns. The letter focused on issues of basic sustenance, intimating indirectly that those who could afford to eat in restaurants or attend the theatre were not fully representative of the Black community. In contrast, Carrie M. Best, the forty-three-year-old Black editor of *The Clarion*, believed that the question of racial segregation in public facilities was extremely important to the entire Black population. She wrote back defending those who would challenge such discrimination:

It is sometimes said that those who seek to serve are 'looking for trouble.' There are some who think it better to follow the line of least resistance, no matter how great the injury. Looking for trouble? How much better off the world would be if

men of good will would look for trouble, find it, and while it is merely a cub, drag
it out into the open, before it becomes the ferocious lion. Racial and Religious
hatred is trouble of the gravest kind. It is a vicious, smouldering and insidious
kind of trouble, born of fear and ignorance. It often lays dormant for years until
some would be Hitler, Bilbo or Rankin emerges to fan the flame into an uncon-
trollable catastrophe.

It is heartening to know how many trouble shooters have come to the aid of *The
Clarion* since the disgraceful Roseland incident. They are convinced, as are we, that
it is infinitely wiser to look for trouble than to have trouble looking for them.[41]

Carrie Best would profile Viola Desmond's treatment on the front
pages of *The Clarion*, denouncing it as a 'disgraceful incident,' and claiming that 'New Glasgow stands for Jim-crowism, at its basest, over the
entire globe.' She also gave prominent placement to a notice from Bernice
A. Williams, NSAACP secretary, announcing a public meeting to solicit
contributions for the Viola Desmond Court Fund. *The Clarion* urged
everyone to attend and give donations: 'The NSAACP is the Ladder to
Advancement. Step on it! Join today!' Money began to trickle in from
across the province, with donations by whites and Blacks alike.[42]

Carrie Best, who was born and educated in New Glasgow, was well
acquainted with the egregious forms of white racism practised there. A
woman who defined herself as an 'activist' against racism, she did not
mince words when she claimed there were 'just as many racists in New
Glasgow as in Alabama.'[43] She was thrown out of the Roseland Theatre
herself in 1942, for refusing to sit in the balcony, and tried unsuccessfully
to sue the theatre management for damages then.[44]

Nor was she a stranger to the heroism of Black resisters. One of her
most vivid childhood memories involved a race riot that erupted in New
Glasgow at the close of the First World War. An interracial altercation
between two youths inspired 'bands of roving white men armed with
clubs' to station themselves at different intersections in the town, barring
Blacks from crossing. At dusk that evening, Carrie Best's mother was
delivered home from work by the chauffeur of the family who employed
her. There she found that her husband, her younger son, and Carrie had
made it home safely. Missing was Carrie's older brother, who had not yet
returned from his job at the Norfolk House hotel. Carrie described what
ensued in her autobiography, *That Lonesome Road*:

In all the years she lived and until she passed away at the age of eighty-one my

Dr Carrie Best.

mother was never known to utter an unkind, blasphemous or obscene word, nor did I ever see her get angry. This evening was no exception. She told us to get our meal, stating that she was going into town to get my brother. It was a fifteen minute walk.

At the corner of East River Road and Marsh Street the crowd was waiting and as my mother drew near they hurled insults at her and threateningly ordered her to turn back. She continued to walk toward the hotel about a block away when one of the young men recognized her and asked her where she was going. 'I am going to the Norfolk House for my son,' she answered calmly. (My mother was six feet tall and as straight as a ramrod.) The young man ordered the crowd back and my mother continued on her way to the hotel. At that time there was a livery stable at the rear entrance to the hotel and it was there my mother found my frightened older brother and brought him safely home.[45]

This was but one incident in an increasingly widespread pattern of white racism, that exploded with particular virulence across Canada during and immediately following the First World War. White mobs terrorized the Blacks living near New Glasgow, physically destroying their property. White soldiers also attacked the Black settlement in Truro, Nova Scotia, stoning houses and shouting obscenities. Throughout the 1920s, Blacks in Ontario and Saskatchewan withstood increasingly concerted intimidation from the hateful Ku Klux Klan. But race discrimination had a much longer history in Canada.[46]

THE HISTORY OF BLACK SEGREGATION IN CANADA

From the middle of the nineteenth century, Blacks and whites in two provinces could be relegated to separate schools by law.[47] Ontario amended its School Act in 1849 to permit municipal councils 'to authorize the establishing of any number of schools for the education of the children of colored people that they may judge expedient.' The preamble to the statute was quite specific. The legislation was necessary, it admitted, because 'the prejudices and ignorance' of certain Ontario residents had 'prevented' certain Black children from attending the common schools in their district. The statute was amended in 1850, to direct local public school trustees to establish separate schools upon the application of twelve or more 'resident heads of families' in the area. In 1886, the legislature clarified that schools for 'coloured people' were to be set up only after an application had been made by at least five Black families in the community.[48]

Although drafted in permissive language, white officials frequently used coercive tactics to force Blacks into applying for segregated schools.[49] Once separate schools were set up, the courts refused Black children admission to any other schools, despite evidence that this forced many to travel long distances to attend schools they would not have chosen otherwise.[50] Separate schools for Blacks continued until 1891 in Chatham, 1893 in Sandwich, 1907 in Harrow, 1917 in Amherstburg, and 1965 in North Colchester and Essex counties.[51] The Ontario statute authorizing racially segregated education would not be repealed until 1964.[52] As white historian Robin Winks has noted:

The Negro schools lacked competent teachers, and attendance was highly irregular and unenforced. Many schools met for only three months in the year or closed entirely. Most had no library of any kind. In some districts, school taxes were collected from Negro residents to support the [white] common school from which their children were barred ... The education received ... could hardly have been regarded as equal ...[53]

Similar legislation dating from 1865 existed in Nova Scotia, where education authorities were authorized to establish 'separate apartments or buildings' for pupils of 'different colors.'[54] A campaign for racial integration in the schools, organized by leaders of the Black community in 1884, prompted an amendment to the law, stipulating that Black pupils could not be excluded from instruction in the areas in which they lived.[55] The original provisions for segregation within the public school system remained intact until 1950.[56] In 1940, school officials in Lower Sackville, in Halifax County, barred Black children from attending the only public school in the area, and until 1959 school buses would stop only in the white sections of Hammonds Plains. In 1960, there would still be seven formal Black school districts and three additional exclusively Black schools in Nova Scotia.[57]

Beyond the schools, racial segregation riddled the country. The colour bar was less rigidified than in the United States, varying between regions and shifting over time.[58] But Canadian employers commonly selected their workforce by race rather than by merit.[59] Access to land grants and residential housing was frequently restricted by race.[60] Attempts were made to bar Blacks from jury service.[61] The military was rigorously segregated.[62] Blacks were denied equal access to some forms of public transportation.[63] Blacks and whites tended to worship in separate churches, sometimes by choice, other times because white congregations refused membership to Blacks.[64] Orphanages and poor-houses could be segregated by race.[65] Some hospitals refused access to facilities to non-white physicians and service to non-white patients.[66] Blacks were even denied burial rights in segregated cemeteries.[67] While no consistent pattern ever emerged, various hotels, restaurants, theatres, athletic facilities, parks, swimming pools, beaches, dance pavilions, skating rinks, pubs and bars were closed to Blacks across the country.[68]

There were as yet no Canadian statutes expressly prohibiting such behaviour. The first statute to prohibit segregation on the basis of race did not appear until more than a year after Viola Desmond launched her civil suit, when Saskatchewan banned race discrimination in 'hotels, victualling houses, theatres or other places to which the public is customarily admitted.' The 1947 Saskatchewan Bill of Rights Act, which also barred discrimination in employment, business ventures, housing, and education, constituted Canada's first comprehensive human rights legislation. The act offered victims of race discrimination the opportunity to prosecute offenders upon summary conviction for fines of up to $200. The Court of King's Bench was also empowered to issue injunctions to restrain the offensive behaviour.[69] But none of this would assist Viola Desmond in November 1946.

PREPARING FOR LEGAL BATTLE

Had Viola Desmond wished to retain a Black lawyer to advise her on legal options, this would have presented difficulties. Nine Black men appear to have been admitted to the bar of Nova Scotia prior to 1946, but few were available for hire.[70] The only Black lawyer practising in Halifax in 1946 was Rowland Parkinson Goffe. A native of Jamaica, Goffe practised initially in England, taking his call to the Nova Scotia bar in 1920. Goffe travelled abroad frequently, operating his legal practice in Halifax only intermittently. For reasons that are unclear, Viola Desmond did not retain Goffe. He may have been away from Halifax at the time.[71]

Four days after her arrest, on 12 November, Viola Desmond retained the services of a white lawyer named Frederick William Bissett. Rev. William Oliver knew Bissett, and it was he who made the initial arrangements for Viola to see the lawyer. A forty-four-year-old native of St John's, Newfoundland, Bissett graduated in 1926 from Dalhousie Law School with a reputation as a 'sharp debater.' Called to the bar in Nova Scotia that year, he opened his own law office in Halifax, where he practised alone until his elevation to the Supreme Court of Nova Scotia in 1961. A noted trial lawyer, Bissett was acclaimed for his 'persistence and resourcefulness,' his 'keen wit and an infectious sense of humour.' Those who knew him emphasized that, above all, Bissett was 'gracious and charming,' a true 'gentleman.' This last feature of his character would potentially have been very helpful to Viola Desmond and her supporters. Their case would be considerably aided if the courts could be induced to visualize Viola Desmond as a 'lady' wronged by rough and racist men. The affront to customary gender assumptions might have been just the thing to tip the balance in the minds of judges who would otherwise have been reluctant to oppose racial segregation. A 'gentleman' such as Bissett would have been the perfect choice to advocate extending the mantle of white chivalry across race lines to cover Black women.[72]

Bissett's first task was to decide how to frame Viola Desmond's claim within the doctrines of law. One option might have been to mount a

Frederick William Bissett.

direct attack on the racially restrictive admissions policy of the theatre. There was an excellent precedent for such a claim in an earlier Quebec Superior Court decision, *Johnson* v *Sparrow*. In 1899, the court awarded $50 in damages to a Black couple barred from sitting in the orchestra section of the Montreal Academy of Music. Holding that a 'breach of contract' had occurred, a white judge, John Sprott Archibald, reasoned that 'any regulation which deprived negroes as a class of privileges which all other members of the community had a right to demand, was not only unreasonable but entirely incompatible with our free democratic institutions.' The Quebec Court of Queen's Bench affirmed the ruling on appeal, although it focussed exclusively on the breach of contract and held that the issue of racial equality did not need to be directly addressed at the time.[73]

A similar position was taken in British Columbia in 1914, in the case of *Barnswell* v *National Amusement Company, Limited*. The Empress Theatre in Victoria promulgated a 'rule of the house that coloured people should not be admitted.' When the white theatre manager turned away James Barnswell, a Black man who was a long-time resident of Victoria, he sued for breach of contract and assault. The white trial judge, Peter Secord Lampman, found the defendant company liable for breach of contract, and awarded Barnswell $50 in damages for humiliation. The British Columbia Court of Appeal affirmed the result.[74]

A string of other cases had done much to erode these principles. In 1911, a Regina newspaper announced that a local restaurant was planning to charge Black customers double what whites paid for meals, in an effort to exclude them from the local lunch-counter. When William Hawes, a Black man, was billed $1.40 instead of the usual $0.70 for a plate of ham and eggs, he took the white restaurant-keeper, W.H. Waddell, to court one week later. His claim was that Waddell had obtained money 'by false pretences.' The case was dismissed in Regina's Police Court, with the local white magistrates concluding that Hawes had known of the double fare when he entered the restaurant, and that this barred a charge of false pretences.[75]

Another example of judicial support for racial segregation occurred during the upsurge of racial violence at the close of the First World War. In 1919, the majority of the white judges on the Quebec Court of King's Bench held in *Loew's Montreal Theatres Ltd.* v *Reynolds* that the theatre management had 'the right to assign particular seats to different races and classes of men and women as it sees fit.' White theatre proprietors from Quebec east to the Maritimes greeted this ruling with enthusiasm, using it to contrive new and expanded policies of racially segregated seating.[76] In 1924, in *Franklin* v *Evans*, a white judge from the Ontario High Court dismissed a claim for damages 'for insult and injury' from W.V. Franklin, a Black watch-maker from Kitchener, who was refused lunch service in 'The Cave,' a London restaurant.[77] In 1940, in *Rogers* v *Clarence Hotel*, the majority of the white judges on the British Columbia Court of Appeal held that the white female proprietor of a beer parlour, Rose Elizabeth Low, could refuse to serve a Black Vancouver businessman, Edward Tisdale Rogers, because of his race. The doctrine of 'complete freedom of commerce' justified the owner's right to deal 'as [she] may choose with any individual member of the public.'[78]

Fred Christie v *The York Corporation*, ultimately reaching a similar result, wound its way through the Quebec court system right up to the Supreme Court of Canada in 1939. The litigation began when the white manager of a beer tavern in the Montreal Forum declined to serve a Black customer in July 1936. Fred Christie, a resident of Verdun, Quebec, who was employed as a private chauffeur in Montreal, sued the proprietors for damages. Judge Louis Philippe Demers, a white judge on the Quebec Superior Court, initially awarded Christie $25 in compensation for humiliation, holding that hotels and restaurants providing 'public services' had 'no right to discriminate between their guests.' The majority of the white judges of the Quebec Court of King's Bench reversed this ruling, preferring to champion the principle that 'chaque propriétaire est maître chez lui.' This philosophy was endorsed by the majority of the white judges on the Supreme Court of Canada, who agreed that it was 'not a question of motives or reasons for deciding to deal or not to deal; [any merchant] is free to do either.' Conceding that the 'freedom of commerce' principle might be restricted where a merchant adopted 'a rule contrary to good morals or public order,' Judge Thibaudeau Rinfret concluded that the colour bar was neither.[79]

In contrast, a series of judges dissented vigorously throughout these cases. In *Loew's Montreal Theatres Ltd.* v *Reynolds*, white judge Henry-George Carroll took pains to disparage the situation in the United States, where law was regularly used to enforce racial segregation. Stressing that social conditions differed in Canada, he insisted: 'Tous les citoyens de ce pays, blancs et noirs, sont soumis à la même loi et tenus aux mêmes obligations.' Carroll spoke pointedly of the ideology of equality that had suffused French law since the revolution of 1789, and reasoned that Mr Reynolds, 'un homme de bonne éducation,' deserved compensation for the humiliation that had occurred.[80]

In *Rogers* v *Clarence Hotel*, Judge Cornelius Hawkins O'Halloran wrote a lengthy and detailed rebuttal to the majority decision. Noting that the plaintiff was a British subject who had resided in Vancouver for more than two decades, with an established business in shoe-repair, O'Halloran insisted that he should be entitled to obtain damages from any beer parlour that barred Blacks from admission. 'Refusal to serve the respondent solely because of his colour and race is contrary to the common law,' claimed the white judge. 'All British subjects have the same rights and privileges under the common law – it makes no difference whether white or coloured; or of what class, race or religion.'[81]

In *Christie* v *The York Corporation*, the first dissent came from Antonin Galipeault, a white judge of the Quebec Court of King's Bench. Pointing out that the sale of liquor in Quebec taverns was already extensively regulated by law, he concluded that the business was a 'monopoly or quasi-monopoly' that ought to be required to service all members of the public. Galipeault noted that if tavern-keepers could bar Blacks, they could also deny entry to Jews, Syrians, the Chinese, and the Japanese. Bringing the matter even closer to home for the majority of Quebecers, he reasoned that 'religion' and 'language' might constitute the next grounds for exclusion. Galipeault insisted that the colour bar be struck down.[82]

At the level of the Supreme Court of Canada, Henry Hague Davis expressly sided with Galipeault, concluding that racial segregation was 'contrary to good morals and the public order.' 'In the changed and changing social and economic conditions,' wrote the white Supreme Court justice, 'different principles must necessarily be applied to new conditions.' Noting that the legislature had developed an extensive regulatory regime surrounding the sale of beer, Davis concluded that such vendors were not entitled 'to pick and choose' their customers.[83]

What is obvious from these various decisions is that the law was unsettled, as Judge Davis frankly admitted: 'The question is one of difficulty, as the divergence of judicial opinion in the courts below indicates.'[84] Where the judges expressly offered reasons for arriving at such different results, their analysis appears to be strained and the distinctions they drew arbitrary. Some tried to differentiate between a plaintiff who had prior knowledge of the colour bar and one who did not. Some considered the essential point to be whether the plaintiff crossed the threshold of the premises before being ejected. *Ad nauseam* the judges compared the status of theatres, restaurants, taverns, and hotels. They argued over whether public advertisements issued by commercial establishments constituted a legal 'offer' or merely 'an invitation to buy.' They debated whether a stein of beer had sufficient 'nutritive qualities' to be regarded as food.

Despite the endless technical arguments, the real issues dividing the judges appear to be relatively straightforward. There were two fundamental principles competing against each other: the doctrine of freedom of commerce and the doctrine of equality within a democratic society. Although the judges seem to have believed that they were merely applying traditional judicial precedents to the case at hand, this was something of a smoke screen. Some judges were choosing to select precedents extolling freedom of commerce, while others chose to affirm egalitarian principles. There was nothing which irretrievably compelled them to opt for one result over the other except their own predilections. A white law professor, Bora Laskin, made this explicit in a legal comment on the *Christie* case, written in 1940: 'The principle of freedom of commerce enforced by the Court majority is itself merely the reading of social and economic doctrine into law, and doctrine no longer possessing its nineteenth century validity.'[85]

Furthermore, no court had yet ruled on the validity of racial segregation in hotels, theatres, or restaurants in the province of Nova Scotia. A cautious lawyer, one easily cowed by the doctrinal dictates of *stare decisis*, might have concluded that the 'freedom of commerce' principle enunciated by the majority of judges in the Supreme Court of Canada would govern. A more adventuresome advocate might have surveyed the range of judicial disagreement and decided to put the legal system to the challenge once more.

The reform-minded lawyer could have gone back to the original decisions in *Johnson* v *Sparrow* and *Barnswell* v *National Amusement Co.*, which most of the judges in the later cases had curiously ignored.[86] Quebec Judge John Sprott Archibald, in particular, laid a firm foundation in *Johnson* v *Sparrow*, eloquently proclaiming the right of Canadians of all races to have equal access to places of public entertainment. Roundly criticizing the policy of racially segregated seating, he explained:

This position cannot be maintained. It would perhaps be trite to speak of slavery in this connection, and yet the regulation in question is undoubtedly a survival of prejudices created by the system of negro slavery. Slavery never had any wide influence in this country. The practice was gradually extinguished in Upper Canada by an act of the legislature passed on July 9th, 1793, which forbade the further importation of slaves, and ordered that all slave children born after that date should be free on attaining the age of twenty-one years. Although it was only in 1834 that an act of the imperial parliament finally abolishing slavery throughout the British colonies was passed, yet long before that, in 1803, Chief Justice Osgoode had declared slavery illegal in the province of Quebec. Our constitution is and always has been essentially democratic, and does not admit of distinctions of races or classes. All men are equal before the law and each has equal rights as a member of the community.[87]

Judge Archibald's recollection of the legal history of slavery in Canada is something of an understatement. The first Black slave arrived in Quebec in 1628, with slavery officially introduced by the French into New France on 1 May 1689.[88] After the British Conquest in 1763, the white general Jeffery Amherst confirmed that all slaves would remain in the possession of their masters.[89] In 1790, the English Parliament expressly authorized individuals wishing to settle in the provinces of Quebec and Nova Scotia to import 'negroes' along with other 'household furniture, utensils of husbandry or cloathing' free of duty.[90] In 1762, the Nova Scotia General Assembly gave indirect statutory recognition to slavery when it explicitly adverted to 'Negro slaves' in the context of an act intended to control the sale of liquor on credit.[91] In 1781, the legislature of Prince Edward Island (then Île St-Jean) passed an act declaring that the baptism of slaves would not exempt them from bondage.[92]

The 1793 Upper Canada statute, of which Judge Archibald was so proud, countenanced a painfully slow process of manumission. The preamble, noting that it was 'highly expedient to abolish slavery in this province, so far as the same may gradually be done without violating private property,' said it all. The act freed not a single slave. Although the statute did ensure that no additional 'negro' slaves could be brought into the province, it confirmed the existing property rights of all current slave-owners. Furthermore, children born of 'negro mother[s]' were to remain in the service of their mothers' owners until the age of twenty-five years (not twenty-one years, as Judge Archibald had noted). The act may actually have discouraged voluntary manumission, by requiring slave-owners to post security bonds for slaves released from service, to cover the cost of any future public financial assistance required.[93] Confronted with litigants who contested the legal endorsement of slavery, white judges in Lower Canada, Nova Scotia, and New Brunswick dispatched inconsistent judgments.[94] Portions of the area that was to become Canada remained slave territory under law until 1833, when a statute passed in England emancipated all slaves in the British Empire.[95] Slavery persisted in British North America well after it was abolished in most of the northern states.[96] Even after abolition, Canadian government officials approved the extradition of fugitive African Americans who escaped from slavery in the United States and sought freedom in Canada.[97]

However, Judge Archibald's ringing declaration that the constitution prohibited racial discrimination was an outstanding affirmation of equality that could potentially have been employed to attack many of the racist practices currently in vogue. Long before the enactment of the Canadian Bill of Rights or the Canadian Charter of Rights and Freedoms, here was a judge who took hold of the largely unwritten, amorphous body of constitutional thought and proclaimed that the essence of a democracy was the legal eradication of 'distinctions of races or classes.' A thoughtful attorney could have created an opening for argument here, reasoning that the 'freedom of commerce' principle should be superseded by equality rights as a matter of constitutional interpretation. These arguments had apparently not been fully made to the Supreme Court of Canada when the *Christie v York Corporation* case was litigated. There should have been room for another try.

In addition, the Supreme Court had expressly admitted that 'freedom of commerce' would have to give way where a business rule ran 'contrary to good morals or public order.' No detailed analysis of the ramifications of racial discrimination was ever presented in these cases. A concerted attempt to lay out the social and economic repercussions of racial segregation might have altered the facile assumptions of some of the judges who could find no fault with colour bars. So much could have been argued. There was the humiliation and assault on dignity experienced by Black men, women, and children whose humanity was denied by racist whites. Counsel could have described the severe curtailment of Black educational and occupational opportunities that placed impenetrable restrictions upon full participation in Canadian society. The distrust bred of racial segregation had triggered many of the instances of interracial mob violence that marred Canadian history. A creative lawyer might have contended that rules that enforced racial divisions undeniably fomented immorality and the disruption of public peace.

Similar arguments had been made before the Ontario Supreme Court in 1945, in the landmark case of *Re Drummond Wren*. The issue there was the legality of a restrictive covenant registered against a parcel of land, enjoining the owner from selling to 'Jews or persons of objectionable nationality.' Noting that there were no precedents on point, Judge John Keiller Mackay, a white Gentile, quoted a legal rule from *Halsbury*: 'Any agreement which tends to be injurious to the public or against the public good is void as being contrary to public policy.' Holding that the covenant was unlawful because it was 'offensive to the public policy of this jurisdiction,' Mackay stated:

In my opinion, nothing could be more calculated to create or deepen divisions between existing religious and ethnic groups in this Province, or in this country, than the sanction of a method of land transfer which would permit the segregation and confinement of particular groups to particular business or residential areas ... It appears to me to be a moral duty, at least, to lend aid to all forces of cohesion, and similarly to repel all fissiparous tendencies which would imperil national unity. The common law courts have, by their actions over the years, obviated the need for rigid constitutional guarantees in our polity by their wise use of the doctrine of public policy as an active agent in the promotion of the public weal. While Courts and eminent Judges have, in view of the powers of our Legislatures, warned against inventing new heads of public policy, I do not conceive that I would be breaking new ground were I to hold the restrictive covenant impugned in this proceeding to be void as against public policy. Rather would I be applying well-recognized principles of public policy to a set of facts requiring their invocation in the interest of the public good.

The common law was not carved in stone. Nor was the judicial understanding of 'public policy,' which as Judge Mackay stressed, 'varies from time to time.'[98]

In assessing his strategy in the *Desmond* case, Bissett had to consider many factors: the wishes of his client, the resources available to prepare and argue the case, the social and political climate within which the case would be heard, and the potential receptivity of the bench. Viola Desmond would have been soundly behind a direct attack on racial segregation. She had come seeking public vindication for the racial discrimination she had suffered. The community support and funding from the NSAACP would have strengthened her claim. The Halifax beautician would have been viewed as a conventionally 'good' client, a successful business entrepreneur, a respectable married woman who had proved to be well mannered throughout her travails. The traditional assumptions about race relations were also under some scrutiny. Although white Nova Scotians continued to sponsor racial segregation in their schools, housing, and workforce, the unveiling of the Nazi death camps towards the end of the Second World War riveted public attention upon the appalling excesses of racial and religious discrimination. In October 1945, the Canadian Parliament entertained a motion to enact a formal Bill of Rights, guaranteeing equal treatment before the law, irrespective of race, nationality, or religious or political beliefs. Public sentiment might have been sufficiently malleable to muster support for more racial integration. Viola Desmond's case potentially offered an excellent vehicle with which to test the capacity of Canadian law to further racial equality.[99]

But Frederick William Bissett decided not to attack the racial segregation directly. Perhaps he simply accepted the Supreme Court of Canada ruling in *Christie* v *York Corporation* as determinative. Perhaps he could not imagine how to push the boundaries of law in new, more socially progressive directions. Perhaps he was intimately acquainted with the white judges who manned the Nova Scotia courts, and knew their predilections well. Whatever the reason, Bissett settled upon a more conventional litigation strategy. That he would fail, even in this more limited effort, may suggest that a more dramatic challenge would have fallen far short of the goal. I prefer to think that the stilted narrowness of the vision dictated an equally narrow response.

REX V DESMOND

Bissett issued a writ on Wednesday, 14 November 1946, naming Viola Desmond as plaintiff in a civil suit against two defendants, Harry L. MacNeil and the Roseland Theatre Co. Ltd. Bissett alleged that Harry MacNeil acted unlawfully in forcibly ejecting his client from the theatre. He based his claim in intentional tort, a legal doctrine that contained little scope for discussion of race discrimination. The writ stipulated that Viola Desmond was entitled to compensatory damages on the following grounds: 1 / assault; 2 / malicious prosecution; and 3 / false arrest and imprisonment. Bissett did not add a fourth and lesser-known tort, 'abusing the process of the law,' which might have offered more scope for raising the racial issues that concerned his client. The three grounds he did enunciate were all advanced in racially neutral terms.[100]

Whether there would have been an opportunity to address the issue of race discrimination indirectly within the common-law tort actions will never be known. The civil claim apparently never came to trial, and the archival records contain no further details on the file. Why Bissett decided not to pursue the civil actions is unclear. Perhaps he felt that the tort claim would be difficult to win. The common-law principle of 'defence of property' might have been invoked to justify the use of force by property owners against trespassers. The defendants would also have been entitled to raise the defence of 'legal authority,' asserting that they were within their rights in removing someone who had breached the tax provisions of the Theatres Act. The conviction registered against Viola Desmond bolstered this line of argument, confirming that at least one court had upheld the defendants' actions. It also served as a complete defense to the claim for 'malicious prosecution.' Upon reflection, Bissett may have decided that he needed to overturn the initial conviction before taking any further action upon the civil claim.[101]

On 27 December 1946, Bissett announced that he would make an application for a writ of *certiorari* to ask the Supreme Court of Nova Scotia to quash Viola Desmond's criminal conviction. There was 'no evidence to support' the conviction, he contended, and the magistrate lacked the 'jurisdiction' to convict her. Bissett filed an affidavit sworn by Viola Desmond, outlining how she had asked for a downstairs ticket and been refused, describing in detail her physical man-handling by the theatre manager and police officer, and documenting the failings in the actual trial process itself. Nothing in the papers filed alluded directly or indirectly to race. Viola Desmond, Reverend W.P. Oliver, and William

Allison (a Halifax packer) jointly committed themselves to pay up to two hundred dollars in costs should the action fail.[102]

A writ of *certiorari* allowed a party to transfer a case from an inferior tribunal to a court of superior jurisdiction by way of motion before a judge. In this manner, the records of proceedings before stipendiary magistrates could be taken up to the Supreme Court for reconsideration. The availability of this sort of judicial review was restricted, however. Parties dissatisfied with their conviction could not simply ask the higher court judges to overrule it because the magistrate's decision was wrong. Instead, they had to allege that there had been a more fundamental denial of justice or that there was some excess or lack of jurisdiction.[103]

There is no written record of what Bissett argued when he appeared before Nova Scotia Supreme Court Justice Maynard Brown Archibald on 10 January 1947.[104] But the white judge was clearly unimpressed. A native of Colchester County, Nova Scotia, Judge Archibald had studied law at Dalhousie University and was called to the Nova Scotia bar in 1919. He practised law in Halifax continuously from 1920 until his appointment to the bench in 1937. Although he was an erudite lecturer in Dalhousie's law school, Archibald did not choose to elaborate upon legal intricacies in his decision in the *Desmond* case. Viola Desmond had no right to use the process of *certiorari*, he announced, and he curtly dismissed her application on 20 January. The cursory ruling of less than two pages contained a mere recitation of conclusion without any apparent rationale. 'It is clear from the affidavits and documents presented to me that the Magistrate had jurisdiction to enter upon his inquiry,' Archibald noted. 'This court will therefore not review on *certiorari* the decision of the Magistrate as to whether or not there was evidence to support the conviction.'[105]

The best clue to deciphering the decision is found in the judge's final paragraph:

It was apparent at the argument that the purpose of this application was to seek by means of *certiorari* proceedings a review of the evidence taken before the convicting Magistrate. It is obvious that the proper procedure to have had such evidence reviewed was by way of an appeal. Now, long after the time for appeal has passed, it is sought to review the Magistrate's decision by means of *certiorari* proceedings. For the reasons that I have already given, this procedure is not available to the applicant.[106]

A part-time stipendiary magistrate for a brief period during his days of

Maynard Brown Archibald, Dalhousie Law Graduating Class, 1925.

law practice, Judge Archibald was concerned that lower court officials be free from unnecessary, burdensome scrutiny by superior court judges. Earlier Nova Scotia decisions had reflected similar fears, suggesting that access to judicial review be restricted to prevent 'a sea of uncertainty' in which the decisions of inferior tribunals were subjected to limitless second-guessing. The proper course of action, according to Archibald, would have been to appeal Magistrate MacKay's conviction to County Court under the Nova Scotia Summary Convictions Act.[107]

Why Bissett originally chose to bring a writ of *certiorari* rather than an appeal is not clear. The Summary Convictions Act required litigants to choose one route or the other, not both. An appeal permitted a full inquiry into all of the facts and law surrounding the case, with the right to call witnesses and adduce evidence, and the appeal court entitled to make a completely fresh ruling on the merits. Although an appeal would seem to have offered greater scope to the defence, Bissett may have preferred to make his arguments before the more elevated Nova Scotia

Supreme Court, which heard applications for *certiorari*, rather than the County Court, which heard appeals from summary convictions. Or he may simply have missed the time limit for filing an appeal, which was set as ten days from the date of conviction. He issued the civil writ a mere five days after the initial conviction, but the writ of *certiorari* was not filed until almost a full month afterwards. Possibly by the time Bissett turned away from the civil process to canvas his options with respect to the criminal law, it was already too late for an appeal.[108]

Since the limitation period for appeals had already run, Bissett had no other option but to seek to overturn Archibald's ruling before the full bench of the Nova Scotia Supreme Court.[109] The case was set down for argument on 13 March. Jack Desmond refused to accompany his wife to court, since he continued to oppose Viola's actions and blamed her for stirring up trouble. The tensions within the marriage were increasing by the day, and would ultimately result in the couple's permanent marital separation.[110] Carrie Best, who did accompany Viola Desmond to court, acknowledged in *The Clarion* that it was an emotionally tense experience to sit through the hearing, 'hoping against hope that justice will not be blind in this case.' Carrie Best admitted that she 'watched breathlessly as the calm, unhurried soft spoken Bissett argued his appeal.' Bissett conceded that the time to lodge the original appeal had 'inadvertently slipped by,' but that this should not bar the court from reviewing on *certiorari*. 'The appellant is entitled to the writ,' claimed Bissett, 'whether she appealed or not, if there has been a denial of natural justice.'[111]

The affidavit Viola Desmond filed to support her case set out in detail the many ways she felt the trial had been procedurally unfair. She had not been told of her right to counsel or her right to seek an adjournment. She did not understand that she was entitled to cross-examine the prosecution witnesses. She was sentenced without any opportunity to make submissions to the court. These several omissions would have more than sufficed to constitute a denial of natural justice, as lawyers understand the meaning of that term in the latter half of the twentieth century. But at the time of the *Desmond* appeal the concept of due process was much less clear. Judge John Doull, who issued his decision on this case on 17 May 1947, even disputed the use of the term 'natural justice.' A former attorney general of Nova Scotia, Doull wrote:

A denial of justice apparently means that before the tribunal, the applicant was not given an opportunity of setting up and proving his case. (The words 'natural justice' were used in some of the opinions of the judges but I doubt whether that is a good term.) At any rate a denial of the right to be heard is a denial of a right which is so fundamental in our legal practice that a denial of it vitiates a proceeding in which such denial occurs.[112]

The white judge conceded that if a 'denial of justice' was established in Viola Desmond's affidavit, the failure to appeal would no longer suffice to bar her claim. But then Judge Doull, a former mayor of New Glasgow, concluded that there had been no such procedural omissions in the present case. None of the other white Supreme Court judges differed from this view.[113]

Bissett's other argument, on the lack of jurisdiction, was vigorously disputed by respondent's counsel, Edward Mortimer Macdonald, Jr, KC. Harry MacNeil's lawyer was a forty-seven-year-old white New Glasgow resident who had received degrees from Dalhousie University, Bishop's College, and McGill. He practised law in Montreal from 1924 to 1930, then returned to practice in his birth province of Nova Scotia, where he served as the town solicitor for New Glasgow. 'The magistrate [had] jurisdiction, [and] tried the case on the evidence before him,' asserted Macdonald. 'The sole objection remaining to the appellant is that the evidence does not support a conviction. The proper remedy therefore is by way of appeal.'[114]

Bissett did not argue that it was beyond the jurisdiction of a magistrate to apply the Nova Scotia Theatres, Cinematographs and Amusements Act to enforce racial segregation. He should have. Courts had long held that it was an abuse of process to bring criminal charges as a lever to enforce debt collection. Here the theatre manager was not trying to help the province collect tax, but to bring down the force of law upon protestors of racial segregation. That Bissett might have drawn an analogy to the abuse of process decisions was suggested months later in a *Canadian Bar Review* article written by J.B. Milner, a white professor at Dalhousie Law School. Calling the *Desmond* case 'one of the most interesting decisions to come from a Nova Scotia court in many years,' Milner asserted that Harry MacNeill was prosecuting Viola Desmond 'for improper reasons.' MacNeill's 'desire to discriminate between negro and white patrons of his theatre' transformed the criminal proceeding into 'a vexatious action,' Milner argued.[115]

None of this was addressed before the court. Instead, Bissett confined his jurisdictional point to the insufficiency of evidence at trial, leaving himself wide open to procedural critique. Judge Robert Henry Graham emphasized that the evidentiary matters in this case did not relate to jurisdiction: 'A justice who convicts without evidence is doing something that he ought not to do, but he is doing it as a Judge and if his jurisdiction to entertain the charge is not open to impeachment, his subsequent error, however grave, is a wrong exercise of a jurisdiction which he has, and not a usurpation of a jurisdiction which he has not.' There could be no question 'raised as to the jurisdiction of the stipendiary magistrate' in this case, concluded Judge Graham, himself another former white mayor and stipendiary magistrate from New Glasgow. Furthermore, Judge Graham added, 'no reason except inadvertence was given to explain why the open remedy of appeal was not taken.' William Francis Carroll and William Lorimer Hall, the other two white judges who delivered concurring opinions in the case, agreed that *certiorari* was not procedurally available to overturn the conviction.[116]

Three of the judges, however, felt inclined to make some comment about the sufficiency of evidence at trial. Graham's view was that the charge had been substantiated: '[Viola Desmond] knew that the ticket she purchased was not for downstairs and so that she had not paid the full tax.' Carroll disagreed: 'the accused did actually pay the tax required by one purchasing such a ticket as she was sold.' Hall, the only judge to make even passing reference to the racial issues, was most explicit:

Had the matter reached the Court by some method other than *certiorari*, there might have been opportunity to right the wrong done this unfortunate woman.

One wonders if the manager of the theatre who laid the complaint was so zealous because of a *bona fide* belief there had been an attempt to defraud the Province of Nova Scotia of the sum of one cent, or was it a surreptitious endeavour to enforce a Jim Crow rule by misuse of a public statute.[117]

Despite their differing opinions, all four judges took the position that Viola Desmond's efforts to overturn Magistrate MacKay's original ruling should be denied. Her conviction would stand.

The decision to apply for *certiorari* rather than to appeal had cost Viola Desmond dearly. Respondent's counsel, E.M. Macdonald, laid the blame squarely at Bissett's feet. 'The appellant had full benefit of legal advice before the expiry of the delays for appeal,' he insisted at the Supreme Court hearing. More than five days before the expiration of the time for appeal, Bissett was actively on the case, having already launched the civil action for assault, malicious prosecution, and false arrest and imprisonment. His decision to opt for judicial review rather than an appeal of the original conviction proved disastrous. He chose to argue the case in a conservative and traditional manner, relegating the race issues to the sidelines of the legal proceeding. Even within this narrow venue, Bissett failed to deliver.

THE AFTERMATH

What must Viola Desmond have thought of the ruling? Although she left no letters or diaries reflecting her views, her sisters recall something of her feelings at the time. Wanda Robson, Viola's younger sister, explains:

The day she came back from the court, knowing she had lost the case, she was very disappointed. A person like my sister never liked to lose. A person like my sister, who was such a hard worker, had always been told if you do hard work, you're going to win. If you're Black or Negro or whatever, you're going to work hard, get that scholarship and win. We forgot about our colour and educated ourselves. She felt that she should have won the case, and she was bitterly disappointed.[118]

Viola Desmond must have been appalled, not only by the ruling, but by the way her attempt to seek legal protection from racial discrimination was turned into a purely technical debate over the intricacies of criminal procedure. None of the judges even noted on the record that she was Black. The intersection of 'white male chivalry' with 'Black womanhood' lay completely unexamined. Nor was there any direct reference to the Roseland Theatre's policy of racially segregated seating. Judge Hall was the only one to advert to the 'Jim Crow rule,' a reference to the practices of racial segregation spawned in the United States after the abolition of slavery. Even Judge Hall's professed concern did not dissuade him from reaching the same conclusion as his brothers on the bench: that the court was powerless to intervene.

Professor Milner took up this very point in his review of the case; 'discrimination against colour,' he noted, took place 'outside the sphere of legal rules.' The theatre manager 'apparently violated no law of human rights and fundamental freedoms in this free county in refusing admission to part of his theatre to persons of negro extraction.' What struck Milner as particularly unfair was that the manager not only removed Viola Desmond, 'as our democratic law says he may,' but also successfully prosecuted her for violating a quasi-criminal provision in a provincial statute.[119]

The Clarion's coverage of the 'disappointing' decision, on 15 April 1947, was muted. Politely expressing appreciation for 'the objective manner in which the judges handled the case,' the editor noted: 'It would appear that the decision was the only one possible under the law. While in the moral sense we feel disappointed, we must realize that the law must be interpreted as it is. The Clarion feels that the reason for the decision lies in the manner in which the case was presented to the Court. This was very strongly implied by the Supreme Court. This is a regrettable fact.'[120]

Bissett, who is not mentioned by name, is clearly taking the fall here. It was his choice of an application for *certiorari*, rather than appeal, which was singled out as the reason for the legal loss. His conservative strategy of camouflaging race discrimination underneath traditional common-law doctrines, his decision not to attack the legality of racial segregation with a frontal assault, was not discussed.

The Clarion did, however, take some solace from Judge Hall's 'Jim Crow' remarks, which it quoted in full, adding:

The Court did not hesitate to place the blame for the whole sordid affair where it belonged. […] It is gratifying to know that such a shoddy attempt to hide behind the law has been recognized as such by the highest Court in our Province. We feel that owners and managers of places of amusement will now realize that such practices are recognized by those in authority for what they are, – cowardly devices to persecute innocent people because of their outmoded racial biases.[121]

Some Blacks believed the whole incident better left alone. There were accusations that Viola Desmond had caused all the trouble by trying to 'pass' for white, that her mother's white heritage caused her to put on airs and sit where she ought never to have sat. Walter A. Johnston, a Black Haligonian employed as a chef with the Immigration department, made a point of criticizing Viola Desmond at an Ottawa national convention of the Liberal party in October 1948. Viola Desmond had been 'censured by the Halifax colored group' for her activism, he advised. 'We told her she was not helping the New Glasgow colored people by motoring over there to cause trouble.' Johnston complained of racial 'agitators' who would 'increase the racial problem and set back the progress towards good feeling.' The policy he counselled: to 'shrug … off the trouble we met' with a 'soft-answer-that-turneth-away-wrath.'[122]

James Calbert Best, Carrie Best's son and the associate editor of *The Clarion*, had an entirely different perspective. Calling for legislation that would put the right to racial equality above the privileges of those in business, he claimed: 'People have come to realize that the merchant, the restaurant operator, the theatre manager all have a duty, and the mere fact that such enterprises are privately owned is no longer an excuse for discrimination on purely racial grounds. [...] Here in Nova Scotia, we see the need of such legislation every day.'[123]

Comparing the situation of Blacks in Nova Scotia with those in the American South, Best castigated Canadians for their complacency:

We do have many of the privileges which are denied our southern brothers, but we often wonder if the kind of segregation we receive here is not more cruel in the very subtlety of its nature. [...]

True, we are not forced into separate parts of public conveyances, nor are we forced to drink from separate faucets or use separate washrooms, but we are often refused meals in restaurants and beds in hotels, with no good reason.

Nowhere do we encounter signs that read 'No Colored' or the more diplomatic little paste boards which say 'Select Clientele,' but at times it might be better. At least much consequent embarrassment might be saved for all concerned.[124]

Bolstered by the apparent inability of the courts to stop racial discrimination, Canadian businesses continued to enforce their colour bars at whim. The famous African-American sculptress Selma Burke was denied service in a Halifax restaurant in September 1947. 'We had expected to find conditions in Canada so much better than in the States,' explained her white companion, 'but I'm sorry to say we were mistaken.'[125] Grantley Adams, the Black prime minister of Barbados, was refused a room in a Montreal hotel in 1954 because the hotel had 'regulations.'[126] The racial intolerance in New Glasgow intensified and spread to other groups. In September 1948, a gang of hooded marauders burned a seven-foot cross on the front lawn of the home of Joe Mong, the Chinese proprietor of a New Glasgow restaurant. Police investigated but pronounced themselves sceptical that the incident had 'anything to do with K.K.K. activities.' It was simply 'a private matter,' they concluded.[127] Akin to 'freedom of commerce.'

After her loss in court, Viola Desmond seems to have withdrawn from public gaze and taken steps to consolidate her business. Her younger sister recalls that Viola sought advice from her father: 'She was wondering what she should do, and my father said: "Viola, I think you've gone as far as you should go. It's time to get on and put this behind you. I won't say that nothing's been gained. Something has, but at what cost?

Viola Desmond relaxing at the Hi-Hat Club in Boston, with her sister and brother-in-law, July 1955. Left to right: Wanda (Davis) Neal, Viola Desmond, Milton Neal.

Your business is sliding." So she set her lips, and got back to her business.'[128] But even the business seems to have lost some of its lustre. Angry at the failure of the legal system to erase her conviction, Viola Desmond set aside her plans to establish franchise operations throughout Canada. She began to invest her money in real estate, believing that this represented greater security in a racially torn society. She bought up homes, renovated them, and rented them out to Black families. Eventually she closed up her shop and moved to Montreal, where she enrolled in business classes, hoping to become a consultant in the entertainment industry. She moved down to New York City, where she had just begun to establish her business when she fell ill. On 7 February 1965, at the age of fifty, Viola Desmond died in New York of a gastro-intestinal haemorrhage.[129]

As a matter of legal precedent, the *Viola Desmond* case was an absolute failure. The lawsuit was framed in such a manner that the real issues of white racism were shrouded in procedural technicalities. The judges turned their backs on Black claims for racial equality, in certain respects openly condoning racial segregation. But the toll that her battle with racial segregation took on Viola Desmond was not entirely for naught. According to Pearleen Oliver, the legal challenge touched a nerve within the Black community, creating a dramatic upsurge in race consciousness. The funds raised for legal fees were diverted to serve as seed money for the fledgling NSAACP, after Frederick William Bissett declined to bill his client, substantially strengthening the ability of the Black organization to lobby against other forms of race discrimination.[130]

While there were undeniably those who thought the struggle better left unwaged, the leaders of Nova Scotia's Black community felt differently. Asked to reflect on Viola Desmond's actions fifteen years later, Dr William Pearly Oliver tried to explain the enormous symbolic significance of the case. His appreciation for her effort transcends the failures of the legal system, and puts Viola Desmond's contribution in clearer perspective: '... this meant something to our people. Neither before or since has there been such an aggressive effort to obtain rights. The people arose as one and with one voice. This positive stand enhanced the prestige of the Negro community throughout the Province. It is my conviction that much of the positive action that has since taken place stemmed from this ...'[131]

8

Conclusion

Canadians unabashedly portrayed their country's population in the bold colours of 'white,' 'red,' 'black,' and 'yellow' during the first half of the twentieth century. From census takers to legislators, from lawyers to judges, from the press to the general public, people incessantly described racial distinctions in terms of colour. In typical newspaper columns, readers found 'redmen' jostling cheek by jowl with 'palefaces,' 'yellow hordes,' and 'black Negroids.' If the language of colour was becoming more muted in census directions by 1950, the common folk remained eminently comfortable with the vivid, no-nonsense terminology.

When prairie townsfolk invited Aboriginal dancers to their summer fairs, it was 'local colour' that they yearned for, to brighten up their festivities. The spectators thrilled when the 'red-skinned' dancers appeared in showy 'warpaint' colours, beading with perspiration until the paint dripped down to form a 'multicoloured coat.' When Canadians set up barriers between 'yellow' proprietors and 'white women,' it was a florid division of colour that separated the two. Even the Ku Klux Klan confidently proclaimed its credo in the language of colour. Theirs was a 'white man's organization,' crowed the Klansmen. They eschewed the 'colored races.'

There were moments of uncertainty, undeniably. The Japanese were sometimes called 'brown' and other times 'yellow.' Immigrants from India were described as 'black' as well as 'brown.' The 'Eskimos' were equally confusing. Diamond Jenness, the famous Eskimologist, believed their skin to be 'lighter in colour' than that of other aborigines, even 'verging towards a yellowish white.' As science became more rigorous, the experts began to assert that people came in all sorts of rag-tag shades: 'bronze,' 'coppery,' 'burnt coffee,' 'cinnamon,' and so forth. And when it came to labelling specific individuals, allocation could be maddeningly uncertain. Ira Johnson was reputed to be Black. He claimed to be white and red. To some commentators, he looked white, while to others he looked red. No one seemed prepared to point out how absurd the whole colourization scheme really was.

Legal authorities continually found themselves squeezed into tight spots as they tried to make sense of the racial divisions enacted into Canadian law. The intricate definitions in the Indian Act kept gliding and shifting, defying those who demanded definite and ascertainable categories. The racial boundaries of other communities were even more imponderable, with even less legislative guidance. Yet judges seemed oblivious to the foundation of sand upon which race definition was built. In case after case, they ruled particular individuals and communities on one side of the line or the other. Person 'x' was an 'Indian,' while person 'y' was not. The Mohawk were 'a distinct race.' Yee Clun and Quong Wing were 'Chinese.' Russian and German waitresses were 'white.' Although the issue never surfaced in the courtroom, everyone knew that Viola Desmond, from a mixed-race family, was 'Black.'

The 'science' of race definition reached its pinnacle in the decade of the 1920s, after which the endless measuring and testing began to produce skewered data that could not help but unmask the hopelessness of the overall project. The case of *Re Eskimos*, in 1939, provides a unique window into the assumptions and understandings of physical anthropologists as they began to rethink their discipline. The judges of the Supreme Court of Canada listened as experts vied with experts to pronounce upon racial categorization, while at the same time acknowledging rather sheepishly that definitive assessments were impossible to make. Even as the scientists concluded that 'race' was not simply physical, but a multitextured embodiment of cultural attributes, they did not take the next step of insisting that the exercise of racial categorization was nonsensical. And none of their caveats stopped the Court from delivering the edict that 'Eskimos' were 'Indians,' as effortlessly as slipping a hot knife through butter.

The ambiguity and instability of 'race' becomes undeniably apparent when one traces its meandering path through history. The size of one's skull, the pendulousness of one's breasts, the language one spoke, the company one kept, even where one resided could prove determinative. For some, the mere wearing of moccasins could tip the balance. The fiction of 'race' is never so obvious as when one looks backward in time.

Drawing lessons from history, some commentators today insist that we should completely foreclose the use of racial designations in the new millennium. They advance the theory that a modern, race-neutral society should reject racial distinctions for the absurdity they are. The argument asserts that the elimination of all 'racial' designations, discussion, and analysis would constitute one more step towards fostering an egalitarian society. But proponents of 'race-neutrality' neglect to recognize that our society is not a race-neutral one. It is built upon centuries of racial division and discrimination. The legacy of such bigotry infects all of our institutions, relationships, and legal frameworks. To advocate 'colour-blindness' as an ideal for the modern world is to adopt the false mythology of 'racelessness' that has plagued the Canadian legal system for so long. Under current circumstances, it will only serve to condone the continuation of white supremacy across Canadian society.

For all the slipperiness of racial definition in law, it is apparent that dramatic, real-life consequences flowed from racial designations. Falling into the legal category of 'Indian' meant that some participants in ceremonial ritual found themselves behind bars. Falling into the legal category of 'Chinese' meant that some male employers were forbidden to hire the female workers they needed for their businesses. Falling into the category of 'white' meant those same female workers were denied occupational choices. A man reputed to be 'Black' who became engaged to a 'white' woman suffered the procession of white-robed men impaling his lawn with fiery crosses. A woman understood to be 'Black' who insisted upon sitting in a theatre where she could properly see the movie courted the possibility of physical ejection from the premises and a stint in jail.

Racial designations played havoc with legal entitlements throughout this period. The right to vote was explicitly tied by law to race. 'Indians,' 'Chinese,' 'Japanese,' 'Hindu,' 'Mongolian,' and 'other Asiatics' were all denied the suffrage at various points in time, a status that imposed political powerlessness across sweeping categories of racialized communities. Immigration laws blatantly blocked entry by race, in a deliberate and successful endeavour to preserve the overwhelming 'whiteness' of the Canadian population and to marginalize other racial groups. Race dramatically affected the enforceability of international legal principles and diplomatic accords, with the 'white-supremacist' nations of the United States and Europe accorded privileges and respect not extended to the

Mohawk and other Aboriginal nations. Religious, cultural, and linguistic freedom depended on race, with Aboriginal peoples denied their spiritual heritage, the use of their languages, and the freedom to organize their societies in ways that were meaningful to them. Access to education, employment, residence, and business opportunities varied dramatically by race. At times, the right to attend certain schools, to hold specific jobs, to live in particular neighbourhoods, and to enter into entrepreneurial competition was denied some races by legislation. At other times, racist teachers, employers, landholders, and customers accomplished the identical ends without such statutory backing, and the legal authorities stood by and refused to intervene. The right to have one's choice of marriage partner respected by the larger society hinged on questions of race. And race was often pivotal to access to public services such as theatres, restaurants, pubs, hotels, and recreational facilities.

Yet, as deeply rooted, multilayered, and systemic as racism was in Canadian society, it was not monolithic in the sense that historians sometimes purport it to be. The evidence of resistance and protest that surfaces so frequently in the legal records is richly suggestive. There were compelling cross-currents competing for ascendancy inside Canadian courtrooms and without, as individuals stood up to contest the institutionalized laws of racial discrimination. Seizing upon the lack of definition of the words 'Chinese' and 'white' in the 'White Women's Labour Law,' lawyers for Asian-born clients tried to force home the complexity of the definitional exercise. Yee Clun attempted to escape from the strictures of the 'White Women's Labour Law' by capitalizing on his Christianity and his 'exemplary' and 'law-abiding character,' separating himself from the racially stigmatized Chinese community by virtue of his religion and respectability. Factors such as gender and class complicated the assessment still further, as the successful businesswoman Viola Desmond sought to stretch racial boundaries to encompass greater equality in recognition of her femininity and entrepreneurial status. Ira Johnson, targeted by the KKK because of his presumed Blackness, publicly proclaimed that his racial identity was considerably more amorphous and complex. If the courts had consulted the Inuit directly in 1930, they would undoubtedly have interrogated the issue of their racial definition in profoundly different ways than the government experts who offered testimony in *Re Eskimos*.

Wanduta and other Aboriginal spokespersons petitioned government officials and representatives of the British Crown repeatedly, objecting to the use of criminal law to sanction Aboriginal culture and spirituality.

Yee Clun and other Chinese Canadians actively resisted the web of discriminatory legislation that encircled their communities. E. Lionel Cross, Rev. H. Lawrence McNeil, and B.J. Spencer Pitt spoke out on behalf of the Black community when they demanded the prosecution of the Ku Klux Klan. Rabbi Maurice Nathan Eisendrath joined them. Viola Desmond, Pearleen Oliver, William Pearly Oliver, and Carrie Best pressed for an end to racial segregation and insisted that Canadian law be called to account for its role in maintaining racial hierarchies.

It would be a mistake to suggest, however, that the racial beliefs and attitudes of any particular racial group were entirely consistent and uniform. There were stark divisions within the Dakota community, between those who sided with Wanduta's efforts to protect traditional culture and spirituality and those who supported Chief Tunkan Cekiyana's desires for increased acculturation into the world of whites. Black activist E. Lionel Cross differed substantially from other Black spokesmen, Rev. H. Lawrence McNeil and B.J. Spencer Pitt, on the question of racial intermarriage. The Nova Scotia Black community split over the utility of legal challenges to racial segregation in theatres. Opinions varied greatly over the goals of anti-racist work, the best sites for struggle, the rationale for expanding or relaxing racial exclusivity, and the strategies to be used to accomplish such ends. Evidence of such disagreements is sometimes assumed to reflect weakness and lack of resolve on the part of racially subordinated communities. Another interpretation is that it reveals wide-ranging intellectual diversity and substantial freedom of expression within racialized groups.

Nor was it only 'non-white' individuals who lent their energies towards the reduction of racial discrimination. The historical record shows significant efforts from a diverse array of people. Malcolm Turriff and four other white businessmen from Rapid City registered their official protests over the conviction and internment of Wanduta after he performed the Grass Dance in southern Manitoba. George Coldwell, the white Brandon lawyer who represented Wanduta, proclaimed his client's treatment under Canadian law as overtly racist, charging: 'We do not see why any different justice should be meted out to them than to a white man and certainly no white man has been treated in the way this Indian has.' Edward Guss Porter, the white Belleville lawyer who represented Eliza Sero, introduced a private member's bill into the House of Commons to incorporate the Council for the Indian Tribes of Canada. He took Eliza Sero's confiscated fishing net sufficiently seriously that he helped her to launch a lawsuit for tortious damages against the government. Andrew Chisholm, the white London lawyer who joined forces with Porter in the case, mounted a detailed and sophisticated argument for Mohawk sovereignty on behalf of the Six Nations Grand River.

George Blair, the white city solicitor, warned Regina City Council that whether a licence applicant was 'Chinese, Japanese, Irish or Greek did not enter into the question,' adding: 'You have no right in the world to discriminate.' The white Saskatchewan judge Philip Mackenzie interpreted the legislative history of the 'White Women's Labour Law' as 'abolish[ing] the discriminatory principle.' William Templeton, the white editor of the Guelph *Mercury*, decried the intimidatory tactics of the KKK that would 'deny rights to worthy citizens because of their color, their creed and race.' He demanded the intervention of government authorities to bring the full weight of the law down upon the racist organization.

White Quebec judge John Archibald concluded that 'any regulation that deprived negroes, as a class, of privileges which all other members of the community had a right to demand, was not only unreasonable but entirely incompatible with our free democratic institutions.' The white Supreme Court of Canada judge Henry Davis pronounced racial segregation to be 'contrary to good morals and the public order.' When the NSAACP began to raise money to fund Viola Desmond's legal challenge to racial segregation, some of the first donors were white Nova Scotians. And Frederick Bissett, the white Halifax lawyer who ultimately lost Viola Desmond's case, donated his fee back to the anti-racist organization to promote its ongoing struggles.

Some of the whites who resisted racism in these cases were lawyers, who might be thought of merely as 'hired guns,' taking anti-racist positions because they were paid to do so by their clients. And some of the white lawyers who appeared in these cases seem not to have grasped much about the significance of racial hierarchy and domination, judging from the arguments they formulated. Yet there are persuasive indications from the surviving historical records that some whites, at least, were cognizant of the injustice of race discrimination in law. George Coldwell's stinging rebuke to Clifford Sifton concerning the racism inherent in Wanduta's prison sentence is one compelling example. George Blair's impassioned insistence on rooting out racism from the municipal licensing process is another. What is eminently clear from these case studies is that racism did not entirely envelop white Canadian society in an unrelieved manner throughout this period. There were white individuals who took explicitly anti-racist positions at specific moments in time.

The evidence of such thinking and activity places the behaviour of other whites into a different context than has traditionally been articulated. Those who espoused philosophies of white supremacy were not speaking in a moral vacuum. Indian Commissioner David Laird, Indian Agent G.H. Wheatley, and farming instructor E.H. Yeomans used every tool at their command to root out Aboriginal dance in a society where such actions were hotly contested by the First Nations and by some whites. Ontario judge William Renwick Riddell contemptuously dismissed Aboriginal sovereignty claims despite having heard voluminous legal submissions, backed up by detailed documentary evidence, about the historical relations between the British Crown and the Six Nations. The Regina president of the Local Council of Women, Maude Stapleford, and her counsel, Douglas Thom, expounded upon the moral dangers of allowing Yee Clun access to white female employees in the same venue that white teachers from the Regina Chinese Mission insisted that 'any girl would be safeguarded in his company.' Oakville Police chief David Kerr and Mayor J.B. Moat articulated smug complacency over the KKK raid against a backdrop of vocal protests from Black, Jewish, and labour leaders.

The complexity of perspectives and diversity of positions suggests the importance of further research and inquiry into the history of race discrimination in Canadian society and law. The paradigm of white supremacy was undoubtedly dominant over theories of racial equality in this period. But it did not go uncontested. There were acrimonious exchanges and divergent views about how issues of race should play out in the Canadian economic, political, social, and legal systems. Some of the individuals portrayed in the cases in this book chose to accentuate and expand racial inequalities. Others actively fought racial discrimination. While whites dominated the first group, and racially subordinated groups the second, some temporarily crossed racial boundaries in their understandings of race and their responses to racism.

Despite the incontrovertible evidence of racism that pervaded Canadian law and society during the first half of the twentieth century, the spectre of 'racelessness' looms large as a peculiarly Canadian mechanism for responding to racial issues. The pattern of 'racelessness' that pervades Canadian legal history encouraged Canadian citizens to maintain a 'stupefying innocence,' in the words of Dionne Brand, about the enormity of racial oppression. When the Supreme Court of Canada directed its gaze to the question of Eskimo status, no one seems to have thought that it mattered that all of the parties, witnesses, counsel, and judges were white. The unselfconscious whiteness that suffused the courtroom left no space for Aboriginal or Inuit presence. The early Mohawk claims of sovereignty were enthusiastically litigated by all-white counsel and all-white clients before all-white panels of judges, with no understanding that Aboriginal voices were germane to the issue. Because the whiteness of the proceeding was invisible to the participants, the evidence and arguments were seemingly 'raceless.'

The race-neutral name of the statute that plagued Yee Clun was An Act to Prevent the Employment of Female Labour in Certain Capacities. Eventually even the provisions were racially sanitized, so there was no overt reference to 'Chinese' employers and 'white' women and girls, at the same time as the intent of the legislators and the officials who administered the law remained steadfastly racial. The immigration laws set up to impede the entry of Blacks made no reference to skin pigmentation, accomplishing their ends by indirect and informal means. When the authorities prosecuted the Ku Klux Klan, there was no mention of race in the litigation. The Klan was apparently a raceless mob of men, and Isabel Jones was a raceless girl. Ira Johnson, of the contested racial identity, was erased from the narrative completely. When Viola Desmond's lawyer advanced her civil suit challenging racial segregation, he did so on the basis of tort doctrines and a writ of *certiorari* arrayed in racially neutral terms. None of the judges noted on the record that Viola Desmond was Black. No one made reference to the Roseland Theatre's racist seating policy. The trial proceeded as if it related to race-neutral tax evasion.

The 'stupefying innocence' permitted Canadian judges to make sweeping decisions concerning the status of racialized communities without having to consider the ramifications of their views. The legal position of the Inuit in Canadian society was not debated as a question of culture, language, resources, needs, or equity. Instead 'Eskimos' were ruled 'Indians' by judges who believed they were simply sorting out a little constitutional wrinkle. Confronted with similarly crucial questions about the legal status of the Mohawk, Canadian judges disregarded centuries of diplomatic negotiations, preserved in English documents and in wampum, apparently unconcerned about the task of sweeping away troublesome records of military and national affiliations.

Canadian legislators who passed legislation to prohibit Aboriginal dance appear almost addle-brained in their failure to take stock of what the new laws actually meant to Aboriginal communities. Prime Minister Macdonald 'forgot' to take out the mandatory minimum penalty provision. The minister of the Interior mischaracterized the provision as a 'misdemeanour' rather than the far more serious 'indictable' offence that Parliament enacted into law. At least three Indian Affairs officials knew that Wanduta had been convicted by a magistrate who had no jurisdiction, but no one stepped in to rectify the improper proceeding. If such problems caused any anxiety on the part of the authorities, there is not a tad of evidence to show for it.

Canadian legislators did not follow the example of the U.S. governments in passing laws that would prohibit interracial marriage. Instead, they accomplished similar goals by more indirect means. They passed laws preventing Asian men from hiring white women, and even then, they refused to be explicit about their motivations. White women's organizations insisted the law was 'not for the purpose of discriminating against an Oriental race,' but for the 'protection of white girls only.' Judge Mackenzie's order to issue Yee Clun a licence, while couched in the language of equality, did not lambast municipal politicians for their racism. He pretended he was simply requiring them to carry out the racially neutral intent of the legislators.

Professing a distinctively Canadian ethos, the 'Kanadian Knights of the KKK' purported to stand apart from the brutality and violence south of the border. Affixing 'maple leaves' to the insignia on their KKK robes, the 'Ku Klux Klan of Kanada' vowed to use more orderly means to accomplish its goals. The Crown Attorney who prosecuted the Ku Klux Klan insisted that he knew nothing about the Klan, and was 'not arguing against' its policies or right to exist. The only newspaper that made public the razing of Ira Johnson's home by fire added the postscript: 'no thought is expressed that the fire was of incendiary origin.' Reporters characterized the KKK as 'lads of the village,' 'tearing about the countryside in flivvers, adorned with flowing cotton, dancing around fiery crosses.' Canadian critics of the KKK resorted to 'raceless' sarcasm and humour to target the white-supremacist organization.

The deputy attorney general carefully declined to take issue with the KKK opposition to interracial marriage, challenging only its methods and strategies. The Ontario Court of Appeal also sidestepped any analysis of the Klan's ideology. Characterizing the legal issue as 'motive,' an 'immateriality,' Chief Justice Mulock avoided responding to the Klan's direct assertion that the reason for its terrifying raid against Ira Johnson constituted 'lawful excuse' under Canadian law. The widespread efforts of KKK sympathizers to use social and economic pressure to prevent cross-race marriages, the ubiquitous condemnation of such relationships in the press, and the avowed reluctance of many religious leaders to perform such marriage ceremonies were acceptable, legitimate activities according to Canadian officials. The only aspect of the Klan's foray to Oakville that attracted legal sanction was its 'un-Canadian,' mob-like march through public streets.

Canadians enacted no statutes mandating racial segregation in theatres, hotels, restaurants, or other facilities. The 'colour bar' was far more muted and informal, fluctuating over time and place, depending on the proclivities of local proprietors and their white clientele. When Viola Desmond's efforts to subvert racial segregation pulled her into the vortex of state-sanctioned proceedings, the law that was used to resolve the dispute was not one of racial segregation, but a race-neutral provision concerning theatre regulation. As the legal proceedings escalated, the judges who refused to overturn Viola Desmond's conviction took refuge in the finer points of criminal procedure, sanctimoniously concluding that it was a pity that she didn't choose the proper legal avenue for redress. The level of Canadian hypocrisy hit new heights when the manager of the Roseland Theatre publicly denied enforcing a racially segregated seating policy; it was just 'customary for colored persons to sit together in the balcony,' he chided, affecting a pronounced sense of wounded innocence.

The decades of the 1930s and 1940s witnessed some shift in the rhetorical analysis of race. Scientists began to deconstruct racial definitions and categories. Legislators began to enact statutes to prohibit racial and religious discrimination in the insurance industry, in social welfare programs, in the labour movement, in land transactions. The publication and display of racial and religious libel came under legislative attack. The first comprehensive human rights statute was enacted in Saskatchewan in 1947. Public analysis of racial discrimination took on new focus. As Pearleen Oliver stated: 'Hitler was dead and the Second World War was over.'

It was this perceived change in Canadian thought and institutions that caused Pearleen Oliver to urge her friend Viola Desmond to make a test case of her abusive treatment at the hands of the Roseland Theatre and 'take it to court.' The legal response turned out to be a crushing disappointment. No fewer than six white judges refused to rectify the disgraceful use of a tax provision to enforce racial segregation. The *Desmond* decision signified that whatever alterations had been wrought in Canadian law and society, at its essential core the change was only symbolic. The entrenched patterns of racial discrimination, the pervasive mythology of Canadian 'racelessness,' and the 'stupefying innocence' that were all hallmarks of this case, clarified to participants and observers alike that Canadian racism was staying the course.

Notes

Extensive notes with complete details, indicated by an asterisk, can be found under catalogues at the following Web site: www.utpress.utoronto.ca

1: Acknowledgments

1 Constance Backhouse, *Petticoats and Prejudice: Women and Law in Nineteenth-Century Canada* (Toronto: The Osgoode Society and Women's Press, 1991).
2 For references to the writings of Vijay Agnew, Himani Bannerji, Derrick Bell, Dionne Brand, Peggy Bristow, Carol Camper, Linda Carty, Patricia Hill Collins, Afua P. Cooper, Angela Davis, Kari Dehli, Richard Delgado, Sylvia Hamilton, Susan Heald, bell hooks, Gloria I. Joseph, Jill Lewis, Audre Lorde, Mari Matsuda, Kate McKenna, Patricia Monture-Angus, Toni Morrison, Roxanna Ng, M. Nourbese Philip, Sherene H. Razack, Adrienne Shadd, Makeda Silvera, Cornel West, and Patricia Williams, see *
3 For references to the writing of Dionne Brand, Beth Brant, Maria Campbell, Ann du Cille, Lenore Keeshig-Tobias, J. Larbalestier, Ann McGrath, Winona Stevenson, and May Yee on the importance of identity and experience in interpreting historical and other information, see *

1: Introduction

1 Instructions to Officers taking the Dominion Census, Introduction to the Census Report of Canada for 1901, *Fourth Census of Canada 1901*, vol. 1

(Ottawa: S.E. Dawson, 1902), sections 47–54, pp. xviii–xix, as quoted in *In re Coal Mines Regulation Act and Amendment Act, 1903* (1904) 10 B.C.R. 408 (B.C.S.C.), at 427. The census was taken as of midnight, 31 March 1901. The instructions also contain a fifth category: 'Persons of mixed white and red blood – commonly known as "breeds"– will be described by the addition of the initial letters "f.b." for French breed, "e.b." for English breed, "s.b." for Scotch breed, "i.b." for Irish breed … Other mixtures of Indians besides the four above specified are rare, and may be described by the letters "o.b." for other breed.' On the history of the word 'Caucasian' and the classification of races by the colours white, yellow, black, red, and brown, see *

2 For census details and references to colour terminology found in Canadian novels, poetry and historical writing, see *

3 'General Review,' *Ninth Census of Canada, 1951,* vol. 10 (Ottawa: Edmond Cloutier, 1953), at 131–2.

4 For census details, see *

5 For some sources in the voluminous literature on the historical analysis of 'race,' see *

6 For references on the racial ideology that emerged from slave cultures; on the racialization of Saxon, Celtic, Norman, Irish, Welsh, Scottish, and English communities; on the contestation of the 'whiteness' of people from Syria, Armenia, Arabia, India, and the Philippines in American legal doctrine; on the racial depiction of religious intolerance against Jews, Mennonites, and Doukhobours in Canada; and on the 1941 census classification of 'Jewish' and 'Ukrainian' races, see *

7 On the 'outsider' status of the Jewish scientists who offered critical analysis of 'scientific' racial understandings, and the semantic nature of shifting categorizations from 'race' to 'culture,' see *

8 For references to the key United Nations documents and the postwar reversal of values in theory if not in practice, see *

9 On the use of colour to portray racial designations and the tenacious assertions that most people 'know it when they see it,' see *

10 Erica Chung-Yue Tao, 'Re-defining Race Relations – Beyond the Threat of "Loving Blackness",' *Canadian Journal of Women and the Law* 6:2 (1993), 455, notes at 457: 'Language and conventions in writing are integral to internalized colonization. The capitalization of Black and Blackness becomes a disruption in reading, because it breaches the standard way of communicating in textual format. In this way, capitalization of Black represents a perverse usage of the colonizer's language, and is, therefore, a visual and linguistic subversion of white supremacy. At the same time, capitalizing Black also affirms pride and power in group identity. For example, we say

we are Canadians, not canadians. Finally, the word "white" will not be capitalized on the grounds that white and whiteness are the reference points by which all other colours or racially defined groups are measured, named, described, and understood. To capitalize white would be, in effect, to say the obvious and affirm the norm.' For additional reference, see *

11 Ian F. Haney López, *White by Law: The Legal Construction of Race* (New York: New York University Press, 1996), notes at 158, citing Barbara J. Flagg '"Was Blind, But Now I See": White Race Consciousness and the Requirement of Discriminatory Intent,' *Michigan Law Review* 91:5 (1993), 953 at 969, and Trina Grillo and Stephanie M. Wildman, 'Obscuring the Importance of Race: The Implication of Making Comparisons between Racism and Sexism (or Other -Isms),' *Duke Law Journal* 1991: 2(1991), 397 at 405: 'Transparency "may be a defining characteristic of whiteness: to be white is not to think about it" ... "White supremacy makes whiteness the normative model. Being the norm allows whites to ignore race, except when they perceive race (usually some else's) as intruding upon their lives." ... Indeed, for many Whites their racial identity becomes uppermost in their mind only when they find themselves in the company of large numbers of non-Whites, and then it does so in the form of a supposed vulnerability to non-White violence, rendering Whiteness in the eyes of many Whites not a privileged status but a victimized one.' For references to the literature on 'whiteness,' see *

12 Given the repetitive saturation of such commentary in historical literature, I do not think it is productive to cite the specific publications in which such statements appear, or to name the authors involved. Some of these statements come from Canadian historians, others from American and British historians. All seem to share the same perspectives.

13 Evelyn Brooks Higginbotham, 'African-American Women's History and the Metalanguage of Race,' *Signs* 17:2 (Winter 1992), 251 at 267.

14 Kenan Malik, *The Meaning of Race: Race, History and Culture in Western Society* (Basingstoke: Macmillan, 1996), notes at 1 that 'the term "racism" entered the popular language for the first time in the interwar years.' Elazar Barkan, *The Retreat of Scientific Racism* (Cambridge: Cambridge University Press, 1992), notes at 2–3 that the use of 'racism' as a derogatory neologism was first recorded in English in the 1930s. The word 'racialism,' a precursor to 'racism,' denoting prejudice based on race difference, was 'introduced into the language at the turn of the century.'

15 In 1944, the Halifax Colored Citizens Improvement League 'argued that the state should promote better race relations by including materials in the curriculum which represented an accurate history of Africans, including

their contributions to society': Agnes Calliste, 'Blacks' Struggle for Education Equity in Nova Scotia,' in Vincent D'Oyley, ed., *Innovations in Black Education in Canada* (Toronto: Umbrella, 1994), at 25. Carrie M. Best, *That Lonesome Road: The Autobiography of Carrie M. Best* (New Glasgow: Clarion, 1977), describes the absence of Black historical research in Canada, and expresses the importance of redressing the omission. In 1976, the National Congress of Black Women decried the lack of attention to Black history in Canada, and demanded that 'Black history should be included in the curriculum at all levels in the schools.' See Lawrence Hill, *Women of Vision: The Story of the Canadian Negro Women's Association, 1951–1976* (Toronto: Umbrella Press, 1996), at 64–5. The Women's Book Committee of the Chinese Canadian National Council notes that, although Canada's Chinese community possesses a long and rich past in this country, 'little of our history has been recorded,' with Canadian history texts 'ignoring aboriginal peoples' and 'people of other racial and cultural backgrounds.' See The Women's Book Committee, *Jin Guo: Voices of Chinese Canadian Women* (Toronto: Women's Press, 1992), at 11. Aboriginal communities add that, when they have been included in traditional historical materials, the accounts are generally more hurtful than helpful.

16 Howard Adams, a Saskatchewan Métis, is scathing in his indictment of the history written by whites about Aboriginal peoples: 'White social scientists have written extensively on native people, but from the perspective of ethnocentrism and white supremacy. Such ideological writings have little validity in regard to the daily lives of Indians and Métis in their colonized communities […] The native people in a colony are not allowed a valid interpretation of their history, because the conquered do not write their own history. They must endure a history that shames them, destroys their confidence, and causes them to reject their heritage. Those in power command the present and shape the future by controlling the past, particularly for the natives. A fact of imperialism is that it systematically denies native people a dignified history.' See Howard Adams, *Prison of Grass: Canada from a Native Point of View* (Saskatoon: Fifth House, 1989, orig. pub. 1975), at 6, 43. George Erasmus and Joe Sanders, 'Canadian History: An Aboriginal Perspective,' in Diane Engelstad and John Bird, eds., *Nation to Nation: Aboriginal Sovereignty and the Future of Canada* (Concord, Ont.: House of Anansi Press, 1992), 3, note at 6: 'Non-native people have … distorted history. It is very difficult to find a history textbook in any province of this country that accurately tells the story of how our two peoples came together. Instead, there are books in which we are still being called pagans and savages, without an accurate reflection of the solemn agreements that were made and which indicate that

indigenous people were to continue to govern themselves.' James W.St.G. Walker, 'The Indian in Canadian Historical Writing,' *Canadian Historical Association Historical Papers* (Ottawa, 1971), 21, surveyed a cross-section of books on Canadian history published from 1829 to 1970, and found them depicting 'Indians' as 'savage,' 'cruel,' 'treacherous,' 'fiendish,' 'bloodthirsty,' 'superstitious,' and 'grotesque.' See also Georges E. Sioui, *For an Amerindian Autohistory: An Essay on the Foundations of a Social Ethic* (Montreal: McGill-Queen's University Press, 1992), and Bruce G. Trigger, *Natives and Newcomers: Canada's 'Heroic Age' Reconsidered* (Montreal: McGill-Queen's University Press, 1985).

17 Robin W. Winks, *The Blacks in Canada: A History* (New Haven: Yale University Press, 1971).

18 For fuller details, see the bibliography.

19 See, for example, B. Singh Bolaria and Peter S. Li, *Racial Oppression in Canada* (Toronto: Garamond, 1988); Angus McLaren, *Our Own Master Race: Eugenics in Canada, 1885–1945* (Toronto: McClelland & Stewart, 1990); Ormond McKague, *Racism in Canada* (Saskatoon: Fifth House, 1991); Julian Sher, *White Hoods: Canada's Ku Klux Klan* (Vancouver: New Star, 1983); Martin Robin, *Shades of Right: Nativist and Fascist Politics in Canada, 1920–1940* (Toronto: University of Toronto Press, 1992); James W.St.G. Walker, *'Race,' Rights and the Law in the Supreme Court of Canada* (Waterloo: The Osgoode Society and Wilfrid Laurier University Press, 1997).

20 See, for example, the discussion in chapter 3 regarding the failure of local judicial figures to take down evidence and file written references to cases involving the prosecution of Aboriginal dance.

21 On the culling of racialized legal records, see, for example, the destruction of files regarding *Sero v Gault*, discussed in chapter 4.

22 Dionne Brand, *Bread Out of Stone* (Toronto: Coach House Press, 1994), at 178. See also George J. Sefa Dei, 'The Politics of Educational Change: Taking Anti-Racism Education Seriously,' in Vic Satzewich, ed., *Racism and Social Inequality in Canada: Concepts, Controversies and Strategies of Resistance* (Toronto: Thompson Educational Publishing, 1998), 299–314.

2: Race Definitions Run Amuck

1 Richard J. Diubaldo 'The Absurd Little Mouse: When Eskimos Became Indians,' *Journal of Canadian Studies* 16:2 (Summer 1981), 34 at 34.

2 *Re Eskimos*, [1939] 80 S.C.R. 104; [1939] 2 D.L.R. 417.

3 For biographical details on Jenness, see *

4 'Factum on Behalf of the Attorney General of Canada, In the Supreme Court

of Canada, In the Matter of a Reference as to whether the term "Indians" in
Head 24 of Section 91 of the British North America Act, 1867, Includes
Eskimo Inhabitants of the Province of Quebec,' at 26–7 [hereinafter cited as
Canada Factum]; 'Exhibit C-47, Case on Behalf of the Attorney General of
Canada, in the Supreme Court of Canada, In the Matter of a Reference as to
Whether the Term "Indians" in Head 24 of Section 91 of the British North
America Act, 1867, Includes Eskimo Inhabitants of the Province of Quebec'
(Ottawa: King's Printer, 1938) [hereinafter cited as Canada Case], at 303;
Diamond Jenness, *Indians of Canada* (Ottawa: National Museum of Canada,
1932; repub. Ministry of Supply & Services Canada, 1977), at 6.

5 Canada Factum, at 19–20. Jenness was not the first to draw a comparison
between the English and the Italians, on one hand, and the Indians and
Eskimos, on the other. In 1927, W.H.B. Hoare, a Department of the Interior
fieldman living in the Barren Lands, had written to his superior, O.S. Finnie,
the first director of the Northwest Territories Branch of the Department of
the Interior, arguing that 'the Inuit could not treated or dealt with like the
Indians, as they were as widely different from one another as is the Englishman from the Italian. [...] The Indian is of low mentality, and seems a dour,
discontented fellow with no ambition to better his conditions either materi-
ally or intellectually. [...] The Eskimo looks upon himself as the equal of
any white man.' See Public Archives of Canada, RG22/253/40-8-1/1.

6 On the group cohesiveness of Englishmen, Scotsmen, Welshmen, and
Ulstermen who emigrated to Canada, and the development of the pan-
British identity in North America, see Ross McCormack, 'Cloth Caps and
Jobs: The Ethnicity of English Immigrants in Canada 1900–1914,' in J.M.
Bumsted, *Interpreting Canada's Past: Vol. II, After Confederation* (Toronto:
Oxford University Press, 1986), at 175–91. For biographical details on the
judges, and the racial and ethnic make-up of the Supreme Court of Canada,
see *

7 'Exhibit C-47,' Canada Case, at 303, citing Jenness, *Indians of Canada*, at 6.

8 Jenness, *Indians of Canada*, at 405.

9 For statutory reference, see *

10 For statutory reference, see *

11 For statutory reference, see *

12 For federal statutory references on Indian status from 1869 to 1951, see *

13 For federal statutory references on Indian status from 1876 to 1951, see *

14 For the 1876 statutory reference to the status of Indian women, and legislation from 1869 to 1951, see *

15 For the 1876 statutory reference to the status of illegitimate Indian children
and Indians who resided in a foreign country, and legislation up to 1951,
see *

16 For federal statutory references to 'half-breeds' from 1876 to 1951, see *

17 For the 1876 statutory provision, relevant sections of legislation in force until 1951, and a judicial opinion on this point, see *

18 For the 1887 statutory reference, the provision re-enacted in 1927, and legal commentary on the problems posed by the implementation of this rule, see *

19 George Manuel and Michael Posluns, *The Fourth World: An Indian Reality* (Don Mills, Ont.: Collier-Macmillan Canada, 1974), note at 21 that 'the Indian Act ... was passed into law by Parliament without any reference to the realities of Indian life as Indian spokesmen might have explained them.' Critiquing the narrowing of definition, they state at 22: 'It was no longer a question of a person being "reputed to be an Indian," a phrase that could be taken to mean accepted by the band as a member, rather than a strict tracing of male blood line, an English way of tracing lineage not accepted by very many Indian societies.' Manuel and Posluns add at 241: 'Indian customs of inheritance and for defining identity have varied from nation to nation according to political and economic structure and religious beliefs. Many trace through the mother's line, some through the father's. My own [i.e., Manuel's] people [Shushwap Nation] work through a mixture of both, as do many of our neighbours.'

20 For the British Columbia provisions of 1903–4 and 1920, see * For a full account of the electoral restrictions for First Nations peoples, see discussion of *Sero* v *Gault* in chapter 4.

21 For the 1922 British Columbia provision, see *

22 For the 1923 British Columbia provision, see *

23 For the 1950 British Columbia provision, see *

24 Robert Berkhofer, *The White Man's Indian: Images of the American Indian from Columbus to the Present* (New York: Knopf, 1978), suggests that, as Europeans developed the idea of 'Indian,' they collapsed into a single group all of the diverse cultures, societies, language groups, and identities of indigenous peoples of the Americas – people who did not think of themselves as one group or one continental people when they were first encountered.

25 For the Saskatchewan provisions of 1908 and 1930 and the Alberta provisions of 1909 and 1946, see *

26 For the 1938 Alberta provision, see * Some individuals of mixed white and Aboriginal ancestry appear to have identified primarily with either their First Nations or their European inheritance. Others established a unique racial identity described as 'Métis,' especially in the fur-trade areas of Rupert's Land and the Great Lakes region. On the creation of the separate Métis identity in Canada, see *

27 For the 1940 Alberta provision, see *

28 For the 1927 and 1946 Ontario provisions, see *

29 *Rex* v *Tronson* (1931), 57 C.C.C. 383 (B.C. County Ct.).

30 *Rex* v *Tronson*, at 518–21.

31 For sources that consider the impact of alcohol upon Aboriginal communities, see *

32 For a more detailed account of the legislation regarding alcohol and First Nations peoples, which was punitive in its effect and failed miserably in its capacity to offer support to First Nations communities, see Constance Backhouse, '"Your Conscience Will Be Your Own Punishment": The Racially-Motivated Murder of Gus Ninham, Ontario, 1902,' in Blaine Baker and Jim Phillips, eds., *Essays in the History of Canadian Law* (Toronto: The Osgoode Society, 1999). The provincial and federal statutes enacted between 1777 and 1951 are listed at *

33 *Regina* v *Howson* (1894), 1 Terr. L.R. 492.

34 *Regina* v *Howson*, at 493–6.

35 For the 1894 provision, which remained in force until 1951, as well as an 1867 liquor ordinance from British Columbia that failed to define 'Indian' at all, see *

36 *The Queen* v *Mellon* (1900), 7 C.C.C. 179.

37 *The Queen* v *Mellon*, at 180–1. On the *mens rea* requirements for the offence, see *Rex* v *Brown* (1930), 55 C.C.C. 29 (Toronto Police Ct.), where it is stated at 32–3: 'Under the decisions, *mens rea* must be proved … The evidence must amount to positive knowledge on the part of the accused as to the nationality of the purchaser, no matter how stupid he may have been.' For additional judicial references, see *

38 *The King* v *Pickard* (1908), 14 C.C.C. 33.

39 *The King* v *Pickard*, at 33–5. *Rex* v *Bennett* (1930), 55 C.C.C. 27 (Ont. County Ct.), would tangle with the issue of deceptive appearances as well. The accused had been convicted of selling wine to Jack Post, an 'Indian.' On appeal, the defence argued that the accused 'did not know or believe or suspect him to be an Indian,' but thought he 'was a Japanese.' The appeal court adjourned the hearing so that the judge might take a look at the individual concerned. 'He is typically Indian in appearance,' pronounced the presiding judge, 'and I do not see how the accused could have very well taken him for other than an Indian. Certainly his appearance would at least cause the accused to suspect him to be an Indian.'

40 *The King* v *Pickard*, at 33–5.

41 *Rex* v *Verdi* (1914), 23 C.C.C. 47.

42 Emma LaRoque states that 'there are some words that are not reclaimable and "squaw" is one of them,' representing 'rapist imagery, where rape and murder merge [and] the grossest acts of the objectification of human beings.' Harmut Lutz notes that one of the definitions of 'squaw' from the *Oxford*

English Dictionary is 'a kneeling figure used for target practice,' and also 'a certain position in which a barrel is held when it is tapped,' so that it is 'a term denoting sexual penetration and violence.' See the text of this conversation in Harmut Lutz, *Contemporary Challenges: Conversations with Canadian Native Authors* (Saskatoon: Fifth House, 1991), at 191–2, 201–2.

43 *Rex* v *Verdi*, at 48–9. The court held: 'The fact that this man voted last summer and did not since resign from the tribe, together with the other facts in evidence, satisfy me that he is an "Indian".'

44 Pauktuutit, *The Inuit Way: A Guide to Inuit Culture* (Ottawa: Pauktuutit, Inuit Women's Association, 1989), at 4; David Damas, 'Arctic,' in William C. Sturtevant, ed., *Handbook of North American Indians*, vol. 5 (Washington: Smithsonian Institution, 1984), at 6–7. Marie Wadden, *Nitassinan: The Innu Struggle to Reclaim Their Homeland* (Vancouver: Douglas & McIntyre, 1991), notes at 26: 'According to [ethnolinguist] José Mailhot, it was the Innu, in conversation with the Basques, who coined the term *aiskimeu* to refer to their Inuit neighbours. She believes the word meant "those who speak a strange language," not "eaters of raw meat" as is popularly believed. The Innu word was eventually spelled "esquimaux" by the French and "eskimo" by the English.' Damas also suggests another possible First Nations source: the Ojibwa 'e-skipot.' Damas mentions additional alternative spellings: Esquimawes, Esquimaud, Esquimos, Eskemoes, Eskima, Eskimeaux, Esquimeaux, Excomminquois, Exquimaux, Ehuskemay, Uskemau, Uskimay, Eusquemay, and Usquemow.

45 Pauktuutit, *The Inuit Way*, at 4. Damas, 'Arctic,' notes at 7 that the commonest self-designation within the Canadian Arctic is 'Inuit,' with several other terms also in use: 'Inupiat (for those of North Alaska), Yupik (southwestern Alaska), and Yuit (Siberia and Saint Lawrence Island).' The 1977 Inuit Circumpolar Conference in Barrow, Alaska, officially adopted 'Inuit' as a designation for all, regardless of local usages.

46 For the 1919 Quebec provision, see *

47 For the 1930 Northwest Territories ordinance, see *

48 For the 1934 provision and a later 1938 provision, see *

49 For the 1948 ordinance, see *

50 For the 1882 provision, see * A later provision passed in 1924 and in force through 1952 (see *) altered the wording to prohibit sales of alcoholic liquor 'to any Esquimaux or Indian.' Surprisingly, the 1882 statute would be the only one cited by the Supreme Court of Canada in its ultimate decision: *Re Eskimos* at 114. The judges ignored the 1924 amendment to the Newfoundland statute separating 'Esquimaux' from 'Indian.'

51 The Minister of the Interior, Hon. Charles A. Stewart, initially proposed to add the following section to the Indian Act: 'The Superintendent General of

Indian Affairs shall have the control and management of the lands and property of the Eskimos in Canada and the provisions of Part I of the Indian Act shall apply to the said Eskimo in so far as they are applicable to their condition and mode of life, and the Department of Indian Affairs shall have the management, charge and direction of Eskimo affairs.' Stewart's explanation was that, with the expansion of the fur trade, there was increasing connection between whites and Eskimos, police posts were being set up in the North, and there was need to establish greater governmental coordination in dealing with the Eskimo. Several legislators objected to the draft provision. One questioned whether 'any request had been made to the government by the Eskimos through their chiefs that they be brought within the provisions of the Indian Act.' No answer was forthcoming. The Leader of the Opposition, Arthur Meighen, objected strenuously to equating Eskimos with Indians, arguing that decades of governmental wardship had not improved the status of Indians, and that there was no need to 'put our wings all around [the Eskimo's] property and tell him he is our ward and that we will look after him. [...] My own opinion would be to leave them alone – make them comply with our criminal law and give them all the benefit of our civil law; in other words, treat them as everybody else is treated. I should not like to see the same policy precisely applied to the Eskimos as we have applied to the Indians.' Meighen's position carried the day, and the provision was shortened to state only that the superintendent general should have charge of Eskimo affairs. See Canada, House of Commons, *Parliamentary Debates* [Hansard; hereinafter cited as *Debates*], 10 June 1924, at 2992–3; 30 June 1924, at 3823–7; 14 July 1924, at 4409–13.

52 *An Act to amend the Indian Act*, S.C. 1924, c.47, s.1; *Debates* 14 July 1924, at 4409.

53 *An Act to amend the Indian Act*, S.C. 1930, c.25, s.1. *The Indian Act*, S.C. 1951, c.29, s.4(1), provides: 'This Act does not apply to the race of aborigines commonly referred to as Eskimos.' *Debates*, 31 March 1930, at 1091–1101.

54 *Debates*, 31 March 1930, at 1092. The 'Scotch' reference was supplied by the Hon. Charles A. Dunning, Minister of Finance.

55 Diamond Jenness, *Eskimo Administration: II. Canada* (Montreal: Arctic Institute of North America, 1964), at 10, 22; Bobbie Kalman and Ken Faris, *Arctic Whales and Whaling* (New York: Crabtree, 1988).

56 For sources on the sexual intermixture, see *

57 On the eastern Arctic, see 'Factum on Behalf of the Attorney General of the Province of Quebec, In the Supreme Court of Canada, In the Matter of a Reference as to Whether the Term "Indians" in Head 24 of Section 91 of the British North America Act, 1867, Includes Eskimo Inhabitants of the Prov-

ince of Quebec' [hereinafter cited as Quebec Factum], at 24, citing Jenness. On the western Arctic, see Emoke J.E. Szathmary, 'Human Biology of the Arctic,' in Sturtevant, ed., *Handbook of North American Indians*, at 64. Dorothy Harley Eber, *Images of Justice* (Montreal and Kingston: McGill-Queen's University Press, 1997), describes at 51 the travels of Morris Pokiak, 'half Inuk, half black,' who used to trade by boat along the Arctic coast in the 1920s and 1930s.

58 Quebec Factum, at 7. The original reference comes from Jenness, *Indians of Canada*, at 247.

59 For examples of provisions passed within the federal jurisdiction, the North-west Territories, Newfoundland, and Quebec, see *

60 For the 1911 Newfoundland provision, a provision passed in 1916, and some legislative history surrounding these, see *

61 For the 1949 ordinances, see *

62 For the 1951 provision, see *

63 For sources on Inuit migration, see *

64 For sources on Inuit languages, see *

65 Jenness, *Eskimo Administration*, at 25, 146; 'Exhibit C-47,' Canada Case, at 305–20. This heroic portrayal ought to be juxtaposed with some of the other passages Jenness concocted, which were distinctly patronizing and dismiss-ive in tone. See, for example, at 128: '[The Eskimo] are a fragmented, amor-phous race that lacks all sense of history, inherits no pride of ancestry, and discerns no glory in past events or past achievements. Until we Europeans shattered their isolation four centuries ago they were more rigidly confined than the dwellers in Plato's cave: no shadowy figures from the outer world ever flickered on their prison wall to provoke new images and new ideas, and not even a Mohammed could have drawn them out of that prison to unite them into a nation.' For a critical assessment of Jenness's contributions to Inuit culture, see Sidney L. Harring, 'The Rich Men of the Country: Canadian Law in the Land of the Copper Inuit, 1914–1930,' *Ottawa Law Review* 21:1 (1989), 1 at 30–9.

66 For sources on contact between whites and the Inuit, see *

67 For references, see *

68 For references, see *

69 Zebedee Nungak, 'Quebecker?? Canadian? ... Inuk!' in Bruce W. Hodgins and Kerry A. Cannon, eds., *On the Land: Confronting the Challenges to Aborigi-nal Self-Determination in Northern Quebec and Labrador* (Toronto: Betelgeuse, 1995), at 19. Mary Ellen Turpel-Lafond notes in 'Oui the People? Conflicting Visions of Self-Determination in Quebec,' in Hodgins and Cannon, eds., *On the Land*, 43 at 66, that these land transfers fly in the face of Inuit national

heritage: 'The Inuit in Quebec have stated that they are part of one Inuit nation in Canada and part of a larger Inuit nation in the Circumpolar Region.' See also the comments of Grand Chief Matthew Coon Come in 'Clearing the Smokescreen,' in Hodgins and Cannon, eds., *On the Land*, 7 at 8–9; Resolution of the Nunavik Leaders Conference, Montreal, 8 December 1994.

70 For reference, see *

71 For references, see *

72 Jenness, *Eskimo Administration*, at 52. Unofficially, the federal Department of Indian Affairs had been providing some relief to Inuit deemed destitute since about 1880. Jenness notes at 32–3 and 40 that the police and traders from the Hudson's Bay Company and Revillon Frères, who served as intermediaries, distributed approximately $4,700 annually for medical attention and education at mission schools on Herschel Island between 1918 and 1923. A full-time physician was installed on Baffin Island in 1926.

73 The estimated total Inuit population of the Canadian Arctic was 6,250; Canada Factum, at 6, citing the Dominion Bureau of Statistics, based on 1935 data.

74 For references, see *

75 For references, see *

76 Jenness, *Eskimo Administration*, at 52, citing Canada Department of the Interior Annual Report, 1933–4, at 35, and W.C. Bethune, *Canada's Eastern Arctic, Its History, Resources, Population and Administration* (Ottawa: Department of Interior, 1934), filed as Exhibit Q-3 in 'Case on Behalf of the Attorney General of Quebec, in the Supreme Court of Canada, In the Matter of a Reference as to Whether the Term "Indians" in Head 24 of Section 91 of the British North America Act, 1867, Includes Eskimo Inhabitants of the Province of Quebec' (Ottawa: King's Printer, 1938) [hereinafter cited as Quebec Case], at 161. Jenness also notes that the five hundred green buffalo hides that were distributed in addition to the meat 'were too thick for clothing, but made tolerable bed-robes, rather heavy, however, to carry on the back during the summer months.'

77 Jenness, *Eskimo Administration*, at 40; Richard Diubaldo, *The Government of Canada and the Inuit: 1900–1967* (Ottawa: Research Branch, Corporate Policy, Indian and Northern Affairs Canada, 1985), at 37. On the starvation along the Ungava coast, which continued well into the 1940s, see Dorothy Mesher, *Kuujjuaq: Memories and Musings* (Duncan, B.C.: Unica, 1995), at 36.

78 30–1 Vict., c. 3 (U.K.)

79 For provisions on the reference power enacted between 1875 and 1927, see *

80 Barry L. Strayer, *The Canadian Constitution and the Courts: The Function and Scope of Judicial Review*, 3d ed. (Toronto: Butterworths, 1988), at 313.

81 Notice of the reference was apparently given to the Provinces of Quebec, Ontario, Manitoba, Alberta, and Saskatchewan. Why these provinces were singled out is not indicated. Quebec Factum, at 1.

82 In the 1930s, most Inuit were dispersed throughout the North, with a small number living at the missions and the Hudson's Bay Company outposts. Those most knowledgeable about Inuit history, culture, and perspective would have been the elders, shamans, and camp leaders drawn from among the most successful hunters. The Inuit Tapirisat of Canada was first formed as an association separate from the Indian Brotherhood of Canada in 1971.This information was drawn from interviews with Inuit elders – Emile Immaroituk, Mariano Aupilarjuk, Marie Tulemaaq, and Akeeshoo Joamie – during the 'Traditions Seminar' of the Legal Studies Program, Nunavut Arctic College, Nunatta Campus, Iqaluit, N.T., 20 July–2 August 1997, and an interview with Paul Quassa, negotiator for the Nunavut Land Claim Agreement, Iqaluit, N.T., 11 September 1997. See also Peter Pitseolak and Dorothy Harley Eber, *People from Our Side: A Life Story with Photographs and Oral Biography* (Montreal and Kingston: McGill-Queen's University Press, 1993), at 77, where Peter Pitseolak notes: 'Before the [Hudson's] Bay [Company] arrived, there was no real boss in an area. Each camp would have a leader – the biggest man and the best hunter would be head. He'd be respected. After the Bay came ... [t]he white men made their own appointments. Sometimes the white men picked a man we didn't like too well. But ... I have always thought that the white men picked a boss who could talk well, who had a good mind. The white men looked for the reliable man.' Pauktuutit, *The Inuit Way*, notes at 15: 'Inuit society was largely egalitarian with no hierarchy or formal authority. Individuals were largely free to do as they wished as long as their actions did not disturb others. The basic system of making decisions for the group was based on consensus. Major decisions affecting the group would be discussed among the adults. People would voice their view and compromise the final decision to ensure that everyone accepted it. People with special skills, talents or knowledge, such as a respected hunter, an elder or a shaman, could be solicited for their opinion on a particular issue but their advice was not binding. Their ability to influence others was limited by the degree to which people chose to follow their advice.'

83 Jenness, *Eskimo Administration*, at 17, 30, 43, 49, 55, 90. One of the few exceptions, according to Jenness, at 23, was the first director of the Northwest Territories Branch of the Department of the Interior, O.S. Finnie.

84 'Stewart, James McGregor,' in H.E. Durant, *National Reference Book on Canadian Business Personalities*, 10th ed. (Canadian Newspaper Service, 1954), at

96–7. Stewart was assisted in the case by C.P. Plaxton, KC, the federal deputy minister of Justice.

85 'Desilets, Auguste, Q.C.,' in Durant, *National Reference Book*, at 698–700. Desilets was assisted in the case by C.A. Seguin, KC, and Edouard Asselin, deputy attorney general of the Province of Quebec.

86 'Order of Reference by the Deputy of the Governor General in Council, dated the 2nd day of April, 1935' (P.C. 867). According to federal counsel C.P. Plaxton, KC, the delay in scheduling the first hearing was largely attributable to Quebec. See Canada Case, at 31.

87 Quebec Factum, at 3, 31. See also the comment at 6: 'Of course, in this as in a great many other matters relating to science, there is no absolute unanimity. Nowhere else than in the field of science does the axiom *tot capita tot sententiae* receive a more frequent application.' The factum takes issue at 23 with Dr Hooton, apologizing at the outset for 'lacking reverence to such an eminent scientist.' See 55 for one reference to 'our humble opinion.'

88 Quebec Factum, at 23–4, 27, 53–4.

89 See, for example, Canada Factum, at 4, 7, 19–21, 23; Correspondence from Stewart to C.P. Plaxton, QC, 18 September 1934, Department of Justice files, Ottawa, as cited in Diubaldo, *Government of Canada and the Inuit*, at 40.

90 Canada Factum, at 16–20.

91 Canada Factum, at 20–3; Canada Case, at 96.

92 Quebec Factum, at 32–4.

93 Quebec Factum, at 35–53.

94 Quebec Factum, at 46–51.

95 Quebec Factum, at 22, 52; 'Exhibit Q-180,' Quebec Case, at 591–4. Diamond and Eileen Jenness were married in 1919, and raised three sons in Ottawa: see William E. Taylor, Jr., 'Foreword,' in Jenness, *Indians of Canada*, at p. v.

96 Eileen Jenness, *The Indian Tribes of Canada* (Toronto: Ryerson Press, 1933), at 6, 9, 102–4. The extract from 'Exhibit Q-180,' Quebec Case, at 594, ends after the first paragraph of this quote.

97 Quebec Factum, at 2–3, 22.

98 Quebec Factum, at 31.

99 Otto Klineberg, *Race Differences* (New York: Harper, 1935), at 17. On Klineberg's Canadian origins and his intellectual career, see *

100 For sources on the history of the word 'race,' see *

101 'Exhibit C-100,' Canada Case, at 384, citing C. Linnaeus, *Systema Naturae*, 5th ed. (London, 1747).

102 Klineberg, *Race Differences*, at 20, citing J.F. Blumenbach, *Anthropological Treatises* (London, 1865); J.C. Nott and G.R. Gliddon, *Types of Mankind* (Philadelphia, 1854); M. Muller, *Lectures on the Science of Language* (London,

1864); M. Muller, *Biographies of Words and the Home of the Aryas* (London, 1888); and J. Deniker, *The Races of Man* (New York, 1900). For reference to Blumenbach's research, see 'Exhibit C-46,' Canada Case, at 267–302; 'Exhibit C-100,' Canada Case, at 384. For reference to Nott and Gliddon's text, see Canada Factum at 24 and 27, and extracts produced in 'Exhibit C-99,' Canada Case, at 383; 'Exhibit C-114,' Canada Case, at 397–9.

103 For references on the evolution of racial ideology, see *

104 For references on the critique of Herbert Spencer's work, see *

105 Minnie Aodla Freeman, 'Living in Two Hells,' in Penny Petrone, ed., *Northern Voices: Inuit Writing in English* (Toronto: University of Toronto Press, 1988), at 241. Freeman, born in 1936 on Cape Horn Island in James Bay, adds, at 241–2: 'Over the years scientists have always been very welcome in Inuit communities. Some have been adopted by Inuit – in fact I adopted one permanently. […] As scientists are often willing to admit, Inuit have clothed them, fed them, taken them to wherever they wanted to go to do their studies. Often Inuit have taken chances, in matters of life and death, because they felt responsible for a particular scientist. We Inuit have met many different kinds of scientists, in terms of personality as well as what they wanted to study. We have studied them while they studied us. […] Personally I have been involved with scientists since I was born. […] But that doesn't mean I have to like everything scientists do – does it? […] My question is, when are you scientists going to start to include in your budgets funds to have the information you gather translated into *inuktitut* and send back north?'

106 See, for example, H.L. Shapiro, *The Alaskan Eskimo: A Study of the Relationship between the Eskimo and the Chipewyan Indians of Central Canada* (New York: The American Museum of Natural History, 1931).

107 Griffith Taylor, *Environment, Race and Migration* (Toronto: University of Toronto Press, 1945), at 252. See also 'Extract from M'Culloch Geographical Dictionary (London, 1866), Exhibit Q-138,' at 444; 'Extract from Encyclopedia Americana (1919), Exhibit Q-169,' at 549, from Quebec Case. Bruce G. Trigger, *Natives and Newcomers: Canada's 'Heroic Age' Reconsidered* (Montreal and Kingston: McGill-Queen's University Press, 1985), notes at 14–15 that distinctions in skin colour reflected the degree of racial prejudice operating within society: '… in the early days of European exploration and settlement, there was little evidence of racial prejudice against the Indians. They were often described as physically attractive, and their skin colour was not perceived to be notably different from that of Whites. It was widely maintained that they were born white and became sun-tanned or dyed themselves brown. […] As disputes over land rights envenomed

relations between English settlers and native peoples ... [t]hey were increasingly referred to as tawny pagans, swarthy Philistines, copper-coloured vermin, and by the end of the eighteenth century redskins.'

108 John Beddoe's formula, 'D + 2ND + 2N - R - F = Index,' is described in Alfred C. Haddon, *The Study of Man* (London: Bliss Sands, 1989), at 22–40. For reference to Haddon's research, published as *The Races of Man* in 1924, see Canada Factum, at 27.

109 Thomas F. Gossett, *Race: The History of an Idea in America* (Dallas: Southern Methodist University Press, 1963), at 69, citing Paul Broca, who founded the Anthropological Society in Paris in 1859.

110 See, for example, 'Exhibit C-125, Extract from "The Polar Regions" by Sir John Richardson (1861) at 298–303,' in Canada Case, at 138; and 'Exhibit C-100, Extract from "Crania Americana"; or a Comparative View of the Skulls of Various Aboriginal Nations of North and South America: to which is prefixed An Essay on the Varieties of the Human Species, by Samuel George Morton, M.C. (1839),' also from Quebec Case, at 385, where he notes that 'the color' of 'the Polar family' is 'brown, lighter or darker, but often disguised by accumulated filth.'

111 Canada Factum, at 25; Quebec Factum, at 13–19; Shapiro, *The Alaskan Eskimo*. See also Taylor, *Environment, Race and Migration*, who notes at 51: 'The most obvious, but least satisfactory, of these physical criteria is the colour of the skin. For scientific purposes this should be judged on the inside of the forearm and not from the face.' See also extracts of Shapiro's work produced as 'Exhibit Q-190,' Quebec Case, at 663–72; 'Exhibit Q-192,' Quebec Case, at 694; 'Exhibit Q-193,' Quebec Case, at 695–700.

112 For reference to the hair classification, see *

113 For reference to skull measurement, see *

114 Canada Factum, at 24; 'Exhibit C-100,' Canada Case, at 384–7; 'Exhibit C-114,' Canada Case, at 397–9; Stephen Jay Gould, 'American Polygeny and Craniometry before Darwin: Blacks and Indians as Separate, Inferior Species,' in Sandra Harding, ed., *The 'Racial' Economy of Science* (Bloomington: Indiana University Press, 1993), at 99–102. Klineberg, *Race Differences*, notes at 36 that 'from the hindsight of our present knowledge that up to 80 percent of the brain's volume is extracellular space and that preserving ... methods are particularly vulnerable in the amount of shrinkage which they cause, we are able to see how extremely unreliable was all of this early data on brain weight and volume.'

115 For reference to the cranial research, see *

116 Klineberg, *Race Differences*, at 36, 77. Although Klineberg recognized the illogical nature of such conclusions, he was unable to refrain from ethno-

centric judgments himself: 'It is interesting ... to note that the largest brains, on the average, were found among the Eskimo, whose culture is comparatively simple.' See also William I. Thomas, 'The Scope and Method of Folk-Psychology,' *American Journal of Sociology* vol. 1 (November 1895), 434 at 436–7, where he notes that the five heaviest brains recorded by Topinard were those of Tourgenieff (2,020 grams), a day labourer (1,925 grams), a brickmason (1,900 grams), a person with epilepsy (1,830 grams), and the illustrious Georges Cuvier (1,830 grams). When the idol of French anthropologists, Gambetta, died and willed them his brain, they were mortified to find it weighed only 1,100 grams, 'just 100 grammes above the point of imbecility.'

117 Kaj Birket-Smith, *The Eskimos* (London: Methuen, 1959, orig. pub. 1936, 1st Danish edition 1927), at 42; H.L. Shapiro, 'Extract from Some Observations on the Origin of the Eskimo (Toronto, 1934), Exhibit Q-190,' at 665; Shapiro, 'Monograph on the Indian Origin of the Eskimo (New York, 1937), Exhibit Q-193,' at 698, both in Quebec Case.

118 Paul Broca, 'Sur les proportions relatives du bras, de l'avant bras et de la clavicule chez les nègres et les européens,' *Bulletin Société d'Anthropologie Paris* 3:2 (1862), 1 at 11. See A. Fullerton & Co., 'Extracts from Gazetteer of the World (London, 1857) Exhibit Q-133,' in Quebec Case, at 401, for reference to the 'diminutive stature' of 'Eastern Esquimaux' attributed to 'their mode of living, which continually exposes them to every hardship and privation.'

119 'Exhibit C-47,' Canada Case, at 304; and citing Jenness, *Indians of Canada*, at 247.

120 Canada Factum, at 27, citing Birket-Smith, *The Eskimos,* at p. vi. Birket-Smith notes at 43–4 that 'most pure-blooded Indians, both in North and South America, belong to the O-type in an overwhelming degree, whereas among the Japanese and a North Asiatic tribe such as the Tungusian Orok less than one-third are O.' See also extracts from Birket-Smith's work produced in 'Exhibit C-98,' Canada Case, at 382, and 'Exhibit Q-191,' Quebec Case, at 673–93.

121 For references on serological studies, see *

122 Birket-Smith, *The Eskimos,* at 30–1.

123 For reference to Cuvier's racial research, see 'Exhibit C-100,' Canada Case, at 384. For further details regarding Saartje Baartman, and the exhibition of 'far-distant peoples' as popular culture, see *

124 'Exhibit C-48,' Canada Case, at 327–42; Klineberg, *Race Differences,* at 25. The absurdity of the search for the pure racial prototype is underscored by an account of a late nineteenth-century exchange between two white

anthropologists, as described by George W. Stocking, Jr, in *Race, Culture and Evolution* (New York: Free Press, 1968), at 58: 'In the thirty-five years after Paul Broca founded the Société d'Anthropologie de Paris in 1859, twenty-five million Europeans were subjected to anthropometric measurement; yet when William Z. Ripley wrote to Otto Ammon asking for a photograph of a "pure" Alpine type from the Black Forest, Ammon was unable to provide one. "He has measured thousands of heads, and yet he answered that he really had not been able to find a perfect specimen in all details. All his round-headed men were either blond, or tall, or narrow-nosed, or something else that they ought not to be".'

125 For references on racial mixing, see *

126 The exhibits submitted by counsel in the case point this out; see, for example, 'Exhibit C-129, Extracts from "Report on Explorations in the Labrador Peninsula" by A.P. Low, Geological Survey of Canada, Ottawa (1896),' published in Canada Case, at 148: 'Along the Atlantic coast, as far north as Hopedale, few or none of the Eskimo are pure blooded. [...] In Ungava Bay and on Hudson Bay there are, around the Hudson Bay posts, many half-breeds, the result of marriage between the employees and Eskimo women.' 'Exhibit C-146, Extracts from Address Entitled "Life in Labrador" by Rev. Henry Gordon, of Cartwright Labrador,' at 172, adds: 'The first serious attempt to settle the coast of Labrador dates from the opening up of trade relations by Mayor Cartwright, some one hundred and fifty years ago. During sixteen years of varying fortunes, Cartwright did much to establish very friendly relations with the natives, and it may be said that from his day dates the gradual cross-breeding of English and Esquimaux which has produced the modern Labrador "Livyere." Out of a total population of some four thousand it is very doubtful if now one third is of pure Esquimaux blood, and the day will not be very long before the Esquimaux stock is totally eliminated from the coast.'

127 Taylor, *Environment, Race and Migration*, at 257. For another example, see Birket-Smith, *The Eskimos*, at 176–7, where he mentions the musings of anthropologist Collins concerning photographs of the Caribou Eskimo: 'He even writes that my photographs "leave no doubt of the considerable amount of white [*sic*] blood present among the Caribou Eskimos," although it seems rather puzzling how it should have been introduced.' See also 'Exhibit Q-169' in Quebec Case and 'Extract from Encyclopedia Americana: North America (Indians) (1919),' at 551, which notes: 'The Eskimo of Greenland have intermarried with the whites (Danish fathers, native mothers), so that except in the parts remote from settlements no pure-blood Eskimo exists; and the same is true of a good deal of Labrador, where the contact has been with fishermen of English descent.'

128 Birket-Smith, *The Eskimos*, at 36–7. For an early reference to 'flaxen'-haired Eskimo, see 'Exhibit Q-88,' in Quebec Case, at 216: Thomas Jeffreys, 'Extract from the Natural and Civil History of the French Dominions in North and South America … (London, 1760).'

129 As recounted by Birket-Smith in *The Eskimos*, at 30.

130 Taylor, *Environment, Race and Migration*, at 257.

131 For references on racial classifications and passing, see *

132 For references, see *

133 Jack Forbes, 'The Manipulation of Race, Caste and Identity: Classifying Afro-Americans, Native Americans and Red-Black People,' *The Journal of Ethnic Studies* 17:4 (Winter 1990), 1 at 37–8. Audrey Smedley, *Race in North America: Origin and Evolution of a Worldview* (Boulder: Westview, 1993), notes at 288 that even the most up-to-date research on genetics has failed to differentiate racial groupings:'[T]here is greater variation among peoples within a geographical race … than there is between them. Indeed, some experts have discovered that only a minor amount of variation in known genetic traits exists between the major "racial" groups.' Smedley concludes that the study of genes has also failed to explain how previous generations transmit 'racially' distinct characteristics: 'We know comparatively little about the mode of inheritance of such polymorphic traits (determined by more than a single gene or position on the DNA) as skin color, hair form, nose shape, and so forth.'

134 Diamond Jenness, 'The Problem of the Eskimo,' in Diamond Jenness, *The American Aborigines: Their Origin and Antiquity* (Toronto: University of Toronto Press, 1933), at 374.

135 'Exhibit C-47,' Canada Case, at 303–4, citing Jenness, *Indians of Canada*, at 246–7.

136 Birket-Smith, *The Eskimos*, at 44. Extracts of this publication are quoted in 'Exhibit Q-191,' Quebec Case, at 673–93.

137 The most up-to-date analysis from the Smithsonian Institution chronicles continuing debate. Damas, 'Arctic,' at 2 notes that there is still 'controversy over whether or not Eskimos are an identifiable racial type.' Lawrence Oschinsky, 'Facial Flatness and Cheekbone Morphology in Arctic Mongoloids: A Case of Morphological Taxonomy,' *Anthropologica* 4:2 (1962), 349–77, has posited an Arctic Mongoloid racial type to be separated from New World and Old World Mongoloid types. Emoke J.E. Szathmary, 'Genetic Markers in Siberian and Northern North American Populations,' *Yearbook of Physical Anthropology*, vol. 24 (1981), 37–73, sees the Reindeer Chukchi, all Eskimo populations (but not the Aleut, for whom comparable data are lacking), and Athapaskan speakers as forming a definite cluster in genetic traits as distinct from Algonquian speakers. Szathmary sees considerable

continuity within Eskimo groups and maintains that, although 'Eskimos do not seem to have any gene that is unique to them, with the exception of variants in the GC (Group Specific a-Globulin) system,' Eskimos are 'genetically identifiable.' Keith J. Crowe, *A History of the Original Peoples of Northern Canada* (Montreal and Kingston: McGill-Queen's University Press, 1974), notes at 8: 'We do not know whether Indians and Eskimos were once the same people. We do not know whether the people of the northern forests and barrens 10,000 years ago were the ancestors of the present Indians, though it is likely. All that the stone tools and fires tell us is that the prehistoric peoples worked out several main cultures.'

138 Canada Factum, at 23, 27; Quebec Factum, at 2, 22, 25, 62.

139 Jenness, *Eskimo Administration*, at 40.

140 *Re Eskimos*, at 123, per Kerwin, J. The selection of 1867 as the pivotal point was something both counsel had conceded early on in their arguments, when they agreed that it was important to assess the question according to the original intent of the legislators who penned the phrase 'Indians and lands reserved for Indians.' (See Quebec Factum, at 60; Canada Factum, at 4–6, 10, in part quoting Strong, J, in *St. Catharines Milling and Lumber Co.* v *The King* (1887), 13 S.C.R. 577 at 606–7.) A more progressive perspective was articulated by the English Privy Council in the celebrated 1930 case *Edwards* v *Attorney-General of Canada*, where the Law Lords decided it was wrong to apply rigid judicial reasoning of earlier centuries to changing perspectives and circumstances.'The British North America Act planted in Canada a living tree capable of growth and expansion within its natural limits,' they noted, and the courts 'must take care not to interpret legislation meant to apply to one community by a rigid adherence to the customs and traditions of another': *Edwards* v *Attorney-General of Canada*, [1930] A.C. 136 (P.C.). That case was based on an application by five Canadian feminists to have the word 'person' interpreted to include 'women' for the purpose of appointment to the Canadian Senate. The decision of the Supreme Court of Canada to refuse the application was overruled by the Judicial Committee of the Privy Council.

141 *Re Eskimos*, at 117, per Cannon, J.

142 *Re Eskimos*, at 114, citing an 1849 report from the Bishop of Newfoundland that was published in London for the Society for the Propagation of the Gospel by the Bishop of London, 'Exhibit Q-197' of the Quebec Case.

143 Quebec Factum, at 63–4. On the perceived importance of the 1879 correspondence, see Diubaldo, 'Absurd Little Mouse,' at 38–9.

144 Jenness, *Eskimo Administration*, at 40. Debates also occurred before the North West Territories Council; see Diubaldo, *Government of Canada and the*

Inuit, at 48–9, citing PAC RG85/1676/250-1-1/2A, Extracts of Minutes of 92nd Session of the N.W.T. Council, 27 April 1939, 9 January 1940, 15 February 1940, 2 April 1940. See also RG85/1870/540-1/2, 8 November 1946, 17 July 1947; RG85/1234/250-1-1-4A, 14 June 1950. *The Indian Act*, S.C. 1951, c.29, s.4(1) provides: 'This Act does not apply to the race of aborigines commonly referred to as Eskimos.' See also *The Indian Act*, R.S.C. 1970, c.149, s.5(4)(1).

145 Diubaldo, *Government of Canada and the Inuit*, notes at 51–2 that federal government Inuit policy witnessed a 'take-off' period after the Department of Northern Affairs and Natural Resources was created in 1953. Louis-Jacques Dorais, *Quaqtaq: Modernity and Identity in an Inuit Community* (Toronto: University of Toronto Press, 1997), notes at 32 that the Quebec government refused to have anything to do with the Nunavik Inuit until the election of the provincial Liberals in 1960, on a platform of increased economic and social autonomy for Quebec. Due to Nunavik's mineral base and hydro-electric potential, the new government considered it to be a strategic area. In 1960, the Quebec Provincial Police replaced the RCMP in Kuujjuaq and Great Whale River (Kuujjuaraapik), and in 1961 the Direction Générale du Nouveau-Québec was set up under the Minister of Natural Resources, René Lévesque. In time, the issue would become entangled in the ongoing debates over secession and sovereignty-association, with the two levels of government taking positions quite contrary to the ones they adopted in *Re Eskimos*.

146 Jenness, *Eskimo Administration*, at 40–1.

3: 'Bedecked in Gaudy Feathers'

1 Rapid City Historical Book Society, *Rapid City and District: Our Past for the Future* (Altona, Man.: D.W. Friesen & Sons, 1978), at 1–23, 82. For references on the history of agricultural fairs in Western Canada and the immigration patterns of the white prairie settlers, see *

2 Rapid City Historical Book Society, *Rapid City*, at 7, 22–5, 69. On the development of prairie towns, see *

3 Peter Douglas Elias, *The Dakota of the Canadian Northwest: Lessons for Survival* (Winnipeg: University of Manitoba Press, 1988), describes at 71–115 some of the agricultural history of the area.

4 Rapid City Historical Book Society, *Rapid City*, at 8–25. On the significance of festivals in the cultural anthropological sense, see Alessandro Falassi, ed., *Time Out of Time: Essays on the Festival* (Albuquerque: University of New Mexico Press, 1987).

5 Rapid City Historical Book Society, *Rapid City*, at 8, 14, 21, 35, 136–7, 363–4.
For discussion of prairie towns, the emerging social and economic divisions
among the residents and the 'boosterism' of 'founding fathers,' see *

6 Although some whites employed First Nations people on a casual basis as
waged labourers, most encountered the Aboriginal people only when they
came into town to trade, selling wild strawberries in the summer, and frozen
fish, woven baskets, and beaded buckskin moccasins in the winter: Rapid
City Historical Book Society, *Rapid City*, at 18, 134. For discussion of itiner-
ant circuses and their role in constructing racial divisions, see *

7 Ken Coates and Fred McGuinness, *Pride of the Land: An Affectionate History of
Brandon's Agricultural Exhibitions* (Winnipeg: Peguis Publishers, 1985), at 29;
Jon Whyte, *Indians in the Rockies* (Banff: Altitude Publishing, 1985), at 71–80;
Keith Regular, 'On Public Display,' *Alberta History* 34:1 (1986), at 1–10.
Edward Ahenakew, *Voices of the Plains Cree* (Regina: Canadian Plains Re-
search Center, University of Regina, 1995), describes at 86 the diversions of
prairie fairs, 'to which the Indians were always invited, with special camp-
ing privileges at the grounds.' Rapid City Historical Book Society, *Rapid
City*, notes at 34 that Malcolm Turriff was 'one of [Chief] J. Antoine's earliest
acquaintances.'

8 Rapid City Historical Book Society, *Rapid City*, at 34 describes Antoine's
funeral: 'A most amazing personality, James Antoine, one of the oldest
members of the Oak River Sioux Reserve, was buried with sombre pomp
and ceremony. Granting his request, the citizens of Rapid City who realized
his unique contribution, laid him to rest in the King's uniform and wrapped
in a Union Jack.'

9 Rapid City Historical Book Society, *Rapid City*, notes at 7–8 the participation
of the 'Indians of the region' at the Dominion Day celebrations in the late
1870s. G.F. Barker, *Brandon: A City, 1881–1961* (Altona, Man.: D.W. Friesen
& Sons, 1977), describes at 9 (in a patronizing tone) the presence of the Oak
River Dakota in Brandon during the summer of 1885: 'Now, the Northwest
uprising quelled and its leaders under arrest, Indians of the Oak River
reserve, attired in bright colors, feathers, beads and war-paint, descended on
the City. Bearing a Union Jack and "accompanied by tom-tom martial
music," the mounted band paused before the "boss of the town (Mayor
Smart)" while their two chiefs – using an interpreter – sought permission to
express, through a pow-wow, their allegiance to the Queen. A reporter
described the performance as an "effort unsurpassed by anything *ever
attempted here* ... the monotonous beating of the drums by musicians
seated in a circle ... dancers moving, barking, hooting." Of course, the hat

was passed around a few times, with remarkable success.' See also Sarah Carter, 'Agriculture and Agitation on the Oak River Dakota Reserve, 1875–1895,' *Manitoba History* 6:2 (Fall 1983), at 4.

10 Hopper, born in 1883, recounts this memory in Rapid City Historical Book Society, *Rapid City*, at 127. Dave McNaught recollects at 134: '[The Indians] always came on Citizens Day in the summer and put on a pow-wow on the corner, where the Union Bank was built afterwards, singing and dancing to the steady beat of the drum.'

11 Rapid City Historical Book Society, *Rapid City*, at 24–5.

12 See, for example, 'The Sun Dance: Thrilling Scenes among the Indians of the Assiniboine Reserve,' Qu'Appelle *Progress*, 16 June 1887; 'Frightful Cruelties at the Manufacture of Braves: A Sun Dance, Revolting Scenes,' Regina *Leader*, 26 July 1883, and similar discussion in Regina *Leader*, 14 June 1894; 'Indians Perishing: Dying from the Practices of Their Heathen Religion,' Ottawa *Evening Journal*, 9 December 1896; 'Red Men Observe Weird Ceremony' and 'Scene in Hall Where Indians Dance Continuously for Forty-Eight Hours Beggars Description: Former Barbarous Custom of Initiating Braves Left Out,' Edmonton *Journal*, 21 July 1923.

13 *Lethbridge Herald*, 23 August 1911. Equally indicative of these conflicting emotions are the number of white authority figures who seem to have been captivated by Aboriginal ceremonies. For one account, see the reference in Fine Day, *My Cree People* (Invermere, B.C.: Good Medicines Books, 1973), at 26, describing how the chief of police wanted to witness a Sun Dance ceremony. The chief 'quietly encouraged' Fine Day to go ahead with it, although the Indian Agent threatened to imprison Fine Day for seven months and Thunderchild for three months. The Sun Dance was held near Battleford. Fine Day does not give the date.

14 W. Keith Regular, '"Red Backs and White Burdens": A Study of White Attitudes towards Indians in Southern Alberta, 1896–1911,' MA thesis (University of Calgary, 1985), notes at 41 and 152 that during the first decade of the twentieth century, as the First Nations began to move out of the 'reserves,' the greater contact with whites in surrounding towns led to a realization by some segments of white society that 'Indians were a resource that could be exploited, especially to the benefit of the numerous local fairs and exhibitions.'

15 On the population of the Oak River Dakota and the presence of the whole community at the fair, see *

16 The details of the dance at the annual fair are drawn from Public Archives of Canada, RG10, vol. 3825, file 60-511-1 [hereinafter cited as PAC file 60-

511-1]. Why the Dakota did not charge admission directly themselves is not clear. At least some First Nations communities had considered their own admission fees in the past: see the Qu'Appelle *Vidette*, 11 August 1887, which intimated that the Blood talked of charging admission at their Sun Dance on the 'Blood Reserve' that year: 'They say that, when the Whites have a show, they charge admission, and, as this is their great circus, they do not see why they should not do the same.' On the intermingling of Dakota and whites in athletic competitions at the fair, see *

17 Patricia Monture-Angus, *Thunder in My Soul: A Mohawk Woman Speaks* (Halifax: Fernwood Publishing, 1995), at 211. Pat Deiter McArthur, *Dances of the Northern Plains* (Saskatoon: Saskatchewan Indian Cultural Centre, 1987), notes at p. xii that 'knowledge [about the various stages and steps that are followed in a ceremony] is reserved for men who have received this right either through a vision or from an elder wishing to pass his knowledge on.' On the 'beauty,' 'costumes,' and 'picturesqueness' of the Grass Dance, see Gontran LaViolette, OMI, *The Sioux Indians in Canada* (Regina: Saskatchewan Historical Society, 1944), at 126–7; James Howard, *The Canadian Sioux* (Lincoln: University of Nebraska Press, 1984), at 146–69.

18 *An Act further to amend 'The Indian Act, 1880',*' S.C. 1884, c.27, s.3, provides: 'Every Indian or other person who engages in or assists in celebrating the Indian festival known as the "Potlach": or in the Indian dance known as the "Tamanawas" is guilty of a misdemeanour, and shall be liable to imprisonment for a term of not more than six nor less than two months in any gaol or other place of confinement; and any Indian or other person who encourages, either directly or indirectly, an Indian or Indians to get up such a festival or dance, or to celebrate the same, or who shall assist in the celebration of the same is guilty of a like offence, and shall be liable to the same punishment.' On the origin of the terms 'Potlatch' and 'Tamanawas,' and for references on the suppression of the West Coast dances, see *

19 *An Act further to amend the Indian Act*, S.C. 1895, c.35, s.6, 114.

20 The exchange of horses is described in a letter from David Laird, Indian Commissioner, Winnipeg, to Secretary, Department of Indian Affairs, Ottawa, 28 February 1903. George Coldwell, the lawyer who would later act for the Dakota, conceded that blankets were also given away: Letter from George Coldwell, KC, to Clifford Sifton, Minister of the Interior, Ottawa, 20 February 1902, PAC file 60-511-1.

21 *An Act respecting Indians*, R.S.C. 1886, c.43, s.112, provides: 'Every one who incites any Indian to commit any indictable offence is guilty of felony and liable to imprisonment for any term not exceeding five years.' Alternative charges might have been laid under section 111, which provides:

Whoever induces, incites or stirs up any three or more Indians, non-treaty
Indians, or half-breeds apparently acting in concert
(a) to make any request or demand of any agent or servant of the Government in a riotous, disorderly or threatening manner, or in a manner
calculated to cause a breach of the peace; or
(b) to do an act calculated to cause a breach of the peace
is guilty of a misdemeanour and shall be liable to be imprisoned for any
term not exceeding two years, with or without hard labor.

For statutory references to earlier provisions passed for Upper Canada in
1853 and 1859, and federal provisions in force between 1884 and 1953, see *

22 *An Act further to amend the Indian Act*, S.C. 1895, c.35, s.114. The proviso was
originally drafted to read: 'Always provided that the foregoing shall not
apply to any agricultural show or exhibition at which prizes are given to the
best exhibits thereat.' Prime Minister Mackenzie Bowell argued for the
deletion of this clause, noting that, if it remained, 'it will permit all these
iniquities we are trying to prevent being performed at an agricultural show.
The reason for making an exception of agricultural fairs was that it was
thought that if the clause was passed without a proviso, it might prevent the
giving of prizes at these exhibitions where the Indians compete, as they do
in the North-west, for prizes.' The prime minister moved that the original
wording be deleted, and the more restricted proviso was substituted. See
Canada, Senate of Canada, *Parliamentary Debates* [Hansard], 31 May 1895,
at 194.

23 Wilson D. Wallis, *The Canadian Dakota* (New York: AMS Press, 1947), at 42,
quotes George Catlin, *Letters and notes on the manners, customs and conditions
of North American Indians*, vol. 1, 3d ed. (London, 1842), at 245: 'I saw so
many of their different varieties of dances among the Sioux that I should
almost be disposed to denominate them the *"dancing Indians"*.' Elias, *Dakota
of the Canadian Northwest*, notes at 73 that 1879 marked the first year after
settlement in which 'anyone had anything to give away.' On the construction of the round house, see Carter, 'Agriculture and Agitation,' at 4. On the
meaning of spiritual dances to First Nations people, see Stan Cuthand, 'The
Native Peoples of the Prairie Provinces in the 1920's and 1930's,' in Ian
Getty and Donald Smith, eds., *One Century Later: Western Canadian Reserve
Indians since Treaty 7* (Vancouver: University of British Columbia Press,
1978), 31 at 39.

24 For commentary, recorded in the annual reports of Indian Agents Markle
and Wheatley, regarding the reluctance of the Oak River Dakota to convert
to Christianity, see *. Elias, *Dakota of the Canadian Northwest*, notes at 114 that

'most of the [Dakota] at Birdtail were confirmed churchgoers by [the turn of the century] ... but at Oak River, the band was divided amongst the Christians and the pagans, as the non-Christians were called ... The clear favouritism that Indian-department officials showed the Christians, as well as the scorn heaped on the pagans, added to the political divisions in the communities, but for the first few years of the decade, there was largely a live and let live attitude on the part of the different groups.'

25 See A. Blair Stonechild, who writes at p. x in Katherine Pettipas, *Severing the Ties that Bind: Government Repression of Indigenous Religious Ceremonies on the Prairies* (Winnipeg: University of Manitoba Press, 1994): '[A]n attack on First Nations spirituality is an attack on the core of First Nations identity, since spirituality pervades all aspects of the First Nations lifestyle.' Jacqueline Gresko, 'White "Rites" and Indian "Rites": Indian Education and Native Responses in the West, 1870–1910,' in A.W. Raporich, ed., *Western Canada Past and Present* (Calgary: McClelland & Stewart West, 1974), 163, notes at 175 that annual Sun Dance gatherings constituted 'the core of cultural resistance among the Cree, Assiniboine, Saulteaux, and Sioux. The sun dance presented a parallel educational system designed to oppose that of the government and missionaries.' For additional references, see *

26 Dr Edward Ahenakew, a Sandy Lake Cree who became an Anglican theologian, recounts in Ruth M. Buck, ed., *Voices of the Plains Cree* (Regina: Canadian Plains Research Center, 1995), at 86, the views of Old Keyam, a fictional, semi-autobiographical character, who steadfastly refused to attend local fairs, resenting the gaze of curious spectators and 'sensitive to offence, however unintentional.' On the insensitivity of whites who observed Aboriginal dances, see *

27 Sidney L. Harring, *Crow Dog's Case: American Indian Sovereignty, Tribal Law and United States Law in the Nineteenth Century* (Cambridge: Cambridge University Press, 1994), describes at 179 the famous Dakota leader Sitting Bull's brief tour with Buffalo Bill's Wild West Show. Harring also notes at 274 that, in the United States, after most Indian Agents outlawed traditional ceremonies and enforced this ban with arrests, Aboriginal communities 'used every possible white-sanctioned occasion for traditional rituals, including cattle fairs, church services, and Fourth of July celebrations.'

28 Cuthand, 'Native Peoples,' at 38. For accounts of Cree elders regarding the importance of dances to the survival of their religion and culture, see statements of Pierre Lewis (Onion Lake), Pat Paddy, George Albert (Sandy Lake), and Alec Simaganis in *Kataayuk: Saskatchewan Indian Elders* (Saskatchewan: Saskatchewan Indian Cultural College, 1976), n.p.; Norma Sluman and Jean Goodwill, *John Tootoosis: A Biography of a Cree Leader* (Ottawa: Golden Dog Press, 1982), at 141–3. For comments of anthropologists, see *

29 Pettipas, *Severing the Ties that Bind*, at 54–9. On the economic and social reciprocity inherent in Give-Away Dances, see *

30 Introducing the bill in his role as superintendent of Indian Affairs, Prime Minister Macdonald added: '[T]he departmental officers and all clergymen unite in affirming that it is absolutely necessary to put this practice down. [...] At these gatherings they give away their guns and all their property in a species of rivalry, and go so far as to give away their wives ...' See Canada, House of Commons, *Debates* [Hansard], 24 March 1884, at 1063; 7 April 1884, at 1399.

31 Canada, Senate of Canada, *Debates*, 15 April 1884, at 625; 17 April 1884, at 654. For additional comments of senators, see *

32 For biographical details on Senator Almon, see *. When he spoke of Highland dancers, Senator Almon may well have been thinking back to the sixteenth century in Scotland, to a period when traditional May Day celebrations featuring Morris and sword dances were outlawed as 'superstitious rites.' See George S. Emmerson, *Scottish Country Dancing: An Evolutionary Triumph* (Oakville, Ont.: Galt, 1997).

33 Third reading in both the House of Commons and the Senate was completed, and royal assent granted, between 17 and 19 April 1884. Speaking on behalf of the government in the Senate, Sir Alexander Campbell insisted that the statute 'would only be enforced in a spirit of mercy.' Senate of Canada, *Debates*, 17 April 1884, at 654. On the inappropriateness of the minimum penalty see *Sessional Papers* (1897), vol. XXXII, no. 12, paper 15, in which John Cotton, a white superintendent of the Northwest Mounted Police, reports that he sentenced three Cree men (Thunderchild, Enu, and Wa-pa-ha) to the minimum two months' penalty, and that this was 'a very severe sentence and not unlikely to be injurious to health.' 'I and the magistrate sitting with me regretted exceedingly that we were precluded from inflicting a much lighter sentence,' continued Cotton, concluding: 'I think experience has shown that the minimum sentence to be awarded in such cases should be lighter. I trust the Indian Act may be so amended during the coming session of Parliament.'

34 For more detailed discussion of the application for *habeas corpus* in the case of Hamasak, a Kwakiutl chief of the Mamalillikulla, who was tried for conducting a Potlatch in 1889, see *

35 Pettipas, *Severing the Ties that Bind*, notes at 104 that, prior to the 1895 amendment, there had been at least one attempt to use the original Potlatch law to prosecute individuals conducting a Sun Dance on the prairies. In 1893 several Aboriginal people from Hobbema, Saddle Lake, and Stoney Plains were arrested by D.L. Clink, the white Hobbema Indian Agent, for conducting a ceremony on a 'Half-breed settlement' on the Battle River.

Clink also arranged to have the ceremonial lodge torn down. Officials from the Department of Indian Affairs advised Clink that they thought he was mistaken in treating the Sun Dance as identical to the Potlatch, and warned him to exercise 'extreme caution' in making further arrests. Those arrested were released with a reprimand. Department of Indian Affairs to the Indian Commissioner, 12 July 1893; D.L. Clink to Indian Commissioner, 19 June 1893, PAC file 60-511-1, at 1.

36 I am indebted to Tracey Lindberg for pointing out how words such as 'wounding' and 'mutilation' reveal substantial cross-cultural misunderstandings. Senate of Canada, *Debates*, 27 May 1895, at 139–41. For details of the prime minister's statements in the Senate, see *

37 House of Commons, *Debates*, 5 July 1895, at 3935; Senate of Canada, *Debates*, 31 May 1895, at 194–5. The bill received royal assent on 22 July 1895.

38 Cuthand 'Native Peoples,' at 38–9. For discussion of the federal policy of cultural suppression in the prairie region, see E. Brian Titley, *A Narrow Vision: Duncan Campbell Scott and the Administration of Indian Affairs in Canada* (Vancouver: University of British Columbia Press, 1986); Gresko, 'White "Rites" and Indian "Rites"'; Jacqueline Judith (Gresko) Kennedy, 'Qu'Appelle Industrial School: White "Rites" for the Indians of the old North-West,' MA thesis (Carleton University, 1970); Regular, 'Red Backs and White Burdens'; Regular, 'On Public Display.'

39 Carter, 'Agriculture and Agitation,' at 6–8, citing PAC RG10, vol. 3895, file 97, 456; Letter from Rev. J.A. Therien of Onion Lake, P.P. Moulin of Hobbema, P. Lebre of Rivière qui Barre, V. Gabillon of Sacred Heart, W. Comire of Good Fish Lake, F.V. Le Goff and H. Delmas of Duck Lake, and ten others to D.C. Scott, 23 July 1923, PAC RG10, vol. 3827, file 60-511-4B; Pettipas, *Severing the Ties that Bind*, at 3–4. Elias, *Dakota of the Canadian Northwest*, notes at 117 that Reverend John Thunder, the white Presbyterian minister at the nearby Dakota community of Oak Lake, objected to the dances, and in particular to the Give-Aways. Thunder corresponded with David Laird in 1907, requesting the criminal prosecution of traditional dancers.

40 Sarah Carter, 'Categories and Terrains of Exclusion: Constructing the "Indian Woman" in the Early Settlement Era in Western Canada,' *Great Plains Quarterly*, vol. 13 (Summer 1993), 147 at 149–50, citing Canada, Annual Report of the Superintendent General of Indian Affairs for the year ending 30 June 1898, *Sessional Papers*, p. xix; for the year ending 31 December 1899, pp. xxiii, xxviii, 166. See also (Gresko) Kennedy, 'Qu'Appelle Industrial School,' who notes at 194 that 'the Indian Department disliked the dances which stirred up dust from the dirt or wooden floors of Indian

homes and usually took place indoors in winter, so that the ventilation of the hovels became even worse by the dust stirred up.' Sarah Carter, *Capturing Women: The Manipulation of Cultural Imagery in Canada's Prairie West* (Montreal and Kingston: McGill-Queen's University Press, 1997), describes at 158–93 the negative images perpetuated by whites of Aboriginal women as 'slovenly and unclean in their personal habits as well as their housekeeping.'

41 Frank Pedley to T. Cory, Indian Agent at Carlyle, Saskatchewan, 9 March 1902 (PAC RG10, vol. 3826, file 60-511-3), at 1; letter of W.H. Lomas, Indian Agent, Cowechan Indian Agency, Maple Bay, B.C., 5 February 1884, as read in the Senate by Sir Alexander Campbell, Senate of Canada, *Debates*, 15 April 1884, at 622.

42 Sergeant Albert Mountain to Officer Commanding, Battleford, 23 March 1894 (PAC file 60-511-1), at 2; Pettipas, *Severing the Ties that Bind*, at 160–1, quoting William Graham to Secretary, 29 October 1928 (PAC RG10, vol. 3827, file 60-511-4B), at 1.

43 See Brief, Bill No. 114, Amendments to the Indian Act, 1914 (PAC RG10, vol. 6809, file 470-2-3, part 6), at 18–22; Annual Report of the Department of Indian Affairs for the Year Ending 31 December 1881, *Sessional Papers* (Ottawa: Queen's Printer, 1882), at 82.

44 House of Commons, *Debates*, 8 May 1914, at 3482. For biographical details about Frank Oliver, see *

45 For details of the prosecution of Hamasak, see *

46 For details regarding the prosecution of Matoose for 'inciting the Indians to commit a breach of the peace,' see *

47 For details, see *

48 For details of the prosecutions of Chief Thunderchild, Wa-pa-ha, Enu, Paddy, and O-ka-nu (the latter two being released on suspended sentences because of their youth), see *

49 Chief Thunderchild, 'The Sun Dance,' as transcribed and translated in Ahenakew, *Voices*, at 46–7 and 50. Chief Thunderchild (1849–1927), whose Cree name was Peyasiw-awasis, became one of the most knowledgeable and respected Aboriginal storytellers on the prairies, revered for his life as a warrior and hunter. Dr Edward Ahenakew recorded many of Chief Thunderchild's stories in written form in 1923.

50 For details, see *

51 For details, see *

52 For details of this and earlier prosecutions against Piapot, his removal as chief by the Department of Indian Affairs, and his community's continuing resistance, see *

53 Pettipas, *Severing the Ties that Bind*, at 122. Pettipas also recounts at 107–25 that, in addition to criminal prosecution, informal methods were used to deter ceremonial dancing, such as persuasion and threats by Indian Agents and local police, refusal to issue 'passes' for travel off-reserve, withholding of Indian Agency food rations, the confiscation of sacred offerings, and the dismantling of ceremonial lodges. My extensive archival search has led me to conclude that most of the written legal records for the prosecutions no longer survive. Some have been destroyed by archivists who deemed the files 'historically insignificant.' Others were never fully documented by the prosecuting and judicial authorities in the first place. For further discussion of the paucity of reported Aboriginal cases, see Sidney L. Harring, '"The Liberal Treatment of Indians": Native People in Nineteenth-Century Ontario Law,' *Saskatchewan Law Review*, vol. 56 (1992), 297–371. It will be important to determine whether there are any oral-history memories of such cases within Aboriginal communities. On the Aboriginal oral tradition, see *

54 Correspondence from Indian Agent G.H. Wheatley to the Indian Commissioner, referenced in letter from David Laird to the Secretary, Department of Indian Affairs, 28 February 1903, PAC file 60-511-1.

55 Rapid City Historical Book Society, *Rapid City*, at 8, 34, 363. Copies of Turriff's letterhead are located in the files of the Public Archives of Canada.

56 David Laird was born in New Glasgow, Prince Edward Island, in 1833, the fourth child of Alexander Laird and Janet Orr (Laird). He graduated from theological college in Truro, Nova Scotia, and became the publisher of a Charlottetown paper, eventually known as the *Patriot*. Married to Mary Louisa Owen of Charlottetown in 1864, he was elected as Liberal provincial MLA in 1871 and as Liberal MP for Queen's County, P.E.I., in 1873. During the 1870s, he served as Minister of the Interior, Lieutenant-Governor of the Northwest Territories, and Indian Commissioner, and then returned to Charlottetown in 1882, where he resumed editorship of the *Patriot*. He was appointed Indian Commissioner for Manitoba and the Northwest Territories in 1899, several years after the death of his wife, and he moved to Winnipeg to take up this post, where he lived with two of his six children. Although he returned to Ottawa in 1909, Laird continued to work for the Department of Indian Affairs well into his seventies. He died of pneumonia in 1914 at the age of eighty. For biographical details, see John W. Chalmers, *Laird of the West* (Calgary: Detselig, 1981), who notes at 200 that Laird was passionately interested in the Greek and Hebrew languages and spent much of his spare time reading and studying them.

57 Telegraph from David Laird to the Secretary of the Department of Indian Affairs, 10 January 1903, PAC file 60-511-1; Report of the Indian Commis-

sioner, Manitoba and the Northwest Territories, *Sessional Papers* (1902), vol. XXXVII, no. 11, paper 27, at 188–9. Laird's concern over the need to 'civilize' the First Nations apparently did not provoke him to extend much concern over incidents of abuse perpetrated against Aboriginal children at residential school. Suzanne Fournier and Ernie Crey, *Stolen From Our Embrace: The Abduction of First Nations Children and the Restoration of Aboriginal Communities* (Vancouver: Douglas & McIntyre, 1997), note at 57 that, as early as 1889, 'the people of St. Peter's Reserve in Manitoba complained officially to Indian Commissioner David Laird about the principal of Rupert's Land Industrial School near Selkirk, Manitoba. Young girls of eight or nine still bore bruises on their bodies several weeks after being strapped, they said. During an investigation, the Anglican principal admitted he fed the children rancid butter and crept into the dormitories at night to kiss little girls, but he was reprimanded, not removed.'

58 For references to Wheatley's career at Indian Affairs, see *

59 Elias, *Dakota of the Canadian Northwest*, at 104, quoting John A. Markle (writing in 1895), who also added: 'The Sioux are particularly fond of dancing and spend entirely too much of their time and earnings at "pow-wowing"… ' In his 1897 report, Markle adds: 'Although [the Oak River Dakota] earn considerable money, they are very indiscreet in the spending of it. They cling tenaciously to their ancient custom of dancing and feasting, and in this way waste a great deal of their earnings': *Sessional Papers* (1898), vol. XXXII, no. 11, paper 14, at 124. Markle was transferred to Alberta to serve as Indian Agent in the Blackfoot Agency in 1900: *Sessional Papers* (1901), vol. XXXVI, no. 11, paper 27, at 240.

60 Regular, 'Red Backs and White Burdens,' at 152; Regular, 'On Public Display,' at 1-2. Wheatley's renewed energy may have been bolstered by a pay raise. His annual salary at his new posting totalled $1,200, a full $200 raise from his previous departmental stipend: *Sessional Papers* (1899), vol. XXXIV, no. 11, paper 14, at 607; *Sessional Papers* (1901), vol. XXXVI, no.11, paper 27, at 237; *Sessional Papers* (1904), vol. XXXVIII, no. 11, paper 27, at 169.

61 For these and other comments by Wheatley and his predecessor Markle about the reluctance of the Dakota to send their children to school, see *

62 On 9 September 1902, Wheatley wrote: 'Owing to the number of summer fairs held in the province during the summer months, the inducements held out to the Indians, by some of the towns, to come and hold "pow-wows" or heathen dances for exhibition purposes to amuse the public, tend to draw the Indians in large numbers to the towns, where on account of the large number of people present, liquor is easily obtainable by them. It is a difficult matter to locate those who give them the liquor and to get sufficient evi-

dence to convict, when located, as the Indians can seldom identify them. Could these dances be prohibited altogether, it would lessen the danger to a great extent': *Sessional Papers* (1902), vol. XXXVII, no. 11, report 27, at 123. The next year, he filed similar comments: 'The numerous fairs held in the towns during the summer and fall months are a temptation to the Indians, as they invariably attend all in the vicinity of their reserves, and those who are addicted to the liquor habit generally manage to get some': *Sessional Papers* (1903), vol. XXXVIII, no. 11, paper 27, at 145. For reference to fairs being 'handy to bootleggers,' see (Gresko) Kennedy, 'Qu'Appelle Industrial School,' at 196.

63 On the lack of qualifications of farming instructors and the allegations that many abused their position, see *

64 Farming Instructor R.W. Scott left the position in 1896, and the *Sessional Papers* for that year note: 'The band is now under the direct supervision of Mr. Richard Joynt, who is a practical farmer of long experience in this province.' By 1897, John Taylor had been appointed to the position, which he held until he resigned on 31 December 1899 to accept a commission in the 2nd Contingent of Canadian Volunteers to South Africa. He was replaced by Mr Thomas Ryan, described in the *Sessional Papers* as 'now the resident moral and industrial guide to the Oak River band.' Ryan held the position until Yeomans was appointed in 1901: *Sessional Papers* (1896), at 144, 461; (1897), at 490; (1900), at 135; (1901), at 127. At least one of these individuals was fired by the department. Elias, *Dakota of the Canadian Northwest*, notes at 99–104 that Farmer Scott left the reserve and was replaced by 'a man whose corruption was so obvious that even the Indian department found him unsatisfactory, and terminated him on very much the same grounds as those presented by the Dakota concerning Scott.' Elias does not specify which farming instructor met this ignominious end, but notes that the misconduct involved officious interference in the activities of Aboriginal farmers, exceeding authority, excessive rudeness, and incompetence.

65 *Sessional Papers* (1901), at 127; (1902), at 161. In a later posting as the Indian Agent at the Peigan Agency in Alberta, Yeomans decried Aboriginal attendance at white fairs, insisting that it caused work interruption, intoxication, and 'immorality.' Letter of E.H. Yeomans to D.C. Scott, 27 October 1910. PAC file 60-511-2.

66 Details of the prosecution of Wanduta are drawn from PAC file 60-511-1 and Pettipas, *Severing the Ties that Bind*, at 119. On the Heyoka, sometimes translated as 'Sacred Clown,' see Howard, *Canadian Sioux*, at 100–6, 172–3; Raymond J. DeMallie and Douglas R. Parks, *Sioux Indian Religion: Tradition and Innovation* (Norman: University of Oklahoma Press, 1987), at 37. Wilson

Wallis, a white anthropologist who conducted field research among the Canadian Dakota several decades later, recognized Wanduta's expertise when he sought him out to solicit information about his religion and culture. Wallis noted that Wanduta was credited with diagnosing and healing an individual from the Dakota community near Portage la Prairie around 1917. The recovered individual reported that the cause of his illness had been hidden from all but Wanduta, advising: 'Other medicine have difficulty in finding out things, but a clown medicineman can find out anything.' Wallis continues: 'It was the custom of a Clown named Wandu'ta to announce after the War dance held by the Dakota who assemble at Brandon, Manitoba, each year during the week of the exposition, the number of spirits that he had seen during the dance. This was a forecast of the number of Dakota to die during the coming year. In 1914 he declined to do this; he said he did not wish to make them feel badly. Some Dakota explained his refusal as owing to the fact that each man and woman would think he or she might be one of those who were destined to die, and a pall would rest over all of them.' Wallis recounts at 126–7 and 130–2 several conversations with Wanduta, whom he describes as 'an old Clown then living on the Griswold reservation,' concerning Wanduta's abilities to diagnose accurately whether specific Dakota who were ill would recover and his abilities to utilize spiritual forces to forecast the coming of game. Wanduta gave Wallis an eye-witness account of the activities in 1866 of a number of Heyoka who sought to eliminate the evil spirit preventing a successful buffalo hunt. Although Wanduta's age is not specified in any of the records, based on these secondary documents it would seem that the youngest that Wanduta could have been in the year of his prosecution is probably mid-forties. Wanduta advised Wallis that, during the twenty years he had been in Canada, he had killed 101 moose. See also Pettipas, *Severing the Ties that Bind*, at 119; Katherine Ann Pettipas, 'Severing the Ties That Bind: The Canadian Indian Act and the Repression of Indigenous Religious Systems in the Prairie Region, 1896–1951,' PhD thesis (University of Manitoba, 1989), at 250; Wallis, *Canadian Dakota*, at 111; Wilson D. Wallis, 'Canadian Dakota Sun Dance,' *Anthropological Papers of the American Museum of History*, vol. XVI, part IV (New York, 1919), at 325.

67 Mahpiyahdinape (Enoch) spent part of the winter of 1896 at Birdtail writing a history of his Dakota community, but according to Elias, *Dakota of the Canadian Northwest*, at 232, the manuscript seems to have been lost. For details about surviving written records on the history of the Canadian Dakota; the three main divisions into Dakota, Nakota, and Lakota (collectively called 'Dakota'); and the Santee, see *

68 On migration patterns and racial intermixing, see *

69 I have placed the word 'reserve' in quotation marks in recognition of concerns that the concept does not capture the Aboriginal understanding of the nature of their claim to traditional lands, and that it is misleading in its suggestion that lands traditionally held by the First Nations could be 'reserved' for their use by the federal government. On the negotiations between the Dakota and the Canadian government, the double-dealing of Canadian and American authorities in their relations with the Dakota, and the resulting arrangements made about the Oak River land, see *

70 Carter, 'Agriculture and Agitation,' at 4, citing Inspector Wadsworth's Report of the Birtle Agencies (1890), PAC RG10, vol. 3844, file 73, 406-2.

71 The individual appointed was W.R. Scott: Carter, 'Agriculture and Agitation,' at 4–5; Sarah Carter, *Lost Harvests: Prairie Indian Reserve Farmers and Government Policy* (Montreal and Kingston: McGill-Queen's University Press, 1990), at 226–9.

72 On the pass system and permit system, see *

73 Carter, 'Agriculture and Agitation,' at 5–8; Carter, *Lost Harvests*, at 226–9. Carter notes that three residents of Oak River – Harry Hotain, Mahpiyaska, and Kinyanyahan – travelled to Ottawa to meet with Indian Commissioner Hayter Reed. The three Dakota were advised that they had violated departmental regulations by leaving the reserve without a permit and were sent home without relief. The department also took steps to prosecute white grain buyers who were dealing with the Dakota; white grain buyers William Chambers of Ogilvie Milling Co. and Alexander and William Forrest of Leitch Bros. at Oak Lake were convicted of buying grain from Indians without permits in 1893. Additional petitions of protest, signed by forty-two Dakota, were forwarded in 1894. Facing the indomitable bureaucracy at Indian Affairs, the Oak River Dakota were unable to work themselves free of the restrictive policies. The majority reconciled themselves to small-scale farming, forcibly prevented from accessing the grain-centred cash economy of the white settlers around them.

74 *Sessional Papers* (1902), vol. XXXVII, no. 11, paper 27, at 121–4; *Sessional Papers* (1901), vol. XXXVI, no. 11, paper 27, at 126. The local press seemed drawn to accounts that suggested successful acculturation. For several examples, see *

75 Elias, *Dakota of the Canadian Northwest*, notes at 98 and 102 that it was Indian Agent John A. Markle who made the appointment of Tunkan Cekiyana (whose name is also spelled 'Tukancikeyana'), an individual held in disdain by many in his community for his propensity to side with the Department of Indian Affairs. In meetings with governmental officials, some Dakota

refused to call Tunkan Cekiyana by his Dakota name, and referred to him contemptuously as 'Chief Pat.' This appears to be the name by which he was known in the white community. Griswold United Church Women, *Bridging the Years, 1867–1967: Griswold Centennial Booklet* (n.p.: Souris Plaindealer Limited, n.d.), notes at 32 that Chief Pat was the son of the (unnamed) man who had been chief when the Dakota came to Canada following the 1862 uprising, adding: 'Chief Pat had worked at the Pratt's Landing in Portage cutting wood. The Indians often took the names of the people for whom they worked and he took the name of Pratt which at first was mistakenly called "Pat." Chief Pat was called to Regina where he was made chief by the Canadian Government and presented with a medal.' On the history of the interference of Canadian officials in the selection of Dakota chiefs in Manitoba, see *

76 George Manuel and Michael Posluns, *The Fourth World: An Indian Reality* (Don Mills: Collier-Macmillan Canada, 1974), note at 43: 'Our ideal of leadership is closely related to developing to a fine art the life-way of giving. Spiritual and material power have never been wholly separated in the Indian world as they seem to have been elsewhere. In many Indian societies, especially those with a less formal structure, a leader may better be described as a person who gives well and who gives often. Even within the most highly structured Indian societies, in which one could earn a title or office only through routes which combined family lines with outstanding ability, there were few nations that based status solely on family lines. There was something basically democratic in the recognition of status through giving. Anyone of sufficient ability and generosity could achieve a status that would almost rival that of an office holder.' See also Wallis, *Canadian Dakota*, at 15; Catherine Price, 'Lakotas and Euroamericans: Contrasted Concepts of "Chieftainship" and Decision-Making Authority,' *Ethnohistory* 41:3 (Summer 1994), 447–64; Menno Boldt and Anthony Long, 'Tribal Traditions and European-Western Political Ideologies: The Dilemma of Canada's Native Indians,' in Menno Boldt and Anthony Long, eds., *The Quest for Justice* (Toronto: University of Toronto Press, 1985), 335–9; Harring, *Crow Dog's Case*, at 179 and 273.

77 For reference, see *

78 For details of the provisions of the 1869 federal statute, and the interference of the Department of Indian Affairs in the selection of chiefs, see *

79 For legislative details concerning the 1876 statute, and later provisions enacted in 1880, 1884, 1886, and 1894, see *

80 For details of the provisions in the 1895 statute, and later provisions enacted in 1898 and 1906, see *

81 Chiefs such as Piapot and Walter Ochapowace, convicted of dancing, were removed from office by departmental officials, while Chief Thunderchild was threatened with the loss of his status as chief if he continued to support ceremonial dancing; see Pettipas, *Severing the Ties that Bind*, at 116–17 and 158–9. Headmen John Asham, Jr, and Ka Ka Kesick were deposed at the Qu'Appelle Agency as promoters of dances, and councillors at the Touchwood Agency, Portage la Prairie, File Hills, and Assiniboine Agency were deposed for similar reasons; see Vic Satzewich and Linda Mahood, 'Indian Affairs and Band Governance: Deposing Indian Chiefs in Western Canada, 1896–1911,' *Canadian Ethnic Studies* 26:1 (1994), 40 at 51.

82 For discussion of the practice of the Department of Indian Affairs, see *

83 Pettipas, *Severing the Ties that Bind*, at 117.

84 Pettipas, *Severing the Ties that Bind*, at 133; J.D. McLean to Indian Commissioner, 5 January 1903, PAC file 60-511-1. The educational facilities available to the Oak River Dakota children also included one day school on the Keeseekoowenin territory (the Okanase day school) and a boarding school in the town of Birtle, which taught rudimentary domestic science, gardening, and the care of stock animals. Other Dakota children attended the Regina, Elkhorn, Brandon, and Qu'Appelle industrial schools and the Pine Creek and Cowessess boarding schools. Indian Agent Wheatley reported in 1903 that the Dakota 'object to the distance the schools are from their reserves and the length of time the children have to stay,' concluding petulantly that 'the Indians as a whole are not interested in the education of their children': *Sessional Papers* (1904), vol. XXXVIII, no. 11, paper 27, at 144.

85 For details and sources on the history of Aboriginal education, and a description of the provincial and federal legislation in force from 1829 to 1951, see *

86 John Tootoosis, born in 1899, explained that his father was 'very troubled by the idea of sending his sons to residential school,' but 'wanted them to learn to read, write and count and be able to speak the language of the white man ... He did not have these skills himself, had often needed them and knew that Indian people would have a better chance in the future if they had them': Sluman and Goodwill, *John Tootoosis*, at 95–7. See also John S. Milloy, 'The Early Indian Acts: Developmental Strategy and Constitutional Change,' in Ian A.L. Getty and Antoine S. Lussier, eds., *As Long as the Sun Shines and Water Flows: A Reader in Canadian Native Studies* (Vancouver: University of British Columbia Press, 1983), at 60; Penny Petrone, *First People, First Voices* (Toronto: University of Toronto Press, 1983).

87 (Gresko) Kennedy, 'Qu'Appelle Industrial School,' notes at 200 that Principal T. Ferrier joined with several prairie religious leaders to write letters

recommending that the department abolish such dances. The correspondence was forwarded by Commissioner Laird to Ottawa in December 1903. Fournier and Crey, *Stolen from Our Embrace*, note at 59 that some of the religious leaders at the residential schools 'reserved their most harsh punishments' for Aboriginal children who insisted upon expressing their cultural and spiritual identity by 'making Indian dances.'

88 Pettipas, *Severing the Ties that Bind*, at 133; J.D. McLean to Indian Commissioner, 5 January 1903, PAC file 60-511-1. Wanduta's son was not the only industrial-school student to participate in the campaign to preserve Aboriginal dance. Gresko, 'White "Rites" and Indian "Rites",' describes at 177–8 how Daniel Kennedy, an Assiniboine who had graduated from Qu'Appelle Industrial School and the Saint Boniface College, not only joined his elders in the dances, but played an active role in the drafting of petitions to Ottawa. Levi Thompson, a lawyer from Wolseley, Saskatchewan, who was retained by the Assiniboine to carry forward their petition to Ottawa in 1906, remarked: 'the leaders of this movement seem to be among the best-educated and most intelligent of them.' See letter to the Hon. F. Oliver, 19 March 1903, PAC file 60-511-2. Charles Nowell used the writing skills he acquired in an Alert Bay residential school to record information about lineage, clan positions, and dancing lore, all vital to the preservation of the Kwagiulth Potlatch; J.R. Miller, *Shingwauk's Vision: A History of Native Residential Schools* (Toronto: University of Toronto Press, 1996), at 358.

89 Letter from David Laird, Indian Commissioner, Winnipeg, to J.D. McLean, Secretary of the Department of Indian Affairs, Ottawa, 9 January 1903, PAC file 60-511-1.

90 Gary Clayton Anderson and Alan R. Woolworth, *Through Dakota Eyes: Narrative Accounts of the Minnesota Indian War of 1862* (St Paul: Minnesota Historical Society Press, 1988), describe at 4 the earlier role of the War of 1862 in ripping apart the social and cultural fabric of Dakota society and fostering deep divisions between segments of the community. They note at 6 that 'perhaps as many as one-fourth of the Dakota people' were attempting 'to adjust to a Euro-American lifestyle' by 1862, moving from their villages onto farms, adopting whites' clothing, and converting to Christianity. They quote at 21–7 comments from Jerome Big Eagle (Wamditanka), born in 1827 at Black Dog's village on the south bank of the Minnesota River, who stated in 1894: '... a little while before the outbreak there was trouble among the Indians themselves. Some of the Indians took a sensible course and began to live like white men. The government built them houses, furnished them tools, seeds, etc., and taught them to farm. [...] Others staid [*sic*] in their tepees. There was a white man's party and an Indian party. We had politics

among us and there was much feeling. [...] The "farmers" were favored by the government in every way. They had houses built for them, some of them even had brick houses, and they were not allowed to suffer. The other Indians did not like this. [...] They called them "cut-hairs," because they had given up the Indian fashion of wearing the hair, and "breeches men," because they wore pantaloons, and "Dutchmen," because so many of the settlers on the north side of the river and elsewhere in the country were Germans.' Mary-Ellen Kelm also notes that Aboriginal people who supported the ban on traditional dance reflect significant disunity within First Nations communities, blurring distinctions between resistant and compliant, between colonizer and colonized. See her book review of Pettipas, *Severing the Ties that Bind*, in *Canadian Historical Review* 78:1 (March 1997), at 171–3.

91 Letter from Chief Tunkan Cekiyana, Griswold, to Department of Indian Affairs, Ottawa, 10 January 1903, PAC file 60-511-1. John Noel, who acted as interpreter so that Chief Tunkan Cekiyana's letter could be written in English, was a Dakota who had refused to take sides in the factionalization which beset the Oak River community over the agricultural regulations of the Department of Indian Affairs in the mid 1890s: see Carter, 'Agriculture and Agitation,' at 7.

92 Sluman and Goodwill, *John Tootoosis*, writing at 201 of the growing involvement of Cree women in Aboriginal political life in the past several decades, note: 'It was something of a surprise at first, especially perhaps among the plains tribes to have women emerging as dynamic and effective leaders as traditionally they had been more or less "silent partners" in the old way of life. (and we can hear a lot of Cree men laughing at *that* statement).' See also Elias, *Dakota of the Canadian Northwest*, at 106. Carter, 'Constructing the "Indian Woman",' notes that, despite the hostility directed against Aboriginal women from the white community, Aboriginal oral and documentary sources record that the work of the women was vital in providing material and spiritual resources to Aboriginal communities during the upheaval in the late nineteenth century.

93 Letter from Chief Tunkan Cekiyana, Griswold, to Department of Indian Affairs, Ottawa, 10 January 1903, PAC file 60-511-1.

94 Letter from Frank Pedley, Ottawa, to Chief Tunkan Cekiyana, Griswold, 27 January 1903; letter from David Laird, Indian Commissioner, to J.D. McLean, Secretary of Indian Affairs, 9 January 1903, PAC file 60-511-1. For biographical details on Pedley, see *

95 PAC file 60-511-1. I have been unable to locate any biographical information on Magistrate Lyons. Police magistrates were appointed by the lieutenant

governor-in-council: RSM 1902, c.104, s.2. Rarely legally trained, such appointees usually came from the ranks of retired officers of the North West Mounted Police or businessmen who had served as justices of the peace. The town of Griswold, in the western judicial district, was located 158 miles west of Winnipeg and 26 miles west of Brandon. By 1905, its population was 325. The hotel where the trial was held was destroyed by fire on 10 December 1903. See n.a., *Bridging the Years: Griswold Centennial*, at 248; Griswold United Church Women, *Bridging the Years, 1867–1967: Griswold Centennial Booklet* (n.p.: Souris Plaindealer Limited, n.d.), at 8, 26.

96 A search of the Griswold *Ledger*, the Marquette *Reporter*, and the Brandon *Western Sun* located not one reference to the dance of the Dakota, the trial, the conviction, or the subsequent efforts to procure the release of Wanduta. To the extent that there was any press coverage of similar prosecutions, the reports were fleeting. For details of these, see *

97 For some discussion of the ethnicity of the population that immigrated to Manitoba during this period, see *

98 Letter from Malcolm Turriff, Rapid City, to S. Stewart, Esq., Department of Indian Affairs, Ottawa, 30 January 1903, PAC file 60-511-1.

99 Elias, *Dakota of the Canadian Northwest*, quoting Markle at 104, citing *Sessional Papers* (1895), no. 12, part I, at 59–60; and letter from J.A. Markle to Secretary, Department of Indian Affairs, 3 August 1909, RG10, vol. 3825, file 60-511-2. Elias describes at 81 the consternation of the Indian Commissioner when he read in a local newspaper in 1888 that a committee of 'respectable citizens' had announced plans for a Dominion Day celebration featuring a 'war dance' by the Dakota. The Department of Indian Affairs itself was not above pandering to similar white appetites, as indicated by the Canadian Exhibit at the Chicago World's Fair in 1893. For details on this, see *

100 Thomas Mayne Daly, the Minister of the Interior who introduced the 1895 amendment to the House of Commons, emphasized the need to 'enlarge the law so as to meet several cases that have arisen where it appears that the Indians themselves were not responsible for getting up these dances, but outsiders encouraged them to do it.' *Debates*, House of Commons, 5 July 1895, at 3935.

101 Report of the Indian Commissioner, Regina, A. Forget, to the Honourable Superintendent General, 22 September 1896 (*Sessional Papers*, 1897, no. 14, 287–302); comments of the Deputy Minister of Indian Affairs in the annual reports of 1926 and 1928, as quoted in Sluman and Goodwill, *John Tootoosis*, at 141. For details of governmental efforts to prevent agricultural societies from sponsoring Aboriginal dances at their exhibitions, see *

102 Letter from David Laird, Indian Commissioner, Winnipeg, to Secretary, Department of Indian Affairs, Ottawa, 28 February 1903, PAC file 60-511-1. For details about religious leaders who took similar positions against clemency, see *

103 Letter from David Laird, Indian Commissioner, Winnipeg, to Secretary, Department of Indian Affairs, Ottawa, 28 February 1903, PAC file 60-511-1.

104 *Sessional Papers* (1901), vol. XXXVI, no. 11, paper 27, at 127 notes: 'I might mention … Harry Hotanina, Itoyetuanka, Caske Hanske and Kinyan-wakan, of the Oak River Sioux, who have fields averaging from fifty to ninety acres each, besides small fields of oats and garden stuff.'

105 For details about the firm of Coldwell and Coleman and information about the admission to the Manitoba bar of the first Aboriginal lawyer in 1974, see *

106 For biographical details on Coldwell and Daly, see *

107 For details concerning the Aboriginal deployment of legal counsel and a partial listing of cases in which lawyers represented those accused of illegal dancing, see *

108 *An Act to amend the Indian Act*, S.C. 1926–7, c.32, s.6, provides: 'Every person who, without the consent of the Superintendent General expressed in writing, receives, obtains, solicits or requests from any Indian any payment or contribution or promise of any payment or contribution for the purpose of raising a fund or providing money for the prosecution of any claim which the tribe or band of Indians to which such Indian belongs, or of which he is a member, has or is represented to have for the recovery of any claim or money for the benefit of the said tribe or band, shall be guilty of an offence and liable upon summary conviction for each such offence to a penalty not exceeding two hundred dollars and not less than fifty dollars or to imprisonment for any term not exceeding two months.' See also *Indian Act*, R.S.C. 1927, c.98, s.141. The prohibition on fundraising was not removed until the enactment of *The Indian Act*, S.C. 1951, c.29. For details concerning the genesis of the prohibition, see *

109 On the Dakota financial situation, see Elias, *Dakota of the Canadian North-west*, at 114–15, who also notes that during this decade the Dakota commanded high wages as skilled and trained workers in a number of fields, often earning 'more than the going rate for the labour in their localities.'

110 For details of the federal statutory provisions regarding appeals, see *

111 For details regarding these two writs, see *

112 Statutory Declarations of Akisa, Pazaiyapa, Wasticaka, Kiyewakan, and Hoksidaska, 'In the Matter of Wanduta, an Indian,' 9 February 1903. David Ross, the interpreter, is identified as a 'Manitoba Farmer' of the 'Indian Village near Portage La Prairie,' PAC file 60-511-1.

113 D.J. Hall, *Clifford Sifton: A Lonely Eminence, 1901–1929*, 2 vols. (Vancouver: University of British Columbia Press, 1981 and 1985); W. Leland Clark, *Brandon's Politics and Politicians* (Altona, Man.: D.W. Friesen & Sons, 1981), at 13, 16, 31–4.
114 Letter from George Coldwell, KC, Brandon, to Clifford Sifton, Minister of the Interior, Ottawa, 20 February 1903, PAC file 60-511-1.
115 Rapid City Historical Book Society, *Rapid City*, at 14–33, 83, 116, 345–6.
116 Statutory Declarations of Edward Soldan, John Bowen Mowatt Dunoon, Edmund Cecil Gosset Jackson, and Alexander McKellar, 'In the Matter of Wanduta, an Indian,' 27 February 1903, PAC file 60-511-1.
117 Gresko, 'White "Rites" and Indian "Rites",' notes at 180 that 'public opinion was often on their [the Aboriginal] side and can be measured in the popularity of Indian festivals at town fairs, or the convivial wish that the chiefs and their braves be allowed their "social dances" or "canoe races".'
118 For a discussion of state of undress, see (Gresko) Kennedy, 'Qu'Appelle Industrial School,' at 219, where she recounts Indian Agent Markle's depiction of 'war dances' in which 'Indians ... appear in public in nude attire [Markle had underlined 'half-naked' in the clipping] with little on them except paint and feathers ...'
119 For details regarding the debate over whether to protest against Aboriginal dance, and the ensuing motion passed by the National Council of Women of Canada in 1901, see *
120 Barker, *Brandon*, notes at 165 that in 1915 the Brandon Imperial Order Daughters of the Empire (IODE) had bestowed the Union Jack upon ninety-year-old Antoine Hoka, something he had vowed to 'possess for the rest of my life and wrap around my body at death.'
121 A letter to the editor titled 'Indian Circle Dances,' written by J.H.S. of Plymouth England, published in the *Indian Head Vidette* on 20 May 1903, eulogizes religious liberty, but makes clear that this concept was not applicable to Aboriginal peoples: 'Religious liberty needs to be jealously guarded, but liberty to practice idolatrous rites in a professed Christian country is dangerous to the community at large. It is the opinion of many that the infamous truckling to and protection and patronage of Hindoo idolatry led to the Indian mutiny with its nameless horrors. Idolators naturally seek every opportunity to destroy all Christian government and impurity may soon lead to open insurrection. The evil needs to be promptly dealt with.' See also Allison M. Dussias, 'Ghost Dance and Holy Ghost: The Echoes of Nineteenth-Century Christianization Policy in Twentieth-Century Native American Free Exercise Cases,' *Stanford Law Review*, vol. 49 (1997), 773 at 775, where she notes that even in the American

setting, where the concept of freedom of religion had constitutional standing, 'freedom of religion meant freedom to practice the Christian religion. The government was deemed to have the authority to suppress traditional religious practices and establish Christianity among the Indians, the Constitution notwithstanding.' For a noteworthy exception to the generalization that whites did not imbue Aboriginal peoples with the right to religious freedom, see Regular, 'On Public Display,' regarding the activities of Rev. John McDougall, the Methodist missionary to the Stoney at Morley, Alberta, who campaigned against the prohibition of Aboriginal dance on the basis of First Nations 'religious liberty.'

122 'The Indian Is Naturally Lazy,' Brandon *Western Sun*, 5 June 1903. For further details about this feature, which profiled a Dakota man from Oak River, see *

123 In her book review of Pettipas's *Severing the Ties that Bind* in *Canadian Journal of Law and Society* 10:2 (Fall 1995), 277 at 279, Tina Loo notes: 'In an example of one of capitalism's many ironies, practices that were outlawed because they prevented Indians from learning the proper habits of industry – from internalizing a capitalist work ethic – persisted in commodified form because of their newly-created economic value.' See also Regular, 'Red Backs and White Burdens,' who notes the tensions displayed in Alberta newspaper articles during the second decade of the twentieth century regarding the appropriateness of 'Indian displays' at fairs.

124 The Statutory Declarations of Edward Soldan, John Bowen Mowatt Dunoon, Edmund Cecil Gosset Jackson, and Alexander McKellar, 'In the Matter of Wanduta, an Indian,' 27 February 1903, PAC file 60-511-1, all state: '[On 17 July] a holiday was being observed in Rapid City and races and other amusements were being held there and as part of the entertainment, I and other citizens of Rapid City arranged with the Indians of the Oak River reserve to attend at Rapid City and give a dance for the amusement of the people visiting the town at that time.'

125 Despite a thorough review, I could locate no reported cases on the prosecution of illegal dances against Aboriginal or non-Aboriginal persons in any of the published series of Canadian law reports. Prosecutions against Aboriginal individuals are mentioned in the archival records of the Department of Indian Affairs, but I have found no discussions of any charges laid against non-Aboriginal persons. To be absolutely certain that no prosecutions were ever launched against white individuals, it would be necessary to complete a full review of all the Canadian court records held in various provincial archives. My initial efforts to locate such records in the archives of the Prairie provinces have produced so little documentation that it

would seem that the prospect of completing such a task with any sense of fullness and accuracy may be of dubious practicality.

126 Regular, 'Red Backs and White Burdens,' at 152–4.

127 'Indian Chief Talks to the Governor-General,' Brandon *Western Sun*, 16 October 1902.

128 After completion of a tour of Western Canada in the fall of 1902, Governor-General Lord Minto did present certain Aboriginal grievances to Prime Minister Sir Wilfrid Laurier. The repression of the Sun Dance was one of the concerns Minto mentioned, and he took issue with the 'want of human sympathy' between white officials at Indian Affairs and Aboriginal peoples, and with the 'somewhat narrow religious sentiments' expressed by the former. See PAC Laurier Papers, vol. 248, at 69214–20, Minto to Laurier, 16 January 1903. Sifton had long been irked by Minto's 'gratuitous interference in the administration of Indian Affairs' and this submission appears to have caused a further deterioration in the relationship between the two men; see Hall, *Clifford Sifton*, vol. 2, at 90. However, it appears to have wrought no change in governmental policy.

129 Telegraphs between David Laird and J.D. McLean, 9–10 January 1903; David Laird to Agent James Wilson of the Blackfoot Agency, 11 July 1898, PAC file 60-511-1.

130 Legal Opinion 'The King v. Wanduta,' directed to the Deputy Superintendent General, Department of Indian Affairs, undated [early March 1903], PAC file 60-511-1.

131 As a general rule in indictable offences, justices of the peace (and police magistrates) had only the power to hear the preliminary inquiry, to ascertain if there was sufficient evidence to put the accused on trial, and then to commit the accused for trial before a higher court (such as the Manitoba Court of King's Bench or the Court of General or Quarter Sessions of the Peace, when presided over by a Superior Court judge or a County or District Court judge): James Crankshaw, *A Practical Guide to Police Magistrates and Justices of the Peace* (Montreal: Theoret, 1905), at 115–17.

132 Legal Opinion 'The King v. Wanduta,' directed to the Deputy Superintendent General, Department of Indian Affairs, undated [early March 1903], PAC file 60-511-1.

133 Letter from Frank Pedley, Deputy Superintendent General of Indian Affairs, to E.L. Newcombe, KC, Deputy Minister of Justice, 10 March 1903; letter from Frank Pedley to Mr Collier, Ottawa, 12 March 1903, PAC file 60-511-1.

134 Letter from D.M.J. [full name not indicated], Secretary, Department of Justice, to Frank Pedley, Deputy Superintendent of Indian Affairs, 15 May

1903; Draft letter, from J.D. McLean, Secretary of Indian Affairs, to Messrs Coldwell & Coleman, 15 May 1903, PAC file 60-511-1.

135 On 1 April 1903, David Laird cabled the Secretary of Indian Affairs to advise that the Indian agent on the Peigan reserve had sentenced an Indian to two months under section 114. 'Has he exceeded his jurisdiction in awarding summery [sic] punishment instead of committing accused for trial?' queried Laird. 'Police have raised question,' he noted. J.D. McLean replied the same day: 'If prima facie case under Section 114 Indian Act Agent should have committed for trial. No jurisdiction to try summarily': PAC file 60-511-1.

136 For references to Clifford Sifton's leadership at Indian Affairs, see *

137 Archbishop Langevin wrote to Sifton on 26 December 1903 recommending that the government 'amend the law' if necessary to eradicate the Aboriginal dances that furnished the First Nations with 'the means of opposing all efforts made by the Government and the Missionaries to civilize the Indians ... to earn a living by farming or by raising cattle.' Langevin complained about whites who favoured Aboriginal dances, describing them as 'greedy skimmers' who sought out dancers 'for the sake of lucre' and as 'gentlemen ... in the romantic view of "amateurs".' Clifford Sifton's reply to Archbishop of Saint Boniface, 31 December 1903, is also located in PAC file 60-511-1.

138 Letter from Coldwell & Coleman to Minister of the Interior and Department of Indian Affairs, Ottawa, 20 May 1903, PAC file 60-511-1.

139 Rapid City Historical Book Society, *Rapid City*, at 8, 24–5.

140 'Indians and Live Stock,' Marquette *Reporter*, 20 August 1903. For particulars of the press account, which is characteristically demeaning to Aboriginal communities, see *

141 Barker, *Brandon*, at 96; for particulars of Barker's condescending commentary, see *. Elias, *Dakota of the Canadian Northwest*, notes at 118 that, under David Laird's instructions, the Department of Indian Affairs hired detectives to attend the Brandon Fair in 1907 to 'see that the law is obeyed ...'

142 For details of the prosecutions of Shave Tail, Standing Buffalo, Commodore, and Joe Smith in 1903; Taytapasahsung in 1904; Fineday, Johnny Bagwany, and Ned Harris in 1914; Chief Joseph Kenemotayo, Charles Tott, Seeahpwassum Kenemotayo, Big Chief Face, and Cessaholis in 1915; eight men from Alert Bay in 1920; George Tanner, Mayzenahweeshick, Blackbird, and forty-three Nootka individuals in 1921; forty-nine Kwakiutl in 1922; Chief Red Dog, Cotasse, Adelard Starblanket, Allen Starblanket, and Buffalo Bull in 1932; individuals from the Sakimay First Nation and Goose Lake in 1933; a Kwakiutl in 1935; Chief Mark Shaboqua, Councillor

Pitchenesse, and George Gilbert in 1938, see * In innumerable cases, although formal charges were not laid, the police and Indian Department officials intervened to withhold rations and refuse passes for individuals involved, dismantle dance lodges, confiscate sacred objects, and terminate ceremonial dancing. For further details, see *

143 The enactment was also equally specific about the reach of the criminal law with respect to those who organized stampedes and exhibitions. Any one who 'induced' or 'employed' an 'Indian' to take part in such a performance was deemed just as guilty as those who danced. For details of the 1914 federal statute, see * It is apparent from the legislative debates that the white MPs and senators had no inkling of the wide-ranging sweep of the criminal prohibition already in place. In both parliamentary houses, objections were raised to the prospect of using criminal law to prohibit the traditional customs, festivals, and ceremonies of Aboriginal people, where these were held within the sanctity of Aboriginal communities. Prime Minister Robert Laird Borden erroneously insisted that 'there will be no difficulty at all about the Indians participating in these ceremonials upon their own reserves.' William James Roche, the white Superintendent General of Indian Affairs, was asked whether the new section prohibited the interchanges of visits among reserves for the purpose of attending festival and ceremonial dances, and replied: 'No, it does not.' Yet the new bill did nothing to repeal the earlier sections that had criminalized just such activities. The ignorance of the legislators about something so fundamentally important to the survival of Aboriginal culture is breathtaking. For further details of the legislative debates and examples of other whites who exhibited similar ignorance, see *

144 Arthur Meighen, the white Minister of the Interior, announced that the reason justices of the peace or Indian agents standing in their stead would process all such cases in future was simply 'to avoid the expense of proceeding by indictment.' He said nothing about how such a change in procedure would relegate all these prosecutions to hearings before individuals who had little training in law, and substantially insulate their actions from legal challenges. During the same discussion, Meighen also indicated that he felt that 'the Indians of this country have been liberally and generously dealt with' and that this was the 'spirit' underlying the act. For details of the 1918 provision and the House of Commons debates, see *

145 Allan Webster Neill, the independent white MP from Comos–Alberni, raised the question of exactly what the term 'in aboriginal costume' had meant in the first place. The Minister of the Interior, Thomas Gerow Murphy, replied in an offhand manner: 'I believe the hon. member would

find the accepted definition in any standard dictionary.' For details of the
House of Commons debates and the 1933 statutory provision, see *

146 For details of the House of Commons debates, see *

147 For details of the legal challenge mounted in 1903 by Etchease, a Saulteaux
from the Muscowpetung First Nation in Saskatchewan, see *

148 For details of the efforts of a group of Dakota to evade prosecution in 1917
and the innovative strategies adopted by Aboriginal communities to take
advantage of legal loopholes, see *

149 For details about petitions drafted to protest the legal attack on religious
and spiritual practices by Chief Thunderchild, O-ka-nu, Charles Fineday,
Joe Ma-ma-gway-see, Chief Red Dog, Blackbird, Chief Ermineskin, Chief
Matoose, Chief Day Walker, and others from across Manitoba, Saskatchewan, and Alberta, see * For commentary on the post–First World War
efforts of F.O. Loft, the work of the League of Indians of Canada, the
League of Indians in Western Canada, and the post–Second World War
efforts of the Protective Association for Indians and Their Treaties, the
Indian Association of Alberta, and the Union of Saskatchewan Indians,
see *

150 For biographical details about Pauline Johnson and her performances in
Rapid City in 1896 and 1899, and nearby Alexander, Manitoba, in 1902,
see *

151 E. Pauline Johnson, *The Moccasin Maker* (Toronto: Ryerson Press, 1913), at
139–43. The essay was first published in the London *Daily Express* on 3
August 1906. Johnson equates the firekeeper of the Iroquois council to the
bishop – 'his garb of fringed buckskin and ermine was no more grotesque
than the vestments worn by the white preachers in high places'– and
describes the ceremony of the 'White Dog Sacrifice,' a major rite of the
Midwinter Ceremony of the Six Nations.

152 For details of Pauline Johnson's connections with Sir Clifford Sifton and
Indian Affairs official Duncan Campbell Scott, see * For another cross-
cultural critique concerning dance, written by Dr Edward Ahenakew, a
Sandy Lake Cree who was also an Anglican priest, see *

153 For details of the statutory provision of 1951 and the parliamentary debates, see *

154 Wallis would ultimately publish a fifty-seven-page anthropological paper
describing the 'Canadian Dakota Sun Dance' in 1919. See Wallis, *Canadian
Dakota*, at 126; Wallis, 'Canadian Dakota Sun Dance,' at 323–80; Wilson D.
Wallis, 'Beliefs and Tales of the Canadian Dakota,' *Journal of American Folk-
Lore* 36 (1923), at 36; Pettipas, 'Severing the Ties that Bind,' at 250.

155 Wallis, *Canadian Dakota*, at 126; Wallis, 'Canadian Dakota Sun Dance,' at

331–2. For details of the conversation Wallis recounts having with the recovered individual, see *

156 Wallis, *Canadian Dakota*, at 332–5. For details of the ongoing disputes between the Oak River Dakota and the Indian Agent, and commentary regarding the persistence of traditional dancing from another white anthropologist, James Howard, who conducted research at each of the eight Canadian 'Sioux reserves' in 1972, see *

4: 'They Are a People Unaquainted with Subordination'

1 Details of the legal proceeding are drawn from *Sero v Gault* (1921), 64 D.L.R. 327, 50 O.L.R. 27, 20 O.W.N. 16 (Ont. S.C.); 'Indians Have Not Additional Rights,' Belleville *Daily Intelligencer*, 5 March 1921, p. 1; 'Indians Have Not Additional Rights,' Kingston *British Whig Standard*, 5 March 1921, p. 1. The actual court documents for this case no longer survive. The Ontario attorney general's file 'was not among those selected for retention in 1965,' and no further records remain within the premier's correspondence or the Department of Natural Resources: Notes from discussion with archivist John Choles, Archives of Ontario, 10 June 1994. On the operation of the seine net, see the description by Judge Riddell in *Sero v Gault*, at 328.

2 For sources on the history of the fishing industry on the Great Lakes and the Bay of Quinte, see *

3 'Deseronto News,' Kingston *British Whig Standard*, 22 March 1921, p. 5.

4 For references to the applicable federal and provincial legislation, and similar enactments in force between 1821 and 1914, see *

5 For references concerning the federal and provincial statutes in force between 1823 and 1914 that provided exceptions for 'Indians,' see *

6 'Indians Have Not Additional Rights,' Belleville *Daily Intelligencer*, 5 March 1921, p. 1; 'Indians Have Not Additional Rights,' Kingston *British Whig Standard*, 5 March 1921, p.1.

7 For sources regarding the history of the Iroquois generally and Tyendinaga in particular, see *

8 The date of the founding of the confederacy is unsettled. Historians and anthropologists have made estimates that range from 1450 to 1660, with First Nations tradition following the earlier date. The Iroquois Confederacy initially consisted of five nations – Mohawk, Oneida, Onondaga, Cayuga, and Seneca. The sixth nation, the Tuscarora, joined the confederacy after being driven from North Carolina around 1713. The harmonious political union forged by the League of the Hodenosaunee would continue for four centuries, despite inevitable tensions and stresses, a feat no other league of

nations has ever been able to duplicate. Darlene M. Johnston, 'The Quest of the Six Nations Confederacy for Self-Determination,' *University of Toronto Faculty of Law Review*, vol.44 (Spring 1986) 1, notes at 9 that the richness of this democratic tradition has prompted commentators to conclude that 'politically, there was nothing in the Empires and kingdoms of Europe in the fifteenth and sixteenth centuries to parallel the democratic constitution of the Iroquois Confederacy, with its provisions for initiative, referendum and recall, and its suffrage for women as well as for men.' Lewis H. Morgan, *League of the Ho-De-No-Sau-Nee or Iroquois* (Rochester: Sage, 1851), noted at 51-2, 133, that the Ho-De-No-Sau-Nee was 'perhaps the only league of nations ever instituted among men, which can point to three centuries of uninterrupted domestic unity and peace.' See also M.P.P. Simon, 'The Haldimand Agreement: A Continuing Covenant,' *American Indian Culture and Research Journal*, vol.7 (1983) 27 at 28; Daniel K. Richter, *The Ordeal of the Longhouse: The Peoples of the Iroquois in the Era of European Colonization* (Chapel Hill: University of North Carolina, 1992), at 1, 30; Mary A. Druke, 'Iroquois and Iroquoian in Canada,' in R. Bruce Morrison and C. Roderick Wilson, eds., *Native Peoples: The Canadian Experience* (Toronto: McClelland & Stewart, 1986), 302 at 309; Matthew Dennis, *Cultivating a Landscape of Peace: Iroquois–European Encounters in Seventeenth-Century America* (Ithaca, N.Y.: Cornell University Press, 1993).

9 Druke, 'Iroquois and Iroquoian,' at 302. For information on the history and settlement patterns of Iroquoian-speaking peoples, see *

10 Druke, 'Iroquois and Iroquoian,' refers at 304 to Jacques Cartier's meeting. Barbara Graymont, *The Iroquois in the American Revolution* (Syracuse, N.Y.: Syracuse University Press, 1972), notes at 6 that 'the identity of these Laurentian Iroquois has always been debatable. They have been variously classed as Huron, Petun, Tuscarora, Mohawk, Seneca, Oneida, and Onondaga by puzzled scholars. For information on the movements and settlement patterns of the Iroquois, see *

11 Druke, 'Iroquois and Iroquoian,' at 309; Gerald E. Boyce, *Historic Hastings* (Belleville: Ontario Intelligencer Ltd, 1967), at 19–20, describing the Mohawk community as of the late eighteenth century. Graymont, *The Iroquois*, notes at 147 that many of the Fort Hunter Mohawks 'lived in far better circum- stances than their white neighbors ... They had considerable livestock, great quantities of Indian corn, potatoes, turnips, and cabbage, sturdy houses and barns, wagons, sleighs, and farm implements. Many of the houses were also comfortably furnished and even had window glass – a rare item on the frontier.'

12 Tehanetorens, *Wampum Belts* (Ohsweken, Ont.: Iroqrafts, 1993), at 10–11, has a detailed explanation of the history of wampum belts and their significance. The origin of the 'Covenant Chain' dates back to the formal alliance struck between the British and the Iroquois at Fort Albany in 1664: Andrea Green, 'Land, Leadership, and Conflict: The Six Nations' Early Years on the Grand River,' MA thesis (University of Western Ontario, 1984), at 12. Ella Cork, *The Worst of the Bargain* (San Jacinto, Calif.: Foundation for Social Research, 1962), describes the wampum at 52: 'This is a band possibly thirty inches long and four inches wide of polished shell beads in natural colours strung and stitched together on deer sinew. There is a red man and a white man joined by two black chains running parallel to show their joint status as "separate and equal".' Cork also notes that the wampum, originally kept at Onondaga, was brought to Grand River, and produced by the Six Nations of Grand River in litigation in 1959 (see discussion of the *Logan* case in the longer Web site* version of the note 81). For sources on the diplomatic negotiations of the Iroquois, see *

13 For sources on Johnson's and Claus's statements, and the sovereignty status of the Iroquois in their relations with the French in the eighteenth century, see *

14 Mohawk historian Amy Huggard, *Ty-En-Din-Aga* (n.p., n.d.), Collection of Anglican Diocese of Ontario Archives, Kingston, Ontario (Box 4T-1, item 33), notes at 29: '… the Mohawks fought so fiercely and effectively under the leadership of William Johnson that the purpose of the French campaign was completely thwarted and in 1763 Canada was ceded to England. In gratitude, England knighted William Johnson and referred to Canada as "England's gift from her loyal Mohawks".' See also Morgan, *Ho-De-No-Sau-Nee*, at 10–11 and 22; G. Elmore Reaman, *The Trail of the Iroquois Indians* (London: Frederick Muller, 1967), at 30–59.

15 On the military negotiations between the Six Nations and the British, and biographical references for Brant and Deserontyon, see *

16 For sources on the war and the treaty, see *

17 For references, see *

18 For information on the British purchase of land from the Mississauga and the subsequent relations between the Mohawks and the Mississauga, see *

19 For information and sources on the division of the two communities, and the oral history accounts of Deganwidah, see *

20 For details about the allotment of land and subsequent surrenders of some portions, and sources describing the Tyendina settlement, see *

21 Letter from Joseph Brant to unidentified correspondent, 1807, quoted in

Annette Rosenstiel, *Red and White: Indian Views of the White Man, 1492–1982* (New York: Universe Books, 1983), at 113. For information on the patterns of acculturation as well as resistance to acculturation, see *

22 For information on the status of women in Iroquois society, see *

23 Comments of Pauline Johnson, published in 'The Lodge of the Law-Makers,' London *Daily Express*, Summer 1906, n.p., as reprinted in E. Pauline Johnson, *The Moccasin Maker* (Tucson: University of Arizona Press, 1987; orig. pub. 1913 by Ryerson Press, Toronto), at 232. For a more detailed discussion of Johnson, see her comments on Aboriginal dance in chapter 3.

24 For sources on the detrimental impact that European colonization had upon gender equality within Iroquois culture, see *

25 Information about Eliza (Brant) Sero has been constructed from the surviving records of the Diocese of Ontario Archives, Anglican Church of Canada, Kingston, Ontario, Tyendinaga Parish Registers, 4-T-9, 4-T-10. Her birth records are not available, as fire destroyed all the Anglican baptism records for the period 1852–76. Genealogy records compiled by G. Ronald Green of Belleville, Ontario, have enabled me to confirm information about Eliza's parents and siblings. Eliza's father was Jacob Oak Brant (Jacobus 'Cobus' Brant). Eliza's mother, Margaret Brant, may have been Margaret Powles prior to her marriage, since Ron Green has records of a marriage on 20 October 1840 between Margaret Powles and Cobus Brant. Eliza's siblings include Catherine Brant, Betsy Oak (Lizzie), Alva, Hugh, Elizabeth, and possibly one additional brother. Information about Eliza Sero's clan is derived from descendants of her sister, Catherine. Catherine Brant had a daughter, Josephine Brant, whose daughter was Helena (*née* Sero) Pfefferle. Helena Pfefferle is a member of the Turtle Clan, and since clans descend matrilineally, Eliza (Brant) Sero would have come from the Turtle Clan as well. Ron Green was unable to locate information about Eliza's Mohawk name, since none of the Mohawk names were registered in written records during this period. The Anglican Diocese of Ontario retains the marriage certificate, 5 October 1882, which lists two witnesses: Lydia Maracle and I.G. Culbertson. Israel Sero's name is listed as Israel Sero/Moses and Israel Scero on some later documents. His occupation is listed as 'labourer' on the baptism certificates for the children. See also notes from Constance Backhouse, 'Interview with David Maracle, Centre for Iroquoian Studies, University of Western Ontario,' London, 22 June 1994; Constance Backhouse, 'Interview with William Isaac "Ike" Hill (born 22 September 1901),' Tyendinaga Territory, 3 September 1994; Constance Backhouse, 'Interview with Audrey (*née* Green) Chisholm, great granddaughter of Eliza Sero,' Belleville, 21 September 1994.

26 Baptism certificates survive for Clara Bella, Theresa, Earl Reuben, Annie
   Elfreda (also spelled 'Alfreda'), and James. The birth years of Maud and
   Nelson Lorne have been constructed from their subsequent marriage certificates. Census records (1901) held by the Tyendinaga Library (copy on file
   with the author) list an additional daughter, Rosa (Rose), three years
   younger than Theresa. Backhouse, 'Interview with Audrey Chisholm';
   Backhouse, 'Interview with Ike Hill.'
27 Tyendinaga Library census records list the date of Israel Sero's death. Karen
   Lewis, Tyendinaga Librarian, advises that the census records kept there note
   that Reuben died in France in 1917: telephone conversation, 25 August 1994.
   The Anglican Diocese of Ontario burial register lists Israel Scero's date of
   burial as 23 November 1914. A plaque in the Anglican Christ Church, Royal
   Chapel of the Mohawks, Tyendinaga Reserve, dedicated to the war dead of
   1914–19, lists Reuben Sero among the deceased soldiers. For details of the
   mixed response of the Six Nations to military service and the racial discrimination within the military, see * The Anglican Diocese of Ontario retains
   three marriage certificates for Eliza Sero's daughters. Theresa Sero, age
   twenty, resident of Tyendinaga, was married on 15 August 1905 to Peter
   Green, the son of William Green and Elizabeth Brant. Peter is described as a
   twenty-eight-year-old labourer, born at Tyendinaga but currently residing
   in Deseronto. Maud Scero, age nineteen, a resident of the Mohawk Reserve,
   was married on 8 August 1911 to William Hill, the son of Solomon Hill and
   Catherine Brant. William is listed as a twenty-six-year-old resident of
   Tyendinaga and a labourer. Tyendinaga Library census records suggest that
   Rose was also married by this time. Her married name was Rose Pinn.
   Nelson Lorne Sero, age eighteen, born in Deseronto but living at
   Tyendinaga and listed as a labourer, was married on 7 September 1928 to
   Clealah Brant. Clealah Brant was twenty years old, and had been born and
   raised at Tyendinaga, the daughter of David S. and Eliza Brant. The wit-
   nesses to the latter marriage were James Sero of Tyendinaga and Hilda Sero
   of Deseronto. Ike Hill describes the net as a 'costly' one, since it was made
   with expensive twine, corks, netting, rope, and jacks: Backhouse, 'Interview
   with Ike Hill.'
28 On the effect of the First World War and the activities of Chief
   Thunderwater and Frederick Ogilvie Loft, see E. Brian Titley, *A Narrow
   Vision: Duncan Campbell Scott and the Administration of Indian Affairs in
   Canada* (Vancouver: University of British Columbia Press, 1986), at 94–109;
   Olive Patricia Dickason, *Canada's First Nations* (Toronto: McClelland &
   Stewart, 1992), at 326–8.
29 Titley, *A Narrow Vision*, at 94–109; Dickason, *Canada's First Nations*, at 326–8.

See also the account of the political organizing efforts of Deskaheh (Levi General) from Six Nations Grand River in Barbara Graymont, ed., *Fighting Tuscarora: The Autobiography of Chief Clinton Rickard* (Syracuse, N.Y.: Syracuse University Press, 1973), at 58-66.

30 Edward Guss Porter, KC, was born on 28 May 1859 at Consecon, Prince Edward County, Ontario. He was educated at Albert University, and married in 1883 to Annie Morrow. A Presbyterian by religion, Porter was first returned to the House of Commons in 1901, and re-elected in 1904, 1908, 1911, 1917, and 1921. See Col. Ernest J. Chambers, ed., *The Canadian Parliamentary Guide 1924* (Ottawa, 1925), at 187. On 3 April 1918, as a consequence of a petition signed by 176 First Nations individuals from all the major reserves in Southern Ontario and Quebec (including Tyendinaga), E. Gus Porter introduced a private member's bill into the House of Commons to incorporate a Council for the Indian Tribes of Canada. Arthur Meighen and Prime Minister Borden placed concerted pressure upon Porter to withdraw the bill after first reading. He did so. See Titley, *A Narrow Vision*, at 93–101.

31 *Black's Law Dictionary*, 6th ed. (St. Paul, Minn.: West Publishing, 1990), at 1508, defines 'trover' as follows: 'In common law practice, the action of trover (or trover and conversion) is a species of action on the case, and originally lay for the recovery of damages against a person who had *found* another's goods and wrongfully converted them to his own use. Subsequently the allegation of the loss of the goods by the plaintiff and the finding of them by the defendant was merely fictitious, and the action became the remedy for any wrongful interference with or detention of the goods of another. In form a fiction; in substance, a remedy to recover the value of personal chattels *wrongfully* converted by another to his own use. Common-law form of action to recover value of goods or chattels by reason of an alleged unlawful interference with possessory right of another, by assertion or exercise of possession or dominion over chattels, which is adverse and hostile to rightful possessor.'

32 Samuel Robinson Clarke, *A Treatise on Criminal Law as Applicable to the Dominion of Canada* (Toronto: Carswell, 1872), recommended at 457 binding 'Indian witnesses' according to whatever ceremonies were traditionally used in Native cultures, 'however strange and fantastic the ceremony might be.' For good measure, he also recommended swearing them in 'on the New Testament' if they believed 'in a supreme being who created all things and in a future state of reward and punishment according to their conduct in this life.' For examples of statutes that expressly permit Aboriginal witnesses to testify, see *

33 For details of the federal statutory provisions in force between 1874 and

1927, British Columbia enactments between 1867 and 1948, and a series of judicial rulings on these issues, see *

34 Bayly appeared for the Crown in *The King v Beboning* (1908), 13 C.C.C. 405, 12 O.W.R. 484, 17 O.L.R. 23 (Ont. C.A.), in which he convinced the court to hold that the theft provisions of the Criminal Code could be enforced against 'Indians' on a 'reserve.' For more details on Edward Bayly, who appeared on behalf of the Crown in the prosecution of the Ku Klux Klan in 1930, see discussion of *R. v Phillips* in chapter 6.

35 *Sero v Gault*, at 328–30.

36 Born on 29 March 1863, Chisholm joined the 7th Fusilliers as a lieutenant while still a law student, and served in the Northwest Rebellion in 1885. A Conservative party member, Chisholm was given the party nomination in 1885, just after Prime Minister Sir John A. Macdonald (briefly) extended the franchise to Indians. Chisholm's political campaigning among his First Nations constituents did not lead to electoral success, and he was defeated in the election. It did, however, lead to a heightened appreciation of Aboriginal concerns. Chisholm was described in his newspaper obituary as an individual who 'took a special interest in [Indian] welfare,' and 'one of the best informed persons in the Dominion on Indian rights and treaties.' Chisholm was called to the bar in 1888, made a KC in 1921, and practised law continuously in London as a sole practitioner until his death at the age of seventy-nine on 11 January 1943. He was predeceased by his wife, Alice Southworth, and survived by two sons, Gilbert and W.G.H. Chisholm, and two daughters, Doris and Constance. For biographical information on Chisholm, see * Chisholm provided legal services to the Chief Deskeheh (Levi General) and the Six Nations Grand River on the topic of sovereignty between 1919 and 1921, as discussed in Titley, *A Narrow Vision*, at 114–17. He compiled 'historical evidence in support of the claim,' made representations before the committee of the House of Commons to oppose the proposed legislation on compulsory enfranchisement, submitted a petition to the governor general, and lobbied for a reference to the Supreme Court of Canada on the question of Six Nations sovereignty. For details about Chisholm's other litigation on behalf of Aboriginal clients, see *

37 I have been unable to locate any copies of Chisholm's petition, which one scholar suggests may have been as long as 180 pages: Sidney L. Harring, '"The Liberal Treatment of Indians": Native People in Nineteenth Century Ontario Law,' *Saskatchewan Law Review*, vol. 56 (1992), 297. If the original petition was filed with the court records, it would have been destroyed when the Archives of Ontario culled the case file in 1965. No copies have been located in the premier's correspondence or the Department of Natural

Resources files held by the Archives of Ontario. A search of the Public
Archives of Canada, 'Correspondence, Accounts, Reports etc. Regarding the
Political Status of the Six Nations,' RG10, vol.2285, 57-169-1A and 1B, has
likewise not elicited the missing petition. The Six Nations Grand River Band
Office at Ohsweken has not been able to locate the petition among their
records. Consequently, I have attempted to reconstruct the arguments that
would have been included in the petition from the following sources: A.G.
Chisholm, Solicitor for Six Nations, 'The Case of the Six Nations,' London
Free Press, 20 March 1920, p. 4; letter by A.G. Chisholm, 'Explanation of
Unrest of Six Nations,' Brantford *Expositor*, 29 March 1921, p. 11; 'Memorandum as to National Status of the Indians in Canada, with particular reference to the case of The Six Nations,' a twenty-nine-page document signed
by Chisholm in London, Ontario, 8 October 1920, Public Archives of Canada
[hereinafter cited as PAC], RG10, vol.2285, 57-169-1A, Pt. 2; 'Memorandum
on the Relation of the Dominion Government of Canada with the Six Nations of the Grand River,' a fifteen-page document submitted at London by
Chief Deskaheh to the Colonial Office, August 1921, PAC RG10, vol. 2285,
57-169-1A, Pt. 2; Correspondence from Deskaheh, Speaker of the Ho-De-No-
Sau-Nees Confederation of the Grand River to His Majesty King George the
Fifth, 22 October 1924, PAC RG10, vol. 2285, 56-169-1A, Pt. 2. For details of
similar arguments made by the Six Nations Confederacy at this time to
oppose the supplanting of traditional forms of government by an elected
council under the Indian Act, see *

38 The lengthy text of the Six Nations position, written by Chief J.S. Johnson,
was published as 'Six Nations Indians Protest Against Compulsory Enfranchisement,' Brantford *Expositor*, 16 March 1921, p. 3. The article claims that
the Six Nations status rests, in part, upon their position as 'aborigines of this
country.' It refers specifically to rape and theft as two categories of criminal
law ceded to the Canadian government, but later notes that 'three crimes'
had been conceded. Presumably the offence of murder was the third. Cork,
Worst of the Bargain, notes at 109–10 that Governor General Sir Guy Carleton
issued an administrative directive in 1775 regarding the resolution of disputes between whites and whites, or between whites and 'Indians' on their
'reserves.' The directive apparently adverted to a concession from First
Nation local councils that they 'should not try to punish the crimes of
murder or theft as these crimes would be under the jurisdiction of the
Province.' Harring, 'The Liberal Treatment of Indians,' notes at 352–3 that
the Grand River Iroquois continued to operate a highly organized legal
system, with dozens of recorded cases dealing with constitutional law, land
law, Indian citizenship and inheritance. Harring adds at 370–1: 'Native
legal, social and political histories exist in twentieth century Ontario, just as

they existed in the nineteenth. The legal history of the Grand River Iroquois spans both centuries ...'

39 For reference to the multiple petitions, see *

40 For references concerning the disdainful repudiation of the earlier negotiations, see *

41 For details of Deserontyon's requests and a full text of the land grant, see *

42 'Indians Have Not Additional Rights,' Belleville *Daily Intelligencer*, 5 March 1921, p. 1; 'Indians Have Not Additional Rights,' Kingston *British Whig Standard*, 5 March 1921, p. 1. Similar sentiments were voiced by white Alberta MP Frank Oliver, himself a former minister of the Interior, in the House of Commons seven years earlier, when he argued that the Six Nations were 'in a different legal position from any Indian bands who are native to the country. These Indian bands on the Grand river ... were given lands under a special treaty, not as subjects of Great Britain, but as allies of Great Britain ...': Canada, House of Commons, *Parliamentary Debates* [Hansard], 11 May 1914, at 3537.

43 For references to the emerging historical literature on the legal clash between European and First Nations communities see *

44 *The King* v *Phelps*, [1823] U.C.K.B. 47 at 52–4. The decision merely notes at 54: 'Judgment in favour of the Crown.' In argument, Esther Phelps's white counsel referred to the Mohawk as 'the faithful and attached allies' of the king, and put forth the claim of sovereignty in clear, if patronizing, terms: 'The foundation of the title from General Haldimand is evidently a treaty, and as such must be recognized by the court ... The Indians must be considered a distinct, though feudatory people; they were transported here by compact; they are not subject to mere positive laws, to statute labour, or militia duty, though perhaps to punishment for crimes against the natural law, or law of nations. It may be considered as a ridiculous anomaly, but it appears ... that these sort of societies, resident within and circumscribed by another territory, though in some measure independent of it, frequently exist, and that the degree of independence may be infinitely varied; and however barbarous these Indians may be considered, the treaty under which they migrated to and reside in this country is binding.' The white solicitor general, Henry John Boulton, insisted that 'the Indians are bound by the common law,' and argued: 'The supposition that the Indians are not subject to the laws of the country is absurd; they are as much so as the French loyalists who settled here after the French revolution, who came to this province from a country perfectly independent, and of which the independence was never doubted.' See also William Renwick Riddell, 'Esther Phelps,' *The University Magazine*, vol. 12 (Montreal, October 1913), at 466–71.

45 *Doe D. Sheldon* v *Ramsay et al.* (1852), 9 U.C.Q.B. 105 at 123 and 133. On the
matter of Haldimand's original land grant, Chief Justice Robinson took issue
with the form of the instrument under which the grant was purportedly
made, and with the nature of the organization receiving the grant (at 122–3):
'In the first place, the Six Nations of Indians took no legal estate under the
instrument given by General Sir Frederick Haldimand. He did not own the
land in question, and could convey no legal interest by any instrument
under *his seal et arms*. Being Governor of Canada, he could have made a
grant of Crown lands by letters patent under the great seal of the province,
which would have been a matter of record; but he could no more grant this
large tract on the Grand River, by an instrument under his seal at arms, than
he could have alienated the whole of Upper Canada by such an instrument.
But secondly, if such an instrument had been made under the great seal, in
the ordinary and proper manner, it could pass no legal interest for want of a
grantee or grantees, properly described and capable of holding. It grants
nothing to any person or persons by name, and in their natural capacity.
General Haldimand could not have incorporated the Six Nations of Indians,
if he had attempted to do it expressly, by an instrument under *his seal et
arms*, and still less could he do it in such a manner incidentally and indirectly by implication. A grant "to the Mohawks Indians, and such others of
the Six Nations as might wish to settle on the Grand River, of a tract of land,
to be enjoyed by them and their posterity forever," could not have the effect
upon any principle of the law of England of vesting a legal estate in anybody. It could amount to nothing more than what it was well understood
and intended to be, a declaration by the government that it would abstain
from granting those lands to others, and would reserve them to be occupied
by the Indians of the Six Nations. It gave no estate in fee, or for life, or for a
term of years, which the Indians could individually or collectively transmit.'
On the question of the applicability of British law, Judge Robert Easton
Burns, who wrote a concurring opinion in this case, concluded at 133–4: 'It
can never be pretended that these Indians while situated within the limits of
this province, as a British province at least, were recognized as a separate
and independent nation, governed by laws of their own, distinct from the
general law of the land, having a right to deal with the soil as they pleased;
but they were considered as a distinct race of people, consisting of tribes
associated altogether distinct from the general mass of inhabitants, it is true,
but yet as British subjects, and under the control of and subject to the general law of England. As regards these lands on the Grand River, the Indians
had no national existence, nor any recognized patriarchal or other form of
government or management, so far as we see in any way … Although they

are distinct tribes as respects their race, yet that gave them no corporate powers or existence ...' For a more detailed analysis of Robinson's judicial position, see Sidney Harring, '"The Common Law Is Not Part Savage and Part Civilized": Chief Justice John Beverley Robinson, Canadian Legal Culture, and the Denial of Native Rights in Mid-Nineteenth-Century Upper Canada,' unpublished manuscript, 1995. Harring notes at 44 that 'many of the members of the family compact, including Robinson, were involved in land speculations of dubious legality, and much of this land was clouded by "Indian title".' Harring concludes at 61 that 'at the core of Robinson's jurisprudence was the denial of aboriginal sovereignty and land rights, aboriginal rights that impeded the orderly European settlement of Upper Canada.' For an example of similar judicial reasoning in the 1928 Nova Scotia County Court case of *Rex* v *Syliboy* and several other cases, see *

46 Dickason, *Canada's First Nations*, at 176; Olive Patricia Dickason, *The Myth of the Savage and the Beginnings of French Colonialism in the Americas* (Edmonton: University of Alberta Press, 1984). William B. Newell (Ta-io-wah-ron-ha-gai), *Crime and Justice among the Iroquois Nations* (Montreal: Caughnawaga Historical Society, 1965), provides detailed, contradictory evidence about the complex social, political, and legal regime developed by Iroquois nations. For some sense of the countervailing perspectives developed by the First Nations about the white European colonizers, see Rosenstiel, *Red and White: Indian Views of the White Man.*

47 Hilary Bates Neary, 'William Renwick Riddell: A Bio-Bibliographical Study,' MA thesis (University of Western Ontario, 1977), at 1–9, 20, 34–8; 'Riddell, Hon. Wm. Renwick'; Henry James Morgan, ed., *The Canadian Men and Women of the Time*, 2d ed. (Toronto: William Briggs, 1912), at 941; 'Riddell, Hon. William Renwick,' in B.M. Greene, ed., *Who's Who and Why: 1921* (Toronto: International Press, 1921), at 94; W. Stewart Wallace, ed., *The Macmillan Dictionary of Canadian Biography*, 3d ed. (Toronto: Macmillan, 1963), at 628; and obituaries: '39 years in Supreme Court – Mr. Justice Riddell dies,' *Toronto Daily Star*, 19 February 1945; 'Justice W.R. Riddell dies soon after wife,' Toronto *Globe and Mail*, 19 February 1945.

48 Neary, 'Riddell,' at 5–6, 8–9, 20. For a full listing of the bibliography, see Neary at 54–161. The reference to 'slang' is found in Morgan, 'Riddell,' at 941. The reference to the hearing aid is from Lita-Rose Betcherman, *The Little Band: The Clashes between the Communists and the Canadian Establishment, 1928–1932* (Ottawa: Deneau, 1983), at 39, citing her interview with Harvey McCullogh, QC, 18 November 1978.

49 On Riddell's involvement with *The Dawn of Tomorrow* see Neary, 'Riddell,' at 27; see also William Renwick Riddell, 'The Slave in Canada,' *Journal of*

Negro History 5:3 (1920), 261. On Riddell's insensitivity to racism see Carolyn Strange, *Toronto's Girl Problems: The Perils and Pleasures of the City, 1880–1930* (Toronto: University of Toronto Press, 1995), at 250, citing Robin W. Winks, *The Blacks in Canada: A History*, 2d ed. (Montreal and Kingston: McGill-Queen's University Press, 1997), at 298. On Riddell's judicial role in the trial of a Black man, Frank Roughmond, who was convicted of murdering a white woman in Stratford in 1908, see *

50 Canadian Social Hygiene Council, *Social Health* 1:11 (Midsummer number, 1925), lists William Renwick Riddell as president and Dr Gordon Bates, a well-known eugenicist, as general secretary. An article published in that volume is titled 'To Advocate the Knowledge and Practice of Social Hygiene as the One Way to Racial Improvement,' with a subheading: 'The Race is to the Strong.' I am indebted to John McLaren for providing me with this information. On the Canadian Social Hygiene Council and the eugenics reform movement in Canada, see Angus McLaren, *Our Own Master Race: Eugenics in Canada, 1885–1945* (Toronto: McClelland & Stewart, 1990).

51 William Renwick Riddell, 'Administration of Criminal Law in the Far North of Canada,' *Journal of Criminal Law, Criminology and Police Science* 20:2 (August 1929), 294–302 at 294. The article promotes the importance of extending English criminal law to northern areas, and begins with the following passage: 'When in 1869, the Dominion of Canada acquired at the cost of £300,000 Sterling, the enormous territory known as Rupert's Land from the Hudson Bay Company, she was not blind to the very great responsibilities she was assuming. While there was a magnificent stretch of land in the southern part, fitted for the highest kind of agriculture, and certain to attract the highest form of immigrant of the White Race, there was also known to be toward the North, an expanse of territory, apparently fit for nothing but the trapper and such forms of humanity and grades of civilization as were represented by the Esquimaux and the wandering Indian tribes. These had little conception of government by law, and seldom considered themselves to be bound by anything but their own desires. Amongst them, too, were degenerate members of the higher race, generally playing on their savage appetites and making profit of their vices.'

52 For a listing of articles that touch on First Nations matters, see *

53 'Esther Phelps,' *The University Magazine*, at 466–7, 470–1.

54 William Renwick Riddell, 'The Sad Tale of an Indian Wife,' *The Canadian Law Times*, vol. 40 (Toronto, 1920), 983; republished in *Journal of Criminal Law and Criminology*, vol. 13 (May 1922), 82–9; 'Esther Phelps,' *The University Magazine*, at 466.

55 For an account of the episode concerning Clara Brett Martin, see Constance

Backhouse, *Petticoats and Prejudice: Women and Law in Nineteenth-Century Canada* (Toronto: Women's Press and the Osgoode Society, 1991), at 308. Riddell later wrote in 'Women as Practitioners of Law,' in *Journal of Comparative Legislation*, vol. 18 (1918), 201 at 206: 'I do not think that the most fervent advocate of women's rights could claim that the admission of women to the practice of law has had any appreciable effect on the Bar, the practice of law, the Bench or the people ... [T]he admission of women is regarded with complete indifference by all but those immediately concerned.' See also 'An Old-Time Misogynist,' Toronto *Canadian Magazine* 58:5 (March 1922), at 379–80.

56 *Jones* v *Grand Trunk R.W. Co.* (1904), 3 O.W.R. 705 (Ont. Div. Ct.); *Jones* v *Grand Trunk R.W. Co.* (1905), 5 O.W.R. 611 (Ont. C.A.). For details of the action, see *

57 The Mississauga claim in *Henry* v *The King* (1905), 9 Ex.C.R. 417 (Exchequer Ct. of Can.) was only partially successful, since the court also ruled that it had no authority to review the manner in which the federal government and the Superintendent General of Indian Affairs managed First Nations lands and finances, the supervisory authority belonging solely to Parliament. Riddell's decision against Chisholm is reported in *Chisholm* v *Herkimer* (1909), 19 O.L.R. 600 (Ont. Weekly Ct.).

58 *Sero* v *Gault*, at 33. Riddell's judgment expressly notes his archival research into the issues in dispute. On Riddell's 'cavalier attitude towards the use of such facilities,' and the efforts of various librarians and archivists to retrieve documents he borrowed years earlier, see Neary, 'Riddell,' at 33.

59 *Sero* v *Gault*, at 330–1. Although Riddell gives no source for Judge Powell's statement, it is presumably based upon a memorandum signed by Powell, later Chief Justice of Upper Canada, recording a conversation with Joseph Brant, which notes: 'My personal opinion was ever in favour of the entire Independence of the Indians in their villages.' The reference is quoted in Malcolm Montgomery, 'The Legal Status of the Six Nations Indians in Canada,' *Ontario History* 55:2 (1963), 93 at 93, citing PAC Q283, p. 94, 3 January 1737; the current PAC reference is RG10, vol.2285, 57-169-1A, Pt. 2. Although Riddell did not specify the precise nature of the retraction he attributes to Powell, he seems to justify his argument by reference to a murder trial in 1822: 'Shawanakiskie, of the Ottawa Tribe, was convicted at Sandwich of the murder of an Indian woman in the streets of Amherstburg, and sentenced to death. Mr. Justice Campbell respited the sentence, as it was contended that Indians in matters between themselves were not subject to white man's law, but were by treaty entitled to be governed by their own customs – Canadian Archives, Sundries, U.C., September 1822. It was said

that Chief Justice Powell had in the previous year charged the grand jury at Sandwich that the Indians among themselves were governed wholly by their own customs. Powell, when applied to by the lieutenant-governor, denied this, and sent a copy of his charge, which was quite to the contrary – id., October, 1822.' For more details on this case, see Dennis Carter-Edwards, 'Shawanakiskie,' *Dictionary of Canadian Biography*, vol. 6 (Toronto: University of Toronto Press, 1987), at 705–6.

60 *Sero* v *Gault*, at 331. Riddell cited neither case, but refers to documents in the Canadian Archives relating to the former, a murder trial of Shawanakiskie, in Sandwich in 1822, which was upheld in 1826 by the lieutenant-governor, to whom the Crown Law Officers had written to report that there was 'no basis for the Indian's claim to be treated according to his customary law.' Curiously, Riddell did not cite another 1820 murder conviction of Negaunausing, a ten-year-old First Nations boy who shot a European boy of about the same age. Riddell must have been aware of this District of Newcastle case, since he documented the conviction and subsequent pardon in his article 'A Criminal Circuit in Upper Canada: A Century Ago,' *Canadian Law Times*, vol. 40 (Toronto, 1920), 711 at 716–17.

61 *Rex* v *Hill* (1907), 15 O.L.R. 406, 11 O.W.R. 20 (Ont. C.A.), at 410. A white informant, Charles Rose, accused George Hill, an unenfranchised treaty Indian residing upon the 'reserve,' of 'attending upon and prescribing for' two white women off the 'reserve.' The court notes: 'He is no more free to infringe an Act of the Legislature than to disregard a municipal by-law, the general protection of both of which he enjoys when he does not limit the operations of his life to his reserve, but though unenfranchised, seeks a wider sphere.' The precise issue of sovereignty is never broached in the case, which was argued instead on the constitutional division of powers. The defendant's argument, that 'Indians' are 'wards of the Dominion, and subject in all relations of life only to federal legislation,' failed. For several later cases, see *

62 *Rex* v *Martin* (1917), 29 C.C.C. 189, 41 O.L.R. 79, 13 O.W.N. 187 (Ont. C.A.). Judge Riddell actually sat on this case, and concluded at 192: 'We are bound by *Rex* v. *Hill* ... to hold that an unenfranchised Indian is subject to provincial legislation in precisely the same way as a non-Indian, at least where, as here, he is out of his reservation.'

63 See, for example, *Sanderson* v *Heap* (1909), 11 W.L.R. 238, 19 Man. R. 122 (K.B.) and the broadly worded application of *Hill* found in *Dion* v *La Compagnie de la Baie D'Hudson* (1917), 51 Que. C.S. 413.

64 *The King* v *Beboning* (1908), 13 C.C.C. 405, 12 O.W.R. 484, 17 O.L.R. 23 (Ont. C.A.), in which the Aboriginal accused was charged with stealing hay on the West Bay Indian 'Reserve' in the district of Manitoulin. The argument of the

accused was that the matter was more properly dealt with under the federal *Indian Act*, R.S.C. 1906, c.81.

65 *Rex* v *Jim* (1915), 26 C.C.C. 236, 22 B.C.R. 106 (B.C.S.C.), notes at 237-8: 'By the British North America Act, 1867, that is to say, by subsection (24) of section 91, Indians and lands reserved for the Indians are reserved for the exclusive jurisdiction of the Dominion Parliament. The Dominion Parliament has enacted a lengthy Act known as the Indian Act ... [I]n fact, by section 51 it is expressly enacted "that all Indian lands ... shall be managed, leased and sold as the Governor-in-Council directs." [...] I would say that the word "management" would, at all events, include the question of regulation and prohibition in connection with fishing and hunting upon the reserves.' For examples of later cases, see *

66 *Dion* v *La Compagnie de la Baie D'Hudson* (1917), 51 Que. C.S., 413 at 416: 'Le fait qu'il y a dans notre province des réserves pour les Indiens n'a pas pour effet de rendre inconstitutionnelle la loi de chasse; ils y sont soumis comme tous les autres:

Indians in Canada are British subjects and entitled to all the rights and privileges of such, except so far as those rights are restricted by statute, and notwithstanding sub-sect. 24 of sect. 91 of the B.N.A. Act, 1867, they are sub-sect [*sic*] to all provincial laws which the province has power to enact.' For details of a 1909 Manitoba case, *Sanderson* v *Heap*, see *

67 Several land-dispute cases that touch on Aboriginal title, while not explicitly focusing upon sovereignty, illustrate these points. For example, the case of *St Catharines Milling Company* involves a dispute between the Ontario and federal governments over the right of a lumbering company to cut timber on the lands south of Wabigoon Lake. The Ontario government was seeking to enjoin the cutting of the timber. The lumber company claimed it obtained its timber rights from the federal government, which acquired title to the land from the Aboriginal inhabitants. The Ontario government argued that there was 'no Indian title at law or in equity.' Once again, the Aboriginal peoples were not present at the hearing, or canvassed for their positions on the legal issues before the court. This did not stop the court from issuing what would come to be considered the definitive ruling on Aboriginal title. In *Regina* v *St. Catharines Milling Co.* (1885), 10 O.R. 196 (Ont. Chancery Ct.), at 204-30, the court is patronizing in its dismissal of Aboriginal claims. For further details, see *

68 William Blackstone, *Commentaries on the Laws of England*, vol. 1, orig. pub. 1765-69 (republished Chicago: University of Chicago Press, 1979), at 354, 357. On Riddell's expertise in international law, see Neary, 'Riddell,' at 8 and 16.

69 Riddell also cites *Halsbury's Laws of England*, vol. 1 at 302-3: 'Persons born

within the allegiance of the Crown include every one who is born within the dominions of the Crown whatever may be the nationality of either or both of his parents ...' This passage provides no further assistance than the quotation from Blackstone, since it fails to settle the question of whether Eliza Sero had been born 'within the dominions of the Crown.' For details of the 1919 federal statute on naturalization, see *

70 The right to exercise the suffrage is distinct from the concept of 'enfranchise-ment,' a process that allowed First Nations people to apply to the federal government for title to land in 'fee simple' and the erasure of their 'Indian' status in law. For federal legislative on enfranchisement in force between 1869 and 1951, see * The Six Nations Confederacy opposed 'enfranchisement' for multiple reasons, not least of which was their claim to be 'allies' not 'subjects' of the British monarch. For an analysis of the coercive and colonialist under-pinnings of enfranchisement, see Darlene Johnston, 'First Nations and Cana-dian Citizenship,' in William Kaplan, ed., *Belonging: The Meaning and Future of Canadian Citizenship* (Montreal and Kingston: McGill-Queen's University Press, 1993), at 349–67. For legislation concerning the right of 'Indians' to exercise their federal suffrage, in force between 1885 and 1960, see *

71 For details of the Ontario legislation between 1908 and 1954, see *

72 For details of the legislation in British Columbia between 1872 and 1949, the case of *Tomey Homma*, the legislation in force in Manitoba between 1892 and 1952, in Saskatchewan between 1908 and 1960, in Prince Edward Island between 1913 and 1963, in New Brunswick between 1889 and 1963, in Alberta between 1909 and 1965, in the Northwest Territories in 1905, and in Quebec between 1915 and 1969, see *

73 *Sero* v *Gault*, at 332–3. On Iroquoian Huron and Six Nations agricultural expertise, see *

74 *Sero* v *Gault*, at 333. For references on the history of Aboriginal use of seine fishing nets, see *

75 *Sero* v *Gault*, at 330–3, citing 'an official letter' from Robinson to Robert Wilmot Horton, Under-Secretary of State for War and Colonies, 14 March 1824, located in the Canadian Archives, Q.337, pt.II, pp.367–8. Like many judges who refused to support legal claims of racialized peoples during this period, Riddell added a caveat to his conclusion: 'Of course, I deal only with the law as I find it, and express no opinion as to the generosity, wisdom, or advisability of the legislation.' For a critique of the alienating norms im-posed upon First Nations communities by Euro-centric visions of justice, see *

76 PAC RG10, vol.2285, file 57-169-1A, Pt.2. I am indebted to Sheila Staats for bringing this correspondence to my attention.

77 Paul Tennant, *Aboriginal Peoples and Politics* (Vancouver: University of British Columbia Press, 1990), notes at 93, 111–13, that Duncan Campbell Scott proposed in 1924 to prohibit the right of Aboriginal people to pay their lawyers to pursue claims without government approval. *An Act to amend the Indian Act*, S.C. 1926–7, c.32, s.6, provides: 'Every person who, without the consent of the Superintendent General expressed in writing, receives, obtains, solicits or requests from any Indian any payment or contribution or promise of any payment or contribution for the purpose of raising a fund or providing money for the prosecution of any claim which the tribe or band of Indians to which such Indian belongs, or of which he is a member, has or is represented to have for the recovery of any claim or money for the benefit of the said tribe or band, shall be guilty of an offence and liable upon summary conviction for each such offence to a penalty not exceeding two hundred dollars and not less than fifty dollars or to imprisonment for any term not exceeding two months.' See also *Indian Act*, R.S.C. 1927, c.98, s.141. The prohibition on fundraising is not removed until the enactment of *The Indian Act*, S.C. 1951, c.29.

78 Irving Powless, Jr, 'The Sovereignty and Land Rights of the Houdenosaunee,' in Christopher Vecsey and William A. Starna, *Iroquois Land Claims* (Syracuse, N.Y.: Syracuse University Press, 1988), at 155–61. For information about Six Nations sovereignty claims south of the border, and an Aboriginal critique of the racist ethnocentricity of the dominant legal culture, see *

79 Patricia Monture-Angus, *Thunder in My Soul: A Mohawk Woman Speaks* (Halifax: Fernwood Publishing, 1995), states at 211: 'Traditional Mohawk people assert that we have never lost or surrendered our sovereignty. Sovereignty has a meaning that is not synonymous with western definition. To be sovereign is one's birthright. It is simply to live in a way which respects our tradition and culture. Sovereignty must be lived, and that is all.' Quoting Oren Lyons, a member of the Hodenosaunee Confederacy, Monture-Angus continues at 229: 'Sovereignty – it's a political word. It's not a legal word. Sovereignty is the act. Sovereignty is the do. You act. You don't ask. There are no limitations on sovereignty. You are not semi-sovereign. You are not a little sovereign. You either are or you aren't': quoted in Richard Hill, 'Oral History of the Haudenosaunee: Views of the Two Row Wampum,' in Jose Bartreiro, ed., *Indian Roots of American Democracy* (New York: Akweikon Press, 1992), at 175. See also Sidney L. Harring, *Crow Dog's Case: American Indian Sovereignty, Tribal Law, and United States Law in the Nineteenth Century* (New York: Cambridge University Press, 1994), at 292, where he notes: 'The vitality of nineteenth-century Indian law lies in the

reality that the tribes never let their sovereignty be determined by any case or trusted that question to any judge. The way that the federal courts analyzed the doctrine of federal Indian law was of great concern to the tribes, but they never let those outcomes define tribal sovereignty. The tribes have resisted in every conceivable way. They lost often and lost badly. [...] But these cases do not have to be cited as precedents in U.S. law to have legal meaning to Indian people. These cases are remembered: the people who remember them know that they stand for tribal sovereignty.'

80 Anglican Diocese of Ontario burial records show the date of burial for Eliza Sero, age sixty-eight, of Tyendinaga, as 19 January 1937.

81 Another Tyendinaga Mohawk fisherman, William Isaac 'Ike' Hill, was charged in the fall of 1950 for possessing a seine net on the Tyendinaga Territory without a licence, contrary to the provincial Game and Fisheries Act. Although convicted in the first instance, Ike Hill was able to secure an acquittal on the ground that there was no supporting federal legislation prohibiting the possession of that type of net. Ike Hill's defence was argued, in part, on the claim of Mohawk sovereignty, and his lawyer reminded the court of the Simcoe Deed of 1793, noting that Lord Dorchester made provision to outfit the Six Nations allies with seine nets in 1789, several years after they settled into their new Upper Canadian homes. The following passages from the 'Argument,' His Worship Magistrate T.Y. Wills, in *Rex v Hill* (document in possession of William Isaac 'Ike' Hill, copy on file with the author) makes the sovereignty arguments: Quoting from Niagara Historical Society No. 40, 1884–90, by Brigadier General E.A. Cruikshank, Letter from Lord Dorchester to Sir John Johnson, Quebec, 28 June 1789. 'It is not in our power to supply the Indians at the Grand River and at Buffalo Creek with provisions as we are in great want ourselves but I approve of a seine being given to each of those settlements if you think it reasonable. [...] It is quite clear that the Mohawk Indians were given a territory that the south side has never been determined. They were allowed to fish with seines as a net was given to each of the Six Nations. To the present day the Dominion Government has never made it clear to the Indians how they are to fish. The Ontario Government has been infringing little by little on the rights of the Indians that were given for services rendered with the understanding that they and their descendants would have a sanctuary. I submit, further, that it is unfair to have this matter decided in the courts as it leaves such a responsibility on the shoulders of the Magistrate because if the right of an Indian, a member of the Band, on his own reserve cannot have a net of any kind without it being seized they have no rights of any kind and it is a mockery to have a reserve. [...] To take away the few privileges that the Indians

have, after it was so clearly given to them, for all time is breaking the word of the King to them and if the people who gave the land to the Indians as a sanctuary were here today and could give their decision I feel sure there would be no doubt as to the result.' Although the outcome in Hill's case was a positive one, the court decided the case on the constitutional division of powers. The judge ignored the sovereignty arguments, cited the *Sero* case, and even went so far as to eulogize William Renwick Riddell as 'a very eminent Judge.' See *R. v Hill* (1951), 14 C.R. 266 (Ont. Co. Ct.). The Six Nations of Grand River remained adamant about their sovereignty, and continued to raise the issue in various domestic and international forums. For details of the claims through 1921 to 1959, see *

5: 'Mesalliances' anf the 'Menace to White Women's Virtue'

1 Earlier versions of this chapter are found in Constance Backhouse, 'White Female Help and Chinese-Canadian Employers: Race, Class, Gender and Law in the Case of Yee Clun, 1924,' *Canadian Ethnic Studies* 26:3 (1994), 34–52; republished in revised format in Wendy Mitchinson et al., eds., *Canadian Women: A Reader* (Toronto: Harcourt Brace, 1996), 280–99.
2 For references on the history of Regina, see *
3 *Sixth Census of Canada, 1921*, Vol. 1: *Population* (Ottawa: King's Printer, 1924), at 542–3, identifies Regina's largest ethnic populations as 25,515 British, 2,902 German, 860 Hebrew, 774 Roumanian, 762 Austrian, 700 French, 536 Russian, several other identified groups, and 250 Chinese.
4 For details of the discriminatory legislation, see Constance Backhouse, 'Gretta Wong Grant: Canada's First Chinese-Canadian Female Lawyer,' *Windsor Yearbook of Access to Justice*, vol. 15 (1996), 3–46. For reference to the anti-Chinese immigration and other laws enacted in British Columbia between 1884 and 1908, federal immigration laws that discriminated against the Chinese between 1885 and 1903, immigration legislation in Newfoundland between 1906 and 1926, legal cases interpreting such provisions and secondary sources, see *
5 David Chuenyan Lai, *Chinatowns: Towns Within Cities in Canada* (Vancouver: University of British Columbia Press, 1988), describes the prairie Chinatowns at 87–95. Regarding Regina, Lai notes: 'Regina did not have a Chinatown, partly because of the small Chinese population and partly because of the mutual agreement made by early Chinese settlers that they would avoid competition by not setting up businesses close to each other. In 1907, for example, there were four Chinese laundries, two Chinese restaurants, and one Chinese grocery store in Regina, scattered throughout the

city's downtown area. The Chinese population in Regina was only eighty-nine in 1911. By 1914, the number of Chinese laundries had increased to twenty-nine, but the number of Chinese grocery stores had only increased to two, and there were still only two Chinese restaurants. These were not confined to one particular street or locality. After the 1920s the Chinese hand laundry business declined steadily, and by 1940, only eight laundries remained in the city. In 1941, Regina had a Chinese population of only 250.' On the social construction of 'Chinatowns,' the impact of residential and business segregation on the 'racialization' of the Chinese community, and the strategies of accommodation and resistance employed by the Chinese, see *

6 'Bylaws Like Piecrust Made to Be Broken,' Regina *Leader*, 12 October 1911, p. 12; 'Regina May Have Segregated Chinese Colony,' Regina *Daily Province*, 14 November 1912, p. 3; 'Chinese Object to Segregation,' Regina *Daily Province*, 15 November 1912, p. 11. Mack Sing, depicted as the 'wealthiest and by far the most influential Chinaman in the city,' objected to the proposal on behalf of the Chinese community of Regina. 'Our population here are law abiding and pay their bills,' he explained, noting that the proposed measure would be very injurious to the business of Chinese laundrymen. There is no further press coverage on the outcome or implementation of this particular scheme. But see also the statement of Regina's white police magistrate, William Trant, and Rev. M. MacKinnon, the white pastor of Knox Church, who defended Chinese laundrymen against a campaign to impose burdensome taxes on their businesses: Regina *Evening Leader*, 24 May 1914, p. 1.

7 For reference to the press articles, which also use unflattering childish characterizations, see *

8 For references to the 'brown' and 'yellow' designations for people from Japan, see *

9 S.S. 1912, c.17, s.1. The word 'Chinaman' seems awkwardly placed alongside the adjectives 'Japanese' and 'Oriental.' The decision to use the word 'Chinaman' instead of 'Chinese' may be an indication of particular disdain. Madge Pon notes that the term 'Chinaman' has been used 'as a euphemism describing ineptitude and incompetence, as evident in the phrase "a Chinaman's chance".' See Madge Pon, 'Like a Chinese Puzzle: The Construction of Chinese Masculinity in Jack Canuck,' in Joy Parr and Mark Rosenfeld, *Gender and History in Canada* (Toronto: Copp Clark, 1996), 88 at 100.

10 For examples of such statutory designations, see *

11 Although this appears to be the first legislative articulation of the concept of the 'white' race, a subsequent Alberta statute purporting to define 'Métis'

utilizes the same word. *An Act Respecting the Métis Population of the Province*, S.A. 1938 (2nd Sess.), c.6, s.2(a), defines 'Metis' as 'a person of mixed white and Indian blood but does not include either an Indian or a non-treaty Indian as defined in *The Indian Act*.' See also *An Act to Amend and Consolidate The Métis Population Betterment Act*, S.A. 1940, c.6, s.2(a). The only other statutes that purport to make reference to the dominant "white" race do so in different terms. *An Act for the better protection of the Lands and Property of the Indians in Lower Canada*, S.Prov.C. 1850, c.42, s.1, refers to 'persons of European descent.' For reference to the 'Caucasian race,' see *An Act Respecting Liquor Licences and the Traffic in Intoxicating Liquors*, S.B.C. 1910, c.30, s.25-6; and R.S.B.C. 1911, c.142, s.24-5, enacted in the context of taking a count of the population to determine whether liquor licences should be issued. See also *An Act to amend the 'Provincial Elections Act'*, S.B.C. 1907, c.16, s.2 and *An Act respecting Elections of Members of the Legislative Assembly*, S.B.C. 1920, c.27, s.2(1), defining 'Hindu' as 'any native of India not born of Anglo-Saxon parents and shall include such person whether a British subject or not.'

12 'Legislators are Working Overtime Now,' Regina *Morning Leader*, 2 March 1912, p. 9. For biographical details on Turgeon, see * For a fuller account of the genesis of the legislation and the Quong Wing and Quong Sing trials that preceded Yee Clun's litigation, see Constance Backhouse, 'The White Women's Labor Laws: Anti-Chinese Racism in Early Twentieth-Century Canada,' *Law and History Review* 14:2 (Fall 1996), 315–68, and James W.St.G. Walker, *'Race,' Rights and the Law in the Supreme Court of Canada* (Waterloo: The Osgoode Society and Wilfrid Laurier University Press, 1997), ch. 2. On the prohibition of interracial marriage and the absence of any laws similar to the 'White Women's Labour Law' in the United States, see *

13 'Legislators Are Working Overtime Now,' Regina *Morning Leader*, 2 March 1912, p. 9. Turgeon suggested that the new measure was pre-emptive, rather than designed to address an actual problem, hinting that extra-provincial events (no details of which were ever provided) had motivated the legislature. In contrast, Lai notes in *Chinatowns* at 93, that the act was precipitated by the arrest in 1912 of a Moose Jaw Chinese restaurant owner, after his employee, a white waitress, lodged an assault complaint against him. Although he states that the case was widely publicized in local newspapers, Lai gives no reference to the case or the press coverage. My search of the Saskatchewan newspapers has not elicited any record of such an arrest in 1912. However, in September 1911, Charlie Chow was charged with committing an indecent assault on a young white girl, who was tarrying in a Moose Jaw Chinese restaurant (possibly the C.E.R. Restaurant) unsuper-

vised, long after she was due home from Sunday school. No conviction appears to have been registered, after evidence was adduced that there was a large crowd in the restaurant, and that the girl's aunt may have induced a false complaint by pressuring the youngster: see 'Child Was Reluctant,' Moose Jaw *Evening Times*, 1 September 1911, p. 1; 'Assault Case Dismissed,' Moose Jaw *Evening Times*, 30 September 1911, p. 10. 'Assault Case Against Chinaman Was Dismissed,' Moose Jaw *Evening Times*, 5 March 1912, p. 7, makes reference to a fist-fight in the Royal Restaurant between a white man, Alfred Essrey, and Charlie Quong. Although the fight appears to have been provoked by Essrey taking pork chops from the kitchen, reference is made to Essrey's having 'reprimanded a Chinaman for assaulting his sweetheart [Miss Jean McLeod], who was a waitress in the Royal restaurant.' All charges were dismissed. Marjorie Norris, *A Leaven of Ladies: A History of the Calgary Local Council of Women* (Calgary: Detselig, 1995), describes at 165–7 the 1913 criminal trial in Calgary of Tai Loy, a Chinese storekeeper charged with sexually assaulting a Polish schoolgirl. The accused man was acquitted after a jury trial before the criminal assize of the Supreme Court.

14 For an account of the formal demands made by Saskatchewan TLC delegates and the Typographical Union, newspaper reports that the provincial government would accede to the request, and the references to the lobby role of organized labour, see *

15 For examples of anti-Asian sentiments on the part of organized labour, see *

16 For references, see *

17 For a copy of the resolution, and references and press accounts on the TLC lobby, see *

18 On the role of Retail Merchants' Associations in Saskatchewan and more generally, see *

19 'Chinese Think Laundry Tax Is Too High,' Moose Jaw *Evening Times*, 21 February 1914, p. 14, and Regina *Evening Leader*, 24 May 1914, p. 1, indicate that the white managers of steam laundries felt they were unable to compete with the long hours worked by Chinese laundrymen. On restaurant prices see, for example, 'Celestials Who Are Now Citizens of Earthly Moose Jaw,' Moose Jaw *Evening Times*, 6 September 1913, p. 7: '[T]he only enemies who oppose [the Chinese] with any degree of reason are firms which are in daily opposition to him in his particular line of business. It is a remarkable fact that in any city where there are a number of Chinese restaurants, the price of "raw material" be what it may, meals are procurable at a very reasonable figure. The Chinaman is essentially an economist, and seems able to supply food for less money than can any other countryman. The European argues and the very contention has been raised in Moose Jaw – that this is because

he is satisfied with less gain, and should therefore be barred from competition.'

20 On the provincial and municipal laws in Saskatchewan, British Columbia, and Ontario, and a series of judicial decisions on their validity, see *

21 For nineteenth-century examples, see the discussion of the restrictions on women's and Asian men's employment in the mines, as well as other female labour restrictions, in Constance Backhouse, *Petticoats and Prejudice: Women and Law in Nineteenth-Century Canada* (Toronto: The Osgoode Society and Women's Press, 1991), ch. 9. For discussion of the modern context see Peter S. Li, 'Race and Gender as Bases of Class Factions and Their Effects on Earnings,' *The Canadian Review of Sociology and Anthropology* 29:4 (November 1992), 488.

22 See the testimony of Rev. Canon Beanlands, Church of England, a white resident of Victoria, as given in the *Report of the Royal Commission to Investigate Chinese and Japanese Immigration* 1902, at 27: 'I have never seen a Chinese man employ a white man ...'

23 The legislation impeding Asian immigration has been described earlier (in note 4) * For sources about the restrictions upon Black immigration and the discriminatory attitudes and restrictions of the 'pass' system that impeded First Nations employment, see *

24 For sources on the comparative pay scales of white women and Asian men, see *

25 The quote is from Mah Po, owner of the King George Restaurant in Regina, 'Japanese Consul General in Regina,' Regina *Morning Leader*, 14 May 1912, p. 2. Anne Elizabeth Wilson, 'A Pound of Prevention – or an Ounce of Cure,' *Chatelaine*, December 1928, p. 12, concedes in her article on the employment of women by Chinese entrepreneurs that white women were the group at risk 'inasmuch as Orientals have not Oriental women in this country.'

26 White restaurant and steam laundry proprietors in British Columbia often advertised that they employed only white help. The reference to stomachs of refined persons is taken from a Victoria restaurant that changed its name and replaced its Chinese cooks with Germans to cater to racist clientele. White men who established laundries 'advertised the whiteness of their employees as much as the whiteness of their linen'; see Patricia E. Roy, *A White Man's Province: British Columbia Politicians and Chinese and Japanese Immigrants, 1858-1914* (Vancouver: University of British Columbia Press, 1989), at 32 and 243.

27 'Shocking Fate of White Girls,' Regina *Morning Leader*, 5 September 1912, p. 9. I am indebted to Kenneth Leyton-Brown for informing me of the existence of this letter.

28 See, for example, 'Chinese a Stagnant Race: The Real Yellow Peril,' Moose
   Jaw *Evening Times*, 21 February 1912, p. 10. 'Chinamen Arrive,' Moose Jaw
   Evening Times, 8 September 1909, p. 1, notes: 'Chinamen pay heavily for
   living in this country, and they deserve to. They take a lot of money from it
   and leave nothing in return, unless it is bitter memories amongst former
   customers of laundry spoiled or digestions ruined.' See also W. Peter Ward,
   *White Canada Forever: Popular Attitudes and Public Policy Toward Orientals in
   British Columbia*, 2d ed. (Montreal and Kingston: McGill-Queen's University
   Press, 1990), at 7–14; F.W. Howay [a judge of the County Court of Westminster, B.C.], *British Columbia: The Making of a Province* (Toronto: Ryerson,
   1928), at 263; Howard Palmer, *Patterns of Prejudice: A History of Nativism in
   Alberta* (Toronto: McClelland & Stewart, 1982), at 43. Mariana Valverde, *The
   Age of Light, Soap and Water: Moral Reform in English Canada, 1885–1925*
   (Toronto: McClelland & Stewart, 1991), notes at 17 that social-purity activists appealed to Canadian nationalism through symbols of 'snowy peaks'
   and 'pure white snow.' For an illustration of the forcefulness of 'cleanliness'
   imagery in the racial context, see Robert Edward Wynne, *Reaction to the
   Chinese in the Pacific Northwest and British Columbia, 1850–1910* (New York:
   Arno Press, 1978), at 182, citing a late nineteenth-century American clergyman who argued that unsanitary Chinese laundries would besmirch the
   purity of white women: 'the dainty garments of white women puddled
   around in suds that reeked with dirt ...'
29 For newspaper articles attributing passage of the act to the Social and Moral
   Reform group, see * On the founding of the Saskatchewan Social and Moral
   Reform Council and its membership, see Regina *Morning Leader*, 14 December 1907, and Erhard Pinno, 'Temperance and Prohibition in Saskatchewan,'
   M.A. thesis (University of Saskatchewan, 1971), at 11–12. Pinno lists the
   following member organizations: Church of England in Canada (Dioceses of
   Saskatchewan and Qu'Appelle), Methodist Church of Canada (Saskatch-
   ewan Conference), Presbyterian Church of Canada (Synod of Saskatch-
   ewan), Saskatchewan Branch of the Baptist Convention, the Roman Catholic
   Church, Evangelical Association, Union Church Conference, Mennonite
   Church, the Saskatchewan Sunday School Federation, Royal Templars of
   Temperance, Trades and Labor Council of Saskatchewan, the Woman's
   Christian Temperance Union, Great War Veterans' Association, Army and
   Navy Veterans' Association, North-West Commercial Travellers, Retail
   Merchants' Association, Dental Association, Medical Association, Educa-
   tional Association, Citizens' Educational Board, Local Council of Women,
   the YMCA, and YWCA. Members of the Legal Committee included: Rever-
   end George Exton Lloyd (Principal of Emmanuel Theological College in

Saskatoon), James Balfour (Barrister and Solicitor, Alderman and Mayor of Regina), Mr H.E. Sampson (Crown Prosecutor for the Regina Judicial District) and Mr C.B. Keenleyside.

30 For references to the 'ladies' debate' and the anti-Chinese statements of Macdonald and other Canadian prime ministers, see *

31 For more details concerning the activities of religious leaders and missionaries, as well as a judicial opinion on whether Chinese plural marriage should be recognized under a will in Canadian law, see *

32 For contemporary newspaper references and secondary sources concerning the conditions for women in China, see *

33 For further discussion of the linkages between Western feminism and imperialism, see *

34 Veronica Jane Strong-Boag, *The Parliament of Women: The National Council of Women of Canada, 1893–1929* (Ottawa: National Museum of Man, 1976), at 186 and 248, citing the National Council of Women of Canada *Yearbook* (1912), at 81–2. Norris, *Leaven of Ladies*, notes at 81 that the Calgary Council of Women debated calling for a 'prohibition of white help in restaurants run by black or yellow people' during their April 1914 meeting. For more recent manifestations of the organized women's movement's problematic positions regarding anti-Asian governmental policies and racism generally, see *

35 Vron Ware, *Beyond the Pale: White Women, Racism and History* (London: Verso, 1992), at 37–8. The ideological focus on motherhood of the 'first wave' of the women's movement, often categorized as 'maternal feminism,' facilitated claims that combined reproduction and racism: see Valverde, *The Age of Light, Soap and Water*, at 60–1.

36 For sources on the alleged link between skin colour and sexuality, see *

37 For references, see *

38 'The Yellow Peril in Toronto,' *Jack Canuck*, 28 October 1911, p. 11. See also 1:4 (16 September 1911). On the stigmatization of the 'partition metaphor,' see Pon, 'Construction of Chinese Masculinity.'

39 Shearer was the head of the council's subcommittee, the National Committee for the Suppression of the White Slave Traffic: see Valverde, *The Age of Light, Soap and Water*, at 54–7, 86; 'Dr. Shearer Gives Regina Bouquet,' Regina *Daily Province*, 16 March 1911, p. 5; 'Rev. Dr. Moore on Social Evil,' Regina *Daily Province*, 21 June 1912, p. 1, reporting on the 'white slavery' investigatory tour of Victoria, Edmonton, Moose Jaw, and Winnipeg undertaken by Dr Moore, secretary of the Methodist temperance and moral reform board; 'Gambling and White Slavery Canada's Menace,' Regina *Daily Province*, 6 November 1912, p. 10. In 1910, the white police staff inspector in charge of Toronto's morality division complained about Chinese men:

'The lure of the Chinaman is ... developing among [young] girls, to their utter demoralization in many instances': Valverde at 111, citing Staff Inspector Kennedy, *Annual Report of the Chief Constable*, 1910, at 31. No statistical data exist to suggest that the Chinese were disproportionately involved in operating brothels in Canada, or that they represented any numerical threat as 'white slavers.' Not surprisingly, however, in view of the rhetoric and stereotyping, there were some prostitution-related criminal charges laid against Chinese men. For some examples, see *

40 'White Girls in Chinese Cafes,' Regina *Leader*, 25 September 1912, p. 12; 'White Women and Chinese Employers,' Regina *Daily Province*, 24 September 1912, p. 7.

41 I am indebted to Erica Tao for her suggestion about the importance of including material on the genesis of the opium trade in China. On the British opium trade, see *

42 'Spreading the Drug Habit,' Regina *Morning Leader*, 7 April 1922, p. 4; 'Chinatown at Vancouver to Get Cleanup,' Regina *Morning Leader*, 3 October 1924, p. 1; 'Seek to Have Drug Peddler Deported Soon,' 6 November 1924,Regina *Morning Leader*, p. 9; Kay J. Anderson, *Vancouver's Chinatown: Racial Discourse in Canada, 1875–1980* (Montreal and Kingston: McGill-Queen's University Press, 1991), at 101; Mariana Valverde, '"When the Mother of the Race Is Free": Race, Reproduction, and Sexuality in First-Wave Feminism,' in Franca Iacovetta and Mariana Valverde, eds., *Gender Conflicts: New Essays in Women's History* (Toronto: University of Toronto Press, 1992), 3 at 14; Ward, *White Canada Forever*, at 9, citing the *Victoria Times*, 25 June 1908. For details concerning testimony before the Royal Commission on Chinese Immigration in 1885, and comparative references to the American and British context, see * While legal records are not a reliable indication of whether these concerns were based upon anything other than racist conjecture, several reported decisions and newspaper accounts of cases suggest there was little factual foundation for the linkage between narcotics and sexual exploitation. For examples, see *

43 Emily F. Murphy, *The Black Candle* (orig. pub. Toronto: Thomas Allen, 1922; repub. Toronto: Coles, 1973), at 17, 28, 233–4, 303–4, 306. But see also 234–9, where she discusses situations in which white women are the aggressors. Emily Murphy's fears were exaggerated further by one Methodist moral reform organization, which insisted that even 'occasionally visiting Chinese restaurants' could lead to the demise of unsuspecting white women. Valverde, *The Age of Light, Soap and Water*, at 97–9, citing a 1911 Methodist annual report, lists the dangerous places catalogued in early tywentieth-century white-slavery narratives as invariably including 'chop suey pal-

aces.' She also notes at 122 that Ethel West, who headed up Presbyterian services for immigrant women in Toronto after 1911, sought to keep under surveillance and rescue Scottish women who 'went to work where Chinamen were employed.'

44 Murphy, *The Black Candle*, picture opposite p. 30, and 188, 210. See also the picture opposite p. 46, which shows a dark-skinned man and white woman with heads touching, and is captioned: 'Once a woman has started on the trail of the poppy, the sledding is very easy and downgrade all the way.' See also 45, 107, 122, 128, 166, 186–9, 196–8, 210, 302–3, and Palmer, *Patterns of Prejudice*, at 84–5. For other passages denoting Emily Murphy's ambivalence about the extent of Chinese designs towards racial superiority, see * Responding to Murphy's provocative prose, the National Council of Women of Canada expressed its consternation over increasing numbers of female and male drug addicts. Its solution: 'further restrictions on oriental immigration were proposed as one means of cutting off the opium supply': see Strong-Boag, *The Parliament of Women*, at 382.

45 Helen Gregory MacGill was one of Canada's first female juvenile court judges, appointed in British Columbia. MacGill travelled to Japan to report on political and social conditions during her earlier career as a journalist. She and her husband, Jim MacGill, also maintained a social relationship with a Vancouver Chinese merchant named Yip Quong, a classical scholar and graduate of Oxford, who was married to a white woman: Elsie Gregory MacGill, *My Mother, The Judge* (Toronto: Ryerson, 1955), at 70–4, 100. MacGill was quite knowledgeable about the history of legislative discrimination against the Chinese, as she had written a detailed essay titled 'Anti-Chinese Immigration Legislation of British Columbia, 1876–1903' (Vancouver, 1925) in which she took a critical perspective on the 'race prejudice' directed against the Chinese. I am grateful to Robert Menzies, School of Criminology, Simon Fraser University, for bringing this paper to my attention. For details of this essay and a later article by MacGill, see *

46 Wilson, 'A Pound of Prevention,' *Chatelaine*, 12 at 13. On the history of the sexual coercion and sexual harassment of women workers in Canada, see, for example, Constance Backhouse and Leah Cohen, *The Secret Oppression: Sexual Harassment of Working Women* (Toronto: Macmillan of Canada, 1978), ch. 3.

47 Report of the Committee on Trades and Professions for Women, National Council of Women of Canada, *The Yearbook of the National Council of Women of Canada, 1927* (Ottawa, 1927), at 88; 'Trades and Professions,' *The Yearbook of the National Council of Women of Canada, 1928* (Ottawa: 1928), at 97; Wilson, 'A Pound of Prevention,' *Chatelaine*, at 12.

48 Wilson, 'A Pound of Prevention,' *Chatelaine*, at 12. The article notes that a recent report of the National Council of Women found female employees suffering from 'wrongful treatment from the white patrons of restaurants kept by Orientals.'

49 In 1911, women made up only 3.5 per cent of the Chinese population across Canada. It would take until the 1960s until the sex ratio began to reach a balance: for references on Chinese-Canadian women, see * James Young of Nanaimo testified before the Royal Commission on Chinese and Japanese Immigration as follows: 'Wherever I have known any considerable number of men deprived of female society for any length of time, the inevitable result has been that they become coarser. The intellect is depraved, the whole moral tone is lowered, and men rush into a greater depth of wicked-ness and vice than would otherwise have been possible.' See *Report of the Royal Commission on Chinese Immigration*, 1885, at 89. See also *Rex v Hung Gee (No. 1)* (1913), 13 D.L.R. 44; 21 C.C.C. 404; 24 W.L.R. 605; 6 Alta. L.R. 167; [1913] 4 W.W.R. 1128 (Alta. S.C.), which gives legal expression to commonly held racist thinking, while overturning the conviction of a Chinese Calgarian for keeping a common gaming house: 'The learned police magis-trate concludes [with] some remarks that suggest an abnormal amount of immorality among the Chinese in this country, and attributes this to the fact that "these people are here without their women." No doubt, he is voicing a common view both as to the fact and its cause.'

50 Anthony B. Chan, *Gold Mountain* (Vancouver: New Star Books, 1983), notes at 80 that white prostitutes in Victoria outnumbered Chinese prostitutes by 150 to 4 in 1902, but it was the Chinese women who were attacked for immorality. For further references, see * In 1898, the National Council of Women wrote to Prime Minister Wilfrid Laurier, demanding an investiga-tion into the 'female slavery' of Chinese-Canadian prostitutes. The request was initially put forward by the Local Councils of Women in Vancouver and Victoria, who hoped that such a study would correct the impression of visitors from Eastern Canada who praised 'the sobriety, the industry, and the peaceableness of the Celestials': Roy, *White Man's Province*, at 17–18, citing National Council of Women to Wilfrid Laurier, 20 August 1898, Laurier Papers, no. 25897-8. In an era when women were touted as the moral guardians of the community, the racist categorization of Chinese women as sexually promiscuous gave increased fuel to the fears that Chinese men were predisposed to improper sexual behaviour. For the comments of the Canadian legislators, see Canada, House of Commons, *Debates* [Hansard], 12 May 1882, at 1471; 30 April 1883, at 905; 8 May 1922, at 1555–6.

51 For references on the hostility towards interracial marriage on the part of both the white and Chinese communities, see *

52 The comment on 'coffins' is found in Roy, *White Man's Province*, at 18, citing the Nanaimo *Free Press*, 5 April 1904. A British Columbia journal sums it up: 'It is when we contemplate these unnatural unions that we find the kernel of the Asiatic problem – the mixing of the races. Race mixture is the essential danger of the Asiatic occupation of this country for race mixture means race deterioration.' On the American marriages, see 'Twelve White Women Brides of Orientals,' Regina *Leader*, 11 November 1911, p. 4, which recounts one of the wedding nuptials as follows: 'When they entered the office of the justice of the peace [the couple] sat down side by side and neither looked at the other for five minutes, while the justice was filling out papers. He studied the design of the linoleum, while she looked far away out of the window ... When the two stood up and clasped hands, [the male bride-groom] was silent and looked straight ahead into vacancy. He did not answer the questions asked. [The bride] merely laughed her assent.' The report emphasizes that the women concerned were widows, one significantly older than the man she was marrying, and that none would agree to having their pictures taken. One bride, it notes, 'seemed to be the financial agent of her husband and carried the family purse in a large wallet.' The 'Don't Wed' headline appeared on Regina *Morning Leader*, 8 January 1912, p. 2, quoting a recently divorced white American woman: 'I know ... enough to give advice to other American girls, and it is never to marry people of Oriental origin or with Oriental strains in the blood. They can never understand each other and the woman will be the one who suffers.'

53 'Shocking Fate of White Girls,' Regina *Morning Leader*, 5 September 1912, p. 9. Clayton James Mosher, *Discrimination and Denial: Systemic Racism in Ontario's Legal and Criminal Justice Systems, 1892–1961* (Toronto: University of Toronto Press, 1998), describes at 79–80 the criminal conviction of missionary Robert Brown, after he conducted a marriage ceremony between a Chinese man and a white woman, on charges that he had no qualifications to perform the service because the 'First Christian Chinese Church, Toronto' was not a properly qualified religious denomination. See also the air of astonishment which attends the report that an Ottawa cleric spoke positively about racial intermarriage: 'Advocates That Whites Should Marry Orientals,' Moose Jaw *Evening Times*, 11 March 1914, p. 12.

54 'Girl Wanted to Wed a Chinaman – But Lethbridge Police Locked Up the Would-Be Couple,' Regina *Leader*, 19 September 1911, p. 14. The two travelled to Lethbridge to wed, and booked a room in a local lodging house. The article states that Mah Wing, proprietor of a Chinese restaurant at Diamond

City, was arrested at the Vendomme Block on 17 September. Janet Given, a twenty-three-year-old 'white girl of Scotch descent' who had been employed by Mah Wing as a waitress for several months, was taken from the same room to the police station. The white acting chief of police, Silliker, determined that the couple had travelled to Lethbridge to be married, but upon their arrival Mah Wing changed his mind and took his fiancée to a lodging house instead. Janet Given was reportedly reluctant to speak to the police, and told them that 'she did not consider it anyone's business if she wanted to be the sweetheart of a Chinaman. Since I have been in Wing's employ, he has treated me better than I have been used to. He has promised to marry me and that is the reason that we made the trip to Lethbridge.' The news report hastened to point out that Miss Given was 'of rather prepossessing appearance' and 'during her rambling conversation made the statement that she came to this country for the purpose of marrying as soon as possible.' There is no legal report of further proceedings, but presumably the police arrested Mah Wing on the theory that he could be charged with some sort of procuring offence, after he booked a hotel room with a woman who was not yet his wife. The interracial nature of the relationship clearly motivated the arrest, revealing how authorities could manufacture indirect legal impediments to interracial marriage when direct legal bars were not available. In 1930, the Halifax police arrested a Chinese man and his white bride after the bride's mother alleged her daughter's name was forged on the marriage certificate. Lee Chong and his 'girl bride,' Dorothy Isabel Dauphinee, were arrested a few days after their wedding at their home on 89 Maitland Street. Police believed the young woman was not yet eighteen years old, and both were later charged with forgery; Halifax *Herald*, 8 and 28 November 1930. I am indebted to Michael Boudreau for bringing the Halifax news item to my attention.

55 Gunter Baureiss, 'The Chinese Community in Calgary,' *Alberta Historical Review* 22:2 (Spring 1974), 1 at 8; Gunter Baureiss, 'Discrimination and Response: The Chinese in Canada,' in Rita M. Bienvenue and Jay E. Goldstein, eds., *Ethnicity and Ethnic Relations in Canada*, 2d ed. (Toronto: Butterworths, 1985), 241 at 251. Walker, *'Race,' Rights and the Law*, notes at 82–3 that *Saturday Night* magazine published an editorial praising American legal prohibitions on racial intermarriage and calling for the federal government to replicate such laws in Canada (citing 15 August 1925).

56 For details of the passage of the act and the press coverage, see *

57 Kenneth B. Leyton-Brown, 'Discriminatory Legislation in Early Saskatchewan and the Development of Small Business,' in Terry Wu and Jim Mason, eds., *Proceedings of the Eighth Annual Conference of the International Council for Small Business – Canada (ICSB)* (Regina: International Council for Small

Business, 1990), 253. The Moose Jaw *Evening Times*, 1 May 1912, p. 1, announced that the Chinese held a mass meeting to discuss the act, and intended to keep on their white female employees until legal advice could be obtained. Frank Yee, the Grand Master of the Chinese Masonic Order in Western Canada, enlisted the support of Dr Sun Yat-sen, the successful leader of the 1911 Chinese Revolution, who wrote to Yee from China. Portions of Dr Sun Yat-sen's letter were published in the Regina *Leader* on 13 May 1912, promising that the Chinese consul from Ottawa would visit Regina soon to investigate the situation. The letter threatened that if the act were enforced, Chinese cities would boycott Canadian goods and Pacific shipping would be decimated by the withdrawal of Chinese labour: 'Dr. Sun Urges Fight Against White Help Law,' Regina *Leader*, 13 May 1912, p. 1; Regina *Morning Leader*, 8 January 1912, p. 9; Regina *Daily Province*, 13 May 1912, p. 1. For further details concerning Sun Yat-sen and the ineffectiveness of these threats, see * The press reported that the Japanese residents of Moose Jaw were also ready to fight the legislation, which they saw as a 'curtailment of their liberties' under 'international law'; 'Moose Jaw Japs to Fight Labor Laws,' Regina *Morning Leader*, 10 May 1912, p. 1; 'Japs at Moose Jaw to Test Labor Law,' Saskatoon *Star-Phoenix*, 10 May 1912, p. 7; 'Moose Jaw Japs Fight Labor Law,' Regina *Daily Province*, 10 May 1912, p. 1. Mr N. Nakane, Japanese proprietor of the Carlton Cafe in Moose Jaw, wrote to Attorney General Turgeon on 5 March 1912 to complain about the Saskatchewan enactment as an 'insult to the honour of Japan.' Turgeon replied on 28 March 1912: 'It is certainly regrettable that any law of the Province should be found objectionable by any portion of the respectable citizens of the Province. However, general conditions some time require things to be done which cannot be agreeable to everybody. In the present case this law was put through, in so far at least as some of the people affected by it were concerned, not so much to remedy an existing state of affairs, but to prevent the growing up of conditions which have arisen elsewhere.' Turgeon Papers, S.A.B., General Correspondence 1911–12, 'N,' box 9, 325–8. Nakane sought an amendment to remove the Japanese from the legislation on the ground that there were 'fewer than twenty Japanese in the whole of Saskatchewan,' too few to pose any serious threat, and that they were not generally in a position to employ white women. He described himself as a naturalized British subject who had lived in Moose Jaw for seven years, and employed only men in his restaurant; 'Employment by Orientals,' Moose Jaw *Evening Times*, 29 April 1912, p. 1. For a rare example of a complaint against the act by a non-Asian individual, Dr Stephens of Yellow Grass, Saskatchewan, see *

58 On Dr Yada's efforts, see 'Japanese Consul General in Regina,' Regina

Morning Leader, 14 May 1912, p. 2; New York *Herald*, 23 April 1913, p. 6. The amendment was passed as *An Act to amend An Act to Prevent the Employment of Female Labour in Certain Capacities*, S.S. 1912-13, c.18, and given royal assent 11 January 1913. For the rationale behind the amendment, see *

59 For reference to the legislation, the failure to proclaim it, similar provisions under the Winnipeg City Charter, and the history of Winnipeg's Chinatown, see *

60 For reference to the enactment, its proclamation on 1 December 1920 after representations from organized labour, the confusion that ensued when many provincial and federal officials seemed unaware of the proclamation, the subsequent campaign to remove the proclamation, and information concerning Ontario enforcement, see *

61 For specifics of the lobby campaign spearheaded by organized labour and the Retail Merchants' Association, and details of the British Columbia statute, see *

62 Despite the legislative inaction, there was substantial evidence of hostility towards the Chinese in Alberta; for further details and statutory references to other racially discriminatory measures in Alberta, see * For reference to anti-Chinese discrimination in Quebec, legislation imposing higher licence fees upon the Chinese, and Quebec cases concerning this, see *

63 For reference to statements of a Halifax alderman concerning a proposed bill, and incidents of anti-Chinese violence and discrimination in the Atlantic provinces, see *

64 A full account of these cases is found in Backhouse, 'The White Women's Labor Laws: Anti-Chinese Racism in Early Twentieth-Century Canada'; Walker, '*Race*,' *Rights and the Law*, ch. 2.

65 See discussion in the introductory chapter of this volume, and regarding *Re Eskimos* in chapter 2; Peter Fryer, *Black People in the British Empire: An Introduction* (London: Pluto Press, 1988), at 61–2; M.F. Ashley Montagu, *Man's Most Dangerous Myth: The Fallacy of Race* (New York: Columbia University Press, 1942); B. Singh Bolaria and Peter S. Li, *Racial Oppression in Canada*, 2d ed. (Toronto: Garamond Press, 1988), at 13–25; F. James Davis, *Who Is Black? One Nation's Definition* (University Park: Pennsylvania State University Press, 1991); Audrey Kobayashi and Peter Jackson, 'Japanese Canadians and the Racialization of Labour in the British Columbia Sawmill Industry,' *B.C. Studies*, vol. 108 (Autumn 1994), 33–58; Audrey Kobayashi, 'Viewpoint: A Geographical Perspective on Racism and the Law,' *Canadian Law and Society Bulletin*, vol. 11 (Spring 1991), 4–6; Audrey Kobayashi, 'Racism and Law in Canada: A Geographical Perspective,' *Urban Geography* 11:5 (October 1970), at 447–73; A. Sivanandan, 'Challenging Racism: Strategies for the 80s,' *Race*

and Class, vol. 25 (1983), i–ii; Peter Jackson, 'The Idea of "Race" and the Geography of Racism,' in Peter Jackson, ed., *Race and Racism* (London: Unwin Hyman, 1987), at 3–21; Ronald T. Takaki, *Iron Cages: Race and Culture in Nineteenth-Century America* (New York: Knopf, 1979); Gloria A. Marshall, 'Racial Classifications: Popular and Scientific,' in Sandra Harding, ed., *The 'Racial' Economy of Science: Toward a Democratic Future* (Bloomington: University of Indiana Press, 1993), at 116.

66 Robert Miles, *Racism* (London: Tavistock, 1989); Anderson, *Vancouver's Chinatown*, at 3–18.

67 For more details on the appeals, see *

68 The case is not reported in the law reports, and the only records come from the Saskatoon *Daily Star*: 'What Is White Woman? Definition Puzzled Magistrate and Lawyers in Case of Orientals in Court,' 14 August 1912, p. 3; 'Counsel for Defence in Orientals Case Questions Authority of Provincial Legislature to Pass Act,' 15 August 1912, p. 3.

69 Angus McLaren, *Our Own Master Race: Eugenics in Canada, 1885–1945* (Toronto: McClelland & Stewart, 1990), at 25; James W.St.G. Walker, '"Race" Policy in Canada: A Retrospective,' in O.P. Dwivedi et al., *Canada 2000: Race Relations and Public Policy* (Guelph: University of Guelph, 1989), at 14; Ruth A. Frager, 'Class, Ethnicity, and Gender in the Eaton Strikes of 1912 and 1934,' in Iacovetta and Valverde, *Gender Conflicts*, 189 at 209.

70 For the 'nigger' reference, see Fryer, *Black People*, at 53, citing H.J.S. Cotton, *New India or India in Transition* (London: Kegan Paul, Trench, 1885), at 37, 41–2. The white British imperialist Cecil Rhodes identified peoples from Africa and Asia as sharing the same skin pigmentation, referring to 'the dark-skinned myriads of Africa and Asia': Fryer, at 68, citing W.T. Stead, ed., *The Last Will and Testament of Cecil John Rhodes ...*, *Review of Reviews Office* (1902), at 140. For an 'Oriental' reference, see Vancouver *Sun*, 18 and 19 June 1907, as quoted in Ted Ferguson, *A White Man's Country: An Exercise in Canadian Prejudice* (Toronto: Doubleday Canada, 1975), at 46: 'Right-thinking people know that the natives of Hindustan ... should not be allowed in this country, except for circus purposes ... We do not think as Orientals do. That is why the East Indians and other Asiatic races and the white race will always miscomprehend each other.' Howay, *British Columbia*, also refers at 266 to Hindu immigrants from India as 'Oriental.'

71 The 'Italian' reference is from Richard Marpole, Vancouver, white general superintendent of the Pacific Division of the Canadian Pacific Railway, *Report of the Royal Commission on Chinese and Japanese Immigration*, 1902, at 194. The white Saskatchewan historian John Hawkes, the provincial legislative librarian and self-acclaimed 'pro-foreigner,' makes the statement re-

garding Slovaks and other specified groups in John Hawkes, *The Story of Saskatchewan and Its People*, vol. 3 (Chicago and Regina: S.J. Clarke, 1924), at 681; see also 690.

72 Hawkes, *Saskatchewan and Its People*, at 1397–8. See also Liz Curtis, *Nothing But the Same Old Story: The Roots of Anti-Irish Racism* (London: Information on Ireland, 1984), at 55, where she notes that the Celts have been labelled racially distinct from Anglo-Saxons, and the British working classes have been considered a 'race apart' from the British upper classes. On the racial construction of the Irish in the American context, see Noel Ignatiev, *How the Irish Became White* (New York: Routledge, 1995); David R. Roediger, *The Wages of Whiteness: Race and the Making of the American Working Class* (London: Verso, 1991), at 133–4; and Marshall, 'Racial Classifications: Popular and Scientific,' at 122–4.

73 Saskatoon *Daily Star*, 'Letters to the Editor: The White Help Question,' Regina *Morning Leader*, 19 August 1912, p.3.

74 'Judge Finds Law Valid in Oriental Help Case and Gives Decision Against Chinamen and Jap Which Counsel Announces He Will Appeal,' Saskatoon *Daily Star*, 21 August 1912, p.3.

75 *An Act to prevent the Employment of Female Labour in Certain Capacities*, S.S. 1918–19, c.85; 'Municipalities Will Decide on Employment,' Regina *Leader*, 18 January 1919; 'Employment Agencies to Vanish Now,' Regina *Leader*, 22 January 1919.

76 For statutory references concerning the 1923 British Columbia amendment and similar legislation, and details of the continuing racialized enforcement, see * The inclusion of 'Indian women and girls' may have been a belated response to concerns occasionally voiced about 'half-breed and Indian women being enticed into opium dens and supplied with opium and liquor, and being ravished by any number of the inmates'; see testimony of William Moresby, the white gaoler at New Westminster, British Columbia, *Report of the Royal Commission on Chinese Immigration*, 1885, at 108. Other accounts appear at 62 and 67. See also Roy, *White Man's Province*, at 274, note 10, citing the *Columbian*, 13 September 1882; Vancouver *World*, 31 January 1908; and *District Ledger*, 14 November 1908, quoting the *World*. The inclusion of Aboriginal women most certainly was not an attempt to equate white women with First Nations women in law, since the province retained numerous discriminatory provisions affecting First Nations women, ranging from the franchise to liquor licensing: see discussion of *Sero* v *Gault* in chapter 4 and *Re Eskimos* in chapter 2.

77 For some examples of alternate spellings, and the tendency of Canadian reporters to ridicule Chinese names, see *

78 The Henderson Directories for Regina show Yee Clun as residing initially in
an apartment on Rose Street, just down from his restaurant. By 1923, Yee
Clun took up residence at 1821 Osler, near the headquarters of the Chinese
Nationalist Party; he remained at that address until 1930, the last year he is
listed in the directory. I am indebted to Elizabeth Kalmakoff of the Saskatchewan Archives Board for the Henderson Directory information. For details
of Chinese settlement on the prairies, and the paucity of Chinese-Canadian
women in Regina and across Canada, see *

79 Yee Clun was the 'prime mover' in securing 'larger and more modern
quarters' for the Chinese National Party, a brick building at 1809 Osler
Street, to furnish community meeting rooms and residential accommodation
for 'bachelor' Chinese residents: 'Allow White Female Help in Chinese
Restaurants,' Regina *Morning Leader*, 8 August 1924, p. 1; 'Council Turns
Down Request of Yee Klung,' 8 October 1924, p. 3; 'Chinese National Party
Reorganizes,' 29 December 29, 1922, p. 9; 'Chinese Society to Move Quarters,' 16 December 1922, p. 17. The Henderson Directory for Regina first lists
Yee Clun as the proprietor of the Exchange Grill in 1917. By 1920, Jow Tai
has joined Yee Clun as the proprietor, and the two are listed jointly or
alternately as proprietors until 1930, when Yee Clun disappears and Jow Tai
carries on the business by himself. I am indebted to Elizabeth Kalmakoff of
the Saskatchewan Archives Board for the Henderson Directory information.
On the importance of the housing facilities that Chinese restaurants offered
to Chinese immigrants on the prairies, see Peter S. Li, 'Chinese Immigrants
on the Canadian Prairie, 1910–1947,' *Canadian Review of Sociology and Anthropology*, vol. 19 (1982), 527 at 534–5.

80 'Allow White Female Help in Chinese Restaurants,' Regina *Morning Leader*,
8 August 1924, p. 1. For reference to the restrictive immigration act of 1923
and its devastating impact on Chinese communities in Canada, see *

81 In one of a series of civil suits launched in 1908, Mack Sing, the proprietor of
a store on Osler Street since 1905, was successful in claiming false arrest and
imprisonment: *Mack Sing v Smith* (1908), 9 W.L.R. 28; 1 Sask. R. 454 (Sask.
S.C.). The white Judge Prendergast released the white mayor, J.W. Smith,
from liability due to his peripheral involvement in the raid. R.J. Harwood
(Regina's white chief of police), A.J. Hogarth and Charles E. Gleadow
(Regina's white constables), and C.H. Hogg (a white corporal in the Royal
North-West Mounted Police) were held liable for $25 in damages. The low
penalty was partly due to the lack of 'malice' on the part of the defendants.
It also reflects the court's anti-Chinese bias: 'As to the quantum of damages,
I think they should be assessed low. […] Their habits, their customs, their
mode of living, make it safe to say that in the circumstances they have not

been injured in their reputation, neither with their own compatriots nor with the general community of this city ...' Although some of the Chinese individuals arrested were clearly intent upon challenging the abuse of police authority, others were apparently anxious to cooperate and not obstruct the police during their raid. The judge notes that some police officers testified that the Chinese men arrested were 'willing (one of the witnesses for the defence said, 'even anxious') to assist the police by shewing them where the Chinese residences were and accompanying them to the city hall, to facilitate the carrying out of the method of search they had adopted.' The court concludes, however, that 'what was called their acquiescence and readiness was undoubtedly the effect of a sense of their helplessness. They knew it was useless to offer opposition, they did not wish to take the responsibility of resisting peace officers, and consequently they submitted.'

82 'Regina May Have Segregated Chinese Colony,' Regina *Daily Province*, 14 November 1912, p. 3, quoting Police Chief Zeats.

83 'Allow White Female Help in Chinese Restaurants,' Regina *Morning Leader*, 8 August 1924, p. 1.

84 'Protest White Girl Help in Chinese Restaurants,' Regina *Morning Leader*, 12 August 1924, p. 1; 'Women Object to Yee Clun's Application,' Regina *Morning Leader*, 13 August 1924, p. 1. On the WCTU in Western Canada, see *

85 'Protest White Girl Help in Chinese Restaurants,' Regina *Morning Leader*, 12 August 1924, p. 1; 'City Women Oppose White Female Help for Chinese,' Regina *Morning Leader*, 24 September 1924, p. 9; 'Is Not Alarmed at Inter-Marriages,' Regina *Morning Leader*, 29 October 1924, p. 2. See also Janet Harvey, 'The Regina Council of Women, 1895–1929,' MA thesis (University of Regina, 1991), at 127; Saskatchewan Local Council of Women, *Minute Books*, S.A.B. S-B82 I.3, 21 March 1921, at 3–4; 14 April 1921, at 1; 28 April 1921, at 1–2; *Minute Books*, S.A.B. S-B82 I.4, 3 April 1926, at 24; 18 December 1927, at 81; 25 April 1930, at 191; 27 May 1930, at 193; Georgina M. Taylor, 'Grace Fletcher, Women's Rights, Temperance, and "British Fair Play" in Saskatoon, 1885–1907,' *Saskatchewan History* 46:1 (Spring 1994), 3–21.

86 Harvey, 'Regina Council of Women'; N.E.S. Griffiths, *The Splendid Vision: Centennial History of the National Council of Women of Canada, 1893–1993* (Ottawa: Carleton University Press, 1993), at 48, 70, 96, 184; Saskatchewan Labour Women's Division, *Saskatchewan Women, 1905-1980* (n.d., n.p.).

87 Canadian Publicity Co., *Pioneers and Prominent People of Saskatchewan* (Toronto: Ryerson Press, 1924), at 80; Provincial Council of Women of Saskatchewan, *History of the Provincial Council of Women of Saskatchewan, 1919–1954* (Regina: Commercial Printers, 1955); Harvey, 'Regina Council of Women,' at 56–7; Elizabeth Kalmakoff, 'Naturally Divided: Women in Saskatchewan

Politics, 1916–1919,' *Saskatchewan History* 46:2 (Fall 1994), 3–18. Nadine Small, 'The "Lady Imperialists" and the Great War: The Imperial Order Daughters of the Empire in Saskatchewan, 1914–1918,' in David De Brou and Aileen Moffatt, eds., *'Other' Voices: Historical Essays on Saskatchewan Women* (Regina: Canadian Plains Research Center, University of Regina, 1995), 76, alludes at 78 to the racial exclusiveness of at least one of Stapleford's women's clubs: 'Until at least the end of the Great War, the membership lists of the IODE in Saskatchewan did not contain names of women of Asian, south European or east-central European descent. […] IODE members called all non-British immigrants "foreigners" whether or not they were naturalized citizens. Foreign-born female immigrants who were not completely Canadianized did not qualify to become members of the Order because the Order did not consider them to be loyal British subjects. […] IODE members even questioned the loyalty of British women who married foreigners.'

88 'May Not Treat Chinese Apart from Others,' Regina *Morning Leader*, 20 August 1924, p. 1.

89 'City Women Oppose White Female Help for Chinese,' Regina *Morning Leader*, 24 September 1924, p. 9; 'Resolution Refused to Women's Labour Leagues,' *Labour Gazette*, October 1924, p. 852. For sources on the Women's Labour League, see *

90 'Women Object to Yee Clun's Application,' Regina *Morning Leader*, 13 August 1924, p. 1; 'May Not Treat Chinese Apart from Others,' Regina *Morning Leader*, 20 August 1924, p. 1. Although the paper reports the name Mrs W.J. Vennele, this is probably a misprint, as no such name is listed in the Regina Henderson's Directory for 1924. The proper spelling must have been 'Vennels,' for William J. Vennels, a news superintendent at the Leader Publishing Company, was active in the Regina Trades and Labor Congress in 1924.

91 Harvey, 'Regina Council of Women,' at 140; 'May Not Treat Chinese Apart from Others,' Regina *Morning Leader*, 20 August 1924, p. 1.

92 'Spreading the Drug Habit,' Regina *Morning Leader*, 7 April 1922, p. 4; 'Chinatown at Vancouver to Get Cleanup,' Regina *Morning Leader*, 3 October 1924, p. 1; 'Seek to Have Drug Peddler Deported Soon,' Regina *Morning Leader*, 6 November 1924, p. 9; Anderson, *Vancouver's Chinatown*, at 101. I have been unable to determine anything further about Mrs Reninger and Mrs Armour. The Henderson Directory for Regina lists several entries under these names during the relevant period. Mrs Margaret W. Armour, the widow of Robert Armour (previously a wholesale and retail butcher and the secretary-treasurer of Hugh Armour & Co. Ltd.), resided at 1876 Rose Street from 1920 to 1926, and may be the individual concerned. The 'Armour

Block' at South Railway and Board Street is across the back alley from the Exchange Grill. I am indebted to Elizabeth Kalmakoff of the Saskatchewan Archives Board for the Henderson Directory information. For further references concerning fears about the intermingling of Chinese men and white, female Sunday school teachers, see *

93 'May Not Treat Chinese Apart From Others: Blair Throws Bomb to Alderman in City Council,' Regina *Morning Leader*, 20 August 1924, p. 1.

94 On Blair's life and career, see 'G.F. Blair Taken by Death While Sitting at Desk,' Regina *Morning Leader*, 2 March 1926, p. 2. On Rev. MacKinnon's earlier position, see Regina *Evening Leader*, 24 May 1914, p. 1.

95 'May Not Treat Chinese Apart from Others,' Regina *Morning Leader*, 20 August 1924, p. 1; 'G.F. Blair Taken by Death While Sitting at Desk,' Regina *Morning Leader*, 2 March 1926, p. 2. On the location of the Chinese YMCA in the club-room of the Chinese National Party, see 'Chinese National Party Reorganizes,' Regina *Morning Leader*, 29 December 1922, p. 9.

96 'Lawyer Marks 80th Birthday,' Regina *Leader-Post*, 4 June 1959; 'Prominent City Lawyer Passes,' Regina *Leader-Post*, 14 March 1964; Osgoode Society Oral History Transcript of Interview with Stuart Thom (Douglas J. Thom's son), 6 November 1981, at 5–35; 'Thom, Douglas J. KC,' *Who's Who in Canada, 1938–39* (Toronto: International Press, 1939), at 1312; James M. Pitsula, *Let the Family Flourish: A History of the Family Service Bureau of Regina, 1913–1982* (Regina: n.p., 1982), at 35–6. Douglas Thom was born in 1879 in Norwood, Ontario, the son of Rev. James and Mattie M. (Simmons) Thom. He obtained a BA from the University of Toronto, Victoria College. His law firm had a substantial commercial practice that included real estate and mortgages, collections, civil litigation, wills, and machine company business. Thom published 'a definitive work on land titles in Western Canada' titled *Thom's Canadian Torrens System*. Thom was trustee of the Regina Collegiate Institute Board, active as a Mason, and belonged to the Assiniboia Club. He was president of the Canadian Club, president of the Board of Trade, vice-consul in Saskatchewan for the Netherlands, president of the Regina Orchestral Society, president of the Community Chest, and vice-president of the Canadian Bar Association. Mabel Thom, the daughter of Rev. E.A. Chown, was born near Petrolia, Ontario. She met her husband at university, and later moved out west to join him. There were four children born of the marriage. Mrs Thom's son described her 'two major interests' as the Council of Women and the University Women's Club, noting that she once travelled to an international conference in Sweden to represent the National Council of Women of Canada. 'She was quite active. She also enjoyed it,' he adds, noting at 43–6: 'She enjoyed jousting with her friends

and politicking for office and this kind of thing. She was no little mouse. She wasn't a little domestic housewife, she was a much more outgoing woman than that ...' Mary Kinnear, *In Subordination: Professional Women, 1870–1970* (Montreal: McGill-Queen's University Press, 1995), notes at 157 that Mabel Thom served as the president of the Canadian Federation of University Women in the 1930s, where she argued against restrictions on the professional lives of women with families.

97 For statutory references to the federal immigration provisions passed in 1885, 1900, and 1903, see *

98 For references to the statutory provisions of 1923, their repeal in 1947, and continuing discriminatory rules in effect until 1956, see *

99 For references to the British Columbia legislation enacted between 1872 and 1949 that impeded Asians from running for election or voting in provincial elections, municipal elections, public school elections, water improvement elections, and petitions for liquor licences, see * Most provinces excluded First Nations voters as well; for details, see discussion of the *Sero* v *Gault* case in chapter 4.

100 For statutory references excluding the Chinese from voting in Saskatchewan between 1908 and 1944, and the provisions in force in Manitoba between 1901 and 1904, see * For comparable details regarding restrictions on the First Nations franchise, see discussion of the *Sero* v *Gault* case in chapter 4.

101 For details of the relevant federal provisions between 1885 and 1948, see *

102 For details of the enactments between 1877 and 1948 and judicial rulings on these provisions, see *

103 British Columbia passed some of the earliest 'contract compliance' legislation in the country, in this case designed not to reduce racial discrimination against minority populations but to enhance it. Various statutes prohibit the employment of Asian workers by companies or persons that receive 'any property, rights or privileges' from the legislature. Others bar provincial assistance to businesses hiring workers unable to read in a language of Europe. For details of the provisions and their judicial interpretation, see *

104 For a thorough analysis, see Bruce Ryder, 'Racism and the Constitution: The Constitutional Fate of British Columbia Anti-Asian Legislation, 1872–1922,' unpublished manuscript, who notes at 125 that, between 1885 and 1907, the British Columbia legislature inserted a clause prohibiting the hiring of Asian labour in fifty-seven acts incorporating private companies, of which only a few were disallowed. For a listing of the legislation between 1885 and 1902, see *

105 Some require higher licensing fees from Chinese applicants than from

others. Some expressly deny licences to the Chinese, while still others do so indirectly through a discriminatory application of facially neutral policies. Others operate by restricting licences to persons on the voters' list, from which Asians are excluded. For examples of these provisions and their judicial interpretation, see *

106 Enrolment as a student-at-law and articled law clerk, and registration as a certified pharmacist's apprentice, were both limited to those entitled to be placed on the voters' list under the Provincial Elections Act: Rule 39 of the Law Society of British Columbia, passed pursuant to the *Legal Professions Act*, S.B.C. 1895, c.29, s.37; s.15 of the Pharmacy By-Laws, passed pursuant to the *Pharmacy Act*, S.B.C. 1891, c.33. The law society rule resulted from a petition in 1918 by Vancouver law students seeking to prohibit 'Asiatics' from becoming lawyers: see Victor Lee, 'The Laws of Gold Mountain: A Sampling of Early Canadian Laws and Cases that Affected People of Asian Ancestry,' *Manitoba Law Journal*, vol. 21 (1992), 301 at 312, citing A. Watts, *Lex Liberorum Rex: History of the Law Society of British Columbia, 1869–1973* (Vancouver: Law Society of British Columbia, 1973), at 36; Ryder, 'Racism and the Constitution'; H.F. Angus, 'The Legal Status in British Columbia of Residents of Oriental Race and Their Descendents,' in Norman MacKenzie, ed., *The Legal Status of Aliens in Pacific Countries* (London: Oxford University Press, 1937), 77 at 83; Joan Brockman, 'Exclusionary Tactics: The History of Women and Visible Minorities in the Legal Profession in British Columbia,' in Hamar Foster and John McLaren, eds., *Essays in the History of Canadian Law: British Columbia and the Yukon*, vol. 6 (Toronto: The Osgoode Society, 1995), 508 at 519–25.

107 For details, see *

108 'The Narcotics Traffic,' Regina *Morning Leader*, 30 December 1922, p. 16; 'Council Turns Down Request of Yee Klung,' Regina *Morning Leader*, 8 October 1924, p. 3.

109 For details, see Backhouse, 'Gretta Wong Grant.'

110 'MacKinnon, Andrew G.,' *Who's Who in Canada, 1936–37* (Toronto: International Press, 1937), at 208. For reference to MacKinnon's public denunciation of the Klan, see Martin Robin, *Shades of Right: Nativist and Fascist Politics in Canada, 1920–1940* (Toronto: University of Toronto Press, 1992), at 67–72; William Calderwood, 'Pulpit, Press and Political Reactions to the Ku Klux Klan in Saskatchewan,' in Susan M. Trofimenkoff, ed., *The Twenties in Western Canada* (Ottawa: National Museums of Canada, 1972), 191. The Klan's efforts to take root in Saskatchewan, its most successful base outside of the United States, peaked in several waves, in 1927 and 1929. Although Catholics were the main targets, the Klan also denounced inter-

marriage between the Chinese, Blacks, and whites, and supported the strict enforcement of the white women's labour law. Robin notes at 33 that Klansmen elected to the Moose Jaw city council insisted upon banning 'the employment of white girls in Chinese restaurants.' For references on the Klan, see * Although Klan support was of great assistance to the Conservative party during the 1926 federal election in Saskatchewan, MacKinnon, a Klan adversary who ran for the Conservatives, was not elected. Both Robin (at 72) and Calderwood (at 211) suggest that the political manoeuvring of the Klan directly affected MacKinnon's political fortunes.

111 'Council Turns Down Request of Yee Klung,' Regina *Morning Leader*, 8 October 1924, p. 3.

112 The application for judicial review appears to have requested declaratory relief and a 'mandamus' requiring the defendant to grant Yee Clun's licence. 'Council Turns Down Request of Yee Klung,' Regina *Morning Leader*, 8 October 1924, p. 3; 'Court to Decide Chinese Rights,' Regina *Morning Leader*, 22 October 1924, p. 9; *Yee Clun v City of Regina* (1925), 20 Sask. L.R. 232 (Sask. K.B.).

113 Judge Mackenzie (whose name also appears as 'MacKenzie') was the son of Philip and Elizabeth MacKenzie. He was educated at the London Collegiate Institute and the University of Toronto, where he received his BA in 1893 and an LLB in 1895. He 'read law' with Mowat, Donney and Langton in Toronto. In London, he practised with Magee, McKillop and Murphy from 1896 to 1901. In Regina, he practised with McCraney, Mackenzie and Hutchinson. He received the designation KC in 1913, and would be elevated to the Saskatchewan Court of Appeal in 1927. In 1922, he became a governor of the University of Saskatchewan and later served as chair of the board of governors. See *Who's Who in Canada, 1938–39* (Toronto: International Press, 1939), at 1476; *Who's Who in Canada, 1945–46*, at 918; W.H. McConnell, *Prairie Justice* (Calgary: Burroughs, 1980), at 217. I am indebted to Elizabeth Kalmakoff of the Saskatchewan Archives Board for information concerning Judge Mackenzie.

114 *Yee Clun v City of Regina*, [1925] 4 D.L.R. 1015; 3 W.W.R. 714; (1925), 20 Sask. L.R. 232 (Sask. K.B.), at 234–7.

115 For details of the rule excluding parliamentary history and its rationale, see *

116 *Yee Clun v City of Regina*, [1925] 4 D.L.R. 1015; 3 W.W.R. 714; (1925), 20 Sask. L.R. 232 (Sask. K.B.), at 234–7.

117 *Rex v Quong Wing*, [1913] 4 W.W.R. 1135, (1913), 12 D.L.R. 656, 24 W.L.R. 913, 21 C.C.C. 326, 6 Sask. R. 242 (Sask. S.C.); *Quong Wing v The King* (1914), 49 S.C.R. 440, [1914] 6 W.W.R. 270, (1914), 18 D.L.R. 121, 23 C.C.C. 113; leave to appeal to the Privy Council refused 19 May 1914.

118 On the issue of suffrage, *In Re the Provincial Elections Act and in Re Tomey Homma, A Japanese* (1900), 7 B.C.R. 368 (Co. Ct.) initially held the electoral exclusions in the *Provincial Elections Act*, R.S.B.C. 1897, c.67, s.8, to be *ultra vires*, a ruling that was upheld in *In Re the Provincial Elections Act and In Re Tomey Homma, A Japanese* (1901), 8 B.C.R. 76 (B.C.S.C.). The Privy Council reversed this on appeal, declaring the discriminatory franchise provisions to be constitutional: *Cunningham v Tomey Homma*, [1903] A.C. 151. See also Ryder, 'Racism and the Constitution,' unpublished manuscript, at 141–66.

119 For further details of these cases, see *

120 For details of *Union Colliery Co. of B.C. v. Bryden*, [1899] A.C. 580, and other decisions of the Privy Council, see *

121 John P.S. McLaren, 'The Early British Columbia Supreme Court and the "Chinese Question": Echoes of the Rule of Law,' in Dale Gibson and W. Wesley Pue, eds., *Glimpses of Canadian Legal History* (Winnipeg: Legal Research Institute, University of Manitoba, 1991), at 111.

122 Bruce Ryder, 'Racism and the Constitution: The Constitutional Fate of British Columbia Anti-Asian Immigration Legislation, 1884–1909,' *Osgoode Hall Law Journal*, vol. 29 (1991), at 619; Ryder, 'Racism and the Constitution'; Alan Grove and Ross Lambertson, 'Pawns of the Powerful: The Politics of Litigation in the Union Colliery Case,' *BC Studies*, vol. 103 (Autumn 1994), 3.

123 *An Act respecting the Employment of Female Labour*, S.S. 1925–6, c.53. Robert Moon, *This Is Saskatchewan* (Toronto: Ryerson, 1953), notes at 46 that Moose Jaw city council refused licences to all Chinese restaurateurs wishing to hire white women. Moon credits the impetus for this to the Ku Klux Klan, which was active in Saskatchewan from the mid-1920s.

124 *Rex ex rel Eley v Yee Clun and Yee Low*, [1929] 1 D.L.R. 194; 3 W.W.R. 558; (1928), 50 C.C.C. 440; 23 Sask. L.R. 170, as heard by white Saskatchewan Court of King's Bench Judge Bigelow. Yee Clun is listed as carrying on business with Yee Low, under the firm name of 'Sam Mon Coffee and Tea Co.' The conviction was quashed on the ground that the prosecution had failed to put into evidence the regulations under which the accused was charged. The Henderson Directory for Regina shows Yee Clun continued to serve as the proprietor of the Exchange Grill (Cafe) in 1929 and 1930, but he is not listed thereafter. I am indebted to Elizabeth Kalmakoff for the Henderson Directory information.

125 'Regina Mourns Loss of Late G.F. Blair, K.C.,' Regina *Morning Leader*, 6 March 1926.

126 For details of the repealing statutes, see *

127 For details of the repealing legislation and the impact of the Saskatchewan

Bill of Rights Act, 1947, see * Prior to the repeal, the continued monitoring efforts of the Regina Local Council of Women resulted in the 1930 prosecution of three Chinese restaurant proprietors from Saskatoon, for indecent and common assault upon three white women, all former employees of the accused; for details, see *

6: 'It Will Be Quite an Object Lesson'

1 The cross burning took place at Main (Colborne) and Third streets: see 'Ku Klux Klan Cohorts Parade into Oakville and Burn Fiery Cross,' Toronto *Globe*, 1 March 1930, p. 1; 'To Investigate K.K.K. Burnings,' London *Free Press*, 1 March 1930, p. 1; 'Klan Took Oakville Girl from Negro Home,' Toronto *Daily Star*, 1 March 1930, p. 1.

2 'Klan Separates Oakville Negro and White Girl,' Hamilton *Spectator*, 1 March 1930, p. 7. On the Oakville police, see Frances Robin Ahern, *Oakville: A Small Town, 1900–1930* (Erin, Ont.: Boston Mills Press, 1981), at 130.

3 'Klan Separates Oakville Negro and White Girl,' Hamilton *Spectator*, 1 March 1930, p. 7; 'Ku Klux Klan Cohorts Parade into Oakville and Burn Fiery Cross,' Toronto *Globe*, 1 March 1930, p. 1; 'To Investigate K.K.K. Burnings,' London *Free Press*, 1 March 1930, p. 1; 'Klan Took Oakville Girl from Negro Home,' Toronto *Daily Star*, 1 March 1930, p. 1; 'Klansmen of Hamilton Defend Their Conduct in "Raid" at Oakville,' Toronto *Globe*, 3 March 1930, pp. 1, 3; 'One Klansman Fined and Two Are Freed,' Toronto *Daily Star*, 10 March 1930; 'Hamilton Klan Member Fined,' Toronto *Globe*, 11 March 1930, p. 9; 'Ku Klux Klan Here on Business,' Oakville *Star and Independent*, 7 March 1930, p. 8. The *Daily Star* uses the name 'Ira Johnston' throughout much of its reporting, and 'Alice' rather than 'Isabel' Jones. Isabel Jones's age is given as twenty and twenty-one, and Captain Broome is identified as 'Captain Broom' and 'Captain Brown' in different reports. Mrs Jones, a domestic 'in service,' was unable to accommodate her daughter, which is why she called upon the assistance of the Salvation Army, the institution to which she was affiliated by religion. Reporters advise that Ira Johnson and Isabel Jones met through their mothers, who both belonged to the Salvation Army and were friends. Isabel allegedly 'suffered a nervous breakdown' and her mother brought her to live with Ira Johnson's mother. Some press accounts suggest that Mrs Jones initially gave her consent to the marriage, but later retracted this. There is some speculation that the retraction was due to Ira Johnson's lack of steady employment. The community disapproval of the interracial marriage and the pressure of the Klan may also have been a factor: see 'Klan Took Oakville Girl from Negro

Home,' Toronto *Daily Star*, 1 March 1930, pp. 1–3. Captain Broome appears to have been ideologically opposed to racial intermarriage, having made earlier efforts to forestall the union. Asked by a reporter whether Mrs Jones asked for his help 'in breaking off the match,' Broome replied: 'Yes, she did. I went to the house and spoke to the girl. I told her that she must think of the children and their position in life as the result of the marriage between races of different colors.' Broome would later tell the press that he hoped the Oakville raid 'might bring about a law to prevent intermarriage between races.' 'Believe Klan …,' Toronto *Daily Star*, 8 March 1930, pp. 1–2. For more details on the class and racial composition of the Salvation Army, which had only twenty-six members in Oakville, see *

4 'Klansmen of Hamilton Defend Their Conduct in "Raid" at Oakville,' Toronto *Globe*, 3 March 1930, pp. 1, 3; 'Klan Took Oakville Girl from Negro Home,' Toronto *Daily Star*, 1 March 1930, p. 2; 'The KKK Visits Oakville,' Oakville *Journal*, clipping held by the Oakville Historical Society, identifies Ira Johnson's uncle as Mr Salt. The Toronto *Daily Star* ('K.K.K. Oakville Raid Has Sequel at Altar,' 24 March 1930, p. 1) identifies his aunt as Mrs Violet Salt. Later clippings use the spelling 'Sault' and also the name 'Stuart.' The Hamilton *Spectator* apparently mistakenly identifies the elderly couple as Ira Johnson's parents: 'Klan Separates Oakville Negro and White Girl,' Hamilton *Spectator*, 1 March 1930, p. 7. The *Dawn of Tomorrow*, a Black newspaper published by J.F. Jenkins in London, Ontario, indicates in an editorial titled 'Oakville and the K.K.K.' (24 March 1930, p. 2) that Johnson 'was ordered to leave town forthwith, which orders he obeyed …' If Johnson did leave Oakville, he returned within a short period of time, as later events clarify.

5 While these events were taking place, Ollie Johnson, one of Oakville's most prominent Black residents, had been searching frantically for Police Chief Kerr. By day, Ollie Johnson operated a dry-cleaning and pressing shop. In his off-hours, his versatile athletic ability as a runner and baseball player had made him a popular figure in Oakville. Ollie Johnson's prowess as the short-stop for the Oakville baseball team was legendary, and his reputation within the white community may have made him a good emissary for seeking help. On Johnson's occupation and stature, see Ahern, *Oakville*, at 126, 172.

6 'Local Klansman is Fined at Oakville,' Hamilton *Spectator*, 11 March 1930, p. 15; 'Klan Separates Oakville Negro and White Girl,' Hamilton *Spectator*, 1 March 1930, p. 7; 'Ku Klux Report Held from Council at Crown's Request,' Toronto *Globe*, 4 March 1930, p. 1.

7 'Ku Klux Klan Cohorts Parade into Oakville and Burn Fiery Cross,' Toronto *Globe*, 1 March 1930, p. 1; 'Klan Separates Oakville Negro and White Girl,'

Hamilton *Spectator*, 1 March 1930, p. 1; 'To Investigate K.K.K. Burnings,' London *Free Press*, 1 March 1930, p. 1.

8 'Ku Klux Klan Here on Business,' Oakville *Star and Independent*, 7 March 1930, p. 8; 'Klan Took Oakville Girl from Negro Home,' Toronto *Daily Star*, 1 March 1930, pp. 2–3; 'Klan Separates Oakville Negro and White Girl,' Hamilton *Spectator*, 1 March 1930, p. 1; 'To Investigate K.K.K. Burnings,' London *Free Press*, 1 March 1930, p. 1; 'If the Ku Klux Klan,' Milton *Canadian Champion*, 6 March 1930, p. 3; 'If the Ku Klux Klan,' Milton *Canadian Champion*, 13 March 1930, p. 3, citing the Brampton *Banner*; 'The KKK Visits Oakville,' clipping of the Oakville *Journal* held by the Oakville Historical Society, quoting unidentified clipping from the Toronto *Daily Star*; 'Klan Took Oakville Girl from Negro Home,' Toronto *Daily Star*, 1 March 1930, p. 1; 'Ku Klux Klan Cohorts Parade into Oakville and Burn Fiery Cross,' Toronto *Globe*, 1 March 1930, p. 1.

9 By the turn of the century, many residents of Oakville used the town as a commuting base, travelling daily by train to work in Toronto and Hamilton. When the highway from Toronto was paved out to Oakville in 1915, the commuting trend accelerated. Oakville's small base of light industry included a basket factory, tire factory, sheet music publisher, yacht-maker, auto sales and service, and fruit farming: see Hazel C. Mathews, *Oakville and the Sixteen: The History of an Ontario Port* (Toronto: University of Toronto Press, 1953), at 4–5, 376–7, 446; Ahern, *Oakville*, at 21, 33–40, 52–3. On the impact of the Depression in southwestern Ontario, see Marjorie Freeman Campbell, *A Mountain and a City: The Story of Hamilton* (Toronto: McClelland & Stewart, 1966), at 223.

10 'Klan Took Oakville Girl from Negro Home,' Toronto *Daily Star*, 1 March 1930, pp. 1–2. Oakville's population stood at 3,298 in 1921, and 3,857 by 1931: *Seventh Census of Canada, 1931* (Ottawa: J.O. Patenaude, 1933), at 68. The racial breakdowns (at 406–7) show 3,582 British, 46 German, 32 Dutch, 28 French, 23 Scandinavian, 20 Chinese and Japanese, 15 Hebrew, 8 Indian and Eskimo, 7 Austrian, 5 Italian, 4 Finnish, 3 Russian, 2 Czech and Slovak, 1 Belgian, and 79 'others.' The religious breakdowns recorded in the 1931 census (at 614–15) show 1,680 Anglicans, 969 United Church, 687 Presbyterians, 336 Roman Catholics, 58 Baptists, 26 Christian Scientists, 21 Lutherans, 15 Jews, 4 Adventists, 2 Pentecostal, and 32 'other.'

11 For further information on the immigration of Blacks, see * On the history of slavery in Canada, see the discussion of Viola Desmond's case, chapter 7.

12 For reference to Nova Scotia legislation barring the entry of liberated slaves from the Caribbean in 1834, and sources describing white resistance to Black immigration in mid-nineteenth-century Ontario and early twentieth-century Western Canada, see *

13 For references, see *

14 For details of the 1910 legislation and later enactments in 1919 and 1921, see *
15 For further details, see *
16 For details, see *
17 The 1861 census shows thirty-seven Blacks living in Oakville: Michael
   Wayne, 'The Black Population of Canada West on the Eve of the American
   Civil War: A Reassessment Based on the Manuscript Census of 1861,' in
   Franca Iacovetta et al., eds., *A Nation of Immigrants: Women, Workers, and
   Communities in Canadian History, 1840s–1960s* (Toronto: University of Toronto Press, 1998), 58 at 72. One of the first Black Oakville residents, James
   Wesley Hill, was a former slave who took up farming on the 9th Line,
   became an agent for the Underground Railroad, and travelled back and
   forth from Canada to the Southern states, assisting hundreds of fellow
   Blacks to escape. Robert Wilson, a white Oakville resident and captain of a
   small grain vessel, made it a practice to secret escaping slaves in the hold of
   his ship. To mark their gratitude, for years Blacks from all over southwestern Ontario would gather annually at Captain Wilson's home, on Dundas
   Street North, to celebrate Emancipation Day. Joe Wordsworth, who ran a
   barbershop and clothes-cleaning business, appears to have been the first
   Black to set up in business in Oakville. Mathews notes that Wordsworth was
   'much plagued by sailors, who threw all his barber's tools' into the Sixteen
   Mile Creek. Other first families include those of James Wesley Hill, the
   Johnsons, the Wallaces, the Strothers, William Holland, Benedict Duncan,
   Lloyd Brown, Samuel Adams, and Christopher Columbus Lee. The British
   Methodist Episcopal Church of Oakville, established in 1875, was reorgan-
   ized in 1891 as the Turner African Methodist Episcopal Church. Mathews,
   Oakville, at 247–8, 419–20; Ahern, *Oakville*, at 117–18; Robin W. Winks, *The
   Blacks in Canada: A History*, 2d ed. (Montreal: McGill-Queen's University
   Press, 1997), at 245. For references on the Underground Railroad and the
   role of Black women in southwestern Ontario, see *
18 'Klan Took Oakville Girl from Negro Home,' Toronto *Daily Star*, 1 March
   1930, p. 2; 'To Investigate K.K.K. Burnings,' London *Free Press*, 1 March
   1930, p. 1. The press describes Ethelbert Lionel Cross as a 'negro barrister of
   British birth.' 'Klansmen's Names Demanded of Price by Negro Barrister,'
   Toronto *Globe*, 17 March 1930, pp. 13–14. He was initially called to the bar in
   Nova Scotia on 12 December 1923, and then moved to Toronto, where he
   articled with E.F. Singer. Admitted to the Ontario bar on 20 March 1924,
   Cross appears to have been the only Black called between 1900 and 1923.
   Three Blacks preceded him. The first Black lawyer in Ontario, Robert Suth-
   erland, a Jamaican of African origin, was admitted to the bar in 1855. Suth-
   erland appears to have been of mixed race, with a Scottish father from

Jamaica, but he was identified as 'coloured' when he attended Queen's
University in Kingston from 1849 to 1852, graduating with honours in
classics and mathematics. He studied law at Osgoode Hall in 1852, and set
up a practice in Walkerton, southwest of Owen Sound, after his call. Delos
Rogest Davis, who is often wrongly credited with being the first Black
lawyer in Canada, was called to the bar in Ontario as a solicitor in 1885 and
as a barrister in 1886. Born in Colchester Township near Amherstburg,
Ontario, in 1846, Davis taught school for four years before receiving an
appointment as commissioner of affidavits in 1871. Two years later he
became a public notary. After studying law for eleven years, Davis was
unable to find a white lawyer willing to hire a Black legal apprentice. He
applied to the Ontario legislature in 1884 for admission as a solicitor under
special statute. In 1886, again by special statute and over the protests of the
Law Society of Upper Canada, Davis became a barrister. Davis became the
first Black King's Counsel in 1910. Davis's son, Frederick Homer Alphonso
Davis, graduated from Osgoode Hall in 1900, and the two men established
their firm of Davis and Davis in Amherstburg. According to Lance C.
Talbot, E. Lionel Cross was the next Black admitted, after a hiatus of twenty-
three years. Talbot credits B.J. Spencer Pitt as following Cross, noting that
'during the 1940s and 1950s, the number of Black lawyers in Ontario, practising mostly in Toronto, numbered no more than five.' The first Black
woman called to the bar in Ontario, Myrtle Blackwood Smith, a Montrealer
with a BA from Sir George Williams University, was not admitted until
1960: see Lance C. Talbot, 'History of Blacks in the Law Society of Upper
Canada,' *Law Society of Upper Canada Gazette* 24:1 (March 1990), 65–70; Ian
Malcolm, 'Robert Sutherland: The First Black Lawyer in Canada?' *Law
Society of Upper Canada Gazette* 26:2 (June 1992), 183–6; Robin W. Winks, *The
Blacks in Canada: A History*, 2d ed, (Montreal and Kingston: McGill–Queen's
University Press, 1997), at 328; *An Act to authorize the Supreme Court of
Judicature for Ontario to admit Delos Rogest Davis to practice as a solicitor*, S.O.
1884, c.94; *An Act to authorize the Law Society of Upper Canada to admit Delos
Rogest Davis as a Barrister-at-Law*, S.O. 1886, c.94; Daniel G. Hill, *The Freedom-
Seekers: Blacks in Early Canada* (Agincourt, Ont.: Book Society of Canada,
1981), at 215; Barry Cahill, 'The "Colored Barrister": The Short Life and
Tragic Death of James Robinson Johnston, 1876–1915,' *Dalhousie Law Journal*,
vol. 15 (1992), 326 at 345; Constance Backhouse, *Petticoats and Prejudice:
Women and Law in Nineteenth-Century Canada* (Toronto: The Osgoode Society
and Women's Press, 1991), at 326 and 439. I am indebted to Susan
Lewthwaite of the Law Society of Upper Canada Archives for information
on Cross. For comparative American sources on Black lawyers, see *

19 On the history of the First Baptist Church, see *

20 Bertrand Joseph Spencer Pitt was born on 8 September 1892, the sixth of
twelve children of a 'prosperous Grenada planter and trader' named Louis
Pitt, and Elizabeth Thomas. Pitt chose to study at Dalhousie under the
misapprehension that its degree would entitle him to practise law anywhere
in the British empire. When he learned that the Dalhousie degree permitted
practice only in Nova Scotia, Pitt requalified at the Middle Temple in London, studying international law and constitutional history: 'Was Bill Newell
Guilty?' Montreal *Standard*, 28 February 1942, p. 4. Talbot, 'History of Blacks
in the Law Society,' notes at 68 that it was difficult for Blacks to find
articling positions, and that such positions were generally available only
with Black and Jewish lawyers. Pitt appears to have been the fifth Black man
to practise law in Ontario. The *Standard* describes Pitt as a 'brilliant Negro
lawyer' with 'an unusually varied practise that has included everything
from criminal cases to cases of involved business litigation.' Talbot also
notes at 67 that 'the bulk of his clients were Canadians of Polish descent.'
His wife was Mary Lee Pitt. Talbot indicates at 68 that Pitt 'acted as a men-
tor to many young Blacks and provided free legal services to many members of the black community.' Blacks who articled with Pitt include James
Watson, QC, who became the Solicitor for the City of Windsor; Myrtle Smith
(*née* Blackwood), who appears to have been Ontario's first Black woman
lawyer; and George Carter, who became Ontario's second Black judge on
the Ontario Provincial Court. (Maurice Alexander Charles, appointed in
1969 to the Provincial Court Criminal Division was first.) Pitt also provided
'personal and professional encouragement' to Julius Alexander Isaac, who
was later named Chief Justice of the Federal Court of Canada. Pitt's failing
health forced him to retire in 1957. He died in Corona, New York, in 1961.
See Lance Carey Talbot, 'The Formation of the Black Law Students' Association (Canada),' *Law Society of Upper Canada Gazette* 26:2 (June 1992), 187 at
192; Cecil Foster, *A Place Called Heaven: The Meaning of Being Black in Canada*
(Toronto: HarperCollins, 1996), at 78. I am also indebted to Susan
Lewthwaite of the Law Society of Upper Canada Archives for locating
information about B.J. Spencer Pitt.

21 'Negroes of Toronto Ask Prosecution,' London *Free Press*, 5 March 1930, p. 3;
'Hears Delegation Against the Klan,' London *Advertiser*, 6 March 1930, p. 4;
'Klansmen of Hamilton Defend Their Conduct in "Raid" at Oakville,'
Toronto *Globe*, 3 March 1930, pp. 1, 3; 'Province Probes Klan Activities,'
London *Advertiser*, 1 March 1930, p. 1. 'Klan Took Oakville Girl from Negro
Home,' Toronto *Daily Star*, 1 March 1930, p. 2, notes that Dr D.A. Wyke,
'negro graduate of the University of Toronto,' also spoke at the meeting. 'All

Negro Population to Protest Klan Act,' Toronto *Daily Star*, 3 March 1930,
indicates that other speakers included Rev. Dr T.H. Henderson of the Grant
AME church, Rev. T.H. Jackson of the St James's BME church, and Rev. Dr
W. Constantine Perry.

22 'Has No Negro Blood, Klan Victim Declares,' Toronto *Daily Star*, 5 March
1930, p. 1; 'Johnson Claims Indian Descent; No Negro Blood in Him, Klan
Victim States.' Hamilton *Spectator*, 6 March 1930, p. 22.

23 'Has No Negro Blood, Klan Victim Declares,' Toronto *Daily Star*, 5 March
1930, p. 1; 'Johnson Claims Indian Descent; No Negro Blood in Him, Klan
Victim States,' Hamilton *Spectator*, 6 March 1930, p. 22. Trying to wade
through the complexity of the evidence, the *Spectator* recounts that Ira
Johnson's paternal grandmother was 'a Cherokee Indian half-breed,' and
that his paternal grandfather was 'of the same race, having married an Irish
woman.' Whether the 'Irish' factor was the other half of the 'half-breed'
designation, or whether the Irish wife preceded or succeeded Johnson's
paternal grandmother is not specified.

24 'Klan Took Oakville Girl from Negro Home,' Toronto *Daily Star*, 1 March
1930, pp. 1–3; 'Johnson Claims Indian Descent; No Negro Blood in Him,
Klan Victim States,' Hamilton *Spectator*, 6 March 1930, p. 22; 'Klansmen's
Names Demanded of Price by Negro Barrister,' Toronto *Globe*, 17 March
1930, p. 13. On the combined history of the Cherokee Nation and Blacks in
the United States, and the complexity of designations regarding Black and
Aboriginal communities, see *

25 Individuals named 'Johnson' who associated with members of the Black
community in Oakville may have been linked with Ollie Johnson, Oakville's
famous Black athlete. Several of the first Black families to settle in Hamilton
were also named 'Johnson'; see Hill, *Freedom-Seekers*, at 58–9, citing Henry
Johnson, Lewis Miles Johnson, and Edward Johnson.

26 'Has No Negro Blood, Klan Victim Declares,' Toronto *Daily Star*, 5 March
1930, p. 1; 'Klan Took Oakville Girl from Negro Home,' Toronto *Daily Star*, 1
March 1930, pp. 1–3; 'Johnson Claims Indian Descent; No Negro Blood in
Him, Klan Victim States,' Hamilton *Spectator*, 6 March 1930, p. 22;
'Klansmen's Names Demanded of Price by Negro Barrister,' Toronto *Globe*,
17 March 1930, p. 13. The *Daily Star* does not mention that the Six Nations
sold Black slaves to settlers in the Niagara region, or that Joseph Brant, the
Mohawk chief who originally established the Six Nations Territory at
Brantford, kept thirty to forty Black slaves: see Hill, *Freedom-Seekers*, at 52;
Ken Alexander and Avis Glaze, *Towards Freedom: The African-Canadian
Experience* (Toronto: Umbrella Press, 1996), at 47. Ahern, *Oakville*, describes
at 40 the company that employed Ira Johnson as a mechanic. A. & G.

Hillmer's Livery Service became completely motorized in 1914–15, and expanded into automobile sales and service for the McLaughlin motor car and later the Model T. Ford. Their sales room and parts department occupied their building on Colborne Street (no. 145 Lakeshore), and they operated a garage in their newly constructed building on Church Street (no. 147). Johnson must have been laid off from Hillmer Bros. shortly before the KKK raid; the press reported that Johnson had recently left Hillmer Brothers, and was working 'with building contractors in this vicinity.'

27 'Believe Klan ...,' Toronto *Daily Star*, 8 March 1930, p. 1.

28 'No Country for a Ku Klux,' Toronto *Globe*, 3 March 1930, p. 4; see also 'The Oakville Case,' Toronto *Daily Star*, 12 March 1930, pp. 1–2.

29 'Clansmen of Hamilton,' Toronto *Globe*, 3 March 1930, p. 3.

30 'Klansmen of Hamilton Defend Their Conduct in "Raid" at Oakville,' Toronto *Globe*, 3 March 1930, pp. 1–3. The name of Ira Johnson's parents is given in 'Klan Took Oakville Girl from Negro Home,' Toronto *Daily Star*, 1 March 1930, p. 2.

31 'No Country for a Ku Klux,' Toronto *Globe*, 3 March 1930, p. 4; 'Senators, Members Are in Ku Klux Klan, Claims Klan Letter,' Toronto *Globe*, 6 March 1930, pp. 1–2; 'Three Must Appear in Oakville Court Because of "Raid",' Toronto *Globe*, 8 March 1930, pp. 1–2. Tom M. Henson, 'Ku Klux Klan in Western Canada,' *Alberta History* 25:4 (Autumn 1977), 1 at 6, notes that some of the members of Parliament accused of Klan membership in the late 1920s were F.W. Turnbull (Regina), Samuel Gobeil (Compton), W.D. Cowan (Long Lake), John Evans (Rosetown), M.C.H. Cahan (St Lawrence–St George), and A.U.G. Bury (East Edmonton).

32 Wyn Craig Wade, *The Fiery Cross: The Ku Klux Klan in America* (London: Simon and Schuster, 1987), at 33–5; Lenwood G. Davis and Janet L. Sims-Wood, *The Ku Klux Klan: A Bibliography* (Westport, Conn.: Greenwood Press, 1984), at p.xiii; Patsy Sims, *The Klan* (New York: Stein and Day, 1982), at 3–4; Kathleen M. Blee, *Women of the Klan: Racism and Gender in the 1920s* (Berkeley: University of California Press, 1991), at 13.

33 Wade, *The Fiery Cross*, at 35–62.

34 Wade, *The Fiery Cross*, at 62; Blee, *Women of the Klan*, at 13–14.

35 The Ku-Klux Act permitted any United States citizen to sue in a federal court persons who had 'deprived him of rights, privileges and immunities' guaranteed by the U.S. Constitution. It created a new crime of 'conspiracy to deprive one of his civil rights.' The offence of 'going in disguise' required proof of intent to deprive someone 'of the right to vote or testify in court,' or to deny anyone twenty other rights secured by the U.S. Constitution. It authorized the president to call out the military to put down civil distur-

bances that deprived citizens of their constitutional rights. It compelled jurors to take an oath that they were not in any way beholden to the Klan. See Wade, *The Fiery Cross*, at 88.

36 Susanna Moodie, *Roughing It in the Bush* (Ottawa: 1988, orig. pub. London, 1852), at 224–5. For details on Moodie's life, see Alison Prentice et al., *Canadian Women: A History* (Toronto: Harcourt, Brace, Jovanovich, 1988), at 69–70. Wayne, 'The Black Population of Canada West,' notes at 69 that racial intermarriage was not entirely uncommon: 'It is noteworthy that 385 black men listed in the census had white wives, mainly immigrant women from Europe or the British Isles. This represented approximately one out of every seven black married men ...'

37 This passage is intended as a description of the Klan's original phase between 1865 and the early 1870s. The column 'Month to Month,' written by Sir John Willison, originally appeared in *The Canadian Magazine* (February 1923), 312–16, and is reprinted in 'The Ku Klux Klan,' *The Canadian Annual Review* (1923), at 82. The columnist takes issue with the activities of the Klan in its later phase, suggesting that the organization 'fell away from the ideals of its founders.'

38 Winks, *Blacks in Canada*, notes at 320 that the original Klan 'may have had a few followers in the united counties of Leeds and Grenville in Ontario, but if so, they were not active.' Gerald Stevens, *The United Counties of Leeds and Grenville* (Brockville: n.p., 1961), states at 22: 'The area has had its nineteenth century witches and rustlers, religious sects, and the K.K.K.; and the steady progress ensured by descendants of Loyalist blood.'

39 Orlo Miller, *This Was London: The First Two Centuries* (Westport, Ont.: Butternut Press, 1988), at 130–3. The decision of the U.S. government to back down is attributed to a treaty recently signed between the United States and Great Britain, and the fact that it was an American presidential election year. Due to Dr Bratton's release, the outstanding charges of murder in South Carolina were never proceeded with, and he was awarded damages for wrongful arrest and imprisonment. After Dr Bratton's 'triumphant return to Canada,' he practised medicine in London for some time, eventually going back to South Carolina, where he died in 1897. Miller notes that London's deputy clerk of the peace, Isaac Bell Cornwall, was convicted in London, Ontario on 17 July 1872 of kidnapping Dr Bratton, based on his role in assisting the American detectives.For details on the response to the Bratton incident by Prime Minister Macdonald and George Brown's Toronto *Globe*, see *

40 'Father and Mother Arrived in London as Runaway Slaves; Distinguished Actor Who Was Born in the City, and spent Boyhood Here, Is Officially

Honored with Freedom of City at Rotary Club Luncheon,' London *Adver-tiser*, 30 October 1937. There may be confusion about the dates, since Richard Harrison was apparently born in London on 29 September 1864. If the house-buring occurred when he was seventeen, it would have taken place in 1881. See also 'A Famous Native of London,' 'Richard B. Harrison in His Home Town,' R.B. Harrison Returns Home,' *London Scrapbooks*, Microfilm Red Series, vol. 26, R971.326L on Reel no. 4, and 'Notes Gathered by Dr Seaborn Re: Characters and Locations of Early London,' in Edwin Seaborn Collection, Reminiscences, at 468–75, London Room, London Public Library. I am indebted to Christopher Doty for advising me of this incident; see Christopher Doty, 'From London to Broadway Stardom,' London *Free Press*, 7 February 1999, p. B2.

41 Wade notes that cross-burning, which did not occur during the first phase of the KKK's activities but became a universal KKK calling-card in its second phase, was entirely attributable to the 'exotic imagination of Thomas Dixon, whose fictional Klansmen had felt so much tangible pride in their Scottish ancestry, they revived the use of burning crosses as signal fires from one clan to another.' *The Birth of a Nation* has been described as 'the first motion-picture blockbuster – one that would gross well over $60 million, establish movies as a major American industry, and enshrine Hollywood, the dull, parched countryside where the film had been shot, as *The Motion Picture Capital of the World*': Wade, *The Fiery Cross*, at 119–46; David M. Chalmers, *Hooded Americanism: The History of the Ku Klux Klan* (New York: Franklin Watts, 1965), at 26; Nancy MacLean, *Behind the Mask of Chivalry: The Making of the Second Ku Klux Klan* (New York: Oxford University Press, 1994), at 12.

42 Wade, *The Fiery Cross*, at 140–69, 252; MacLean, *Behind the Mask of Chivalry*, at 13–19; Chalmers, *Hooded Americanism*, at 297.

43 On the composition of the Klan membership, the WKKK, and Junior Klans for boys and girls, see *

44 Chalmers, *Hooded Americanism*, at 279. Willison's column, 'Month to Month,' originally appeared in *The Canadian Magazine* (February 1923), at 312–16, and is reprinted in 'The Ku Klux Klan,' *The Canadian Annual Review* (1923), at 82.

45 On Klan splinter groups, see Wade, *The Fiery Cross*, at 191; Sims, *The Klan*, at 7. On the three Canadian groups and their goals, see P.M. Richards, 'How the Ku Klux Klan Came to Canada,' *Saturday Night*, 26 June 1926, at 1–2; Julian Sher, *White Hoods: Canada's Ku Klux Klan* (Vancouver: New Star, 1983), at 19–61; Martin Robin, *Shades of Right: Nativist and Fascist Politics in Canada, 1920–1940* (Toronto: University of Toronto Press, 1992), at 2–59. On the qualifications for membership, see Knights of the Ku Klux Klan of

Kanada, *Provisional Constitution and Laws of the Invisible Empire* (n.p. 1925); *Kloran: Knights of the Ku Klux Klan of Kanada* (Toronto: n.p., 1925). On the membership profile, see Robin, *Shades of Right*, at 45–6; William Calderwood, 'The Rise and Fall of the Ku Klux Klan in Saskatchewan,' MA thesis (University of Saskatchewan, 1968), at 144–5; Regina *Morning Leader*, 11 May 1928.

46 Blee, *Women of the Klan*, at 86; MacLean, *Behind the Mask of Chivalry*, at 143–4; Knights of the KKK of Kanada, *Provisional Constitution*, at 19; *Kloran: Knights of the Ku Klux Klan of Kanada*. There is no ban on mixed race marriages at common law, so legislation was needed to accomplish this. Peggy Pascoe, 'Miscegenation Law, Court Cases, and Ideologies of "Race" in Twentieth-Century America,' *Journal of American History*, vol. 83 (June 1996), 44, notes at 49 that forty-one American colonies and states enacted such laws. Sixteen statutes were still on the book in 1967, when the U.S. Supreme Court ruling in *Loving* v *Virginia*, 388 U.S. 1 (1967), held such laws unconstitutional for violation of the equal protection laws, because they were intended to maintain white supremacy. On the history of miscegenation law in the United States, see *

47 Montreal *Daily Star*, 1 October 1921, cited in Robin, *Shades of Right*, at 11; Henson, 'Ku Klux Klan,' at 2.

48 Henson, 'Ku Klux Klan,' at 1–2, citing Edmonton *Journal*, 20 October 1929, and *The British Columbia Federationist*, 24 November 1922, at 2.

49 Robin, *Shades of Right*, at 11; Arthur T. Doyle, *Front Benches and Back Rooms: A Story of Corruption, Muckraking, Raw Partisanship and Intrigue in New Brunswick* (Toronto: Green Tree Publishing, 1976), at 217–18, 252, 257–8.

50 Robin, *Shades of Right*, at 11. 'Ku Klux Klan Diminishes in U.S.,' *Saturday Night*, 16 October 1926, at 1–2, reports that Lord 'abandoned his responsible duties in New Brunswick without troubling to inform his constituents of his intention … in order to accept the post of "Imperial Klaliff" of the Ku Klux Klan of Kanada.' See also P.M. Richards, 'Claims of the Ku Klux Klan,' *Saturday Night*, 17 July 1926, at 1.

51 Michael Boudreau, 'Crime and Society in a City of Order: Halifax, 1918–1935,' PhD thesis (Queen's University, 1996), notes at 415–16 that these incidents occurred on two successive nights in October 1932. 'Police officials reported that they knew the identity of the Klan leaders and would monitor their activities.' No further action ensued.

52 Allan Bartley, 'A Public Nuisance: The Ku Klux Klan in Ontario 1923–27,' *Journal of Canadian Studies* 30:3 (Fall 1995), 156 at 159.

53 Bartley, 'Public Nuisance,' at 161, citing anonymous, confidential sources.

54 Bartley, 'Public Nuisance,' at 162; 'Ku Klux Rears Head in City of Hamilton

with 32 Initiations,' Toronto *Globe*, 19 November 1924, pp. 1–2; 'Ku Klux Organizer Found Guilty of Carrying Revolver,' Toronto *Globe*, 20 November 1924; "Detective Warned in Note Signed K.K.K.,' Toronto *Globe*, 22 November 1924; Canadian Security Intelligence Service, *Right Wing Extremist Groups in Canada and the United States*, 14 November 1988 (Solicitor General's file no. VF2115, Solicitor General of Canada, Library and Reference Centre, Ottawa), at 19.

55 'Three Must Appear in Oakville Court Because of "Raid",' Toronto *Globe*, 8 March 1930, pp. 1–2.

56 Richards, 'How the Ku Klux Klan Came to Canada,' at 1; Canadian Security Intelligence Service, *Right Wing Extremist Groups*, at 19–20.

57 Bartley, 'Public Nuisance,' at 164; 'Klansmen Balked by Minister,' London *Evening Advertiser*, 29 June 1925; 'Klan Fiery Cross Burned at Dresden,' London *Free Press*, 1 August 1925; 'Fiery Cross of K.K.K. Burned at Wallaceburg,' London *Free Press*, 20 August 1925; 'Klan Meeting Breaks Up,' London *Free Press*, 2 September 1925.

58 The sermon was given at the Hyatt Avenue United Church by B.C. Eckhardt, a lay preacher from Nilestown. Rev. R.J. McCormick refused to allow the Klansmen admittance wearing gowns, and they had to sit with their gowns and hoods folded under their arms. Eckhardt later announced that his sermon had been 'a Klan address.' See 'Klansmen Balked by Minister,' London *Evening Advertiser*, 29 June 1925.

59 'Klan Spokesman Outlines Aims,' London *Free Press*, 3 August 1925, pp. 1–2. 'The Ku Klux Klan,' *The Canadian Annual Review* (1923), reports at 82–3 that the London mayor professed hostility to the Klan: 'London needs no Ku Klux Klan or other order that seeks to gain unjust ends by a cowardly parade of masks and mystery ... As Mayor of London, I will use all the power of my office to rid the city of the verminous missionaries of an order that seeks to terrify citizens who may differ from these so-called Knights of the Ku Klux Klan in race, colour, religion, or ability to succeed.'

60 'Klan Meeting Breaks Up When Hawkins Declines to Answer Questions,' London *Free Press*, 2 September 1925.

61 'Ku Klux Klan Holds First Open Air Ceremony in Canada,' London *Free Press*, 15 October 1925, p. 2.

62 'First Canadian Ku Klux Burial,' London *Free Press*, 21 January 1926, p. 1.

63 Robin, *Shades of Right*, at 13.

64 Robin, *Shades of Right*, at 19–21; Henson, 'Ku Klux Klan,' at 4.

65 Saskatchewan was organized by three white American Klansmen: Hugh F. 'Pat' Emmons, Lewis A. Scott, and Harold Scott. Howard Palmer, *Patterns of Prejudice: A History of Nativism in Alberta* (Toronto: McClelland & Stewart,

1982), estimates at 101 that the Saskatchewan Klan membership reached 20,000 in the summer of 1928, a number 'four times that of Klan membership in bordering northern states with comparable populations.' Robert Moon, *This Is Saskatchewan* (Toronto: Ryerson, 1953), estimates at 45–7 that at its peak there were 40,000 KKK members in Saskatchewan. See also Robin, *Shades of Right*, at 28–35, 41–6; William Calderwood, 'Religious Reactions to the Ku Klux Klan in Saskatchewan,' *Saskatchewan History* 26:3 (1973), 103; William Calderwood, 'The Decline of the Progressive Party in Saskatchewan, 1925–1930,' *Saskatchewan History* 21:3 (Autumn 1968), 81; James W.St.G. Walker, *'Race,' Rights and the Law in the Supreme Court of Canada* (Toronto: The Osgoode Society, 1997); James Gray, *Roar of the Twenties* (Toronto: Macmillan, 1975), at 267–73; Patrick Kyba, 'Ballots and Burning Crosses – The Election of 1929,' in Norman Ward and Duff Spafford, eds., *Politics in Saskatchewan* (Toronto: Longmans, 1968), at 105–23; Henson, 'Ku Klux Klan,' at 1–8. On Canadian attitudes towards and experience with interracial marriages, see discussion of Yee Clun's case in chapter 5 and discussion of Viola Desmond's case in chapter 7.

66 Henson, 'Ku Klux Klan,' at 4–5; Raymond J.A. Huel, 'J.J. Maloney: How the West was Saved from Rome, Quebec and the Liberals,' in John E. Foster, ed., *The Developing West* (Edmonton: University of Alberta Press, 1983), at 221–41. Palmer, *Patterns of Prejudice*, at 101–10, 198–9, identifies the driving force of Alberta's KKK as Hamilton-born J.J. Maloney, and notes that there were Klan activities in Arrowwood, Bashaw, Blackie, Bow Island, Cadomin, Calgary, Camrose, Carmangay, Carstairs, Chauvin, Clandonald, Claresholm, Coleman, Didsbury, Edmonton, Edson, Erskine, Forestburg, Fort Saskatchewan, Gibbons, Innisfail, Irma, Jarrow, Killam, Lacombe, Lomond, Marwayne, Medicine Hat, Milo, Nanton, Newbrook, Olds, Pincher Creek, Ponoka, Red Deer, Retlaw, Sterco, Stettler, Stoney Plain, Taber, Tofield, Turner Valley, Vermilion, Vulcan, Wainwright, and Wetaskiwin. Palmer estimates this totals 'about one-eighth of the approximately four hundred cities, towns, and villages in the province that might have been large enough to sustain fraternal orders.'

67 Robin, *Shades of Right*, notes at 11 that 'allegations that Klansmen had set the blazes' were not silenced by official denials from Atlanta authorities. Henson, 'Ku Klux Klan,' notes at 2 that the blazes were 'preceded by messages of warning signed by the K.K.K.'

68 Robin, *Shades of Right*, at 16; Henson, 'Ku Klux Klan,' at 2.

69 Robin, *Shades of Right*, at 23–5; Henson, 'Ku Klux Klan,' at 2.

70 The Thorold incident occurred in December 1922. 'The Ku Klux Klan,' *The Canadian Annual Review* (1923), at 82–3; Bartley, 'Public Nuisance,' at 160.

71 'The Ku Klux Klan,' *Canadian Annual Review*, at 82–3; Bartley, 'Public Nuisance,' at 160.

72 Canadian Security Intelligence Service, *Right Wing Extremist Groups*, at 20; Robin, *Shades of Right*, at 14–15.

73 Robin, *Shades of Right*, at 14–15; 'Clan Bigotry Crops Up in Belleville,' *Saturday Night*, 30 October 1926, p. 2; Richards, 'Claims of the Ku Klux Klan,' at 1.

74 Bartley, 'Public Nuisance,' at 161, citing anonymous, confidential sources.

75 Karen Dubinsky, *Improper Advances: Rape and Heterosexual Conflict in Ontario, 1880–1929* (Chicago: University of Chicago Press, 1993), at 124, citing District Court Judges' Criminal Court, Algoma District, 1927. The reference to the cross burning appears in court records describing the 'depraved family' members who were charged with running a brothel and using their daughters as prostitutes. On the Klan's efforts to police sexual 'misbehaviour' among whites, see Blee, *Women of the Klan*, at 82.

76 Henson, 'Ku Klux Klan,' at 6. The efforts of the KKK to seek the removal of Mr Bilodeau, a francophone Catholic postmaster in Lafleche, are also described in House of Commons, *Parliamentary Debates* [Hansard], vol.3 (9 June 1928), at 4077–8.

77 Palmer, *Patterns of Prejudice*, at 102.

78 Palmer, *Patterns of Prejudice*, at 106, citing a telephone interview with Archie Keyes, the columnist concerned, in Calgary, May 1978.

79 Robin, *Shades of Right*, at 23–7, citing Allan Seager, 'A History of the Mine Workers' Union of Canada, 1925–1936,' MA thesis (McGill University, 1977), at 151–4. Fred Doberstein, the Lacombe blacksmith who was apparently 'prone to amorous escapades,' was also threatened with death. On the Klan's efforts to police philandering husbands, see Blee, *Women of the Klan*, at 82.

80 'Klan Spokesman Outlines Aims,' London *Free Press*, 3 August 1925, pp. 1–2, notes that 'the meeting passed off without disturbance and the two police constables held nothing more than a watching brief ...' 'Fiery Cross of K.K.K. Burned at Wallaceburg,' London *Free Press*, 20 August 1925, notes that 'Fire Chief Best was called to the scene, and after an investigation concluded there was no danger of fire.' The scene was a burning cross, about twelve feet by six feet, which 'burned brightly' between midnight and three o'clock.

81 See, for example, the disclaimer of responsibility issued by Klan officials from their Atlanta headquarters when the Quebec cathedral and Sulpician rest-house were burned in 1922. Other examples include the Atlanta-based denial from the Imperial Wizard that the KKK was responsible for the burning of St Boniface College, and the denials from the American and

Canadian Klan that it was responsible for the explosion in St Mary's Roman
Catholic church in Barrie: Robin, *Shades of Right*, at 11, 16, 165–6. The same
tendency to claim KKK linkages as 'purported' or 'alleged,' despite the
existence of letters signed 'KKK' and fiery crosses burning at the site, shows
up in the accounts of some historians of the Klan. See, for example, Bartley,
'Public Nuisance,' at 160; Winks, *Blacks in Canada*, at 322; Henson, 'Ku Klux
Klan,' at 6.

82 Chalmers, *Hooded Americanism*, at 280; Robin, *Shades of Right*, at 15; Bartley,
'Public Nuisance,' at 165–6; 'Ku Klux Klan Accused of Dynamite Outrage in
the Town of Barrie,' Toronto *Globe*, 22 June 1926, pp. 1–2; 'Two More
Klansmen Arrested at Barrie Following Outrage,' Toronto *Globe*, 23 June
1926, p. 1; Archives of Ontario [hereinafter cited as AO], RG4-32, Department of Attorney-General for Ontario, File 1526/1926, *Rex vs. Skelly, Lee and
Butler*.

83 When contacted for comment about the trial, white American Klan leaders
also attempted to absolve themselves of any connection with the Canadian
organization. For his part, Skelly claimed that, the day after the bombing, he
had been taken to meet with a lawyer acting for the Klan, who 'induced him
to sign a statement absolving the Ku Klux Klan from all responsibility for
the act. […] [H]e stated that he was afraid that they would do away with
him if he did not sign it.' See 'Two More Klansmen Arrested at Barrie
Following Outrage,' Toronto *Globe*, 23 June 1926, p. 3; Bartley, 'Public
Nuisance,' at 165–6, citing Barrie *Examiner*, 17 June 1926, 24 June 1926, 21
October 1926; and AO RG4-32, Department of Attorney-General for Ontario,
File 1526/1926, *Rex v Skelly, Lee and Butler*; Winks, *Blacks in Canada*, at 322.

84 'Three Must Appear in Oakville Court Because of "Raid",' Toronto *Globe*, 8
March 1930, pp. 1–2; 'Summonses Served on Alleged Klan Raiders,' London
Free Press, 8 March 1930, p. 5; 'Klansmen Fined $50 and Costs, Two Others
Found Not guilty; Did Not Wear Masks in Raid,' Toronto *Globe*, 11 March
1930, pp. 1, 3. The press describes Dr Phillips variously as 'William H.,'
'William A.,' 'William E.,' 'William J.,' and 'H.A.' 'William H.' is the information contained in the Archives of Ontario, Transcript of Jail Register
Entry, Milton Jail, RG20, Series F-23, vol. 7, no. 162, from which the other
biographical details were obtained. I have preferred 'William A.' because
this is the listing that appears continuously in the Vernon City of Hamilton
Directories from 1929 to 1932. Harold Orme is listed as an assistant to
chiropractor Dr S.J. Albin until 1932, when he is listed as a 'labourer.' Orme
was married to a woman named Viola, and they roomed at 64 Bay Street
South. Some of the press accounts designate Harold Orme as 'Dr. Orme.'
Ernest Taylor was married to a woman named Eva, and owned a home at

154 Gibson Avenue. Phillips is referred to throughout the written records on this case as 'Dr. Phillips,' a designation that may have been based on his chiropractic occupation. When the case was before the Ontario Court of Appeal, Judge Mulock questioned the designation 'Dr.' as applied to a chiropractor, asking: 'Who calls him a doctor, then?' Phillips's defence counsel, Reid Bowlby, agreed that 'there was no justification for the title.' '"Had No Lawful Excuse" Judge Says of K.K.Klan,' Toronto *Daily Star*, 1 April 1930, pp. 1–2. On the history of chiropractic, see *

85 *Criminal Code*, R.S.C. 1927, c.36, s.464(c).

86 For details of the original 1861 English statute, the enactment of a similar provision in Canada in 1869, and the placement of the offence in the Criminal Code in 1892, see *

87 'Klansmen's Names Demanded of Price by Negro Barrister,' Toronto *Globe*, 17 March 1930, pp. 13–14; 'K.K.K. Drops All Interest in Oakville Couple's Affairs,' Toronto *Daily Star*, 24 March 1930, pp. 1–2; 'Earlscourt Labor Protests Activities of Ku Klux Klan,' Toronto *Globe*, 21 March 1930, p. 14. For further analysis of why these suggestions were unlikely to have been useful see *

88 For details of these charges, which might all have been utilized in the circumstances, see *

89 'Acted on Mother's Request Klan Statement Now Claims,' undated clipping held by the Oakville Historical Society. For details of the offence of 'watching and besetting,' see *

90 'Tear Off the Mask from Kowardly Klans,' Guelph *Evening Mercury and Advertiser*, 5 October 1926.

91 'Tear Off the Mask from Kowardly Klans,' Guelph *Evening Mercury and Advertiser*, 5 October 1926. Templeton also sent a telegram to the Ontario attorney general, enclosing copies of his articles from the *Mercury* and demanding to know what legal action could be taken against the Klan. For details of Deputy Attorney General Edward J. Bayly's response, see *

92 For details of the proactive charges regarding peace bonds and 'loitering by night,' see *

93 For the relevant statutory provision regarding 'defamatory libel,' see *

94 For legislative details of the defences, see *

95 For the *Saturday Night* reference, see 'Girls Be Careful Whom You Marry,' 15 August 1925, as cited in Walker, *'Race,' Rights and the Law in the Supreme Court of Canada*, at 82–3. There are many examples of prominent Canadian figures who endorsed the Klan's hostility towards racial intermarriage. See, for example, the comments of white Toronto lawyer A.R. Hassard, who, while castigating the Klan's tactics in the Oakville raid, enthusiastically

endorsed their goal: 'From what I have read my sympathies are strongly with the girl and her mother, but unfortunately the law is the other way. If this practice of intermarrying whites and negroes be extensively carried on, some society ought to secure the enactment of a uniform law throughout Canada on the subject. If the Klansmen are really in earnest, they would be the proper people to do that. There is no law against whites and blacks intermarrying, but I think there should be. I think that neither the marriage license issuer nor a minister who has any respect for himself would, except under the gravest conditions, assist in the marriage of a white and a black. The same should be said of the marriage of a white girl and a Chinese. I remember many years ago a large negro out near Dufferin St. was married to a white woman and the children, five or six of them, were of all colors, ranging from black, gray to white. I think that those children would be subject to a good deal of torment in the public schools. A negro child of black parents is generally not subjected to indignity in school.' 'Has No Negro Blood, Klan Victim Declares,' Toronto *Daily Star*, 5 March 1930, p. 2. Ruth I. McKenzie, 'Race Prejudice and the Negro,' *Dalhousie Review* vol.20 (1940), notes at 201 that 'intermarriage [of Blacks] with whites is not approved.'

96 For legislative details of the group defamation law, see *
97 For further details regarding the Nationalist Party of Canada, the campaign for the enactment of the law organized by Marcus Hyman, a Jewish immigrant from Britain who was a lawyer and law lecturer at the Manitoba Law School, and the legislative and prosecutorial history of the new law, see *
98 For details of the 1944 legislation and the lobby campaign that generated the new law, see *
99 This book will not attempt to chronicle the various municipal by-laws that contributed to racist practices, nor those that attempted, beginning in the 1940s, to reduce racist behaviour. The discussion which follows is limited to provincial and federal enactments. For details of the 1932 Ontario provision and its genesis, see *
100 For legislative details of the 1931, 1932, 1933, and 1945 provisions, see *
101 For legislative details of the 1950 provision, see *
102 For legislative details of the provisions enacted in Ontario and Manitoba in 1950, see *
103 For legislative details, see *
104 For details of the 1919 provision, which was repealed in 1936, see *
105 For details of the lobby campaign, see *
106 The individuals concerned about discrimination and inequities in Cana-

dian society were, perhaps, reluctant to adopt the sorts of measures that had been used to attack left-wing organizations such as the Communist Party. A white CCF member of Parliament, J.S. Woodsworth, spoke out against the KKK in the House of Commons in 1926, but explicitly refrained from endorsing such tactics: 'I had placed in my hands a short while ago one of the [KKK] circulars sent to a friend of mine summoning a meeting of this organization. […] I shall not go into the literature which I hold in my hand, nor am I going to urge the Department of Justice to summarily deport these people. I would remind them however that the machinery is there and has been used in the case of much more worthy people. I am not strong however, on repressive measures; I hope we shall soon have fewer of these measures than are now in force in this country. I do think, though, that we should do everything in our power to lessen the influence of such an organization as this, because if we allow such bodies as the Ku Klux Klan, the latest American importation, to engender a spirit of intolerance in this country, we are bound to have a serious time ahead of us.' See House of Commons, *Debates*, vol.1 (29 January 1926), at 573.

107 For details of the prosecutions, see *

108 For legislative details concerning the riot provisions, see *

109 For some expressions of concern about this, published in contemporary periodicals, see *

110 The Ontario Supreme Court records for this case were 'destroyed due to extensive culling' (correspondence from Joseph Solovitch, Archives of Ontario, 30 March 1995), as were the files from the attorney general and the provincial police: Milton: W.I. Dick re Ku Klux Klan demonstration #1946 (destroyed); Phillips, W.A. General #2489 (destroyed); Sentences, Dr W.A. Phillips, Being Masked at Night (Ku Klux Klan) #638 (destroyed); correspondence from Joseph Solovitch, Archives of Ontario, 14 March 1995. I have relied upon the reported decision, *Rex v Phillips* (1930), 55 C.C.C. 49 (Ont. C.A.); the Benchbooks of Sir William Mulock, Book 14, 14 January 1929–3 June 1930, Court of Appeal of Ontario Archives, Box 412, Shelf 23, Bay 4, Aisle Book 14, p. 309, and the newspaper coverage of the case. The designation of the Oakville trial as 'the first' is somewhat problematic, given the three Barrie Klansmen who were convicted in 1926.

111 'Local Klansman Is Fined at Oakville,' Hamilton *Spectator*, 11 March 1930, p. 15; 'Klansman Fined $50 and Costs, Two Others Found Not Guilty; Did Not Wear Masks in Raid,' Toronto *Globe*, 11 March 1930, pp. 1, 3; 'Three Klansmen on Trial Today,' London *Advertiser*, 10 March 1930, p. 1; 'One Klansman Fined and Two Are Freed,' Toronto *Daily Star*, 10 March 1930; 'Klansmen on Trial Here,' Oakville *Star and Independent*, 14 March 1930, p.

1. Mathews, *Oakville*, mentions at 248 that the Wallaces were one of the first Black families to settle in Oakville.

112 'Klansmen of Hamilton Defend Their Conduct in "Raid" at Oakville,' Toronto *Globe*, 3 March 1930, pp. 1, 3. Ahern, *Oakville*, notes at 131 that McIlveen's store was the last shop on Main Street, no. 126.

113 'W.I. Dick, Crown Attorney for 45 Years,' Toronto *Globe*, 24 April 1962, p. 4.

114 'Klansman Fined $50 and Costs, Two Others Found Not Guilty; Did Not Wear Masks in Raid,' Toronto *Globe*, 11 March 1930, pp. 1, 3; 'Klansman Fined $50 and Costs, Plans to Appeal,' London *Advertiser*, 11 March 1930, p. 3; 'Tear Off the Mask from Kowardly Klans,' Guelph *Evening Mercury and Advertiser*, 5 October 1926; 'That Freedom,' Guelph *Evening Mercury and Advertiser*, 8 October 1926. The Guelph paper also suggests that a number of city councillors were active Klan members.

115 'Local Klansman Is Fined at Oakville,' Hamilton *Spectator*, 11 March 1930, p. 15.

116 Charles William Reid Bowlby was born in 1892 in Tapleytown, Ontario, to Charles Bowlby and Anna Cross. He served in the First World War in the 26th Battalion from 1915 to 1917. After receiving war injuries, he returned to Ontario and articled with the Hamilton firm of Nesbit, Gauld, Langs. He was called to the Ontario bar in 1919. He practised with Washington, Martin, Bowlby & Griffin at 7 Hughson South, and resided at 525 Dundurn South. His wife was Mary Elsie Dixon and he was a member of the United Church. I am indebted to Susan Lewthwaite of the Law Society of Upper Canada Archives for this information.

117 'Klansman Fined $50 and Costs, Two Others Found Not Guilty; Did Not Wear Masks in Raid,' Toronto *Globe*, 11 March 1930, pp. 1, 3; 'Local Klansman Is Fined at Oakville,' Hamilton *Spectator*, 11 March 1930, p. 15; 'One Klansman Fined and Two Are Freed,' Toronto *Daily Star*, 10 March 1930.

118 'Klansmen of Hamilton Defend Their Conduct in "Raid" at Oakville,' Toronto *Globe*, 3 March 1930, pp. 1, 3; 'Klansman Fined $50 and Costs, Two Others Found Not Guilty; Did Not Wear Masks in Raid,' Toronto *Globe*, 11 March 1930, pp. 1, 3; 'Local Klansman Is Fined at Oakville,' Hamilton *Spectator*, 11 March 1930, p. 15; 'One Klansman Fined and Two are Freed,' Toronto *Daily Star*, 10 March 1930.

119 'Klansman Fined $50 and Costs, Two Others Found Not Guilty; Did Not Wear Masks in Raid,' Toronto *Globe*, 11 March 1930, pp. 1, 3; 'Local Klansman Is Fined at Oakville,' Hamilton *Spectator*, 11 March 1930, p. 15; 'One Klansman Fined and Two Are Freed,' Toronto *Daily Star*, 10 March 1930.

120 'Klansman Fined $50 and Costs, Two Others Found Not Guilty; Did Not Wear Masks in Raid,' Toronto *Globe*, 11 March 1930, pp. 1, 3; 'Local Klansman Is Fined at Oakville,' Hamilton *Spectator*, 11 March 1930, p. 15; 'One Klansman Fined and Two Are Freed,' Toronto *Daily Star*, 10 March 1930.

121 The Toronto *Daily Star* would raise some question about this verdict in an editorial 'The Oakville Case,' 12 March 1930, pp. 1–2. Recognizing that the two men discharged by McIlveen had not had their faces coloured and had not worn masks, the *Star* queried whether this was sufficient to warrant an acquittal. Weren't Taylor and Orme still 'disguised,' given their garb of the 'white gowns and hoods of this secret society'? The offence required proof that the individual charged have 'his face masked or blackened, or be ... otherwise disguised, by night.' The use of the disjunctive 'or' suggests that, even with faces uncovered, there might have been some argument that Taylor and Orme were 'disguised.' The *Star* urged the Crown to 'carry these two cases to a higher court.' No appeal was ever mounted.

122 'Klansman Fined $50 and Costs, Two Others Found Not Guilty; Did Not Wear Masks in Raid,' Toronto *Globe*, 11 March 1930, pp. 1, 3; 'Local Klansman Is Fined at Oakville,' Hamilton *Spectator*, 11 March 1930, p. 15; 'One Klansman Fined and Two Are Freed,' Toronto *Daily Star*, 10 March 1930.

123 'Klansman Fined $50 and Costs, Two Others Found Not Guilty; Did Not Wear Masks in Raid,' Toronto *Globe*, 11 March 1930, pp. 1, 3; 'Local Klansman Is Fined at Oakville,' Hamilton *Spectator*, 11 March 1930, p. 15; 'One Klansman Fined and Two Are Freed,' Toronto *Daily Star*, 10 March 1930.

124 'Klansman Fined $50 and Costs, Two Others Found Not Guilty; Did Not Wear Masks in Raid,' Toronto *Globe*, 11 March 1930, pp. 1, 3; 'Local Klansman Is Fined at Oakville,' Hamilton *Spectator*, 11 March 1930, p. 15; 'One Klansman Fined and Two Are Freed,' Toronto *Daily Star*, 10 March 1930.

12 5'Klansman Fined $50 and Costs, Two Others Found Not Guilty; Did Not Wear Masks in Raid,' Toronto *Globe*, 11 March 1930, pp. 1, 3; 'Local Klansman Is Fined at Oakville,' Hamilton *Spectator*, 11 March 1930, p. 15. 'Hamilton Klan Member Fined,' London *Free Press*, 11 March 1930, p. 9, notes that the costs were $33, and that in lieu of payment the convicted man would have had to serve thirty days.

126 'K.K.K. Prosecutions Ended with One Conviction Won,' Toronto *Daily Star*, 11 March 1930, p. 2.

127 'K.K.K. Prosecutions Ended with One Conviction Won,' Toronto *Daily Star*,' 11 March 1930, p. 2.

128 'Oakville and the K.K.K.,' *Dawn of Tomorrow*, 24 March 1930, p. 2. The
    Dawn of Tomorrow was edited and published by James Jenkins in London,
    Ontario, from 1923 to 1931, the time of his death. His widow, Christine
    Jenkins, continued the operation. For details see Rella Braithwaite and
    Tessa Benn-Ireland, *Some Black Women: Profiles of Black Women in Canada*
    (Toronto: Sister Vision, 1993), at 65. 'The Oakville Case,' Toronto *Daily Star*,
    12 March 1930, pp. 1–2, also raises queries about the acquittals of Taylor
    and Orme.

129 The KKK wrote to Cross and to Rev. Maurice Eisendrath (for further
    information see further discussion in this chapter) several letters it released
    to the press, demanding 'retraction' of statements 'against the Klan' and
    threatening 'immediate action' for slander. The letter to Cross also states:
    'It is very apparent that you sadly misunderstood the notice prompting the
    Klan's action at Oakville, or that you were determined to discredit the fact
    that we acted in a lawful manner, or that you were making much of an
    opportunity to gain for yourself free public advertisement. [While it may
    be your legal privilege to marry] a Chinese, a Jewess, a white woman or
    any other nationality, as [you are] quoted as saying, the Klan believes it
    would be a sad state of affairs if mixed marriages and racial impurity were
    to gain favor. 'Klan May March Again in Answer to Appeals,' Toronto
    Daily Star, 26 March 1930, pp. 1–2; 'Ku Klux Klan Will Appeal Court
    Decision,' London *Advertiser*, 15 March 1930, p. 1.

130 'House Raided by K.K.K. Is Burned,' London *Free Press*, 18 March 1930, p. 1.

131 Cross's letter to the attorney general reads: 'I take it that this is a veiled
    threat and disguised intimidation aimed at me by the spokesman of this
    outlaw body. May I suggest to you that an organization which vauntingly
    proclaims "we will do what the law cannot do," and in spite of the convic-
    tion of one of its members recently, with brazen defiance still maintains
    that it will continue to invade the rights and liberties of the citizen who
    falls foul of its tenets, is eminently a fit subject for your attention and
    should be shorn of some of its arrogance.' 'K.K.K. Drops All Interest in
    Oakville Couple's Affairs,' Toronto *Daily Star*, 24 March 1930, pp. 1–2;
    'Complaint Is Made of Ku Klux Claims,' Toronto *Globe*, 24 March 1930, p.
    1; 'Four Face Charges,' Toronto *Daily Star*, 7 March 1930, p. 1; 'Believe Klan
    ...,' Toronto *Star*, 8 March 1930, p. 1; 'Indian Marries Oakville Girl,' Lon-
    don *Free Press*, 24 March 1930, p. 15. On the KKK's tactics of intimidation
    against Black lawyers south of the border, see *

132 'Klansmen's Names Demanded of Price by Negro Barrister,' Toronto *Globe*,
    17 March 1930, pp. 13–14. Closer to home, it appears that racial mixture
    between Blacks and whites was also endemic. Michael Power and Nancy

Butler, *Slavery and Freedom in Niagara* (Niagara-on-the-Lake: Niagara Historical Society, 1993), note at 71 that by 1871 most of the Blacks in the Niagara area were 'of mixed race. The pure-blooded African was fading away in Niagara – in fact and in memory.' Power and Butler also note at 61 that there were many mixed marriages of Blacks and whites in nineteenth-century Niagara.

133 'Klansmen's Names Demanded of Price by Negro Barrister,' Toronto *Globe*, 17 March 1930, pp. 13–14; 'K.K.K. Drops All Interest in Oakville Couple's Affairs,' Toronto *Daily Star*, 24 March 1930, pp. 1–2; 'Earlscourt Labor Protests Activities of Ku Klux Klan,' Toronto *Globe*, 21 March 1930, p. 14. On the exploitative and forced sexual relations between white men and Black women see Angela Y. Davis, *Women, Race and Class* (New York: Random House, 1983).

134 'Klan Took Oakville Girl from Negro Home,' Toronto *Daily Star*, 1 March 1930, p. 2.

135 'Has No Negro Blood, Klan Victim Declares,' Toronto *Daily Star*, 5 March 1930, p. 2; 'Declares Negro Blood Improves White Race,' Toronto *Daily Star*, 1 April 1930, p. 2. Pitt stated: 'Of course I do not know what the results of intermarriage would be from a biological standpoint … but I am inclined to think that it would be a forced condition. The theory seems to me to be mere speculation. I would rather not discuss the matter further, as I do not think it would do my own race any good to begin a controversy on the color question. Whenever in the past there has been a discussion of the "evils" of mixed marriages, the censure has always been passed against the colored party and not the white.' Pitt's comments are in response to a speech given by Dr Edwin Grant Conklin, a professor of biology from Princeton University, to the Canadian Club on 31 March 1930. There Conklin stated that the only solution to the colour problem in the United States was 'the losing of the distinctiveness of the negro by blending with other racial elements in the process of time.' Recognizing the inevitability of racial mixing, Conklin stated: 'It has never happened that two races, no matter how distinct, have inhabited the same territory for a thousand years without losing their distinctiveness and blending their traits.' Conklin was not, however, a racial egalitarian. He was a charter member of the racist Galton Society in New York and he advocated reducing the birth rate 'among inferior races' and increasing it 'among superior peoples.' 'Savant Would Blend Negroes with Whites,' Toronto *Daily Star*, 1 April 1930, p. 9; Hamilton Cravens, *The Triumph of Evolution* (Philadelphia: University of Pennsylvania Press, 1978), at 115–17.

136 On the history of Black nationalism within Canada, see * For more detailed

analysis of racial discrimination in employment, housing, and access to public facilities, see discussion of Viola Desmond's case in chapter 7.

137 'Declares Negro Blood Improves White Race,' Toronto *Daily Star*, 1 April 1930, p. 2. These remarks were made in the context of responding to Professor Conklin's lecture, prompting Cross to note: 'Dr. Conklin in his observations on race blending is in line with science on this question.' Cross continued his advocacy of Black genetic input by adding: 'His virility combined with the mental sharpness of the white man would give a better race.'

138 'Klansmen's Names Demanded of Price by Negro Barrister,' Toronto *Globe*, 17 March 1930, pp. 13–14; 'K.K.K. Drops All Interest in Oakville Couple's Affairs,' Toronto *Daily Star*, 24 March 1930, pp. 1–2; 'Earlscourt Labor Protests Activities of Ku Klux Klan,' Toronto *Globe*, 21 March 1930, p. 14. Another group that supported Cross's position was the International League for Peace and Freedom, represented by Mrs Alice Lowe: see 'Has No Negro Blood, Klan Victim Declares,' Toronto *Daily Star*, 5 March 1930, pp. 1–3. For more details concerning racial segregation in Canada see the discussion of Viola Desmond's case in chapter 7.

139 'Rabbi Calls K.K.K. Lawless Body,' Hamilton *Spectator*, 24 March 1930, p. 19; 'K.K.K. Drops All Interest in Oakville Couple's Affairs,' Toronto *Daily Star*, 24 March 1930, pp. 1–2. On the friendships and political connections forged between Jewish and Black communities see Alexander and Glaze, *Towards Freedom*, at 191–2. For further details regarding Rabbi Eisendrath, see *

140 'Earlscourt Labor Protests Activities of Ku Klux Klan,' Toronto *Globe*, 21 March 1930, p. 14.

141 'No Country for a Ku Klux,' Toronto *Globe*, 3 March 1930, p. 4. 'The Oakville Case,' Toronto *Daily Star*, 12 March 1930, pp. 1–2, notes: 'The kind of people who allow their inclinations and preferences to guide them, instead of their reason, may condone what was done at Oakville. But even though they condone that which was done, they should be able to perceive that the instrument used in the doing of it is one that cannot be tolerated in Ontario or in Canada or in any British country. [...] The night-riding, the uniform, the invasion of a private dwelling, the removal of an individual from one place to another – all this was lawlessness, in contempt of the Crown and all our lawful institutions. [...] It is all well enough for such an organization to profess good intentions, but no secret court of self-elected persons can be permitted to carry on in this province in defiance of our lawful institutions.' Some newspapers were less affable. William Templeton's Guelph *Mercury* was one of the most oppositional: see earlier

discussion in this chapter. 'A Menace to Law and Order,' Regina *Morning Leader*, 29 November 1922, p. 4, also states: 'The moment ... any ... organizing official of the Ku Klux Klan steps across the border he should be booted back over it. Canada has enough problems on her hands at the present time without being stirred up by the lawlessness for which the "invisible empire" stands. [...] It seeks to establish "the solidarity of the Protestant Gentile white race not only in the United States but throughout the world." This brands it as anti-Catholic and anti-Semitic and sets it against every race but the Caucasian – a strange program to be promulgated at this late date in human history, when co-operation among all races and religions is beginning to show itself far more profitable to the world than division, dissension and conflict. [...] [T]he authorities in Canada should be prompt to act against the menace the moment it rears its mischievous head in this country. We have here, as the United States has, Catholics and Protestants, Gentiles and Jews, whites and blacks and browns and reds and yellows, all living in increasing harmony one with the other. Setting one against another would be fatal to that ideal of Canadian unity toward which all sections of the country are now working ...' A few periodicals were equally antagonistic. 'The Ku Klux Klan,' *The Canadian Annual Review* (1923), at 82–3, cites the threats of violence associated with Klan activities and claims that Canada 'would not prove a suitable field for the Klan's operations.' 'The Ku Klux Klan,' *The Canadian Forum*, vol. 9 (April 1930), at 233, states:'The Klan spirit is rooted in intolerance and can bear only evil fruit. [...] There is no place for it in Canada.'

142 A.D. Monk, 'Knights of the Knightshirt,' *The Canadian Magazine*, vol. 66 (October 1926), at 31, also adds: '[O]ne wonders that a plan so utterly un-Canadian and un-British should find root in our soil.'

143 For two noteworthy exceptions, see the discussion regarding William Templeton, the white editor of the Guelph *Mercury*, discussed above, and 'A Menace to Law and Order,' Regina *Morning Leader*, 29 November 1922, p. 4.

144 On the $4 commission rate, see Wade, *The Fiery Cross*, at 154. The charter of the Canadian Klan provided that the three original organizers should be the 'Imperial officers,' with the right to 'share equally in the income' and 'determine the salaries' paid. Richards, 'Claims of the Ku Klux Klan'; 'Ku Klux Klan Diminishes in U.S.,' *Saturday Night*, 16 October 1926, pp. 1–2; Monk, 'Knights of the Knightshirt,' at 31. The reference to the Welland *Tribune-Telegraph* is from the *Canadian Magazine* article; no date or page reference is given. Similar preoccupation with the finances of the Klan appears in the debates of the House of Commons: see, for example, House of Commons, *Debates*, vol.1 (24 March 1931), at 252–3.

145 Monk, 'Knights of the Knightshirt,' at 31. Richards, 'How the Ku Klux Klan
Came to Canada,' at 1–2, uses the phrase 'queer happenings' to describe
cross-burnings, the dynamiting of Roman Catholic buildings, the shooting
of bullets, and campaigns to prevent the employment of individuals based
on their 'racial' heritage. This characterization considerably downplays the
violent hate-mongering of the Klan. Even the Regina *Morning Leader*, in an
editorial that is adverse to the Klan on explicitly anti-racist and egalitarian
principles ('A Menace to Law and Order,' 29 November 1922, p. 4), makes
light of Klan connections to violent deeds: 'The suspicion that the Ku Klux
Klan is responsible for the fire that destroyed St. Boniface College last
Saturday is probably unfounded and silly enough ...' See also 'The Ku
Klux Klan,' *The Canadian Forum*, vol. 9 (April 1930), at 233, which refers to
the 'offensive buffoonery of the Ku Klux Klan in Canada.' The Edmonton
Journal, 25 September 1933, quotes the particularly bizarre comments of an
Alberta judge, who describes some activities of the Klan as reminding him
of 'boys who go into the woods to play Indians.' These statements were
made in the context of a trial that found Klan organizer J.J. Maloney guilty
of theft and conspiracy in connection with the removal of legal documents
from the office of an Edmonton lawyer.

146 'Klan Spokesman Outlines Aims,' London *Free Press*, 3 August 1925, pp. 1–
2; 'At Altar of the Klan,' London *Advertiser*, 25 October 1925; Richards,
'Claims of the Ku Klux Klan'; House of Commons, *Debates*, vol. 2 (29 April
1930), at 1557. Henson, 'Ku Klux Klan,' reports at 6 that Evans was one of
the MPs accused of being a Klan member in the 1920s. See also Robin,
Shades of Right, at 14, who notes that the Ontario Klansmen 'remained, for
the most part, mundane fraternalists eager to disassociate themselves from
the reputation of violence and lawlessness, tar and feathers, that plagued
their American relatives.'

147 For some examples, see Wade, *The Fiery Cross*, at 63–84.

148 'Klansman Argues Sentence Appeal,' London *Advertiser*, 16 April 1930, p.
17; 'Klansman and U.S. Gangsters Feel Teeth of Canadian Law,' Toronto
Globe, 17 April 1930, pp. 13–14; 'Klansman Appealed Only to Be Jailed,'
Toronto *Daily Star*, 17 March 1930; 'Klansman Loses Appeal Against
Oakville Fine and Must Go to Jail,' London *Advertiser*, 17 April 1930, p. 3;
'"Had No Lawful Excuse" Judge Says of K.K.Klan,' Toronto *Daily Star*, 16
April 1930, pp. 1–2. No court transcripts or files survive, but Chief Justice
Sir William Mulock's Benchbook 14, Court of Appeal of Ontario Archives,
at 309, contains the judge's notes of counsel's argument. Judge David Inglis
Grant was born in 1872 in Ingersoll, Ontario, the son of Rev. Robert Neil
Grant of Orillia and Mary McMullen Grant of Woodstock. He was called to
the bar 'with honours and the silver medal' in 1895, obtained his KC in

1921, and practised law in Orillia until 1911 and Toronto until his appointment to the High Court in 1925. The 'scholarly' judge was elevated to the Court of Appeal in 1927: see 'Grant, Hon. David Inglis,' *Who's Who in Canada, 1930–31* (Toronto: International Press, 1932), at 838.

149 'Grant, Hon. David Inglis,' *Who's Who in Canada, 1930–31*, at 838. Grant is also listed as a member of the Ancient Free and Accepted Masons.

150 'Klansman Argues Sentence Appeal,' London *Advertiser*, 16 April 1930, p. 17; 'Klansman and U.S. Gangsters Feel Teeth of Canadian Law,' Toronto *Globe*, 17 April 1930, pp. 13–14; 'Klansman Appealed Only to Be Jailed,' Toronto *Daily Star*, 17 March 1930; 'Klansman Loses Appeal Against Oakville Fine and Must Go to Jail,' London *Advertiser*, 17 April 1930, p. 3; '"Had No Lawful Excuse" Judge Says of K.K.Klan,' Toronto *Daily Star*, 1 April 1930, pp. 1–2; Chief Justice Sir William Mulock's Benchbook 14, Court of Appeal of Ontario Archives, at 309. Inexplicably, the benchbook indicates that Bowlby argued that 'the men were not masked.' While this was a finding made at trial with respect to Taylor and Orme, Bowlby had expressly conceded in the earlier proceeding that Dr Phillips was masked. It is difficult to understand what Bowlby intended by this argument. If he meant to suggest Dr Phillips was not masked, he had little basis for doing so. If he meant to suggest that others in Dr Phillips's party were not masked, this would conceivably place his client at a disadvantageous contrast with the other marchers. Chief Justice Mulock's benchbook notes that Bowlby also made an alternative argument, that if his client were masked he had 'lawful excuse.' The judge's notes indicate that both counsel also made arguments of statutory interpretation, with Bowlby arguing that section 455(c) should be read as part of the larger offence of housebreaking, while Bayly argued on behalf of the Crown that 'words of limitation are not to be read into a statute if it can be avoided.' Bayly also queried what 'lawful excuse' there could be 'for burglary or housebreaking.' Judge William Edward Middleton was born in Toronto, the son of William and Mary A. (Norerre) Middleton, called to the bar in 1885, and appointed to the court in 1910. Elevated to the Court of Appeal in 1928, Judge Middleton was reputed to be 'brilliant,' a 'recognized authority in procedural matters,' and someone who 'looked at law through a microscope,' operating 'within a narrow frame of reference.' On Middleton, see 'Middleton, Hon. Mr. Justice William Edward,' *Who's Who in Canada, 1930–31*, at 548; Lita-Rose Betcherman, *The Little Band: The Clashes between the Communists and the Canadian Establishment, 1928–1932* (Ottawa: Deneau, 1983), at 82, citing her interview with W.B. Common, QC, 9 June 1980.

151 Bartley, 'Public Nuisance,' at 162, 167–70. Bartley adds, however, that

Bayly 'was reluctant to challenge the Klan except on the most narrow legal grounds. To do otherwise would contribute to the Klan's publicity efforts and erode the credibility of the legal system.'

152 On the *Sero* v *Gault* case, see chapter 4. Edward J. Bayly was born in London, Ontario, in 1865, the son of a merchant/manufacturer, William Bayly, and his wife, Susan Wilson Bayly. A graduate of Trinity College School and University of Toronto, Bayly was called to the bar in 1890, and served as an examiner of the Law Society of Upper Canada from 1896 to 1899. He won the Canada Cup sailing for Aemilius Jarvis's Royal Canadian Yacht Club crew in Toledo in 1896, was the 'star' of the University of Toronto football team, Osgoode Hall's 'star' left halfback, and the president of the Canadian Rugby Union and the Ontario Rugby Football Union. Bayly carried on a private law practice with James Haverson, KC, Edmond Bristol, KC, Seymour Corley, KC, and Mr Justice Eric Armour until his appointment as a full-time solicitor for the attorney general's department in Toronto in 1907. His friendship with Attorney General Price stretched back to Price's stint as a law student in Bayly's law office. Described as a 'noted conversationalist,' who could 'discourse at great length on an amazing range of subjects with authority,' Bayly was acknowledged as 'perhaps the best known member of the civil service.' He also served as the president of the Ontario Civil Service Association. His junior colleagues at the attorney general's office recalled him 'in full sail,' seated behind his 'treasured walnut desk,' waxing eloquent about his past exploits in football, boating, and driving his big Pierce Arrow. Bayly is described as a 'heavy set figure, often clad in a frock coat' in his obituary. Betcherman provides details of Bayly's physical description, adding that in his later years the 'noiseless, effortless glide of the ex-athlete was becoming somewhat jerky.' 'He was in the habit of writing memos to himself,' she adds, 'which he stuck into his hat-band, and as he "shuffled" to Queen's Park, whenever he doffed his hat to an acquaintance, bits of paper would flutter in his wake.' Henry James Morgan, ed., *The Canadian Men and Women of the Time*, 2d ed. (Toronto: William Briggs, 1912), at 70; 'Edward Bayly, K.C., Stricken Suddenly in Sixty-Ninth Year,' Toronto *Globe*, 30 January 1934, pp. 4–5; 'Edward Bayly, K.C. Suddenly Stricken,' Toronto *Daily Star*, 30 January 1934, p. 3; Betcherman, *Little Band* at 51, 163, 221, citing author's interviews with Harvey McCullogh, QC, 18 November 1978 and W.B. Common, QC, 9 June 1980.

153 'Klansman Argues Sentence Appeal,' London *Advertiser*, 16 April 1930, p. 17; 'Klansman and U.S. Gangsters Feel Teeth of Canadian Law,' Toronto *Globe*, 17 April 1930, p. 13.

154 Bayly's obituary would describe him as 'particularly proud of his Welsh ancestry.' 'Edward Bayly, K.C., Stricken Suddenly in Sixty-Ninth Year,' Toronto *Globe*, 30 January 1934, pp. 4–5. On the Klan's claim that it was no different from other fraternal lodges on the matter of racial exclusivity, see Blee, *Women of the Klan*, at 18.

155 *Rex* v *Phillips* (1930), 55 C.C.C. 49 (Ont. C.A.), at 50–1. For details of similar judicial comments from the Ontario Supreme Court bench in 1926, upon the conviction of a Black man for rape, see *

156 *Rex* v *Phillips*, at 51. For press commentary see 'Klansman and U.S. Gangsters Feel Teeth of Canadian Law,' Toronto *Globe*, 17 April 1930, pp. 13–14; 'Impose Jail Sentence on Klan Masker,' Saskatoon *Star-Phoenix*, 17 April 1930, p. 1.

157 'Mulock, The Rt. Hon. Sir William, P.C., K.C.M.G.,' *Who's Who in Canada, 1936–37*, at 483–4. Mulock was the son of Mary Cawthra and Dr Thomas Homan Mulock. Mulock's wealth came from his mother's side, for Mary Cawthra was descended from Toronto's first millionaire family. The early death of his doctor father, Thomas Homan Mulock, precipitated some financial constraint in his student years, but in later life Mulock made a fortune speculating in real estate and the stock market. Called to the bar in 1868, he received his KC in 1890. His brilliant negotiation and organizational skills are credited with the consolidation of nine separate colleges and professional schools into the University of Toronto, and the development of a telecommunications cable linking Canada, Britain, Australia, and New Zealand. His religious affiliation was Anglican. Sources note that no amount of ageing seemed to curtail Mulock's relish for rye whisky and his trademark Havana cigars. On Mulock's physical appearance, finances, and reputation, see Betcherman, *Little Band*, at 207–8, citing Herbert Bruce, *Varied Operations* (Toronto, 1958), at 274–80; R.T.L. [Charles Vining], *Bigwigs, Canadian and Otherwise* (Toronto, 1935), at 120; Ross Harkness, *J.E. Atkinson of The Star* (Toronto, 1963), at 84–5; Toronto *Daily Star*, 6 September 1929. Betcherman also describes, at 207–8, Mulock's antipathy to the Communist Party and its leaders, whom he convicted of violating section 98 of the Criminal Code in 1932: 'Of men in public life, none … was as outspokenly anti-Communist as Sir William Mulock, Chief Justice of Ontario. Communism sought to eradicate everything he had achieved in a long life that far exceeded the allotted biblical span.' In what surely constitutes a noteworthy footnote to his historical legacy, Mulock also hired Clara Brett Martin, Canada's first white female lawyer, to work as an articling student for his law firm in the 1890s, despite the considerable controversy evoked by her presence in the legal profession. His sponsor-

ship of Clara Brett Martin is usually attributed to his daughter's friendship with the budding young female lawyer, and not to any principled endorsement of women's rights generally. On the link with Clara Brett Martin, see Backhouse, *Petticoats and Prejudice*, at 309. On Clara Brett Martin's career generally, see *

158 *Rex* v *Phillips*, at 50: 'These facts show illegal interference with her liberty. The motive of the accused and his companions is immaterial. Their action was unlawful and it is the duty of this Court to pronounce the appropriate punishment.' The reporter for the *Canadian Criminal Cases* added an introductory paragraph to help readers make sense of the decision: 'The case arises out of the methods adopted by members of a secret organization who without physical force induced a white girl to leave the house of the aunt of a man with whom she was friendly who was not of white origin.' The reporter's note is the only reference to race, designating the 'whiteness' of Isabel Jones. The debate over Ira Johnson's purported First Nations and Black origins is delicately sidestepped by classifying him as 'not of white origin.' The KKK is still not mentioned, and remains a mysterious 'secret organization.' The failure to advert to the KKK may be partly attributed to discussion during the appeal, in which Judge Hodgins asked whether the men from Hamilton 'formed an organization of any kind.' Since it is unlikely that the judges could have missed the extensive press commentary on the case, and the widespread acknowledgment of KKK involvement, this must have been an effort to get counsel to implicate the KKK formally for the record. Defence counsel Bowlby replied that the men 'had been referred to as the Ku Klux Klan, but that there was no ground for that assertion in the evidence.' '"Had No Lawful Excuse" Judge Says of K.K. Klan,' Toronto *Daily Star*, 1 April 1930, pp. 1–2. Bowlby's reply was clearly erroneous, since Harold Orme had admitted his Klan membership on the stand at trial. Dr Phillips testified that the gown and hood he was wearing belonged to the 'order' to which he belonged. Since he and Orme wore the same garb, it was stretching matters to suggest that there was no evidence from the trial concerning Klan involvement. On the proclivity of Canadian courts to avoid racial designation in racialized litigation, see also discussion of Viola Desmond's case in chapter 7.

159 'Appeal Is Talked by Klan,' London *Advertiser*, 17 April 1930, p. 1. For the rules concerning criminal appeals to the Supreme Court of Canada, see *

160 'Appeal Is Talked by Klan,' London *Advertiser*, 17 April 1930, p. 1. Bowlby's apparent growing sense of unease over his client's activities was also apparent when he appeared before the Ontario Court of Appeal on behalf of Dr Phillips. Reid Bowlby pressed his client's case forcefully, but

admitted in open court that 'he held no brief for the Klan.' See 'Klansman Appealed Only to Be Jailed,' Toronto *Daily Star*, 17 March 1930.

161 'Appeal Is Talked by Klan,' London *Advertiser*, 17 April 1930, pp. 1–2; 'No Further Appeal in Phillips Case,' London *Advertiser*, 18 April 1930, p. 1.

162 'Hamilton Klansman Begins Term in Jail,' Toronto *Globe*, 24 April 1930, p. 2.

163 'Still on Strike,' Milton *Canadian Champion*, 8 May 1930, p. 3; 'Klansman Tries Hunger Strike,' Acton *Free Press*, 8 May 1930, p. 8; Transcript of Jail Register Entry, Milton Jail, AO RG20, Series F-23, vol.7, entry no. 162.

164 Robin, *Shades of Right*, notes at 15 that the 'Klan's desultory attempts at intimidation and skirmishes with the law, duly reported by a press seeking sensational linkages with their American cousins, seriously hampered the Ontario organizational campaign.' Winks, *Blacks in Canada*, notes at 324–5 that 'the glare of publicity, the prompt provincial action, and a continuing rumor that the Klan was an American conspiracy to set Canadians against each other, put an end to Klan activities in Ontario.'

165 Sher, *White Hoods*, notes at 60 that internally the Klan 'was weakened by constant bickering among its leaders and scandals which saw some of them brought to trial for fraud, theft and other charges.' He notes that the failure of the Canadian Klan to develop a truly national structure consigned the smaller, provincial associations to a fractured and less effective movement. Sher also cites 'external opposition' from labour, French Catholics, and some individual newspaper editors as a factor in the downturn of KKK power.

166 Sher, *White Hoods*, notes at 60 that the Klan in Canada faded in the late 1920s and virtually disappeared for almost half a century. See also Winks, *Blacks in Canada*, at 324–5.

167 'This and That,' Acton *Free Press*, 15 May 1930, p. 6.

168 Vernon *City of Hamilton Directories* (Hamilton: Vernon Directories, 1930, 1931, and 1932) show William A. Phillips as continuing to operate his chiropractic office from 127 1/2 King Street E., and residing with his wife, Laura, on Burlington Street West.

169 The date of disbarment is 21 January 1937. The grounds for disbarment are listed in Law Society of Upper Canada 'Convocation Proceedings,' vol. 8, and the press release in the Law Society of Upper Canada Archives Member File of Ethelbert Lionel Cross no. 675-3300, specifying 'misappropriation of funds.' It is also indicated that Cross did not appear and went unrepresented at his disciplinary hearing. Talbot, 'History of Blacks in the Law Society,' states at 66: '[Cross's] career was short-lived when, in 1937, after encountering professional difficulties, he left the practice of law. The reasons [for] this are unclear but there can be little doubt that the Great

Depression may have had a great influence.' Disbarment appears to have plagued Black lawyers disproportionately to their numbers, and further research would be necessary to assess the ways in which race discrimination affected such outcomes. Talbot notes at 68 that, of the five Black lawyers practising in Ontario in the 1940s and 1950s, 'two were disbarred, one in 1948 and the other in 1953.' On the disciplinary vigilance that the Law Society showed towards Black lawyers, who were accused of 'touting' and 'conduct unbecoming,' see Oral History Transcript of Mr Charles Roach, The Osgoode Society, interviewed by Christine J.N. Kates, November–December 1989.

170 Talbot, 'History of Blacks in the Law Society,' recounts the police assault in February 1942 at 67–8, indicating that it 'illustrates some of the hazards faced by a Black lawyer.' Talbot also indicates that Pitt's most famous case was his defence of Bill Newell, who was convicted of murdering his wife, Anne Newell, in October 1940, on Centre Island. The internationally based Universal Negro Improvement Association was founded in 1914 by Marcus Mosiah Garvey, a Jamaican-born Black who sought to 'organize the 400 million Negroes of the world into a vast organization to plant the banner of freedom on the great continent of Africa.' Garvey advocated Black pride; Black nationalism; economic self-help; and economic, political, and cultural independence from whites. The first Canadian unit opened in Montreal in 1919. The Montreal, Halifax, and Toronto chapters were the most active. Pitt is credited with holding the Toronto chapter together into the 1940s. During the 1940s, when Black patrons and musicians were barred from many night clubs, they congregated in the Toronto UNIA building on College Street for evening jazz sessions, which became a venue for remarkable musical talent. The UNIA also functioned as a centre for Black culture and political strategizing. See Winks, *Blacks in Canada*, at 414–16; Alexander and Glaze, *Towards Freedom*, at 128–33. Alexander and Glaze note at 133 that 'Garvey's statements about racial purity and attacks on light-skinned blacks alienated many, for inter-racial marriages between blacks and whites, and blacks and Indians were quite common at the time.' Given Pitt's public position against interracial marriages, he may have had less difficulty with this than other UNIA adherents.

171 Campbell, *Hamilton*, at 155 records Reid Bowlby's elevation to the bench. Bowlby died on 8 April 1952 in Hamilton. I am indebted to Susan Lewthwaite of the Law Society of Upper Canada Archives for the information on Bowlby.

172 'Edward Bayly, K.C. Suddenly Stricken,' Toronto *Daily Star*, 30 January 1934, p. 3.

173 'Mulock, The Rt. Hon., Sir William, P.C., K.C.M.G.,' *Who's Who in Canada, 1936–37*, at 483.

174 Dan La Forme, described as a 'Chippewa Indian of Oakville,' who had been a personal friend of Ira Johnson's for over twenty years, made arrangements for the marriage venue and acted as a witness to the ceremony. Despite having secured a letter of consent from Isabel Jones's mother, Ira Johnson had some difficulty locating a pastor who would perform the service, and at least one refused to conduct the ceremony. Captain Broome continued to maintain his public opposition to interracial marriages, but indicated that he had no objection to Ira Johnson personally, and wished him luck. Contacted by the *Star* for his opinion, Harold Orme, acting as spokesman for the Hamilton Ku Klux Klan, conceded defeat. Pronouncing the matter now closed, Orme stated: 'We will not put asunder what God hath joined together.' Ira Johnson requested some measure of privacy from continuing press scrutiny: 'We are only human,' he told the *Star*, 'and I wish the people would leave us alone.' 'Indian Marries Oakville Girl,' London *Free Press*, 24 March 1930, p. 15; 'K.K.K. Drops All Interest in Oakville Couple's Affairs,' Toronto *Daily Star*, 24 March 1930, pp. 1–2; 'K.K.K. Oakville Raid Has Sequel at Altar,' Toronto *Daily Star*, 24 March 1930, pp. 1–2.

7: 'Bitterly Disappointed' at the Spread of 'Colour-Bar Tactics'

1 Details surrounding the arrest are taken from 'Affidavit of Viola Irene Desmond,' 29 January 1947, *His Majesty the King* v *Viola Irene Desmond*, Public Archives of Nova Scotia (hereinafter cited as PANS), RG39 'C' Halifax, v. 937, Supreme Court of Nova Scotia no. 13347; 'Negress Alleges She Was Ejected from Theatre,' Halifax *Chronicle*, 30 November 1946, p. 2; 'Ban All Jim Crow Rules Is Comment on N.S. Charge,' Toronto *Daily Star*, 30 November 1946, p. 3. Material from this chapter was presented as the Seventh Annual Gibson-Armstrong Lecture in Law and History at Osgoode Hall Law School in February 1994, and an earlier version was published as 'Racial Segregation in Canadian Legal History: Viola Desmond's Challenge, Nova Scotia 1946,' *Dalhousie Law Journal* 17:2 (Fall 1994), 299–362.

2 On the history of the Roseland Theatre and the racist nature of *The Birth of a Nation* (film) and Black-face minstrelsy, see *

3 For details concerning a number of Canadian cases that set historical precedents for Viola Desmond's direct-action approach, see *

4 On MacNeil and his theatre, see *

5 'Negress Alleges She Was Ejected from Theatre,' Halifax *Chronicle*, 30 November 1946, p. 2; 'Affidavit of Viola Irene Desmond,' PANS. For the reference to the gloves and posture, see the notes of the researcher who assisted with the compilation of material for this chapter: Tanya Hudson, 'Interview with Dr. Pearleen Oliver,' Halifax, 28 August 1995.

6 For biographical details on MacKay, see 'Former Magistrate Dies at 84 [Obituary],' Halifax *Chronicle-Herald*, 29 September 1961, p. 2.

7 See R.S.N.S. 1923, c.162, s.8(8), 9, 10, 14. The initial enactment is *Theatres and Cinematographs Act*, S.N.S. 1915, c.9, as amended.

8 For details of the statutory provision and the pricing arrangement at the Roseland, see *

9 'Record,' Rod G. MacKay, Stipendiary Magistrate for the Town of New Glasgow, County of Pictou, 9 November 1946 *R.- (Inf. Henry MacNeil)* v *Viola Desmond*, PANS; 'Affidavit of Viola Desmond,' PANS.

10 'Record,' Rod G. MacKay, PANS. The ultimate disposition of the costs is unclear. One handwritten document signed by Magistrate MacKay indicates that the accused was to pay Harry MacNeil, 'the Informant herein, the sum of six dollars for his costs in this behalf.' Another handwritten document signed by the magistrate indicates that the costs were broken down: $2.50 to be paid to himself as magistrate, and $3.50 to Police Chief Elmo C. Langille.

11 'Affidavit of Viola Desmond,' PANS; R.S.N.S. 1923, c.162, s.8(3), 8(10). *Saturday Night* raises this point in its coverage of the trial, 7 December 1946, p. 5: '[T]he action of the magistrate in fining the lady in question for defrauding the province, when she had most expressly tendered to the box office the proper price, including tax, of the seat in which she later insisted on sitting, is a travesty of justice.'

12 'Negress Alleges She Was Ejected from Theatre,' Halifax *Chronicle*, 30 November 1946, p. 2. On the historical use of the terms 'Negro' and 'Negress' and the preference of the Black community for the word 'coloured,' see *

13 'Ban All Jim Crow Rules Is Comment on N.S. Charge,' Toronto *Daily Star*, 30 November 1946, p. 3. MacNeil continued: 'We have a large colored patronage at our theatre and we don't permit color discrimination to be a determining factor. It would be poor policy for us to set up a color bar. [...] There was no discrimination.'

14 This raises the important question of how many other trials lie buried, lost to historical scrutiny, because the real issues relating to racial divisions were (consciously?) unspoken or camouflaged with unrelated legal matters. On the tendency to delete references to race in evidence filed on racial- discrimination matters, see Robin W. Winks, *The Blacks in Canada: A History*, 2d ed.

(Montreal: McGill-Queen's University Press, 1997), at 424, discussing the 1920 hearing under the Industrial Disputes Investigation Act into the racially motivated discharges of thirty-six Black porters from the CPR. On a comparative note, see the discussion of the appeal of the conviction of Rosa Parks in the Montgomery bus boycott in Alabama in 1955, which never mentioned the Alabama bus segregation statute or racial segregation. 'One reads the opinion in vain trying to understand the issue that her appeal raised,' notes Robert Jerome Glennon in 'The Role of Law in the Civil Rights Movement: The Montgomery Bus Boycott, 1955–1957,' *Law and History Review*, vol. 9 (1991), 59 at 88.

15 Viola Desmond's older sister recalls her sister's actions as unpremeditated: 'I think it was a spontaneous action. She was aware of prejudice, but she had not been exposed to that kind of prejudice. In Halifax, you could sit where you liked in the theatre. So I think it came as a shock to her. She was well-known in Halifax, she felt herself to be an entrepreneur, she paid taxes, and she was part of the city. She knew people at different levels, so it was more of a shock for her. She acted spontaneously and I truly believe she never thought she would be physically mishandled. I think she was more shocked than surprised.' See Constance Backhouse, 'Interview with Mrs S.A. (Emily) Clyke, Viola Desmond's older sister,' Montreal, 28 April 1995. For reference to Viola Desmond as 'well known throughout the province,' see *The Clarion* 1:1 (December 1946), PANS Reel 4340.

16 Constance Backhouse, 'Interview with Wanda Robson, Viola's younger sister,' North Sydney, 22 March 1995; Backhouse, 'Interview with Mrs S.A. (Emily) Clyke.' Judith Fingard, 'Race and Respectability in Victorian Halifax,' *Journal of Imperial and Commonwealth History* 20:2 (May 1992), 169, notes at 180–2, 185, that the Davises were well-established members of the Black elite in Halifax. For information on the racial segregation of barbershops and the niche that Black barbers established in Canada, see *

17 James Albert Davis managed the sizeable family real estate holdings of his own family and that of his wife until the Depression knocked the bottom out of the market. At that point, James Davis became the service manager of the Argyle Street Garage. He continued to cut hair for family and friends in his home throughout his life; Backhouse, 'Interview with Wanda Robson'; Backhouse, 'Interview with Mrs S.A. (Emily) Clyke.' Viola Desmond's grandfather secured a position as a letter carrier when he retired from barbering. Viola's uncle (and godfather), John Davis, also obtained employment in the Post Office Division in Halifax. On the rarity of Blacks achieving the status of civil-service or post-office employees, see correspondence from Beresford Augustus Husbands, President of the Colored Men's Conserva-

tive Social and Athletic Club, to the mayor of Halifax, 17 May 1937, protesting that 'there is no representative of the colored race in any of the local civic departments': PANS RG35-102 (3B) v.7, no. 42; W.P. Oliver, 'Cultural Progress of the Negro in Nova Scotia,' *Dalhousie Review* 29:3 (1949), at 297–8, reprinted in George Elliott Clarke, ed., *Fire on the Water: An Anthology of Black Nova Scotian Writing*, vol. 1 (Lawrencetown Beach, N.S.: Pottersfield Press, 1991), at 129–33.

18 Henry Johnson was born in Richmond, Virginia. Full information concerning his parents is not available, although Wanda Robson was able to provide the following details: 'His father was a white plantation owner … I can't tell you about his mother – I don't know. This is where the mixed race comes in. Henry Walter Johnson was maybe seven-eighths white – who is white, who is Black, I don't know. Henry was a Baptist minister in New Haven, Connecticut, and he also was at Cornwallis Street Baptist Church in Halifax for one year. While in New Haven, he worked as a businessman. He was a real estate entrepreneur who also sold antiques. He married Gwendolin's mother, Susan Smith, who was a white woman born in Connecticut. Henry bought property when living in Halifax. Gwendolin inherited those properties.' See Backhouse, 'Interview with Wanda Robson.' For biographical details on Viola Desmond's parents, who married on 9 March 1908, see PANS Micro.: Churches: Halifax: Trinity Anglican: Baptisms no. 735, 736, 844; RG32 Marriages: Halifax County: 1908: no. 92, at p.249; Notes of the researcher who assisted with the compilation of material for this chapter, Allen B. Robertson, 'Interview with Pearleen Oliver,' Halifax, July 1993.

19 Canadians appear to have accepted that any known Black ancestry resulted in a racial classification as 'Black.' For one example, see *Gordon* v *Adamson* (1920), 18 O.W.N., 191 at 192 (Ont. High Ct.), in which Judge Middleton describes the child of a 'white' mother and a 'negro' father as 'coloured.' Judith Fingard notes in 'Race and Respectability in Victorian Halifax,' at 170, that 'regardless of skin colour,' members of 'the Afro-Nova Scotia community were universally identified as "coloured".' W. Burton Hurd, 'Racial Origins and Nativity of the Canadian People,' *Census of Canada 1931*, vol. 13 (Ottawa: Supply and Services, 1942), notes at p.vii that the instructions given to Canadian enumerators for the 1931 census were as follows: 'The children begotten of marriages between white and black or yellow races will be recorded as Negro, Chinese, Japanese, Indians, etc., as the case may be.' James W.St.G. Walker, *Race,' Rights and the Law in the Supreme Court of Canada* (Waterloo: The Osgoode Society and Wilfrid Laurier University Press, 1997), notes at 18 that these instructions contradicted the provisions of the Indian Act at the time: see discussion of *Re Eskimos* in chapter 2. On the

extensiveness of racial intermixing (some voluntary and some coercive) and the accepted rules of racial designation in the United States, see *

20 At the turn of the century, interracial marriages appear to have been on the decline: Fingard, 'Race and Respectability in Victorian Halifax,' at 179. Ruth I. McKenzie, 'Race Prejudice and the Negro,' *Dalhousie Review*, vol.20 (1940), notes at 201 that 'intermarriage [of Blacks] with whites is not approved.' Wanda Robson discusses Viola Desmond's racial identification in the following terms: 'Would Viola have defined herself as "mixed race"? Of course. Would you be wrong in describing her as Black? Not as far as I am concerned. I am of the generation that was raised to be proud of being Black. Viola is clearly Black. I know what I am, she is my sister.' See Backhouse, 'Interview with Wanda Robson.' On the experience of claiming mixed-race heritage in Canada see Carol Camper, ed., *Miscegenation Blues: Voices of Mixed Race Women* (Toronto: Sister Vision, 1994). James and Gwendolin Davis produced twelve children. See PANS Micro.: Churches: Halifax: Trinity Anglican: Baptisms no. 735, 736, 844; Robertson, 'Interview with Pearleen Oliver.' Viola's obituary in the Halifax *Chronicle-Herald*, 10 February 1965, p. 26, lists nine surviving siblings. There were five sisters and one brother in Montreal: Gordon Davis, Emily (Mrs S.A. Clyke), Eugenie (Mrs F.L. Parris), Helen (Mrs B.W. Fline), Constance (Mrs W. Scott), Olive (Mrs A. Scott). There were two brothers and one sister in Halifax: John Davis, Alan Davis, Wanda (Mrs W. Neal). See also the obituary in Halifax *Mail Star*, 10 February 1965, p. 8.

21 During the depression, Viola worked after school as a mother's helper in order to make ends meet; Notes of the researcher who assisted with the compilation of material for this chapter, Allen B. Robertson, 'Interview with Jack Desmond,' Halifax, 16 June 1993 and 23 June 1993; Backhouse, 'Interview with Wanda Robson'; Backhouse, 'Interview with Mrs S.A.(Emily) Clyke.' For details on the large number of Black women who chose teaching, and the expansion of occupational opportunities in hairdressing, see *

22 Viola's sister, Wanda Robson, recalls that Viola Desmond lived at the 'Y' and worked part-time as a cigarette girl at Small's Paradise nightclub in Harlem to make ends meet. Viola Desmond took great pains to conceal her Harlem employment from her mother, because she knew her parents would not have approved. While in New York, she also worked as an agent for musicians, and obtained copyright for some lyrics for her clients. See notes of David Woods, who assisted with the compilation of material for this chapter, 'Interview with Wanda Robson,' North Sydney, October 1995; Backhouse, 'Interview with Mrs S.A. (Emily) Clyke'; Robertson, 'Interview with Jack Desmond'; Brigdlal Pachai, *Beneath the Clouds of the Promised Land:*

The Survival of Nova Scotia's Blacks (Halifax: Lancelot Press for Black Educators Association of Nova Scotia, 1991), at 152–3, 297; Backhouse, 'Interview with Wanda Robson.' For details on the specific services that Black women sought from hairdressers and the spectacular career of Madame C.J. Walker, see *

23 Jack's father, Norman Mansfield Desmond, was a hack driver for John Church's Livery Stable and a founding deacon of the New Glasgow Black Baptist Church. Jack Desmond's mother, Annie Williams, worked as a domestic servant. Both Jack's parents were born into farming families in Tracadie in Antigonish County: Robertson, 'Interview with Jack Desmond'; Pachai, *Beneath the Clouds*, at 152–4, 297; New Glasgow *Clarion* 1:1 (December 1946); *Halifax-Dartmouth City Directories* (Halifax: Might Directories Atlantic, 1938–46). On the emigration of Blacks to Nova Scotia, see *

24 Jack Desmond's sister, Amelia, married a Black barber, Sydney Jones, who initially offered Jack the opportunity to take up barbering. Wanda Robson recalls that Jack Desmond's customers were approximately 80 per cent Black and 20 per cent other races. She also notes that he was 'easy-going' and not nearly as hard-working as Viola. Jack Desmond worked from his shop on Gottingen Street continuously until his retirement. When he closed his barber shop, he sold the site to Frank Sobey, who ultimately sold the store to Foodland groceries. Jack Desmond continued to work for both of the new owners, and to cut hair in people's homes for many years after: 'Jack's Got All the Answers: King of Gottingen,' Halifax *Mail-Star*, Saturday insert in *The Leader*, 31 May 1986, p. 13; Backhouse, 'Interview with Wanda Robson'; Pachai, *Beneath the Clouds*, at 152–4; Robertson, 'Interview with Jack Desmond.' On the residence patterns of Black Haligonians and the importance of Gottingen Street to the Black community, see *

25 The precise opening date for Vi's Studio of Beauty Culture is unclear, with various sources suggesting 1937, 1940, and 1941. See Backhouse, 'Interview with Wanda Robson'; Backhouse, 'Interview with Mrs S.A.(Emily) Clyke'; Tanya Hudson, 'Interview with Clara Adams,' Halifax, 24 July 1995; Tanya Hudson, 'Interview with Barbara Bowen,' Halifax, 26 July 1995; Woods, 'Interview with Pearleen Oliver'; Backhouse, 'Interview with Mrs S.A. (Emily) Clyke.'

26 Robertson, 'Interview with Pearleen Oliver'; Constance Backhouse, 'Interview with Gwen Jenkins,' London, March 1995; Hudson, 'Interview with Clara Adams'; 'Takes Action,' New Glasgow *Clarion* 1:1 (December 1946); advertisements for her business in New Glasgow *Clarion* 2:4 (28 February 1947) and 11:5 (15 March 1947); 'Beauty School Graduation,' Truro *Clarion* 2:9 (2 July 1947); Pachai, *Beneath the Clouds*, at 153; Robertson, 'Interview

with Jack Desmond'; *Halifax-Dartmouth City Directories*, 1938–46; Elaine
McCluskey, 'Long-Established Minority Still Excluded from Power,' Halifax
Chronicle-Herald, 16 March 1989, p. 41.

27 Backhouse, 'Interview with Wanda Robson'; Robertson, 'Interview with
Pearleen Oliver.' On the employment patterns of middle-class Black women
and the resulting gender tensions, see *

28 Graduates of the school included: Nora Dill, Rose Gannon, Rachel Kane,
Verna Skinner, Joyce Lucas, Helen Davis, Bernadine Bishop, Bernadine
Hampden, Evelyn Paris, Vivian Jackson, Ruth Jackson, Maddie Grosse,
Gene States, Patricia Knight, Mildred Jackson, and Barbara Bowen. Students
were required to pay tuition of $40 a month, and to sign on for a minimum
of six months' training. They were taught shampoo, press and curl, mani-
cures, and hygiene: Backhouse, 'Interview with Mrs S.A. (Emily) Clyke';
Hudson, 'Interview with Barbara Bowen'; Hudson, 'Interview with Clara
Adams'; David Woods, 'Interview with Rose Gannon-Dixon,' Halifax,
August 1995.

29 For details regarding Viola Desmond's reputation in Nova Scotia, see 'Takes
Action,' New Glasgow *Clarion* 1:1 (December 1946). On the restricted business opportunities available to Black Nova Scotians, and the predominantly
middle-class status of Blacks who contested racial segregation in Canadian
courts, see * The issue of class designation is complex, especially when
overlaid by race. Within the Black community, Viola Desmond would
probably have been viewed as upper-class. From the vantage point of
whites, a married woman who worked outside the home as a beautician
would probably have been classified as working-class. Class definitions,
when examined through distinct racial perspectives, can become as slippery
as race definitions themselves. On the complex racial dynamics associated
with the promulgation of and resistance to white middle-class culture
within the African-American community, see Evelyn Brooks Higginbotham,
*Righteous Discontent: The Women's Movement in the Black Baptist Church,
1880–1920* (Cambridge, Mass.: Harvard University Press, 1993).

30 See for example 'Takes Action,' New Glasgow *Clarion* 1:1 (December 1946);
Pachai, *Beneath the Clouds*, at 152–5; McCluskey, 'Long-Established Minority'; Robertson, 'Interview with Pearleen Oliver'; Hudson, 'Interview with
Barbara Bowen'; Hudson, 'Interview with Clara Adams'; Backhouse, 'Interview with Wanda Robson.' Although there were a number of cases brought
by Black men earlier, and a few brought by Black couples (see further
discussion in this chapter), Viola Desmond appears to have been the first
Black woman in Canada to take legal action against racially segregated
seating practices independently in her own right. This claim is based upon

an appraisal of reported cases only. There may have been others whose cases were unreported, or whose cases do not reveal on the face of the documents that race was the issue. For details of similar challenges brought by Black women in the United States, see *

31 Evelyn Brooks Higginbotham, 'African-American Women's History and the Metalanguage of Race,' *Signs* 17:2 (Winter 1992), 251 at 254, 257, 261. For further analysis and references on the racialized configuration of gender, see *

32 McCluskey, 'Long-Established Minority'; Pachai, *Beneath the Clouds*, at 154.

33 'Negress Alleges She Was Ejected from Theatre,' Halifax *Chronicle*, 30 November 1946, p. 2.

34 Hudson, 'Interview with Pearleen Oliver'; Ken Alexander and Avis Glaze, *Towards Freedom: The African-Canadian Experience* (Toronto: Umbrella Press, 1996), at 155. Prior to her marriage to Jack Desmond, Viola belonged to the racially mixed congregation of the Trinity Anglican Church. She switched affiliations to her husband's church upon marriage.

35 For biographical details on Pearleen (Borden) Oliver, whose own attempts to enter the nursing profession were barred because of race, see Doris McCubbin, 'The Women of Halifax,' *Chatelaine*, June 1954, p. 16; Colin A. Thomson, *Born with a Call: A Biography of Dr William Pearly Oliver, C.M.* (Dartmouth, N.S.: Black Cultural Centre, 1986); George Elliott Clarke, ed., *Fire on the Water*, vol. 1 (Lawrencetown Beach, N.S.: Pottersfield Press, 1991), at 171; reference by Frances Early in her review of 'Rethinking Canada: The Promise of Women's History,' *Resources for Feminist Research* 21 (Spring 1992), at 25, to oral interviews of Pearleen Oliver, held by Saint Mary's University Library, Halifax; Alexander and Glaze, *Towards Freedom*, at 155. For reference to Pearleen Oliver's public-speaking campaign in the 1940s to publicize cases of Black women refused admission to nursing schools see Agnes Calliste, 'Women of "Exceptional Merit": Immigration of Caribbean Nurses to Canada,' *Canadian Journal of Women and the Law*, vol. 6 (1993), 85 at 92. For reference to Pearleen Oliver's interest in discrimination against Black women, see Clarke, ed., *Fire on the Water*, at 146, where he notes that Pearleen Oliver's *One of His Heralds* (Halifax: Pearleen Oliver, n.d.) discusses the situation of Agnes Gertrude Waring (1884–1951), whose attempt to receive ordination to preach at the Second Baptist Church in New Glasgow was refused by the Maritime Baptist Convention because she was female. For reference to the 'Little Black Sambo' campaign see correspondence from Beresford Augustus Husbands to the Mayor of Halifax, following Pearleen Oliver's address on 26 January 1944, in PANS. Helen Campbell Bennerman's *Story of Little Black Sambo*, first published in 1899, became a

Canadian classic, according to Robin Winks, 'still selling well in its sixteenth printing in 1969': Winks, *Blacks in Canada*, at 295.

36 Born in 1912, Rev. Oliver grew up in a predominantly white community in Wolfville, Nova Scotia, and graduated from Acadia University with a BA in 1934, and a Masters of Divinity in 1936. For biographical details on Rev. W.P. Oliver (who would later become the chair of the Black United Front) see Thomson, *Born with a Call*; 'Halifax Cleric Elected,' Halifax *Chronicle-Herald*, 3 September 1960, p. 13; Clarke, ed., *Fire on the Water*, vol. 1, at 171; Marjorie Major, 'The Negroes in Nova Scotia,' PANS Mg1, v. 1767, no. 42K; Oliver, 'Cultural Progress of the Negro,' at 134; W.P. Oliver, 'Urban and Rural Life Committee of The African United Baptist Association of Nova Scotia,' PANS Mg1, v.1767, no. 42L; Winks, *Blacks in Canada*, at 350–2; Robin W. Winks, 'Negroes in the Maritimes: An Introductory Survey,' *Dalhousie Review* 48:4 (1969), 453 at 469; Nancy Lubka, 'Ferment in Nova Scotia,' *Queen's Quarterly* 76:2 (1969), 213–28.

37 Viola Desmond sought medical treatment from a physician from the West Indies who resided in the same building as her parents and maintained an office on the corner of Gottingen and Gerrish streets. Being Black, this physician had no access to city hospitals and had to perform all procedures in his office: Robertson, 'Interview with Pearleen Oliver.' Wanda Robson believes the doctor's name may have been F.B. Holder, a British Guiana–born Black physician practising in Halifax at this time; Backhouse, 'Interview with Wanda Robson.'

38 Pearleen Oliver sought support from a number of other Black organizations: the Halifax Coloured Citizens Improvement League, the president of the Ladies' Auxiliary of the Cornwallis Street Baptist Church, and the president of the Missionaries' Society. She was disappointed how few people came to the meeting, and discouraged by the reluctance many expressed to 'make trouble': Hudson, 'Interview with Pearleen Oliver'; Robertson, 'Interview with Pearleen Oliver.' For the mission statement of the NSAACP, a list of its charter members, and information about predecessor organizations, see *

39 'Negress Alleges She Was Ejected from Theatre,' Halifax *Chronicle*, 30 November 1946, p. 2. This position was supported by Mrs M.H. Spaulding, chair of the emergency committee for civil rights of the Civil Liberties League, whose views are quoted in 'Ban All Jim Crow Rules Is Comment on N.S. Charge,' Toronto *Daily Star*, 30 November 1946, p. 3: '"Jim Crow practices, such as segregating Negroes or any other group in certain sections of theatres, or in keeping them out of hotels, have no place in Canada and should be forbidden by law. There is no place for second-class citizenship in this country," said Mrs. Spaulding. She added there had been instances of

the same sort of racial discrimination in other parts of Canada. The practice is that when Negroes try to buy a ticket at a theatre they are told the only seats available are in the balcony, she asserted. "When Paul Robeson was in Toronto in 'Othello' at the Royal Alexandra he said he would not appear if there was any discrimination against colored people, and they were seated in all parts of the house.'"

40 New Glasgow, N.S., *The Clarion* 1:1 (December 1946). For information on *The Clarion* and other Black newspapers in Canada, see *

41 'Editorial, Taking Inventory,' New Glasgow, N.S., *The Clarion* 2:4 (28 February 1947), p. 2.

42 'Takes Action' and 'Viola Desmond's Appeal,' New Glasgow, N.S., *The Clarion* 1:1 (December 1946), p. 1; 'Editorial: A New Year's Message,' *The Clarion* 2:1 (January 1947). The latter article notes that 'one of New Glasgow's leading business men' (race unspecified) donated ten dollars to the case, leading the editor to applaud him for his 'courage and generosity.' Pearleen Oliver recalls that money came in from all over the province, in amounts both large and small, with more white donors than Black: Robertson, 'Interview with Pearleen Oliver.' On the origins and meaning of the American phrase 'Jim Crow,' see *

43 PANS, SMI Division, CBC Radio, Collection Ar2265-2268 and 2279, Carrie Best Interview. Dr Carrie M. Best, whose birth name was Carrie Prevoe, was born in New Glasgow in 1903, and completed high school in New Glasgow. She married Albert Theophilus Best, a Barbadian-born Black porter for the Canadian National Railway, and had one son, J. Calbert Best. Carrie Best was an editor and publisher of several Black newspapers, founding the *Clarion* in 1946, and publishing the nationally circulated *The Negro Citizen* in 1949. In 1956, she began to write columns in the Pictou *Advocate* on matters of human rights, and produced and narrated radio shows for five stations for twelve years. In 1970, she was awarded the Lloyd McInnes Memorial Award for her contribution to social betterment. She received the Order of Canada in 1974 and an honorary degree from St Francis Xavier University in 1975. Her son, Calbert Best, became national president of the Civil Service Association of Canada in Ottawa in 1960, and an assistant deputy minister for Manpower and Immigration in 1970. See Dr Carrie M. Best, *That Lonesome Road: The Autobiography of Carrie M. Best* (New Glasgow, N.S.: Clarion Publishing, 1977); Clarke,ed., *Fire on the Water*, vol. 1, at 171; Winks, *Blacks in Canada*, at 405, 408; 'Albert Best Dies Sunday,' New Glasgow *Evening News*, 5 August 1971; 'The Gracious Activist,' *The Novascotian*, 10 April 1982, cover story and pp. 3–4; 'Nova Scotians Best, Buckler Honored,' Halifax *Chronicle-Herald*, 21 December 1974; 'St. FX Confers Honorary Degrees on Two N.S.

Women, N.B. Lawyer,' New Glasgow *Evening News*, 12 May 1975; 'Three Honorary Doctorates to Be Awarded at Convocation,' New Glasgow *Evening News*, 24 April 1975, p. 9; 'Two to Receive Decorations in Order of Canada Tonight,' New Glasgow *Evening News*, 16 April 1980; 'J.C. Best Accepts New Post,' Halifax *Chronicle-Herald*, 19 January 1966; 'Cal Best Re-elected Civil Servants' Chief,' Halifax *Chronicle-Herald*, 1 October 1960.

44 On 18 February 1942, Carrie Best issued a writ of summons against Norman W. Mason and the Roseland Theatre Co. Ltd, for ejecting her and her son, Calbert, from the theatre on 29 December 1941. The event was a deliberate, planned attack on the policy of racial segregation that the theatre began to impose in the 1940s, apparently at the request of some white patrons. Carrie Best wrote to Mason, the white owner of the theatre, challenging him on the policy and advising that she and her son intended to sit on the main floor on 29 December 1941. When she tried to do so that afternoon, she was asked to leave by the white assistant manager, Erskine Cumming, white police officer George S. Wright, and white police chief Elmo Langille. When she refused to leave, Officer Wright placed his hands under Mrs Best's arms and raised her from her seat. She apparently announced: 'That's all I wanted you to do, put your hands on me. I will fix you for this.' Then she and her son left the theatre. Carrie Best retained James Hinnigar Power, a white New Glasgow lawyer, and commenced litigation, claiming assault and battery and breach of contract. She sought $4 in repairs to her coat, $5,000 in general damages for the assault and battery, and $500 general damages for the wrongful revocation of the licence given to her to witness the performance. Trial was held on 12 May 1942, in the Pictou Court House, before Robert Henry Graham of the Supreme Court of Nova Scotia, the same judge who would later hear Viola Desmond's case. The white judge charged the all-white jury to answer the following questions, to which they responded:

1. Did the Defendant Company's ticket seller sell any tickets to the Plaintiff? No.

2. Did the Defendant ticket seller sell her a downstairs ticket? No.

3. Did the Plaintiff know the Defendant Company would not sell her a downstairs ticket? Yes.

4. Had the Plaintiff any reasonable grounds for thinking the ticket seller sold her a downstairs ticket? No.

5. Did the Plaintiff do as she did because she knew Defendant Company's ticket seller would not sell her a downstairs ticket? Yes.

6. Was any more force used to remove the plaintiff than was necessary? No.

7. What damage, if any, did the Plaintiff sustain? None.

Upon the return of these findings, Judge Graham dismissed Carrie Best's action, and charged her with the Defendant's bill of costs, which amounted to $156.07. See *Best* v *Mason and Roseland Theatre*, PANS RG39 'C' (PI) 1986-550/099, file A4013 (1942); 'Case Dismissed against Mason and Roseland Theatre,' New Glasgow *Evening News*, 15 May 1942; 'Case Dismissed,' New Glasgow *Eastern Chronicle*, 19 May 1942; 'Two Sentences Are Imposed in Supreme Court,' Pictou *Advocate*, 21 May 1942; 'Jury Dismisses Suit for Damages,' Halifax *Herald*, 15 May 1942; 'Colored Woman's Action Dismissed,' Halifax *Chronicle*, 15 May 1942. For a fuller account, see Constance Backhouse, '"I Was Unable to Identify with Topsy": Carrie M. Best's Struggle against Racial Segregation in Nova Scotia, 1942,' *Atlantis* 22:2 (Spring 1998), 16–26. I am indebted to Barry Cahill for bringing the archival file to my attention.

45 Best, *That Lonesome Road*, at 43–4. The Norfolk House, where Carrie's brother worked, had a history of refusing to support the practices of racial discrimination so common in the area. The Halifax *Eastern Chronicle*, 28 May 1885, noted that Mr H. Murray, a white man, refused to close his Norfolk hotel to the Fisk Jubilee Singers, a Black choir group. Members of the choir had earlier been refused admission to hotels in Pictou and Halifax.

46 Truro, which would earn itself the designation 'the Alabama of Canada' and 'Little Mississippi,' also maintained a 'Whites Only' waiting room in the railway station: Lubka, 'Ferment in Nova Scotia,' at 215; Winks, *Blacks in Canada*, at 319–25, 420; Winks, 'Negroes in the Maritimes,' at 466–7; Thomson, *Born with a Call*, at 467. On the activities of the KKK, see discussion of *R.* v *Phillips* in chapter 6.

47 Although similar legislation was not passed in provinces other than Ontario and Nova Scotia, New Brunswick's legislature enacted two statutes giving explicit recognition to the existence of Black schools. For details of the 1842 and 1843 New Brunswick provisions, and information about more informal segregation methods used in other provinces, see * For a comparison with the segregated schooling offered First Nations children, see discussion of *R.* v *Wanduta* in chapter 3.

48 For legislative details of the 1849, 1850, 1859, and 1886 provisions, see *

49 Winks, *Blacks in Canada*, at 365–76; Robin W. Winks, 'Negro School Segregation in Ontario and Nova Scotia,' *Canadian Historical Review* 50:2 (1969), 164 at 174, 176; Jason H. Silverman and Donna J. Gillie, 'The Pursuit of Knowledge under Difficulties: Education and the Fugitive Slave in Canada,' *Ontario History*, vol. 74 (1982), at 95; Claudette Knight, 'Black Parents Speak: Education in Mid-Nineteenth-Century Canada West,' *Ontario History*, vol. 89 (1997), at 269. For some discussion of the resistance offered by Blacks to

these practices see Peggy Bristow, '"Whatever you raise in the ground you can sell it in Chatham": Black Women in Buxton and Chatham, 1850–65,' in Peggy Bristow et al., *'We're Rooted Here and They Can't Pull Us Up': Essays in African-Canadian Women's History* (Toronto: University of Toronto Press, 1994), 69 at 114–16; Afua P. Cooper, 'Black Women and Work in Nineteenth-Century Canada West: Black Woman Teacher Mary Bibb,' in Bristow et al., *We're Rooted Here*, at 148–68.

50 *Washington v The Trustees of Charlotteville* (1854), 11 U.C.Q.B. 569 (Ont. Q.B.), held that school authorities could not exclude Black children unless alternative facilities for 'colored pupils' had been established, but *In re Dennis Hill v Schools Trustees of Camden and Zone* (1854), 11 U.C.Q.B. 573 (Ont. Q.B.), ruled that Black children could be forced to attend separate schools located miles away from their homes and outside of their school sections. *An Act to Amend the Act respecting Common Schools in Upper Canada*, S.O. 1868-69, c.44, s.9, provides 'that no person shall be deemed a supporter of any separate school for coloured people, unless he resides within three miles in a direct line of the site of the school house for such separate school; and any coloured child residing farther than three miles in a direct line from the said school house shall be allowed to attend the common school of the section within the limits of which the said child shall reside.' These provisions are continued by *An Act respecting Separate Schools*, R.S.O. 1877, c.206, s.2–5; *The Separate Schools Act*, R.S.O. 1897, c.294. After the amendment, several cases acknowledged that race should not be the sole ground for exclusion from common schools, but then accepted the testimony of school authorities regarding overcrowding and 'insufficient accommodation,' using this to defeat the claims of Black parents to register their children in non-segregated schools: see *In re Hutchison and School Trustees of St. Catharines* (1871), 31 U.C.Q.B. 274 (Ont. Q.B.); *Dunn v Board of Education of Windsor* (1884), 6 O.R. 125 (Ontario Chancery Division). For two examples of cases where the efforts of education officials to bar Black children from common public schools were challenged successfully, see *Simmons and the Corporation of Chatham* (1861), 21 U.C.Q.B. 75 (Ont. Q.B.), quashing for uncertainty a by-law which purported to enlarge substantially the geographic catchment area of a separate school, and *Stewart and Schools Trustees of Sandwich* (1864), 23 U.C.Q.B. 634 (Ont. Q.B.), which accepted evidence that the separate school operated only intermittently as a reason to overrule the common school's refusal to register a Black female student. See also Winks, *Blacks in Canada*; Winks, 'Negro School Segregation,' at 175–82; Knight, 'Black Parents Speak.'

51 Winks, *Blacks in Canada*; Winks, 'Negro School Segregation,' at 182, 190.

52 For legislative details of the specific provisions relating to 'coloured people' between 1887 and 1964, see *

53 Winks, 'Negro School Segregation,' at 177.

54 For legislative details of the 1865 and 1873 provisions, see *

55 For legislative details of the 1884 provision, see *

56 For legislative details of the provisions in force between 1900 and 1950, see *

57 In Lower Sackville, Mrs Pleasah Lavinia Caldwell, a Black Nova Scotian, responded by opening a 'kitchen school' in her home, which educated Blacks in the area until her death in 1950: Helen Champion, 'School in a Kitchen,' unlabelled clipping dated 9 November 1949, PANS, Mg1, v.1767 no. 42a. In 1964, four such districts continued: Beechville, Hammond Plains, Lucasville, and Cherry Brook, all in Halifax County: Winks, *Blacks in Canada*, at 376–80. For details of the lack of funding and difficulties recruiting teachers and obtaining equipment, premises, and transportation in Nova Scotia see Winks, 'Negro School Segregation,' at 186–91.

58 Winks, *Blacks in Canada*, comments at 325 on the 'formlessness of the racial barrier,' noting at 326: 'In the United States the Negro was somewhat more sure – sure of where he could and could not go, of when to be meek and when to be strong. In Canada he was uncertain.'

59 Oliver, 'Cultural Progress of the Negro,' notes at 129–35 that most Black males could not find work except in the heaviest and most poorly paid jobs: agriculture, mining, lumbering, steel, railway, and shipping industries. In most cases, they were also barred from membership in unions. Business ventures were limited to barber shops, beauty parlours, taxi business, trucking, shoe-making, a newspaper, and one co-operative store. See also James W.St.G. Walker, *Racial Discrimination in Canada: The Black Experience* (Ottawa: Canadian Historical Association, 1985), at 15, where he notes that, during the inter-war years, Black men were concentrated in the following jobs: waiters, janitors, barbers, and labourers. The elite among the men worked as railway waiters and porters: see Stanley G. Grizzle, *My Name's Not George: The Story of the Brotherhood of Sleeping Car Porters in Canada* (Toronto: Umbrella Press, 1998); Judith Fingard, 'From Sea to Rail: Black Transportation Workers and Their Families in Halifax, c.1870–1916,' *Acadiensis* 24:2 (Spring 1995), 49–64; Agnes Calliste, 'The Struggle for Employment Equity by Blacks on American and Canadian Railroads,' *Journal of Black Studies* 25:3 (January 1995), 297–317; Agnes Calliste, 'Blacks on Canadian Railways,' *Canadian Ethnic Studies* 20:2 (1988), 36–52; Agnes Calliste, 'Sleeping Car Porters in Canada: An Ethnically Submerged Split Labour Market,' *Canadian Ethnic Studies* 19:1 (1987), 1–20. Prior to the Second World

War, Black females were limited to teaching school or domestic work. On the pervasive restriction to domestic work, Suzanne Morton, 'Separate Spheres in a Separate World: African-Nova Scotian Women in late-19th-Century Halifax County,' *Acadiensis* 22:2 (Spring 1993), 61, notes at 67: 'African-Nova Scotian women had virtually no legal wage-earning opportunities outside domestic service, taking in laundry, or sewing. Regardless of the status in the community, property holdings or occupation of the husband, married women and widows charred, and young women were servants.' Dorothy W. Williams, *Blacks in Montreal, 1628–1986: An Urban Demography* (Cowansville, Que.: Yvon Blais, 1989), notes at 45 that the superintendent of nurses of the Montreal General Hospital admitted in the 1930s that Black nurses could not find employment in Montreal, 'since there were not enough Black patients to care for in the hospitals (and White patients would not allow Black nurses to touch them).' See also 'Girl Barred by Color from Nurses Training Course,' New Glasgow, N.S., *The Clarion* 2:15 (6 October 1947), p. 1, recounting race barriers against Black women throughout Ontario. The nursing field opened to women in Nova Scotia in 1949, when two Blacks graduated as registered nurses. See also Dionne Brand, *No Burden to Carry: Narratives of Black Working Women in Ontario, 1920s to 1950s* (Toronto: Women's Press, 1991), at 155, 184, 207. Williams notes at 45 that Blacks were barred from doing medical internships in Montreal between 1930 and 1947. The Faculty of Medicine at McGill University arranged instead for Blacks to serve their internships with Howard University in Washington, D.C. Donald H. Clairmont and Dennis W. Magill, 'Nova Scotia Blacks: Marginality in a Depressed Region,' in W.E. Mann, ed., *Canada: A Sociological Profile* (Toronto: Copp Clark, 1971), 177 at 179, 183, quote P.E. MacKerrow, *A Brief History of the Colored Baptists of Nova Scotia* (Halifax, 1895): 'the United Sates with her faults, which are many, has done much for the elevation of the coloured race. Sad and sorry are we to say that is more than we can boast of here in Nova Scotia. Our young men as soon as they receive a common school education must flee away to the United States and seek employment. Very few ever receive a trade from the large employers, even in the factories, on account of race prejudices ...' Rev. Adam S. Green, MS, *The Future of the Canadian Negro* (1904), PANS V/F v.144 no. 11, at 17, notes: 'How many negroes do you find as clerks, book-keepers, or stenographers within the provinces? I know of but *one* ... Our people are excluded from such lucrative positions, not so much from disqualification, as from race-prejudice.'

60 On the history of residential segregation by race across Canada, see *

61 Although there was no legislation explicitly barring Blacks from jury serv-

ice, some legal officials took steps to eliminate their names in the empanel-
ling of jury lists. Winks, *Blacks in Canada*, at 251, 284–6, notes that a challenge to Black jurors and jury foremen in Toronto in 1851 was unsuccessful,
but that Blacks were excluded from jury service in Victoria between 1864
and 1872. James W.St.G. Walker, *The Black Identity in Nova Scotia: Community
and Institutions in Historical Perspective* (Halifax: Black Cultural Centre for
Nova Scotia, 1985), notes at 8 that Blacks 'could not serve on juries or claim
a jury trial.' See also James M. Pilton, 'Negro Settlement in British Columbia,' MA thesis (University of Victoria, 1951); 'Colored Men as Jurors,'
Victoria *Colonist*, 7 May 1872, p. 3; 'Colored Jurors,' Victoria *Colonist*, 21
March 1872, p.3; 27 November 1872, p. 3; 'Have Them Right,' New Westminster *Times*, 18 February 1860.

62 On the history of military segregation, see *

63 For a case documenting the resistance of a Black man to racial segregation
on a Chatham steamer in the 1850s, see *

64 Winks, 'Negroes in the Maritimes,' at 466; Winks, *Blacks in Canada*, at 286,
325; Daniel G. Hill, *The Freedom-Seekers: Blacks in Early Canada* (Agincourt,
Ont.: Book Society of Canada, 1981), at 104.

65 On the racial segregation of orphans and paupers in Nova Scotia, see *

66 On the denial of hospital services to Blacks in Halifax and Edmonton, see *

67 On segregated cemeteries, see *

68 Winks, *Blacks in Canada*, notes at 248, 283–4, 286, 325 that hotels in Hamilton,
Windsor, Chatham, and London refused admission to Blacks in the mid-
nineteenth century. In the 1860s in Victoria, the chief theatre refused Blacks
access to the dress circle or to orchestra seats, the Bank Exchange Saloon
refused service to Blacks, and they were also excluded from Queen Victoria's birthday ball and from the farewell banquet for Governor James Douglas. The colour line remained visible in British Columbia in restaurants and
places of entertainment prior to the First World War. Blacks were not admitted to the boy scout troops or the YMCA in Windsor, and Black musicians
had to establish their own orchestra in Owen Sound. Winks notes at 325–6,
388, 420, 457: 'In 1924 the Edmonton City Commissioner barred Negroes
from all public parks and swimming pools – and was overruled by the city
council; in Colchester, Ontario, in 1930, police patrolled the parks and
beaches to keep blacks from using them. In Saint John all restaurants and
theatres closed their doors to Negroes in 1915; two years later the chief
theatres of Hamilton also did so. [...] In 1929, when the World Baptist
Conference was held in Toronto, Negro delegates were denied hotel rooms.
[...] Only one hotel in Montreal could be depended upon not to turn
Negroes away in 1941. [...] Many dance pavilions, skating rinks and

restaurants made it clear that they did not welcome blacks; and several pubs in Saskatchewan and British Columbia insisted that Negroes sit in corners reserved for them.' Even into the 1960s, Black residents were virtually barred from community restaurants, and Windsor barkeepers designated separate 'jungle rooms' for Blacks until 1951. See also 'Hotels Refuse to Take Negroes,' Vancouver *Province*, 13 August 1945, p. 2, recounting how Black members of the cast of *Carmen Jones* were denied hotel accommodation in Vancouver; and 'Color Bar Said Drawn in Local Pub,' Vancouver *Sun*, 30 July 1948, p. 1. Howard Lawrence, New Glasgow, N.S., *The Clarion* 2:2 (December 1946), urged the Black community to establish a community centre because 'every place is closed to us.' Anna-Maria Galante, 'Ex-Mayor Lewis Broke New Ground,' *Afro-Nova Scotian Portraits* (Halifax: Chronicle-Herald and Mail-Star, 19 February 1993), at P7, quotes Daurene Lewis stating that the dances in Annapolis Royal were always segregated (*circa* 1940s and 1950s) and attempts were made to segregate the movie house as well. McKenzie, 'Race Prejudice and the Negro,' notes at 201 that '[Negroes] are not always served in the best restaurants, nor admitted to high-class hotels. They are restricted, in cities, to the poorer residential districts, and are not accepted socially.' See also Daniel G. Hill, 'Black History in Early Ontario,' *Canadian Human Rights Yearbook* (Ottawa: Human Rights Research and Education Centre, University of Ottawa, 1984–5), at 265; Grizzle, *My Name's Not George*, at 54–5; Winks, 'Negroes in the Maritimes,' at 467; Winks, 'Negro School Segregation,' at 189; Allen P. Stouffer, *The Light of Nature and the Law of God: Antislavery in Ontario, 1833–1877* (Montreal and Kingston: McGill-Queen's University Press, 1992), at 200–1; Brand, *No Burden to Carry*, at 134, 149–50, 153, 210–11, 278. For reference to comparable treatment of First Nations peoples, see George Manuel and Michael Poslums, *The Fourth World: An Indian Reality* (Don Mills: Ontario: Collier-Macmillan Canada, 1974), at 101.

69 For legislative details regarding the 1947 and 1949 Saskatchewan provisions, and similar legislation enacted in Ontario in 1951 and 1954 on the heels of a concerted lobby campaign, see *

70 On the admission of Black lawyers (including James Robinson Johnston, Joseph Eaglan Griffith, Frederick Allan Hamilton, and George W.R. Davis) to the bar of Nova Scotia, to the bar of British Columbia (Joshua Howard), and to the bar of New Brunswick (Abraham Beverly Walker), see * For details concerning Ontario, see chapter 6.

71 Barry Cahill, 'The "Colored Barrister": The Short Life and Tragic Death of James Robinson Johnston, 1876–1915,' *Dalhousie Law Journal*, vol. 15 (1992), 326, notes at 373 that Goffe was admitted to Gray's Inn in 1905, and called to

the bar by Gray's Inn in 1908. He practised at the English bar for six years, and 'was employed in various government departments' during and after the First World War. He died in 1962 in his ninetieth year.

72 For biographical details on F.W. Bissett, the son of Frederick W. Bissett and Ethel Gray (Smith) Bissett, see 'Bissett, Frederick William, B.A., LL.B.,' *Maritime Reference Book: Biographical and Pictorial Record of Prominent Men and Women of the Maritime Provinces* (Halifax: Royal Print, 1931), at 34; 'Bench Vacancy Filled,' Halifax *Chronicle-Herald*, 11 March 1961; 'Mr. Justice F.W. Bissett,' Halifax *Mail-Star*, 11 November 1978, p. 6; 'Mr. Justice Bissett, 76, Dies in Halifax,' Halifax *Mail-Star*, 10 November 1978, pp. 1–2; 'Tributes Paid to Mr. Justice F.W. Bissett,' Halifax *Mail-Star*, 11 November 1978, pp. 1–2. Apart from Rev. Oliver's recommendation, it remains unclear why Viola Desmond selected F.W. Bissett. She seems to have been familiar with at least some other white members of the legal profession prior to this. Earlier, in November 1946, she retained Samuel B. Goodman, a white lawyer from Halifax, to issue a writ against Philip Kane, the white car dealer who sold her the 1940 Dodge, for overcharging her in violation of the Wartime Prices and Trade Board Order. See *Viola Desmond v Philip Kane*, PANS RG39 "C" Halifax v.936, no. S.C. 13304.

73 *Johnson v Sparrow* (1899), 15 Que. S.C. 104 (Quebec Superior Court), at 108. For details of Judge Archibald's decision, see * When the case went on appeal to the Quebec Court of Queen's Bench, Judge Bossé refused to equate a hotel and a theatre under the common-law rule, but upheld the $50 damage award based on the breach of contract. The court did not overturn Judge Archibald's explicit racial analysis, but stated that it was unnecessary to decide the question of whether Blacks were entitled to the same rights of admission as whites in this case; *Johnson v Sparrow* (1899), 8 Que. Q.B. 379. Walker, *'Race,' Rights and the Law*, suggests at 146 that 'in dismissing Justice Archibald's reasoning the appeal decision undermined any general application of the non-discriminatory principle.' With respect, this is arguably an overreading of the appeal decision. Judge Bossé adverts to the legislation in the United States endorsing racial segregation, explicitly questions whether these enactments might be unconstitutional as violating the principle of equality, notes that similar legislation has not been enacted in Canada, and then concludes that the present dispute, which can be resolved on a purely contractual basis, does not require any further rulings on racial discrimination. This does not appear to be an overt rejection of Judge Archibald's analysis on racial equality, but a reluctance to rule on the matter in the present case. For further discussion of the common-law duty to serve, and another Ontario case that followed *Johnson v Sparrow*, see * Several earlier

cases premised on an innkeeper's duty to serve the public were brought by Jacob Francis, an English-born Black saloon-keeper in Victoria. In the spring of 1860, Francis was refused service of two bottles of champagne in a billiard saloon at Yates and Government streets. On 20 April 1860, a civil jury heard his claim for forty shillings in damages in *Francis v Miletich*, Archives of British Columbia (hereinafter cited as ABC) C/AA/30.3D/2, Vancouver Island, Supreme Court of Civil Justice, Rule and order book, 1859–61, at 63, 69; C/AA/30.3P/5, Vancouver Island, Supreme Court of Civil Justice, at 118–19, 123; GR848, Vancouver Island, Charge Books; 'Refusing a Drink to a Coloured Man,' Victoria *Gazette*, 21 April 1860, p. 3. The jury held that Miletich was an innkeeper, that Francis was refused liquor but not received as a guest, and that Francis sustained no injury and was not entitled to damages. In 1862, Jacob Francis was refused service at the Bank Exchange Saloon in Victoria, and again sought legal relief. According to newspaper accounts, a white Victoria police magistrate, Augustus F. Pemberton, ruled that saloons that refused service to Black men would either not get a licence or would be fined and their licence not renewed when it expired. According to the charge book, the case was dismissed by Magistrate Pemberton on 4 July 1862. See *Jacob Francis v Joseph Lovett*, ABC GR848, Charge books, vol.3; 'Wouldn't Let Him Drink,' Victoria *Colonist*, 26 June 1862, p. 3; 'Shall a Black Man Drink at a White Man's Bar?' Victoria *Colonist*, 28 June 1862, p. 3; 'The Vexed Question Settled,' Victoria *Colonist*, 5 July 1862, p. 3; 'Shall a Colored Man Drink at a White Man's Bar?' Victoria *British Colonist*, 5 July 1862, p. 3. For more details on Francis, who was earlier denied the right to take up an elected seat in the colonial Legislative Assembly because of his race, see Pilton, 'Negro Settlement in British Columbia'; S. Stott, 'Blacks in B.C.,' ABC NW/016.325711/B631. For a similar case in 1913, see *Moses Rowden v J.B. Stevens, Prop., Stratford Hotel*, ABC GR1651, British Columbia County Court (Vancouver) Plaint and procedure books, 1886–1946 [B7314–B7376]; GR1651, British Columbia County Court (Vancouver), Indexes to plaint and procedure books, 1886–1946 [B7897–B7901]; GR1418, British Columbia County Court (Vancouver), Judgments 1893–1940 [B2611–B2643]; 'Negro Sues Because Color Line Is Drawn,' Vancouver *Province*, 4 October 1913, p. 15; 'Hotel Bar Refused to Serve Negro,' Vancouver *Province*, 10 July 1913, p. 17; 'Enters Suit for Damages for Being Refused Drink,' Vancouver *Sun*, 1 October 1913, p. 1. Rowden sought relief before the city's licence commissioners, who refused to intervene. He then claimed $500 damages on the basis that Stevens failed to meet his common-law obligation as an innkeeper to serve travellers. The outcome of the case is unclear from the surviving documentation.

74 *Barnswell* v *National Amusement Company, Limited* (1914), 21 B.C.R. 435,
[1915] 31 W.L.R. 542 (B.C.C.A.). See also 'Suit Against Theatre,' Victoria
Times, 30 May 1914, p. 18; 'Damages Are Awarded,' Victoria *Times*, 10
December 1914, p. 16; 'Legal Intelligence,' Victoria *Daily Colonist*, 10 December 1914, p. 3. For further details, see *

75 'Colored Patrons Must Pay Double,' Regina *Leader*, 9 October 1911, p. 7,
announces: 'One of the city's restaurants has decided to draw the colored
line and in future all colored patrons will pay just double what their white
brothers are charged. This, of course, is not a money-making venture, but is
a polite hint to these people that their patronage is not wanted. It is understood that the change is made at the urgent request of some of the most
influential patrons, and not on the initiative of the management. It is an
innovation in the running of hotels, cafes and restaurants of the city and the
experiment will be watched with interest.' The exact basis for the ruling,
which is not reported in the published legal reports, is somewhat difficult to
reconstruct from the press account in 'May Charge Double Price,' Regina
Leader, 16 October 1911, p. 7. The newspaper specifies that the case was 'a
charge of obtaining money under false pretences' laid against W.B. Waddell
by William Hawes. There was some factual dispute over whether Hawes
had been notified of the double charge prior to ordering, with Hawes
claiming he had not, and Waddell claiming he had. White magistrates
Lawson and Long concluded that Hawes had, and held that therefore there
was no case of false pretences. The press seems to have been less convinced,
claiming that the case stood for the proposition that 'a restaurant keeper has
the right to exclude colored patrons by charging double prices without,
however, taking proper steps to make the charge known to those whom he
proposes to exclude.' The press report also hints that the claim may have
been rooted in breach of contract, recounting that the plaintiff tried to show
that Hawes 'had no knowledge of [the double price] arrangement when he
gave his order, and that the bill of fare from which he ordered constituted a
contract ...' The contract issues appear to have been ignored by the court.
Counsel for Hawes, Mr Barr, sought leave to appeal, but this was denied.
For another example of a case where Blacks were charged extra, see *R.* v *J.D.
Carroll*, ABC GR419, B.C. Attorney General Documents, Box 1, file 21/1860,
and 'Police Court,' Victoria *Colonist*, 14 January 1860, p. 3, where William
Bastion, a Black man, charged J.D. Carroll, a white innkeeper, with extortion
after he charged him $1.50 for three drinks he had already consumed on 10
January 1860. Charles Jackson and Arthur Wiggins, white men who were
with Bastion at the time, testified that they had never been charged more
than 12 1/2 cents per drink. Carroll was committed for trial by Magistrate

Augustus Pemberton in Victoria Police Court on 12–13 January 1860, but the outcome of the case is not clear from the surviving records. The Victoria *Colonist*, 19 January 1860, suggests that the case was dismissed because Carroll was a spirit dealer and not an innkeeper; see Diba B. Majzub, '"A God Sent Land for the Colored People"? The Legal Treatment of Blacks in Victoria, 1858–1865,' unpublished manuscript, at 23.

76 *Loew's Montreal Theatres Ltd.* v *Reynolds* (1919), 30 Que. K.B. 459 (Quebec King's Bench) per John-Edward Martin, J., at 466; Winks, 'Negroes in the Maritimes,' at 467; 'Court Says Color Line Is Illegal; All Equal in Law,' Montreal *Gazette*, 5 March 1919, p. 4. For details of the case, and a 1912 case in Edmonton that reached a more informal, but similar resolution, see *

77 *Franklin* v *Evans* (1924), 55 O.L.R. 349, 26 O.W.N. 65 (Ont. High Court). See also 'Dismisses Suit of Colored Man,' London *Evening Free Press*, 15 March 1924, which gives the name as W.K. Franklin. Strangely, neither *Johnson* v *Sparrow* nor *Barnswell* was cited in the legal decision, and Judge Haughton Lennox concluded that there were no authorities or decided cases in support of the plaintiff's contention. Most of the decision centred on common-law rules requiring hotel-keepers to supply 'accommodation of a certain character, within certain limits, and subject to recognized qualifications, to all who apply.' Contrasting restaurants with innkeepers, Lennox held that the common-law obligations did not apply to the defendant. The white judge did, however, seem to have been ambivalent about the result he reached in this case. Disparaging the conduct of the white restaurant owner and his wife, whose attitude towards the plaintiff Lennox described as 'unnecessarily harsh, humiliating, and offensive,' Lennox contrasted their situation with that of the plaintiff: 'The plaintiff is undoubtedly a thoroughly respectable man, of good address, and, I have no doubt, a good citizen, and I could not but be touched by the pathetic eloquence of his appeal for recognition as a human being, of common origin with ourselves.' Lennox then expressly ducked the issue: 'The theoretical consideration of this matter is a difficult and decidedly two-sided problem, extremely controversial, and entirely outside my sphere in the administration of law – law as it is.' Lennox dismissed the action without costs. Curiously, the account in the local Black newspaper, *The Dawn of Tomorrow*, suggests that the plaintiff won: 'W.V. Franklin Given Damages,' London *Dawn of Tomorrow*, 2 February 1924, p. 1; 'Mr. W.V. Franklin's Victory,' London *Dawn of Tomorrow*, 16 February 1924, p. 2. This coverage appears erroneous in asserting that 'the jury took only 20 minutes to decide that Mr. Franklin should be awarded damages,' since the law report notes that there was no jury, and that the claim was dismissed. However, the Black press, unlike the white press, did recount the plaintiff's

testimony in valuable detail: 'When Mr. Franklin was called to the witness box for the defence counsel [and asked], "Have you any ground for damages?" Mr. Franklin's eloquent and polished reply was: "Not in dollars and cents, but in humiliation and inhuman treatment at the hands of this fellow man, yes. Because I am a dark man, a condition over which I have no control, I did not receive the treatment I was entitled to as a human being. God chose to bring me into the world a colored man, and on this account, defendant placed me on a lower level than he is."' Reference was also made in the Black press, on 16 February 1924, to the views of the Black community on the necessity of bringing the case: 'In a recent article in our paper we stated that the colored people of London stood solidly behind Mr. Franklin. On the whole we did stand behind him but a few there were who doubted the wisdom of his procedure, believing, as they expressed it, that his case would cause ill feeling between the races. [… N]othing in respect is ever gained by cringing or by showing that we believe ourselves to be less than men. Nothing will ever be gained by submitting to treatment which is less than that due to any British subject.' The financial cost of bringing such an action was acknowledged by the *Dawn of Tomorrow*, which made an express appeal to readers to contribute money to assist Mr Franklin in defraying the costs of the case, since 'the monetary damages awarded him by the courts is far below the actual cost to him.'

78 *Rogers* v *Clarence Hotel et al.*, [1940] 2 W.W.R. 545, (1940), 55 B.C.R. 214 (B.C.C.A.).

79 *Christie and Another* v *York Corporation* (1937), 75 Que. C.S. 136 (Que. Superior Court); rev'd *York Corporation* v *Christie* (1938), 65 Que. B.R. 104 (Que. K.B.); leave to appeal granted *Fred. Christie* v *The York Corporation*, [1939] 80 S.C.R. 50 (S.C.C.); upheld *Fred Christie* v *The York Corporation*, [1940] 81 S.C.R. 139 (S.C.C.). For a more detailed account of this case, see *

80 *Loew's Montreal Theatres Ltd.* v *Reynolds* (1919), 30 Que. K.B. 459 (Quebec King's Bench), at 462–3.

81 *Rogers* v *Clarence Hotel et al.*, [1940] 2 W.W.R. 545, (1940), 55 B.C.R. 214 (B.C.C.A.); ABC GR1570, British Columbia Supreme Court (Vancouver), Judgments, 1893–1947 [B6321] v.39, p. 257; GR1727, British Columbia Bench books, v.368, pp.319–25; 'Court Rules Beer Parlor Must Serve Colored Patron,' Vancouver *Province*, 23 February 1940, p. 11; 'Owner's Right: May Refuse to Serve Beer,' 22 February 1940, Vancouver *Province*, p. 2; 'Negro Suing Proprietor of Beer Parlor,' Vancouver *Sun*, 22 February 1940, p. 1; 'Negro Wins Right to Use Beer Parlor,' Vancouver *Sun*, 23 February 1940, p. 17. For a more detailed account of the case, see *

82 *York Corporation* v *Christie* (1938), 65 Que. B.R. 104 (Que. K.B.), at 125–39.

83 *Fred Christie* v *The York Corporation*, [1940] S.C.R. 139 (S.C.C.), at 147, 152.
84 *Fred Christie* v *The York Corporation*, [1940] S.C.R. 139 (S.C.C.), at 152. On the significance of the many dissenting judges, see Frank R. Scott *Essays on the Constitution* (Toronto: University of Toronto Press, 1977), at 333.
85 Bora Laskin, 'Tavern Refusing to Serve Negro – Discrimination,' *Canadian Bar Review*, vol. 18 (1940), 314 at 316. See also Frank R. Scott, *The Canadian Constitution and Human Rights* (Toronto: Canadian Broadcasting Company, 1959), at 37.
86 None of the later cases mentioned *Barnswell* v *National Amusement Co.* The reluctance of Canadian judges to discuss matters of race explicitly may have had something to do with this. County Court Judge Lampman's trial decision in *Barnswell* was the only portion of the judgment that mentioned the plaintiff's race. In the report of the decision in the *Western Law Reporter*, Lampman's trial decision is not included, even in summary form. Since the appeal rulings make no express mention of race, a legal researcher would have been hard-pressed to conclude that the case was an anti-discrimination precedent. The report in the *British Columbia Reports*, however, does make the issue of race explicit. *Johnson* v *Sparrow* was mentioned briefly, in *Loew's Montreal Theatres Ltd.* v *Reynolds*, which distinguished it on two rather peculiar grounds: that the plaintiff in *Johnson* had already purchased a ticket prior to the refusal of entry while the plaintiff in *Reynolds* had not, and that the plaintiff in *Johnson* had been unaware of the colour bar, whereas the plaintiff in *Reynolds* was deliberately challenging the policy. Although the Quebec Court of King's Bench in *Christie* v *York Corporation* also cited *Johnson* v *Sparrow*, the Supreme Court ruling made no mention of the decision, nor did the other cases discussed above. The curious erasure of the earlier anti-discrimination rulings is underscored by the comments of Judge Lennox in *Franklin* v *Evans*, who noted that counsel for the Black plaintiff, Mr Buchner, 'could find no decided case in support of his contention.' A scholarly article written years later, Ian A. Hunter, 'Civil Actions for Discrimination,' *Canadian Bar Review*, vol. 55 (1977), 106, also fails to mention the *Johnson* v *Sparrow* case or the *Barnswell* v *National Amusement Co.* case, although the author discusses the others in detail. See also D.A. Schmeiser, *Civil Liberties in Canada* (London: Oxford University Press, 1964), at 262–74, who erroneously refers to *Loew's Montreal Theatres* as 'the earliest reported Canadian case in this area,' ignores *Johnson* v *Sparrow* and *Barnswell* v *National Amusement Co.*, and then concludes: 'The foregoing cases clearly indicate that the common law is particularly barren of remedies guaranteeing equality of treatment in public places or enterprises ...'
87 *Johnson* v *Sparrow* (1899), 15 Que. S.C. 104 (Superior Court), at 107.

88 On the history of slavery under the French regime, see *

89 For reference to the clause in the 1763 Treaty of Paris, see *

90 For the 1790 English provision, see *

91 For details of the 1762 legislative provision, see *

92 For details of the 1781 legislative provision, which was repealed in 1825, see *

93 For details of the 1793 provisions and their re-enactment through 1897, see *

94 For details of the judicial cases, see *

95 For details of the 1833 English provision, see *

96 On the tenacity of slavery in Canada, see *

97 For details of the 1842 decision to permit the extradition of Nelson Hackett and the 1860–1 extradition of John Anderson, see *

98 *Re Drummond Wren*, [1945] O.R. 778 (Ont. Supreme Court), at 780–3, and quoting 7 Halsbury, 2d ed. 1932, at 153–4. See also *Essex Real Estate* v *Holmes* (1930), 37 O.W.N. 392 (Ont. High Court), in which the court took a narrow interpretation of the following restrictive covenant: 'that the lands shall not be sold to or occupied by persons not of the Caucasian race nor to Europeans except such as are of English-speaking countries and the French and the people of French descent,' holding that a Syrian was not excluded by such a clause. See also *Re Bryers & Morris* (1931), 40 O.W.N. 572 (Ont. High Court). One year after the *Desmond* litigation, another set of white, Gentile judges would disagree with Judge Mackay's ruling. In *Re Noble and Wolf*, [1948] 4 D.L.R. 123, O.W.N. 546 (Ont. High Court), affirmed [1949] O.R. 503, O.W.N. 484, 4 D.L.R. 375 (Ont. C.A.), they explicitly upheld a restrictive covenant prohibiting the sale or lease of a summer resort property to 'any person of the Jewish, Hebrew, Semitic, Negro or coloured race or blood.' Fearful of 'inventing new heads of public policy' that would impede 'freedom of association,' the judges espoused racial exclusivity as an obvious social right. Ontario Court of Appeal Chief justice Robert Spelman Robertson wrote: 'It is common knowledge that, in the life usually led at such places, there is much intermingling, in an informal and social way, of the residents and their guests, especially at the beach. That the summer colony should be congenial is of the essence of a pleasant holiday in such circumstances. The purpose of [the restrictive covenant] here in question is obviously to assure, in some degree, that the residents are of a class who will get along well together. To magnify this innocent and modest effort to establish and maintain a place suitable for a pleasant summer residence into an enterprise that offends against some public policy, requires a stronger imagination than I possess. […] There is nothing criminal or immoral involved; the public interest is in no way concerned. These people have simply agreed

among themselves upon a matter of their own personal concern that affects property of their own in which no one else has an interest.' This ruling was later overturned, *Annie Maud Noble and Bernard Wolf* v *W.A. Alley et al.*, [1951] 92 S.C.R. 64, 1 D.L.R. 321 (S.C.C.). The Supreme Court justices made no explicit comment on the public policy reasoning of the earlier decisions. Instead they held the covenant void for uncertainty: 'it is impossible to set such limits to the lines of race or blood as would enable a court to say in all cases whether a proposed purchaser is or is not within the ban.' See also *Re McDougall and Waddell*, [1945] O.W.N. 272 (Ont. High Court), where the court considered a restrictive covenant that prohibited the sale or occupation of lands 'by any person or persons other than Gentiles (non-semetic [*sic*]) of European or British or Irish or Scottish racial origin.' The court held that such provisions did not violate the newly enacted Ontario Racial Discrimination Act, and that there were no legal restrictions to affect their implementation. For the first legislation to ban racially restrictive covenants on land, see *An Act to amend The Conveyancing and Law of Property Act*, S.O. 1950, c.11; *An Act to amend The Law of Property Act*, S.M. 1950, c.33. These statutes are discussed in more detail in chapter 6.

99 The debate on the motion, which failed to lead to the incorporation of a Bill of Rights in the British North America Act is recorded in *Hansard Parliamentary Debates* 10 October 1945, at 900.

100 See *Viola Irene Desmond* v *Henry L. McNeil and Roseland Theatre Co. Ltd.*, PANS RG39 'C' Halifax, v.936-37, Supreme Court of Nova Scotia, no. 13299, filed 14 November 1946. On 12 December 1946, Bissett filed a notice of discontinuance against the Roseland Theatre Company Ltd, along with a writ alleging the same claim against the parent corporation: *Viola Irene Desmond* v *Odeon Theatres of Canada Ltd. and Garson Theatres Ltd.*, PANS RG39 'C' Halifax v.936-37, Supreme Court of Nova Scotia, no. 13334. For details concerning the law of 'assault,' 'battery,' 'false imprisonment,' 'malicious prosecution,' and the tort of 'abuse of process,' see * Under the latter cause of action, Bissett could have argued that MacNeil invoked summary criminal prosecution under The Theatres Act, a process not unlawful in itself, for the collateral and improper motive of enforcing racial segregation. The conviction would have become irrelevant, with the sole focus being whether racial segregation constituted an 'unjustifiable' ulterior motive for the theatre manager's acts, which necessitated harm to others.

101 For details of the common law defence, see *

102 'Recognizance for Certiorari,' 24 December 1946; 'Notice of Motion,' 27 December 1946; and 'Affidavit of Viola Irene Desmond,' PANS. The notice

was served upon Rod G. MacKay and Harry MacNeil on 30 December 1946. Litigants were required to put up financial sureties before filing actions for judicial review.

103 For information on the availability of *certiorari* applications, see *

104 There is no published report of the case brought before Judge Archibald, and the press coverage contains no further details: see 'Supreme Court Ruling Sought,' Halifax *Herald*, 10 January 1947, p. 18. The 'Notice of Motion' lists three grounds, although the vagueness of the claims permits little analysis: 1. That there is no evidence to support the aforesaid conviction. 2. That there is evidence to show that the aforesaid Viola Irene Desmond did not commit the offence hereinbefore recited. 3. That the information or evidence did not disclose any offence to have been committed within the jurisdiction of the convicting Magistrate. The report of the appeal of Judge Archibald's ruling, *The King* v *Desmond* (1947), 20 M.P.R. 297, at 298 and 300 (N.S.S.C.), suggests that Bissett also tried at first instance to make a technical argument that the prosecution failed to allege the location where the offence took place. Apparently he abandoned this claim when the original information, stipulating that the acts occurred 'in the Town of New Glasgow,' was located.

105 'Decision of Archibald, J.,' 20 January 1947, PANS; *The King* v *Desmond* (1947), 20 M.P.R. 297 (N.S.S.C.), at 298–9. Judge Archibald was born in Manganese Mines, Colchester County, to John H. Archibald and Mary Alice (Clifford) Archibald. He was educated at public schools in Truro and received his LLB from Dalhousie in 1915. A Liberal in politics and United Church by religion, Judge Archibald lectured in Criminal and Statute Law at Dalhousie in the mid-1920s. He was appointed to the Supreme Court in 1937, and in 1948 he was appointed to the Exchequer Court of Canada, a post he held until his death in 1953. See 'Archibald, The Hon. Maynard Brown,' *Who's Who in Canada, 1945–46* (Toronto: International Press, 1946), at 1042; *Who's Who in Canada, 1951–52*, at 612; *Maritime Reference Book*, at 23–4; *Annals – North British Society: 1950–1968* (Kentville, N.S.: Kentville Publishing, 1969), at 58–9; and obituary, 'Prominent Jurist Held Many Important Posts,' Halifax *Chronicle-Herald*, 10 July 1953, pp. 1, 6.

106 'Decision of Archibald, J.,' PANS, at p. 2; *The King* v *Desmond*, at 299.

107 For earlier Nova Scotia decisions see, for example, *The Queen* v *Walsh* (1897), 29 N.S.R. 521 (N.S.S.C.), at 527. See also *The Nova Scotia Summary Convictions Act*, S.N.S. 1940, c.3, s.58.

108 S.N.S. 1940, c.3, s.59, 60, 62, 66, as amended S.N.S. 1945, c.65.

109 'Notice of Appeal,' 20 January 1947, and 'Entry of Appeal,' 21 February 1947, PANS. See also 'Reserve Appeal Decision in Desmond Case,' Halifax

Herald, 14 March 1947, p. 18. For details of the appellant's and respondent's arguments, see *The King* v *Desmond* (1947), 20 M.P.R. 297 (N.S.S.C.), at 299–301.

110 Some cite the couple's disagreement over the case as the main source of the marital breakdown: Hudson, 'Interview with Pearleen Oliver.' Others suggest that there were long-standing, additional strains within the marriage caused by Jack Desmond's drinking and his distrust of Viola's ambitious business prospects: Woods, 'Interview with Gannon-Dixon'; Backhouse, 'Interview with Wanda Robson.'

111 'Clarion Went A-Visiting!' New Glasgow, N.S., *The Clarion* 2:5 (15 March 1947), p. 2.

112 *The King* v *Desmond* (1947), 20 M.P.R. 297 (N.S.S.C.), at 307. Other reports of the case appear as (1947), 89 C.C.C. 278, 4 C.R. 200, [1947] 4 D.L.R. 81. For biographical details on Doull, who was born in New Glasgow on 1 November 1878, see Halifax *Chronicle-Herald,* 1 October 1960, p. 32; *Who's Who in Canada, 1945–46,* at 474.

113 Doull's comment is found at 309. Doull served as mayor of New Glasgow in 1925. Judge Robert Henry Graham noted at 304 that Bissett had argued a denial of natural justice, relying on *R.* v *Wandsworth,* [1942] 1 All E.R. 56, in which the court overturned the conviction of a defendant who had been denied the opportunity to defend himself. Judge Graham, however, made no reference to Viola Desmond's detailed affidavit alleging similar treatment and refused to find a denial of natural justice in the present case.

114 The son of a New Glasgow lawyer and politician Hon. Col. Edward Mortimer Macdonald, PC, Macdonald, Jr, was born in Pictou, called to the bar of Quebec in 1924, and the Nova Scotia bar in 1929. He practised with the law firm of Macdonald & MacQuarrie, with offices in Pictou and New Glasgow. He was a Liberal and a Presbyterian. See *Maritime Reference Book,* at 11; 'Macdonald, E.M.: Death: Town Solicitor for New Glasgow Dies,' PANS MG1, v.2022 no. 20; Charles G.D. Roberts and Arthur J. Tunnell, *The Canadian Who's Who,* vol. 2 (1936–7) (Toronto: Murray Printing, 1936), at 660.

115 J.B. Milner, 'Case and Comment,' *Canadian Bar Review,* vol. 25 (1947), 915 at 915–22. Interestingly, Milner did not believe that the trial decision to convict Viola Desmond was incorrect, describing it at 919 as 'technically perfect.' For biographical details about Milner and further details concerning his article, see *

116 For Judge Graham's ruling, see *The King* v *Desmond* (1947), 20 M.P.R.297 (N.S.S.C.), at 305, quoting in part Viscount Caldicott in *Rex* v *Nat Bell Liquors Limited,* [1922] 2 A.C. 128 (H.L.), at 151. For biographical details on

Judge Graham, who was born in New Glasgow on 30 November 1871, the son of John George Graham and Jane (Marshall) Graham, see obituary, 'Mr. Justice Graham Dies at Age 85,' Halifax *Mail-Star*, 28 May 1956, pp. 1, 6; *Who's Who in Canada, 1945–46*, at 466; *The Canadian Who's Who*, vol. 4 (Toronto: Trans-Canada Press, 1948), at 380; *Catalogue of Portraits of the Judges of the Supreme Court of Nova Scotia and other Portraits* (Halifax: Law Courts, n.d.), PANS F93C28, at 110. Graham received a BA and LLB from Dalhousie, was called to the Nova Scotia bar in 1894, and named a KC in 1913. He served as town councillor in New Glasgow in 1898, mayor from 1899 to 1900, and represented Pictou County as a Liberal in the House of Assembly between 1916 and 1925. He served as stipendiary magistrate from 1906 to 1910, and was appointed puisne judge of the Supreme Court in 1925.

117 *The King* v *Desmond* (1947), 20 M.P.R. 297 (N.S.S.C.), at 305–7. Unlike Doull and Graham, Judge Carroll was not born in New Glasgow, but in Margaret Forks, Nova Scotia, on 11 June 1877. Educated at St Francis Xavier College in Antigonish and at Dalhousie University, he was called to the bar of Nova Scotia in 1905, serving several terms as a Liberal MP. For biographical details, see obituary, Halifax *Chronicle-Herald*, 26 August 1964, p. 16; *Who's Who in Canada, 1945–46*, at 666. The decision on file at the archives, 'Decision of Hall, J.,' PANS, shows that the original typed version reads: 'Had the matter reached the Court by some method other than *certiorari*, there might have been opportunity to right the wrong done this unfortunate woman, *convicted on insufficient evidence*' (emphasis added). The latter phrase was crossed out by pen, initialled by Judge Hall, and did not appear in the reported version of the decision. Judge Hall was born in Melvern Square, Annapolis County, in 1876 to Rev. William E. and Margaret (Barss) Hall. He was educated at Acadia and Dalhousie University and admitted to the bar in 1900. He practised law in Liverpool, N.S., from 1902 to 1918, and then became Halifax Crown Prosecutor. Active in the Conservative party, he was elected to the provincial legislature and served as attorney general in 1926. He was also an active worker for welfare organizations in Halifax. Judge Hall was appointed to the Nova Scotia Supreme Court in 1931. For biographical details see *Prominent People of the Maritime Provinces* (St. John: McMillan, 1922), at 77–8; obituary, 'Veteran Jurist Dies at 81,' Halifax *Mail-Star*, 27 May 1958, p. 3; PANS Biographical Card File, MG9, v.41, p. 262; *Who's Who in Canada, 1945–46*, at 1494–5.

118 Backhouse, 'Interview with Wanda Robson.' Similar reactions were expressed by Ida B. Wells, the famous African-American campaigner against

lynching, after she lost a lawsuit in Memphis, Tennessee, in the late nine-teenth century, when she was denied accommodation in the 'ladies' only' (white) railway carriage. Ida B. Wells's diary entry reads: 'I felt so disap-pointed because I had hoped such great things for my people generally. I have firmly believed all along that the law was on our side and would, when we appealed to it, give us justice. I feel shorn of that belief and utterly discouraged, and just now, if it were possible, would gather my race in my arms and fly away with them': Alfreda M. Duster, ed., *Crusade for Justice: An Autobiography of Ida B. Wells* (Chicago: University of Chicago Press, 1970), at p. xvii.

119 Milner, 'Case and Comment,' at 915–16, 922.

120 'The Desmond Case,' Truro, N.S., *The Clarion* 2:15 (April 1947), p. 2, and 'Dismisses Desmond Application,' Truro, N.S., *The Clarion* 2:15 (April 1947), p. 4.

121 'The Desmond Case,' Truro, N.S., *The Clarion* 2:15 (April 1947), p. 2. *The Clarion* would later reprint a 15 July 1947 (p. 1) editorial from *Maclean's* magazine, in which the *Desmond* case is described and critiqued: 'In a free country one man is as good as another – any well-behaved person may enter any public place. In Nova Scotia a Negro woman tried to sit in the downstairs section of a theatre instead of the Jim Crow gallery. Not only was she ejected by force, but thereafter she, not the theatre owner, was charged and convicted of a misdemeanour. Most Canadians have been doing a fair amount of grumbling lately about the state of our fundamental freedoms. Maybe it's time we did more than grumble.' See 'Is This a Free Country?' Truro, N.S., *The Clarion* 2:12 (15 August 1947), p. 2.

122 On the allegations that Viola Desmond might have been trying to 'pass,' see Backhouse, 'Interview with Wanda Robson.' For Johnston's comments see 'N.S. Negroes Libelled by Attack,' Truro, N.S., *The Clarion* 3:8 (13 October 1948), p. 1.

123 'Toronto Leads the Way,' Truro, N.S., *The Clarion* 2:12 (15 August 1947), p. 2. The same paper reports that the City of Toronto Board of Police Com-missioners passed a regulation (inserted in a city by-law governing the licensing of public places) providing a penalty of licence cancellation for any hall, rink, theatre, or other place of amusement in the city which refused to admit anyone because of race, colour, or creed. See 'Toronto Law Against Discrimination' and 'Toronto Leads the Way,' Truro, N.S., *The Clarion* 2:12 (15 August 1947), pp. 1–2.

124 'No Discrimination,' Truro, N.S. *The Clarion* 2:12 (15 August 1947), p. 2. *Saturday Night* also draws a comparison with the United States, on 7 December 1946, p. 5: 'Racial segregation is so deeply entrenched in what

the American people are accustomed to call their way of life that the problems which it raises in a democracy (it raises none in a totalitarian state) will not be solved in the United States without a good deal of conflict. Canada is in a position to avoid most of that conflict if she avoids getting tied into the American way of life in that respect, and now is the time to take action to avoid it.'

125 'American Artists Score Racial Discrimination,' Halifax *Chronicle*, 15 September 1947, PANS Mg15, vol. 16, no. 18; 'More Discrimination,' Truro, N.S., *The Clarion* 2:14 (1 November 1947), p. 2. Selma Burke's female companion was A.F. Wilson, a noted American author of several books on race discrimination. *The Clarion* reports in 2:11 (1 August 1947), pp. 1–2, that a New Glasgow restaurant refused service to a young West Indian student working with the provincial Highways department. The same article notes that a Black couple, Mr and Mrs A.T. Best, was also refused seating in a small fruit store and fountain in New Glasgow.

126 Esmerelda Thornhill, 'So Often Against Us: So Seldom for Us, Being Black and Living with the Canadian Justice System,' Plenary Presentation to the IXth Biennial Conference of the Congress of Black Women of Canada, Halifax, 1989, at 3 (copy on file with the author).

127 'New Glasgow,' Truro, N.S., *The Clarion* 3:6 (8 September 1948), p. 3. For further discussion of the KKK, see chapter 6.

128 Backhouse, 'Interview with Wanda Robson.'

129 Backhouse, 'Interview with Wanda Robson'; Backhouse, 'Interview with Mrs. S.A. (Emily) Clyke'; Obituaries in the Halifax *Chronicle-Herald*, 10 Feb. 1965, p. 26, and Halifax *Mail Star*, 10 February 1965, p. 8.

130 Robertson, 'Interview with Pearleen Oliver.' Paula Denice McClain, *Alienation and Resistance: The Political Behavior of Afro-Canadians* (Palo Alto: R. & E. Research Associates, 1979), notes at 59 that the NSAACP was responsible for integrating barbershops in Halifax and Dartmouth, sponsoring the first Blacks for employment in Halifax and Dartmouth stores, integrating the nurses' training and placement programs, persuading insurance companies to sell Blacks policies other than industrial insurance, and initiating a controversy that resulted in the Dartmouth school board hiring Blacks.

131 Thomson, *Born with a Call*, at 84.

Bibliography

A. BOOKS

Adams, Howard. *Prison of Grass: Canada from a Native Point of View.* Saskatoon: Fifth House, 1989, orig. pub. 1975.

Addison, C.G. *A Treatise on the Law of Torts.* Edited by H.G. Wood, vol. 2. Jersey City, N.J.: Frederick D. Linn, 1881.

Agnew, Vijay. *Resisting Discrimination: Women from Asia, Africa, and the Caribbean and the Women's Movement in Canada.* Toronto: University of Toronto Press, 1996.

Ahenakew, Edward. *Voices of the Plains Cree.* Edited by Ruth M. Buck. Regina: Canadian Plains Research Center, University of Regina, 1995.

Ahern, Frances Robin. *Oakville: A Small Town, 1900–1930.* Erin, Ont.: Boston Mills Press, 1981.

Alexander, Ken, and Avis Glaze. *Towards Freedom: The African-Canadian Experience.* Toronto: Umbrella Press, 1996.

Allen, Theodore W. *The Invention of the White Race.* London: Verso, 1994.

Almaguer, Tomas. *Racial Fault Lines: The Historical Origins of White Supremacy in California.* Berkeley: University of California Press, 1994.

Anderson, Gary Clayton, and Alan R. Woolworth. *Through Dakota Eyes: Narrative Accounts of the Minnesota Indian War of 1862.* St Paul: Minnesota Historical Society Press, 1988.

Anderson, Karen. *Chain Her by One Foot: The Subjugation of Women in Seventeenth-Century New France.* London: Routledge, 1991.

Anderson, Kay J. *Vancouver's Chinatown: Racial Discourse in Canada, 1875–1980.* Montreal and Kingston: McGill-Queen's University Press, 1991.

Andracki, Stanislaw. *Immigration of Orientals into Canada, with Special Reference to Chinese.* New York: Arno Press, 1978.

Archer, John H. *Saskatchewan: A History.* Saskatoon: Western Producer Prairie Books, 1980.

Ashworth, William. *The Late, Great Lakes: An Environmental History.* New York: Knopf, 1986.

Assembly of First Nations. *Breaking the Silence, An Interpretive Study of Residential School Impact and Healing as Illustrated by the Stories of First Nations Individuals.* Ottawa: First Nations Health Commission, 1994.

Augstein, Hanna Franziska, ed. *Race: The Origins of an Idea, 1760–1850.* Bristol: Thoemmes Press, 1996.

Avery, Donald. *Dangerous Foreigners: European Immigrant Workers and Labour Radicalism in Canada, 1896–1932.* Toronto: McClelland & Stewart, 1979.

Backhouse, Constance. *Petticoats and Prejudice: Women and Law in Nineteenth-Century Canada.* Toronto: Women's Press and The Osgoode Society, 1991.

Backhouse, Constance, and Leah Cohen. *The Secret Oppression: Sexual Harassment of Working Women.* Toronto: Macmillan of Canada, 1978.

Banner, Lois W. *American Beauty.* New York: Alfred A. Knopf, 1983.

Bannerji, Himani. *Returning the Gaze: Essays on Racism, Feminism and Politics.* Toronto: Sister Vision Press, 1993.

– *Thinking Through: Essays on Feminism, Marxism and Anti-Racism.* Toronto: Women's Press, 1995.

Bannerji, Himani, Linda Carty, Kari Dehli, Susan Heald, and Kate McKenna, eds. *Unsettling Relations: The University as a Site of Feminist Struggles.* Toronto: Women's Press, 1991.

Banton, Michael. *Racial and Ethnic Competition.* Cambridge: Cambridge University Press, 1983.

Barkan, Elazar. *The Retreat of Scientific Racism.* Cambridge: Cambridge University Press, 1992.

Barker, G.F. *Brandon: A City, 1881–1961.* Altona, Man.: D.W. Friesen & Sons, 1977.

Barman, Jean. *The West beyond the West: A History of British Columbia.* Toronto: University of Toronto Press, 1991.

Barman, Jean, Yvonne Hebert, and Don McCaskill. *Indian Education in Canada,* Vol. 1: *The Legacy.* Vancouver: University of British Columbia Press, 1986.

Beaudoin, Gerald A. *The Supreme Court of Canada: Proceedings of the October 1985 Conference.* Cowansville, Que.: Editions Y. Blais, 1986.

Bederman, Gail. *Manliness and Civilization: A Cultural History of Gender and Race in the United States, 1880–1917.* Chicago: University of Chicago Press, 1995.

Bell, Derrick. *And We Are Not Saved: The Elusive Quest for Racial Justice*. New York: Basic Books, 1989.
– *Faces at the Bottom of the Well: The Permanence of Racism*. New York: Basic Books, 1992.
– *Race, Racism and American Law*, 2d ed. Boston: Little, Brown, 1980.
Bennet, Jr., Lerone. *Before the* Mayflower. Baltimore: Penguin, 1966.
Bennett, John W., and Seena B. Kohl. *Settling the Canadian-American West, 1890–1915*. Lincoln: University of Nebraska Press, 1995.
Berkhofer, Robert. *The White Man's Indian: Images of the American Indian from Columbus to the Present*. New York: Knopf, 1978.
Best, Dr Carrie M. *That Lonesome Road: The Autobiography of Carrie M. Best*. New Glasgow, N.S.: Clarion Publishing, 1977.
Betcherman, Lita-Rose. *The Little Band: The Clashes between the Communists and the Canadian Establishment, 1928–1932*. Ottawa: Deneau, 1983.
Bethune, W.C. *Canada's Eastern Arctic: Its History, Resources, Population and Administration*. Ottawa: Department of the Interior, 1934.
Bigelow, Melville Madison. *The Law of Torts*, 7th ed. Boston: Little, Brown, 1901.
Birket-Smith, Kaj. *The Eskimos*. London: Methuen, 1959; orig. pub. 1936; 1st Danish ed. 1927.
Black's Law Dictionary, 6th ed. St Paul, Minn.: West Publishing, 1990.
Blackstone, William. *Commentaries on the Laws of England*, vol. 1. Chicago: University of Chicago Press, 1979; orig. pub. 1765–9.
Blee, Kathleen M. *Women of the Klan: Racism and Gender in the 1920s*. Berkeley: University of California Press, 1991.
Boas, Franz. *The Social Organization and the Secret Societies of the Kwakiutl Indians*. Report of the United States National Museum for 1895. Washington, D.C.: Government Printing Office, 1897.
Bolaria, B. Singh, and Peter S. Li. *Racial Oppression in Canada*, 2d ed. Toronto: Garamond, 1988.
Boyce, Gerald E. *Historic Hastings*. Belleville: Ontario Intelligencer, 1967.
Braithwaite, Rella, and Tessa Benn-Ireland. *Some Black Women: Profiles of Black Women in Canada*. Toronto: Sister Vision, 1993.
Brand, Dionne. *Bread Out of Stone*. Toronto: Coach House Press, 1994.
– *No Burden to Carry: Narratives of Black Working Women in Ontario 1920s to 1950s*. Toronto: Women's Press, 1991.
Brant, Beth (Degonwadonti). *Mohawk Trail*. Toronto: Women's Press, 1985.
Brant, Beth. *I'll Sing 'til the Day I Die: Conversations with Tyendinaga Elders*. Toronto: McGilligan, 1995.
Brennan, J. William, and Ian E. Wilson. *Regina before Yesterday: A Visual History, 1882–1945*. Regina: Centax, 1978.
Bristow, Peggy, Dionne Brand, Linda Carty, Afua A. Cooper, Sylvia Hamilton,

and Adrienne Shadd, eds. *We're Rooted Here and They Can't Pull Us Up: Essays in African-Canadian Women's History*.Toronto: University of Toronto Press, 1994.

Brode, Patrick. *The Odyssey of John Anderson*. Toronto: The Osgoode Society, 1989.

Brown, Jennifer S.H. *Strangers in Blood: Fur Trade Company Families in Indian Country*. Vancouver: University of British Columbia Press, 1980.

Bushnell, Ian. *The Captive Court: A Study of the Supreme Court of Canada*. Montreal: McGill-Queen's University Press, 1992.

Cameron, James M. *About New Glasgow*. New Glasgow, N.S.: Hector Publishing, 1962.

– *More About New Glasgow*. Kentville, N.S.: Kentville Publishing, 1974.

Campbell, Marjorie Freeman. *A Mountain and a City: The Story of Hamilton*. Toronto: McClelland & Stewart, 1966.

Campbell, Robert A. *Demon Rum or Easy Money: Government Control of Liquor in British Columbia from Prohibition to Privatization*. Ottawa: Carleton University Press, 1991.

Camper, Carol, ed. *Miscegenation Blues: Voices of Mixed-Race Women*. Toronto: Sister Vision, 1994.

Canada. Department of Indian Affairs. *Indian Treaties and Surrenders*, vol. 1. Ottawa: Queen's Printer, 1891.

Canadian Publicity Co. *Pioneers and Prominent People of Saskatchewan*. Toronto: Ryerson Press, 1924.

Carley, Kenneth. *The Sioux Uprising of 1862*. St Paul: Minnesota Historical Society, 1976.

Carter, Francis. *The Middlesex Bench and Bar*. London: Middlesex Law Association, 1969.

Carter, Sarah. *Capturing Women: The Manipulation of Cultural Imagery in Canada's Prairie West*. Montreal and Kingston: McGill-Queen's University Press, 1997.

– *Lost Harvests: Prairie Indian Reserve Farmers and Government Policy*. Montreal and Kingston: McGill-Queen's University Press, 1990.

Carter, V., and W.L. Akili. *The Window of Our Memories*, vol. 1. St Albert, Alta.: Black Cultural Research Society of Alberta, 1981.

Cartwright, H., ed. *The Canadian Law List*. Toronto: Imrie and Graham, 1900.

Chalmers, David M. *Hooded Americanism: The History of the Ku Klux Klan*. New York: Franklin Watts, 1965.

Chalmers, John W. *Laird of the West*. Calgary: Detselig, 1981.

Chambers, Major Ernest J., ed. *The Canadian Parliamentary Guide, 1915*. Ottawa: Gazette Printing, 1915.

Chambers, Col. Ernest J., ed. *The Canadian Parliamentary Guide, 1924*. Ottawa: Gazette Printing, 1925.

Chan, Anthony B. *Gold Mountain*. Vancouver: New Star Books, 1983.

Charlesworth, Hector, ed. *A Cyclopaedia of Canadian Biography*. Toronto: Hunter Rose, 1919.

Cheng, Tien-Feng. *Oriental Immigration to Canada*. Shanghai: Commercial Press, 1931.

Chin, Frank, Jeffrey Paul Chan, Lawson Fusao Inada, and Shawn Hsu Wong, eds. *Aiiieeee! An Anthology of Asian-American Writers*. New York: Penguin, 1991.

Chrisjohn, Roland, and Sherri Young, with Michael Maraun. *The Circle Game: Shadows and Substance in the Indian Residential School Experience in Canada*. Penticton, B.C.: Theytus, 1997.

Clark, W. Leland. *Brandon's Politics and Politicians*. Altona, Man.: D.W. Friesen & Sons, 1981.

Clarke, George Elliott, ed. *Fire on the Water: An Anthology of Black Nova Scotian Writing*, 2 vols. Lawrencetown Beach, N.S.: Pottersfield Press, 1991 and 1992.

Clarke, Samuel Robinson. *The Magistrates' Manual*, 3d ed. Toronto: Carswell, 1893.

– *A Treatise on Criminal Law as Applicable to the Dominion of Canada*. Toronto: Carswell, 1872.

Clutesi, George. *Potlatch*. Sidney, B.C.: Gray's Publishing, 1969.

Coates, Ken, and Fred McGuinness. *Pride of the Land: An Affectionate History of Brandon's Agricultural Exhibitions*. Winnipeg, Peguis Publishers, 1985.

Codere, Helen. *Fighting with Property: A Study of Kwakiutl Potlatching and Warfare, 1792–1930*. New York: J.J. Augustus, 1950.

Cole, Douglas, and Ira Chaikin. *An Iron Hand upon the People: The Law against the Potlatch on the Northwest Coast*. Vancouver: Douglas & McIntyre, 1990.

Collins, Patricia Hill. *Black Feminist Thought*. Boston: Unwin Hyman, 1990.

Cork, Ella. *The Worst of the Bargain*. San Jacinto, Calif.: Foundation for Social Research, 1962.

Côté, Pierre-André. *The Interpretation of Legislation in Canada*, 2d ed. Cowansville, Que.: Yvon Blais, 1991.

Craies, William Feilden. *A Treatise on Statute Law*, 3d ed. Toronto: Carswell, 1923.

Craig, Terrence. *Racial Attitudes in English-Canadian Fiction, 1950–1980*. Waterloo: Wilfrid Laurier University Press, 1987.

Crankshaw, James. *A Practical Guide to Police Magistrates and Justices of the Peace*. Montreal: Theoret, 1905.

Cravens, Hamilton. *The Triumph of Evolution, American Scientist and the Heredity–Environment Controversy, 1900–1941*. Philadelphia: University of Pennsylvania Press, 1978.

Crowe, Keith J. *A History of the Original Peoples of Northern Canada*. Montreal and Kingston: McGill-Queen's University Press, 1974.

Cumming, Peter, and Neil H. Mickenberg. *Native Rights in Canada*, 2d ed. Toronto: The Indian–Eskimo Association of Canada, 1972.

Curtis, Liz. *Nothing But the Same Old Story: The Roots of Anti-Irish Racism*. London: Information on Ireland, 1984.

Davis, Angela Y. *Women, Race and Class*. New York: Random House, 1981.

Davis, F. James. *Who Is Black? One Nation's Definition*. University Park: Pennsylvania State University Press, 1991.

Davis, Lenwood G., and Janet L. Sims-Wood. *The Ku Klux Klan: A Bibliography*. Westport, Conn.: Greenwood Press, 1984.

Degler, Carl N. *In Search of Human Nature: The Decline and Revival of Darwinism in American Social Thought*. New York: Oxford University Press, 1991.

Delgado, Richard, ed. *Critical Race Theory: The Cutting Edge*. Philadelphia: Temple University Press, 1995.

DeMallie, Raymond J., and Douglas R. Parks. *Sioux Indian Religion: Tradition and Innovation*. Norman: University of Oklahoma Press, 1987.

Dennis, Matthew. *Cultivating a Landscape of Peace: Iroquois–European Encounters in Seventeenth-Century America*. Ithaca, N.Y.: Cornell University Press, 1993.

Dickason, Olive Patricia. *Canada's First Nations*. Toronto: McClelland & Stewart, 1992.

– *The Myth of the Savage and the Beginnings of French Colonialism in the Americas*. Edmonton: University of Alberta Press, 1984.

Diubaldo, Richard. *The Government of Canada and the Inuit: 1900–1967*. Ottawa: Research Branch, Corporate Policy, Indian and Northern Affairs Canada, 1985.

Dorais, Louis-Jacques. *Quaqtaq: Modernity and Identity in an Inuit Community*. Toronto: University of Toronto Press, 1997.

Doyle, Arthur T. *Front Benches and Back Rooms: A Story of Corruption, Muckraking, Raw Partisanship and Intrigue in New Brunswick*. Toronto: Green Tree Publishing, 1976.

Driedger, E.A. *The Construction of Statutes*. Toronto: Butterworths, 1974.

Drinnon, Richard. *Facing West: The Metaphysics of Indian-Hating and Empire-Building*. Minneapolis: University of Minnesota Press, 1980.

Drucker, Philip, and Robert F. Heizer. *To Make My Name Good: A Re-examination of the Southern Kwakiutl Potlatch*. Berkeley: University of California Press, 1967.

Dubinsky, Karen. *Improper Advances: Rape and Heterosexual Conflict in Ontario, 1880–1929*. Chicago: University of Chicago Press, 1993.

Durant, H.E. *National Reference Book on Canadian Business Personalities*, 10th ed. Montreal: Canadian Newspaper Service, 1954.

Duster, Alfreda M., ed. *Crusade for Justice: The Autobiography of Ida B. Wells*. Chicago: University of Chicago Press, 1970.

Dyer, Thomas G. *Theodore Roosevelt and the Idea of Race*. Baton Rouge: Louisiana State University Press, 1980.

Eber, Dorothy Harley. *Images of Justice*. Montreal and Kingston: McGill-Queen's University Press, 1997.

Eisendrath, Maurice N. *The Never Failing Stream*. Toronto: Macmillan, 1939.

Elias, Peter Douglas. *The Dakota of the Canadian Northwest: Lessons for Survival*. Winnipeg: University of Manitoba Press, 1988.

Emmerson, George S. *Scottish Country Dancing: An Evolutionary Triumph*. Oakville: Galt, 1997.

Falassi, Alessandro, ed. *Time Out of Time: Essays on the Festival*. Albuquerque: University of New Mexico Press, 1987.

Ferguson, Ted. *A White Man's Country: An Exercise in Canadian Prejudice*. Toronto: Doubleday Canada, 1975.

Fidler, Chief Thomas, and James R. Stevens. *Killing the Shaman*. Moonbeam: Penumbra Press, 1985.

Fine Day. *My Cree People*. Invermere, B.C., Good Medicines Books, 1973.

Fisher, Robin. *Contact and Conflict: Indian–European Relations in British Columbia, 1774–1890*. Vancouver: University of British Columbia Press, 1977.

Flexner, Stuart Berg. *I Hear America Talking*. London: Van Nostrand Reinhold, 1976.

Forbes, Jack D. *Black Africans and Native Americans: Race, Class and Color in the Evolution of Red-Black Peoples*. Oxford: Basil Blackwell, 1988.

Foster, Cecil. *A Place Called Heaven: The Meaning of Being Black in Canada*. Toronto: HarperCollins, 1996.

Foster, Michael K., Jack Campisi, and Marianne Mithun, eds. *Extending the Rafters: Approaches in Iroquoian Studies*. Albany: State University of New York Press, 1984.

Fournier, Suzanne, and Ernie Crey. *Stolen from Our Embrace: The Abduction of First Nations Children and the Restoration of Aboriginal Communities*. Vancouver: Douglas & McIntyre, 1997.

Fowler, David H. *Northern Attitudes towards Interracial Marriage: Legislation and Public Opinion in the Middle Atlantic and the States of the Old Northwest, 1780–1930*. New York: Garland, 1987.

Frankenberg, Ruth. *White Women, Race Matters: The Social Construction of Whiteness*. Minneapolis: University of Minnesota Press, 1993.

Frederickson, George M. *The Black Image in the White Mind: The Debate on Afro-American Character and Destiny, 1817–1914.* New York: Harper & Row, 1971.

Frideres, James S. *Aboriginal Peoples in Canada: Contemporary Conflicts,* 5th ed. Scarborough: Prentice-Hall, 1998.

Friesen, Gerald. *The Canadian Prairies: A History.* Toronto: University of Toronto Press, 1987.

Frost, Stanley. *The Challenge of the Klan.* New York: Negro Universities Press, 1924.

Fryer, Peter. *Black People in the British Empire: An Introduction.* London: Pluto Press, 1988.

Gates, L.F. *Land Policies of Upper Canada.* Toronto: University of Toronto Press, 1968.

Giddings, Paula. *When and Where I Enter: The Impact of Black Women on Race and Sex in America.* New York: William Morrow, 1984.

Gilman, Sander. *Difference and Pathology: Stereotypes of Sexuality, Race and Madness.* Ithaca, N.Y.: Cornell University Press, 1985.

– *Sexuality: An Illustrated History.* New York: John Wiley, 1989.

Gisborne, F.H., and A.A. Fraser. *Correspondence, Reports of the Minister of Justice and Orders in Council: Upon the Subject of Provincial Legislation, 1896–1920,* vol. 2. Ottawa: F.A. Acland, 1922.

Goldberg, David Theo. *Racial Subjects: Writing on Race in America.* New York: Routledge, 1997.

Gossett, Thomas F. *Race: The History of an Idea in America.* Dallas: Southern Methodist University Press, 1963.

Gould, Stephen Jay. *The Flamingo's Smile: Reflections in Natural History.* New York: Norton, 1985.

Grant, Agnes. *No End of Grief: Indian Residential Schools in Canada.* Winnipeg: Pemmican Publications, 1996.

Gray, James. *Roar of the Twenties.* Toronto: Macmillan, 1975.

Graymont, Barbara. *The Iroquois in the American Revolution.* Syracuse, N.Y.: Syracuse University Press, 1972.

– ed. *Fighting Tuscarora: The Autobiography of Chief Clinton Rickard.* Syracuse, N.Y.: Syracuse University Press, 1973.

Greaves, Ida. *The Negro in Canada.* Orillia, Ont.: Packet-Times Press, 1930.

Green, Rayna. *Women in American Indian Society.* New York: Chelsea House, 1992.

Greenberg, Jack. *Race Relations and American Law.* New York: Columbia University Press, 1959.

Griffiths, N.E.S. *The Splendid Vision: Centennial History of the National Council of Women of Canada, 1893–1993.* Ottawa: Carleton University Press, 1993.

Griswold United Church Women. *Bridging the Years, 1867–1967, Griswold Centennial Booklet.* n.p.: Souris Plaindealer, n.d.

Grizzle, Stanley G. *My Name's Not George: The Story of the Brotherhood of Sleeping Car Porters in Canada.* Toronto: Umbrella, 1998.

Gronewold, Sue. *Beautiful Merchandise: Prostitution in China, 1860–1936.* New York: Haworth, 1982.

Guillaumin, Collette. *Racism, Sexism, Power and Ideology.* London: Routledge, 1995.

Guy-Sheftall, Beverly. *Daughters of Sorrow: Attitudes toward Black Women, 1880–1920.* Brooklyn, N.Y.: Carlson Publishing, 1990.

Haddon, Alfred C. *The Study of Man.* London: Bliss Sands, 1989.

Haig-Brown, Celia. *Resistance and Renewal: Surviving the Indian Residential School.* Vancouver: Tillacum, 1988.

Hall, D.J. *Clifford Sifton: A Lonely Eminence, 1901–1929,* 2 vols. Vancouver: University of British Columbia Press, 1981 and 1985.

Haller, Jr, John S. *Outcasts from Evolution: Scientific Attitudes of Racial Inferiority, 1859–1900.* Urbana: University of Illinois Press, 1971.

Hannaford, Ivan. *Race: The History of an Idea in the West.* Baltimore, Md.: Johns Hopkins University Press, 1996.

Harding, Sandra, ed. *The 'Racial' Economy of Science.* Bloomington: Indiana University Press, 1993.

Harper, Fowler Vincent. *A Treatise on the Law of Torts.* Indianapolis: Bobbs-Merrill, 1938.

Harring, Sidney L. *Crow Dog's Case: American Indian Sovereignty, Tribal Law, and United States Law in the Nineteenth Century.* New York: Cambridge University Press, 1994.

– *White Man's Law: Native People in Nineteenth-Century Canadian Jurisprudence.* Toronto: The Osgoode Society and University of Toronto Press, 1998.

Hawkes, John. *The Story of Saskatchewan and Its People,* vol. 3. Chicago and Regina: S.J. Clarke, 1924.

Hawkins, Freda. *Canada and Immigration: Public Policy and Public Concern,* 2d ed. Montreal and Kingston: McGill-Queen's University Press, 1988.

Helly, Denise. *Les Chinois de Montréal, 1877–1951.* Quebec: Institut québécois de recherche sur la culture, 1987.

Henry, Frances, et al. *The Colour of Democracy: Racism in Canadian Society.* Toronto: Harcourt Brace, 1994.

Higginbotham, Evelyn Brooks. *Righteous Discontent: The Women's Movement in the Black Baptist Church, 1880–1920.* Cambridge, Mass.: Harvard University Press, 1993.

Hill, Daniel G. *The Freedom-Seekers: Blacks in Early Canada.* Agincourt, Ont.: Book Society of Canada, 1981.

Hill, Lawrence. *Women of Vision: The Story of the Canadian Negro Women's Association, 1951–1976*. Toronto: Umbrella Press, 1996.

Hohn, Marek. *Dope Girls: The Birth of the British Drug Underground*. London: Lawrence & Wishart, 1992.

hooks, bell. *Ain't I A Woman: Black Women and Feminism*. Boston: South End Press, 1981.

– *Black Looks: Race and Representation*. Toronto: Between the Lines, 1992.

– *Feminist Theory: From Margin to Center*. Boston: South End Press, 1984.

– *Teaching to Transgress: Education as the Practice of Freedom*. New York: Routledge, 1994.

– *Yearning: Race, Gender and Cultural Politics*. Toronto: Between the Lines, 1990.

Hornby, Jim. *Black Islanders: Prince Edward Island's Historical Black Community*. Charlottetown: Institute of Island Studies, 1991.

Horsman, Reginald. *Race and Manifest Destiny: The Origins of American Racial Anglo-Saxonism*. Cambridge, Mass.: Harvard University Press, 1981.

Howard, James. *The Canadian Sioux*. Lincoln: University of Nebraska Press, 1984.

Howay, F.W. [a judge of the County Court of Westminster, B.C.]. *British Columbia: The Making of a Province*. Toronto: Ryerson Press, 1928.

Hunter, A.T. *Canadian Edition of the Law of Torts by J.F. Clerk and W.H.B. Lindsell*. Toronto: Carswell, 1908.

Ignatiev, Noel. *How the Irish Became White*. New York: Routledge, 1995.

Indian Self-Government in Canada: Report of the Special Committee. House of Commons, Canada, 32nd Parliament, 1st Sess. 1983.

Jaine, Linda, ed. *Residential Schools: The Stolen Years*. Saskatoon: University of Saskatchewan, 1993.

Jenness, Diamond. *The American Aborigines: Their Origin and Antiquity*. Toronto: University of Toronto Press, 1933.

– *Eskimo Administration: II. Canada*. Montreal: Arctic Institute of North America, 1964.

– *Indians of Canada*. Ottawa: National Museum of Canada, 1932; repub. Ministry of Supply & Services Canada, 1977.

Jenness, Eileen. *The Indian Tribes of Canada*. Toronto: Ryerson Press, 1933.

Johnson, E. Pauline. *The Moccasin Maker*. Tucson: University of Arizona Press, 1987; orig. pub. Ryerson Press, 1913.

Johnston, Basil H. *Indian School Days*. Toronto: Key Porter, 1988.

Johnston, C.M. *Valley of the Six Nations*. Toronto: University of Toronto Press, 1964.

Johnston, Sheila M.F. *Buckskin and Broadcloth: A Celebration of E. Pauline Johnson - Tekahionwake, 1861-1913*. Toronto: Natural Heritage Books, 1997.

Jones, Jacqueline. *Labor of Love, Labor of Sorrow: Black Women, Work and the Family, From Slavery to the Present*. New York: Vintage Books, 1986.

Joseph, Gloria I. and Jill Lewis. *Common Differences: Conflicts in Black & White Feminist Perspectives*. Boston: South End Press, 1981.

Kalman, Bobbie and Ken Faris. *Arctic Whales & Whaling*. New York: Crabtree, 1988.

Kataayuk: Saskatchewan Indian Elders. Saskatchewan: Saskatchewan Indian Cultural College, 1976.

Kelsay, Isabel T. *Joseph Brant, 1743-1807: Man of Two Worlds* .Syracuse. New York: Syracuse University Press, 1984.

Kingston, Maxine Hong. *China Men*. New York: Alfred A. Knopf, 1977.

Kinnear, Mary. *In Subordination: Professional Women, 1870-1970*. Montreal and Kingston: McGill-Queen's University Press, 1995.

Klineberg, Otto. *Race Differences*. New York: Harper, 1935.

Knockwood, Isabelle with Gillian Thomas. *Out of the Depths, The Experience of Mi'kmaq Children at the Indian Residential School at Shubenacadie, Nova Scotia*. Lockeport, N.S.: Roseway, 1992.

Konvitz, Milton R. *The Alien and the Asiatic in American Law*. Ithaca, N.Y.: Cornell University Press, 1946.

Krauter, Joseph F., and Morris Davis. *Minority Canadians: Ethnic Groups*. Toronto: Methuen, 1978.

La Forest, G.V. *Disallowance and Reservation of Provincial Legislation*. Ottawa: Department of Justice, 1955.

Lai, David Chuenyan. *Chinatowns: Towns within Cities in Canada*. Vancouver: University of British Columbia Press, 1988.

LaViolette, Forrest. *The Struggle for Survival: Indian Cultures and the Protestant Ethic in British Columbia*. Toronto: University of Toronto Press, 1973.

LaViolette, Gontran, OMI. *The Sioux Indians in Canada*. Saskatchewan Historical Society: Regina, 1944.

Lemert, Edwin M. *Alcohol and the Northwest Coast Indians*. Berkeley: University of California Press, 1954.

Leonard, William Torbert. *Masquerade in Black*. Metuchen, N.J.: Scarecrow Press, 1986.

Lerner, Gerda, ed. *Black Women in White America*. New York: Vintage Books, 1973.

Lodwick, Kathleen L. *Crusaders against Opium: Protestant Missionaries in China, 1874–1917*. Lexington: University of Kentucky Press, 1996.

López, Ian F. Haney. *White by Law: The Legal Construction of Race*. New York: New York University Press, 1996.

Lorde, Audre. *Sister Outsider: Essays and Speeches*. Trumanburg, N.Y.: Crossing Press, 1984.

Lutz, Harmut. *Contemporary Challenges: Conversations with Canadian Native Authors*. Saskatoon: Fifth House, 1991.

Lydekker, J.W. *The Faithful Mohawks*. Cambridge, Eng., 1939.

MacGill, Elsie Gregory. *My Mother, The Judge*. Toronto: Ryerson, 1955.

MacLean, Nancy. *Behind the Mask of Chivalry: The Making of the Second Ku Klux Klan*. New York: Oxford University Press, 1994.

MacLeod, D. Peter. *The Canadian Iroquois and the Seven Years' War*. Ottawa: Canadian War Museum and Dundurn Press, 1996.

Malik, Kenan. *The Meaning of Race: Race, History and Culture in Western Society*. Basingstoke: Macmillan, 1996.

Mancall, Peter C. *Deadly Medicine: Indians and Alcohol in Early America*. Ithaca, N.Y.: Cornell University Press, 1995.

Mangan, J.A., ed. *The Imperial Curriculum: Racial Images and Education in the British Colonial Experience*. London: Routledge, 1993.

Manuel, George, and Michael Posluns. *The Fourth World: An Indian Reality*. Don Mills, Ont.: Collier-Macmillan Canada, 1974.

Marks, Lynne. *Revivals and Roller Rinks: Religion, Leisure and Identity in Late-Nineteenth-Century Small-Town Ontario*. Toronto: University of Toronto Press, 1996.

Martin, Tony. *Race First: The Ideological and Organizational Struggles of Marcus Garvey and the Negro Improvement Association*. Westport, Conn.: Greenwood, 1976.

Mathews, Hazel C. *Oakville and the Sixteen: The History of an Ontario Port*. Toronto: University of Toronto Press, 1953.

Matsuda, Mari. *Where Is Your Body? And Other Essays on Race and Gender in the Law*. Boston: Beacon Press, 1996.

May, Katja. *African Americans and Native Americans in the Creek and Cherokee Nations, 1830s to 1920s*. New York: Garland, 1996.

McArthur, Pat Deiter. *Dances of the Northern Plains*. Saskatoon: Saskatchewan Indian Cultural Centre, 1987.

McClain, Paula Denice. *Alienation and Resistance: The Political Behavior of Afro-Canadians*. Palo Alto, Calif.: R. & E. Research Associates, 1979.

McConnell, W.H. *Prairie Justice*. Calgary: Burroughs, 1980.

McCullough, A.B. *The Commercial Fishery of the Canadian Great Lakes*. Ottawa: Canadian Parks Service, Environment Canada, 1989.

McKague, Ormond. *Racism in Canada*. Saskatoon: Fifth House, 1991.

McLaren, Angus. *Our Own Master Race: Eugenics in Canada, 1885–1945*. Toronto: McClelland & Stewart, 1990.

McMillan, Alan D. *Native Peoples and Cultures of Canada*. Vancouver: Douglas & McIntyre, 1988.

Mears, Eliot Grinnell. *Resident Orientals on the American Pacific Coast: Their Legal and Economic Status.* New York: Institute of Pacific Relations, 1927.

Mesher, Dorothy. *Kuujjuaq: Memories and Musings.* Duncan, B.C.: Unica, 1995.

Meyer, Ron W. *History of the Santee Sioux: United States Indian Policy on Trial.* Omaha: University of Nebraska Press, 1967.

Miles, Robert. *Racism.* London: Tavistock, 1989.

Miller, J.R. *Shingwauk's Vision: A History of Native Residential Schools.* Toronto: University of Toronto Press, 1996.

Miller, Orlo. *This Was London: The First Two Centuries.* Westport, Ontario: Butternut Press, 1988.

Miller, Stuart Creighton. *The Unwelcome Immigrant: The American Image of the Chinese, 1785–1882.* Berkeley: University of California Press, 1969.

Mills, Donald L. 'A Brief History of Chiropractic, Naturopathy and Osteopathy in Canada: Appendix I.' *Royal Commission on Health Services: A Study of Chiropractors, Osteopaths, and Naturopaths in Canada.* Ottawa: Queen's Printer, 1966.

Montagu, M.F. Ashley. *Man's Most Dangerous Myth: The Fallacy of Race.* New York: Columbia University Press, 1942.

Montour, Enos T. *The Feathered U.E.L.* Toronto: United Church of Canada Division of Communication, 1973.

Monture-Angus, Patricia. *Thunder in My Soul: A Mohawk Woman Speaks.* Halifax: Fernwood Publishing, 1995.

Moodie, Susanna. *Life in the Clearings versus the Bush.* London: Richard Bentley, 1853.

– *Roughing It in the Bush.* Ottawa: Carleton University Press, 1988; orig. pub. London, 1852.

Moon, Robert. *This Is Saskatchewan.* Toronto: Ryerson, 1953.

Moore, J. Stuart. *Chiropractic in America: The History of a Medical Alternative.* Baltimore, Md.: Johns Hopkins University Press, 1993.

Morgan, Henry James, ed. *The Canadian Men and Women of the Time*, 2d ed. Toronto: William Briggs, 1912.

Morgan, Lewis H. *League of the Ho-De-No-Sau-Nee or Iroquois.* Rochester, N.Y.: Sage, 1851.

Morrison, Toni. *Playing in the Dark: Whiteness and the Literary Imagination.* Cambridge, Mass.: Harvard University Press, 1993.

– ed. *Race-ing Justice, En-gendering Power: Essays on Anita Hill, Clarence Thomas, and the Construction of Social Reality.* New York: Pantheon, 1992.

Morrison, William R. *Under the Flag: Canadian Sovereignty and the Native People in Northern Canada.* Ottawa: Indian and Northern Affairs Canada, 1984.

Morse, Bradford W., ed. *Aboriginal Peoples and the Law.* Ottawa: Carleton University Press, 1985.

Morton, Patricia. *Disfigured Images: The Historical Assault on Afro-American Women*. New York: Greenwood, 1991.

Mosher, Clayton James. *Discrimination and Denial: Systemic Racism in Ontario's Legal and Criminal Justice Systems, 1892–1961*. Toronto: University of Toronto Press, 1998.

Murphy, Emily F.. *The Black Candle*. Toronto: Coles, 1973; orig. pub. Toronto, 1922.

National Council of Women of Canada. *Yearbook*. Ottawa, 1901.

Newell, William B. Ta-io-wah-ron-ha-gai. *Crime and Justice among the Iroquois Nations*. Montreal: Caughnawaga Historical Society, 1965.

Ng, Roxanna. *The Politics of Community Service: Immigrant Women, Class and State*. Toronto: Garamond, 1986.

Noel, Jan. *Canada Dry: Temperance Crusades before Confederation*. Toronto: University of Toronto Press, 1995.

Noon, John A. *The Laws and Government of the Grand River Iroquois*. Viking Publications no.18. New York: Johnson Reprint, 1964; orig. pub. 1949.

Norris, Marjorie. *A Leaven of Ladies: A History of the Calgary Local Council of Women*. Calgary: Detselig, 1995.

O'Brien, Brendan. *Speedy Justice: The Tragic Last Voyage of His Majesty's Vessel 'Speedy'*. Toronto: The Osgoode Society, 1992.

O'Callaghan, E.B. *Documents Relative to the Colonial History of New York*, vol. 7. Albany, N.Y., 1856–83.

Omatsu, Maryka. *Bittersweet Passage: Redress and the Japanese Canadian Experience*. Toronto: Between the Lines, 1992.

Onondaga Historical Association. *Official Record of Indian Conference*. Syracuse, N.Y., 1919.

Osterhout, Stephen Scott. *Orientals in Canada: The Story of the Work of the United Church of Canada with Asiatics in Canada*. Toronto: Ryerson Press, 1929.

Pachai, Brigdlal. *Beneath the Clouds of the Promised Land: The Survival of Nova Scotia's Blacks*. Halifax: Lancelot Press for Black Educators Association of Nova Scotia, 1991.

Palmer, Howard. *Patterns of Prejudice: A History of Nativism in Alberta*. Toronto: McClelland & Stewart, 1982.

Pascoe, Peggy. *Relations of Rescue: The Search for Female Moral Authority in the American West, 1874–1939*. New York: Oxford University Press, 1990.

Pauktuutit. *The Inuit Way: A Guide to Inuit Culture*. Ottawa: Pauktuutit, Inuit Women's Association, 1989.

Pearce, Roy Harvey. *Savagism and Civilization: A Study of the Indian and the American Mind*. Baltimore, Md.: Johns Hopkins University Press, 1965.

Peterson, Jacqueline, and Jennifer S.H. Brown. *The New Peoples: Being and*

Becoming Métis in North America. Winnipeg: University of Manitoba Press, 1985.

Petrone, Penny, ed. *First People, First Voices*. Toronto: University of Toronto Press, 1983.

– *Northern Voices: Inuit Writing in English*. Toronto: University of Toronto Press, 1988.

Pettipas, Katherine. *Severing the Ties that Bind: Government Repression of Indigenous Religious Ceremonies on the Prairies*. Winnipeg: University of Manitoba Press, 1994.

Philip, M. Nourbese. *Frontiers: Essays and Writings on Racism and Culture*. Stratford, Ont.: Mercury Press, 1992.

Pitseolak, Peter, and Dorothy Harley Eber. *People from Our Side: A Life Story with Photographs and Oral Biography*. Montreal and Kingston: McGill-Queen's University Press, 1993.

Pitsula, James M. *Let the Family Flourish: A History of the Family Service Bureau of Regina, 1913–1982*. Regina: n.p., 1982.

Pittard, Eugene. *Race and History: An Ethnological Introduction to History*. New York: Alfred A. Knopf, 1926.

Power, Michael, and Nancy Butler. *Slavery and Freedom in Niagara*. Niagara-on-the-Lake, Ont.: Niagara Historical Society, 1993.

Prentice, Alison, Paula Bourne, Gail Cuthbert Brandt, Beth Light, Wendy Mitchinson, and Naomi Black. *Canadian Women: A History*. Toronto: Harcourt, Brace, Jovanovich, 1988.

Prosser, William L. *Handbook of the Law of Torts*. St Paul, Minn.: West Publishing, 1941.

Province of British Columbia. *Report on Oriental Activities within the Province*. Victoria: Charles F. Banfield, King's Printer, 1927.

Provincial Council of Women of Saskatchewan. *History of the Provincial Council of Women of Saskatchewan, 1919–1954*. Regina: Commercial Printers, 1955.

Prucha, F.P. *American Indian Policy in the Formative Years*. Cambridge, Mass.: Harvard University Press, 1962.

Quarles, Benjamin. *The Negro in the Making of America*, 3d ed. New York: Collier, 1987.

Rapid City Historical Book Society. *Rapid City and District: Our Past for the Future*. Altona, Man.: D.W. Friesen, 1978.

Rasing, W.C.E. *'Too Many People': Order and Nonconformity in Iglulingmiut Social Process*. Nijmegen: Katholieke Universiteit, Faculteit Der Rechtsgeleerdheid, 1994.

Ray, Arthur. *Indians in the Fur Trade*. Toronto: University of Toronto Press, 1974.

Razack, Sherene H. *Looking White People in the Eye: Gender, Race, and Culture in Courtrooms and Classrooms*. Toronto: University of Toronto Press, 1998.

Reaman, G. Elmore. *The Trail of the Iroquois Indians*. London: Frederick Muller, 1967.

Report of the Royal Commission on Aboriginal Peoples. *Looking Forward, Looking Back*, vol. 1. Ottawa: Minister of Supply and Services Canada, 1996.

Richter, Daniel K. *The Ordeal of the Longhouse: The Peoples of the Iroquois in the Era of European Colonization*. Chapel Hill: University of North Carolina Press, 1992.

Riddell, W.A. *Regina from Pile O'Bones to Queen City of the Plains*. Burlington, Ont.: Windsor Publications, 1981.

Robin, Martin. *Shades of Right: Nativist and Fascist Politics in Canada, 1920–1940*. Toronto: University of Toronto Press, 1992.

Roediger, David. *Towards the Abolition of Whiteness: Essays on Race, Politics and Working Class History*. London: Verso, 1994.

– *The Wages of Whiteness: Race and the Making of the American Working Class*. London: Verso, 1991.

Rogers, A.W., ed. *Tremeear's Annotated Criminal Code*, 4th ed. Toronto: Burroughs, 1929.

Rosenberg, Louis. *Canada's Jews: A Social and Economic Study of Jews in Canada in the 1930s*. Montreal and Kingston: McGill-Queen's University Press, 1993; orig. pub. 1939.

Rosenstiel, Annette. *Red and White: Indian Views of the White Man, 1492–1982*. New York: Universe Books, 1983.

Roy, Patricia E. *A White Man's Province: British Columbia Politicians and Chinese and Japanese Immigrants, 1858–1914*. Vancouver: University of British Columbia Press, 1989.

Russett, Cynthia Eagle. *Sexual Science: The Victorian Construction of Womanhood*. Cambridge, Mass.: Harvard University Press, 1989.

Sahrhage, Dietrich, and Johannes Lundbeck. *A History of Fishing*. New York: Springer-Verlag, 1992.

St Pierre, Mark, and Tilda Long Soldier. *Walking in the Sacred Manner: Healers, Dreamers, and Pipe Carriers–Medicine Women of the Plains Indians*. New York: Simon & Schuster, 1995.

Saunders, Charles R. *Share & Care: The Story of the Nova Scotia Home for Colored Children*. Halifax: Nimbus, 1994.

Saxton, Alexander. *The Rise and Fall of the White Republic: Class Politics and Mass Culture in Nineteenth-Century America*. London: Verso, 1990.

Schiebinger, Londa. *Nature's Body: Gender in the Making of Modern Science*. Boston: Beacon Press, 1993.

Schmeiser, D.A. *Civil Liberties in Canada*. London: Oxford University Press, 1964.

Scholefield, E.O.S., and F.W. Howay. *British Columbia from the Earliest Times to the Present*. Vancouver: S.J. Clark, 1914.

Scott, Frank R. *The Canadian Constitution and Human Rights*. Toronto: Canadian Broadcasting Company, 1959.

– *Essays on the Constitution*. Toronto: University of Toronto Press, 1977.

Shapiro, H.L. *The Alaskan Eskimo: A Study of the Relationship between the Eskimo and the Chipewyan Indians of Central Canada*. New York: The American Museum of Natural History, 1931.

Shepard, R. Bruce. *Deemed Unsuitable: Blacks from Oklahoma Move to the Canadian Prairies in Search of Equality in the Early 20th Century Only to Find Racism in Their New Home*. Toronto: Umbrella Press, 1997.

Sher, Julian. *White Hoods: Canada's Ku Klux Klan*. Vancouver: New Star, 1983.

Shimony, Annemarie A. *Conservatism among the Grand River Iroquois*. New Haven, Conn.: Yale University Press, 1961.

Shkilnyk, Anastasia. *A Poison Stronger than Love: The Destruction of an Ojibwa Community*. New Haven, Conn.: Yale University Press, 1985.

Sickels, Robert J. *Race, Marriage, and the Law*. Albuquerque: University of New Mexico Press, 1972.

Silvera, Makeda. *Silenced*. Toronto: Williams-Wallace, 1983.

Silverman, Jason. *Unwelcome Guests: Canada West's Response to American Fugitive Slaves, 1800–1865*. Millwood, N.Y.: Associated Faculty Press, 1985.

Sims, Patsy. *The Klan*. New York: Stein and Day, 1982.

Sioui, Georges E. *For an Amerindian Autohistory: An Essay on the Foundations of a Social Ethic*. Montreal and Kingston: McGill-Queen's University Press, 1992.

Sluman, Norma, and Jean Goodwill. *John Tootoosis: A Biography of a Cree Leader*. Ottawa: Golden Dog Press, 1982.

Smedley, Audrey. *Race in North America: Origin and Evolution of a Worldview*. Boulder, Colo.: Westview, 1993.

Smith, Dan. *The Seventh Fire: The Struggle for Aboriginal Government*. Toronto: Key Porter Books, 1993.

Smith, Jr., J. Clay. *Emancipation: The Making of the Black Lawyer, 1844–1944*. Philadelphia: University of Pennsylvania Press, 1993.

Solomon, Barbara. *Ancestors and Immigrants*. Cambridge, Mass.: Harvard University Press, 1956.

Spittal, William Guy. *Iroquois Women: An Anthology*. Ohsweken, Ont.: Iroqrafts, 1990.

Stallybrass, W.T.S. *Salmond's Law of Torts*. Toronto: Carswell, 1945.

Stepan, Nancy. *The Idea of Race in Science*. Hamden, Conn,: Archon Books, 1982.

Sterling, Dorothy, ed. *We Are Your Sisters: Black Women in the Nineteenth Century*. New York: W.W. Norton, 1984.

Stevens, Gerald. *The United Counties of Leeds and Grenville*. Brockville: n.p., 1961.

Stewart, W.P. *My Name Is Piapot*. Maple Creek: Butterfly Books, 1981.

Stocking, George W. *Victorian Anthropology*. New York: Free Press, 1987.

Stocking, Jr., George W. *Race, Culture and Evolution*. New York: Free Press, 1968.

Stone, William Leete. *Life of Joseph Brant – Thayendanegea*, 2 vols. New York, 1838.

Stouffer, Allen P. *The Light of Nature and the Law of God: Anti-Slavery in Ontario, 1833–1877*. Montreal and Kingston: McGill-Queen's University Press, 1992.

Strange, Carolyn. *Toronto's Girl Problems: The Perils and Pleasures of the City, 1880–1930*. Toronto: University of Toronto Press, 1995.

Strayer, Barry L. *The Canadian Constitution and the Courts: The Function and Scope of Judicial Review*, 3d ed. Toronto: Butterworths, 1988.

Strong-Boag, Veronica Jane. *The Parliament of Women: The National Council of Women of Canada, 1893–1929*. Ottawa: National Museum of Man, 1976.

Takaki, Ronald T. *Iron Cages: Race and Culture in Nineteenth-Century America*. New York: Knopf, 1979.

Tarnopolsky, Justice Walter Surma, and William F. Pentney. *Discrimination and the Law*. Don Mills, Ont.: Richard De Boo, 1985.

Taylor, Griffith. *Environment, Race and Migration*. Toronto: University of Toronto Press, 1945.

Tehanetorens. *Wampum Belts*. Ohsweken, Ont.: Iroqrafts, 1993.

Tennant, Paul. *Aboriginal Peoples and Politics*. Vancouver: University of British Columbia Press, 1990.

Thomson, Colin A. *Blacks in Deep Snow: Black Pioneers of Canada*. Don Mills, Ont.: J.M. Dent, 1979.

– *Born with a Call: A Biography of Dr William Pearly Oliver, C.M.* Dartmouth, N.S.: Black Cultural Centre, 1986.

Titley, E. Brian. *A Narrow Vision: Duncan Campbell Scott and the Administration of Indian Affairs in Canada*. Vancouver: University of British Columbia Press, 1986.

Tobach, Ethel, and Betty Rosoff, eds. *Challenging Racism and Sexism: Alternatives to Genetic Explanations*. New York: The Feminist Press, 1994.

Trigger, Bruce G. *Natives and Newcomers: Canada's 'Heroic Age' Reconsidered*. Montreal and Kingston: McGill-Queen's University Press, 1985.

Troper, Harold. *Only Farmers Need Apply*. Toronto: Griffin House, 1972.

Trudel, Marcel. *L'esclavage au Canada français*. Quebec: Presses universitaires Laval, 1960.

Valverde, Mariana. *The Age of Light, Soap and Water: Moral Reform in English Canada, 1885–1925*. Toronto: McClelland & Stewart, 1991.

Van Kirk, Sylvia. *'Many Tender Ties': Women in Fur-Trade Society, 1670–1870*. Winnipeg: Watson & Dwyer, 1980.

Vecsey, Christopher, and William A. Starna. *Iroquois Land Claims*. Syracuse, N.Y.: Syracuse University Press, 1988.

Vincent, Theodore. *Black Power and the Garvey Movement*. Berkeley: Ramparts, 1971.

Wadden, Marie. *Nitassinan: The Innu Struggle to Reclaim Their Homeland*. Vancouver: Douglas & McIntyre, 1991.

Wade, Wyn Craig. *The Fiery Cross: The Ku Klux Klan in America*. London: Simon and Schuster, 1987.

Waley, Arthur. *The Opium War through Chinese Eyes*. London: Unwin, 1958.

Walker, Alice. *In Search of Our Mothers' Gardens*. New York: Harcourt, Brace, Jovanovich, 1983.

Walker, James W.St.G. *The Black Identity in Nova Scotia: Community and Institutions in Historical Perspective*. Halifax: Black Cultural Centre for Nova Scotia, 1985.

– *The Black Loyalists: The Search for a Promised Land in Nova Scotia and Sierra Leone, 1783–1870*. Toronto: University of Toronto Press, 1992.

– *'Race,' Rights and the Law in the Supreme Court of Canada*. Waterloo: The Osgoode Society and Wilfrid Laurier University Press, 1997.

– *Racial Discrimination in Canada: The Black Experience*. Ottawa: Canadian Historical Association, 1985.

Wallace, A.F.C., with the assistance of Sheila C. Steen. *The Death and Rebirth of the Seneca*. New York: Knopf, 1970.

Wallis, Wilson D. *The Canadian Dakota*. New York: AMS Press, 1947.

Ward, W. Peter. *White Canada Forever: Popular Attitudes and Public Policy toward Orientals in British Columbia*, 2d ed. Montreal: McGill-Queen's University Press, 1990.

Wardwell, Walter I. *Chiropractic: History and Evolution of New Profession*. St Louis: Mosby Year Book, 1992.

Ware, Vron. *Beyond the Pale: White Women, Racism and History*. London: Verso, 1992.

Watetch, Abel. *Payepot and His People*. Saskatoon: Modern Press, 1959.

Weaver, Sally M. *Medicine and Politics among the Grand River Iroquois: A Study of the Non-conservatives*. Ottawa: National Museums of Canada, 1972.

Wei, William. *The Asian American Movement*. Philaldelphia: Temple University Press, 1993.

West, Cornel. *Race Matters*. New York: Vintage, 1994.

Whyte, Jon. *Indians in the Rockies*. Banff, Alta.: Altitude Publishing, 1985.

Wickberg, Edgar, et al. *From China to Canada: A History of the Chinese Communities in Canada*. Toronto: McClelland & Stewart, 1982.

Williams, David R. *Duff: A Life in the Law*. Vancouver: University of British Columbia Press, 1984.

Williams, Dorothy W. *Blacks in Montreal, 1628–1986: An Urban Demography*. Cowansville, Que.: Yvon Blais, 1989.

Williams, Patricia J. *The Alchemy of Race and Rights*. Cambridge, Mass.: Harvard University Press, 1991.

– *The Rooster's Egg: On the Persistence of Prejudice*. Cambridge, Mass.: Harvard University Press, 1995.

Wilson, Edmund. *Apologies to the Iroquois*. Syracuse, N.Y.: Syracuse University Press, 1992.

Winfield, P.H. *A Text-Book of the Law of Tort*. Toronto: Carswell, 1946.

Winks, Robin W. *The Blacks in Canada: A History*, 2d ed. Montreal and Kingston: McGill-Queen's University Press, 1997.

Wolfe, Alexander. *Earth Elder Stories*. Saskatoon: Fifth House, 1988.

Women's Book Committee, Chinese Canadian National Council. *Jin Guo: Voices of Chinese Canadian Women*. Toronto: Women's Press, 1992.

Woods, David. *Native Song*. Porters Lake, N.S.: Pottersfield Press, 1990.

Woodward, C. Vann. *The Strange Career of Jim Crow*, 3d rev. ed. New York: Oxford University Press, 1974.

Wright, J.F.C. *Saskatchewan: The History of a Province*. Toronto: McClelland & Stewart, 1955.

Wright, Richard. *Native Son*. New York: Harper, 1993, orig. pub. 1940.

Wu, Cheng-Tsu. *'Chink!'* New York: World Publishing, 1972.

Wynne, Robert Edward. *Reaction to the Chinese in the Pacific Northwest and British Columbia, 1850–1910*. New York: Arno Press, 1978.

Yee, Paul. *Saltwater City: An Illustrated History of the Chinese in Vancouver*. Vancouver: Douglas & McIntyre, 1988.

Yee, Paul. *Struggle and Hope: The Story of Chinese Canadians*. Toronto: Umbrella Press, 1996.

York, Geoffrey. *The Dispossessed: Life and Death in Native Canada*. Toronto: Lester & Orpen Dennys, 1989.

Zack, Naomi. *Race and Mixed Race*. Philadelphia: Temple University Press, 1993.

B. ARTICLES

Adilman, Tamara. 'A Preliminary Sketch of Chinese Women and Work in British Columbia, 1858-1950.' In Barbara K. Latham and Roberta J. Pazdro, eds., *Not Just Pin Money*. Victoria: Camosun College, 1984.

Allen, Robert S. 'The British Indian Department and the Frontier in North America, 1755–1830.' In *Canadian Historic Sites*. Ottawa: Indian and Northern Affairs, 1975.

Angus, Henry F. 'Canadian Immigration: The Law and Its Administration.' In Norman MacKenzie, ed., *The Legal Status of Aliens in Pacific Countries*. London: Oxford University Press, 1937.

Angus, H.F. 'The Legal Status in British Columbia of Residents of Oriental Race and Their Descendants.' In Norman MacKenzie, ed., *The Legal Status of Aliens in Pacific Countries*. London: Oxford University Press, 1937.

Applebaum, Harvey M. 'Miscegenation Statutes: A Constitutional and Social Problem.' *Georgia Law Journal*, vol .53 (1964).

Archibald, Jo-Ann. 'Resistance to an Unremitting Process: Racism, Curriculum and Education in Western Canada.' In J.A. Mangan, ed., *The Imperial Curriculum: Racial Images and Education in the British Colonial Experience*. London: Routledge, 1993.

Artibise, Alan F.J. 'Boosterism and the Development of Prairie Cities, 1871–1913.' In R. Douglas Francis and Howard Palmer, eds., *The Prairie West: Historical Readings*. Edmonton: University of Alberta Press, 1985.

Backhouse, Constance. 'Clara Brett Martin: Canadian Heroine or Not?' and 'Response.' *Canadian Journal of Women and the Law* 5:2 (1992).

– 'Gretta Wong Grant: Canada's First Chinese-Canadian Female Lawyer.' *Windsor Yearbook of Access to Justice*, vol. 15 (1996).

– '"I Was Unable to Identify with Topsy": Carrie M. Best's Struggle Against Racial Segregation in Nova Scotia, 1942.' *Atlantis* 22:2 (Spring 1998).

– 'Racial Segregation in Canadian Legal History: Viola Desmond's Challenge, Nova Scotia, 1946.' *Dalhousie Law Journal* 17:2 (Fall 1994).

– 'To Open the Way for Others of My Sex: Clara Brett Martin's Career as Canada's First Woman Lawyer.' *Canadian Journal of Women and the Law* 1:1 (1985).

– 'White Female Help and Chinese-Canadian Employers: Race, Class, Gender and Law in the Case of Yee Clun, 1924.' *Canadian Ethnic Studies* 26:3 (1994); republished in a revised version in Wendy Mitchinson et al., eds., *Canadian Women: A Reader*. Toronto: Harcourt Brace, 1996.

– 'The White Women's Labor Laws: Anti-Chinese Racism in Early Twentieth-Century Canada.' *Law and History Review* 14:2 (Fall 1996).

– '"Your Conscience Will Be Your Own Punishment": The Racially-Motivated Murder of Gus Ninham, Ontario, 1902.' In Blaine Baker and Jim Phillips, eds., *Essays in the History of Canadian Law*. Toronto: The Osgoode Society, 1999.

Ball, Milner S. 'Stories of Origin and Constitutional Possibilities.' (1989) 87 *Michigan Law Review*.

Banton, Michael. 'The Classification of Races in Europe and North America: 1700–1850.' *International Social Science Journal* 39:1 (February 1987).

Barron, Laurie. 'The Indian Pass System in the Canadian West, 1882–1935.' *Prairie Forum* 13:1 (1988).

Bartlett, Richard H. 'Citizens Minus: Indians and the Right to Vote.' *Saskatchewan Law Review*, vol.44 (1980/1).

Bartley, Allen. 'A Public Nuisance: The Ku Klux Klan in Ontario, 1923–27.' *Journal of Canadian Studies* 30:3 (Fall 1995).

Barton, Brad, and Anne Moynihan. 'The Black Community's Struggle for Quality Education in Nova Scotia.' In Vincent D'Oyley, ed., *Innovations in Black Education in Canada*. Toronto: Umbrella Press, 1994.

Baskin, Cindy. 'Women in Iroquois Society.' *Canadian Woman Studies* 4:2 (Winter 1982).

Baureiss, Gunter. 'The Chinese Community in Calgary.' *Alberta Historical Review* 22:2 (Spring 1974).

– 'Discrimination and Response: The Chinese in Canada.' In Rita M. Bienvenue and Jay E. Goldstein, eds., *Ethnicity and Ethnic Relations in Canada*, 2d ed. Toronto: Butterworths, 1985.

Beaton, Elizabeth. 'An African-American Community in Cape Breton, 1901–1904.' *Acadiensis* 24:2 (Spring 1995).

Beauchamp, W.M. 'The Journal of American Folk-Lore' (1900). Republished in William Guy Spittal, *Iroquois Women: An Anthology*. Ohsweken, Ont.: Iroqrafts, 1990.

Beaver, George. 'Early Iroquoian History in Ontario.' *Ontario History* 75:3 (September 1993).

Bell, D.G. 'Slavery and the Judges of Loyalist New Brunswick.' *University of New Brunswick Law Journal*, vol. 31 (1982).

Bieder, Robert E. 'Scientific Attitudes toward Indian Mixed-Bloods in Early Nineteenth-Century America.' *Journal of Ethnic Studies*, vol.8 (1980).

Bilharz, Joy. 'First among Equals? The Changing Status of Seneca Women.' In Laura F. Klein and Lillian A. Ackerman, *Women and Power in Native North America*. Norman: University of Oklahoma Press, 1995.

Boisseau, T.J. '"They Called Me *Bebe Bwana*": A Critical Cultural Study of an Imperial Feminist.' *Signs: Journal of Women in Culture and Society* 21:1 (1995).

Boldt, Menno, and Anthony Long. 'Tribal Traditions and European-Western Political Ideologies: The Dilemma of Canada's Native Indians.' In Menno Boldt and Anthony Long, eds., *The Quest for Justice*. Toronto: University of Toronto Press, 1985.

Bourgeois, Donald J. 'The Six Nations: A Neglected Aspect of Canadian Legal History.' *The Canadian Journal of Native Studies* 6:2 (1986).

Brand, Dionne. 'Black Women and Work: The Impact of Racially Constructed Gender Roles on the Sexual Division of Labour.' *Fireweed*, vol. 26 (Winter/Spring 1987).

– '"We weren't allowed to go into factory work until Hitler started the war":
The 1920s to the 1940s.' In Peggy Bristow et al., eds., *Essays in African Canadian Women's History*. Toronto: University of Toronto Press, 1994.

Brant, Beth, 'From the Inside – Looking at You.' *Canadian Woman Studies* 14:1
(Fall 1993).

Bristow, Peggy. '"Whatever you raise in the ground you can sell it in
Chatham": Black Women in Buxton and Chatham, 1850–65.' In Peggy
Bristow et al., *'We're Rooted Here and They Can't Pull Us Up': Essays in African-
Canadian Women's History*. Toronto: University of Toronto Press, 1994.

Broca, Paul. 'Sur les proportions relatives du bras, de l'avant bras et de la
clavicule chez les nègres et les européens.' *Bulletin Société d'Anthropologie
Paris* 3:2 (1862).

Brockman, Joan. 'Exclusionary Tactics: The History of Women and Visible
Minorities in the Legal Profession in British Columbia.' In Hamar Foster and
John McLaren, eds., *Essays in the History of Canadian Law: British Columbia and
the Yukon*, vol. 6. Toronto: The Osgoode Society, 1995.

Brouwer, Ruth Compton. 'A Disgrace to "Christian Canada": Protestant Foreign Missionary Concerns about the Treatment of South Asians in Canada,
1907–1940.' In Franca Iacovetta et al., *A Nation of Immigrants: Women, Workers,
and Communities in Canadian History, 1840s–1960s*. Toronto: University of
Toronto Press, 1998.

Brown, Jennifer S.H. 'Women as Centre and Symbol in the Emergence of Métis
Communities.' *Canadian Journal of Native Studies*, vol. 3 (1983).

Brown, Judith K. 'Economic Organization and the Position of Women Among
the Iroquois.' In William Guy Spittal, *Iroquois Women: An Anthology*.
Ohsweken, Ont.: Iroqrafts, 1990.

Brown-Kubisch, Linda. 'The Black Experience in the Queen's Bush Settlement.'
Ontario History 88:2 (June 1996).

Brownlie, Robin, and Mary-Ellen Kelm. 'Desperately Seeking Absolution:
Native Agency as Colonialist Alibi?' *Canadian Historical Review* 75:4 (December 1994).

Bundles, A'Lelia Perry. 'Walker, Madam C.J. (Sarah Breedlove), 1867–1919.' In
Darlene Clark Hine, *Black Women in America: An Historical Encyclopedia*, vol. 2.
Brooklyn: Carlson Publishing, 1993.

Cahill, Barry. 'The "Colored Barrister": The Short Life and Tragic Death of
James Robinson Johnston, 1876–1915.' *Dalhousie Law Journal*, vol. 15 (1992).

– 'Slavery and the Judges of Loyalist Nova Scotia.' *University of New Brunswick
Law Journal*, vol. 43 (1994).

Calderwood, William. 'The Decline of the Progressive Party in Saskatchewan,
1925–1930.' *Saskatchewan History* 21:3 (Autumn 1968).

– 'Pulpit, Press and Political Reactions to the Ku Klux Klan in Saskatchewan.'

In Susan M. Trofimenkoff, ed., *The Twenties in Western Canada*. Ottawa: National Museums of Canada, 1972.
- 'Religious Reactions to the Ku Klux Klan in Saskatchewan.' *Saskatchewan History* 26:3 (1973).
Calliste, Agnes. 'Blacks on Canadian Railways.' *Canadian Ethnic Studies* 20:2 (1988).
- '"Blacks" Struggle for Education Equity in Nova Scotia.' In Vincent D'Oyley, ed., *Innovations in Black Education in Canada* Toronto: Umbrella Press, 1994.
- 'Race, Gender and Canadian Immigration Policy: Blacks from the Caribbean, 1900–1932.' *Journal of Canadian Studies* 28:4 (Winter 1993/4).
- 'Sleeping Car Porters in Canada: An Ethnically Submerged Split Labour Market.' *Canadian Ethnic Studies* 19:1 (1987).
- 'The Struggle for Employment Equity by Blacks on American and Canadian Railroads.' *Journal of Black Studies* 25:3 (January 1995).
- 'Women of "Exceptional Merit": Immigration of Caribbean Nurses to Canada.' *Canadian Journal of Women and the Law*, vol. 6 (1993).
Carr, Lucien. 'On the Social and Political Position of Woman among the Huron-Iroquois Tribes.' In William Guy Spittal, *Iroquois Women: An Anthology*. Ohsweken, Ont.: Iroqrafts, 1990.
Carter, Sarah. 'Agriculture and Agitation on the Oak River Dakota Reserve, 1875–1895.' *Manitoba History* 6:2 (Fall 1983).
- 'Categories and Terrains of Exclusion: Constructing the "Indian Woman" in the Early Settlement Era in Western Canada.' *Great Plains Quarterly*, vol. 13 (Summer 1993).
- 'Controlling Indian Movement: The Pass System.' *NeWest Review*, May 1985.
Chan, Anthony B. 'The Myth of the Chinese Sojourner in Canada.' In K. Victor Ujimoto and Gordon Hirabyashi, eds., *Visible Minorities and Multiculturalism: Asians in Canada*. Toronto: Butterworths, 1980.
Clairmont, Donald, and Fred Wien. 'Blacks and Whites: The Nova Scotia Race Relations Experience.' In Douglas F. Campbell, ed., *Banked Fires: The Ethnics of Nova Scotia*. Port Credit, Ont.: Scribblers' Press, 1978.
Clark, B.L. 'Diamond Jenness, 1886–1969.' In *Development of Caribou Eskimo Culture: A Diamond Jenness Memorial Volume*. Ottawa: National Museum of Canada, 1977.
Coates, K.S., and W.R. Morrison. 'More than a Matter of Blood: The Federal Government, the Churches and the Mixed Blood Populations of the Yukon and the Mackenzie River Valley, 1890–1950.' In F.Laurie Barron and James B. Waldram, eds., *1885 and After: Native Society in Transition*. Regina: Canadian Plains Research Center, 1986.

Collette, Christine. 'For Labour and for Women: The Women's Labour League, 1906–18.' *Labour/Le Travail*, vol. 26 (1990).

Collison, Gary. '"Loyal and Dutiful Subjects of Her Gracious Majesty, Queen Victoria": Fugitive Slaves in Montreal, 1850–1866.' *Quebec Studies*, vol. 19 (1995).

Coon Come, Grand Chief Matthew. 'Clearing the Smokescreen.' In Bruce W. Hodgins and Kerry A. Cannon, eds., *On the Land: Confronting the Challenges to Aboriginal Self-Determination in Northern Quebec and Labrador*. Toronto: Betelgeuse, 1995.

Cooper, Afua P. 'Black Women and Work in Nineteenth-Century Canada West: Black Woman Teacher Mary Bibb.' In Peggy Bristow et al., *We're Rooted Here and They Can't Pull Us Up: Essays in African- Canadian Women's History*. Toronto: University of Toronto Press, 1994.

Cottam, S. Barry. 'Indian Title as "Celestial Institution": David Mills and the *St. Catharines Milling* Case.' In Kerry Abel and Jean Friesen, eds., *Aboriginal Resource Use in Canada: Historical and Legal Aspects*. Winnipeg: University of Manitoba Press, 1991.

Creese, Gillian. 'Exclusion or Solidarity? Vancouver Workers Confront the "Oriental Problem".' *BC Studies*, vol. 80 (Winter 1988/9).

– 'Immigration Policies and the Creation of an Ethnically Segmented Working Class in British Columbia, 1880–1923.' *Alternate Routes*, vol. 17 (1984).

– 'Organizing Against Racism in the Workplace: Chinese Workers in Vancouver before the Second World War.' *Canadian Ethnic Studies* 19:3 (1987).

Crenshaw, Kimberle Williams. 'Race, Reform, and Retrenchment: Transformation and Legitimation in Antidiscrimination Law.' *Harvard Law Review*, vol. 101 (1988).

Cruikshank, Brig.-General E.A. 'The Coming of the Loyalist Mohawks to the Bay of Quinte.' *Ontario History*, vol. 26 (1930).

Cuthand, Stan. 'The Native Peoples of the Prairie Provinces in the 1920's and 1930's.' In Ian Getty and Donald Smith, eds., *One Century Later: Western Canadian Reserve Indians Since Treaty 7*. Vancouver: University of British Columbia Press, 1978.

Damas, David. 'Arctic.' In William C. Sturtevant, ed., *Handbook of North American Indians*, vol. 5. Washington, D.C.: Smithsonian Institution, 1984.

D'Anglure, Bernard Saladin. 'Inuit of Quebec.' In William C. Sturtevant, ed., *Handbook of North American Indians*. Washington, D.C.: Smithsonian Institution, 1984.

Dawson, J. Brian. 'The Chinese Experience in Frontier Calgary, 1885–1910.' In A.W. Rasporich and Henry Klassen, eds., *Frontier Calgary: 1875–1914*. Calgary: University of Calgary Press, 1975.

de Groot, Joanna. '"Sex" and "Race": The Construction of Language and Image in the Nineteenth-Century.' In S. Mendes and J. Rendall, eds., *Sexuality and Subordination*. London: Routledge, 1989.

Dei, George J. Sefa. 'The Politics of Educational Change: Taking Anti-Racism Education Seriously.' In Vic Satzewich, ed., *Racism and Social Inequality in Canada: Concepts, Controversies and Strategies of Resistance*. Toronto: Thompson Educational Publishing, 1998.

Dickason, Olive Patricia. 'For Every Plant There Is a Use.' In Kerry Abel and Jean Friesen, eds., *Aboriginal Resource Use in Canada: Historical and Legal Aspects*. Winnipeg: University of Manitoba Press, 1991.

– 'From "One Nation" in the Northeast to "New Nation" in the Northwest: A Look at the Emergence of the Métis.' In Jacqueline Peterson and Jennifer S.H. Brown, eds., *The New Peoples: Being and Becoming Métis in North America*. Winnipeg: University of Manitoba Press, 1985.

Dickinson, John A. 'Native Sovereignty and French Justice in Early Canada.' In Jim Phillips, Tina Loo, and Susan Lewthwaite, eds., *Crime and Criminal Justice: Essays in the History of Canadian Law*. Toronto: The Osgoode Society, 1994.

Diubaldo, Richard J. 'The Absurd Little Mouse: When Eskimos Became Indians.' *Journal of Canadian Studies* 16:2 (Summer 1981).

Donovan, Kenneth. 'Slaves and Their Owners in Île Royale, 1713–1760.' *Acadiensis* 25:1 (Autumn 1995).

Doyle-Bedwell, Patricia E. 'The Evolution of the Legal Test of Extinguishment: From *Sparrow* to *Gitskan*.' *Canadian Journal of Women and the Law*, vol. 6 (1993).

Druke, Mary A. 'Iroquois and Iroquoian in Canada.' In R. Bruce Morrison and C. Roderick Wilson, eds., *Native Peoples: The Canadian Experience*. Toronto: McClelland & Stewart, 1986.

du Cille, Ann. 'The Occult of True Black Womanhood: Critical Demeanor and Black Feminist Studies.' *Signs* 19:3 (Spring 1994).

Duclos, Nitya. 'Disappearing Women: Racial Minority Women in Human Rights Cases.' *Canadian Journal of Women and the Law*, vol. 6 (1993).

Dussias, Allison M. 'Ghost Dance and Holy Ghost: The Echoes of Nineteenth-Century Christianization Policy in Twentieth-Century Native American Free Exercise Cases.' *Stanford Law Review*, vol. 49 (1997).

Edmunds, R. David. '"Unacquainted with the Laws of the Civilized World": American Attitudes toward the Métis Communities in the Old Northwest.' In Jacqueline Peterson and Jennifer S.H. Brown, eds., *The New Peoples: Being and Becoming Métis in North America*. Winnipeg: University of Manitoba Press, 1985.

Erasmus, George, and Joe Sanders. 'Canadian History: An Aboriginal Perspective.' In Diane Engelstad and John Bird, eds., *Nation to Nation: Aboriginal*

Sovereignty and the Future of Canada. Concord, Ont.: House of Anansi Press, 1992.

Fenton, William N. 'Iroquoian Culture History: A General Evaluation.' In W.N. Fenton and J. Gulick, eds., *Symposium on Cherokee and Iroquois Culture.* Smithsonian Institution, Bureau of American Ethnology Bulletin, no. 180. Washington, D.C.: U.S. Government Printing Office, 1961.

Fingard, Judith. 'From Sea to Rail: Black Transportation Workers and Their Families in Halifax, c. 1870–1916.' *Acadiensis* 24:2 (Spring 1995).

– 'Race and Respectability in Victorian Halifax.' *Journal of Imperial and Commonwealth History* 20:2 (May 1992).

Finkelman, Paul. 'The Anderson Case and Rights in Canada and England.' In Louis A. Knafla and Susan W.S. Binnie, eds., *Law, Society and the State: Essays in Modern Legal History.* Toronto: University of Toronto Press, 1995.

Flagg, Barbara. '"Was Blind, But Now I See": White Race Consciousness and the Requirement of Discriminatory Intent.' *Michigan Law Review*, vol. 91 (1993).

Forbes, Jack. 'The Manipulation of Race, Caste and Identity: Classifying Afro-Americans, Native Americans and Red-Black People.' *The Journal of Ethnic Studies* 17:4 (Winter 1990).

Forkey, Neil S. 'Maintaining a Great Lakes Fishery: The State, Science, and the Case of Ontario's Bay of Quinte, 1870–1920.' *Ontario History* 87:1 (March 1995).

Foster, Hamar. '"The Queen's Law Is Better Than Yours": International Homicide in Early British Columbia.' In Jim Phillips, Tina Loo, and Susan Lewthwaite, eds., *Crime and Criminal Justice: Essays in the History of Canadian Law.* Toronto: The Osgoode Society, 1994.

– 'Sins against the Great Spirit: The Law, the Hudson's Bay Company, and the Mackenzie's River Murders, 1835–1839.' *Criminal Justice History: An International Annual*, vol. 10 (1989).

Foster, John E. 'The Origins of the Mixed Bloods in the Canadian West.' In Lewis H. Thomas, ed., *Essays on Western History, in Honour of Lewis Gwynne Thomas.* Edmonton: University of Alberta Press, 1976.

Foster, John E. 'The Métis: The People and the Term.' *Prairie Forum*, vol. 3 (1978).

– 'The Plains Métis.' In Bruce Morrison and R.C. Wilson, eds., *Native Peoples: The Canadian Experience.* Toronto: McClelland & Stewart, 1986.

– 'Some Questions and Perspectives on the Problem of Métis Roots.' In Jacqueline Peterson and Jennifer S.H. Brown, eds., *The New Peoples: Being and Becoming Métis in North America.* Winnipeg: University of Manitoba Press, 1985.

Foster, Martha Harroun. 'Lost Women of the Matriarchy: Iroquois Women in the Historical Literature.' *American Indian Culture and Research Journal* 19:3 (1995).

Foster, Michael K. 'On Who Spoke First at Iroquois-White Councils: An Exercise in the Method of Upstreaming.' In Michael K. Foster et al., eds., *Extending the Rafters: Approaches in Iroquoian Studies*. Albany, N.Y.: State University of New York Press, 1984.

Frager, Ruth A. 'Class, Ethnicity, and Gender in the Eaton Strikes of 1912 and 1934.' In Franca Iacovetta and Mariana Valverde. eds., *Gender Conflicts: New Essays in Women's History*. Toronto: University of Toronto Press, 1992.

Freeman, Minnie Aodla. 'Living in Two Hells.' In Penny Petrone, ed., *Northern Voices: Inuit Writing in English*. Toronto: University of Toronto Press, 1988.

Gilman, Sander L. 'Black Bodies, White Bodies: Toward an Iconography of Female Sexuality in Late Nineteenth-Century Art, Medicine, and Literature.' In Henry Louis Gates, Jr, ed., *'Race,' Writing, and Difference*. Chicago: University of Chicago Press, 1986.

Glennon, Robert Jerome. 'The Role of Law in the Civil Rights Movement: The Montgomery Bus Boycott, 1955–1957.' *Law and History Review*, vol. 9 (1991).

Good, E. Reginald. 'Mississauga–Mennonite Relations in the Upper Grand River Valley.' *Ontario History* 87:2 (1995).

Gould, Stephen Jay. 'American Polygeny and Craniometry before Darwin: Blacks and Indians as Separate, Inferior Species.' In Sandra Harding, ed., *The 'Racial' Economy of Science*. Bloomington: Indiana University Press, 1994.

Grant, John N. 'Black Immigrants into Nova Scotia, 1776–1815.' *Journal of Negro History* 58:3 (July 1973).

Green, Gretchen. 'Molly Brant, Catherine Brant, and Their Daughters: A Study in Colonial Acculturation.' *Ontario History* 81:3 (September 1989).

Gresko, Jacqueline. 'White "Rites" and Indian "Rites": Indian Education and Native Responses in the West, 1870–1910.' In A.W. Raporich, ed., *Western Canada Past and Present*. Calgary: McClelland and Stewart West, 1974.

Grobsmith, Elizabeth S. 'The Lakhota Giveaway: A System of Social Reciprocity.' *Plains Anthropologist* 24:84 (1979).

Grove, Alan, and Ross Lambertson. 'Pawns of the Powerful: The Politics of Litigation in the Union Colliery Case.' *BC Studies*, vol. 103 (Autumn 1994).

Hall, Anthony J. *'The St. Catharines Milling and Lumber Company versus the Queen*: Indian Land Rights as a Factor in Federal-Provincial Relations in Nineteenth-Century Canada.' In Kerry Abel and Jean Friesen, eds., *Aboriginal Resource Use in Canada: Historical and Legal Aspects*. Winnipeg: University of Manitoba Press, 1991.

Hall, D.J. 'Clifford Sifton: Immigration and Settlement Policy 1896–1905.' In R.

Douglas Francis and Howard Palmer, eds., *The Prairie West: Historical Readings*. Edmonton: University of Alberta Press, 1985.

Hamilton, Sylvia. 'Our Mothers Grand and Great: Black Women of Nova Scotia.' *Canadian Woman Studies* 4:2 (Winter 1982).

Harley, Sharon. 'For the Good of Family and Race: Gender, Work, and Domestic Roles in the Black Community, 1880–1930.' *Signs* 15:2 (1990).

Harring, Sidney L. '"The Liberal Treatment of Indians": Native People in Nineteenth-Century Ontario Law.' *Saskatchewan Law Review*, vol. 56 (1992).

– 'The Rich Men of the Country: Canadian Law in the Land of the Copper Inuit, 1914–1930.' *Ottawa Law Review* 21:1 (1989).

Harris, Cheryl. 'Whiteness as Property.' *Harvard Law Review*, vol. 106 (1993).

Hartlen, Gary C. 'Bound for Nova Scotia: Slaves in the Planter Migration, 1759–1800.' In Margaret Conrad, ed., *Making Adjustments: Change and Continuity in Planter Nova Scotia, 1759–1800*. Fredericton: Acadiensis Press, 1991.

Henson, Tom M. 'Ku Klux Klan in Western Canada.' *Alberta History* 25:4 (Autumn 1977).

Herrington, M. Eleanor. 'Captain John Deserontyou and the Mohawk Settlement at Deseronto.' *Queen's Quarterly*, vol. 29 (1921/2).

Higginbotham, Evelyn Brooks. 'African-American Women's History and the Metalanguage of Race.' *Signs* 17:2 (Winter 1992).

Hill, Asa R. (Secretary, Six Nations Council). 'The Historical Position of the Six Nations.' *Ontario Historical Society*, vol. 19 (1922).

Hill, B.E. 'The Grand River Navigation Company and the Six Nations Indians.' *Ontario History* 63:1 (1971).

Hill, Daniel G. 'Black History in Early Ontario.' *Canadian Human Rights Yearbook*. Ottawa: Human Rights Research and Education Centre, University of Ottawa, 1984–5.

Hill, Richard. 'Oral History of the Haudenosaunee: Views of the Two Row Wampum.' In Jose Bartreiro, ed., *Indian Roots of American Democracy*. New York: Akweikon Press, 1992.

Horton, James Oliver. 'Freedom's Yoke: Gender Conventions among Antebellum Free Blacks.' *Feminist Studies* 12:1 (Spring 1986).

Hudson, Nicholas. 'From "Nation" to "Race": The Origin of Racial Classification in Eighteenth-Century Thought.' *Eighteenth-Century Studies* 29:3 (1996).

Huel, Raymond J.A. 'J.J. Maloney: How the West Was Saved from Rome, Quebec and the Liberals.' In John E. Foster, ed., *The Developing West*. Edmonton: University of Alberta Press, 1983.

Hunter, Ian A. 'Civil Actions for Discrimination.' *Canadian Bar Review*, vol. 55 (1977).

Ireland, Ralph R. 'Some Effects of Oriental Immigration on Canadian Trade Union Ideology.' *American Journal of Economics and Sociology*, vol. 19 (1960).

Jackson, Peter. 'The Idea of "Race" and the Geography of Racism.' In Peter Jackson, ed., *Race and Racism*. London: Unwin Hyman, 1987.

Jefferson, Robert. 'Fifty Years on the Saskatchewan.' *Canadian Northwest Historical Society: Publications*, vol. 1: 1926–31. Battleford, Sask.: Canadian Northwest Historical Society, 1931.

Jennings, John. 'The North West Mounted Police and Indian Policy after the 1885 Rebellion.' In F. Laurie Barron and James B. Waldram, eds., *1885 and After: Native Society in Transition*. Regina: Canadian Plains Research Center, 1986.

Johnston, Charles M. 'Joseph Brant, the Grand River Lands and the Northwest Crisis.' *Ontario History* 55:4 (1963).

– 'To the Mohawk Station: The Making of a New England Company Missionary – the Rev. Robert Lugger.' In Michael K. Foster et al., eds., *Extending the Rafters: Approaches in Iroquoian Studies*. Albany, N.Y.: State University of New York Press, 1984.

Johnston, Darlene M. 'First Nations and Canadian Citizenship.' In William Kaplan, ed., *Belonging: The Meaning and Future of Canadian Citizenship*. Montreal: McGill-Queen's University Press, 1993.

– 'The Quest of the Six Nations Confederacy for Self-Determination.' *University of Toronto Faculty of Law Review*, vol. 44 (Spring 1986).

Judd, Carol M. 'Moose Factory Was Not Red River: A Comparison of Mixed-Blood Experiences.' In Duncan Cameron, ed., *Exploration in Canadian Economic History: Essays in Honour of Irene M. Spry*. Ottawa: University of Ottawa Press, 1985.

Kalmakoff, Elizabeth. 'Naturally Divided: Women in Saskatchewan Politics, 1916–1919.' *Saskatchewan History* 46:2 (Fall 1994).

Kelm, Mary-Ellen. 'Book review of Pettipas, *Severing the Ties that Bind*.' *Canadian Historical Review* 78:1 (March 1997).

Kirby, Percival. 'The Hottentot Venus.' *Africana Notes and News*, vol. 6 (1949).

– 'More about the Hottentot Venus.' *Africana Notes and News*, vol. 10 (1953).

Knight, Claudette. 'Black Parents Speak: Education in Mid-Nineteenth-Century Canada West.' *Ontario History*, vol. 89 (1997).

Kobayashi, Audrey. 'Racism and Law in Canada: A Geographical Perspective.' *Urban Geography* 11:5 (October 1970).

– 'Viewpoint: A Geographical Perspective on Racism and the Law.' *Canadian Law and Society Bulletin*, vol. 11 (Spring 1991).

Kobayashi, Audrey, and Peter Jackson. 'Japanese Canadians and the Racialization of Labour in the British Columbia Sawmill Industry.' *BC Studies*, vol. 108 (Autumn 1994).

Kyba, Patrick. 'Ballots and Burning Crosses –The Election of 1929.' In Norman Ward and Duff Spafford, eds., *Politics in Saskatchewan*. Toronto: Longmans, 1968.

Lai, David Chuenyan. 'The Issue of Discrimination in Education in Victoria, 1901–23.' *Canadian Ethnic Studies* 19:3 (1987).

Landon, Fred. 'The Anti-Slavery Society of Canada.' *Ontario History*, vol. 48 (1956).

– 'The Negro Migration to Canada After the Passing of the Fugitive Slave Act.' *Journal of Negro History*, vol. 5 (1920).

Larbalestier, J. 'The Politics of Representation: Australian Aboriginal Women and Feminism.' *Anthropological Forum*, vol. 6 (1990).

Laskin, Bora. 'Tavern Refusing to Serve Negro –Discrimination.' *Canadian Bar Review*, vol. 18 (1940).

Lee, Victor. 'The Laws of Gold Mountain: A Sampling of Early Canadian Laws and Cases that Affected People of Asian Ancestry.' *Manitoba Law Journal*, vol. 21 (1992).

Leyton-Brown, Kenneth B. 'Discriminatory Legislation in Early Saskatchewan and the Development of Small Business.' In Terry Wu and Jim Mason, eds., *Proceedings of the Eighth Annual Conference of the International Council for Small Business – Canada (ICSB)*. Regina: International Council for Small Business, 1990.

Li, Peter S. 'Chinese Immigrants on the Canadian Prairie, 1910–1947.' *Canadian Review of Sociology and Anthropology*, vol. 19 (1982).

Li, Peter S. 'The Economic Cost of Racism to Chinese-Canadians' *Canadian Ethnic Studies* 19:3 (1987).

– 'Immigration Laws and Family Patterns: Some Demographic Changes among Chinese Families in Canada, 1885–1971.' *Canadian Ethnic Studies* 12:1 (1980).

– 'Race and Gender as Bases of Class Factions and Their Effects on Earnings.' *The Canadian Review of Sociology and Anthropology* 29:4 (November 1992).

Lindstrom-Best, Varpu. 'Finnish Socialist Women in Canada, 1890–1930.' In Linda Kealey and Joan Sangster, eds., *Beyond the Vote: Canadian Women and Politics*. Toronto: University of Toronto Press, 1989.

Loo, Tina. 'Book Review of Pettipas's *Severing the Ties that Bind*.' *Canadian Journal of Law and Society* 10:2 (Fall 1995).

– 'Don Cranmer's Potlatch: Law as Coercion, Symbol and Rhetoric in British Columbia, 1884–1951.' In Tina Loo and Lorna R. McLean, eds., *Historical Perspectives on Law and Society in Canada*. Toronto: Copp Clark Longman, 1994.

Lubka, Nancy. 'Ferment in Nova Scotia.' *Queen's Quarterly* 76:2 (1969).

MacGill, H.G. 'The Oriental Delinquent in the Vancouver Juvenile Court.' *Sociology and Social Research* 22:5 (May-June 1938).

MacNair, Peter. 'From Kwakiutl to Kwakwa ka'wakw.' In R. Bruce Morrison and C. Roderick Wilson, eds., *Native Peoples: The Canadian Experience*. Toronto: McClelland & Stewart, 1986.

Madill, Dennis F.K. 'Riel, Red River, and Beyond: New Developments in Métis History.' In Colin G. Calloway, ed., *New Directions in American Indian History*. Norman: University of Oklahoma Press, 1988.

Makahonuk, Glen. 'Craft Unionism and the 1912 Strike Wave.' *Saskatchewan History* 44:2 (Spring 1992).

Malcolm, Ian. 'Robert Sutherland: The First Black Lawyer in Canada?' *Law Society of Upper Canada Gazette* 26:2 (June 1992).

Marks, Lynne. 'The "Hallelujah Lasses": Women and the Salvation Army in English Canada, 1882–1892.' In Franca Iacovetta and Mariana Valverde, eds., *Gender Conflicts: Essays in Women's History*. Toronto: University of Toronto Press, 1992.

– 'The Knights of Labor and the Salvation Army: Religion and Working-Class Culture in Ontario, 1882–1890.' *Labour/Le Travail*, vol. 28 (1991).

Marshall, Gloria A. 'Racial Classifications: Popular and Scientific.' In Sandra Harding, ed., *The 'Racial' Economy of Science: Toward a Democratic Future*. Bloomington: University of Indiana Press, 1993.

Mathias, Chief Joe, and Gary R. Yabsley. 'Conspiracy of Legislation: The Suppression of Indian Rights in Canada.' *BC Studies*, vol. 89 (1991).

McCormack, Ross. 'Cloth Caps and Jobs: The Ethnicity of English Immigrants in Canada, 1900–1914.' In J.M. Bumsted, ed., *Interpreting Canada's Past*, vol. 2: *After Confederation*. Toronto: Oxford University Press, 1986.

McEvoy, F.J. 'A Symbol of Racial Discrimination: The Chinese Immigration Act and Canada's Relations with China, 1942–1947.' *Canadian Ethnic Studies* 14:3 (1982).

McGrath, Ann, and Winona Stevenson. 'Gender, Race and Policy: Aboriginal Women and the State in Canada and Australia.' *Labour/Le Travail*, vol. 38 (Fall 1996).

McKenzie, Ruth I. 'Race Prejudice and the Negro.' *Dalhousie Review*, vol. 20 (1940).

McLaren, John P.S. 'The Early British Columbia Supreme Court and the "Chinese Question": Echoes of the Rule of Law.' In Dale Gibson and W. Wesley Pue, eds., *Glimpses of Canadian Legal History*. Winnipeg: Legal Research Institute, University of Manitoba, 1991.

Meyer, Roy W. 'The Canadian Sioux: Refugees from Minnesota.' *Minnesota History* 41:1 (1968).

Milloy, John S. 'The Early Indian Acts: Developmental Strategy and Constitutional Change.' In Ian A.L. Getty and Antoine S. Lussier, eds., *As Long as the*

Sun Shines and Water Flows: A Reader in Canadian Native Studies. Vancouver: University of British Columbia Press, 1983.

Milner, J.B. 'Case and Comment.' *Canadian Bar Review*, vol. 25 (1947).

Mitchell, Marjorie, and Anna Franklin. 'When You Don't Know the Language, Listen to the Silence: An Historical Overview of Native Indian Women in B.C.' In Barbara K. Latham and Roberta J. Pazdro, eds., *Not Just Pin Money*. Victoria: Camosun College, 1984.

Molot, Henry L. 'The Duty of Business to Serve the Public: Analogy to the Innkeeper's Obligation.' *Canadian Bar Review*, vol. 46 (1968).

Montgomery, Malcolm. 'The Legal Status of the Six Nations Indians in Canada.' *Ontario History* 55:2 (1963).

– 'The Six Nations Indians and the Macdonald Franchise.' *Ontario History* 57:1 (1965).

Morrison, William R. 'Canadian Sovereignty and the Inuit of the Central and Eastern Arctic.' *Etudes/Inuit/Studies* 10:1/2 (1986).

Morton, Suzanne. 'Old Women and Their Place in Nova Scotia, 1881–1931.' *Atlantis* 20:1 (1995).

– 'Separate Spheres in a Separate World: African-Nova Scotian Women in late-19th-Century Halifax County.' *Acadiensis* 22:2 (Spring 1993).

Nipp, Dora. '"But Women Did Come": Working Chinese Women in the Inter-war Years.' In Jean Brunet, ed., *Looking into My Sister's Eyes*. Toronto: Multicultural History Society of Ontario, 1986.

Nungak, Zebedee. 'Quebecker?? Canadian? ... Inuk!' In Bruce W. Hodgins and Kerry A. Cannon, eds., *On the Land: Confronting the Challenges to Aboriginal Self-Determination in Northern Quebec and Labrador*. Toronto: Betelgeuse, 1995.

Oliver, W.P. 'Cultural Progress of the Negro in Nova Scotia.' *Dalhousie Review* 29:3 (1949), as reprinted in George Elliott Clarke, ed., *Fire on the Water: An Anthology of Black Nova Scotian Writing*, vol. 2. Lawrencetown Beach, N.S.: Pottersfield Press, 1992.

Oschinsky, Lawrence. 'Facial Flatness and Cheekbone Morphology in Arctic Mongoloids: A Case of Morphological Taxonomy.' *Anthropologica* 4:2 (1962).

Osumi, Megumi Dick. 'Asians and California's Anti-Miscegenation Laws.' In Nobuya Tsuchida, ed., *Asian and Pacific American Experiences: Women's Perspectives*. Minneapolis: University of Minnesota, Asian/Pacific American Learning Resource Center, 1982.

Palmer, Howard. 'Strangers and Stereotypes: The Rise of Nativism 1880–1920.' In R. Douglas Francis and Howard Palmer, eds., *The Prairie West: Historical Readings*. Edmonton: University of Alberta Press, 1985.

Pascoe, Peggy. 'Miscegenation Law, Court Cases, and Ideologies of "Race" in Twentieth-Century America.' *Journal of American History*, vol. 83 (June 1996).

- 'Race, Gender, and Intercultural Relations: The Case of Interracial Marriage.' *Frontiers* 12:1 (Summer 1991).
Peiss, Kathy. 'Beauty Culture.' In Darlene Clark Hine, ed., *Black Women in America: An Historical Encyclopedia*, vol. 1. Brooklyn: Carlson Publishing, 1993.
Peller, Gary. 'Race Consciousness.' *Duke Law Journal* vol. 1990.
Peterson, Jacqueline. 'Many Roads to Red River: Métis Genesis in the Great Lakes Region, 1680–1815.' In Jacqueline Peterson and Jennifer S.H. Brown, *The New Peoples: Being and Becoming Métis in North America*. Winnipeg: University of Manitoba Press, 1985.
- 'Prelude to Red River: A Social Portrait of the Great Lakes Métis.' *Ethnohistory*, vol. 25 (1978).
Pon, Madge. 'Like a Chinese Puzzle: The Construction of Chinese Masculinity in Jack Canuck.' In Joy Parr and Mark Rosenfeld, *Gender and History in Canada*. Toronto: Copp Clark, 1996.
Powless, Jr, Irving. 'The Sovereignty and Land Rights of the Houdenosaunee.' In Christopher Vecsey and William A. Starna,eds., *Iroquois Land Claims*. Syracuse, N.Y.: Syracuse University Press, 1988.
Prestney, Susie. 'Inscribing the Hottentot Venus: Generating Data for Difference.' In Phillip Darby, ed., *At the Edge of International Relations: Postcolonialism, Gender and Dependency*. London: Pinter, 1997.
Price, Catherine. 'Lakotas and Euroamericans: Contrasted Concepts of "Chieftainship" and Decision-Making Authority.' *Ethnohistory* 41:3 (Summer 1994).
Price, Graham. 'The King v. Alikomiak.' In Dale Gibson and Wesley Pue, eds., *Glimpses of Canadian Legal History*. Winnipeg: Legal Research Institute, 1991.
Randle, Martha Champion. 'Iroquois Women, Then and Now.' In William Guy Spittal, *Iroquois Women: An Anthology*. Ohsweken, Ont.: Iroqrafts, 1990.
Regular, Keith. 'On Public Display.' *Alberta History* 34:1 (1986).
- 'Esther Phelps.' *The University Magazine*, vol. 12. Montreal, October 1913.
- 'The Slave in Canada.' *Journal of Negro History* 5:3 (1920).
- 'Women as of Practitioners of Law.' *Journal of Comparative Legislation* (1918).
Riddell, William Renwick. 'Administration of Criminal Law in the Far North of Canada.' *Journal of Criminal Law, Criminology and Police Science* 20:2 (August 1929).
- 'A Criminal Circuit in Upper Canada: A Century Ago.' *Canadian Law Times*, vol. 40 (Toronto, 1920).
- 'Former Indian Treatment for Venereal Disease.' *Urologic and Cutaneous Review*, vol. 32 (November 1928).
- 'Indian Episodes in Early Michigan.' *Michigan History Magazine*, vol. 18 (1934).

- 'Indian War Council Held at Detroit in 1700.' *Transactions of the Royal Society of Canada*, 3d ser., vol.25, Section II (1931).
- 'Medicine of the Indians of Acadia Two and a Quarter Centuries Ago.' *Medical Record: A National Review of Medicine and Surgery*, vol. 140 (July 1934).
- 'An Old-Time Misogynist.' *Canadian Magazine* 58:5 (March 1922).
- 'The Sad Tale of an Indian Wife.' *The Canadian Law Times*, vol. 40 (Toronto, 1920); republished in *Journal of Criminal Law and Criminology*, vol. 13 (May 1922).
- 'Some Indian Medicine 240 Years Ago and Now.' *Medical Record: A National Review of Medicine and Surgery*, vol. 144 (October 1936).
- 'The Status of the Indian.' *Bench and Bar*, vol. 5 (October 1935).
- 'Was Molly Brant Married?' *Ontario Historical Society Papers and Records*, vol. 19 (1922).
Rioux, Marcel. 'Relations between Religion and Government among the Longhouse Iroquois of the Grand River.' In *National Museum of Canada Bulletin 126*. Ottawa: National Museum of Canada, 1972.
Roome, Patricia. 'Amelia Turner and Calgary Labour Women, 1919–1935.' In Linda Kealey and Joan Sangster, eds., *Beyond the Vote: Canadian Women and Politics*. Toronto: University of Toronto Press, 1989.
Roy, Patricia E. 'Protecting Their Pocketbooks and Preserving Their Race: White Merchants and Oriental Competition.' In A.R. McCormack and Ian MacPherson, eds., *Cities in the West*. Ottawa: National Museum of Man, 1975.
Ryder, Bruce. 'Racism and the Constitution: The Constitutional Fate of British Columbia Anti-Asian Immigration Legislation, 1884–1909.' *Osgoode Hall Law Journal*, vol. 29 (1991).
Satzewich, Vic, and Linda Mahood. 'Indian Affairs and Band Governance: Deposing Indian Chiefs in Western Canada, 1896–1911.' *Canadian Ethnic Studies* 26:1 (1994).
Schneider, William. 'Race and Empire: The Rise of Popular Ethnography in the Late Nineteenth Century.' *Journal of Popular Culture* 11:1 (Summer 1977).
Schuh, Cornelia. 'Justice on the Northern Frontier: Early Murder Trials of Native Accused.' *Criminal Law Quarterly*, vol. 22 (1978–80).
Shafer, Ann Eastlack. 'The Status of Iroquois Women.' In William Guy Spittal, ed., *Iroquois Women: An Anthology*. Ohsweken, Ont.: Iroqrafts, 1990.
Sheehan, Nancy M. 'The WCTU on the Prairies, 1886–1930.' *Prairie Forum* 6:1 (1981).
Shepard, R. Bruce. 'The Little "White" Schoolhouse: Racism in a Saskatchewan Rural School.' *Saskatchewan History*, vol. 39 (1986).
- 'Plain Racism: The Reaction Against Oklahoma Black Immigration to the Canadian Prairies.' In Ormond McKague, ed., *Racism in Canada*. Saskatoon: Fifth House, 1992.

Shimony, Annemarie. 'Conflict and Continuity: An Analysis of an Iroquois Uprising.' In Michael K. Foster et al., eds., *Extending the Rafters: Approaches in Iroquoian Studies*. Albany, N.Y.: State University of New York Press, 1984.

Silverman, Jason. 'The American Fugitive Slave in Canada: Myths and Realities.' *Southern Studies*, vol. 19 (1980).

– '"We Shall Be Heard!": The Development of the Fugitive Slave Press in Canada.' *Canadian Historical Review*, vol. 65 (1984).

Silverman, Jason H., and Donna J. Gillie. 'The Pursuit of Knowledge under Difficulties: Education and the Fugitive Slave in Canada.' *Ontario History*, vol. 74 (1982).

Simon, M.P.P. 'The Haldimand Agreement: A Continuing Covenant.' *American Indian Culture and Research Journal*, vol. 7 (1983).

Sivanandan, A. 'Challenging Racism: Strategies for the 80s.' *Race and Class*, vol. 25 (1983).

Small, Nadine. 'The Lady Imperialists and the Great War: The Imperial Order Daughters of the Empire in Saskatchewan, 1914–1918.' In David De Brou and Aileen Moffatt, eds., *'Other' Voices: Historical Essays on Saskatchewan Women*. Regina: Canadian Plains Research Center, University of Regina, 1995.

Smandych, Russell, and Rick Linden. 'Co-existing Forms of Native and Private Justice: An Historical Study of the Canadian West.' In Kayleen M. Hazlehurst, ed., *Legal Pluralism and the Colonial Legacy: Indigenous Experiences of Justice in Canada, Australia, and New Zealand*. Aldershot, UK: Avebury Press, 1995.

Smith, Donald B. 'The Dispossession of the Mississauga Indians: A Missing Chapter in the Early History of Upper Canada.' *Ontario History* 73:2 (1981).

Speisman, Stephen. 'Antisemitism in Ontario: The Twentieth Century.' In Alan Davies, ed., *Antisemitism in Canada: History and Interpretation*. Waterloo: Wilfrid Laurier University Press, 1992.

Spry, Irene M. 'The Métis and Mixed-Bloods of Rupert's Land before 1870.' In Jacqueline Peterson and Jennifer S.H. Brown, eds., *The New Peoples: Being and Becoming Métis in North America*. Winnipeg: University of Manitoba Press, 1985.

Stanley, George F.G. 'The Six Nations and the American Revolution.' *Ontario History* 56:4 (1964).

Starna, William A. 'Aboriginal Title and Traditional Iroquois Land Use: An Anthropological Perspective.' In Christopher Vecsey and William A. Starna, *Iroquois Land Claims*. Syracuse, N.Y.: Syracuse University Press, 1988.

Stepan, Nancy. 'Race, Gender, Science and Citizenship.' *Gender & History* 10:1 (April 1998).

Strange, Carolyn, and Tina Loo. 'Spectacular Justice: The Circus on Trial, and the Trial as Circus, Picton, 1903.' *Canadian Historical Review* 77:2 (1996).

Surtees, Robert J. 'The Iroquois in Canada.' In Francis Jennings et al., eds., *The History and Culture of Iroquois Diplomacy.* Syracuse, N.Y. : Syracuse University Press, 1985.

Szathmary, Emoke J.E. 'Genetic Markers in Siberian and Northern North American Populations.' *Yearbook of Physical Anthropology,* vol. 24 (1981).

Szathmary, Emoke J.E. 'Human Biology of the Arctic.' In William C. Sturtevant, ed., *Handbook of North American Indians.* Washington, D.C.: Smithsonian Institution, 1984.

Taggart, Michael. 'The Province of Administrative Law Determined?' In Michael Taggart, ed., *The Province of Administrative Law.* Oxford: Hart Publishing, 1997.

Talbot, Lance Carey. 'The Formation of the Black Law Students' Association (Canada).' *Law Society of Upper Canada Gazette* 26:2 (June 1992).

– 'History of Blacks in the Law Society of Upper Canada.' *Law Society of Upper Canada Gazette* 24:1 (March 1990).

Tao, Erica Chung-Yue. 'Re-defining Race Relations – Beyond the Threat of "Loving Blackness".' *Canadian Journal of Women and the Law* 6:2 (1993).

Taylor, Georgina M. 'Grace Fletcher, Women's Rights, Temperance, and "British Fair Play" in Saskatoon, 1885–1907.' *Saskatchewan History* 46:1 (Spring 1994).

Thomas, William I. 'The Scope and Method of Folk-Psychology.' *American Journal of Sociology,* vol. 1 (November 1895).

Tooker, Elizabeth. 'On the New Religion of Handsome Lake.' *Anthropological Quarterly* 41:4 (October 1986).

Torok, C.H. 'The Tyendinaga Mohawks.' *Ontario History* 57:2 (1965).

Troper, Harold Martin. 'The Creek-Negroes of Oklahoma and Canadian Immigration, 1909–11.' *Canadian Historical Review* 53:3 (September 1972).

Tulchinsky, Gerald. 'The Jewish Experience in Ontario to 1960.' In Roger Hall et al., eds., *Patterns of the Past: Interpreting Ontario's History.* Toronto: Dundurn Press, 1988.

Turpel-Lafond, Mary Ellen. 'Oui the People? Conflicting Visions of Self-Determination in Quebec.' In Bruce W. Hodgins and Kerry A. Cannon, eds., *On the Land: Confronting the Challenges to Aboriginal Self-Determination in Northern Quebec and Labrador.* Toronto: Betelgeuse, 1995.

Vachon, André. 'L'eau-de-vie dans la société indienne.' Canadian Historical Association *Annual Report.* Ottawa: CHA Public Archives, 1960.

Valverde, Mariana. '"When the Mother of the Race Is Free": Race, Reproduction, and Sexuality in First-Wave Feminism.' In Franca Iacovetta and Mariana Valverde, eds., *Gender Conflicts: New Essays in Women's History.* Toronto: University of Toronto Press, 1992.

van den Berghe, Pierre L. 'The African Diaspora in Mexico, Brazil, and the

United States.' In Audrey W. Bonnett and G. Llewellyn Watson, eds., *Emerging Perspectives on the Black Diaspora*. London: University Press of America, 1990.

Van Kirk, Sylvia '"What If Mama Is an Indian?" The Cultural Ambivalence of the Alexander Ross Family.' In Jacqueline Peterson and Jennifer S.H. Brown, eds., *The New Peoples: Being and Becoming Métis in North America*. Winnipeg: University of Manitoba Press, 1985.

Vizkelety, Beatrice. 'Discrimination, the Right to Seek Redress and the Common Law: A Century-Old Debate.' *Dalhousie Law Journal*, vol. 15 (1992).

Voisey, Paul. 'The Urbanization of the Canadian Prairies, 1871–1916.' In R. Douglas Francis and Howard Palmer, eds., *The Prairie West: Historical Readings*. Edmonton: University of Alberta Press, 1985.

Wagner, Sally Roesch. 'The Iroquois Confederacy: A Native American Model for Non-Sexist Men.' In William Guy Spittal, ed., *Iroquois Women: An Anthology*. Ohsweken, Ont.: Iroqrafts, 1990.

– 'The Root of Oppression Is the Loss of Memory: The Iroquois and the Early Feminist Vision.' In William Guy Spittal, ed., *Iroquois Women: An Anthology*. Ohsweken, Ont.: Iroqrafts, 1990.

Walker, James W.St.G. 'The Indian in Canadian Historical Writing.' *Canadian Historical Association Historical Papers*. Ottawa, 1971.

– '"Race" Policy in Canada: A Retrospective.' In O.P. Dwivedi et al., eds., *Canada 2000: Race Relations and Public Policy*. Guelph: University of Guelph Press, 1989.

Wallace, W. Stewart, ed. 'Jenness, Diamond.' *The Macmillan Dictionary of Canadian Biography*, 4th ed. Toronto: Macmillan of Canada, 1978.

Wallis, Wilson D. 'Canadian Dakota Sun Dance.' *Anthropological Papers of the American Museum of History*, vol. 16, Part IV. New York: American Museum of History, 1919.

Wallis, Wilson D. 'Beliefs and Tales of the Canadian Dakota.' *Journal of American Folk-Lore*, vol. 36 (1923).

Ward, W. Peter. 'The Oriental Immigrant and Canada's Protestant Clergy, 1858–1925.' *BC Studies*, vol. 22 (Summer 1974).

Wayne, Michael. 'The Black Population of Canada West on the Eve of the American Civil War: A Reassessment Based on the Manuscript Census of 1861.' In Franca Iacovetta et al., eds., *A Nation of Immigrants: Women, Workers, and Communities in Canadian History, 1840s–1960s*. Toronto: University of Toronto Press, 1998.

Welke, Barbara Y. 'When All the Women Were White, and All the Blacks Were Men: Gender, Class, Race and the Road to *Plessy*, 1855–1914.' *Law and History Review* 13:2 (Fall 1995).

Wenxiong, Gao. 'Hamilton: The Chinatown that Died.' *The Asianadian: An Asian Canadian Magazine*, vol. 1 (Summer 1978).

Wickberg, Edgar. 'Chinese and Canadian Influences on Chinese Politics in Vancouver 1900–47.' *BC Studies*, vol. 45 (Spring 1980).

Williams, Paul. 'Oral Tradition on Trial.' In *Gin Das Winan: Documenting Aboriginal History in Ontario*. Toronto: Champlain Society, 1996.

Williams, Jr, Robert A. 'The Algebra of Federal Indian Law: The Hard Trail of Decolonizing and Americanizing the White Man's Indian Jurisprudence.' *Wisconsin Law Review*, vol. 3 (1986).

Winks, Robin W. 'The Canadian Negro: A Historical Assessment.' *Journal of Negro History* 53:4 (October 1968).

– 'Negro School Segregation in Ontario and Nova Scotia.' *Canadian Historical Review* 50:2 (1969).

– 'Negroes in the Maritimes: An Introductory Survey.' *Dalhousie Review* 48:4 (1969).

Wright, Roland. 'The Public Right of Fishing, Government Fishing Policy, and Indian Fishing Rights in Upper Canada.' *Ontario History* 84:4 (December 1994).

Yee, May. 'Finding the Way Home Through Issues of Gender, Race and Class.' In Himani Bannerji, ed., *Returning the Gaze: Essays on Racism, Feminism and Politics*. Toronto: Sister Vision Press, 1993.

Yee, Shirley. 'Gender Ideology and Black Women as Community-Builders in Ontario, 1850–70.' *Canadian Historical Review* 75:1 (March 1994).

Zorn, Roman J. 'Criminal Extradition Menaces the Canadian Haven for Fugitive Slaves, 1841–1861.' *Canadian Historical Review*, vol. 38 (1957).

C. UNPUBLISHED MANUSCRIPTS

Bagnall, John C. 'The Ontario Conservatives and the Development of Anti-Discrimination Policy, 1944–1962.' PhD thesis, Queen's University, 1984.

Benincasa, James E. 'Cultural Divisions and the Politics of Control: The Canadian Removal of the Six Nations' Hereditary Council in 1924.' MA thesis, University of Western Ontario, 1994.

Boudreau, Michael S. 'Crime and Society in a City of Order: Halifax, 1918–1935.' PhD thesis, Queen's University, 1996.

Calderwood, William. 'The Rise and Fall of the Ku Klux Klan in Saskatchewan.' MA thesis, University of Saskatchewan, 1968.

Coates, K.S. 'Furs Along the Yukon: Hudson's Bay Company–Native Trade in the Yukon River Basin, 1830–1893.' MA thesis, University of Manitoba, 1979.

Green, Andrea. 'Land, Leadership, and Conflict: The Six Nations' Early Years on the Grand River.' MA. thesis, University of Western Ontario, 1984.

Hall, Anthony J. 'The Northwest Territories of North America: A Place or a Procedure for the Extinguishment and Privatization of Indian country?' Unpublished manuscript, 1998.

Hamori-Torok, Charles. 'The Acculturation of the Mohawks of the Bay of Quinte.' PhD thesis, University of Toronto, 1966.

Harring, Sidney. '"The Common Law Is not Part Savage and Part Civilized": Chief Justice John Beverley Robinson, Canadian Legal Culture, and the Denial of Native Rights in Mid-nineteenth Century Upper Canada.' Unpublished manuscript, 1995.

Harvey, Janet. 'The Regina Council of Women, 1895–1929.' MA thesis, University of Regina, 1991.

Imai, Shin. 'Canadian Immigration Law and Policy: 1867–1935.' LLM thesis, York University, 1983.

Jennings, John. 'The Northwest Mounted Police and Canadian Indian Policy, 1873–1896.' PhD thesis, University of Toronto, 1979.

Kennedy, Jacqueline Judith Gresko. 'Qu'Appelle Industrial School: White "Rites" for the Indians of the old North-West.' MA thesis, Carleton University, 1970.

Majzub, Diba B. '"A God Sent Land for the Colored People"? The Legal Treatment of Blacks in Victoria, 1858–1865.' Unpublished manuscript, 1997.

Marks, Lynne Sorrel. 'Ladies, Loafers, Knights and "Lasses": The Social Dimensions of Religion and Leisure in Late Nineteenth-Century Small-Town Ontario.' PhD thesis, York University, 1992.

Martyn, Byron Curti. 'Racism in the United States: A History of the Anti-Miscegenation Legislation and Litigation.' PhD thesis, University of Southern California, 1979.

McGovern, Marcia A. 'The Woman's Christian Temperance Union Movement in Saskatchewan, 1886–1920: A Regional Perspective on the International White Ribbon Movement.' MA thesis, University of Regina, 1977.

Mosher, J.F. 'Liquor Legislation and Native Americans: History and Perspective.' University of California, Boalt Hall School of Law, 1975.

Neary, Hilary Bates. 'William Renwick Riddell: A Bio-Bibliographical Study.' MA thesis. University of Western Ontario, 1977.

Nipp, Dora. 'Canada-Bound: An Exploratory Study of Pioneer Chinese Women in Western Canada.' MA thesis. University of Toronto, 1983.

Patterson, E. Palmer. 'Andrew Paull and Canadian Indian Resurgence.' PhD thesis, University of Washington, 1962.

Peterson, Jacqueline. 'The People in Between: Indian–White Marriage and the Genesis of a Métis Society and Culture in the Great Lakes Region, 1680–1830.' PhD thesis, University of Chicago, 1981.

Pettipas, Katherine Ann. 'Severing the Ties that Bind: The Canadian Indian Act and the Repression of Indigenous Religious Systems in the Prairie Region, 1896–1951.' PhD thesis, University of Manitoba, 1989.

Pettit, Jennifer. 'From Longhouse to Schoolhouse: The Mohawk Institute, 1834–1940.' MA thesis, University of Western Ontario, 1993.

Pilton, James M. 'Negro Settlement in British Columbia.' MA thesis, University of Victoria, 1951.

Price, Graham. 'Remote Justice: The Stipendiary Magistrate's Court of the Northwest Territories, 1905–55.' LLM thesis, University of Manitoba, 1986.

Price-Jones, K. Shelley. 'Emerging from the Shadows: The Life of Captain John Deserontyou, circa 1742–1811, Founder of the Bay of Quinte Mohawk Village.' MA thesis, Queen's University, 1993.

Regular, W. Keith. '"Red Backs and White Burdens": A Study of White Attitudes towards Indians in Southern Alberta, 1896–1911.' MA thesis, University of Calgary, 1985.

Ryder, Bruce. 'Racism and the Constitution: The Constitutional Fate of British Columbia Anti-Asian Legislation, 1872–1922.' Unpublished manuscript.

Seager, Allan. 'A History of the Mine Workers' Union of Canada, 1925–1936.' MA thesis, McGill University, 1977.

Walker, Barrington. 'Gender, Sexual Transgressions, and Representations of Black Masculinity in Judicial Discourse: The John Paris and William McCathern Trials in 1920s Canada.' Unpublished manuscript.

Welke, Barbara Y. 'Gendered Journeys: A History of Injury, Public Transport and American Law, 1865–1920.' PhD thesis, University of Chicago, 1995.

Picture Credits

Case on Behalf of the Attorney General of Canada, in the Supreme Court of Canada, Re Indian-Eskimo Reference (King's Printer: Ottawa): Morton's drawings of skulls, 398

Audrey Chisholm, Belleville, Ontario: Eliza Sero's house; Reuben Sero; Clara Brant

Audrey Chisholm and Gloria Smith, Belleville, Ontario: Clara Brant, Eliza Sero, and Theresa Green

Mrs S.A. (Emily) Clyke, Montreal, Quebec: Viola after high school; grade three class; confirmation class; diplomas; souvenir calendar; Desmond Beauty Studio graduation; Desmond School of Beauty Culture graduation

Chronicle-Herald and the *Mail-Star*, Halifax, N.S.: Dr Carrie Best; F.W. Bissett

Berthe G. Crête, Grand-Mère, Quebec: Auguste Desilets

Law Society of Upper Canada Archives, Special Collections: Riddell, S264

London Public Library: 'First Canadian Ku Klux Burial'

G. Macdonald, carto [ ] praxis, as printed in Bruce W. Hodgins and Kerry A. Cannon, *On the Land: Confronting the Challenges to Aboriginal Self-Determination in Northern Quebec and Labrador* (Toronto: Betelgeuse Books, 1995): map of Northern Quebec and Labrador

Shirley A. Maracle, Deseronto, Ontario, and Shirley Bennett, Belleville, Ontario: Eliza Sero

Vivian S. Morrison: James McGregor Stewart

National Archives of Canada: Photographs by L.T. Burwash from the Historical Photographs Collection, Avataq Cultural Institute: Pijausuittuq, A-PA-099301; Lucassie Uvua, A-PA-099370; Qajakjuaq, A-PA-099344; unidentified Inuk, A-PA-099614; Photograph by J.L. Robinson: Inuit children, A-PA-102211; Klansmen with burnt cross, PA-87848

Provincial Archives of Manitoba and Rapid City District and Historical Society: Rapid City collection: aerial view, photographer Carl Nettekoven; store-fronts, photographer W.A. Martel; Indians 17 collection: Pow Wow, N7569; Morris, Edmund collection: Grass Dance, 294, N16561; Wanduta, 127, N16264; Laird, David collection: Laird, 2, N10451; Coldwell, George Robson collection: Coldwell, 1; Sifton, Clifford collection: Sifton, 1; Indians–Sioux 5 collection: Dakota at Brandon Fair, N105; Brandon Fair 1916-1 collection: First Nations and fair organizers

Public Archives of Nova Scotia: M.B. Archibald, Gauvin and Gentzel Collection, 1987-267 #41

Rapid City District and Historical Society: Agricultural Society Exhibition

Wanda Robson, North Sydney, N.S.: James and Gwendolyn Davis; relaxing at the Hi-Hat Club

Saskatchewan Archives Board: Two Chinese men, R-A15649; Turgeon, R-A251; Chinese family, R-B7329; Stapleford, R-A17103; Sunday school banquet, R-D729; McKinnon, R-A8000; Mackenzie, R-B4536

J.J. Talman Regional Collection, D.B. Weldon Library, University of Western Ontario: Andrew Chisholm

Toronto Reference Library: *Phillips* trial, *Toronto Daily Star*, 11 March 1930, p. 21; 'Pastor Receives Warning,' *Toronto Daily Star*, 7 March 1930, p. 3; 'Guarded by Police in Edward St. Home,' *Toronto Daily Star*, 8 March 1930, p. 2; *Phillips* trial, *Toronto Daily Star*, 24 March 1930, p. 3

Index

W.H. Morrow, ed., *Northern Justice: The Memoirs of Mr Justice William G. Morrow*

Beverley Boissery, *A Deep Sense of Wrong: The Treason. Trials and Transportation to New South Wales of Lower Canadian Rebels after the 1838 Rebellion*

1996 Carol Wilton, ed., *Essays in the History of Canadian Law: Volume VII – Inside the Law: Canadian Law Firms in Historical Perspective*

William Kaplan, *Bad Judgment: The Case of Mr Justice Leo A. Landreville*

F. Murray Greenwood and Barry Wright, eds., *Canadian State Trials: Volume I – Law, Politics, and Security Measures, 1608–1837*

1997 James W. St.G. Walker, *'Race,' Rights, and the Law in the Supreme Court of Canada: Historical Case Studies*

Lori Chambers, *Married Women and Property Law in Victorian Ontario*

Patrick Brode, *Casual Slaughters and Accidental Judgments: Canadian War Crimes and Prosecutions, 1944–1948*

Ian Bushnell, *The Federal Court of Canada: A History, 1875–1992*

1998 Sidney Harring, *White Man's Law: Native People in Nineteenth-Century Canadian Jurisprudence*

Peter Oliver, *'Terror to Evil-Doers': Prisons and Punishments in Nineteenth-Century Ontario*

1999 Constance Backhouse, *Colour-Coded: A Legal History of Racism in Canada, 1900–1950*

G. Blaine Baker and Jim Phillips, eds., *Essays in the History of Canadian Law: Volume VIII – In Honour of R.C.B. Risk*